INTERNATIONAL SERIES IN
LIBRARY AND INFORMATION SCIENCE
GENERAL EDITOR G. CHANDLER

VOLUME 3

ECONOMICS OF EDUCATION

THIRD EDITION

INTERNATIONAL SERIES IN LIBRARY AND INFORMATION SCIENCE

General Editor: G. CHANDLER

BAKEWELL, K.G.B.
A Manual of Cataloguing Practice
(Volume 14)

DUREY, P.
Staff Management in University and College Libraries
(Volume 16)

ELLIS, A.
Library Services for Young People in England and Wales 1830-1970
(Volume 13)

HALE, B.
The Subject Bibliography of the Social Sciences and Humanities
(Volume 12)

HODSON, J.H.
The Administration of Archives
(Volume 15)

KIMBER, R.T. and BOYD, A.
Automation in Libraries
(Volume 10)

WHITE, C.M.
Bases of Modern Librarianship
(Volume 1)

ECONOMICS OF EDUCATION

A Selected Annotated Bibliography

BY

M. BLAUG

*Professor of the Economics of Education
and Head of the Research Unit in the Economics of Education,
University of London Institute of Education*

THIRD EDITION

PERGAMON PRESS
OXFORD · NEW YORK · TORONTO · SYDNEY · PARIS · FRANKFURT

U.K.	Pergamon Press Ltd., Headington Hill Hall, Oxford OX3 0BW, England
U.S.A.	Pergamon Press Inc., Maxwell House, Fairview Park, Elmsford, New York 10523, U.S.A.
CANADA	Pergamon of Canada Ltd., 75 The East Mall, Toronto, Ontario, Canada
AUSTRALIA	Pergamon Press (Aust.) Pty. Ltd., 19a Boundary Street, Rushcutters Bay, N.S.W. 2011, Australia
FRANCE	Pergamon Press SARL, 24 rue des Ecoles, 75240 Paris, Cedex 05, France
FEDERAL REPUBLIC OF GERMANY	Pergamon Press GmbH; 6242 Kronberg-Taunus, Pferdstrasse 1, Federal Republic of Germany

First edition 1966
Second edition 1970
Third edition 1978

British Library Cataloguing in Publication Data
Blaug, Mark
Economics of education.
(International series in library and
information science). - 3rd ed.
1. Education - Finance - Bibliography
2. Education - Economic aspects - Bibliography
I. Title II. Series
016.3384'7   Z5814.F5   78-40307
ISBN 0-08-020627-1

In order to make this volume available as economically and as rapidly as possible the author's typescript has been reproduced in its original form. This method unfortunately has its typographical limitations but it is hoped that they in no way distract the reader.

*Printed in Great Britain by William Clowes & Sons Limited
London, Beccles and Colchester*

CONTENTS

Preface to the First Edition   1

Preface to the Second Edition   3

Preface to the Third Edition   4

Abbreviations   5

A. DEVELOPED COUNTRIES

   1. GENERAL SURVEYS   9

   2. THE ECONOMIC CONTRIBUTION OF EDUCATION   18

      (a) Earlier Views   18
      (b) The Production-function Approach   23
      (c) Human Capital Formation   32
      (d) Measurement of Returns   36

   3. THE ECONOMIC ASPECTS OF EDUCATION   86

      (a) Costs and Determinants of Expenditures   86
      (b) Public and Private Finance   100
      (c) Productivity and Efficiency   115
      (d) Technical and Vocational Education   134
      (e) Higher Education   148

   4. EDUCATIONAL PLANNING   173

      (a) General Treatments   174
      (b) Mathematical Models   188

        (c) Manpower Forecasting   194

    5. BRAIN DRAIN AND INTERNATIONAL TRADE   230

    6. SOCIAL MOBILITY AND RESERVES OF TALENT   238

    7. THE POLITICS OF EDUCATION   256

    8. THE ECONOMICS OF HEALTH   263

B. DEVELOPING COUNTRIES

    1. GENERAL SURVEYS   269

    2. THE ECONOMIC CONTRIBUTION OF EDUCATION   273

        (a) Historical Comparative Material   273
        (b) International Comparisons   278
        (c) Case Studies and Special Problems   285

    3. THE ECONOMIC ASPECTS OF EDUCATION   308

        (a) Costs and Finance   308
        (b) Productivity and Efficiency   315
        (c) Technical and Vocational Education   319
        (d) Informal Education   325

    4. EDUCATIONAL PLANNING   335
        (a) General Treatments   335
        (b) Mathematical Models   359
        (c) Manpower Forecasting   362

C. BIBLIOGRAPHIES   379

D. ITEMS RECEIVED TOO LATE FOR CLASSIFICATION   389

Index of Authors   399

Index of Countries   419

PREFACE TO THE FIRST EDITION

It is difficult to define the nature and scope of a subject like the economics of education. It derives its *raison d'être* from the peculiarities of education as an "industry" absorbing material and human resources: in most countries, it is largely collectively provided and financed; although the inputs of teachers and buildings are bought in the market place, the output of students is not sold; its production-cycle is longer than that of most other industries and it consumes a relatively large fraction of its own output; it is not a profit-maximising activity and, indeed, it is not self-evident that it is maximising anything at all; it is both "invest-ment" and "consumption" in so far as it prepares students both to earn a living and to enjoy the fruits of living; its pay-off takes a long time to materialise but it depreciates slowly and rarely becomes entirely obsolete; it serves to diffuse the existing stock of knowledge but it also acts to increase that stock; it both pre-serves and disseminates social values, sometimes fostering and sometimes impeding social and occupational mobility; its economic consequences are complex and so thoroughly intertwined with its social and political effects that any hope of separating them can be made to seem absurd. Since economics is what economists do, perhaps the best definition of the economics of education is simply: the contents of this bibliography.

It may be helpful, however, to say a little more than this. The economic analysis of education centres round such questions as: how much should a country spend on education and how should the expenditure be financed; is education mainly invest-ment or mainly consumption; if investment, how large is its yield in comparison to other forms of investment in people and things; if consumption, how much choice do consumers actually have in demanding more education; what is the optimum combina-tion of inputs employed within the educational system; what is the optimum structure of the educational pyramid (i.e. the different levels and channels of the educational system); what is the optimum mix of formal and informal education (i.e. on the job training and adult education); and, lastly, what contribution does education make to the overall development of human resources and how far can we control the expan-sion of education by systematic planning, particularly in low-income countries? This is a formidable list of topics which demonstrates that the economics of educa-tion forms a bridge between economics (particularly, public finance and labour economics), sociology (particularly, social stratification and industrial sociology), social administration, comparative education, and educational psychology, partaking at the same time of a still wider subject, the economics of human resources.

For that reason it is not easy to know where to stop in a survey of the literature. The present bibliography takes a narrow view of the field, but not so narrow as to exclude aspects of the sociology and politics of education. A bibliography of bibliographies is included to suggest other lines of reading. The classificatory scheme adopted here is necessarily somewhat arbitrary, and many items might have been reported under several headings (the cross-references are designed to meet this problem). There is a vast body of writings concerned with particular countries and areas, only the most important of which are listed below. Our criterion of selec-tion is a simple one: does the country or area study contribute to fundamental generalisation about the economic aspects or economic role of education? For obvious

1

reasons, the literature on developed countries is distinguished from that dealing with the developing nations. No attempt is made to include descriptive material about educational systems in different countries, but an index of countries is included to assist the student of comparative education.

As a field of inquiry in the social sciences, the economics of education is still in its infancy. Recently, Allan Cartter of the American Council on Education, surveying the status of the subject in the United States, wrote: "There are currently a number of centers where economists are engaged in research into various aspects of the economics of education: Schultz and Bowman at Chicago; Weisbrod and Hansen at Wisconsin; Bowen and Machlup at Princeton; Fein and Rivlin at Brookings; Hirsch and others at UCLA; Becker at Columbia; Harris at San Diego; and others too numerous to mention. In the four short years since Schultz's presidential address at the American Economic Association Meeting in St. Louis (see below 108), the economics of education has become a popular enough subject to run the danger now of becoming fashionable."* Indeed, the fashion has crossed the Atlantic and spread throughout Europe and the underdeveloped world of Africa and Asia. In this country, there is a large research unit at the London School of Economics, headed by C. A. Moser, and a smaller one at the University of London Institute of Education, headed by myself, investigating the economic and statistical aspects of British and overseas education; there is Vaizey's work at the Acton Society Trust and the valuable contributions of research organisations like Political and Economic Planning and the Overseas Development Institute. Paris has now become the veritable capital of the world of educational planning, with UNESCO, OECD, and the new International Institute of Economic Planning pouring forth a ceaseless flow of literature, complemented by the works of Debeauvais and Lê Thành Khôi at the *Institut d'étude du développement économique et social,* that of Piatier and Eicher at the *Centre de recherches sur l'économie de l'éducation,* and that of Fourastié and Vimont at the *Institut national d'études demographiques.* Hellmut Becker has put Western Germany on the map with the mammoth *Institut für Bildungsforschung in der Max-Planck Gesellscaft,* where Edding heads a department of economic research. We could mention Bombach at the *Institut für angewandte Wirtschaftsforschung* at the University of Basle, Tinbergen at The Netherlands Economic Institute of Rotterdam, Oteiza at the Economic Research Centre of the *Instituto Torcuato Di Tella,* Buenos Aires, and regional research centres like ILO in Geneva, the East African Institute of Social Research in Uganda, the ECLA Institute for Economic and Social Planning, Santiago de Chile, and the Institute of Applied Manpower Research, New Delhi, but enough has been said to indicate the extraordinary flowering of interest in the economics of education in recent years around the world.

The following bibliogrpahy is largely confined to published literature (in English, French, and German) with the exception of certain mimeographed papers which can be obtained from various international agencies and institutions on request. A chronological rather than an alphabetical listing is adopted in order to demonstrate the development of the subject over the years. There is an alphabetical index of authors for easy reference. It will be apparent that the literature has been growing at an accelerated rate since 1960. As new material is continuously appearing, it is our intention to keep the bibliography up to date by further editions. Indeed, the present one is a very much enlarged edition of an earlier version, circulated in 1964.

A number of recognised experts in the economics of education offered suggestions for items to be included in the bibliography. I especially wish to thank C. A. Anderson, G. S. Becker, M. J. Bowman, C. F. Carter, A. Curle, M. Debeauvais, Mrs. J. Floud, F. H. Harbison, J. Miner, T. W. Schultz, G. Skorov, A. C. R. Wheeler and G. L. Williams for their helpful comments and advice.

*AER, May, 1965, p. 485. If the names mentioned here are unfamiliar to the reader, the bibliography will be useful to him.

PREFACE TO THE SECOND EDITION

The first edition of this bibliography, published in 1966, promised further instalments. The present edition is the first fulfilment of this promise: it brings the literature up to date (July 1969). The fact that the present version contains 1350 items as against some 800 items in the first edition is sufficient testimony to the growth rate of the subject.

This bibliography has been a one-man effort from the start, which accounts for almost all of its limitations. I would like to express my gratitude, however, to Miss. M. A. Woodhall, who has repeatedly brought items to my attention that I would otherwise have missed. If any readers would like to point out other omissions, or commissions, I would appreciate hearing from them.

University of London   MARK BLAUG
Institute of Education

PREFACE TO THE THIRD EDITION

Keeping a bibliography up to date is like smoking cigarettes: once you have started, it is very hard to stop. I like reading and I like making notes on what I
read - that is how this bibliography began. Once having begun, it costs me little
to keep it up. However, the job of classifying the books and articles under different headings for the purposes of readers other than myself has become increasingly onerous with time. The economics of education has come a long way since its
"birth" in the early 1960s and now seems to be bursting its former boundaries.
Some of its traditional concerns, such as the battle between the manpower-requirements approach and rate-of-return analysis, have practically faded away and entirely
new topics, such as earnings functions, screening hypotheses, and educational production functions, have appeared on the horizon. The classificatory scheme I
adopted in the first edition of 1966 seems increasingly inappropriate for the
literature of the last few years. Nevertheless, I have retained the original headings if only to stress certain continuities in the development of the subject. I
dare say that another bibliographer might classify the same material in a totally
different way. My only defence is habit-of-mind and the conviction that all classifications are arbitrary.
 The present edition carries the reader through to September, 1975. It contains
roughly 1,940 items, as against 1,350 in the second edition (1970) and 800 in the
first edition (1966). Lest some readers conclude that the annual growth rate of
the subject is declining, let me point out that I have become more selective as the
years have gone by. In recent years, in particular, it has become increasingly
difficult to decide what constitutes labour economics as distinct from the economics
of education, or international trade theory as distinct from the theory of human
capital, or the sociology and psychology of education as distinct from the economist's investigation of input-output relationships in schools. The economics of
education is threatening to become an approach rather than a branch of economics.
Far from deploring this tendency, I hope that it may in time render unnecessary
bibliographies such as this one.

University of London   MARK BLAUG
Institute of Education

ABBREVIATIONS

AAAPS	*Annals of the American Academy of Political and Social Science*
ABR	*Accounting and Business Research*
AE	*Applied Economics*
AER	*American Economic Review*
AF	*Africa*
AJER	*Alberta Journal of Educational Research*
AJES	*American Journal of Economics and Sociology*
AJPH	*American Journal of Public Health*
AJS	*American Journal of Sociology*
AS	*Advancement of Science*
ASR	*American Sociological Review*
BILD	*Bildungsplanung: Ansätze, Modelle, Probleme Ausgewählte Beiträge*, eds. K. Hufner, J. Naumann. Stuttgart: Ernst Klett Verlag, 1971.
BILS	*Bulletin of the International Institute for Labour Studies*
BJES	*British Journal of Educational Studies*
BJIR	*British Journal of Industrial Relations*
BJS	*British Journal of Sociology*
BOUIES	*Bulletin of the Oxford University Institute of Economics and Statistics*
CATER	*Catholic Educational Review*
CER	*Comparative Education Review*
CERD	*Canadian Education and Research Digest*
CESO	*Centre for the Study of Education in Changing Societies, The Hague*
CJE	*Canadian Journal of Economics*
CJEPS	*Canadian Journal of Economics and Political Science*
CLR	*California Law Review*
CON	*Consommation*
CRAC	*The Journal of the Careers Research and Advisory Centre*
CS	*Current Sociology*
CSSH	*Comparative Studies in Society and History*
CST	*Caribbean Studies*
DBR	*District Bank Review*
EAER	*East African Economic Review*
EAMJ	*East AFrican Medical Journal*
EC	*Economica*
ECOM	*Econometrica*
ECON	*De Economist*
EDCC	*Economic Development and Cultural Change*
EEA	*Explorations in Entrepreneurial History*
EES	*Education, Economy and Society*, eds. A. H. Halsey, J. Floud, C. A. Anderson. Glencoe, Ill.: Free Press, 1961.
EHE	*Economics of Higher Education*, ed. S. J. Mushkin. Washington, D.C.: Government Printing Office, 1962.
EHR	*Economic History Review*
EJ	*Economic Journal*
ENC	*Encounter*

ENHR	*English Historical Review*
ER	*Economic Record*
ERV	*Educational Review*
ESQ	*Economic Studies Quarterly*
ESR	*Economic and Social Review*
ET	*Ekonomisk Tidskrift*
ETR	*Economic Trends*
FAE	*Fundamental and Adult Education*
GER	*German Economic Review*
HBR	*Harvard Business Review*
HE	*Higher Education*
HEB	*Higher Education Bulletin*
HER	*Harvard Educational Review*
HIR	*Higher Education Review*
HR	*Human Relations*
IA	*International Affairs*
IAU	*International Association of Universities*
IDER	*Indian Educational Review*
IDR	*Indian Economic Review*
IEA-EE	*Economics of Education. International Economic Association Conference,* eds. E. A. G. Robinson, J. Vaizey. London: Macmillan, 1966.
IEJ	*Indian Economic Journal*
IER	*International Economic Review*
IJE	*Irish Journal of Education*
IJES	*International Journal of Educational Sciences*
IJSE	*International Journal of Social Economics*
ILR	*International Labour Review*
ILRR	*Industry and Labour Relations Review*
INDR	*International Development Review*
IR	*Industrial Relations*
IRE	*International Review of Education*
IRJ	*Industrial Relations Journal*
ISSJ	*International Social Science Journal*
IUEB	*Indiana University School of Education Bulletin*
JASA	*Journal of the American Statistical Association*
JB	*Journal of Business*
JDE	*Journal of Development Economics*
JDS	*Journal of Development Studies*
JEH	*Journal of Economic History*
JEI	*Journal of Economic Issues*
JEL	*Journal of Economic Literature*
JEP	*Journal of Educational Psychology*
JES	*Journal of Educational Sociology*
JFE	*Journal of Farm Economics*
JGE	*Journal of General Education*
JHE	*Journal of Higher Education*
JHR	*Journal of Human Resources*
JIA	*Journal of International Affairs*
JLE	*Journal of Law and Economics*
JMAS	*Journal of Modern African Studies*
JMF	*Journal of Marriage and the Family*
JMSS	*Journal of the Manchester Statistical Society*
JPBE	*Journal of Public Economics*
JPE	*Journal of Political Economy*
JRSS	*Journal of the Royal Statistical Society*
JSP	*Journal of Social Psychology*
KIK	*Investment in Human Capital,* ed. B. F. Kiker. Columbia, South Carolina: University of South Carolina Press, 1971.

KON	*Konjunkturpolitik*
KYK	*Kyklos*
LBR	*Lloyds Bank Review*
MAS	*Modern Asian Studies*
MER	*Malayan Economic Review*
MET	*Metroeconomica*
MIN	*Minerva*
MJ	*Manpower Journal*
MLR	*Monthly Labor Review*
MS	*The Manchester School*
NJES	*Nigerian Journal of Economic and Social Studies*
NS	*New Society*
NTJ	*National Tax Journal*
NZJE	*New Zealand Journal of Educational Studies*
ODU	*ODU-Journal of African Studies*
OECD–EAHE	*Economic Aspects of Higher Education,* ed. S. E. Harris. Paris: OECD, 1964.
OECD–EGIE	*Policy Conference on Economic Growth and Investment in Education, I: Summary Reports and Conclusions, II: Targets for Education in Europe in 1970, III: The Challenge of Aid to Newly Developing Countries, IV: The Planning of Education in Relation to Economic Growth, V: International Flows of Students.* Paris: OECD, 1962.
OECD–RF	*The Residual Factor and Economic Growth,* ed. J. Vaizey. Paris: OECD, 1964.
OEP	*Oxford Economic Papers*
OP	*Occupational Psychology*
ORE	*Oxford Review of Education*
ORQ	*Operational Research Quarterly*
PA	*Pacific Affairs*
PC	*Problems of Communism*
PDK	*Phi Delta Kappa*
PDR	*Pakistan Development Review*
PEE	*Perspectives on the Economics of Education. Readings in School Finance and Management,* ed. C. S. Benson. Boston: Houghton Mifflin, 1963.
P–EED	*Penguin Modern Economics: Economics of Education, 1, 2,* ed. M. Blaug. London: Penguin Books, 1968, 1969.
PEJ	*Philippine Economic Journal*
PEP	*Political and Economic Planning*
PF	*Public Finance*
PMR	*Productivity Measurement Review*
POP	*Population*
QBFE	*Quarterly Bulletin of Fundamental Education*
QJE	*Quarterly Journal of Economics*
QRAE	*Quarterly Review of Australian Education*
RE	*Revue économique*
REP	*Revue d'économie politique*
RER	*Review of Educational Research*
RES	*Review of Economics and Statistics*
REST	*Review of Economic Studies*
RFP	*Revue Francaise de Pedagogue*
RIW	*Review of Income and Wealth*
RLMA	*Readings in Labor Market Analysis,* eds. J. F. Burton, Jr., L. K. Benham, W. M. Vaughan III. New York: Holt, Rinehart and Winston, 1971.
RRPE	*Review of Radical Political Economics*
SAJE	*South African Journal of Economics*
SE	*Sociology of Education*
SEA	*Social and Economic Administration*
SEJ	*Southern Economic Journal*
SEP	*Socio-Economic Planning Sciences*

SES	*Social and Economic Studies*
SJPE	*Scottish Journal of Political Economy*
SM	*School Management*
SOR	*Sociological Review*
SOV	*Soviet Education*
SPE	*Scientia Paedogogica Experimentalies*
SPS	*Socio-Economic Planning Sciences*
SR	*School Review*
SRM	*Sociological Review Monographs*
SS	*Soviet Studies*
SSR	*Social Service Review*
SWJ	*Swedish Economic Journal*
SZNA	*Schweizerische Zeitschrift für Nachwuchs und Ausbildung*
SZVS	*Schweizerische Zeitschrift für Volkswirtschaft und Statistik*
TAU	*The Australian University*
TBR	*The Three Banks Review*
TCR	*The Centennial Review*
TER	*The Educational Record*
TES	*Times Educational Supplement*
TIP	*Theory into Practice*
TM	*Tiers-Monde. Problèmes des Pays Sous-Développés*
UNESCO-REED	*Readings in the Economics of Education*, eds. M. J. Bowman *et al.* Paris: UNESCO, 1968.
UQ	*Universities Quarterly*
UR	*Urban Review*
URB	*Educational Investment in an Urban Society. Costs, Benefits and Public Policy*, eds. M. R. Levin, A. Shank. New York: Teachers College Press, 1970.
WA	*Weltwirtschaftliches Archiv*
WAJE	*West AFrican Journal of Education*
WD	*World Development*
WEJ	*Western Economic Journal*
WYK-I	*Human Capital Formation and Manpower Development*, ed. R. A. Wykstra. New York: The Free Press, 1971.
WYK-II	*Education and the Economics of Human Capital*, ed. R. A. Wykstra. New York: The Free Press, 1971.
YBESR	*Yorkshire Bulletin of Economic and Social Research*
YEE	*Yale Economic Essays*
ZAK	*Konjunkturpolik, Zeitschrift für angewandte Konjunkturforschung*
ZGS	*Zeitschrift für die gesamte Staatswissenschaft*

A: DEVELOPED COUNTRIES
1. GENERAL SURVEYS

In the second edition of this bibliography (1970), I expressed the view that "the economics of education still lacks a satisfactory introductory textbook for students". Either textbook writers heard my complaint, or else all great minds think alike: in the last five years, as many as eleven different textbooks in the economics of education have appeared on the scene, which together with seven books already in the field in 1970, give students and teachers considerable scope for choice. For those with little economics, it is hard to beat Benson[11] and Rogers and Richlin[20] for American readers, O'Donoghue[19] and Woodhall and Ward[25] for British readers, Freund[13] for German readers, and Hallak[34] for French ones. Schultz[22,114], Perlman[28], Vaizey[27] and Sheehan[30] are perfectly accessible to those with elementary economics. Blaug[15], Thurow[17] and Cohn[23] require a little more than mere acquaintance with elementary economic principles. There is no dearth of spendid survey articles to complement these textbooks, such as Bowman[7,8,14,16,21,32,35,154], Schultz[108,294], Bowen[169], Miller[122], and Rivlin[745]. In addition, there are thirteen anthologies of classic articles (see Abbreviations above), which provide still further sources of readings to supplement a textbook. Lastly, there are now some good and bad Marxist and radical critiques of the subject, such as Gintis[24], Westoby[26], Bowles and Gintis[401], and Carnoy[1278], which can serve as antidotes to the "hidden curriculum".

1961

1 C. S. BENSON, *The Economics of Public Education*. New York: Houghton Mifflin, 1961. Pp. 580.

   This trail-blazing textbook goes beyond the usual treatment of school finance as a branch of school administration, and attempts explicit use of economic reasoning in analysing school expenditures. No prior knowledge of economics is assumed and virtually every aspect of American education is covered: problems of federal, state and local finance; the case for public education; the problem of efficiency in education; trends in teachers' salaries; and the impact of inflation on educational spending. See the book review by F. Shaw, *AER*, December, 1962, pp. 1215-16. (See also 11.)

1962

2   J. VAIZEY, *The Economics of Education*.   London: Faber & Faber, 1962. Pp. 165.

    A brief book, written in a conversational style, which covers almost every
    aspect of the subject. The first chapter on "What Some Economists Said About
    Education" and the third chapter on "The Returns to Education" are reprinted
    in *UNESCO-REED*, pp. 50-56, 592-601 and *URB*, pp. 137-47. Ch. 2 discusses whether
    education is investment or consumption, dealing at the same time with the ques-
    tion of private versus public education. Ch. 4 looks at patterns of national
    expenditures on education. Ch. 5 considers educational finance. Ch. 6 treats
    the productivity or efficiency of education, conceived as an industry. Ch. 7,
    perhaps the best chapter in the book, analyses manpower problems. Ch. 8 deals
    with trends in teachers' salaries. Ch. 9 is concerned with the "pool of
    ability". The last two chapters take up the question of education in under-
    developed countries. A select bibliography is included. See the book review
    by W. G. Bowen, *AER*, September, 1963, pp. 832-35.

3   J. VAIZEY, "The Present State of the Economics of Education", *ISSJ*, XIV, 4,
    1962, pp. 619-33, reprinted in J. Vaizey, *The Control of Education*. London:
    Faber & Faber, 1963, pp. 17-35.

    A brief review of the subject with some pessimistic remarks about the value
    of rate-of-return analysis.

1963

4   H. CORREA, *The Economics of Human Resources*.   Amsterdam: North-Holland Pub-
    lishing Co., 1963. Pp. 262.

    A book which purports to present an integrated treatment of the economics of
    education and health, but in fact covers only part of the field. The most ori-
    ginal part of the book is the penultimate chapter which develops a Harrod-
    Domar-type growth model with specific educational coefficients; the resulting
    system proves to be mathematically insoluble. (See 1736, 1778, 1779 for sub-
    sequent developments of this model.) See the book review by S. J. Hunt, *AER*,
    December, 1964, pp. 1187-89.

5   F. EDDING, *Ökonomie des Bildungswesens. Lehren und Lernen als Haushalt und als
    Investition*. Freiburg: Verlag Rombach, 1963. Pp. 440

    A collection of papers, some of which have never been put in print before,
    and excerpts from various books by the author (see 418, 436, 438, 859, 867)
    which together cover the entire range of subject matter in the economics of
    education. The work includes an excellent bibliography.

1965

6   J. VAIZEY, "Towards a New Political Economy? Or Some Problems of Some Aspects
    of Economics in the Light of 'Human Resource' Concepts", *OECD–RF*, pp. 201-13.

       A wide-ranging re-examination of some of the leading themes of the economics
    of education by an author who now cites himself as having long denied the
    importance of education for economic growth. See the critical comments on this
    paper by J. W. Kendrick and H. G. Johnson, *ibid.*, pp. 213-19, 225-28.

1966

7   M. J. BOWMAN, "The New Economics of Education", *IJES*, I, 1, 1966, pp. 29-46.

       In this first issue of a new journal, the author discusses the factors that
    have led to the emergence of the subject of the economics of education. After
    a brief analysis of the role of literacy in economic development, the bulk of
    the paper is then devoted to an excellent review of recent rate-of-return
    studies of educational investment.

8   M. J. BOWMAN, "The Human Investment Revolution in Economic Thought", *SE*, Spring,
    1966, pp. 111-37, reprinted in *P-EED*, 1, pp. 101-34.

       This review of the literature roams far and wide, covering earlier discus-
    sions of education in the history of economic thought, the burgeoning of edu-
    cational planning concepts since World War II, the increasing use of mathema-
    tical models in educational planning, and a variety of recent findings about
    the economic value of education.

9   C. S. BENSON, *The School and the Economic System*. The Foundations of Education
    Series. Chicago, Ill.: Science Research Associates, 1966. Pp. 117.

       This is a capsule up-to-date version of the author's larger work (see 1).
    The first 60 pages are a straightforward exposition of elementary economics,
    followed by "a review of the economists' latest discoveries about the schools",
    that is, Schultz, Becker, Machlup, Denison, and all that. The context through-
    out is that of American education.

1968

10 G. F. KNELLER, *Education and Economic Thought*. New York: John Wiley, 1968.
    Pp. 139.

       A popular exposition for teachers of the basic principles of economics, the
    history of economic thought, and the economics of education. In the effort to
    do too much, the author necessarily ends up doing it all rather superficially.

11 C. S. BENSON, *The Economics of Public Education*. Boston: Houghton Mifflin,
    2nd ed., 1968. Pp. 368.

    This is not just a new edition but a completely rewritten version, retaining
    only superficial resemblance to the first edition (see 1). New materials
    include chapters on educational planning and programme budgeting in education.
    The book remains an excellent source for statistics on American education, and
    the details of patterns of educational finance in the United States. It is
    primarily addressed, as was the first edition, to school administrators.

1969

12 R. L. JOHNS, E. L. MORPHET, *The Economics and Financing of Education. A
    Systems Approach*. Englewood Cliffs, N.J.: Prentice-Hall, 2nd ed., 1969.
    Pp. 580.

    A textbook addressed to teacher and administrators and focussed on the Ameri-
    can scene. Chapter 3, pp. 66-103, discusses the findings of economists on the
    economic benefits of education.

13 R. FREUND, *Bildungsplanung, Bildunginvestitionen, Bildungsertrag*. Wien:
    Jupiter-Verlag, 1969. Pp. 191.

    A fairly popular account of recent developments in the economics of educa-
    tion, with much more emphasis on German work than is customary in Anglo-
    American books of this kind.

14 M. J. BOWMAN, "Economics of Education", *RER*, 30, 5, Winter, 1969, pp. 641-70.

    A review of recent work in the economics of education, centering around
    measurement problems of the quality of labour, human investment decision theory
    and the application of multivariate analysis to identification problems involv-
    ing education as a crucial variable.

1970

15 M. BLAUG, *An Introduction to the Economics of Education*. London: The Penguin
    Press, 1970. Pp. 363.

    Enough said.

16 M. J. BOWMAN, "An Economist's Approach to Education", *IRE*, XVI, 2, 1970,
    pp. 160-76.

    A characteristically perceptive essay on the basic elements of the economics
    of education.

17 L. THUROW, *Investment in Human Capital*. Belmont, California: Wadsworth Publishing Co., 1970. Pp. 145.

   This book for its size has no competitors: it may be regarded as the first satisfactory elementary introduction to the subject. The context is exclusively American. One of the odd features of the book is the author's attitude to aggregate production functions as against his views on rate-of-return analysis: the assumptions, limitations and strengths of the latter are carefully set out but measurements of aggregate production functions are treated as if they were unproblematic.

1971

18 W. L. PETERSON, *Principles of Economics Micro*. Homewood, Ill.: Richard D. Irwin, 1971, pp.215-36.

   A special chapter on the economics of education marks an innovation in the writing of elementary textbooks in economics.

19 M. O'DONOGHUE, *Economic Dimensions in Education*. Dublin: Gill and Macmillan, 1971. Pp. 223.

   A well argued and lucidly written textbook which assumes no previous knowledge of economics and does justice to all the contending views in the field. Published in 1971, it seems to have been written in 1968, which dates it slightly. Apart from this drawback, it is perfect reading for British A-level and undergraduate courses. An unusual feature of the book is an extended chapter on brain drain, reviewing the contributions of Grubel, Scott, Weisbrod and Thomas (see 1133, 1140).

20 D. C. ROGERS, H. S. RICHLIN, *Economics and Education*. *Principles and Applications*. New York: The Free Press, 1971. Pp. 404.

   This is a book like that of Benson's (see 1): it is addressed to students in education and both teaches economics and illustrates some of its applications. Twelve papers are reprinted at various points in the argument, namely, Campbell and Siegel (see 782); Cartter (see 607); Burns and Chiswick (see 524); Woodhall and Blaug (see 600); Levin (see 633); Riew (see 460); Lee Hansen (see 164); Friedman (see 1256); D. A. Page, "Retraining Under the Manpower Development Act: A Cost-Benefit Analysis", reprinted from *Public Policy*, 1964; parts of Denison (see 62); The University of the State of New York, *The Regents Statewide Plan for the Expansion and Development of Higher Education, 1964*; and Republic of Tanzania, *Tanzania Second Five-Year Plan for Economic and Social Development, 1969-1974*.

21 M. J. BOWMAN, "Economics of Education", *RER*, December, 1971.

   Another survey paper, which moves from (1) Schultz-Denison-Becker-and-all-that to (2) simultaneous equation estimates of the income-education relationship, (3) "work of staff and students at the Comparative Education Center of

the University of Chicago", and (4) papers by Welch. It is a story without
much thread but it is interesting nevertheless.

1972

22 T. W. SCHULTZ, *Human Resources*. Economic Research: Retrospect and Prospect.
    Fiftieth Anniversary Colloquium VI of the National Bureau of Economic Research.
    New York: Columbia University Press, 1972. Pp. 97.

      The author's central aim is to assess achievements to date in the field of
    human capital and to predict future research developments. In consequence, he
    provides an excellent summary of recent work, confining himself entirely to
    American applications but ranging far and wide over published and unpublished
    material. It is difficult to think of a better summary of the outstanding
    strengths and weaknesses of human capital theory as it now stands. The book
    includes a lengthy bibliography and brief comments by A. M. Rivlin and G. G.
    Somers, who disagree about the actual impact of research in human capital on
    American manpower and educational policies.

23 E. COHN, *The Economics of Education*. Lexington, Mass.: D. C. Heath & Co.,
    1972. Pp. 392.

      An undergraduate textbook, American in style and outlook. It suffers perhaps
    from a tendency to reduce the subject to a series of case studies, at the cost
    of developing general principles, but its thorough coverage of the literature
    makes it a valuable addition to other available texts. Particularly noteworthy
    are chs. 5 and 7, which present preçis of a large number of rate-of-return
    studies; ch. 8, which provides superb summaries of recent American work on
    educational production functions; ch. 10, which canvasses new ideas on educa-
    tional finance in the U.S.A., and ch. 11, which deals with econometric and
    paediometric models of educational systems.

24 H. GINTIS, "A Radical Analysis of Welfare Economics and Individual Development",
    QJE, November, 1972, pp. 572-99; "Comment" by T. Parsons with "Reply" by
    Gintis, *ibid.*, May, 1975, pp. 280-302.

      A Marxist attack on neoclassical welfare economics, based on the idea that
    consumer's preferences are socially determined and that education is itself a
    major determinant of these preferences. Parson's comments and Gintis' reply
    take up the question of the multiple functions of higher education.

25 M. WOODHALL, V. WARD, *Economic Aspects of Education*. *A Review of Research in
    Britain*. London: N.F.E.R., 1972. Pp. 127.

      Under headings such as costs and expenditure, cost-benefit analysis, the
    demand for educated manpower, educational planning, the productivity of educa-
    tion, and sources of finance, this booklet provides an excellent review of
    British research in the economics of education for the tyro. Includes a brief,
    selected bibliography of American research.

26 A WESTOBY, "The 'Economics of Education'", *Counter Course. A Handbook for Course Criticism,* ed. T. Pateman, London, Penguin Books, 1972, pp. 182-86.

A brief critique from the standpoint of the New Left. Concentrates largely on private rate-of-return calculations as a manifestation of the general bourgeois tendency to reduce the whole of life to the cash nexus. For a slightly expanded version, adding a few pages on Marxism in words cribbed directly from Marx (as if they were transparently obvious), see his "Economists and 'Human Capital'", *Education or Domination,* ed. D. Holly. London: Arrow Books, 1974.

27 J. VAIZEY, K. NORRIS, J. SHEEHAN, *The Political Economy of Education.* London: Gerald Duckworth & Co., 1972. Pp. 297.

The preface claims that this is "a new book, with added matter, entirely rearranged," but it is only fair to point out that it is in fact identical to three paperbacks published several years ago (see the review by M. Blaug, *EJ,* March, 1973, pp. 341-4. See also 459.) It consists of 22 chapters that fall neatly into six parts: first, a series of analytical essays which examine the theory of human capital from the standpoint of the so-called Cambridge view of capital; second, some chapters that comment on the manpower forecasting approach to educational planning; third, a group of factual chapters on international trends in educational expenditures; fourth, a set of chapters that discuss and illustrate various methods of projecting the costs of education, fifth, two theoretical chapters on measuring the productivity of educational systems, supplemented by two empirical chapters that look at particular aspects of measuring educational inputs; and sixth and last, two chapters that report new work on the demand and supply of teachers in several European countries. In short, what we have here is neither a textbook nor a research monograph, but a collection of essays that falls somewhere in between.

1973

28 R. PERLMAN, *The Economics of Education. Conceptual Problems and Policy Issues.* New York: McGraw-Hill, 1973. Pp. 151.

An introductory text, geared to the American market, which emphasizes the strengths and weaknesses of rate-of-return analysis. The last half of the book is devoted to policy issues, particularly the property tax controversy, the debate on educational vouchers, and the issue of loans and grants for students in higher education.

29 J. VAIZEY, *The Economics of Education.* London: Macmillan, 1973. Pp. 64.

A rapid tour through the subject (in 53 pages) which holds no surprises for those acquainted with the author's many books on the economics of education.

30 J. SHEEHAN, *The Economics of Education.* London: Allen & Unwin, 1973. Pp. 140.

A thoroughly competent and lucid introduction to the field, easier than Blaug, Cohn, Schultz, Thurow and Vaizey, but slightly more demanding than Perlman and O'Donoghue.

31   J. VAIZEY, "Education, Economics Of", *Encyclopaedia Brittanica*, Fifteenth
     Edition. Chicago: Helen Hemingway Benton, 1974, *Macropaedia*, VI, pp. 310-16.

     A balanced, non-technical survey of the subject.

1974

32   M. J. BOWMAN, "Learning and Earning in the Postschool Years", *Review of
     Research in Education*, eds. F. N. Kerlinger, J. B. Carroll. Itasca, Illinois:
     F. E. Peacock Inc., 1974, Vol. 2, pp. 202-44.

     Another superb literature review by an author whose articles over the years
     constitute something like a running commentary on current research efforts in
     the field.

33   J. BURKHEAD, J. MINER, "The Economics of Education in British Perspective -
     A Review Article", *JHR*, Summer, 1974, pp. 390-98.

     A contemptuous dismissal of Blaug's textbook (see 15) as "narrowly neo-
     classical" and Vaizey's recent compendium (see 27) as "useful" but "badly
     mistitled". It is time, the authors conclude, for someone to attempt "the
     Great Synthesis of the economics of education". Perhaps Burkhead and Miner?

34   J. HALLAK, *A qui profite l'école* - Paris: Presses Universitaires de France,
     1974. Pp. 261.

     This book does for France in the 1970s what John Vaizey's *Economics of
     Education* did for Britain in the 1960s: to bring to the general reader a
     flavour of what has been going on in the economics of education, set in the
     context of current policy concerns at home and abroad. This is high-grade
     journalism and judged as such it is highly effective. For the specialist,
     the fascination of a book like this is to see who and what is included, and
     in what order (e.g., the extraordinary observation that the theory of human
     capital has never been systematically presented anywhere, p. 44; the assertion
     that the Bowles intergeneration model neatly solves the nature vs. nurture
     debate, p. 109; etcetera).

1975

35   M. J. BOWMAN, "Education and Opportunity: Some Economic Perspectives", *ORE*,
     I, 1, 1975, pp. 73-84.

     A literature review of recent work on the schooling-ability relationship as
     well as Hansen-Weisbrod-type studies of the finance of higher education (see
     525,528, 529).

36 A. ZIDERMAN, "The Economics of Educational Policy", *Current Issues in Economic Policy*, eds. R. M. Grant, G. K. Shaw. Oxford: Philip Allan, 1975, pp. 129-50.

A splendid introduction to the subject in the context of British educational debates.

2. THE ECONOMIC CONTRIBUTION OF EDUCATION

(a) *Earlier Views*

The economics of education is a relatively new subject with a very old history: economists have been writing on education ever since economics became a self-conscious scientific discipline. For example, the idea that the provision of education is a method of accumulating human capital goes back to the seventeenth century, as Johnson[48], Walsh[132], and Kiker[58] show. The classical period of English political economy was rich in discussion of educational issues, from Adam Smith down to John Stuart Mill. Just what the classical economists believed about education, however, is not immediately self-evident from reading them, and the interested student will find a marked contrast between the fairly standard presentation of Vaizey[2], Baumol[46], and Blitz[47], the revolutionary reinterpretation of West[49,50], [1345], and the somewhat equivocal version of Hollander[56]. Blaug[60] attempts to resolve these differences in interpretation.

The neo-classical period is even more controversial: see e.g. Blandy[55] and Kiker[57] on Marshall, and Tu[59] on such writers as Sidgwick and Pigou. Despite Marshall's brilliant discussion of the economics of industrial training[39], and Nicholson's estimate of the stock of human capital in the United Kingdom[40], the entire subject was sadly neglected in the decades before World War I, as well as in the interwar years; in this connection, Clark[42] supplies ample evidence. Socialist writers, however, never lost sight of the social if not the economic role of education: witness Tawney's famous Hobhouse Memorial Lecture of 1938[44], and the more recent views of British socialists[419].

1841

37 H. MANN, *Fifth Annual Report, Covering the Year 1841*. Washington, D.C.: National Education Association, facsimile ed., 1949, pp. 81-120.

With astonishing prescience, the secretary of the Board of Education of the State of Massachusetts proceeds in the last section of this report to demonstrate "the difference in the productive ability - where natural capacities have been equal - between the educated and the uneducated". He reproduces a number of letters from businessmen, testifying to the superior productivity of educated over uneducated workers in similar occupations, and, in addition, touches on most of the now familiar "indirect benefits" of education. See also his *Twelfth Annual Report Covering the Year 1848* (facsimile ed., 1952), "Intellectual Education as a Means of Removing Poverty, and Securing Abundance", pp. 53-76.

1875

38 H. von THÜNEN, *Der Isolierte Staat*.   Rostock: 3rd ed., 1875, II, pp. 140-52,
    reprinted in English translation in *UNESCO-REED*, pp. 391-96.

    A remarkable early discussion of human capital valuations in connection with
    the economic cost of war.

1890

39 A. MARSHALL, *The Principles of Economics*.   London: Macmillan, 9th ed., 1961,
    Bk. IV, ch. 6, pp. 204-19; Bk. VI, ch. 4, pp. 563-66; Mathematical Note XXIV,
    p. 858, excerpts reprinted in *UNESCO-REED*, pp. 609-12.

    A famous discussion of industrial training in which Marshall argues that
    education may be regarded as a national investment

1891

40 J. S. NICHOLSON, "The Living Capital of the United Kingdom", *EJ*, March, 1891,
    pp. 95-107, reprinted in *UNESCO-REED*, pp. 227-34.

    In this path-breaking article, Nicholson revives Petty's method of valuing
    human capital, arriving at a figure that is five times the value of physical
    capital, and concludes with a plea for further study of the implications of
    this fact.

1908

41 F. T. CARLTON, *Economic Influences upon Educational Progress in the U.S.,
    1820-1850* (1908), reprinted in *Classics in Education, No. 27*.   New York:
    Teachers College Press, Teachers College, Columbia University, 1965. Pp. 165.

    An early history of American education which emphasises the influence of the
    economy on the development of the American public school system, including a
    brief comparison of English and American education in the nineteenth century.

1928

42 H. F. CLARK, "The Economic Effects of Education as Shown by the Statements of
    Economists", *IUEB*, May, 1928, pp. 1-40.

    A collection of quotations from about 60 economists, which shows the lack
    of serious attention to the economics of education by most writers of this
    period (approx. 1875-1920).

1932

43 A. G. B. FISHER, "Education and Relative Wage Rates", *ILR*, June, 1932,
    pp. 743-64.

    An early effort to draw attention to the importance of education as a factor
    in income distribution, particularly in narrowing the margin between skilled
    and unskilled workers since World War I.

1938

44 R. H. TAWNEY, *Some Thoughts on the Economics of Public Education*. L. T.
    Hobhouse Memorial Trust Lectures, No. 8. London: Oxford University Press,
    1938. Pp. 45.

    In this remarkable pamphlet, Tawney advocates expansion of education on the
    grounds that, among other things, education is a way of "investing in human
    beings". Fifteen years before economists turned their attention to what he
    calls "that repulsive hybrid", the economics of education, Tawney grasped most
    of the issues: "Since, in short, economic considerations necessarily carry
    weight, it is important to form some idea, at least, of what they weigh"; "the
    benefit of education to the boys and girls concerned is weighed against the
    loss to employers of their services as errand-boys or little piecers, and to
    parents of their earnings"; England must learn "to depend less on cheap coal
    and more on trained intelligence".

1940

45 Educational Policies Commission, National Education Association of the USA,
    Educational and Economic Well-Being in American Democracy. Washington, D.C.;
    NEA, 1940. Pp. 227.

    An omnibus of socio-economic arguments in favour of more education, addressed
    to the interested layman.

1952

46 W. J. BAUMOL, *Welfare Economics and the Theory of the State*. London: Longmans,
    1952, ch. 12, pp. 140-57.

    This chapter demonstrates the ancient lineage of an economic theory of
    government action based on the distinction between private and public benefits.
    A number of classical economists (Smith, Storch, Say, McCulloch, Mill, Sidge-
    wick, etc.) so defended the provision of education by the State. See also
    L. Robbins, *The Theory of Economic Policy in English Classical Political
    Economy* (London: Macmillan, 1952), pp. 89-93.

1961

47 R. C. BLITZ, "Some Classical Economists and Their Views on the Economics of
    Education", *Economia*, 72-73, 1961, pp. 34-60, excerpts reprinted in *UNESCO-
    REED*, pp. 37-48.

The best general account we have of the economic analysis of education in classical political economy.

1964

48 E. A. J. JOHNSON, "The Place of Learning, Science, Vocational Training and 'Art' in Pre-Smithian Economic Thought", *JEH*, June, 1964, pp. 116-45, reprinted in *UNESCO-REED*, pp. 25-34.

A new article based on the author's study of the *Predecessors of Adam Smith. The Growth of British Economic Thought* (New York: Prentice-Hall, 1937), i.e. Hales, Mun, Petty, King, Hume, Steuart, among others.

49 E. G. WEST, "The Role of Education in Nineteenth-Century Doctrines of Political Economy", *BJES*, May, 1964, pp. 161-73.

The author shows that, contrary to what is usually believed, most classical economists did not attribute direct economic value to education and, on the whole, favoured private rather than public schools. See also the author's "Adam Smith's Two Views on the Division of Labour", *EC*, February, 1964, pp. 23-32.

50 E. G. WEST, "Private versus Public Education: A Classical Economic Dispute", *JPE*, October, 1964, pp. 465-76, reprinted in *The Classical Economists and Public Policy*, ed. A. W. Coats. London: Methuen & Co., 1971, pp. 123-43.

In an elaboration of his earlier article, the author shows that Senior, Mill, and Chadwick, in contradiction of what Adam Smith had taught, went over to "a new kind of educational paternalism" in advocating public education (See 56).

1966

51 K. HÜFNER, *The History of the Measurement of Human Capital*. Berlin: Institut für Bildungsforschung, 1966. Pp. 22, mimeographed.

A history of the concept of human capital, drawing attention to a number of German and French authors.

52 W. L. MILLER, "The Economics of Education in English Classical Economics", *SEJ*, January, 1966, pp. 294-310.

A schematic review of some leading questions posed by the classical economists: (1) education as human investment; (2) the economic objectives of education; (3) the effects of education on income distribution; (4) the scope cf government action in education; and (5) methods of increasing the efficiency of education.

53 B. F. KIKER, "The Historical Roots of the Concept of Human Capital", *JPE*, October, 1966, pp. 481-500, reprinted in *WYK I*, pp. 2-24, and *KIK*, pp. 51-78.

An excellent history of the concept, tracing it back to Petty in the eighteenth century (see also 58).

1967

54 E. G. WEST, "Tom Paine's Voucher Scheme for Public Education", *SEJ*, January, 1967, pp. 378-82.

   An interesting historical note which shows that the roots of Friedman's voucher scheme go back to Paine's *Rights of Man*.

55 R. BLANDY, "Marshall on Human Capital: A Note", *JPE*, December, 1967, pp. 874-75.

   A salutory dissent from the standard misrepresentation of Marshall's attitude to the concept of human capital.

1968

56 S. HOLLANDER, "The Role of the State in Vocational Training: The Classical Economists' View", *SEJ*, April, 1968, pp. 513-25.

   An important article which attempts to explain why the classical economists did not explicitly favour vocational training, although they advocated state support for elementary education. In the course of his argument, the author attacks West (50).

57 B. F. KIKER, "Marshall on Human Capital: Comment", *JPE*, September/October, 1968, pp. 1088-90.

   A defence of the view that Marshall abandoned the idea of human capital formation (see also 55).

58 B. F. KIKER, *Human Capital in Retrospect*. Columbia: University of South Carolina Bureau of Business and Economic Research, 1968. Pp. 142.

   An encyclopaedic account of the concept of human capital valuation in economic thought from the days of William Petty to about 1940. The relevant English, German and French (but not Italian) literature is covered in great detail under such headings as the money value of a man; the money value of a nation's stock of human capital; the loss of human capital from wars; the monetary value of migration; the costs and benefits of health maintenance, and the returns from investment in human capital. The volume lacks an index but the table of contents is more detailed than usual.

1969

59 P. N. V. TU, "The Classical Economists and Education", *KYK*, 1969, XXII, 2, pp. 691-717.

   A compendium of comments on education by Adam Smith and a dozen or so major nineteenth century British economists. The author claims that "qualitatively, they said, though often in general and non-technical language, everything that is to be said about the economics of education".

60 M. BLAUG, "The Economics of Education in English Classical Political Economy: A Re-Examination", *Essays on Adam Smith*, ed. A. F. Skinner, *Bicentenary Edition of the Works of Adam Smith*. Glasgow: Glasgow University Press, 1976, pp. 256-87.

  A re-assessment of both the primary and secondary literature, denying that the classical economists held a theory of human capital in any meaningful sense. A historical appendix examines the relationship between literacy and the Industrial Revolution.

(b) THE PRODUCTION-FUNCTION APPROACH

Of all the branches of the economics of education, this particular method of measuring the contribution of education to economic growth presents the most serious difficulties to the average student: it is quite impossible to understand what it is all about without a knowledge of marginal productivity theory and the concept of a Production Function. Therefore, before plunging into the literature, the reader is well advised to consult the chapter on the theory of production in one of the standard textbooks of economic theory, and, since the concept of a production function is a mathematical one, the relevant pages in a book like R. G. D. Allen, *Mathematical Analysis for Economists* (London: Macmillan, 1949), pp. 315-22. He should not go forward until he feels sure he has understood the properties of linearly homogeneous production functions in one of its simpler varieties, such as the so-called "Cobb-Douglas" function; M. Blaug, *Economic Theory in Retrospect* (London: Heinemann Educational Books, 1968), pp. 446-61, may be helpful here.

The locus classicus in this field is Denison[62]. Aukrust[61] gives a good review of the subject before Denison introduced education explicitly into an aggregate production-function model of the American economy. Earlier Soviet work by Strumilin[63],[130] is in the same direction, although not spelled out in similar formal terms. Denison's way is only one way of dealing with the education variable, as some of Griliches' papers[65],[69],[74] make evident; it has been criticised by Abramovitz[62], Nelson[67],[78],[100], Solow and Eckstein[873], and revised by Bowman[68], Schwartzman[82] and Layard[98], but remains, nevertheless, an impressive effort to quantify education as one of the many sources of growth in a modern economy. It has been applied by Bertram and others to Canada[72],[75], by Bowles to Greece[93], by De Wolff and Ruiter[243] to Holland, by Psacharopoulos to Hawaii[89], by Moreh to Britain[92], and by Selowsky[85] and Denison himself[73],[102] to comparative growth rates of different countries.

Bowles' use of the two-level CES production function to measure the elasticity of substitution between types of educated labour[81] has sparked off a series of attempts to test the manpower-requirement approach to educational planning, that is, the proposition that this elasticity approaches zero: see Dougherty[97], Psacharopoulos[99], Tinbergen[101], and Fallon and Layard[103].

1959

61 O. Aukrust, "Investment and Economic Growth", *PMR*, February, 1959, pp. 35-53; "Some Comments" by R. M. Solow, *ibid.*, November, 1959, pp. 62-68, reprinted in *UNESCO-REED*, pp. 190-204, 209-13, and in *KIK*, pp. 83-108.

  After examining the implications of the constant capital-output-ratio approach to economic growth, the author pleads for more attention to "the human factor", i.e. organisation, professional skills, and technical knowledge, illustrated with reference to an empirical study of Norway. Solow comments on the implications of Aukrust's remarks.

1962

62 E. F. DENISON, *The Sources of Economic Growth in the US and the Alternatives Before Us*. Committee for Economic Development, Supplementary Paper No. 13. New York: CED, 1962, ch. 7, pp. 67-80, reprinted in *PEE*, pp. 33-42.

An ambitious attempt to quantify the contribution of formal education to economic growth in the context of an aggregate production-function model of the US economy. It includes a notable attempt to estimate the growth effects of raising the school-leaving age by one year. See the valuable review article by M. Abramovitz in *AER*, September, 1962, particularly pp. 769-71, concluding that "Denison has probably not been successful in approximating the contribution made by the rise in the level of education to our past growth" on the grounds that he ignored the indirect public benefits. See also E. F. Denison, "Measuring the Contribution of Education to Economic Growth", *OECD-RF*, pp. 13-56, reprinted in *UNESCO-REED*, pp. 315-337, and *WYK I*, pp. 69-80, where the author defends some of his assumptions and applies a similar approach to a comparison between the USA, the UK, and Italy.

63 S. G. STRUMILIN, "The Economics of Education in the USSR", *ISSJ*, XIV, 4, 1962, pp. 633-46.

An explanation of Soviet methods of estimating the contribution of education, which, upon inspection, appears to be the familiar production-function approach travelling in disguise. (See also 130.)

1963

64 E. F. DENISON, "Proportion of Income Differentials Among Education Group 'due to' Additional Education: The Evidence of the Wolfle-Smith Survey", *OECD-RF*, pp. 86-100.

In this important addendum to *The Sources of Economic Growth*, Denison examines new evidence to justify his attribution of three-fifths of the income differentials among males of the same age to formal education. See also his spirited reply to critics in the same volume, pp. 77-86.

65 Z. GRILICHES, "The Sources of Measured Productivity Growth: US Agriculture, 1940-1960", *JPE*, August, 1963, pp. 331-47.

Discarding the traditional production-function approach, the author measures the change in total output by holding the production function constant and attributing the extra output to changes in the quantity and quality of inputs and to economies of scale. He finds that the rise in the educational levels of US farmers accounts for one-third of conventionally measured productivity increases over the last 20 years. See also the author's "Estimates of the Aggregate Agricultural Production Function from Cross-Sectional Data", *JFE*, May, 1963, pp. 419-28.

1964

66 L. J. WALDÉN, "Long Term Manpower Problems II: Research, Education and Economic Development", *ET*, June, 1964, pp. 113-60.

A Harrod–Domar growth model with various labour inputs distinguished by levels of education and various capital inputs distinguished by associated levels of research.

67 R. R. NELSON, "Aggregate Production Functions and Medium-range Growth Projections", *AER*, September, 1964, pp. 575-607.

An outstanding review and critique of growth models based on aggregate production functions, including recent efforts to embody improvements in the quality of capital and labour. The author concludes that "it is misleading to assume that the various factors resulting in the growth of total factor productivity are independent"; in particular, "it is a mistake to try to introduce into the production function variables such as average years of education without an explicit theory that shows *how* that variable should be entered (see also 100)".

68 M. J. BOWMAN, "Schultz, Denison, and the Contribution of 'Eds' to National Income Growth", *JPE*, October, 1964, pp. 450-65.

This important paper examines the bridge between the production-function approach and the rate-of-return approach to educational investment. The author criticises Schultz's estimate of the contribution of education to economic growth, based on multiplying the cost of education by an internal rate of return on investment in education. Schultz's and Denison's calculations are revised by allowing for additional factors ignored by both authors, indicating that about 18-19 per cent, and not 23 per cent as Denison claimed, of the national income growth rate can be credited to the increased education of the labour force. The paper concludes with a defence of aggregate production-function studies, noting, however, that "they do not provide the tools needed for analysis of critical questions concerning factor proportions and investment decisions in development processes".

69 Z. GRILICHES, "Research Expenditures, Education, and the Aggregate Agricultural Production Function", *AER*, December, 1964, pp. 961-75.

This paper extends the author's earlier measurement of an aggregate agricultural production function to cover the years 1954 and 1959. Once again, an educational variable is included in the function; furthermore, the level of public expenditures on agricultural research and extension is explicitly introduced as an additional variable. The findings are that both of these variables affect the level of agricultural output "significantly", the latter earning a gross social rate of return of about 300 per cent.

1965

70 G. H. HILDEBRAND, T. C. LIU, *Manufacturing Production Functions in the United States 1957: An Inter-industry and Interstate Comparison of Productivity.* Ithaca, New York: Cornell University Press, 1965. Pp. 224.

This book provides estimates of Cobb-Douglas-type production functions for 15 two-digit American manufacturing industries in 1957, with separate coefficients for production and nonproduction workers, the former corrected for labour quality improvements on the basis of school years completed by persons

25 years of age and over in each state in 1960. The authors compare the results of using such a "corrected" variable with uncorrected labour input variables and find that the corrected variable gives better results in seven of the fifteen industries.

1966

71 R. R. NELSON, E. S. PHELPS, "Investment in Humans, Technological Diffusion, and Economic Growth", *AER*, May, 1966, pp. 69-76, reprinted in *WYK I*, pp. 93-100.

A model of economic growth based on the assumption that education promotes growth, not by augmenting the productive capacity of the labour force, but by accelerating the rate at which entrepreneurs adopt the best-practice technology.

72 G. W. BERTRAM, *The Contribution of Education to Economic Growth*. Staff Study No. 12. Economic Council of Canada. Ottawa, Canada: Queen's Printer, 1966, Pp. 147.

An important study applying the Denison method of calculating the "sources of growth" to Canada. At various points, and especially in ch. 2, ingenious comparisons are made in levels of educational attainment between Canada and the United States. Among the technical appendices, B-7, B-8, and B-9 are particularly recommended.

1967

73 E. F. DENISON, *Why Growth Rates Differ: Postwar Experience in Nine Western Countries*. Washington, D.C.: The Brookings Institution, 1967. Pp. 494.

In this book, the author applies his aggregate production-function model to the growth rates of the United States and eight Western European countries. For our purposes, most relevant are ch. 8 and App. F, pp. 78-108, 373-403, on education as a factor in determining differential growth rates (see also the summary, ch. 15, pp. 187-200). For another summary of the book, see the author's "Sources of Post-war Growth in Nine Western Countries", *AER*, May, 1967, pp. 325-32.

74 D. W. JORGENSON, Z. GRILICHES, "The Explanation of Productivity Change", *REST*, XXXIV (3), No. 99, 1967, pp. 249-83.

This should be read as an extended commentary on Denison (62), augmenting both capital and labour for quality changes, so that total factor productivity explains only 3-4 per cent rather than 40-50 per cent of American economic growth (see, particularly, pp. 271-75).

75 N. H. LITHWICK, G. POST, T. K. RYMES, "Postwar Production Relationships in Canada", *The Theory and Empirical Analysis of Production*, ed. M. Brown. New York: Columbia University Press, 1967, pp. 139-257.

This study includes a Denison-type measurement of the contribution of education to Canadian economic growth for the period 1929-56, showing a much lower
figure than Denison calculated for the United States over the same period
(see Table 16, p. 195).

76 Z. GRILICHES, "Production Functions in Manufacturing: Some Preliminary
    Results", *ibid.*, pp. 275-322; "Comments" by R. G. Bodkin, J. Popkin, and
    others, and a "Reply" by Griliches, *ibid.*, pp. 322-40.

    Griliches' model treats education, in the manner of Denison, as a purely
    labour-augmenting factor (see pp. 311-13). Popkin's critique and Griliches'
    reply contain interesting comments on the relationship between occupation and
    education and their interaction effects on earnings.

77 M. BROWN, A. H. CONRAD, "The Influence of Research and Education on CES Pro-
    duction Relations", *ibid.*, pp. 341-72; "Comments" by N. E. Erleckyj, B. A.
    Weisbrod, and a "Reply" by Brown and Conrad, *ibid.*, pp. 372-94.

    The authors estimate a CES production function from pooled times series and
    cross-section data for a number of manufacturing firms in the United States
    during the 1950's. Education is taken to be labour-augmenting but is repre-
    sented by years of schooling embodied in the labour force, unweighted by
    earnings differentials (see pp. 352-53). The comments attack the principal
    finding, namely, that the marginal productivity of education and research was
    greater in the group of durables than in the group of industries producing
    nondurables.

78 R. R. NELSON, "Aggregative Production Functions and Economic Growth Policy",
    ibid., pp. 479-94.

    This paper considers the guidance for economic growth policy in the United
    States that is provided by present knowledge of aggregate production functions.
    The pages on education, pp. 482-84, present some doubts on the general treat-
    ment of education as a labour-augmenting factor around the theme of educational
    qualifications serving the employer as cheap discriminants of native intelli-
    gence and achievement drive.

79 R. L. RAIMON, V. STOIKOV, "The Quality of the Labor Force", *ILRR*, April, 1967,
    pp. 391-413.

    The authors construct an index of the quality of the US labour force for the
    period 1956-65, based on a weighting of workers in separate occupations by
    their median full-time earnings in the base year. They find that the index
    increased less than 3 per cent over the decade.

1968

80 L. C. THUROW, "Disequilibrium and the Marginal Productivity of Capital and
    Labor", *RES*, February, 1968, pp. 23-31.

    After estimating an aggregate production function for the American economy
    that covers a wide range of alternative specifications about its form, the

author concludes that the marginal product of labour is larger than the observed compensation of employees, while the marginal product of capital is smaller than the observed returns to capital. Consequently, rates of return on investment in education have been seriously underestimated: the author surmises that the social rate of return on investment in human capital may be 60 per cent larger than the private rate of return, p. 31 (See 87).

81 S. BOWLES, *The Aggregation of Labor Inputs in the Study of Growth and Planning: Experiments with a Two Level CES Function*. Economic Development Report, Center for International Affairs. Cambridge, Mass.: Center for International Affairs, Harvard University, 1968. Pp. 37, mimeographed.

An estimate of the elasticity of substitution between three types of educated labour across all industries taken together in twelve countries (See also 903).

82 D. SCHWARTZMAN, "Education and the Quality of Labor 1929-1963", *AER*, June, 1968, pp. 508-13.

The author recalculates Denison's estimate of the contribution of education to economic growth between 1930 and 1960, using the average hourly earnings of non-agricultural employees by age, sex and years of schooling instead of the annual income of males. His estimate yields 12 per cent as against Denison's figure of 32.6 per cent (See 90).

83 S. M. BESEN, "Education and Productivity in U.S. Manufacturing: Some Cross-Section Evidence", *JPE*, May/June, 1968, pp. 494-97.

Uses a Cobb-Douglas production function with a measure of educational attainment as a separate independent variable to explain interstate productivity differentials in American manufacturing.

84 P. A. NEHER, K. A. J. HAY, "Education and Capital Misallocation in a Growing Economy", *CJE*, August, 1968, pp. 609-18.

A growth model with two production functions and three economic goods, educated labour entering as a separate variable into both production functions. The article explores the equilibrium growth paths of the economy.

1969

85 M. SELOWSKY, "On the Measurement of Education's Contribution to Growth", *QJE*, August, 1969, pp. 449-63.

The article argues that Denison-type measurements have underestimated the contribution of education by excluding the contribution that is due to additions to the labour force with the same education as the existing labour force. The author develops a production function which is Cobb-Douglas for capital but CES for the various types of labour and uses it to generate time series for relative wages in Chile and Mexico where actual data of this kind is lacking. He then recalculates the contribution of education to growth in Chile, Mexico, and India on a variety of assumptions about the parameters of his production function (See also 1374).

86 M. L. SKOLNIK, "An Empirical Analysis of Substitution Between Engineers and Technicians in Canada", *IR*, 25, 2, 1969, pp. 284-300.

After a discussion of the concept of substitution, the author develops derived demand equations from a CES production function fitted to Canadian data. The results reveal a high degree of substitutability between engineers and technicians.

87 L. C. THUROW, *Poverty and Discrimination*. Washington: The Brookings Institution, 1969. Pp. 214.

The book is organised around four main themes: the incidence of poverty in America; the role of education in determining income distribution; the economic effects of various forms of discrimination against Negroes; and the possible levers for policy to eradicate poverty and discrimination. Ch. 3 presents an interstate poverty incidence model using Census data and App. A reworks the Denison results for the U.S.A. with an explicit estimate of the aggregate production function.

88 Z. GRILICHES, "Capital-Skill Complementarity", *RES*, November, 1969, pp. 465-68.

An econometric note to show that there is American evidence which suggests that capital is more complementary with highly educated than with so-called "raw labour".

89 G. PSACHAROPOULOS, *The Anatomy of a Rate of Growth: The Case of Hawaii, 1950-1960*. Honolulu: University of Hawaii, 1969. Pp. 73.

An application of Denison-type growth accounting to the State of Hawaii, concluding that 12 per cent of Hawaiian growth over the decade 1950 to 1960 was due to education.

90 E. F. DENISON, "The Contribution of Education to the Quality of Labor: Comment", *AER*, December, 1969, pp. 935-43; "Reply" by D. Schwartzman, *ibid.*, pp. 944-46.

Denison comments on Schwartzman's new estimate of the contribution of education to American economic growth (see 82) and shows that the small size of this estimate does not, as appeared, stem mainly from the substitution of hourly earnings for annual incomes as quality weights. The discussion involves a detailed re-examination of data sources but Denison's piece is a useful review of his own previous estimates.

1970

91 F. WELCH, "Education in Production", *JPE*, January/February, 1970, pp. 35-59, reprinted in *KIK*, pp. 324-53.

This paper discusses the role of education in production functions as enhancing both the marginal product of educated labour and the efficiency of non-labour inputs. After considering this dual role analytically, the author runs some new tests on U.S. agriculture across the 49 states.

1971

92 J. MOREH, "Human Capital and Economic Growth: United Kingdom, 1951-1961",
    ESR, September, 1971, pp. 73-93.

    This rather tortuously written article applies the Schultz and Denison
    measurements of the contribution of education to economic growth to the case
    of Britain in the 1950's. The author finds that formal education alone con-
    tributed between 10 and 14 per cent of the increase in national income in the
    decade 1951-61, while on-the-job training contributed between 7 and 10 per
    cent. Despite differences in methods of calculation and source of data, the
    author's numbers are remarkably similar to Denison's own estimate of 12 per
    cent.

93 S. BOWLES, "Growth Effects of Changes in Labor Quality and Quantity, Greece:
    1951-1961", *Studies in Development Planning*, ed. H. B. Chenery, Cambridge,
    Mass.: Harvard University Press, 1971, pp. 371-85.

    A Denison-type calculation of the contribution of education to economic
    growth applied to Greece in the 1950's (see also 903).

1972

94 J. Tinbergen, "The Impact of Education on Income Distribution", *RIW*, 1972,
    pp. 255-65.

    Combining data gathered by others on America, Canada and The Netherlands,
    the author calculates regressions of the variance of income on average incomes,
    average years of schooling and the variance of years of schooling. In the
    final section of the paper, he constructs what he calls demand-and-supply equa-
    tions by including the percentage of third-level educated people employed in
    the four leading sectors of the economy.

95 G. PSACHAROPOULOS, "Measuring the Marginal Contribution of Education to Econo-
    mic Growth", *EDCC*, July, 1972, pp. 641-58.

    A Denison-type exercise in growth accounting with a twist: Denison-type
    estimates are compared with Schultz-type estimates and the differences are
    shown to be small.

96 V. A. ZHAMIN, S. L. KOSTAMAN, "Education and Soviet Economic Growth", *IRE*,
    XVIII, 2, 1972, pp. 155-71.

    An updating of Zhamin's earlier article (see 1438) and still very much in
    the old Strumilin tradition.

97 R. S. DOUGHERTY, "Estimates of Labor Aggregation Functions", *JPE*, November/
    December, 1972, pp. 1101-1119.

    This paper estimates a two-level CES production function with labour disaggre-
    gated by occupation and by educational level. The data is for American states

in the year 1960. The main results are estimates for the elasticity of substitution between types of labour that significantly exceed unity, on the
basis of which the author suggests that the manpower requirements approach
should now be abandoned.

1973

98 P. R. G. LAYARD, "Denison and the Contribution of Education to National Income
Growth: A Comment", *JPE*, July/August, 1973, pp. 1013-16.

This note argues that Denison slightly exaggerated the contribution of
education by selecting the wrong base in calculating his index of labour force
quality.

99 G. PSACHAROPOULOS, "Substitution Assumptions Versus Empirical Evidence in
Manpower Planning", *ECON*, 121, 6, 1973, pp. 609-28.

This paper summarizes work by Bowles, Dougherty and the author himself on
the elasticities of substitution between different types of educated labour
(see also 1377).

100 R. R. Nelson, "Recent Exercises in Growth Accounting: New Understanding or
Dead End?", *AER*, June, 1973, pp. 462-68.

This short note attempts to deliver a *coup de grâce* to Denison-and-all-that,
concluding with a few trenchant comments on rate-of-return analysis.

1974

101 J. Tinbergen, "Substitution of Graduate By Other Labour", *KYK*, XXVII, 2, 1974,
pp. 217-26.

Reconsiders the evidence collected by Bowles, Dougherty and Ullman to recalculate the elasticity of substitution between third-level educated and all
other labour. The elasticity is found to be about unity, a figure lower than
that obtained by the three authors cited.

102 E. F. DENISON, *Accounting for United States Economic Growth*. Washington, D.C.:
The Brookings Institution, 1974. Pp. 355.

Reworks earlier work (62), carrying the measurements backwards to 1902 and
forward to 1969, while refining many of the calculations. The measured contribution of education to economic growth, however, remains substantially what
it was before.

1975

103 P. R. FALLON, P. R. G. LAYARD, "Capital-Skill Complementary Income Distribution and Output Accounting", *JPE*, April, 1975, pp. 279-302.

Using international data for 23 countries and two-level CES production functions, the authors show that physical capital is more complementary to educated rather than to raw labour and that previous estimates of the elasticity of substitution between more and less educated labour have erred on the high side. They also demonstrate that intercountry differences in per capita income are due more to differences in physical than in human capital (see 1363).

(c) HUMAN CAPITAL FORMATION

There are essentially two equally correct ways of measuring the current stock of physical capital: cumulating data on past investment in current prices and deflating the total with the aid of a price index (the backward view), and discounting the expected flow of future earnings from currently invested capital (the forward view). In the ideal world of perfect competition, the two measurements would yield identical answers. Needless to say, in the real world the figures will be very different.

Both approaches have their counterpart in the field of human capital: Schultz[106],[107] measures capital formation by education in terms of the backward view; Weisbrod[109] values human capital in terms of the forward view. The backward view appears to be more satisfying conceptually. At any rate, it has far more proponents than the foward view: there are Petty's efforts in the eighteenth century, as described by Kiker[58] and Dublin and Lotka[132], Nicholson's work in the 1890's[40], and examples in recent years from Israel and Japan[1332],[1396]. On the technical problems of measuring human capital, Bowman[113],[115] is virtually definitive

It may not be obvious at first sight what useful purpose is served by measuring the stock of education embodied in the labour force. Schultz[104],[108],[110],[114] makes the case more forcefully than anyone else, but see also Johnson[105]. No student should miss the interesting debate on this question between Schaffer and Schultz[110].

1959

104   T. W. SCHULTZ, "Investment in Man: An Economist's View", *SSR*, June, 1959, pp. 109-17, reprinted in *UNESCO-REED*, pp. 69-75, and *WYK I*, pp. 59-68.

An early statement by the "father" of the concept of human capital.

1960

105   H. G. JOHNSON, "The Political Economy of Opulence", *CJEPS*, 1960, reprinted in *Money, Trade and Economic Growth. Survey Lectures in Economic Theory.* London: Allen & Unwin, pp. 164-80.

This free-wheeling "reconstruction" of economics for the age of opulence closes with the suggestion that all the factors of production should be lumped together as items of capital equipment, created by past investment and rendering current services to production, a treatment which would eliminate a number of self-created problems in the theory of growth. "The masses are becoming capitalists . . . as owners of consumption capital, and as possessors of educated skills." (See also 153).

106 T. W. SCHULTZ, "Capital Formation by Education", *JPE*, December, 1960, pp. 571-84, partly reprinted in *EHE*, pp. 93-102, and in *URB*, pp. 116-36.

   In this fundamental article, Schultz estimates human capital formation in the USA since 1900 as a sum of the earnings foregone by students and the costs of educational services provided by schools.

1961

107 T. W. SCHULTZ, "Education and Economic Growth", *Social Forces Influencing American Education. The Sixtieth Yearbook of the National Society for the Study of Education*, ed. N. B. Henry. Chicago, Ill.: Chicago University Press, 1961, II, pp. 46-88, summary reprinted in *EES*, pp. 50-52, and in *UNESCO-REED*, pp. 277-89, 298-312.

   An exploratory study with many tables of supporting data also presented in other publications of the author.

108 T. W. SCHULTZ, "Investment in Human Capital", *AER*, March, 1961, pp. 1-17, reprinted in *P-EED*, 1, pp. 13-33, *URB*, pp. 43-61, *WYK II*, pp. 23-41, and *KIK*, pp. 3-21.

   An authoritative statement of the concept of human capital which makes a strong case for investigating the returns to investment in human beings.

109 B. A. WEISBROD, "The Valuation of Human Capital", *JPE*, October, 1961, pp. 425-37.

   Estimates the capital value—the net future productivity discounted at 3 per cent and 10 per cent—of US males at various ages and concludes with a figure for 1960 far in excess of the value of physical capital. The article closes with a discussion of the significance of such estimates for public spending policies.

110 H. G. SCHAFFER, "Investment in Human Capital: Comment", *AER*, December, 1961, pp. 1026-35; "Reply" by T. W. Schultz, *ibid.*, pp. 1035-39, reprinted in *P-EED*, 1, pp. 45-64, and *KIK*, pp. 22-39.

   A consistent attack on the concept of human capital on theoretical and practical grounds with a vigorous reply by Schultz.

1962

111 OECD, *Policy Conference on Economic Growth and Investment in Education*, I, Paris: OECD, 1962. Pp. 45.

   Contains, among other things, speeches by Dean Rusk, US Secretary of State, P. H. Coombs, chairman of the conference, and W. H. Heller, Kennedy's Chairman of the Council of Economic Advisors, all of which pay tribute to the concept of "investment in human capital".

112 M. DEBEAUVAIS, "The Concept of Human Capital", *ISSJ*, XIV, 4, 1962, pp. 660-76.

An attempt to place the concept in the mainstream of economic thought.

113 M. J. BOWMAN, "Human Capital: Concepts and Measures", *EHE*, pp. 69-93, reprinted in *UNESCO-REED*, pp. 246-62.

A technical discussion of measurement problems in the area of human capital formation.

1963

114 T. W. SCHULTZ, *The Economic Value of Education*. New York.: Columbia University Press, 1963. Pp. 92.

A useful review of recent American work on the costs and economic benefits of education, with a chapter on "unfinished research" and a comprehensive bibliography of over 200 items under 5 headings.

115 M. J. BOWMAN, "The Costing of Human Resource Development", *IEA-EE*, pp. 421-50, excerpts reprinted in *UNESCO-REED*, pp. 787-89.

A convincing defence of the practice of including foregone earnings in the "real cost" of both formal and informal education.

116 M. DEBEAUVAIS, *L'éducation de la population française et son évolution de 1850 à 1980*. Paris: *Institut d'étude du développement économique et social*, 1963. Pp. 122.

This volume consists of 3 related papers: (1) a brief study, edited by M. Maës, of the length of the school cycle and the gradual increase of enrolment ratios in France from 1850-1961; (2) a method of calculating the stock of education embodied in the French labour force from 1936-61 and of projecting the indicated trend to 1980, edited by M. Panayohakis; and (3) a lengthy study of the distribution of the stock by age, sex, occupation, and profession from 1954-61 with projections up to 1980, edited by J. Pillet.

1965

117 M. R. COLBERG, *Human Capital in Southern Development 1939-1963*. Chapel Hill, N.C.: University of North Carolina Press, 1965. Pp. 136.

An important work that calculates changes in the South's college-educated human capital as a share of all human capital in the United States since 1939, in order to deduce the amount of migration of human capital that has taken place. Along the way, there are interesting discussions of the determination of teachers' salaries in the South and income-education differentials in the South and North.

118   T. W. SCHULTZ, "Investing in Poor People", *AER*, May, 1965, pp. 510-20.

   A discussion of the poverty problem from the standpoint of human capital
   formation.

1966

119   T. W. SCHULTZ, "Public Approaches to Minimize Poverty", *Poverty Amid Affluence*,
   ed. L. Fishman. New Haven, Conn.: Yale University Press, 1966, pp. 165-81.

   A broad treatment of the poverty problem, extending his previous arguments.

120   J. VAIZEY, "Education, Training and Growth", *Economic Growth in Britain*, ed.
   P. D. Henderson. London: Weidenfeld & Nicholson, 1966, pp. 237-61.

   This article estimates the expected rise in the amount of education embodied
   in the British labour force by 1980 as a result of the recent expansion of
   higher education and discusses the implications of this rise for the future
   growth of the British economy. (See also 874).

1967

121   J. K. FOLGER, C. B. NAM, *Education of the American Population. A 1960 Census
   Monograph*. Washington, D.C.: US Government Printing Office, 1967. Pp. 290.

   A description of student enrolments, teacher characteristics and the educational attainments of the American population over time, as revealed by Census
   data and other statistical material. The volume includes appendices that evaluate Census Bureau statistics on education, and discuss the instructions for
   education items in successive American decennial censuses since 1840.

122   W. L. MILLER, "Education as a Source of Economic Growth", *JEI*, December, 1967,
   pp. 280-96.

   Another Bowen-type survey (see 169) concluding with a plea to fellow economists to turn to questions of educational reform.

1968

123   M. J. BOWMAN, "Principles in the Valuation of Human Capital", *RIW*, September,
   1968, pp. 217-46.

   A miscellany of comments on human capital measurement problems, particularly
   from the point of view of the gains and losses of migration. Along the way,
   the author compares American age-earnings profiles with those of Japan for
   1961.

124   O. J. FIRESTONE, "Education and Economic Development - The Canadian Case",
   RIW, December, 1968, pp. 341-85.

A brief version of the author's full-length book, *Industry and Education,
A Century of Canadian Development* (1968), which summarizes a good deal of work
that has been done in Canada on the contribution of education to economic growth
in the framework of a Rostow-stages view of the Canadian economy. It also
includes comparisons with the United States.

1972

125 A. RAZIN, "Investment in Human Capital and Economic Growth", *MET*, May-August,
1972, pp. 101-116.

A formal model of steady-state growth in which households accumulate human
capital as business firms accumulate physical capital. Apart from the usual
results, some policy implications follow with respect to the finance of education.

126 B. F. KIKER, J. BIRKELI, "Human Capital Losses Resulting from U.S. Casualties
of the War in Vietnam", *JPE*, September/October, 1972, pp. 1023-30.

Estimate the total loss in human capital due to the war to lie between $6
and 12 billion, or about 1 per cent of American GNP. See also P. Eden, "U.S.
Human Capital Loss in Southeast Asia", *JHR*, Summer, 1972, pp. 384-93. This
estimates the human capital loss to be $17 billion, an addition of 14 per cent
to the actual budgeted costs of the war.

1973

127 J. MOREH, "Human Capital: Deterioration and Net Investment", *RIW*, September,
1973, pp. 279-302.

The author estimates aggregate net investment in human capital in the United
States in 1960 on the basis of age-earnings profiles for American white males.
He finds that it was about equal to net investment in physical assets
(including consumers' durables).

128 G. LABER, "Human Capital in Southern Migration", *JHR*, Spring, 1973, pp. 223-41.

An estimate of the net gain from intranational migration to the human capital
stock of the American South.·

(d) MEASUREMENT OF RETURNS

If the acquisition of education is a type of investment by the individual in his
own future earning capacity, as economists have been claiming ever since Adam Smith,
it is only reasonable to asK; is it a profitable investment compared to alternative
investment options? To answer that question we have to compare the known stream of
educational costs with the expected stream of future earnings that will accrue to

an educated individual. We can do this either by calculating the internal rate of return which would equate the present value of the costs with the present value of the prospective earnings, after which we can compare this rate of return with the yield of business capital, or by using the yield of business capital as a discount factor to calculate the net present value of a certain amount of education, for subsequent comparison with the net present value of capital projects in industry. In either case, what we are doing is simply cost-benefit analysis, treating the purchase of education as perfectly analogous to the purchase of any capital asset.

Unfortunately, some education is purchased for consumption rather than investment reasons, and the earning streams which we observe to be associated with extra education are not entirely attributable to education; native ability, achievement drive, age, race, sex, social class origins, regional location, and on-the-job training all influence an individual's earning capacity. Furthermore, not all the benefits of education accrue to the educated individual alone. Thus, if we are to calculate the yield of investment in education, we must isolate the investment component, eliminate all the non-educational determinants of differences between individual incomes, and distinguish the private from the social benefits of additional schooling.

The development of the literature in this field has only gradually come to grips with all the difficulties inherent in the rate-of-return approach to educational investment. A glance at Clark[42], Ellis[129], and Strumilin[130] reveals the state of innocence that prevailed until recently. It must be remarked, however, that many of the objections to the approach advanced by recent critics are implied by Marshall[39] and clearly stated in Walsh's prescient article of 1935[132]. With Friedman and Kuznets[134], we enter the modern era of the subject. At first, there was a marked tendency to confine the argument to the benefit side, simply demonstrating that extra education is in fact correlated with higher earnings: see Glick and Miller[137], Houthakker[143], and Miller[136,148,160,174,208]. Following on the earlier work by Fisher[43], the role of occupation as an intervening factor in the relationship between education and income was illuminated by the works of Reder[968], Keat[149], Duncan[152], and Wilkinson[218], Weiss[277], Mayhew[291], and Schweitzer[302], with Mincer[142,270,393], and Becker[206,235] and Chiswick[206,241,256,272] spelling out the implications of rising educational attainment on the distribution of income in the long run, on which see also Jencks[329].

As long ago as 1932, Gorweline[131] drew attention to the role of differential genetic endowment, a point re-emphasised more recently by Bridgeman[144], while Anderson[135], Bowman[190], Fein[190], Lassiter[191,200], Gillman[198], Fogel[212], Ribich[246], Ashenfelter and Taussig[304], Weiss[277], Hines, Tweeten and Redfern[280], Weiss and Williamson[321], Gwartney[331], Blinder[363], Chiswick[366], Welch[221,367,372], Masters[386], Morse[387], and Haworth, Gwartney and Haworth[398] demonstrate the effect of racial and regional differences on individual incomes. Denison[62,64] takes the argument one step further by attributing three-fifths of the observed income differentials among males of the same age to formal education, a hypothesis confirmed by Becker[179] and by Morgan, David, Cohen, and Brazer[161,167], with the aid of an elaborate multiple-regression analysis of family income determination in the United States. Recently, however, it has been argued by Griliches[272] and Griliches and Mason[815] that Denison over-estimated the effects of the non-education variables.

The influence of on-the-job training, and indeed the entire relationship between formal education and labour training, still remains in doubt. The leading theoretical work on this subject is by Becker[179], as extended by Mincer[157,393]. The Becker-Mincer theory of labour training stands or falls on the view taken of labour mobility, in which connection see Bodenhöfer[226], Lansing and Morgan[227], Gallaway[228], Ladinsky[229], Bowman and Myers[231], Benewitz and Zucker[236], Dufty[254], Weiss[300], Rosen[323], and Fisher[374]. Borus[180] has opened up new avenues of study with a cost-benefit analysis of a government-sponsored retraining scheme, now carried further by Weisbrod[215], Main[238], Stromsdorfer[239,245], Somers[245,261], Thomas and Moxham[242], Ziderman[258], and Hughes[266].

The social as distinct from the private benefits of education are discussed in a

purely theoretical sense by Bowman[155] and Blaug[182], and measured, however imper-
fectly, by Becker[145,179], Eicher[146], Weisbrod[158,175], and Hirsch[176].

Most of the work in this field has been done in the United States. There is,
however, the earlier Soviet effort, ably criticised by Kahan[172], and, in more recent
years the yield of educational investment has been estimated for 32 countries, as
surveyed by Psacharopoulos and Hinchliffe[337]. Nevertheless, problems about the
adjustment of earnings for differences in native ability, family background, and
quality of education remain, as witnessed by the recent work of Taubman and
Wales[333,353,809], Hause[297,815], Jencks[329], Bowles[342,815], Morgan and Sirageldin[247],
Weisbrod and Karpoff[248], Hansen, Weisbrod and Scanlon[279], Conlisk[303], Johnson and
Stafford[338], Morgenstern[348], Link[349], Link and Ratledge[406], and Solmon[828]. Recent
years have seen the emergence of the screening hypothesis, or theory of credentialism, challenging human capital theory on its own grounds: see Berg[265], Blaug[311],
Arrow[341], Spence[357,384], Rothschild[365], Wiles[375], Layard and Psacharopoulos[389],
Welch[401], Stiglitz[402], Chiswick[828], and Rawlins and Ulman[843]. In this respect,
evidence on racism and sexism in labour markets take on new meaning: for evidence
on sexism, see particularly Woodhall[340], Sawhile[355], Malkiel and Malkiel[358], Mincer
and Polachnek[377] and Johnson and Stafford[394].

One of the difficulties with rate-of-return estimates is that they have no
policy implications in and of themselves. For purposes of policy decision, what is
wanted is not just the yield of educational investment, but also the yield of every
other type of social expenditure. Similar studies are now being conducted in the
field of water resource development, motorways, medical care, and the like, but the
picture is far from complete. Eckstein[425] and Prest and Turvey[196] survey the entire
field of cost-benefit analysis. Wiseman[190] and Peacock and Wiseman[510] discuss the
pitfalls of arriving at policy decisions in the light of rate-of-return calculations
with particular attention to health, while Blaug[182,209] goes over the same grounds
from the viewpoint of education. The question of student loans for higher education is a striking example of the problem of translating rate-of-return figures into
policy measures: see Van Den Haag[138], Harris[427], and references cited in the section on "Public and Private Finance". The evidence on low and even negative rates
of return to postgraduate education, one of the most subsidised parts of higher
education, continues to throw doubt on the policy implications of rate-of-return
analysis: see Butter[217], Ashenfelter and Mooney[237,263], Danielson[263], Maxwell[278],
Siegfried[293], Weiss[308], Bailey and Schotta[312], Dodge and Stager[319] and Metcalf[334].
See, likewise, evidence on the rate of return to teacher training: Bibby[288],
Hinchliffe[301], Birch and Calvert[362], and Turnbull and Williams[391] .

It is self-evident that there is an intimate connection between the stock of human
capital, the rate of return on investment in education, and the contribution of
education to economic growth. Nevertheless, there are many hurdles to cross in
establishing this connection, as Bowman[68] has shown. We are still far from having
constructed a firm bridge between the three approaches separately discussed in
this bibliography under the heading "The economic contribution of education".

The rate-of-return approach has never lacked critics, among the most outstanding
of which are Schaffer[110], Vaizey[2,3,27,168] Balogh and Streeten[165], Eckaus[159,371],
Daniere[819,872], Merrett[216], Chamberlin[261], Sheehan[451], and Carter[823]. On the side
of the defence, however, see Bowman[154], Lee Hansen[164], and Blaug[182]. The entire
controversy has been reviewed at various stages of the debate by Renshaw[147],
Machlup[162], Bowen[169], Lê Thành Khôi[173], Caine[177], Rivlin[745], Bowman[7], and Blaug[182];
probably the most useful single reference is Bowen[169].

1917

129 A. C. ELLIS, *The Money Value of Education*. Bureau of Education, Bulletin
     No. 22. Washington, D.C.: Government Printing Office, 1917. Pp. 52.

An early effort to prove that education constitutes profitable investment in human capital. Cites a large number of individual studies of the effects of education in different parts of the United States. The discussion of the problem is, however, somewhat naive. A detailed bibliography reveals the status of the subject in 1917.

1924

130 S. G. STRUMILIN, "The Economic Significance of National Education", *Planovoe Khoziaistvo*, Nos. 9-10, 1924, reprinted in English in *UNESCO- REED*, pp. 413-50, and in *IEA-EE*, pp. 267-324.

A classic article based on a sample of Leningrad workers and the very first to attempt to measure the returns to education. (See also 63 and 172).

1932

131 D. E. GORSELINE, *The Effect of Schooling Upon Income*. Bloomington, Ind.: Graduate Council of Indiana University, 1932. Pp. 284.

This remarkable pioneer work, "attempting to separate the effect that schooling has upon income from the combined effects that schooling, inheritance, health, good luck, bad luck, and other factors have upon income", examines a selective sample of about 200 blood brothers educated and gainfully employed in the State of Indiana in 1927. Ch. 2, pp. 16-20, reviews a dozen previous studies of the relation between education and income, noting that all of them failed to make any adjustment for differential ability; by limiting himself to blood brothers, the author hopes to be able to eliminate all the factors other than education that determine personal income. After analysing the sample for differences in age, education, grades attained in school, scores on standardised tests, occupational rank, place of residence, size of family, inherited income, windfall income, and medical expenses, the author concludes that "schooling does add to the income of individuals", and that approximately half of the mean income differentials of the least and the most educated in an average year are attributable to education.

1935

132 J. R. WALSH, "Capital Concept Applied to Man", *QJE*, February, 1935, pp. 255-85, partly reprinted in *UNESCO-REED*, pp. 453-74.

This perceptive article, written long before the current interest in human "capital", considers the returns from formal schooling on the basis of several samples of college graduates. The approach is that of looking at the present value of future returns, discounted at 4 per cent. All the limitations of this type of research are mentioned and briefly discussed. A lengthy footnote cites the relevant literature between 1700 and 1935; for a detailed review of the history of the concept of human capital, see L. I. Dublin, A. J. Lotka, *The Money Value of a Man* (New York: Ronald Press, 2nd ed., 1946), ch. 2, pp. 6-21.

1937

133 H. F. CLARK, *Life Earnings in Selected Occupations in the United States*. New York: Harper & Bros., 1937. Pp. 408.

This study, based on data for the period 1920 to 1936, makes interesting reading in the light of recent interest in rate-of-return analysis. The findings are conveniently summarised in ch. 1. Ch. 2 emphasises the need for better information regarding lifetime earnings. This book probably influenced the American decision to include earnings in the 1939 census.

1946

134 M. FRIEDMAN, S. KUZNETS, *Income From Independent Professional Practice*. New York: National Bureau of Economic Research, 1946. Pp. 594.

A pioneering effort to explain the incomes of doctors and dentists in terms of the discounted value of future net incomes with due allowance for nonpecuniary preferences and monopolistic restraints. For a careful critique of the study, see H. G. Lewis, *Unionism and Relative Wages in the United States: An Empirical Inquiry* (Chicago, Ill.: Chicago University Press, 1963), pp. 114-24.

1955

135 C. A. ANDERSON, "Regional and Racial Differences in Relation Between Income and Education", *SR*, January, 1955, pp. 38-45.

Using American census data, the author shows that the effect of education on earnings differs between whites and non-whites and between different regions in the USA.

136 H. P.MILLER, *Income of the American People*. New York: John Wiley, 1955, pp. 45-46, 65-68.

Brings out the findings of the 1950 Census relating income to education, age, and race, without any formal attempt to measure the returns to education.

1956

137 P. C. GLICK, H. P. MILLER, "Educational Level and Potential Income", *ASR*, June, 1956, reprinted in *The Sociology of Education. A Source Book*, ed. R. R. Bell. Homewood, Ill.: Dorsey Press, 1962, pp. 167-74.

An early attempt (extending P. C. Glick's "Educational Attainment and Occupational Advancement", *Transactions of the Second World Congress of Sociology*. London: 1954, II, pp. 183-93) which produced the oft-cited figure of $100,000 as the lifetime income benefit of attending an American college. The authors deduct educational costs from returns and conclude that investment in college education pays better than most investments.

138 E. VAN DEN HAAG, *Education as an Industry*. New York: Augustus M. Kelley, 1956. Pp. 163.

An early and non-quantitative contribution to the concept of human capital, concluding with an outline of a scheme whereby colleges would invest in the education of their students, taking a share of their future income. The difficulties in such a plan are not squarely faced. See the essay review by D. Riesman, "Who Will and Who Should Pay for Higher Education?", *SR*, Summer, 1958, pp. 218–31.

139 H. F. CLARK, "The Return on Educational Investment", *The Yearbook of Education, 1956*, ed. J. A. Lauwerys. London: Evans Bros., 1956, pp. 495-506, reprinted in *PEE*, pp. 24-32.

A popular treatment, stressing the role of agricultural education in the development of the American economy.

140 D. WOLFLE, J. G. SMITH, "The Occupational Value of Education for Superior High School Graduates", *JHE*, April, 1956, pp. 201-13.

The summary results are reprinted in 736, pp. 178-79: median salaries of a group of students from three states in 1933-38 rose with more college education even after adjustments were made for differences in ability, school performance, and father's occupation. For further discussion of the data, see 64.

1958

141 T. W. SCHULTZ, "The Emerging Economic Scene and Its Relation to High School Education", *The High School in a New Era*, eds. F. S. Chase, C. A. Anderson. Chicago, Ill.: Chicago University Press, 1958, pp. 97-113.

A discursive article which at one point attributes Britain's low rate of growth relative to the USA to lower enrolments in Great Britain.

142 J. MINCER, "Investment in Human Capital and Income Distribution", *JPE*, August, 1958, pp. 281-300.

Discarding stochastic explanations of income distribution, the author develops a model which makes interoccupational differentials in earnings a function of differences in training. He shows that such a model accounts for a number of observed empirical regularities in income distribution. See also the directly related article by A. D. Roy, "The Distribution of Earnings and of Individual Output", *EJ*, September, 1950, pp. 489-505.

1959

143 H. S. HOUTHAKKER, "Education and Income", *RES*, February, 1959, pp. 24-28, reprinted in *WYK II*, pp. 116-25, and *KIK*, pp. 181-89.

A sophisticated attempt to measure the present value of lifetime income from various years of schooling, using 1950 Census data, and concluding with some widely quoted qualifications about this approach to the economic value of education.

1960

144 S. BRIDGEMAN, "Problems in Estimating the Monetary Value of College Education",
     Higher Education in the USA. The Economic Problems, ed. S. E. Harris.
     Cambridge, Mass.: Harvard University Press, 1960, pp. 180-85.

     Reviews the findings of two large-scale studies on ability differences among
     college students, concluding that there is serious danger in exaggerating the
     cash value of a college education because the role of superior ability in gen-
     erating higher incomes has not been adequately recognised.

145 G. S. BECKER, "Underinvestment in College Education", *AER*, May, 1960, pp.
     346-54; "Comments" by H. Villard, *ibid.*, pp. 375-78, reprinted in *WYK II*,
     pp. 105-15.

     Preliminary results of an NBER study (see 179), suggesting.that the private
     rate of return on college education is not very different from the rate of
     return on business capital. This puts the burden of the contention of under-
     investment on the public benefits of education, about which very little is
     known. The author contends that improvements in the quality of college educa-
     tion would raise the returns. Villard's comments deal with the question of
     measuring the public benefits.

146 J.-C. EICHER, "La rentabilité de l'investissement humain", *RE*, July, 1960,
     pp. 577-609, reprinted in English in *UNESCO-REED*, pp. 363-83.

     After discarding measurement of the private rate of return to education, the
     author attempts to measure the social rate of return by a multiple-regression
     analysis of interstate and interregional differences in the USA.

147 E. F. RENSHAW, "Estimating the Returns to Education", *RES*, August, 1960,
     pp. 318-24, reprinted in *UNESCO-REED*, pp. 560-68.

     A critical review of various estimates of the returns to education, a com-
     pendium of the shortcomings in this approach to resource allocation in educa-
     tion and, lastly, new estimates of income differentials due to education.

148 H. P. MILLER, "Annual and Lifetime Income in Relation to Education: 1939-59",
     AER, December, 1960, pp. 962-87, reprinted in *KIK*, pp. 150-80.

     Looking solely at the income side, this study demonstrates that the relative
     income position of college graduates has not declined since 1939, despite the
     rise in college enrolment, apparently because the demand has kept pace with
     the increased supply.

149 P. G. KEAT, "Long-Run Changes in Occupational Wage Structure, 1900-1956", *JPE*,
     December, 1960, pp. 584-600.

     An attempt to explain the decline in relative skill differentials over the
     last 50 years. After reviewing a number of factors, the author concludes that
     changes in the costs and lengths of education and training account for a large
     part of the narrowing of wage differentials.

1961

150 H. M. GROVES, *Education and Economic Growth*. The Committee on Educational
     Finance. National Education Association. Washington, D.C.: NEA, 1961.
     Pp. 58. Excerpts reprinted in *PEE*, pp. 7-12.

     A popular but cogent review of recent American findings about the gains from
     investment in education, and a brief discussion of the problems of manpower
     wastage and educational finance in the USA.

151 J. VAIZEY, "Comparative Notes on Economic Growth and Social Change in Education",
     CER, June, 1961, pp. 7-13; "Education as Investment in Comparative Perspective"
     ibid., October, 1961, pp. 97-105.

     Eclectic comments on the contribution of education to economic growth. In-
     cludes an estimate of the opportunity costs of education in the UK in 1955.

152 O. D. DUNCAN, "Occupational Components of Educational Differences in Income",
     JASA, December, 1961, pp. 783-92.

     Presents a method of making inferences about the role of occupational selec-
     tion in the absence of a simultaneous cross-tabulation of income by occupation
     and education. Concludes that occupation is a major intervening factor in the
     relationship between education and income.

1962

153 H. G. JOHNSON, "The Social Policy of an Opulent Society", *Money, Trade and
     Economic Growth. Survey Lectures in Economic Theory*. London: Allen & Unwin,
     1962, pp. 180-95.

     Some cogent remarks on the meaning and applicability of the rate-of-return
     approach to education. (See also 1410).

154 M. J. BOWMAN, "Converging Concerns of Economists and Educationists", *CER*,
     October, 1962, pp. 111-20, reprinted in *WYK II*, pp. 52-67.

     A vigorous defence of the rate-of-return approach as most likely to lead to
     fruitful interdisciplinary communication between economists and educationists.
     The private and social returns to education are clearly distinguished.

155 M. J. BOWMAN, "Social Returns to Education", *ISSJ*, XIV, 4, 1962, pp. 647-60.

     An analytical clarification of the nature of the public benefits of education.

156 G. S. BECKER, "Investment in Human Capital: A Theoretical Analysis", *JPE*,
     Suppl., October, 1962, pp. 9-50, excerpts reprinted in *UNESCO-REED*, pp. 505-19;
     "Comment" by R. S. Eckaus, *JPE*, October, 1963, pp. 501-4, reprinted in *P-EED*,
     1, pp. 183-214.

     The argument proceeds from a discussion of specific kinds of human capital,
     with particular attention to on-the-job training, to a general theory applying

to any kind of human capital. A fundamental article, full of original insights. Eckaus' comments point out the special assumptions in Becker's argument. For a development of Becker's distinction between "general" and "specific" labour-training investments by firms, with particular reference to the demand for labour in the short run, see W. Y. Oi, "Labor as a Quasi-Fixed Factor", *JPE*, December, 1962, pp. 538-56.

157   J. MINCER, "On the Job Training: Costs, Returns and Some Implications", *JPE*, Suppl., October, 1962, pp. 50-80, reprinted in *UNESCO-REED*, pp. 524-52, and *KIK*, pp. 279-323.

   Estimates the amounts of resources invested in on-the-job training in the USA and the rates of return on such investment, and discusses some of the implications of the findings.

158   B. A. WEISBROD, "Education and Investment in Human Capital", *JPE*, Suppl., October, 1962, pp. 106-24, reprinted in *P-EED*, *1*, pp. 156-82, *WYK II*, p. 68-88, and *KIK*, pp. 228-53.

   Clarifies the measurement of the private benefits of education by consider-ing some elements usually neglected, and contributes fresh ideas on the measure-ment of the social benefits.

159   R. S. ECKAUS, "Education and Economic Growth", *EHE*, pp. 102-29, partly reprinted in *UNESCO-REED*, pp. 571-87.

   After some introductory remarks on the theme stated in the title, various measures of the economic contribution of education are critically reviewed. A number of topics are touched upon and, in every case, the author adds some-thing new to the discussion.

160   H. P. MILLER, "Income and Education: Does Education Pay Off?", *EHE*, pp. 129-47.

   As a warning against hasty generalisations about the private benefits of education, the author discusses two difficult cases to illustrate his point: relatively constant income differentials between whites and non-whites and between veterans and non-veterans, despite differential educational attainments.

161   J. N. MORGAN, M. H. DAVID, W. J. COHEN, H. E. BRAZER, *Income and Welfare in the USA*. New York: McGraw-Hill, 1962. Pp. 531.

   This study of family-income determination by the Survey Research Center of the Institute for Social Research at the University of Michigan is more detailed than any previously attempted. It concludes that "one explanatory factor looms above the others in importance in determining family income: the level of for-mal education of the head and his wife." Of particular interest are the chap-ters on "The Dynamics of Social and Economic Change", pp. 331-87, which seek to isolate the "pure" effect of education, separated from the effects of native intelligence and family background. The section of "Educational Expectations and Attitudes", pp. 387-427, analyses the demand for higher education as a sequential process. One of the chapters in this book was published separately as *Educational Achievement—Its Causes and Effects* by M. David *et al.* (Ann Arbor, Michigan: Survey Research Center, 1961. Pp. 158). See also D. Creamer, "Some Determinants of Low Family Income", *EDCC*, April, 1961, pp. 413-40, for a similar study with similar conclusions for New York State.

162 F. MACHLUP, *The Production and Distribution of Knowledge in the United States.*
     Princeton, N.J.: Princeton University Press, 1962, ch. 4, pp. 51-145.

   Ch. 4 presents a detailed review of all the relevant literature on the costs
of formal education in the USA, together with some discussion of the rate-of-
return approach. Elsewhere in this book, Machlup attempts for the first time
to measure the total costs of all types of informal education in the USA. See
the book reviews by M. J. BOWMAN, *SR*, Summer, 1963, pp. 235-45, and T. W. Schultz,
AER, September, 1963, pp. 836-38.

1963

163 J. BONNER, D. S. LEES, "Consumption and Investment", *JPE*, February, 1963,
     pp. 64-76.

   An effective defence of the concept of human capital. The issue rests essentially on the view taken of the productive process: in the Marshall-Pigou
view of "final output" and the Keynesian view of national income, investment
of any kind appears to be somewhat inconsistently included. It is argued that
the idea of human capital implies a closed input-output model of the economy.

164 W. LEE HANSEN, "Total and Private Rates of Return to Investment in Schooling",
     ibid., April, 1963, pp. 128-41, reprinted in *UNESCO-REED*, pp. 486-500, *P-EED*,
     1, pp. 137-55, *WYK II*, pp. 126-46, and *KIK* , pp. 211-27.

   In a significant contribution, the author presents internal rates of return
to both private and total investment in schooling and defends the rate-of-
return approach as against the conventional additional-lifetime-income method
employed by Miller and Houthakker.

165 T. BALOGH, P. P. STREETEN, "The Coefficient of Ignorance", *BOUIES*, May, 1963,
     pp. 99-107, reprinted in *P-EED*, *1*, pp. 383-95, and *WYK I*, pp. 194-204.

   The article is mainly concerned with unwarranted extensions to underdeveloped
countries of results derived from the experiences of industrialised countries,
but along the way the authors express strong disagreement with American studies
of the economic contribution of education. On the rate-of-return approach they
say: "The American data, which are most used, do not produce evidence as to
whether expenditure on education is a *cause* or an *effect* of superior incomes;
they do not show, even if we could assume it to be a condition of higher
earnings, whether it is a *sufficient* or *necessary* condition of growth, and they
do not separate *monopolistic* and *other forces* influencing differential earnings
which are correlated with, but not caused by, differential education." Similar
views are expressed in an earlier article by Balogh in *TES*, June 8, 1962,
p. 1179.

166 R. VUARIDEL, "Capital humain et économie de l'éducation", *SZVS*, June, 1963,
     pp. 193-219.

   Stresses the importance of the indirect benefits of education which are
likened to consumer durables in contrast to the direct benefits which are in
the nature of producer goods. Seems to deny that the indirect benefits are
associated with increases in national income.

167   J. N. MORGAN, M. H. DAVID, "Education and Income", *QJE*, August, 1963, pp.
      423-38, reprinted in *WYK II*, pp. 177-95.

      Multivariate analysis is used to derive estimates of the effects of education
      on hourly earnings, indicating that the objections to the use of simple aver-
      age earnings of different age and education groups on grounds of spurious corre-
      lation are correct but quantitatively unimportant. See also J. N. Morgan,
      C. Lininger, "Education and Income: Comment", *QJE*, May, 1964, pp. 346-47.

168   J. VAIZEY, "Criteria for Public Expenditures on Education", *IEA-EE*, pp. 451-63.

      After a quick once-over-lightly review of the debate, Vaizey concludes: "I
      am more agnostic on the matter of the contribution of education to economic grow
      than a number of more recent converts to the cause. I am doubtful whether,
      in the long run, the concepts of education as 'investment' will prove much
      of a guide on what 'ought' to be spent on education."

169   W. G. BOWEN, "Assessing the Economic Contribution of Education: An Appraisal
      of Alternative Approaches", *Higher Education. Report of the Committee under
      the Chairmanship of Lord Robbins 1961-63.* London: HMSO, 1963, App. 4,
      pp. 73-96. Cmnd. 2154-IV. Reprinted in *OECD-EAHE*, pp. 177-201, *P-EED, 1*,
      pp. 67-100, and *Economic Aspects of Education. Three Essays* by W. G. Bowen.
      Princeton, N.J.: Industrial Relation Section, Princeton University, 1964,
      pp. 3-41.

      A useful review of the literature divided into (a) the simple-correlation
      approach; (b) the residual approach; (c) the returns-to-education approach;
      and (d) the forecasting-manpower-needs approach.

170   A. O. KRUEGER, "The Economics of Discrimination", *JPE*, October, 1963,
      pp. 481-87.

      Corrects the wage determination model in G. S. Becker's *Economics of Dis-
      crimination* (1957, 2d ed, 1971) by introducing education as an additional
      variable.

171   S. J. HUNT, "Income Determinants for College Graduates and the Return to
      Educational Investment", *YEE*, Fall, 1963, pp. 305-57.

      An attempt to improve estimates of the income benefits of college education
      in the USA by introducing the effect of an improved quality of undergraduate
      education on the yield of investment in graduate education.

172   A KAHAN, "Some Russian Economists on Returns to Schooling and Experience",
      first published in *UNESCO-REED*, pp. 399-410.

      The first systematic history and critique of Russian work on the rate of
      return to investment in education. (See 63, 130, 1438.)

1964

173 LÊ THÀNH KNÔI, "Le rendement de l'éducation", *TM*, janvier-mars, 1964,
     pp. 105-39.

     A careful review of the literature on the residual-factor and rate-of-return
     approaches to the economic value of education.

174 H. P. MILLER, *Rich Man, Poor Man*. New York: Thomas Y. Crowell, 1964, ch. 8,
     pp. 139-65.

     The chapter on "the cash value of education" in this popular book on income
     distribution in the United States presents the chief findings to date on life-
     time earnings differentials from extra education in America.

175 B. A. WEISBROD, *External Benefits of Public Education. An Economic Analysis*.
     Princeton, N.J.: Industrial Relations Section, Princeton University, 1964.
     Pp. 143. Excerpts reprinted in *URB*, pp. 151-71.

     This important and very original book is an extension and elaboration of the
     author's earlier article (see 158). It deals, in particular, with geographical
     spillovers among school districts in the United States and includes a case
     study of a district in Missouri (see 214).

176 W. Z. HIRSCH, E. W. SEGELHORST, M. J. MARCUS, *Spillover of Public Education
     Costs and Benefits*. Los Angeles: University of California Press, 1964.
     Pp. 465.

     A useful discussion of geographical spillovers of both costs and benefits of
     education, together with an ingenious attempt to measure them in one school
     district in Missouri. (See also 175 for a discussion of some of the same data).

177 S. CAINE, "Education as a Factor of Production", *LBR*, April, 1964, pp. 1-17.

     Some critical comments on current investigations of the investment return
     on education and brief discussions of various other topics in the economics
     of education.

178 J. E. MEADE, *Efficiency, Equality and the Ownership of Property*. London:
     Allen & Unwin, 1964, pp. 30-32, 59-63.

     This discussion of the distribution of property in a modern economy touches
     on the equalising tendency of education and analyses the impact of alternative
     educational policies on the distribution of earning power and, through the
     power to accumulate, on the distribution of real wealth.

179 G. S. BECKER, *Human Capital. A Theoretical and Empirical Analysis, with
     Special Reference to Education*. Princeton, N.J.: Princeton University Press,
     1964. Pp. 187. Excerpts reprinted in *URB*, pp. 62-70.

     This *magnum opus*, incorporating and extending earlier studies by the author
     (see 145, 156), develops a general theory of human capital formation and applies

it to such diverse phenomena as interpersonal, interracial, and interregional differences in earnings, the shape of age-earnings and age-wealth profiles, and the rates of return from high school and college education in 1939 and 1949, corrected for variations in native ability and home environment. It is shown that private rates of return on college education exceed those on business capital, but social rates of return are roughly similar to the yield of business capital. A closing section on "future research" sketches further work along similar lines contemplated by the author. See the book review by A. Rees, *AER*, September, 1965, pp. 958-60, and the article review by M. W. Reder, *JHR*, Winter, 1967, pp. 97-104.

180 M. E. BORUS, "A Benefit-Cost Analysis of the Economic Effectiveness of Retraining the Unemployed", *YEE*, Fall, 1964, pp. 371-429.

An attempt to calculate the private and social returns of a government-sponsored retraining programme in Connecticut. After comparing the present value of future income streams of retrained and untrained workers, the author concludes that benefits considerably outweigh costs, and that the social rate of return is higher than the private rate.

181 C. H. FRIEDMAN, "Education of New York City Public School Teachers: An Economic Analysis", *ILRR*, October, 1964, pp. 20-32.

Demonstrates that the rate of return to post-baccalaureate teacher training in the New York City school system is negative relative to teachers with post-graduate preparation. It is argued that this fact accounts for the difficulties that N.Y.C. has experienced in recruiting highly trained teachers.

1965

182 M. BLAUG, "The Rate of Return on Investment in Education in Great Britain", *MS*, September, 1965, pp. 205-62, reprinted in *P-EED*, *1*, pp. 215-59, and in German in *Nutzen-Kosten-Analyse und Programmbudget*, ed. H. C. Recktenwald, Tübingen: J. C. B. Mohr, 1970, pp. 291-302.

Calculates the private and social rate of return on educational investment in secondary and higher education in Great Britain in 1963 and defends rate-of-return analysis against six objections that are current in the literature. The final section of the paper discusses the policy implications of the approach.

183 G. ROUTH, *Occupation and Pay in Great Britain, 1906-60*. National Institute of Economic and Social Research. Cambridge: Cambridge University Press, 1965. Pp. 182.

This detailed study of changes in the composition and pay structure of occupational groups includes a historical analysis of income differentials. There is a very short section on the length of training required in different occupations, and an estimate of the average educational level of the labour force since 1911. But the author's main emphasis is on the importance of institutional factors in determining income differentials.

184 W. LEE HANSEN, "'Shortages' and Investment in Health Manpower", *The Economics of Health and Medical Care*, ed. S. J. Axelrod. Ann Arbor, Mich.: The University of Michigan, 1965, pp. 75-92.

   One of the first articles to use rate-of-return evidence to throw light on shortages of qualified manpower, in this case, physicians and dentists in the United States. The author compares the rates of return of physicians and dentists with those of all male college graduates between 1939 and 1956, showing that the shortage of doctors and dentists has declined since 1949.

185 G. L. REID, D. J. ROBERTSON, eds., *Fringe Benefits, Labour Costs and Social Security*. London: Allen & Unwin, 1965. Pp. 336.

   An attempt to measure the economic importance of fringe benefits for employees in Britain as compared with the United States and Europe. Includes results from a survey in Glasgow on expenditures on fringe benefits for manual workers, including sick pay, redundancy schemes, holidays with pay, pension schemes, and free education. This section provides an analysis of each type of benefit by industry, size of firm, etc. The question whether free education is a fringe benefit for the employee or an investment for the firm is briefly discussed.

186 J. R. PODOLUK, *Earnings and Education* (Advance Release from Census Monograph, *Incomes of Canadians*). Dominion Bureau of Statistics, Central Research and Development Staff. Ottawa: Queen's Printer and Controller of Stationery, 1965. Pp. 82.

   This study analyses the earnings of the Canadian labour force by age, sex, occupation, and years of schooling, and calculates the present value of net earnings by years of schooling at various discount rates. Includes some comparisons with recent United States findings.

187 J. T. TUNES, P. B. JACOBSON, R. J. PELLEGRIN, *The Economic Returns to Education. A Survey of the Findings*. Eugene, Oregon: Center for the Advanced Study of Educational Administration, 1965. Pp. 45.

   A straightforward summary of the work of Schultz, Lee Hansen, Miller, and Denison, with a brief bibliography of rate-of-return literature.

188 Economic Council of Canada, Second Annual Review, *Towards Sustained and Balanced Economic Growth*. Ottawa: Queen's Printer, 1965. Pp. 204.

   Ch. 4, pp. 71-97, of this annual review is devoted to the topic of education and Canadian economic growth, and compares the mean years of schooling and the rates of return on investment in education in Canada and the United States.

189 H.-J. VOSGERAU, "Ueber Kosten und Erträge von Ausbildungsinvestitionen", *KYK*, XVIII, 3, 1965, pp. 434-50.

   A review of American work on the rate of return on investment in college education, with critical remarks on the neglect of the external effects of education.

190 J. W. McKIE, ed., "Education and the Southern Economy", *SEJ*, Suppl., July,
     1965, pp. 1-128.

     The five papers in this volume were originally delivered at a Conference on
     Education and Human Resources sponsored by the Inter-University Committee for
     Economic Research on the South. The first paper, "Cost-Benefit Analysis in
     Education" by J. Wiseman, reprinted in *URB*, pp. 205-23, and *WYK I* , pp. 177-93,
     raises some sceptical questions about the policy implications of rate-of-return
     analysis, which T. W. Schultz answers in a comment, pp. 1-15. W. C. Stubble-
     bine's "Institutional Elements in the Financing of Education", with comments
     by E. F. Renshaw, pp. 15-39, is a path-breaking essay: using a simplified
     analytical model with differences in family preferences for education as a
     function of family shares of the tax base, he tries to show that educational
     systems which combine private and public finance will elicit maximum financial
     support. A. M. Cartter applies the authoritative-opinion principle to the
     ordinal measurement of "Qualitative Aspects of Southern University Education",
     with comments by H. G. Schaller, pp. 39-73. M. J. Bowman's "Human Inequalities
     and Southern Underdevelopment", with comments by A. M. Rivlin, pp. 73-106, is
     concerned with various measures of under-development of the human resources of
     the South. R. Fein supplies additional detail on "Educational Patterns in
     Southern Migration", with comments by W. N. Parker, pp. 106-28.

191 R. L. LASSITER, JR., "The Association of Income and Education for Males by
     Region, Race, and Age", *ibid.*, July, 1965, pp. 15-23.

     Measures the statistical relationship between income and years of school
     completed for males in the South and North of the United States by race and
     age, using the 1960 Census of Population (see 200).

192 M. GISSER, "Schooling and the farm problem", *ECOM*, July, 1965, pp. 582-92.

     This article reports on the results of an econometric study of the relation-
     ship between the level of schooling in American farm areas and the income of
     farm workers. It estimates supply and demand functions for farm labour, incor-
     porating the level of schooling as a predetermined variable, and concludes
     that the net effect of more schooling would be to raise incomes in rural areas
     and to encourage farm out-migration. The closing section estimates the cost
     of raising the level of schooling in rural farm areas from an average of 8 to
     an average of 12 years.

193 M. J. BOWMAN, "The Requirements of the Labour-Market and the Education Explo-
     sion", *The Education Explosion. World Year Book of Education 1965*, eds.
     G. Z. F. Bereday, J. A. Lauwerys. London: Evans Bros., 1965, pp. 64-81.

     Presents and discusses rate-of-return evidence for the United States, India,
     and Mexico, followed by a typology of educational explosions around the world.
     The basic thesis of the article is that the recent expansion in the private
     demand for education is explainable on economic grounds.

194 H. P. MILLER, "Lifetime Income and Economic Growth", *AER*, September, 1965,
     pp. 834-44; "Comment" by Y. Ben-Porath, *ibid.*, September, 1966, pp. 869-72,
     reprinted in *WYK I*, pp. 219-30.

     Argues that the usual methods of estimating lifetime incomes associated with
     education from cross-section surveys of earnings tend to produce underestimates

of the rate of return on investment in education because of the failure to take account of the future growth of income. No reference is made to Becker's book *Human Capital* where this factor is discussed and taken into account.

195 W. Z. HIRSCH, E. W. SEGELHORST, "Incremental Income Benefits of Public Education", *RES*, November, 1965, pp. 392-99.

Using the results of sample survey data collected in 1957 for the St. Louis City County area, the authors calculate regression coefficients representing the net effect of education on income, after adjusting for race, sex, mortality, occupation, self-employment, supervisory status, occupation of father, years of work experience, migration from the Deep South, size of birthplace, and quality of education in terms of per pupil expenditure. They find very high rates of return and compare their results with those of Lee Hansen, Miller, and Becker.

196 A. R. PREST, R. TURVEY, "Cost-Benefit Analyses: A Survey", *EJ*, December, 1965, pp. 683-736, reprinted in *Surveys of Economic Theory,* III. London: Macmillan, 1966, pp. 155-207.

This background paper on rate-of-return analysis surveys the entire field and discusses applications of cost-benefit analysis to water resource planning, transport problems, land usage, health, education, and defence.

197 Committee of the National Science Foundation Report on the Economics Profession, *The Structure of Economists' Employment and Salaries, 1964, AER*, Suppl., December, 1965. Pp. 98.

Some 12,000 American economists are included in the NSF's National Register of 224,000 Scientific and Technical Personnel. The NSF itself will shortly publish a new edition of its *American Science Manpower*, covering the 1964 data for each of the twelve physical and social science professions. This publication is an analysis of the information on economists. The central findings are summarised on pp. 1-6. From the point of view of the manpower forecaster, particular attention is drawn to the discussion of the definition of an economist (the Census counts 10,000 more economists than the NSF), pp. 11-16, the wide range of educational qualifications characterising an economist, p. 19, and the importance of occupation as a factor intervening between education and salary, pp. 34-36. All the evidence needed to calculate rates of return to investment in an economist's education are to be found here (see also 249, 293).

198 H. J. GILMAN, "Economic Discrimination and Unemployment", *ibid.*, December, 1965, pp. 1077-97.

This paper tests the hypothesis that the greater unemployment rate of American nonwhite males over white males is due not just to discriminatory treatment in hiring and firing, but to the occupational and educational characteristics of nonwhite workers. It turns out that occupation does indeed account for almost half of the differential unemployment rates in the 1950's, but that differences in educational attainment as such have little impact on the differential.

1966

199 F. T. JUSTER, *Household Capital Formation and Financing 1897-1962*. New York:
     NBER, 1966. Pp. 146.

     Apart from some useful pages on the investment versus consumption aspects of
     household capital formation, including education, pp. 5-13, there is an impor-
     tant chapter on the structure of consumer capital markets in the United States,
     pp. 51-73, which has implications for the interpretation of private rates of
     return on educational investment.

200 R. L. LASSITER, JR., *The Association of Income and Educational Achievement*,
     University of Florida Monographs Social Sciences No. 30. Gainesville.
     Florida: University of Florida Press, 1966. Pp. 52.

     The first study to examine the relationship between income and education,
     as well as rates of return on investment in education, in the United States
     by race, sex, urban-rural residence, and region for the census years 1949 and
     1959. A linear regression model is employed to estimate the strength of the
     relationships.

201 G. L. REID, L. C. HUNTER, *Industrial Worker Mobility*. Paris: OECD, Director-
     ate for Manpower and Social Affairs, 1966. Pp. 209, mimeographed.

     Although education is hardly mentioned in this study, it provides an able
     summary of a literature (and a bibliography of 280 items) that bears directly
     on some aspects of the economics of education, such as manpower planning and
     the economics of on-the-job training.

202 G. J. STIGLER, *The Theory of Price*. New York: Macmillan, 3rd ed., 1966,
     chs. 16, 18, pp. 257-74, 288-312.

     One of the few texts in microeconomics that discuss the effects of on-the-
     job training on lifetime earnings and the impact of education on the distribu-
     tion of income.

203 W. Z. HIRSCH, M. J. MARCUS, "Some Benefit-Cost Considerations of Universal
     Junior College Education", *NTJ*, March, 1966, pp. 48-57, reprinted in *WYK II*,
     pp. 147-62.

     A rate-of-return analysis of a two-year college programme for the United
     States.

204 F. T. DENTON, *An Analysis of Interregional Differences in Manpower Utilization
     and Earnings*. Staff Study No. 15. Economic Council of Canada. Ottawa,
     Canada: Queen's Printer, 1966. Pp. 62.

     A regression analysis of interregional differences in levels of income in
     Canada which includes educational densities in each region as one of the deter-
     mining factors.

205 R. KLINOV-MALUL, *The Profitability of Investment in Education in Israel*.
     Jerusalem: The Maurice Falk Institute for Economic Research in Israel, 1966.
     Pp. 109.

     An elaboration and refinement of 1395. Calculates the present value of the
     net returns to years of schooling in Israel in 1957 at various discount rates,
     after making allowance for country of origin and length of residence, but not
     for native ability. Comparisons are drawn with the United States, and the
     returns to doctors, lawyers, engineers, and accountants are separately calcu-
     lated.

206 G. S. BECKER, B. CHISWICK, "Education and the Distribution of Earnings",*AER*,
     May, 1966, pp. 358-70.

     The sketch of a theory of personal income distribution based on the effects
     of education and training received by individuals, together with some empirical
     results explaining regional income differences in the United States by varia-
     tions in the amount of schooling.

207 W. G. BOWEN, T. A. FINEGAN, "Educational Attainment and Labor Force Participa-
     tion", *ibid.*, 1966, pp. 567-83.

     A study of the relation in the United States between years of schooling com-
     pleted and the labour force participation rate for both younger and older males
     as well as for married women. See the comments by W. Lee Hansen, pp. 594-6.

208 H. P. MILLER, *Income Distribution in the United States*. *A 1960 Census Mono-
     graph*. Washington, D.C.: US Government Printing Office, 1966. Pp. 306.

     The pivotal chapter in this masterful book is ch. 6 on "Income and Education",
     which estimates age-earnings profiles by years of schooling completed and for
     various occupations in the census years 1939, 1949, and 1959. Other chapters
     consider wage and salary trends for major occupation and skill groups between
     1939 and 1959. The volume includes a valuable appendix that evaluates census
     income data.

209 M. BLAUG, "An Economic Interpretation of the Private Demand for Education",
     EC, May, 1966, pp. 166-82, reprinted in German in *BILD*, pp. 212-34.

     Develops the policy implications of the hypothesis that the demand for educa-
     tion is a function of the private yield of educational investment.

210 R. BARLOW, H. E. BRAZER, J. N. MORGAN, *Economic Behaviour of the Affluent*.
     Washington, D.C.: The Brookings Institution, 1966. Pp. 285.

     Presents the results of a sample survey of high-income individuals in the
     United States with details of their investment behaviour, motives for saving,
     occupational characteristics, etc. The sample had a higher than average level
     of education and the study includes some analysis of investment behaviour with
     respect to education.

211 A. K. SEN, "Education, Vintage, and Learning by Doing", *JHR*, Fall, 1966,
     pp. 3-22.

An important article that constructs and tests a simple "vintage" model of investment in labour quality, relating work experience to formal educational preparation. The model's major predictions—that the rate of increase of productive ability will decline with age and that the productive ability profile will have a single peak—are tested with the aid of data from the US Census of 1960 and the Canadian Census of 1961

212 W. FOGEL, "The Effect of Low Educational Attainment on Incomes: A Comparative Study of Selected Ethnic Groups", *ibid.*, pp. 22-41, reprinted in *WYK I*, pp. 367-82.

Using 1960 US Census data, this study shows that a given educational attainment has less income value for certain minority groups in the United States than for the majority. Educational attainment accounts for less than half of the difference between the 1959 median income of minority groups and the majority.

213 T. BLUMENTHAL, "The Effect of Socio-Economic Factors on Wage Differentials in Japanese Manufacturing Industries", *ESQ*, September, 1966, pp. 53-67.

This article presents a variance-covariance analysis of wage differentials in Japanese manufacturing, taking account of such factors as sex, age, occupation, education and size of firm. Age-education earnings profiles by size of firm are given and education is shown to contribute much less to earnings than sex, age and size of firm.

214 A. G. HOLTMANN, "A Note on Public Education and Spillovers through Migration", *JPE*, October, 1966, pp. 524-26.

A critique of Weisbrod's thesis that migration of educated people constitutes an external effect; the argument is an application of Becker's competitive model in which profit-maximising firms will not bear the cost of general on-the-job training.

215 B. A. WEISBROD, "Conceptual Issues in Evaluating Training Programs", *MLR*, October, 1966, pp. 1091-97.

A clear exposition of the nature of the costs and benefits of training programmes.

216 S. MERRETT, "The Rate of Return to Education. A Critique", *OEP*, November, 1966, pp. 289-303, reprinted in *WYK II*, pp. 196-213.

The author criticises rate-of-return analysis for slighting the interactions between education, income, and native ability. The bulk of the paper is devoted to a simple exposition of the statistical difficulties of unravelling these interactions in multivariate analysis, concluding that "research into the rate of return to education should be discontinued". An appendix deals with the Becker-Mincer method of calculating the returns to labour training.

217 I. H. BUTTER, *Economics of Graduate Education: An Exploratory Study*. US Department of Health, Education and Welfare, Office of Education, Bureau of Research. Final Report. Ann Arbor, Mich.: The University of Michigan, 1966. Pp. 97.

Calculates social rates of return to investment in American graduate education in four fields—physics, zoology, sociology, and english—and compares these
to rates of return at other levels of American higher education.

218   B. W. WILKINSON, "Present Values of Lifetime Earnings for Different Occupations", *JPE*, December, 1966, pp. 556-73, reprinted in *RLMA*, pp. 362-77, and
KIK, pp. 254-78.

This important article calculates some net present values of Canadian lifetime earnings in six different occupations and for three levels of education
within each occupation from the 1961 Canadian Census. It is found that at any
one discount rate, there exists a rough similarity of net present values for
persons with varying amounts of education. The paper concludes with some
comparisons between the findings for 1957 and 1961.

1967

219   L. C. THUROW, "The Causes of Poverty", *QJE*, February, 1967, pp. 39-57.

An econometric analysis of the causes of poverty in the United States which
shows that education alone will significantly reduce the incidence of poverty
in future years. The article closes with some important comments on the ambiguous policy implications of the study.

220   R. A. WYKSTRA, "Some Additional Evidence on Education and Non-participation
in the Labor Force", *WEJ*, June, 1967, pp. 288-93.

Some additional evidence for recent decades on the relationship between
educational attainment and labour force participation rates in the United
States.

221   F. WELCH, "Labor-Market Discrimination: An Interpretation of Income Differences in the Rural South", *JPE*, June, 1967, pp. 225-41, reprinted in *KIK*,
pp. 540-62.

A model of market discrimination, followed by an empirical analysis of
White–Negro income differentials in ten southern American states in 1959, to
determine the separate effects of differences in the ownership of physical
capital, differences in the quantity and quality of education received, and
outright market discrimination against educated labour.

222   T. W. SCHULTZ, "The Rate of Return in Allocating Investment Resources to
Education", *JHR*, Summer, 1967, pp. 293-310.

A stock-taking of recent examples of rate-of-return analysis and a judicious
evaluation of the strengths and weaknesses of the approach as an allocative
guide to investment in education.

223   G. HANOCH, "An Economic Analysis of Earnings and Schooling", *ibid.*, pp. 310-30,
reprinted in *WYK I*, pp. 231-49, and *KIK*, pp. 190-210.

This paper is based on an unpublished thesis that is widely regarded as the most careful of all the efforts to date to estimate private rates of return to educational investment in the United States. The paper concludes with a discussion of the shape of the demand function for investment in education.

224 M. BLAUG, "The Private and the Social Returns on Investment in Education: Some Results for Great Britain", *ibid.*, pp. 330-47.

This paper summarises the results of 182 and 1072.

225 Y. BEN-PORATH, "The Production of Human Capital and the Life Cycle of Earnings", *JPE*, August, 1967, Part I, pp. 352-65, reprinted in *KIK*, pp. 130-49.

A difficult but important theoretical article, which adds a microeconomic production function of human capital to the Schultz-Becker theory of investment of human beings, and then explores some of the implications of the properties of the production function for (1) the life cycle of earnings and (2) the optimal path of accumulation of human capital.

226 H.-J. BODENHÖFER, "The Mobility of Labor and the Theory of Human Capital", *JHR*, Fall, 1967, pp. 431-48, reprinted in *KIK*, pp. 917-36.

A broad theoretical discussion of the returns to labour mobility, as distinct from returns to education and to on-the-job training.

227 J. B. LANSING, J. N. MORGAN, "The Effect of Geographical Mobility on Income", *ibid.*, pp. 449-60.

Empirical evidence is produced to show that the income of migrants in the United States is actually lower than that of nonmigrants, even after standardising for differences in the number of years of schooling. The authors conclude that years of schooling is a poor index of the educational differences between people of different geographic backgrounds.

228 L. E. GALLAWAY, "Industry Variations in Geographic Labor Mobility Patterns", *ibid.*, pp. 461-74.

On the basis of 1957 cross-section data for the United States, the author shows that interindustry movements are positively related to differences in earnings and inversely related to the distance between labour markets.

229 J. LADINSKY, "The Geographic Mobility of Professional and Technical Manpower", *ibid.*, pp. 475-94.

A detailed empirical analysis of the 1960 Census to reveal the determinants of the migration of professional, technical, and kindred workers. Age accounted for most of the explained variance in mobility, followed by income, education, regional location, sex, family size, and marital status. The paper closes with a discussion of the occupational determinants of mobility.

230 A. ZUCKER, "A Note on the Declining Tendency with Age for Investment in Human Capital", *ibid.*, pp. 538-40.

A measurement of the coefficient of variation of rates of return by age on the assumption of a simple investment model and a rate of return of 8 per cent.

231 M. J. BOWMAN, R. G. MYERS, "Schooling, Experience, and Gains and Losses in Human Capital Through Migration", *JASA*, September, 1967, pp. 875-98, reprinted in *WYK I*, pp. 309-35, and *KIK*, pp. 485-516.

A theoretical discussion of human investment models of internal migration within the United States, which reviews the work of Sjaastad, Weisbrod, Grubel and Scott, and Fein, and makes suggestions for new census tabulations that would allow more careful analysis of the determinants of migration.

232 J. J. KAUFMAN, G. N. FARR, J. C. SHEARER, *The Development and Utilization of Human Resources. A Guide for Research.* University Park, Pa.: Institute for Research on Human Resources, The Pennsylvania State University, 1967. Pp. 91.

This is a rather depressing little book which catalogues the vast areas of ignorance about the demand for and supply of human resources, with particular reference to the United States, and concludes with "Suggested Priorities in Research". Bibliographical references, suggesting the little that we do know, might have converted this publication into a really useful contribution.

233 C. J. CIPRIANI, "Hedging in the Labor Market", *SEJ*, October, 1967, pp. 286-92; "Comment" by A. R. Melnik, *ibid.*, January, 1969, pp. 270-72, reprinted in *KIK*, pp. 360-76.

An application of Becker's analysis of human capital formation to the choice of acquiring a second in addition to a first skill as a method of hedging against skill obsolescence.

234 A. B. CARROLL, L. A. IHNEN, "Costs and Returns for Two Years of Post-secondary Technical Schooling: A Pilot Study", *JPE*, December, 1967, pp. 862-73.

This study is based on evidence about 45 graduates of a two-year post-secondary technical school in North Carolina. The income data covered a period of 7-8 years and were standardised for differences in ability, motivation, family background, and a number of other relevant variables. The rate of return on the total investment was found to be 16.5 per cent.

235 G. S. BECKER, *Human Capital and the Personal Distribution of Income. An Analytical Approach.* W. S. Woytinsky Lecture No. 1. Ann Arbor, Mich.: University of Michigan, 1967. Pp. 49. Excerpts reprinted in *KIK*, pp. 40-50.

This important but relatively inaccessible pamphlet develops the opening chapters of the author's *Human Capital* into a general theory of the size distribution of personal income.

1968

236 M. C. BENEWITZ, A. ZUCKER, "Human Capital and Occupational Choice—A Theoretical Model", *SEJ*, January, 1968, pp. 406-9, reprinted in *KIK*, pp. 354-59.

A sketch of a model of occupational choice based on the notion that individuals choose that occupation for which the present value of expected income is
maximised.

237 O. ASCHENFELTER, J. D. MOONEY, "Graduate Education, Ability and Earnings",
     RES, February, 1968, pp. 78-86, reprinted in *WYK I*, pp. 250-62.

     The authors use multiple regression analysis to estimate the money returns
     to graduate education in the USA, after adjusting for variations in native
     ability. One of their central conclusions is that years of graduate study is
     an inadequate measure of graduate educational attainment: degree level and
     field of study account for more of the variance in earnings than years of
     study (see 263).

238 E. D. MAIN, "A Nationwide Evaluation of the M.D.T.A. Institutional Job
     Training", *JHR*, Spring, 1968, pp. 159-70.

     An evaluation of the job-training schemes of the American Manpower Develop-
     ment and Training Act. The principal finding is that MDTA training increased
     the incomes of trainees by helping them to obtain steadier employment rather
     than by raising their wages.

239 E. W. STROMSDORFER, "Determinants of Economic Success in Retraining the Unem-
     ployed: the West Virginia Experience", *ibid.*, pp. 139-58.

     A multivariate analysis of a sample of trainees in a government-sponsored
     retraining programme for the long-term unemployed in West Virginia. During
     the 18-month post-training period, additional earnings exceeded costs, even
     after allowing for variations in associated factors: the rate of return on
     the costs of the programme was as high as 64-90 per cent.

240 *The World Year Book of Education 1968. Education Within Industry,* eds.
     J. A. Lauwerys, D. G. Scanlon, B. Holmes, L. G. Howe, K. E. Thurley. London:
     Evans Bros., 1968. Pp. 382.

     This volume contains 18 useful case studies, but the six theoretical chapters
     and the 14 national surveys are too brief to be of much value. It is extra-
     ordinary that in a book like this the names of Becker and Mincer do not even
     appear and that virtually nothing is said about the recent advances in the
     economics of labour training.

241 B. R. CHISWICK, "Schooling and Intra-Regional Income Inequality", *AER*, June,
     1968, pp. 495-501.

     An attempt to explain the relationship between schooling and regional dif-
     ferences in personal incomes in the United States, based on a calculation of
     the rates of return from schooling for white males in all the 51 states in
     1960.

242 B. THOMAS, J. MOXHAM and J. A. G. JONES, "A Cost-Benefit Analysis of Industrial
     Training", *BJIR*, July, 1969, pp. 231-64.

A case-study of how to measure the costs and benefits of a training scheme
in one British firm, preceded by a lengthy discussion of the analytical framework of cost-benefit analysis at the level of the individual enterprise.

243 L. EMMERIJ, M. FRANK, O. F. STALEMAN, P. DE WOLFF, R. RUITER, *De economie van
het onderwijs*. Vereniging voor de Staathuishondkunde. Den Haag: Martinus
Nijhoff, 1968. Pp. 179.

A major collection of essays, so far available only in Dutch. L. Emmerij
contributes an interesting research-oriented review of recent developments in
the economics of education, with illustrative Dutch, American, and international data, pp. 7-59. M. Frank complements this review with "Some Comments
on the Economics of Education", pp. 60-82. O. F. Staleman attempts to analyse
"The Internal Efficiency of Education" in The Netherlands, pp. 82-110. Lastly,
P. De Wolff and R. Ruiter estimate the rate of return to levels of education
in Holland, the sources of growth in Holland à la Denison, and Layard-Saigal
equations for Dutch industries and occupations, which they then compare with
manpower forecasts up to 1980.

244 H. LYDALL, *The Structure of Earnings*. London: Oxford University Press, 1968.
Pp. 394.

This study attempts to explain both changes in the distribution of earnings
from employment over time and differences in the distribution between countries in recent years. The distribution of education in an economy plays an
important role in the author's theory (see, particularly, pp. 209-15, 254-62).
In addition, the book contains excellent surveys of theories of the size distribution of personal incomes, pp. 12-42, present evidence on the interrelationship between genetic inheritance, home background, and school achievement,
pp. 71-88, and recent efforts to account for occupational earnings differentials by the element of investment in training, pp. 88-102.

245 G. G. SOMERS, ed., *Retraining the Unemployed*. Madison, Wisc.: University of
Wisconsin Press, 1968. Pp. 351.

This volume of nine essays begins with an introductory essay by G. G.
Somers, pp. 3-16, followed by a veritable monograph by H. A. Gribbard and
G. G. Somers, "Government Retraining of the Unemployed in West Virginia",
pp. 17-124; M. E. Borus, "The Effect of Retraining the Unemployed in Connecticut", pp. 125-48; H. A. Chesler, "The Retraining Decision in Massachusetts:
Theory and Practice", pp. 140-70; J. E. Williams, "Retraining in Tennessee",
pp. 171-92; R. J. Solie, "An Evaluation of the Effects of Retraining in
Tennessee", pp. 193-212; L. A. Ferman, S. Harvey, "Job Retraining in Michigan",
pp. 213-56; A. R. Weber, "Experiments in Retraining: A Comparative Study",
pp. 257-98; and G. G. Cain and E. W. Stromsdorfer, "An Economic Evaluation of
Government Retraining Programs in West Virginia", pp. 299-338. For earlier
versions of some of these papers, see 180, 239.

246 T. I. RIBICH, *Education and Poverty*. Washington, D.C.: The Brookings Institution, 1968. Pp. 163. Excerpts reprinted in *URB*, pp. 172-204.

This superb little book applies cost-benefit analysis to job training, dropout prevention and compensatory education in the United States, bringing
together all the available evidence on the likely economic returns from such

programmes. The author shows that these projects to date have yielded very
low rates of return and are, on the whole, not capable of seriously alleviating
the poverty problem in the United States. The book includes a critical appendix on Weisbrod's concept of "option values". (See also 534).

247 J. MORGAN, I. SIRAGELDIN, "A Note on the Quality Dimension in Education", *JPE*,
     September/October, 1968, pp. 1069-77.

   An ingenious attempt to measure differences in the quality of schooling
between American states by removing all the standard effects on earnings of
family heads, and then relating the unexplained residual earnings to the
average expenditures on primary and secondary education years ago in the state
where each person grew up.

248 B. A. WEISBROD, P. KARPOFF, "Monetary Returns to College Education, Student
     Ability, and College Quality", *RES*, November, 1968, pp. 491-97.

   Working with data from a sample of about 7,000 male college graduate
employees of the American Telephone and Telegraph Company, the authors show
that about 25 per cent, or at most 31 per cent, of the observed earnings
differentials of college graduates are due to schooling alone.

249 N. A. TOLLES, E. MELICHAR, *Studies of the Structure of Economists' Salaries
     and Income*, Supplement, *AER*, December, 1968, pp. I-XXXV, 1-153.

   An exhaustive analysis of the data published earlier (197) with comparisons
to other professional salaries and incomes in the United States.

250 "Onderwijs en Economie", *Economisch-Statistische Berichten*, December 18, 1968,
     pp. 1165-99.

   A symposium on the economics of education made up of three articles in
English by J. Vaizey, M. Blaug, and J. King, and five articles in Dutch by
J. Tinbergen, L. Emmerij, P. Ressenaar, P. de Wolff, and W. Drees. The paper
by de Wolff summarises a study (243) which calculated rates of return on educational investment in The Netherlands.

1969

251 D. C. ROGERS, "Private Rates of Return to Education in the United States:
     A Case Study", *YEE*, Spring, 1969, pp. 89-134.

   This is an important contribution to the literature. It is a study of 364
individuals who were in their last year of elementary education in 1935: IQ
data was obtained and longitudinal earnings for the cohort since 1935 were
extrapolated up to 1965 from national data. A multiple regression model was
run with 34 independent variables and private rates of return were calculated
for each level of education. These rates are compared to the results of other
studies. The central finding of the study is that IQ has little effect on
rates of return because it depresses the pure returns from education almost
equally at all levels.

252 R. W. CONLEY, "A Benefit-Cost Analysis of the Vocational Rehabilitation Pro-
     gramme", *JHR*, Spring, 1969, pp. 226-32.

     An estimate of the costs and benefits in the form of enhanced earnings of
     the rehabilitation programme for 170,000 disabled persons, carried out in the
     fiscal year 1967.

253 F. WELCH, "Linear Synthesis of Skill Distribution", *ibid.*, Summer, 1969,
     pp. 311-27.

     This highly original paper attempts to provide a method for linearly combin-
     ing skill categories so as to minimise the number of categories required to
     describe a skill distribution. Making use of American data by states, the
     author shows that three schooling categories suffice to describe the distri-
     bution of earnings by education among the 50 states.

254 N. F. DUFTY, "A Model of Choice in an Australian Labor Market", *ibid.*,
     pp. 328-42.

     An important paper that attempts to construct a model of occupational choice
     with special reference to Australian labour markets.

255 J. MATON, "Experience on the Job and Formal Training as Alternative Means of
     Skill Acquisition: An Empirical Study", *ILR*, September, 1969, pp. 239-55.

     This article estimates iso-skill lines, that is isoquants relating formal
     education to work experience, from a sample of about 300 workers in Belgian
     and Argentinian enterprises.

256 B. CHISWICK, "Minimum Schooling Legislation and the Cross-Sectional Distribu-
     tion of Income", *EJ*, September, 1969, pp. 495-507.

     This is a difficult but significant article which extends the work of
     Mincer, Becker and Chiswick to analyse the effect of compulsory schooling on
     both the distribution of earnings in an economy and the rate of return on
     educational investment. The paper develops a model which is tested on British
     and Dutch data.

257 G. PSACHAROPOULOS, *The Rate of Return on Investment in Education at the
     Regional Level. Estimates for the State of Hawaii.* Honolulu, Hawaii:
     Economic Research Center, University of Hawaii, 1969. Pp. 101.

     Estimates private and social rates of return for Hawaii for the years 1959
     and 1965 and compares these with corresponding rates in the rest of the USA.

258 A. ZIDERMAN, "Costs and Benefits of Adult Retraining in the United Kingdom",
     EC, November, 1969, pp. 363-76.

     A calculation of the rate of return and pay-off period of investment in
     British Government Training Centres.

259 G. L. MANGUM, *The Emergence of Manpower Policies.* New York: Holt, Rhinehart
     and Winston, 1969. Pp. 173.

A popular book on the battery of federally supported manpower policies that grew up in the USA in the 1960's. Ch. 4 reviews some of the work that has been done by American scholars attempting to evaluate these programs.

260 C. S. SMITH, "Benefits to British Employers from Post-Secondary Education", *JRSS*, Pt. 3, 1969, pp. 408-17.

An excerpt of 267. Various industries and firms in British manufacturing are compared in terms of their manpower profiles and various indicators of economic performance with the aid of both correlation and regression analyses (it is not always clear which is being used). Only published data is employed. The findings are almost wholly negative.

261 G. G. SOMERS, W. D. WOOD, eds., *Cost-Benefit Analysis of Manpower Policies*. Kingston, Ontario: Queen's University, 1969. Pp. 272.

This volume comprises nine important papers: (1) B.A. Weisbrod, "Benefits of Manpower Programs: Theoretical and Methodological Issues", pp. 3-15, which briefly takes up the problem of introducing equity considerations into cost-benefit analysis; (2) R. W. Judy, "Costs: Theoretical and Methodological Issues", pp. 16-29, with comments by J. S. MacDonald and H. Raynauld; (3) W. R. Dymond, "The Role of Benefit/Cost Analysis in Formulating Manpower Policy", pp. 42-55; (4) K. J. Arrow, "The Social Discount Rate", pp. 56-75, which throws doubt on the use of observed rate of return as discount rates, with comments by A. Harberger and G. Reuber (Harberger's comments are particularly cogent); (5) E. Hardin, "Benefit-Cost Analysis of Occupational Training Programs: A Comparison of Recent Studies", pp. 97-118; (6) G. G. Cain, R. G. Hollister, "Evaluating Manpower Programs for the Disadvantaged", pp. 119-51, with comments by E. W. Stromsdorfer; (7) R. A. Levine, "Manpower Programs in the War on Poverty", pp. 170-83; (8) R. A. Jenness, "Manpower Mobility Programs", pp. 184-220, with comments by H. S. Parnes and G. H. McKechnie; and (9) N. W. Chamberlin, "Some Further Thoughts on the Concept of Human Capital", pp. 230-48, reprinted in *WYK I*, pp. 205-15, which consists largely of profound misgivings.

1970

262 M. M. G. FASE, *An Econometric Model of Age-Income Profiles. A Statistical Analysis of Dutch Income Data 1958-1967*. Rotterdam: Rotterdam University Press, 1970. Pp. 92.

This book consists essentially of an attempt to describe Dutch age-income-education data in terms of the lognormal distribution, and demands from the reader a good deal of knowledge of mathematical statistics. It closes with an interesting attempt to test the theory that people choose professional occupations with regard to lifetime rather than current earnings, pp. 77-79, as well as estimates of the rate of return to investment in education in The Netherlands in 1965, pp. 79-83.

263 A. L. DANIELSON, "Some Evidence on the Private Returns to Graduate Education: Comment", *SEJ*, January, 1970, pp. 334-38.

A comment on Ashenfelter and Mooney (see 237) which recalculates their data after making adjustments for mortality rates, growth in earnings differentials and the incidence of the personal income tax.

264 P. S. ALBIN, "Poverty, Education and Unbalanced Economic Growth", *QJE*,
     February, 1970, pp. 70-84.

     Combining the fact of rising real costs of education over time with the
     prevailing imperfections of the capital market, the author predicts the likeli-
     hood of chronic poverty in the United States.

265 I. BERG, *Education and Jobs: The Great Training Robbery*. New York: Praeger,
     1970. Pp. 200.

     A book which attempts to marshall American evidence to deny the thesis that
     education makes people more productive. For a review, see Blaug (311) and
     Bowman (534).

266 J. J. HUGHES, *Cost-Benefit Aspects of Manpower Retraining*. Department of
     Employment and Productivity. Manpower Papers No. 2. London: H.M.S.O.,
     1970. Pp. 42.

     An excellent review of American and Swedish research on training and retrain-
     ing schemes.

267 C. S. SMITH, *The Costs of Further Education: A British Analysis*. Oxford:
     Pergamon Press, 1970. Pp. 202.

     Despite its title, this is an exercise in cost-benefit analysis, based on a
     sample survey of colleges for cost data and a mixture of published and unpub-
     lished information for data on earnings. The book seems to have been written
     in 1967, and never revised thereafter, and its present-value approach makes
     for a somewhat clumsy presentation of the evidence.

268 L. MAGLEN, R. LAYARD, "How Profitable is Engineering Education?", *HIR*, Spring,
     1970, pp. 51-67.

     Private and social rates of return to higher qualified manpower in the
     British electrical engineering industry, a chapter of a forthcoming book on
     manpower utilisation in the industry (see 306).

269 R. H. REED, H. P. MILLER, "Some Determinants of Variations in Earnings for
     College Men", *JHR*, Spring, 1970, pp. 177-90.

     Using multiple regression with dummy variables, the authors study the influ-
     ences of age, sex, colour, college rank, field of specialization, father's
     occupation, father's education and region of residence on the earnings of
     American college graduates. The over-all variation explained is surprisingly
     low and family background variables prove to have little effect on earnings.

270 J. MINCER, "The Distribution of Labor Incomes: A Survey. With Special
     Reference to the Human Capital", *JEL*, March, 1970, pp. 1-26.

     This brilliant review concentrates on the human capital approach to the
     analysis of the distribution of personal earnings but stochastic theories of
     income distribution are briefly canvassed. The underlying theory is thoroughly

explored and a large number of empirical studies are interpreted in the light of the theory. The article concludes that the human capital model has been relatively successful in explaining a variety of features in observed distributions of earnings.

271 J. L. COCHRANE, B. F. KIKER, "An 'Austrian' Approach to the Theory of Investment in Human Beings", *SEJ*, April, 1970, pp. 385-89.

This paper develops a simple Böhm-Bawerkian model of an institution that is investing in training in order to maximise the rate of return on its budget, where the returns include the future earnings of trainees.

272 W. LEE HANSEN, ed., *Education, Income and Human Capital*. Studies in Income and Wealth, Vol. 35, Conference on Research in Income and Wealth. New York: Columbia University Press, 1970. Pp. 320

This is obviously going to become a much-quoted book: it contains seven excellent survey-articles with trenchant critiques by several commentators for each article. The seven articles are: (1) S. Bowles, "Towards an Educational Production Function", pp. 11-60, with comments by J. E. Brandl and J. C. Hause; (2) Z. Griliches, "Notes on the Role of Education in Production Functions and Growth Accounting", pp. 71-114, with comments by J. Conlisk and R. R. Nelson; (3) Y. Ben-Porath, "The Production of Human Capital Over Time", pp. 129-46, with comments by J. Mincer and L. Thurow; (4) B. Chiswick, "An Interregional Analysis of Schooling and the Skewness of Income", pp. 157-83, with comments by M. J. Bowman and D. Foley; (5) P. B. Kenen, "Skills, Human Capital, and Comparative Advantage", pp.195-229, with comments by A. O. Krueger R. E. Baldwin and D. J. Daly; (6) A. Scott, "The Brain Drain - Is a Human Capital Approach Justified?", pp. 241-84, with comments by A. G. Holtmann and L. A. Sjaastad; and (7) T. W. Schultz, "The Reckoning of Education as Human Capital", pp. 297-306.

273 B. M. FLEISHER, *Labor Economics. Theory and Evidence*. Englewood Cliffs, New Jersey: Prentice Hall, 1970. Pp. 304.

Of all the recent texts in labour economics, this is perhaps the one most thoroughly coloured by the human investment revolution in economic thought. Certain pages (pp. 92-104, 213-18) deal specifically with human capital and the rate of return, but references to the economics of education occur repeatedly throughout this book. In addition, it takes a strong line in favour of testing neoclassical wage theory and includes a number of judicious reviews of empirical evidence bearing on the validity of competitive wage theory.

274 W. FRANKE, I. SOBEL, *The Shortage of Skilled and Technical Workers. An Inquiry into Selected Occupations in Short Supply*. Lexington, Mass.: Heath Lexington Books, 1970. Pp. 391.

A useful study of labour market adjustments to manpower scarcities, focussing on six professions (nursing, medical technology, tool and die making, tool and die designing, electronic engineering and metalwork engineering) and two labour markets (Chicago and St. Louis). Each of these markets is examined from the demand and from the supply side and alternative policies to facilitate market adjustments are carefully analyzed. One of the surprising findings of this study is that shortages, on a variety of definitions, did not exist in any of the four industrial occupations.

275 H. FOLK, *The Shortage of Scientists and Engineers*. Lexington, Mass.: Heath Lexington Books, 1970. Pp. 364.

There is no doubt that this is the definitive book on the labour market for engineers in the United States. It contains an excellent discussion of the various meanings of the shortage concept (ch. 1), an examination of the demand and supply of engineers and scientists in recent years (chs. 2 and 3), showing quite conclusively that demand is relatively price-elastic but supply is relatively price-inelastic, a calculation of the rate of return to college education by occupational specialisations (ch. 5), and a review of American forecasts for engineers and scientists.

276 B. J. OGILVY, "A Cost Benefit Study of Education in New Zealand", *NZJES*, May, 1970, pp. 33-46.

A study of the private and social rates of return to investment in several levels and types of secondary and higher education in New Zealand in 1966.

277 R. D. WEISS, "The Effect of Education on the Earnings of Blacks and Whites", *RES*, May, 1970, pp. 150-59.

This paper marries the 1/1000 sample of 1960 US Census to information on educational achievement derived form the Coleman Report to test the effect of education on earnings. It shows that achievement explains more of the variance in earnings than does the number of years in school, at least for whites although not for blacks. The article includes an interesting recursive model of income determination which introduces occupation as a variable intervening between education and earnings.

278 L. MAXWELL, "Some Evidence on Negative Returns to Graduate Education", *WEJ*, June, 1970, pp. 186-89.

Using a sample of graduates of the University of Nebraska, ranging in age from 24 to 65, the author calculates rates of return to post-graduate education by sex and region and finds that the private rate of return for males with master's degrees is negative.

279 W. LEE HANSEN, B. A. WEISBROD, W. J. SCANLON, "Schooling and Earnings of Low Achievers", *AER*, June, 1970, pp. 409-18; "Comments" by B. R. Chiswick, S. Masters and T. Ribich; "Reply" by the authors, *ibid*., September, 1972, pp. 752-62.

A regression analysis of the earnings of men aged 17-25 who failed to pass the Armed Forces Qualification Test. Although none of the four regressions that were run "explained" more than 15 per cent of the variance in annual earnings, the authors conclude that years of schooling itself is not a significant determinant of the earnings of low achievers.

280 F. HINES, L. TWEETEN, M. REDFERN, "Social and Private Rates of Return to Investment in Schooling, By Race-Sex Groups and Regions", *JHR*, Summer, 1970, pp. 318-40.

This article calculates average and marginal private and social rates of return by sex, race and region for the USA in 1959, after adjusting earnings for ability, mortality and secular growth.

281   C. S. SMITH, "Costs and Benefit of Further Education: Some Evidence from a
      Pilot Study", *EJ*, September, 1970, pp. 583-604.

      Based on undisclosed sample data, this study of British further education
      compares the present value of earnings with the present value of costs. Some-
      what stronger conclusions are reached than are perhaps warranted by the evi-
      dence (an excerpt of 267).

282   T. JOHNSON, "Returns from Investment in Human Capital", *AER*, September, 1970,
      pp. 546-60.

      Constructs a model of the investment process and uses it to predict life-
      time earnings. These predicted profiles are then used to calculate rates of
      return on educational investment. This is a difficult article in part because
      it is expounded in a peculiarly obscure manner.

283   D. R. WITMER, "Economic Benefits of College Education", *RER*, October, 1970,
      pp. 511-23.

      An uncritical review of American evidence with a bibliography.

284   G. E. JOHNSON, "The Demand for Labour by Educational Category", *SEJ*, October,
      1970, pp. 190-204.

      An analytical formulation of the problem in terms of the traditional theory
      of profit maximisation.

285   A. G. HOLTMANN, A. E. BAYER, "Determinants of Professional Income Among Recent
      Recipients of Natural Science Doctorates", *JB*, October, 1970, pp. 410-18.

      Another multiple regression analysis of earnings, this time of 6,000 science
      doctorates in 1964 who received their Ph.D's between 1957 and 1959. The data
      is analysed by six fields of study and three sectors of employment.

286   R. G. HOLLISTER, *Education and Distribution of Income: Some Exploratory
      Forays. OECD Conference on Policies for Educational Growth. Background Study
      No. 11.* Paris: OECD, 1970. Pp. 40, mimeographed.

      An important paper exploring rate-of-return evidence insofar as it bears on
      the possible effects of education on the distribution of income. As the
      author rightly emphasizes, rate-of-return analysis suggests a significant im-
      pact on income distribution and yet the evidence indicates otherwise: the
      paper discusses the possible resolutions of this apparent conflict.

287   R. G. HOLLISTER, "Education and Income: A Study of Cross-Sections and Cohorts",
      OECD Conference on Policies for Educational Growth. Paris: OECD, 1970,
      pp. 63-136, mimeographed.

      The author shows that cross-sectional age-earnings profiles for the USA in
      1939 or 1949 poorly predict the profiles observed 10 or 20 years later.
      Furthermore, the shift over time in these profiles appears to reflect no
      simple pattern by age or education categories.

288 J. BIBBY, "Rewards and Careers", *HIR*, Autumn, 1970, pp. 9-18.

   One of the first attempts in Britain to compare the age-earnings profiles
of teachers in different educational sectors, contrasting these with earnings
in private industry.

289 A. DANIÈRE, J. MECHLING, "Direct Marginal Productivity of College Education
in Relation to College Aptitude of Students and Production Costs of Institutions", *JHR*, Winter, 1970, pp. 51-70.

   By combining a variety of data sources, the authors obtain tentative estimates of the present values of the expected earnings flows of American students
of different aptitudes entering colleges and universities of different quality.
On the basis of the findings, they advance some criticisms of recent policies
of selecting students for higher education in the USA.

1971

290 G. E. JOHNSON, K. C. YOUMANS, "Union Relative Wage Effects by Age and Education", *ILLR*, January, 1971, pp. 171-79.

   Utilizing multiple regression analysis, this study shows that unions in the
United States benefit less educated workers more than more educated workers
and, in addition, favour the very young and the very old. Some of these
effects are reversed for black rather than white workers.

291 A. MAYHEW, "Education, Occupation and Earnings", *ibid.*, pp. 216-25.

   This important article emphasizes variations in earnings within occupations
in the United States as associated with variations in educational attainment.
Despite the popularity of the notion that more education opens the door to
better-paying jobs, half of the advantage in earnings associated with additional education for men who do not go to college is actually due to higher
earnings within the kind of occupations which are also open to those with less
education.

292 H. N. HEINEMANN, E. SUSNA, "Criteria for Public Investment in the Two-Year
College: A Program Budgeting Approach", *JHR*, Spring, 1971, pp. 171-84.

   A rate-of-return study of a representative American two-year college. Cost
data were obtained from a particular college. Earnings data were obtained
from special surveys with the aid of special assumptions, whose reasonableness
was checked against census evidence. The rate of return was found to be about
13 per cent.

293 J. J. SIEGFRIED, "Rate of Return to the Ph.D. in Economics", *ILRR*, April, 1971,
pp. 420-31.

   Using the Tolles-Jones-Clague data for 1964 (see 197), the author calculates
private and social rates of return to earnings as well as to incomes, cross-
classifying the rates by type of employment, methods of finance and duration
of course. Among the more interesting results are negative rates to the

education sector on the assumption that type of employer is not predetermined when the Ph.D. course is begun; if it is predetermined, quite respectable rates emerge even for the education sector.

294 T. W. SCHULTZ, *Investment in Human Capital. The Role of Education and of Research*. New York: The Free Press, 1971. Pp. 272

Reprints, among others, parts of 107, 108, 110, 118, 222, 272, 534, 788, 815, 1401 but includes new essays on the "Changing Patterns of Earnings Foregone" and on "The Allocation of Resources to Research".

295 R. B. FREEMAN, *The Market for College-Trained Manpower. A Study in the Economics of Career Choice*. Cambridge, Mass.: Harvard University Press, 1971. Pp. 264.

This is clearly an important contribution to the marriage of labour economics and the economics of education. It examines the labour market for engineers, doctorates, and one or two other categories in the United States via regression analysis, supplemented by survey results. Chapters 1 and 2 develop a testable cobweb model of these markets, which are then tested in chapters 4 and 5. Chapter 9 deals with academic labour markets. The upshot of the book is to vindicate the view that college students in America view their education as an investment in future earnings potential and that labour markets in the US do react smoothly to variations in supply with a 3-4 year lag.

296 H. GINTIS, "Education, Technology and the Characteristics of Worker Productivity", *AER*, May, 1971, pp. 266-79.

This important paper argues that better-educated workers earn more, not because education imparts vocational skills, but because it imparts social skills. A variety of data is introduced to lend plausibility to this thesis.

297 J. C. HAUSE, "Ability and Schooling as Determinants of Lifetime Earnings or If You're So Smart, Why Aren't You Rich?", *ibid.*, pp. 289-304.

Re-analyzes the Rogers data (see 251), the Husèn data (see 1237) and evidence from Project Talent to throw light on the relationship between ability and earnings.

298 M. D. HURD, "Changes in Wage Rates Between 1959 and 1967", *RES*, May, 1971, pp. 189-99.

This paper uses new data to study the change in wage rates in the USA between the two dates by race, sex, age and education. Among the interesting findings is the stability of wages by education over the 9-year period.

299 V. MORRIS, A. ZIDERMAN, "The Economic Return on Investment in Higher Education in England and Wales", *ETR*, May, 1971, pp. xx-xxxi.

These calculations of the social rate of return are based on a postal questionnaire sent to 15,000 qualified people in 1968, from which certain persons were unfortunately excluded on the grounds that "extra-educational influences

were important in determining earnings levels". For more information on the
data itself, see Department of Education and Science, Statistics of Education,
Special Series No. 3, *Survey of Earnings of Qualified Manpower in England and
Wales 1966-67* (London: H.M.S.O., 1971. Pp. 44).

300 Y. WEISS, "Learning By Doing and Occupational Specialization", *JET*, June,
1971, pp. 189-98.

   An attempt to develop a model of rational choice which would account, at
one and the same time, for occupational specialization and the tendency to
invest in education at an early age.

301 K. HINCHLIFFE, "Teachers, The Open University and The Rate of Return", *HIR*,
Summer, 1971, pp. 49-56.

   Using teachers' salary scales and various assumptions about age of entry
and the value placed on leisure foregone, the author calculates the private
rate of return to male and female secondary school teachers investing in a
degree course at the Open University in the U.K.

302 S. O. SCHWEITZER, "Occupational Choice, High School Graduation and Investment
in Human Capital", *JHR*, Summer, 1971, pp. 321-32.

   Calculates the rate of return on high school attendance in the USA by occupation and shows that for certain occupations, the private rate of return is
unfavourable. The author uses the results to explain the pattern of high
school drop-outs.

303 J. CONLISK, "A Bit of Evidence on the Income-Education-Ability Interrelation",
ibid., pp. 358-62.

   Examines two new data sources, each with special limitations of its own,
and finds that ability-measures are insignificant in one and very significant
in the other in explaining the variance of earnings.

304 O. ASHENFELTER, M. K. TAUSSIG, "Discrimination and Income Differentials:
Comment", *AER*, September, 1971, pp. 746-750; J. Gwartney, "Reply", *ibid.*,
pp. 751-55.

   This is a critique of Gwartney's results presented in *AER*, June, 1970,
which explained a large portion of Negro-white income differences in the United
States by differences in scholastic achievement levels. The results are ques-
tioned as not resting on any conceptual framework of income determination.
See also V. L. Rawlins, "Discrimination, Achievement, and Payoffs to a College
Degree: A Comment, *JHR*, Summer, 1974, pp. 415-19.

305 C. M. LINDSAY, "Measuring Human Capital Returns", *JPE*, November/December, 1971,
pp. 1195-1215.

   This somewhat obscure article argues that all previous estimates of rates
of return to educational investment have been overestimates owing to the fact
that the expectation of higher lifetime earnings alters the desirable work-

leisure ratio. The precise effect of course depends on the individual utility functions; nevertheless, the author shows the general tendency is always to overstate the rate of return.

306 P. R. G. LAYARD, J. D. SARGAN, M. E. AGER, D. J. JONES, *Qualified Manpower and Economic Performance. An Inter-Plant Study in the Electrical Engineering Industry*. London: Allen Lane The Penguin Press, 1971. Pp. 267.

Despite its almost wholly negative results, this is a path-breaking book, the first ever to compare the educational intensity of firms with their economic performance. The book estimates labour demand functions by occupation and education, production functions for sub-divisions of the British electrical engineering industry, and private and social rates of return to investment in education. Chs. 8 and 9 on the relationship between education and occupation are of particular interest. The reader is warned that chs. 11-13 on production functions are virtually unreadable by all but experts in econometrics.

307 T.-W. HU, M. L. LEE, E. W. STROMSDORFER, "Economic Returns to Vocational and Comprehensive High School Graduates", *JHR*, Winter, 1971, pp. 25-50, reprinted in *WYK II*, pp. 89-102, and *KIK*, pp. 158-75.

A multiple regression analysis of the earnings over six years of employment of some 3,000 graduates of vocational and comprehensive high schools in three major American cities, showing that vocational school graduates earned more than comprehensive school graduates after controlling for IQ and socio-economic background. Although the costs of vocational schools are higher than those of comprehensive schools, even the social rate of return on vocational education exceeds that on comprehensive education.

308 Y. WEISS, "Investment in Graduate Education", *AER*, December, 1971, pp. 835-52.

The author develops a set of earnings functions for eight types of scientific and technical manpower in the USA and then uses these to estimate both average and marginal rates of return to postgraduate education.

1972

309 J. CORINA, *Labour Market Economics. A Short Survey of Recent Theory*. London: Heinemann Educational Books, 1972, ch. 6, pp. 51-61.

One of the chapters in this survey is focussed on "Labour Income Size Distribution and Human Capital". It provides a sceptical and somewhat diffuse survey of the work of Becker, Mincer and Chiswick on the effects of education on income distribution.

310 A. G. HOLTMANN, "On-the-Job Training, Obsolescence, Options, and Retraining", *SEJ*, January, 1972, pp. 414-17.

An analysis of the interrelationships between skill obsolescence, options to invest in training, and retraining, in the context of a human capital optimisation model.

311 M. BLAUG, "The Correlation Between Education and Earnings: What Does It
     Signify?", *HE*, February, 1972, pp. 53-76. "Comment" by A. Westoby and "Reply"
     by Blaug, *ibid.*, November, 1972, pp. 463-76.

     The paper examines three alternative explanations of the basic finding that
     amounts of education and personal earnings are positively correlated in some
     30 countries studied. Arbitrarily labelled, the economic, the sociological
     and the psychological explanation, the three explanations turn out on closer
     examination to be virtually the same explanation. It is denied that the
     "economic explanation" so-called is confined to cognitive knowledge.

312 D. BAILEY, C. SCHOTTA, "Private and Social Rates of Return to Education of
     Academicians", *AER*, March, 1972, pp. 19-31; "Comment" by L. Figa-Talamanca
     and J. A. Tomaske, *ibid.*, March, 1974, pp. 217-24.

     Reports private and social rates of return to American Ph.D.'s in academic
     employment as low as zero to one per cent. The most interesting aspect of the
     analysis is the clear demonstration of the strong effect of additional years
     spent in graduate school.

313 E. COHN, "On the Net Present Value Rule for Educational Investment", *JPE*,
     March/April, 1972, pp. 418-20.

     Another plea in favour of the present value approach which tacitly assumes
     that rates of return are only calculated for private, not for social reasons.
     Most of the author's objections fall to the ground in the case of the social
     rate of return.

314 H. M. LEVIN, *The Costs to the Nation of Inadequate Education*. Select Committee
     on Equal Educational Opportunity, United States Senate. Washington: US Govern-
     ment Printing Office, 1972. Pp. 62.

     A cost-benefit analysis of the provision of high school education for all
     American males aged 25 to 34. The implied rate of return of this policy is
     estimated to be about 600 per cent.

315 A. KLEVMARKEN, *Statistical Methods for the Analysis of Earnings Data, With
     Special Application to Salaries in Swedish Industry*. Stockholm: Industrial
     Institute for Economic and Social Research, 1972. Pp. 271.

     Applies multivariate analysis to Swedish age-earnings profiles for the
     periods 1961-70, using both cross-section and time series data, and calculates
     social rates of return on educational investment in Sweden. A surprising
     finding is the stability of the cross-sectional results over the 10-year
     period.

316 P. M. BLAIR, *Job Discrimination and Education: An Investment Analysis. A
     Case Study of Mexican-Americans in Santa Clara County, California*. New York:
     Praeger, 1972. Pp. 250.

     An analysis of age-earnings profiles, rates of return on educational invest-
     ment and occupational mobility for 160,000 high school and college-educated
     Mexican-Americans.

317 E. F. RENSHAW, "Are We Overestimating the Returns from a College Education?",
     SR, May, 1972, pp. 459-75.

     Throws cold water on rate-of-return studies and illustrates his argument
     with detailed references to the United States.

318 W. T. GARNER, "On the Returns to Higher Education", *ibid.*, pp. 476-82.

     A half-hearted defence in the light of Renshaw's criticisms.

319 D. A. DODGE, D. A. A. STAGER, "Economic Returns to Graduate Study in Science,
     Engineering and Business", *CJE*, May, 1972, pp. 182-98.

     After calculating private and social rates of return to Canadian post-
     graduate education in 1966, the authors compare their findings to rates for
     undergraduate training in Canada, as well as returns to graduate education in
     the USA. Although they make no adjustments for differential abilities, they
     do discuss a number of other qualifications to their results.

320 J. AARRESTAD, "Returns to Higher Education in Norway", *SWEJ*, June, 1972,
     pp. 261-80.

     A calculation of both private and social rates of return to different types
     of secondary and higher education in Norway, using 1966 data.

321 L. WEISS, J. G. WILLIAMSON, "Black Education, Earnings, and Interregional
     Migration: Some New Evidence", *AER*, June, 1972, pp. 372-83.

     The new evidence is for the year 1967 and the results show a significant
     shift in the earnings function of Black Americans over the decade of the
     1960's: education generated returns to blacks in 1967 that were as high as
     those enjoyed by whites in 1960.

322 J. J. SPENGLER, "Economic Malfunctioning in the Educational Industry", *AJES*,
     July, 1972, pp. 225-40.

     A popular article which attacks the certification function of American
     schools and colleges.

323 S. ROSEN, "Learning and Experience in the Labor Market", *JHR*, Summer, 1972,
     pp. 326-42.

     A fully developed model of the Mincer type based on the idea that the
     explicit market for jobs overlaps an implicit market for learning opportunities.
     The final pages of the article develop the implications of the model for occu-
     pational discrimination against minorities of all kinds.

324 R. T. MICHAEL, *The Effect of Education on Efficiency in Consumption*. NBER
     Occasional Paper 116. New York: Columbia University Press, 1972. Pp. 139.

     This monograph develops a Becker-like theory of the household production
     function in which education is viewed as affecting the efficiency of consumption,

conceived as a production process for transforming goods and services into utilities. The theory predicts that an increase in the education of a head of the household will affect consumption in exactly the same way as an increase in money income. This prediction is tested and confirmed on US and Israeli budgetary data (see 336).

325 E. COHN, "Investment Criteria and the Ranking of Educational Investments", *PF*, 27 (3), 1972, pp. 355-60.

Using data reported by Lee Hansen and Houthakker, the author argues once again, wrongly I believe, that the present-value approach might yield different investment rankings in the field of educational investment than the rate-of-return criterion.

326 L. A. JALLADE, "Niveau d'instruction et salaires", *RFP*, Octobre-Novembre, 1972, pp. 40-66.

This is the first serious effort to estimate French age-earnings profiles by levels of education and by occupational categories. The data derives from several sources, referring to the years 1962 and 1968, and regression analysis is used to estimate the profiles.

327 Y. WEISS, "The Risk Element in Occupational and Educational Choices", *JPE*, November/December, 1972, pp. 1203-13.

A pioneering article, which calculates rates of return for American scientists given various degrees of risk aversion. The rates were found to be sensitive to changes in risk aversion; on the other hand, risk differentials among individuals were found to be relatively unimportant (see 385).

328 B. HARRISON, "Education and Underemployment in the Urban Ghetto", *AER*, December, 1972, pp. 796-812.

A study of the determinants of black-white earnings differentials, using regression analysis from which the author draws somewhat stronger conclusions than seem to be justified by the data.

329 C. JENCKS and others, *Inequality: A Re-assessment of the Effect of Family and Schooling in America*. New York: Basic Books, 1972. Pp. 399.

Using the technique of path analysis, by which the effect of family background and IQ genotype on earnings is traced sequentially through schooling and occupational status, the authors throw doubt on the proposition that more and better schooling can be expected to have a significant effect on the distribution of income. The data source is American and the argument is entirely conducted in the American context. The book has attracted wide attention, including rebuttals by J. Coleman and A. Rivlin, with an important reply by the author (see 1250).

330 J. D. GWARTNEY, "Discrimination, Achievement and Payoffs of a College Degree", *JHR*, Winter, 1972, pp. 60-70.

Uses regression analysis to show that discrimination against Negroes is weakest in the market for college-educated people.

331 J. F. O'CONNELL, "The Labor Market for Engineers: An Alternative Methodology",
     ibid., pp. 71-86.

     Analyzes the labour market for American engineers by testing a simultaneous
     equation model, first by ordinary and then by two-stage least squares. Shows
     that the supply of engineers is responsive to absolute wage differences but
     that the demand for engineers is fairly insensitive to relative wage differ-
     ences. The major influence on the demand side is R & D expenditures.

1973

332 J. CREAN, "Foregone Earnings and the Demand for Education: Some Empirical
     Evidence", *CJE*, February, 1973, pp. 23-42.

     Using time-series data on Canadian secondary schools, the author tests a
     regression model of student decision-making, the results of which strongly
     suggest an inverse relationship between foregone earnings and the demand for
     education.

333 J. TAUBMAN, T. J. WALES, "Higher Education, Mental Ability, and Screening",
     JPE, January/February, 1973, pp. 28-55.

     Using an entirely new data source for US Army Air Force volunteers during
     World War II, the authors regress earnings at ages 33 and 47 on respondent's
     education, father's education and a large number of mental ability measures.
     They find that, although ability has little effect on starting salaries, its
     effects grow over time particularly for those with graduate education and high
     ability. Quantitatively, they confirm Denison's 35 per cent alpha-coefficient.
     They then proceed to formulate the screening hypothesis as profit-maximising
     behaviour on the part of employers. Their test of the screening hypothesis,
     however, showing that it accounts for up to 50 per cent of the private returns,
     is not entirely convincing. For a longer version, see 809.

334 D. METCALF, "The Rate of Return to Investing in a Doctorate: A Case Study",
     SJPE, February, 1973, pp. 43-51.

     Calculates the private and social rate of return to a doctorate in univer-
     sity teaching in Britain after prior regression analysis of the relevant earn-
     ings function.

335 R. S. ECKAUS, "Returns to Education with Standardized Incomes", *QJE*, February,
     1973, pp. 121-31.

     The author recalculates private rates of return to American education in
     1960 after adjusting earnings for a standard 40-hour work week, 50 weeks in
     the year. Because of the tendency for annual hours of work to increase with
     education, he finds that rates of return are much lower than the conventional
     estimates for high school but not for college education.

336 R. T. MICHAEL, "Education in Nonmarket Production", *JPE*, March/April, 1973,
     pp. 306-27.

     An article version of parts of his book (324).

337 G. PSACHAROPOULOS, K. HINCHLIFFE, *Returns to Education. An International Comparison.* Amsterdam: Elsevier Scientific Publishing Company, 1973. Pp. 216.

   This is an important book which, for the first time, collates all the available country evidence on rates of return to educational investment: 53 case studies for 32 countries. Its central purpose is to establish systematic patterns in rates of return around the world and to relate these to the economic and educational performance of countries.

338 G. E. JOHNSON, F. P. STAFFORD, "School Returns to Quantity and Quality of Schooling", *JHR*, Spring, 1973, pp. 139-55.

   "Quality of schooling" in this paper refers to interstate differences in the USA in per pupil expenditure on primary and secondary schools. The authors regress an earnings function for 1965 on the standard variables supplemented by a quality-of-schooling variable and use it to calculate rates of return on investment in quality improvements.

339 V. STOIKOV, "The Structure of Earnings in Japanese Manufacturing Industries: A Human-Capital Approach", *JPE*, March/Arpil, 1973, pp. 340-55.

   Multiple regression analysis of the earnings function in Japanese manufacturing, showing that experience outside the firm of current employment is no less important than it is in the West and that it is to some extent substitutable for experience inside the firm. The earnings function is then used to recalculate the rate of return to college education in Japan.

340 M. WOODHALL, "The Economic Returns to Investment in Women's Education", *HE*, 2, 1973, pp. 275-99.

   Presents evidence for nine countries, showing that the rate of return on investment in secondary and higher education are usually, but not invariably, lower for women than for men. This is followed by a discussion of the non-monetary benefits of education as they apply to women's education. For a more popular version of the same article, see the author's "Investment in Women: A Reappraisal of the Concept of Human Capital", *IRE*, XIX, 1, 1973, pp. 9-28, part of an issue which is entirely devoted to the education of women.

341 K. J. ARROW, "Higher Education as a Filter", *JPBE*, 2, 1973, pp. 193-216.

   An important article which subtly expounds the screening hypothesis in all its possible varieties, together with a possibly less than convincing attempt to meet the obvious objections to it.

342 S. BOWLES, "Understanding Unequal Economic Opportunity", *AER*, May, 1973, pp. 346-56.

   A review of some of the author's recent work on American earnings functions, showing that IQ explains little but family background explains much of the variance in individual earnings.

343   J-C. EICHER, "L'éducation comme investissement: la fin des illusions?", *REP*, mai-juin, 1973, pp. 407-32.

A subtle evaluation of rate-of-return analysis in the light of recent evidence about earnings functions whose striking characteristic is differences in the results reached by different studies. The author also considers certain French Marxist objections to the theory of human capital and, in addition, reviews what French evidence there is on earnings functions.

344   Y. COMAY, A. MELNIK, M. A. POLLATSCHEK, "The Option Value of Education and the Optimal Path for Investment in Human Capital", *IER*, June, 1973, pp.297-304.

An application of dynamic programming to the problem of educational choices by individuals, illustrated by an example drawn from US data.

345   A. G. HOLTMANN, "The Timing of Investments in Human Capital: A Case in Education", *PF*, July, 1973, pp. 300-6.

The author develops a rigorous analysis of the problem of calculating rates of return to education at every age in an individual's life and then employs American data for Southern Blacks to demonstrate that postponement of education to a later age may be optimal in certain circumstances.

346   L. LEVY-GARBOUA, "Remunere-t-on les études?", *CON*, 3, 1973, pp. 57-75.

An analysis of the earnings function of a nation-wide sample of 5,000 French male workers under the age of 45. Derives private rates of return for both schooling and post-school formal training by social class. Includes a discussion of the screening hypothesis in the light of the above evidence (see also 369).

347   R. L. BOWLBY, W. R. SCHRIVER, "Academic Ability and Rates of Return to Vocational Training", *ILRR*, April, 1973, pp. 980-90.

Analyzes data for 127 matched pairs of secondary school graduates in the USA and demonstrates an inverse relationship between academic ability and the adjusted private rate of return to vocational education.

348   R. D. MORGENSTERN, "Direct and Indirect Effects on Earnings of Schooling and Socio-Economic Background", *RES*, May, 1973, pp. 225-33.

The first article to estimate both a non-recursive, single-equation earnings function (for the USA) and a recursive model in which years of schooling itself is explained as well as earnings. The results show schooling exerts a strong independent influence on earnings but, on the other hand, socio-economic background exerts direct as well as indirect effects on earnings.

349   C. R. LINK, "The Quantity and Quality of Education and Their Influence on Earnings: The Case of Chemical Engineers", *ibid.*, pp. 241-47.

This paper estimates a 1961 earnings function for self-identified chemical engineers in the USA, paying special attention to the measurement of college quality, length of training received, and ability of individuals.

350   J. E. STIGLITZ, "Approaches to the Economics of Discrimination", *AER*, May, 1973, pp. 287-95.

      This paper hardly mentions education. Nevertheless, a complete theory of earnings differentials would account at one and the same time for the educational as well as the discriminatory determinants of earnings differences. For that reason, the continued discussion of the economics of racism has a bearing on issues in our subject.

351   V. STOIKOV, "Size of Firm, Worker Earnings, and Human Capital: The Case of Japan", *ILRR*, July, 1973, pp. 1095-1106.

      Another attempt by the author to destroy the thesis that workers' earnings are related to size of firm when standardizing for differences in labour quality. The analysis takes the form of estimating a 1967 earnings function for male workers in Japanese manufacturing.

352   A. ZIDERMAN, "Does It Pay To Take A Degree? The Profitability of Private Investment in University Education in Britain", *OEP*, July, 1973, pp. 262-74.

      Despite its title, the paper is concerned with all of post-secondary education in Britain: it calculates average and marginal private rates of return from 1968 earnings data.

353   T. J. WALES, "The Effect of College Quality on Earnings: Results from the NBER-Thorndike Data", *JHR*, Summer, 1973, pp. 306-17.

      Continuing the earlier work of Taubman and Wales (see 333), the author shows that the effect of college quality on earnings in the USA is very large, but this may reflect a return to student ability rather than a return to the college choice because of the relatively high correlation between student ability and college quality.

354   C. M. LINDSAY, "Real Returns to Medical Education", *ibid.*, pp. 331-48.

      This article verifies his earlier theoretical argument that the returns to education are invariably overestimated by ignoring the tendency of the educated to work longer hours.

355   I. V. SAWHILL, "The Economics of Discrimination Against Women: Some New Findings", *ibid.*, pp. 383-95.

      The author finds the key in the role of training-cum-experience and shows that this element alone can account for a considerable portion of the earnings differential between men and women.

356   V. STOIKOV, "Recurrent Education: Some Neglected Economic Issues", *ILR*, August-September, 1973, pp. 187-208.

      A careful rate-of-return comparison between postponed recurrent education and a programme of "investing in older persons", followed by a discussion of some of the problems created by obsolescence of knowledge, uncertainty and the rising quality of education through time.

357 M. SPENCE, "Job Market Signaling", *QJE*, August, 1973, pp. 355-74.

   An interesting attempt to develop a theory of information signals in labour markets with obvious implications for the so-called "screening hypothesis" (see also 384).

358 B. G. MALKIEL, J. A. MALKIEL, "Male-Female Pay Differentials in Professional Employment", *AER*, September, 1973, pp. 693-705.

   This is a fascinating study of salary differentials among 272 professional employees in a single American corporation. The results do not easily generalise, however, as the employees in question appear to be R & D personnel in an engineering firm.

359 A. SCHWARTZ, "Interpreting the Effect of Distance on Migration", *JPE*, September/October, 1973, pp. 1153-69.

   Using data on the flows of American migrants cross-classified by age and education, the author estimates the effect of age and education on the distance elasticity of migration. He shows that the distance elasticity is largely independent of age but is lower, the higher the level of the migrant's education.

360 D. WHIPPLE, "A Generalized Theory of Job Search", *ibid.*, 1973, pp. 1170-88.

   A reworking of the standard job-search model based on expected utility maximisation, noting that its policy conclusions are much more ambiguous than is usually admitted.

361 D. METCALF, "Pay Dispersion, Information, and Returns to Search in a Professional Labour Market", *RESJ*, October, 1973, pp. 491-505.

   This paper applies Stigler's theory of job search to the market in recruits to UK university teaching. It marks an advance on earlier empirical applications of this model by correcting the observed wage dispersion for the heterogeneity of the labour in question.

362 D. W. BIRCH, J. R. CALVERT, "How Profitable is Teaching?", *HIR*, Autumn, 1973, pp. 35-44.

   A valuable rate-of-return study applied to a teaching career in Britain, distinguishing male and female graduates, non-graduates and those who obtain a qualification through the Open University.

363 A. S. BLINDER, "Wage Discrimination: Reduced Form and Structural Estimates", *JHR*, Fall, 1973, pp. 436-55.

   This paper focusses on white-black and male-female wage differentials in the USA and estimates both an earnings function and education functions, occupational functions, etcetera. Both structural and reduced-form equations are estimated and the two sets of estimates are then synthesized. The results give an unusually heavy emphasis to pure discrimination.

364   M. J. GREENWOOD, "The Geographic Mobility of College Graduates", *JHR*, Fall, 1973, pp. 506-15.

      A re-examination of traditional models of interregional migration, utilising data on American college graduates.

365   M. ROTHSCHILD, "Models of Market Organization with Imperfect Information", *JPE*, November/December, 1973, pp. 1283-1308.

      This paper surveys recent theoretical work on markets whose participants act on the basis of incomplete information, including the case of employers choosing between workers with different educational qualifications (pp. 1301-2).

366   B. R. CHISWICK, "Racial Discrimination in the Labor Market: A Test of Alternative Hypotheses", *ibid.*, pp. 1330-1352.

      This paper tests alternative models of labor market discrimination by looking at the variance of the log of incomes among adult white and non-white males in American states when the rate of return on schooling and the distribution of schooling, age and weeks worked are held constant. The only hypothesis to survive the test is the white employee discrimination hypothesis.

367   F. WELCH, "Education and Racial Discrimination", *Discrimination in Labor Markets*, eds. O. Ashenfelter, A. Rees. Princeton, New Jersey: Princeton University Press, 1973, pp. 43-81.

      Presents new evidence on the returns to schooling for black and white workers, using cross-sectional data for 1959 and 1966. Concludes that there has been a significant increase in the rate of return to schooling for black relative to white workers over this period and suggests several explanations for this phenomenon.

368   A. ZIDERMAN, "Rates of Return on Investment in Education: Recent Results for Britain", *JHR*, Winter, 1973, pp. 85-97.

      An improved version of the Morris-Ziderman study (see 299), adding private rates to the previously calculated social rates.

369   L. LÉVY-GARBOUA, *Recherche sur les rendements de l'éducation en France. Exposé des principaux résultats.* Actions thematiques programmees No. 1. Sciences Humaine. Paris: Editions du Centre national de la recherche scientifique, 1973. Pp. 66.

      These are the first results of a rate-of-return exercise which CNRS has been financing since 1971. This publication deals exclusively with age-earnings profiles, estimated from 1962 data but supported by similar evidence for 1971. An interesting feature of the study in the attempt to compare age-earnings profiles by broad occupational categories.

370   K. J. ARROW, "The Theory of Discrimination", *Discrimination in Labor Markets*, eds. O. Ashenfelter, A. Rees. Princeton, New Jersey: Princeton University Press, 1973, pp. 3-33.

The author takes up where Becker left off, adding adjustment costs and imperfect information to Becker's concept of racial hiring preferences, to produce a neoclassical theory of wage differentials between workers who are perfect substitutes in all their non-racial aspects. The same model appears in more technical form in A. H. Pascal, ed., *Racial Discrimination in Economic Life* (Lexington, Massachusetts: D. C. Heath, 1972), chs. 2, 6. See also M. W. Reder's highly pertinent "Comment", pp. 34-42.

371 R. S. ECKAUS, *Estimating the Returns to Education: A Disaggregated Approach*. A Technical Report sponsored by the Carnegie Commission on Higher Education. Berkeley, California. Carnegie Commission on Higher Education, 1973. Pp. 95.

This study consists of three papers. The first, "Estimation of the Returns to Education with Hourly Standardized Incomes", is a longer version of a previously published paper (335). The second, a rate-of-return calculation by occupations for the US, 1960, is an important contribution. The last essay, "On the Identification of the Relations Between Education and Income" is not in fact about disaggregation but rather about the difference between cross-section and a time-series age-earnings profile. In the introduction to the book, the author reiterates his earlier scepticism about rate-of-return analysis in general.

372 F. WELCH, "Black-White Differences in Returns to Schooling", *AER*, December, 1973, pp. 893-907.

The author considers recent American evidence suggesting a significant change in the 1960's towards greater returns to education for blacks. Evidence on the quality of education for blacks and whites is also briefly considered.

373 W. J. HALEY, "Human Capital: The Choice Between Investment and Income", *ibid.*, pp. 929-44.

The article reconsiders the Ben-Porath theoretical rationalisation for observed age-earnings profiles (see 225) and generalizes previous results. The theory is then tested on Mincer's original training data (see 392).

1974

374 M. R. FISHER, "The Human Capital Approach to Occupational Differentials", *IJSE*, I, 1, 1974, pp. 40-62.

A penetrating discussion of the strengths and weaknesses of the human capital explanation of changes in relative occupational wage rates and a review of the evidence, particularly with reference ot Britain.

375 P. WILES, "The Correlation Between Education and Earnings: The External-Test-Not-Content Hypothesis", *HE*, February, 1974, pp. 43-58.

An idiosyncratic examination of hypotheses other than vocational content which are capable of explaining the correlation between education and earnings. An interesting appendix discusses the experiences of the German "politologie" (see 1102).

376 A. BOTTOMLEY, J. DUNWORTH, "Rate of Return on University Education with Economies of Scale", *HE*, February, 1974, pp. 91-102.

   Another nugget out of the Bradford gold-mine and the first estimates for Britain of the rate of return on university education by fields of study, distinguishing average and marginal rates, and calculating the social rate on pretax earnings as well as on tax receipts only.

377 J. MINCER, S. POLACHNEK, "Family Investments in Human Capital: Earnings of Women", *JPE*, March/April, 1974, Part II, *Marriage, Family, Human Capital and Fertility,* pp. 76-108.

   An attempt to produce a complete human capital explanation of female earnings applied to longitudinal data. The argument is complex and seems to depend as much on econometric as on economic theory; see O. D. Duncan's trenchant comments, pp. 109-110.

378 M. NERLOVE, "Household and Economy: Towards a New Theory of Population and Economic Growth", *ibid.*, pp. 200-218.

   This paper may serve as an introduction to the rest of the papers in this volume, as well as the whole of the "new home economics" à la Chicago to which this volume is dedicated. See also Z. Griliches' critical remarks, touching on the alleged "constancy of the rate of return to schooling" in the USA, pp. 219-21.

379 D. O. PARSONS, "The Cost of School Time, Foregone Earnings, and Human Capital Formation", *ibid.*, pp. 251-66.

   The author argues that foregone earnings seriously underestimate the indirect costs of schooling, which in fact take the form of leisure foregone rather than earnings foregone. A simple model is constructed to impute a value to foregone leisure and various rate-of-return calculations are examined to estimate the bias in ignoring foregone leisure. At the college level very little bias results, but at the high school level, the bias is considerable.

380 K. BROOK, F. R. MARSHALL, "The Labor Market for Economists", *AER*, May, 1974, pp. 488-511.

   Prepared for the AEA Committee on Hiring Practices with a view to improving the flow of information in the labour market for economists, this paper is actually a valuable summary of evidence about a particular professional labour market in the United States.

381 G. E. JOHNSON, F. P. STAFFORD, "Lifetime Earnings in a Professional Labor Market: Academic Economists", *JPE*, May/June, 1974, pp. 549-70.

   Compares the earnings of economists by age both cross-sectionally and over time, using National Science Foundation Register data from 1964 to 1970. Casts further light on the role of years of experience as a factor in the determination of lifetime earnings.

382 N. M. GORDON, T. E. MORTON, I. C. BRADEN, "Faculty Salaries: Is there Discri-
     mination by Sex, Race, and Discipline?", *AER*, June, 1974, pp. 419-27.

     An elaborate earnings function is estimated for about 2,000 staff members of
     "a large urban university" in the United States.

383 A. KATZ, "Schooling, Age, and Length of Unemployemnt", *ILRR*, July, 1974,
     pp. 597-605.

     Shows that in the USA, more schooling reduces unemployment, a relationship
     which itself declines with age.

384 A. M. SPENCE, *Market Signaling: Informational Transfer in Hiring and Related
     Screening Processes.* Cambridge, Mass.: Harvard University Press, 1974.
     Pp. 221.

     A difficult but important book on market equilibrium when imperfect informa-
     tion is conveyed via "signals". The argument begins with job markets where
     educational qualifications are used as signals but the argument is extended to
     many other selection and screening problems in economic life. The earlier
     article (357) provides a summary of the content.

385 J. C. HAUSE, "The Risk Element in Occupational and Educational Choices:
     Comment", *JPE*, July/August, 1974, pp. 803-8.

     A rebuttal of Weiss (see 327) respecting the effect of risk aversion on the
     rate of return from educational investment.

386 S. H. MASTERS, "The Effect of Educational Differences and Labor-Market Discri-
     mination on the Relative Earnings of Black Males", *JHR*, Summer, 1974,
     pp. 342-60.

     Using both 1960 and 1967 data, the author tries to show by means of regres-
     sion analysis that labour market discrimination has a larger effect on the
     racial earnings gap than either years of schooling completed or scores on
     scholastic attainment tests.

387 L. D. MORSE, "Schooling and Discrimination in the Labor Markets", *ibid.*,
     pp. 398-407.

     Demonstrates once again that the discrimination component in the racial
     earnings gap in the United States increases with years of schooling attained.

388 T. JOHNSON, F. J. HEBEIN, "Investment in Human Capital and Growth in Personal
     Income, 1956-1966", *AER*, September, 1974, pp. 604-15.

     Estimates the rate-of-growth-of-incomes factor in rate-of-return calculations
     by using a series of cross-sections to derive the results. In the course of
     the analysis, a significant change in age-education-earnings profiles is detect-
     ed for the United States, dating from 1960 or thereabouts.

389 R. LAYARD, G. PSACHAROPOULOS, "The Screening Hypothesis and the Returns to
Education", *JPE*, September/October, 1974, pp. 985-98.

A reply to the Berg-Taubman-Wales formulation of "credentialism" or the
screening-hypothesis explanation of earnings differentials by education. The
reply is effective but only because the ideas under attack constitute weak
versions of "credentialism".

390 N. OULTON, "The Distribution of Education and the Distribution of Income",
EC, November, 1974, pp. 387-402.

An attempt to complete the Becker-Chiswick-Mincer schooling model by explaining the distribution of schooling simultaneously with the distribution of
income. The results, however, fail to explain the unimodal, skewed distribution of income that is actually observed.

391 P. TURNBULL, G. WILLIAMS, "Sex Differentials in Teachers' Pay", *JRSS*, Series A
(General), Vol. 137, Pt. 2, 1974, pp. 245-58.

An earnings function for male and female British school teachers, showing
that single women earn consistently more than married women but less than men,
particularly in primary schools.

392 P. J. MYERS, "Income Distribution and Becker's Model of Human Investment",
Economic Policies and Social Goals, ed., A. J. Culyer. London: Martin
Robertson, 1974, pp. 94-112.

A Marxist critique of Becker's model of training, arguing essentially that
the lifetime conception of the incentives to acquire and provide training does
not mix well with static, competitive theory.

393 J. MINCER, *Schooling, Experience and Earnings*. New York: National Bureau of
Economic Research, 1974. Pp. 152.

The central concept of this important contribution to the literature is the
"overtaking point": if individuals choose occupations so as to equalise the
present value of lifetime earnings, the effect of such post-school investment
decisions among a cohort of individuals with a given level of schooling is to
produce an initial dispersion of earnings by education, followed by a phase of
convergence as the various profiles cross each other. Mincer then shows that
this point of "overtaking" typically occurs about 7-9 years after entry into
the labour force. See the review by M. Blaug, *EDCC*, October, 1975.

394 G. E. JOHNSON, F. P. STAFFORD, "The Earnings and Promotion of Women Faculty",
AER, December, 1974, pp. 888-903.

A human-capital explanation of academic earnings differentials by sex in the
USA. The authors conclude that roughly two-fifths of lifetime earnings differences is attributable to discrimination, three-fifths being due to human capital differences.

395 D. LEVHARI, Y. WEISS, "The Effect of Risk on the Investment in Human Capital",
ibid., pp. 950-63.

A difficult article which develops a simplified model of the effects of uncertainty on human investment decisions.

1975

396 A. B. ATKINSON, *The Economics of Inequality*. Oxford: Clarendon Press, 1975, Ch. 5.

   Ch. 5 of this lucid textbook on the distribution of income and wealth takes up human capital theory, contrasting Becker and Mincer with Bowles and Jencks.

397 T. D. WALLACE, L. A. IHNEN, "Full-Time Schooling in Life-Cycle Models of Human Capital Accumulation", *JPE*, February, 1975, pp. 137-56.

   A re-working of Ben-Porath's life-cycle model of human capital formation (225), with particular reference to the nature of the capital market for human investment.

398 J. G. HAWORTH, J. G. GWARTNEY, C. HAWORTH, "Earnings, Productivity, and Changes in Employment Discrimination During the 1960's", *AER*, March, 1975, pp. 158-68.

   Further evidence of the thesis that employment opportunities in the USA changed drastically in the 1960's in favour of blacks, particularly for younger, better educated blacks. See also C. R. Link, "Black Education, Earnings, and Interregional Migration", *ibid.*, pp. 236-44.

399 R. RAYMOND, M. SESNOWITZ, "The Returns to Investment in Higher Education: Some New Evidence", *JHR*, Spring, 1975, pp. 139-54.

   The latest rate-of-return calculation for American higher education, using 1970 data. Among the findings are the failure of rates to decline over the 1960's and reversal of the usual disparity between the rates for two-years and four-years college.

400 F. WELCH, "Human Capital Theory: Education, Discrimination, and Life Cycles", *AER*, May, 1975, pp. 63-73.

   A review of the present empirical status of the theory, with particular reference to the impact of schooling on lifecycle earnings profiles. The review of race differences in earnings concludes that there is no "human capital theory of discrimination".

401 S. BOWLES, H. GINTIS, "The Problem with Human Capital Theory - A Marxian Critique", *ibid.*, pp. 74-82.

   A preview of their forthcoming book, *Education and Capitalism in the US.*, all the more effective for blandly acknowledging virtually every claim of human capital theory, including the fundamental claim that schooling enhances worker productivity.

402 J. E. STIGLITZ, "The Theory of 'Screening', Education, and the Distribution of Income", *AER*, June, 1975, pp. 283-300.

   An important article which generalizes the screening phenomenon and asks whether a Pareto equilibrium exists under conditions where screening occurs.

403 D. A. WISE, "Academic Achievement and Job Performance", *ibid.*, pp. 350-66.

    A study of 1,300 graduates employed in a large American firm, which looks at the relationship between academic achievement and job performance, the latter unfortunately being measured indirectly. The analysis bears directly on certain controversial aspects of human capital theory.

404 P. TURNBULL, G. WILLIAMS, "Supply and Demand in the Labour Market for Teachers: Qualification Differentials in Teachers' Pay", *BJIR*, July, 1975, pp. 215-22.

    Continuing their earlier work (391), the authors run another earnings function for British school teachers, examining the effects of qualifications on the lifetime earnings of school teachers.

405 T. I. RIBICH, J. L. MURPHY, "The Economic Returns to Increased Educational Spending", *JHR*, Winter, 1975, pp. 56-77.

    Use *Project Talent* data to run a well-specified earnings function with a strong ability but somewhat poor earnings measure. School expenditure is shown to influence earnings via years of schooling but the implied rate of return on educational spending is negative.

406 C. R. LINK, E. C. RATLEDGE, "Social Returns to Quantity and Quality of Education: A Further Statement", *ibid.*, pp. 78-89.

    An American earnings function, paying particular attention to quality measures re. white-black earnings differentials. Work experience is shown to be a critical variable.

1976

407 M. J. BOWMAN, "Postschool Learning and Human Resource Accounting", *RIW*, January, 1976, pp. 483-99.

    After an excellent analysis of the various methods employed to estimate human capital formation in the context of growth accounting, the author goes on to discuss the difficulties inherent in the concept of postschool investment.

3. THE ECONOMIC ASPECTS OF EDUCATION

(a) *Costs and Determinants of Expenditures*

Cost studies of education is one of the oldest recognised branches of the economics of education. There is a wealth of literature measuring costs at all levels of the educational system, attempting to account for differences in the costs of individual schools, differences in educational expenditures between regions of the same country, changes over time in national expenditures on education, and differences between countries in the fraction of the gross national product devoted to education.

Since the bulk of educational expenditure at all levels of the educational system goes to teachers, trends in teachers' salaries have been subjected to repeated investigation. For the United States, see Stigler[411], Ruml and Tickton[413,426], Lieberman[415], and Benson[1]. The related question of teacher supply is discussed by Bibby[288], Hinchliffe[301], Birch and Calvert[362], Turnbull and Williams[391,404], Leite, Lynch, and others[459], and Thomas[475]. The special question of trends in university salaries is dealt with by Harris[427], Bowen[491], Mills[495], Caplow and McGee[740], Robbins[751] and Katz[824].

Cost differentials between individual states in the United States have been studied by Hughes and Lancelot[409], Harris[410,427], Hirsch[421], Shapiro[431], Miner[433], James and others[434,439], and Tolley and Olson[460], all of whom have employed statistical techniques to explain the differences that are observed. Similar methods have been used by the California and Western Conference[568], Calkins[592], and Bowen[441], to account for differences in per student costs between American universities. For a review, see Witmer[468]. The question of economies of scale of high schools has been studied by Riew[440], Kiesling[447], Cohn[448], Louis and McNamara[465], Dawson and Dancey[470], and Cohn and Riew[472].

There are a number of estimates of the total costs of national educational systems: for Great Britain, see Leybourne and White[408], Judges[412], Wiles[414], Peacock and Wiseman[479], and Vaizey[419]; for France, see Institut national de la statistique[420]; for Belgium, see D'Hoogh[432]; for Canada, see Hemphill[446]; and for the United States, see Schultz[106], Machlup[162], and Blitz[429].

Income foregone by students has always been a contentious issue in such estimates; Schultz[106] and Blitz[429] arrive at different figures for the United States; Vaizey[151] once estimated it for Great Britain, but later excluded it from his larger study[419,450,459], and eventually developed the strong conviction that foregone earnings should not be counted[2]. The whole issue has been authoritatively discussed by Bowman[115]. For an interesting forecast of educational costs in Great Britain, see Vaizey and Pratt[1228], supplemented by Vaizey's post mortem on his own forecasts[866].

It is one thing to know how much education actually costs in real terms, and another thing to know how much a country spends on education. Abramovitz and Eliasberg[417], Peacock and Wiseman[424], and Vaizey[419] analyse Britain's total educational expenditures in the past; Benson[1], Miner[433], and McMahon[455] attack the problem with respect to the United States.

There has been little interest in the price elasticity of demand for education, but Benson[1], Harris[422], and Hirsch[423] have estimated the income elasticity of demand for education in the United States, Paterson[441], and Sharples[471] have done so for Canada, and Debeauvais[458] has made similar estimates for all the OECD member countries. See also Olivera[780] and Sacks[886]. Brazer and David[428] deal with the problem closely linked to income elasticity: the intergeneration effect in the demand for education.

The outstanding authority on international comparisons of educational expenditures is Edding[418,436], but also see Vaizey[2], Harris[500], Kaser[437], and Blot and Debeauvais[500]. Comparisons of the fractions of GNP devoted to education in different countries is beset with pitfalls; for some warnings, see Peacock and others[511].

1940

408   G. G. LEYBOURNE, K. WHITE, *Education and the Birth-Rate. A Social Dilemma.*
      London: Jonathan Cape, 1940. Pp. 375.

      An early attempt to estimate the total costs, including income foregone,
      of secondary and university education in Great Britain in the interwar years.
      The authors conclude that the real cost of formal education has been an impor-
      tant influence in reducing the birth rate, and they defend free public educa-
      tion on these grounds.

1946

409   R. M. HUGHES, W. H. LANCELOT, *Education. America's Magic.* Ames, Iowa: Iowa
      State College Press, 1946. Pp. 189.

      The first and most interesting part of this book, pp. 8-87, provides a
      weighted educational ranking of the 48 American states based on (1) enrolment
      figures at various levels; (2) incomes earned per child of school age; (3)
      share of earned incomes devoted to education; (4) educational expenditures per
      pupil; and (5) the average number of school years completed by adults. The
      second part of the book discusses a number of educational problems in America.
      The final chapter, by way of attempting to substantiate the dramatic title of
      this book, includes enrolment data for most countries in the world for the
      period 1931-40.

1948

410   S. E. HARRIS, *How Shall We Pay for Education?* New York: Harper & Bros.,
      1948. Pp. 214.

      The book opens with the sentence: "Economists should pay more attention to
      the economics of education". It is predominantly concerned with the impact
      of inflation on educational expenditures in the USA. Includes historical
      surveys of trends in public spending on education, tuitions, endowments and
      salaries.

1950

411 G. J. STIGLER, *Employment and Compensation in Education*. National Bureau of
Economic Research, Occasional Paper 33. New York: NBER, 1950. Pp. 73.

   An analysis of teachers' salaries since 1900, concluding that the "net
advantages" of college teaching in 1941 exceeded those of dentistry and were
almost equal to those of law and medicine.

1955

412 A. V. JUDGES, "The Social Cost of an Educational Programme", *Looking Forward
in Education*, ed. A. V. Judges. London: Faber & Faber, 1955, pp. 13-38.

   An early rough estimate of the costs of education in Great Britain in 1955.

413 B. RUML, S. G. TICKTON, *Teaching Salaries Then and Now. A 50-Year Comparison
with Other Occupations and Industries*. The Fund for the Advancement of Education, Bulletin No. 1. New York: FAE, 1955. Pp. 93.

   The technical report by S. G. Tickton and the brief review of the evidence
by B. Ruml highlight the relative deterioration of teachers' salaries, particularly at the top, since 1900. This careful study compares both the money
and the real purchasing power of teachers' salaries with money and real wages
in a variety of other industries. (See also 426).

1956

414 P. J. D. WILES, "The Nation's Intellectual Investment", *BOUIES*, November,
1956, pp. 279-90.

   A pioneering estimate of the annual gross expenditure on both formal and
informal education in the UK in 1953, together with a tentative estimate of
net current educational expenditures in that year.

415 M. LIEBERMAN, *Education as a Profession*. Englewood, N.J.: Prentice-Hall,
1956, ch. 12, pp. 373-417.

   The chapter on "The Economic Status of Teachers" contains a survey of trends
in teachers' salaries in the USA since 1900 and a discussion of the determinants of teachers' salaries in America. Other chapters in this penetrating
book, such as ch. 8 on "Teachers and Their Characteristics" and ch. 14 on
"Occupational Status", bear indirectly on issues in the economics of education.

416 West Midland Group, *Local Government and Central Control*. London: Routledge
& Kegan Paul, 1956. Pp. 296.

   A study of local government and the provision of social services in four
English midland counties, including an analysis of local variations in educational expenditures in 1938 and 1951. An attempt is made to analyse the effectiveness of each social service, and various indicators of the quality of

education in the region are examined: pupil-teacher ratios, proportion of
pupils over 15, proportion of school leavers with School Certificates, etc.,
but there is no direct comparison of costs or of the quality of education
provided.

1957

417 M. ABRAMOVITZ, V. F. ELIASBERG, *The Growth of Public Employment in Great
Britain*. National Bureau of Economic Research. Princeton, N.J.: Princeton
University Press, 1957, pp. 116-24.

A useful comparison of employment in public educational institutions in the
USA and the UK for the period 1900-50.

1958

418 F. EDDING, *Internationale Tendenzen in der Entwicklung der Ausgaben für Schulen
und Hochschulen*. Kieler Studien, No. 47. Kiel: Instituts für Weltwirtschaft
an der Universität Kiel, 1958. Pp. 164, 156.

An international comparison of 18 countries over the first half of this
century, relating public spending on education to some key indicators of development, particularly national income. Establishes an income elasticity of
demand for education in excess of unity and shows that 5 per cent seems to be
the ceiling level for the proportion of total income devoted to public education. An English version of the conclusions (pp. 157-64, reprinted in *UNESCO-
REED*, pp. 812-17) and English table-headings in the statistical appendices
make this a valuable source for data, even for those who read no German.

419 J. VAIZEY, *The Costs of Education*. London: Allen & Unwin, 1958. Pp. 256.

A comprehensive analysis of direct private and public expenditures on formal
education in the UK from 1920-55 in both money and real terms, with separate
estimates for England and Wales, Scotland and Northern Ireland, attempting to
explain both variations in the total figure and changes within the total, in
the course of which the author deals expertly with various aspects of British
education—see, e.g. the section on "The Economics of Private Education",
pp. 148-55. See also Vaizey's proposal to convert "public schools" into
"sixth forms": "The Public Schools", *The Establishment*, ed. H. Thomas (London:
A. Blond, 1959), pp. 23-49, and a similar proposal by C. A. R. Crosland, *The
Conservative Enemy*. *A Programme of Radical Reform for the 1960's* (London:
Jonathan Cape, 1962), ch. 11, pp. 167-83; see also "A Labour Educational
Policy", *The Conservative Enemy*, pp. 188-207. But the best statement of the
"socialist case on public schools" is a Young Fabian Pamphlet by H. Glennerster
and R. Pryke, *The Public Schools* (London: Fabian Society, 1964. Pp. 36).
For a new up-dated version of Vaizey's study, see J. Vaizey, J. Sheehan,
*Resources for Education. An Economic Study of Education in the United Kingdom,
1920-1965*. (London: Allen & Unwin, 1968. Pp. 176.)

420 INSEE, *Coût et développement de l'enseignement en France*. Ministère des
affaires économiques et financières. Institut national de la statistique et
des études économiques, Études économiques, N. 3. Paris: Presses universitaires de France, 1958. Pp. 104.

A semi-official study of the costs of education in France in 1955, as well as a forecast of French educational costs in 1966. Along the way, useful comparisons are made of enrolment ratios at all levels of education in various countries around the world: Germany, England, Canada, Spain, Japan, New Zealand, the Netherlands and Sweden.

1959

421   W. Z. HIRSCH, *Analysis of the Rising Costs of Public Education*. Study Papers No. 4, Joint Econ. Comm., Congress of the US. Washington, D.C.: Government Printing Office, 1959, pp. 1-43, excerpts reprinted in *PEE*, pp. 150-62.

Test of a hypothesis that daily current expenditure for primary and secondary education is a function of high school enrolment as a proportion of total enrolment, the percentage of pupils in urban areas, the annual salaries of teachers, and the number of principals per 1000 pupils. Teachers' salaries turned out to be the crucial variable. A succinct summary of the argument is to be found in the author's article: "Determinants of Public Education Expenditure", *NTJ*, March, 1960, pp. 29-41.

1960

422   S. E. HARRIS, *More Resources for Education*. New York: Harper & Bros., 1960. Pp. 86.

A series of lectures, touching on the income elasticity of expenditures on education, the issue of productivity, teachers' salaries, and the pros and cons of federal aid.

1961

423   W. Z. HIRSCH, "Income Elasticity of Public Education", *IER*, September, 1961, pp. 330-40.

An estimate of the income elasticity of primary and secondary education in the USA. The relevant elasticity turns out to be well under unity.

424   A. T. PEACOCK, J. WISEMAN, *The Growth of Public Expenditures in the United Kingdom*. National Bureau of Economic Research. Princeton, N.J.: Princeton University Press, 1961. Pp. 213.

While there are few specific references to education in this volume, it is nevertheless a useful source of explanatory hypotheses about the changing trends in public expenditures on social services. It is the authors' thesis that decisions about public expenditures are essentially political in nature (see ch. 2 on "Determinants of Government Expenditure"). Ch. 6 on "Central and Local Government Expenditure" throws light on controversies about educational finance in Britain.

425   O. ECKSTEIN, "A Survey of the Theory of Public Expenditure Criteria", *Public Finances, Needs, Sources, Utilization*, ed. J. M. Buchanan. Princeton, N.J.: Princeton University Press, 1961, pp. 439-94.

A thorough review of recent work in the theory of public expenditures and a useful reminder that education raises no measurement problems not encountered in cost-benefit analysis of other public services. See also R. N. McKean in the same volume on "Evaluating Alternative Expenditure Programs", *ibid.*, pp. 337-64, and U. Hicks, "Choice, Efficiency and Control in the Public Services", *Public Expenditure Appraisal and Control*, eds. A. T. Peacock, D. J. Robertson (Edinburgh: Oliver & Boyd, 1963), pp. 146-65.

426   S. G. TICKTON, *Teaching Salaries Then and Now—A Second Look*. The Fund for the Advancement of Education. New York: FAE, 1961. Pp. 45.

This report reproduces and brings up to date the statistical tables of 413.

1962

427   S. E. HARRIS, *Higher Education: Resources and Finance*. New York: McGraw-Hill, 1962. Pp. 713.

Covers an extremely wide range of issues and sometimes reads like a personal journal. Pts. 2, 3 and 4 deal with the question of tuition levels and student aid; once an outspoken advocate of very much higher tuition fees, Harris here modifies his views and instead favours increases in scholarship aid, particularly, increases in federal loan funds to be made available on a long-term basis at subsidised rates of interest. The book includes 4 chapters comparing expenditures for higher education, burden, capacity and effort in the 50 American states. The final section is devoted to the micro-economics of higher education—management of endowments, cost economies, and faculty salaries. The findings are summarised by the author in *OECD-EAHE*, pp. 109-17. See also E. F. Renshaw's suggestive review article of the book, *SR*, Winter, 1963, pp. 493-503, dealing with the issue of university fees, and the review by W. G. Bowen, *AER*, September, 1963, pp. 832-35.

428   H. E. BRAZER, M. H. DAVID, "Social and Economic Determinants of the Demand for Education", *EHE*, pp. 21-43.

A nation-wide probability sample of spending units in the USA in 1960 yields the firmest evidence we yet have of the intergeneration effect in the demand for education: children of more educated parents attain more than average education, even after allowing for the better economic situation of the family.

429   R. C. BLITZ, "The Nation's Educational Outlay", *ibid.*, pp. 147-73, 390-404.

A new estimate for the USA, 1955-58, including commercial vocational schools, and formal training for the military. An appendix calculates the incomes foregone by students, arriving at an incredible figure 75 per cent higher than Schultz's previous estimate (see 106).

430   P. H. KARMEL, *Some Economic Aspects of Education*. Melbourne: F. W. Cheshire, 1962. Pp. 25.

After some general remarks on education and economic development, including cogent remarks on manpower planning, the author turns to Australian Census data revealing a rise in educational levels. He notes that Australia ranks high in per capita income but relatively low in the proportion of total income devoted to education, and rejects the view that this denies the contribution of education to Australian development. He closes the pamphlet with a plea for additional expenditures on education.

431 S. SHAPIRO, "Some Socioeconomic Determinants of Expenditures for Education: Southern and Other States Compared", *CER*, October, 1962, pp. 160-66.

A sophisticated statistical exercise designed to throw light on spending patterns between states in the USA.

1963

432 C. D.'HOOGH, *Problèmes économiques de l'enseignement. Contribution à l'étude de l'investissement en capital humain.* Bruxelles: Publications du centre des problèmes sociaux et professionels, 1963. Pp. 223.

A review of the work of Edding, Schultz and Vaizey, and a study of the costs of education in Belgium 1907-38, the demand and supply of teachers 1950-60, and relevant current issues in Belgian educational planning. Includes a trilingual bibliography.

433 J. MINER, *Social and Economic Factors in Spending for Public Education.* The Economics and Politics of Public Education, No. 11. Syracuse, N.Y.: Syracuse University Press, 1963. Pp. 159. Excerpts reprinted in *URB*, pp. 93-107.

An impressive attempt to expound the theory of public expenditures as it relates to education, to review previous American empirical studies of the determinants of public expenditures on education, and to present an ambitious original empirical study, based on a sample of 1100 local school systems in 23 states. A brief concluding chapter summarises the major findings.

434 H. T. JAMES, J. A. THOMAS, H. J. DYCK, *Wealth, Expenditure and Decision-making for Education.* Stanford, California: Stanford University Press, 1963. Pp. 203.

An analysis of some of the determinants of the level and pattern of educational expenditure, and of the relationship between educational inputs and output in various American states. The authors examine the effects of variations in the level of state support and the degree of fiscal autonomy on local expenditure, and also the relation between expenditure and various measures of community wealth. The second part of the study is devoted to the relationship between various input variables and output, as measured by pupil-scores in achievement tests administered as part of *Project Talent*. A relationship between test scores and expected lifetime income is postulated, but not empirically tested.

1965

435 J. SLEEMAN, "Educational Costs and Local Government Structure in Scotland",
     SJPE, November, 1965, pp. 281-92.

     An analysis of the structure of public education costs in Scotland, particu-
     larly as between different local educational authorities.

1966

436 F. EDDING, "Expenditure on Education. An International Survey", *IEA-EE*,
     pp. 24-71.

     An outstanding review of the difficulties of making international comparisons
     in educational expenditures. A wealth of data is conveniently brought together
     in tables and graphs.

437 M. C. KASER, "Education and Economic Progress: Experience in Industrialized
     Market Economies", *ibid.*, pp. 89-174.

     An example of the simple-correlation approach applied to a dozen industrial-
     ised countries, relating GNP per head as well as the growth rate of GNP to
     five separate indicators of educational density, such as student-staff ratios,
     educational expenditures per student, and teachers' salaries.

438 F. EDDING, *Methods of Analysing Educational Outlays*. Statistical Reports and
     Studies. Paris: UNESCO, 1966. Pp. 70.

     A guide to cost analysis of educational expenditures on the institutional,
     regional, and national level.

439 H. T. JAMES, J. A. KELLY, W. I. GARMS, *Determinants of Educational Expenditures
     in Large Cities of the United States*. Stanford, California: Stanford Univer-
     sity School of Education, 1966. Pp. 198.

     An attempt to explain variations in levels of educational expenditure in the
     14 largest city school systems in the United States. Multiple regression
     analysis shows that the most important determinants of educational expenditure
     are socio-economic characteristics of the city population, such as average
     education of adults, the level of unemployment, and the per capita income of
     the city. Argues that this raises serious policy questions, since most large
     American cities are faced with increased demands for educational facilities,
     shrinking local revenue, and a decline in the average level of schooling in
     the adult population.

440 J. RIEW, "Economies of Scale in High School Operation", *RES*, August, 1966,
     pp. 280-88.

     An econometric analysis of the relationship between school size and costs
     per pupil place, based on data for senior high schools in the State of Wiscon-
     sin, concluding that the schools in question operate under conditions of in-
     creasing returns to scale.

1967

441 I. W. PATERSON, "Determinants of Expenditures for Education", *CERD*, June, 1967, pp. 155-69.

    Presents the findings of a Ph.D. dissertation which applies multiple correlation analysis to the determinants of educational expenditures by province in Canada for the years 1941-61. The income elasticity of educational expenditures rose through this period and in 1961 was found to exceed unity.

442 W. J. BAUMOL, "Macroeconomics of Unbalanced Growth: The Anatomy of the Urban Crisis", *AER*, June, 1967, pp. 415-26.

    Despite its title, this article is relevant to the economics of education: it demonstrates rigorously that costs in any labour-intensive sector like education, where the possibilities of productivity improvements are more limited than in the rest of the economy, must rise over time.

443 H. J. KIESLING, "Measuring a Local Government Service: A Study of School Districts in New York State", *RES*, August, 1967, pp. 356-67.

    A study that attempts to explain average school district pupil achievement in basic subjects by per-pupil expenditure, school district size, average pupil intelligence, and a variety of socio-economic attributes of the community in which the school district is located.

444 R. T. FITZGERALD, "Investment in Education: A Study of Recent Trends in Expenditure; The Costs of Schooling: An Analysis of Some Recent Trends", *QRAE*, September, 1967, pp. 1-20.

    An analysis of recent trends in educational expenditures in Australia.

445 E. LOVELESS, "Returns Expected on Investments in Education", *CATER*, October, 1967, pp. 475-83.

    A simple correlation analysis of the relationship in the United States between annual state expenditures on education through 1926-30 and annual per capita state income through 1951-55. The resulting correlations are then used to estimate crude rates of return on state investment in education.

446 H. D. HEMPHILL, "Trends in Educational Finance and the Public Sector, 1946-60" *CERD*, December, 1967, pp. 334-48.

    The first part of the paper provides evidence of the steadily rising trend in educational expenditure and in the proportion of government spending devoted to education in Canada since 1946. In an attempt to discover how this increase was financed, the author then correlates educational expenditure with all major sources of government revenue, and finds that the highest correlations are with property taxes and motor fuel taxes. He concludes that despite a fall in the municipal governments' share in total educational expenditure, "the local tax payer has borne the brunt of the burden of increased education costs".

1968

447 H. J. KIESLING, *High School Size and Cost Factors*. Final Report, Project
No. 6-1590. Washington, D.C.: US Department of Health, Education and Welfare,
Office of Education, 1968. Pp. 134.

A study of the relationship of high school performance to expenditure per
pupil and high school size, using data generated by *Project Talent*. It was
found that expenditure is positively related to performance, as measured by a
dozen or so achievement tests, and that increased size is negatively related
to most measures of performance. Within groups of high schools cross-classified by regions, however, little relationship was found between size and expenditure to performance.

448 E. COHN, "Economies of Scale in Iowa High School Operations", *JHR*, FAll, 1968,
pp. 422-34.

Measuring output of high schools by incremental test scores, the author
estimates unit cost functions and shows that unit costs fall in Iowa high
schools as size grows.

449 W. G. BOWEN, *The Economics of the Major Private Universities*. Berkeley,
Calif.: Carnegie Commission on Higher Education, 1968. Pp. 66.

A study of rising costs per student in American private universities and a
discussion of the reasons for believing that costs will more or less continue
to rise at 7 per cent per annum in the future as they have in the past.

450 M. F. LEITE, P. LYNCH, J. SHEEHAN, J. VAIZEY, *The Economics of Educational
Costing. Inter-Country and Inter-Regional Comparisons*. Vol. 1 - *Costs and Com-
parisons A Theoretical Approach*. Lisbon: Centro de Economia e Financas,
Instituto Gulbenkian de Ciencia, 1968. Pp. 137.

The core of this book is a number of international comparisons of unit costs
in primary education, as well as some Portuguese interregional comparisons.
Before dealing with this problem, however, the authors discuss the methodology
of projecting educational costs. Ch. 2 consists of a series of notes on the
concept of earnings foregone, concluding that it should be ignored in cost
studies. Ch. 5 reviews Denison-and-all-that: it does not fit in with the
rest of the book but it is very interesting nevertheless.

1969

451 M. F. LEITE, P. LYNCH, K. NORRIS, J. SHEEHAN, J. VAIZEY, *The Economics of
Educational Costing. Inter-Country and Inter-Regional Comparisons*. Vol. III -
Capital and Returns in Education. Lisbon: Centro de Economia e Financas,
1969. Pp. 161.

This is a by-product of an ambitious study of educational costs and is
almost wholly concerned with "the human investment revolution in economic
thought", although several chapters also deal with the manpower-requirements
approach to educational planning. Chs. 2-6, by J. Sheehan, provide a sharp
but fair criticism of human capital, rates of return, etcetera. Ch. 7 is
devoted to the "social demand" for places, which the authors themselves favour
as the best approach to educational planning.

452   W. Z. HIRSCH, M. J. MARCUS, "Intercommunity Spillovers and the Provision of
      Public Education", *KYK*, XXII, 4, 1969, pp. 641-60.

        This paper extends the authors' earlier work (see 176) on intercommunity
      spill-overs and their implications for local expenditure decisions in the
      American context. A case study for St. Louis, Missouri provides numerical
      illustration of the theoretical model.

453   J. P. CULLITY, "The Growth of Educational Employment in Three Countries,
      1895-1964", *JHR*, Winter, 1969, pp. 84-92.

        Comparisons of the growth of employment of teachers and educational admini-
      strators in the UK, the USA and Germany.

1970

454   G. WILSON, P. LEWIS, "Cost Studies in Higher Education, *HIR*, Spring, 1970,
      pp. 15-30.

        A discussion of methods of finance of higher and further education in the
      UK and a review of the difficulties these create for unit cost studies.

455   W. MCMAHON, "An Economic Analysis of Major Determinants of Expenditures on
      Public Education", *RES*, August, 1970, pp. 242-52.

        A simultaneous-equation estimate of educational expenditures for 50 American
      states based on both cross-section and time series data for the post-war
      period. The factors influencing demand, production costs, and revenues are
      set out in much greater detail than in previous studies.

456   R. BARLOW, "Efficiency Aspects of Local School Finance", *JPE*, September/
      October, 1970, pp. 1028-40; "Comments and Extensions" by N. M. Edelson,
      Y. Barzel, T. Bergstrom, T. Hogan, R. Sheldon, *ibid.*, January/February, 1973,
      pp. 156-98; "Reply" by Barlow, *ibid.*, pp. 199-202.

        This paper considers the Pareto non-optimality properties of local school
      expenditures associated with the property tax in the USA. The article drew
      a variety of comments relating to the public goods theory of local expenditure

457   J. SHEEHAN, "Economic Aspects", *The Extra Year. The Raising of the School-
      Leaving Age*, ed. T. W. Tibble. London: Routledge & Kegan Paul, 1970,
      pp. 54-69.

        After discussing the financial aspects of the then prospective ROSLA, the
      author attempts to calculate the real costs, including earnings foregone, of
      the extra school year. The final pages of the article discuss the probable
      benefits of the extra year, concluding that little if any case exists for it
      on economic grounds.

458   M. DEBEAUVAIS, *Comparative Study of Educational Expenditure and Its Trends
      in OECD Countries Since 1950. OECD Conference on Policies for Educational
      Growth. Background Study No. 2.* Paris: OECD, 1970. Pp. 38, mimeographed.

A valuable study of the Great Ratio (educational expenditures to GNP) as sell as the composition of expenditures. The income-elasticity of expenditures is estimated from both cross-section and time series data.

459 M. F. LEITE, P. LYNCH, K. NORRIS, J. SHEEHAN and J. VAIZEY, *The Economics of Educational Costing. Inter-Country and Inter-Regional Comparisons.* Vol. II - *Production Functions in Education, Teachers and Their Salaries and Regional Analysis.* Lisbon: Instituto Gulbenkian de Ciencia, Centro de Economia e Financas, 1970. Pp. 160.

This is a collection of unrelated papers on the topics of educational efficiency, trends in resource use, and the economics of teachers' salaries, using data for England and Wales, Ireland and Portugal. The first three chapters on production functions in education hardly begin to explore the recent literature on the topic; they include a lengthy, but rather confusing, critique of Woodhall and Blaug's work on productivity measurements (see 600). Next, there is an interesting chapter on new media, followed by three chapters on trends in expenditures in the three countries. Lastly, there is a chapter on teachers' salaries, a chapter on teacher supply in England and Wales and a chapter on teacher forecasts, again in England and Wales. The whole of this book plus 450 and 451, but omitting chapter 2 of 450 on earnings foregone, has been reprinted as 27.

1971

460 G. S. TOLLEY, E. OLSON, "The Interdependence Between Income and Education", *JPE*, May/June, 1971, pp. 460-80.

This is both an important contribution to the economics of education and a superb illustration of certain standard econometric results. Using evidence for 51 American states, the authors show that a single-equation estimate of the relationship between income and educational expenditures yields biased coefficients; they carry out simultaneous-equations estimates and discover that the source of the bias in single-equation estimates is the relatively large effect of income on education. Their equations include wealth variables, distinguishing human wealth from nonhuman wealth. There are obvious implications of these findings for previous international estimates of the income-education relationship.

1972

461 H. L. HANDA, *Towards a Rational Education Policy. An Econometric Analysis of Ontario, Canada, 1950-65, with Tests 1966-68 and Projections 1969-75.* Toronto: Ontario Institute for Education, Occasional Papers No. 10, 1972. PP. 272.

Another simultaneous-equations estimate of educational expenditures, incorporating student-demand equations, school and college-supply equations and educational budget constraints - but *not* labor demand or supply equations. The results are clearly presented and a didactic chapter on econometric model-building with time series data is included.

1973

462 L. WAGNER, "The Economics of the Open University", *HE*, May, 1972, pp. 159-84,
     "Comment" by C. F. Carter and "Reply" by Wagner, *ibid.*, February, 1973,
     pp. 69-72.

     Attempts to show that the Open University in Britain is bound to be cheaper
     per completed student than the traditional university.

463 H. GLENNERSTER, *Willing The Means. An Examination of the Cost of Reforming
     Our Education System.* London: Council for Educational Advance, 1972. Pp. 35.

     The author crudely calculates the increase in real public expenditures on
     education that will be required in Britain by 1980 to achieve eleven targets
     laid down by the Council for Educational Advance. In the final pages, he
     briefly considers the desirability of these targets and canvasses various means
     of financing the increase in expenditures that will be required. Along the
     way, he describes the principal machinery for financing education in Britain.

464 B. WILLIAMS, "The Escalating Costs of Universities", *IAU*, September, 1972,
     pp. 91-113.

     An examination of real expenditures on Australian universities since 1957
     and the reasons why they have been fairly constant since about 1961.

465 E. COHN, *Public Expenditure Analysis. With Special Reference to Human
     Resources.* Lexington, Mass.: D. C. Heath and Co., 1972. Pp. 157.

     This is a textbook prepared for a course in public expenditure analysis,
     offered to state officials in the USA. It includes an introduction to statis-
     tical concepts, welfare economics and cost-benefit analysis, followed by a
     chapter on education (a summary of the author's book, 23) and a chapter on
     health, both of which simply report on the literature.

466 D. R. WITMER, "Cost Studies in Higher Education", *RER*, Winter, 1972,
     pp. 99-127.

     A summary and bibliography of cost studies of American higher education
     since about 1900.

467 A. V. WARD, *Resources for Educational Research and Development.* London:
     National Foundation for Educational Research, 1973. Pp. 131.

     An interesting attempt to estimate total expenditure on educational research
     in Britain with breakdowns for sources, sponsors, performers and organisations.
     There is also a chapter on educational research expenditure in other countries.

468 L. S. LOUIS, J. F. McNAMARA, "Economies of Scale for a State System of Public
     School Districts", *SEP*, June, 1973, pp. 295-303.

     After a brief review of previous literature, the authors outline a method
     for measuring economies of scale at the American public-school-district level
     and then illustrate its application with reference to school districts in
     Oregon.

469 A. L. GUSTMAN, G. B. PIDOT, Jr., "Interactions Between Educational Spending and Student Enrollment", *JHR*, Winter, 1973, pp. 3-23.

A simultaneous equation model of the relationship between public school expenditures and public school enrolments tested on a sample of 79 urban areas in the United States. The principal finding is that the education budget of a community varies non-linearly with enrolments such that student outlays are lower where the enrolment rate is higher.

1974

470 D. A. DAWSON, K. J. DANCEY, "Economies of Scale in the Ontario Public School Sector", *AJER*, June, 1974, pp. 186-97.

A study of economies of scale in the public secondary schools of Ontario Province. No convincing evidence of increasing returns to scale were found.

471 B. SHARPLES, "Responsiveness of Educational Expenditures to Factors of Economic Growth", *ibid.*, pp. 198-207.

Estimates income and population elasticities of demand for public education in each province of Canada with data for the period 1957-66.

472 E. COHN, J. RIEW, "Cost Functions in Public Schools", *JHR*, Summer, 1974, pp. 408-14.

A discussion of some new findings on economies of scale in public high schools in the United States.

473 B. LAIDLAW, R. LAYARD, "Traditional Versus Open University Teaching Methods: A Cost Comparison", *HE*, November, 1974, pp. 439-67.

Estimates the direct instructional cost of the British Open University teaching methods as against conventional full-time university instruction. The authors show that the variable cost per student-course is almost always lower in the Open University than elsewhere.

1975

474 M. S. FELDSTEIN, "Wealth, Neutrality and Local Choice in Public Education", *AER*, March, 1975, pp. 75-89.

Argues and attempts to refute the hypothesis that local expenditure on education in the USA is a function of the taxable wealth of the local community.

475 R. B. THOMAS, "The Supply of Graduates to School Teaching", *BJIR*, March, 1975, pp. 107-14.

Tests and confirms the hypothesis that the supply of graduates to teaching
in Britain is sensitive to unemployment and to alternative salaries.

(b) PUBLIC AND PRIVATE FINANCE

Educational finance around the world presents a confusing picture: there appear
to be infinite varieties of public and private sources of finance cutting across
different mixtures of public and private provision of education. In America, for
example, there is municipal, state, and federal aid to education, not to mention
fees charged to students and institutional scholarships, and these funds go alike
to public and private schools. In Great Britain, there are private schools, semi-
private schools, state schools and autonomous universities, yet all these, with
the exception of entirely private schools, are heavily dependent on central finance.
Bewildering as are the facts, the principles of educational finance offer little
solace, remaining as they do a subject of controversy among the experts. In this
section we concentrate on the facts; for the controversy, see the section on "The
Politics of Education". The special financial problems of higher education are
also taken up in a later section on "Higher Education".

Benson[1] describes American federal government aid to elementary and secondary
education; Burston[478], Peacock and Wiseman[479], and Lees[480] discuss British central
government aid. On the relations between local and central government finance in
both America and England, see Benson[1,493], Lees[480], the Committee for Economic
Development[481], Renshaw[483] ; Burkhead[489,493], Hirsch[494], Forte[500], and Eckstein[872].

The question of private finance is canvassed by Vaizey[2,419], Van Den Haag[138],
Lansing and others[482], Harris[500], Bowen[518], and Glennerster and Wilson[531].

Harris[427], Vickrey[485], Goode[486], Edding[500], Merrett[508], Prest[499], Jenkins and
Straubenzee[512], Shell and others[515], Glennerster and others[520], Mishan[523], Collins[53?]
Woodhall[535], Rudd[536], Johson[541], Johnstone and Dresch[544], McNulty[546], Peitchinis[552],
and Nerlove[557] write on the knotty problems of making loans to students in higher
education. The more recent proposal to finance primary and secondary schools by
vouchers is discussed by Friedman[1256], Levin[517], Rowley[522], Benson[534], Jenning[539],
La Noue[542], Erickson[543], Wolf[554] and Eysenbach[555]. Hansen and Weisbrod's study of
the distribution of costs and benefits of higher education in California[525] has
sparked off applications to other American states: see Hansen and Weisbrod[528,815],
Pechman[529,815], Windham[545], Hight and Pollock[548], and Crean[558].

Much is to be learned by systematic international comparisons of educational
finance. Lees[487], Bowen[488], and Vogelnik[492] contrast university finance in Britain
and the United States, and Garcia[500] compares the situation in various European
countries. Eide[500] and Embling[500] provide international comparisons of methods of
control over educational expenditures. The problem of finding additional sources
of revenue to finance educational expansion is analysed by Senf, Mushkin, and
Vaizey[500].

For further bibliographical references see Alexander and Covert[1880] and Munse
and Booher[1886].

1929

476 J. CORLETT, *A Survey of the Financial Aspects of Elementary Education.*
     London: P. S. King, 1929. Pp. 227.

An early study of the finance of British primary education in the nineteenth
and twentieth centuries. Various methods of financing education are discussed,

including the "payment by results" scheme of 1871, and block and percentage
grants. The cuts in educational expenditures in the 1920's are examined in
detail.

1939

477 F. H. SWIFT, *European Policies of Financing Educational Institutions. The
Practices of France, Czechoslovkia, Austria, Germany, and England and Wales.*
University of California Publications in Education, vol. 8. Berkeley,
Calf.: California University Press, 1933-39. Pp. 970.

An invaluable source of information about European educational finance in
the interwar period.

1956

478 W. H. BURSTON, "The Incidence of Taxation and of State Provision for Education:
United Kingdom", *The Yearbook of Education, 1956,* ed. J. A. Lauwerys. London:
Evans Bros., 1956, pp. 180-97.

A good description of methods of financing education in the United Kingdom.

479 A. T. PEACOCK, J. WISEMAN, "The Finance of State Education in the UK", *ibid.,*
pp. 305-21.

A pioneer effort to estimate the costs of education in 1954 and to allocate
the burdens and benefits of education between central and local governments
and between broad income classes.

480 D. S. LEES, chairman of Study Group, *Local Expenditure and Exchequer Grants.
A Research Study.* London: Institute of Municipal Treasurers and Accountants,
1956. Pp. 352. Excerpts reprinted in *PEE*, pp. 354-63.

This masterly appraisal of the system of central grants to local authorities
in England and Wales defends "specific or percentage grants" which have
characterised the English grant system for over a century and criticises proposals to replace them by "unit grants" or "general grants". The book is now
somewhat dated owing to the introduction of general or "block grants" in 1959.
The conclusions of the study are conveniently summarised on pp. 281-87. Chs.
10-11, pp. 222-50, deal specifically with grants for education.

1959

481 CED, *Paying for Better Public Schools.* New York: Committee for Economic
Development, 1959. Pp. 90. Excerpts reprinted in *PEE*, pp. 273-85.

This excellent pamphlet on ways of financing projected expansion of elementary and secondary schools through the 1960's includes valuable historical and
current data on expenditures, incomes, and enrolment by states. Ch. 3 on
"The Role of the Federal Government" concludes that further extension of

federal government activities in the field of elementary and secondary education is undesirable. A number of committee members, however, dissented from
this conclusion.

1960

482 J. B. LANSING, T. LORIMER, C. MORIGUCHI, *How People Pay for College*. Survey
     Research Center, Institute for Social Research, Michigan University. Ann
     Arbor, Mich.: SRC, 1960. Pp. 160.

       This study of the costs of higher education borne by American parents is
     based on two special social surveys conducted by the Survey Research Center.
     It examines both the factors influencing the present size of parents' contri-
     butions and those influencing parents' plans to finance college education for
     their children. A particularly important section is ch. V, sect. B on the
     "Factors Influencing Educational Attainment", pp. 119-46.

483 E. F. RENSHAW, "A Note on the Expenditure Effect of State Aid to Education",
     JPE, April, 1960, pp. 170-74.

       A refutation by means of multiple-regression analysis of a popular hypothesis
     in the literature on school finance, namely, that state aid largely substitutes
     for local finance, leaving total local expenditures on education unaffected.
     Cites several other studies of this relationship.

484 Ministry of Education, UK, *Grants to Students*. Reports of the Committee
     Appointed by the Minister of Education and the Secretary of State for Scotland
     in June, 1958. London: HMSO, 1960. Cmnd. 1051. Pp. 135.

       This is the committee that devised the present system of student grants in
     British higher education. The description of the system of student grants
     before 1958, which fills several chapters, the analysis of the conflicting
     opinions in the committee on means tests applied to grants, ch. 7, pp. 44-59,
     and the estimates of the costs of the proposals, ch. 13, pp. 92-94, make
     strange reading ten or fifteen years later. See also the interesting "Notes
     of Reservation", pp. 105-8, where B. Thomas proposes "substantial sixth form
     bursaries" as a preliminary step to the removal of means testing of grants.

1962

485 W. VICKREY, "A Proposal for Student Loans", *EHE*, pp. 268-81.

       A proposal for encouraging students to borrow finance for their education
     by allowing them to repay a percentage of their future income rather than a
     fixed sum with interest.

486 R. GOODE, "Educational Expenditures and the Income Tax", *ibid.*, pp. 281-305,
     reprinted in *KIK*, pp. 563-85.

       A radical proposal to change the tax treatment of education by allowing the
     student to write off the cost of education against his future taxable income
     over a period of years (see 503).

487 D. S. LEES, "Financing Higher Education in the US and in Great Britain", *ibid.*, pp. 328-45.

A useful contrast between the two countries with data for recent years.

1963

488 W. G. BOWEN, "University Finance in Britain and the US: Implications of Financing Arrangements for Educational Issues", *PF*, 1963, pp. 45-83, reprinted in W. G. Bowen, *Economic Aspects of Education. Three Essays*. Princeton, N.J.: Industrial Relations Section, 1964, pp. 41-87.

A comparison of patterns of university finance in Britain and in the USA and an attempt to indicate the educational implications of different methods of finance. Argues the case for a rise in student fees in both countries.

489 J. BURKHEAD, *State and Local Taxes for Public Education*. The Economics and Politics of Public Education, No. 7. Syracuse, N.Y.: Syracuse University Press, 1963. Pp. 110.

An expert appraisal of the adequacy of American state and local taxes for the support of elementary and secondary education, with particular attention to the property tax, its character, burden, economic effects, income elasticity, and administrative patterns. The first chapter of the monograph discusses the possibility of a general theory of intergovernmental finance.

490 A. M. CARTTER, "Tax Reliefs and the Burden of College Costs", *TER*, October, 1963, pp. 424-32.

A discussion of the many bills now before Congress to grant tax credits to parents with children attending college, an arrangement which, the author argues, would really only benefit high-income families.

491 W. G. BOWEN, "University Salaries: Faculty Differentials", *EC*, 1963, pp. 341-60, reprinted in W. G. Bowen, *Economic Aspects of Education. Three Essays*. Princeton, N.J.: Industrial Relations Section, 1964, pp. 87-127.

A study of the pattern of university salaries in Great Britain, demonstrating that science and technology offer higher age-specific salary rates than arts despite the existence of uniform salary scales for all subjects.

1964

492 D. VOGELNIK, "A Comparison Between the Financing of Higher Education in the USA and Yugoslavia", *OECD-EAHE*, pp. 117-33.

The bulk of this article is devoted to the USA, leaving only a few pages for a description of educational finance in Yugoslavia.

493 J. BURKHEAD, *Public School Finance. Economics and Politics*. Syracuse, N.Y.: Syracuse University Press, 1964. Pp. 394.

Eleven of the chapters in this volume are summaries of the monographs published as The Economics and Politics of Public Education Series (see 433, 489,
but not 589). Two chapters were specifically commissioned for this volume:
B. M. Gross, "The Administration of Public Schools", ch. 2, pp. 23-50, and
C. S. Benson, "State Aid Patterns", ch. 9, pp. 205-36. The author contributes
an introductory chapter on "The Economics of School Finance" and a closing
chapter on "Patterns for Resource Mobilization". The total effect of the
volume is, despite efforts to the contrary, somewhat lopsided.

494 W. Z. HIRSCH, "Fiscal Impact of Industrialization on Local Schools", RES, May,
     1964, pp. 191-99.

     A test of the proposition that local industrialisation improves the fiscal
     position of local school districts in the USA.

495 G. MILLS, "Dispersion of Academic Salaries in Great Britain and in the USA",
     BJIR, July, 1964, pp. 251-58.

     Presents measures of dispersion for British and American academic salaries,
     concluding that, contrary to casual impression, salary variation for the pro-
     fession is not greater in the United States than in Great Britain.

1965

496 NEA, Trends in Financing Public Education. Proceedings of the Eighth National
     Conference on School Finance. Washington, D.C.: National Education Associa-
     tion, 1965. Pp. 248.

     Some thirty brief non-technical articles on the broad economic and political
     issues in school support, the development of measures of ability of state and
     local government to support schools, the size-cost structure of school systems,
     the improvement of the property tax, and the decision-making process in school
     finance. Among the leading writers contributing to this volume are A. M.
     Rivlin, C. S. Benson, and J. Burkhead.

497 C. S. BENSON, The Cheerful Prospect: A Statement on the Future of American
     Education. Boston, Mass.: Houghton Mifflin, 1965. Pp. 134.

     A discussion of financial and administrative issues in American education,
     with frequent references to the British system. The author suggests a number
     of reforms, such as reorganisation of school districts and the establishment
     of state salary scales for teachers, which he argues would increase equality
     of educational provision and efficiency of resource allocation.

1966

498 G. KALTON, The Public Schools: A Factual Survey. London: Longmans, Green
     & Co., 1966. Pp. 179.

     This is a purely factual survey of the private sector of the British educa-
     tional system, somewhat thin on financial matters, and a thorough knowledge

of the state sector is essential to make sense of the data that is presented. The book includes an illuminating sociological introduction by R. Lambert.

499 A. R. PREST, *Financing University Education.* London: Institute of Economic Affairs, 1966. Pp. 39.

This reprints the evidence presented by the author to the Robbins Committee (see 751) and adds a postscript which reviews the debate in Britain since 1962 on loan schemes for students in higher education. See the article review by M. Blaug, "Loans for Students?", *NS*, 4 October, 1966, pp. 538-39. See also J. Vaizey, *Higher Education in the Stationary State.* (Liverpool: Liverpool University Press, 1967. Pp. 18.)

500 OECD, Study Group, *Financing of Education for Economic Growth.* Paris: OECD, 1966. Pp. 421.

This volume consists of 6 papers on educational finance in underdeveloped countries and 13 papers on finance in developed countries. A. R. Prest argues the case for public finance and public provision of education versus public subsidies for private provision: "Internal Fiscal Policies and Education Programmes in Developing Nations", pp. 17-31; R. A. Musgrave assembles some "Notes on Educational Investment in Developing Nations", pp. 31-41; R. Goode discusses criteria and possible forms of "External Aid for Investment in Education in Developing Countries", pp. 41-58; The Netherlands Economic Institute employs econometric methods to forecast 1975 levels of educational expenditures in 25 developing countries, "Financial Aspects of Educational Expansion in Developing Regions: Some Quantitative Estimates", pp. 59-73; D. Blot and M. Debeauvais analyse "Educational Expenditures in Developing Areas: Some Statistical Aspects", pp. 73-88.

A. T. Peacock and J. Wiseman lead off in the section on developed countries with an important paper on "Economic Growth and the Principles of Educational Finance in Developed Countries", pp. 89-103, reprinted in *P-EED*, 2, pp. 343-59, in which they demonstrate the ambiguous policy implications of rate-of-return studies and introduce some useful distinctions about the "external benefits" of education. S. E. Harris examines recent trends in "Public Expenditures on Education", pp. 103-52. A. Garcia presents "The Financing of Education under a Centralised System: France", pp. 153-69, followed by "The Financing of Education in France, Great Britain, Norway, and Germany", pp. 197-212. K. Eide and J. Embling then review methods of control over educational expenditures in Norway and in the UK, pp. 169-97. P. Senf writes, with special reference to Western Germany, on the "Financial Implications of the Expansion, by 1970, of Public and Educational Expenditures in Five Countries of the European Economic Community", pp. 337-69, followed by 2 papers on the same subject with reference to the MRP by J. Vaizey, pp. 383-98, and the OECD Secretariat, pp. 369-82. S. J. Mushkin deals with "Financing Secondary School Expansion", pp. 267-98, reprinted in *SE*, Summer, 1965, pp. 267-97. F. Forte considers the implications of "Local and Central Government Problems in the Financing of Education", pp. 299-336. S. E. Harris contrasts "Student Financing and Enrolment in Higher Education" in Western Europe and in the United States, pp. 213-50. Lastly, F. Edding discusses the theory of "Student Aid with the help of detailed figures of aid in Western Germany, pp. 251-67. There are summary reports by A. Williams, J. A. Pechman, K. Eide, and J. Embling, pp. 399-423.

501 Développement des ressources humaines, Rapports des boursiers, *Essai d'analyse du financement de l'enseignement universitaire en Belgique.* Paris: OECD, 1966. Pp. 116.

A study in the finance of higher education in Belgium carried out in 1964.

502 *Public Finance and Education*. Papers and Proceedings of the XXIst Session of
the International Institute of Public Finance, Paris, September, 1965, *PF*,
XXI, 1-2, 1966, pp. 1-325.

The papers include: (1) a veritable handbook on educational finance by
M. Frank, E. Rosselle, "Finances publiques et education", pp. 1-121; (2)
M. Orlowski, Z. Pirozynski, "Problems of Financing Education in Socialist
Countries", with comment by J. B. D. Derksen, pp. 121-70; (3) V. V. Lawrov,
"Socialist Systems of Financing Public Education", pp. 170-84; (4) M. H.
Peston, "The Theory of Spillovers and its Connection with Education", with
comments by M. O'Donoghue, pp. 184-206; (5) L. Faluvégi, "The Planning of
Budgetary Expenditure on Education on the Basis of a Mathematical Model—the
Method Employed in Hungary", with comments by A. T. Peacock, pp. 206-36;
(6) C. D'Hoogh, "Systèmes de financement et optimalisation des dépenses
d'enseignement", pp. 236-58; (7) E. Liefmann-Keil, "Grants in Aid to Students
in a Growing Economy with Technical Progress, A Comment", pp. 258-69; (8)
S. A. Aluko, "Public Finance and Education in Nigeria", with comments by
E. R. Rolph, pp. 269-316; and (9) a summary of the issues raised at the conference by J. Wiseman, pp. 316-25.

503 R. GOODE, "Tax Treatment of Individual Expenditures for Education and Research"
AER, May, 1966, pp. 208-17.

A useful review of the current American tax treatment of educational expenditures with some specific suggestions for reform.

504 J. M. CAROVANO, "Financing Public Higher Education, 1969-70", *NTJ*, June, 1966,
pp. 125-38.

Enrolment in American schools in 1969 is calculated on the assumption that
enrolment in private institutions in each state will increase at the same rate
in the 1960's as in the 1950's; the required income per student is projected
on this basis. Staff salaries are projected on the assumption of unchanged
student-staff ratios and again on the assumption of a one per cent increase
in student-staff ratios with no fall in quality.

505 A. PEACOCK, R. J. LAVERS, "The Social Accounting of Education", *JRSS*, Series
A, Vol. 129, P. 3, 1966, pp. 448-66.

This paper develops a consistent production, consumption, and financing
account for educational services in any country, in the light of which it
discusses the difficulty of measuring the contribution of education to GNP.
The foregoing analysis is then used to evaluate the treatment of education in
the published national accounts of the United Kingdom (see 511).

506 D. SEERS, R. JOLLY, "The Treatment of Education in National Accounting", *RIW*,
September, 1966, pp. 195-209.

Advocates treating educational expenditures as capital formation rather than
as public and private consumption for purposes of drawing up national income
accounts. Most of the article is devoted to the problems of valuing the stock
of educational capital and of estimating the extent of depreciation.

1967

507 M. V. PAULY, "Mixed Public and Private Financing of Education: Efficiency
     and Feasibility", *AER*, March, 1967, pp. 120-30.

     A terse theoretical paper, demonstrating with the aid of the distinction
     between marginal and inframarginal externalities that equal public support
     to each student violates Pareto optimality.

508 S. MERRETT, "Student Finance in Higher Education", *EJ*, June, 1967, pp. 288-303.

     The author analyses the finance of higher education in terms of a stylised
     contrast between a "capitalist" and a "socialist" system.

509 B. MACLENNAN, "The Finance of Grant-Aided Schools in Scotland", *SJPE*, June,
     1967, pp. 156-74.

     An analysis of the current expenditure and cost structure of grant-aided
     Scottish schools, a counterpart to direct-grant schools in England and Wales,
     with some comparisons to education authority schools.

510 ANON, "University Finance: Should Students Pay?", *NS*, June 22, 1967,
     pp. 914-16.

     A brilliant article on the finance of British universities with a plea for
     a rise in fees coupled with loans.

1968

511 A. PEACOCK, H. GLENNERSTER, R. LAVERS, *Educational Finance. Its Sources and
     Uses in the United Kingdom*. London: Oliver & Boyd, 1968.

     A path-breaking attempt to present British educational finance in a consis-
     tent set of social accounts. The raw data used is that for 1962-63. Among
     the more interesting aspects of the book is a revision of the standard figure
     for the contribution of the education "industry" to GDP from 4.8 to 3.0 per
     cent, pp. 21-23, 58-60.

512 S. JENKINS, B. VAN STRAUBENZEE, *Student Loans. Pros and Cons*. London:
     Conservative Political Centre, 1968. Pp. 36.

     An excellent summary of the arguments on both sides as applied to British
     higher education.

513 *Public Schools Commission. First Report*. London: HMSO, 1968, I. Pp. 237.

     The parts of the report relevant in this context are ch. 14, pp. 349-75,
     which is concerned with the nature and magnitude of public subsidies to private
     schools, chs. 15-16, pp. 376-460, which deal with the costs of the commission's
     proposals for integrating independent boarding schools, and J. Vaizey's "Note
     of Reservation", pp. 221-24.

514 *Public Schools Commission. First Report.* London: HMSO, 1968, II: Appendices. Pp. 493.

The appendices include a study of the "Need and Demand for Boarding Education" by R. Lambert and R. Woolfe, pp. 241-79, a report on "The Finances of the Public Schools" by H. Glennerster and G. Wilson, pp. 284-343 (see also 531), and a fascinating compendium of information on the "Careers of Former Public School Pupils", pp. 225-40.

515 K. SHELL, F. M. FISHER, D. K. FOLEY, A. F. FRIEDLANDER, "The Educational Opportunity Bank: An Economic Analysis of a Contingent Repayment Loan Program for Higher Education", *NTJ*, March, 1968, pp. 2-45.

A central feature of EOB is a "contingent repayment loan", which in effect works as a graduate tax. The authors provide a thorough analysis of EOB, its costs, and allocative and distributional effects.

516 R. L. MATTHEWS, "Finance for Education", *TAU*, April, 1968, pp. 59-95.

After summarising the ideas of the classical economists on education, the author analyses the pattern of educational expenditures in Australia in recent years and proceeds to canvass a wide array of policy proposals to tap new sources of finance for higher education.

517 H. M. LEVIN, "The Failure of the Public Schools and the Free Market Remedy", *UR*, June, 1968, pp. 32-37.

A discussion of educational vouchers in the American context and some proposals for ensuring that vouchers will not have divisive effects in respect of class and race.

518 H. R. BOWEN, *The Finance of Higher Education*. Berkeley, Calif.: Carnegie Commission on Higher Education, 1968. Pp. 36.

A discussion of student costs and sources of finance of colleges in the USA and a proposal for a mixed grants-loans system for American higher education.

519 D. COCHRANE, "The Cost of University Education", *ER*, June, 1968, pp. 137-53.

After a general discussion of rate-of-return analysis, the author moves on to an analysis of trends in expenditure on higher education in Australia, concluding with a plea for a rise in fees and a switch to greater reliance on student loans.

520 H. GLENNERSTER, S. MERRETT, G. WILSON, "A Graduate Tax", *HIR*, Autumn, 1968, pp. 26-38; "Comment" by K. F. Wallis, *ibid.*, Spring, 1969, pp. 65-67.

This very useful article calculates the rate of repayment that would be necessary to render a student loans scheme in British higher education self-financing after so many years, on various assumptions about the magnitude of the loan and the level of interest rates.

1969

521 A. T. PEACOCK, A. J. CULYER, *Economic Aspects of Student Unrest*.   London:
     Institute of Economic Affairs, 1969. Pp. 23.

     An economic analysis of student unrest in Britain, and a recommendation to
     finance students rather than institutions.

522 C. K. ROWLEY, "The Political Economy of British Education", *SJPE*, February,
     1969, pp. 152-76.

     An analysis of the economic case for "free" state education and a defence
     of the voucher scheme.

523 E. J. MISHAN, "Some Heretical Thoughts on University Reform", *ENC*, March,
     1969, pp. 3-15.

     A vigorous restatement of the case for cost-covering fees and student loans
     in the context of British higher education.

524 J. M. BURNS, B. R. CHISWICK, "An Economic Analysis of State Support for Higher
     Education", *WEJ*, March, 1969, pp. 84-95, reprinted in *ROG*, pp. 91-7.

     A general discussion of the externality argument and the problem of imper-
     fect markets for human capital. Scholarships, loans and other forms of govern-
     ment subsidies to higher education are reviewed in the light of these consi-
     derations.

525 W. LEE HANSEN, B. A. WEISBROD, *Benefits, Costs, and Finance of Public Higher
     Education*. Chicago: Markham Publishing Co., 1969. Pp. 114.

     After calculating the present value of the earnings differentials of Califor-
     nia graduates and the private as well as the social costs of public higher
     education in the State of California, the authors go on to consider the net
     benefits of higher education to parents of college students after allowing
     for public subsidies and the burden of tax payments. They conclude that the
     general effect of subsidies to higher education in California is to promote
     rather than to discourage inequalities of income. The book closes with a
     valuable essay on optimal financing schemes for higher education. Ch. 4,
     containing the heart of the matter, is reproduced with additional material in
     their article "The Distribution of Costs and Direct Benefits of Higher Educa-
     tion: The Case of California", *JHR*, Spring, 1969, pp. 176-91.

1970

526 J. M. BURNS, B. R. CHISWICK, "Analysis of the Effects of a Graduated Tuition
     Program at State Universities", *JHR*, Spring, 1970, pp. 237-45.

     A general discussion of the possible effects of a change from nominal or
     zero tuition fees to graduated tuition fees (graduated in relation to parental
     income) at public universities in the United States.

527 E. COHN, A. GIFFORD, I. SHARKANSKY, "Benefits and Costs of Higher Education
     and Income Redistribution: Three Comments", *ibid.*, pp. 222-36.

     A discussion of the significance of Hansen and Weisbrod's findings (see 525).

528 W. LEE HANSEN, "Income Distribution Effects of Higher Education", *AER*, May,
     1970, pp. 335-40; "Comments" by W. A. Wallis, *ibid.*, pp. 350-51.

     An extension of his and Weisbrod's work on California to the State of
     Wisconsin.

529 J. PECHMAN, "The Distributional Effects of Public Higher Education in Califor-
     nia", *JHR*, Summer, 1970, pp. 361-70; "Reply" by W. Lee Hansen and B. A.
     Weisbrod, *ibid.*, Summer, 1971, pp. 363-74.

     This note attacks the Hansen-Weisbrod thesis that the finance of higher
     education in California leads to substantial redistribution of income from
     lower to higher income groups. See also R. W. Hartman, "A Comment on the
     Pechman-Hansen-Weisbrod Controversy", *ibid.*, Fall, 1970, pp. 519-23.

530 M. BLAUG, "Raising the School Age: Bribery vs. Compulsion", *HIR*, Autumn,
     1970, pp. 53-58.

     An application of consumer-surplus analysis to the issue of raising the
     school leaving age in Britain from 15 to 16.

531 H. GLENNERSTER, G. WILSON, *Paying for Private Schools*. London: Allen Lane,
     The Penguin Press, 1970. Pp. 183.

     This is the first study of the income, expenditure and costs of private
     schools in Britain based on a questionnaire survey. The book includes an
     estimate of the total level of public support to private education, some his-
     torical data on the expenditure of private schools, and a controversial final
     chapter which considers their probable future.

532 D. COLLINS, "Financing Higher Education: A Proposal", *ER*, Fall, 1970,
     pp. 368-77.

     A proposal for a federally financed and insured revolving loan fund to
     finance the whole of US higher education.

533 K. D. ROOSE, "Aid to Students - or to Institutions", *ibid.*, pp. 355-67.

     An argument in favour of aid to students in the context of US higher educa-
     tion.

534 R. L. JOHNS, I. J. GOFFMAN, K. ALEXANDER, D. STOLLAR, eds. *Economic Factors
     Affecting the Financing of Education*. Gainesville, Florida: National Educa-
     tional Finance Project, 1970. Pp. 372.

     This is a solid collection of 11 papers on the problems of financing educa-
tion in the American context. It begins with a characteristically stimulating paper

by K. E. Boulding, "Factors Affecting the Future Demand for Education",
pp. 1-27. There follow a new paper by T. W. Schultz, "The Human Capital
Approach to Education", pp. 29-57, which summarizes available information on
rates of return in the USA; J. R. Davis, "The Social and Economic Externalities
of Education", pp. 59-81, a standard piece which does little to advance the
debate on externalities; M. J. Bowman, "Education and Economic Growth",
pp. 83-120, which *inter alia* criticizes Berg (265); C. Benson, "Economic Analysis of Institutional Alternatives for Providing Education (Public, Private
Sector)", pp. 121-82, a fascinating discussion of Friedman's voucher plan,
Coleman's contract scheme and family-power-equalising proposals; H. M. Levin,
"The Effect of Different Levels of Expenditure on Educational Output", pp.
173-206, a splendid review of production-function measurements of American
schooling; T. I, Ribich, "The Effect of Educational Spending on Poverty Edu-
cation", pp. 207-34, an up-dated version of his book (see 246); H. E. Brazer,
"Federal, State, and Local Responsibility for Financing Education", pp. 235-63;
J. M. Buchanan, "Taxpayer Constraints on Financing Education", pp. 265-90;
J. F. Due, "Alternative Tax Sources for Education", pp. 291-328; and S. J.
Mushkin and W. Pollak, "Analysis in a PPB Setting", pp. 329-72.

535 M. WOODHALL, *Student Loans. A Review of Experience in Scandinavia and Elsewhere*. London: George Harrap & Co., 1970. Pp. 224.

   The definitive account of Scandinavian experience with student loans, including the economic, social and educational effects of loans on Swedish higher
education. Includes a chapter on student loan schemes in other countries.
For a digest of the book in French, see M. Woodhall, *Systèmes de prêts aux
étudiants en Scandinavie*. Le financement des systèmes éducatifs: études de
cas spécifiques - 2 (Paris: UNESCO-IIEP, 1972. Pp. 42). See also a summary
in English with additional materials, M. Woodhall, "Methods of Financing
Higher Education", *Contemporary Problems in Higher Education. An Account of
Research*, eds. H. J. Butcher, E. Rudd. London: McGraw-Hill, 1972, pp. 347-60.

536 E. RUDD, "Who Pays for Undergraduate Study?", *UQ*, Winter, 1970, pp. 49-58.

   After a brief discussion of the system of student grants in Britain, the
author analyses the case for a loans scheme as a top-up to current maintenance
grants in the light of a survey he has conducted of students at the University
of Essex.

1971

537 E. O. OLSEN, "Some Theorems in the Theory of Efficient Transfers", *JPE*,
January/February, 1971, pp. 166-76.

   This paper proves a few positive theorems about the effects of any voluntary
voucher scheme and then applies these theorems to proposed voucher schemes in
housing and in education.

538 C. A. HICKROD, "Local Demand for Education: A Critique of School Finance and
Economic Research Circa 1959-1969", *RER*, February, 1971, pp. 35-49.

   A quick review of the literature, largely and indeed solely with reference
to the American scene.

539   F. G. JENNING, "Symposium on Educational Vouchers", *TR*, February, 1971,
      pp. 325-404.

         Six essays by J. Areen, C. Jencks, E. Ginzberg and others on the announced
      experiment of the Office of Economic Opportunity with a voucher scheme.

540   S. A. HOENACK, "The Efficient Allocation of Subsidies to College Students",
      AER, June, 1971, pp. 302-11.

         Constructs a university optimisation model that simultaneously achieves
      certain enrolment objectives and a desirable distribution of students from
      various income groups, given a fixed total subsidy available to a university.
      The model is applied to the University of California with some striking
      results.

541   H. G. JOHNSON, "British University Finance: Public and Private", *University
      Independence. The Main Questions,* ed. J. Mon. Scott. London: Rex Collings,
      1971, pp. 33-43.

         A brief, pungent plea for a private British university with cost-covering
      fees and loans for students.

1972

542   G. R. LA NOUE, ed., *Educational Vouchers: Concepts and Controversies.*   New
      York: Teachers College Press, 1972. Pp. 176.

         A collection of papers, congressional reports, and judicial pronouncements
      on education vouchers, mostly in the context of American education. There is
      a new paper by J. Areen and C. Jencks, which takes up the political aspects of
      education vouchers.

543   D. E. ERICKSON, "Education Vouchers: Nature and Funding", *TIP*, April, 1972,
      pp. 108-16.

         A discussion of recent American thinking since Friedman.

544   D. B. JOHNSTONE, S. P. DRESCH, *New Patterns for College Lending: Income
      Contingent Loans.* A Ford Foundation Report. New York: Colombia University
      Press, 1972. Pp. 209.

         A major study of the experience with income contingent loans in American
      higher education, including deferred tuition plans at such major universities
      as Yale and Harvard.

545   D. M. WINDHAM, *Education, Equality and Income Redistribution. A Study of
      Public Higher Education.* Lexington, Mass.: Heath Lexington Books, 1972.
      Pp. 120.

         A slim book (the text runs to only 55 pages), which reproduces the Hansen-
      Weisbrod California finding for the State of Florida.

1973

546 J. K. McNULTY, "Tax Policy and Tuition Credit Legislation: Federal Income Tax Allowances for Personal Costs of Higher Education", *CLR*, January, 1973, pp. 1-80.

   A detailed analysis of the case for income tax allowances of private educational costs, together with a history of the many attempts in recent years to get the US Congress to pass legislation of this kind.

547 S. PELTZMAN, "The Effect of Government Subsidies-in-Kind on Private Expenditures: The Case of Higher Education", *JPE*, January/February, 1973, pp. 1-27.

   The author begins by showing that subsidies-in-kind replace more private consumption of the subsidised good than an equivalent money subsidy; in the limit, subsidies-in-kind may reduce total consumption. He then goes on to test this proposition by examining subsidies-in-kind at American State universities. He shows that equivalent money subsidies would indeed have replaced less consumption and in the final section of the paper he speculates about the political process which has encouraged subsidies-in-kind.

548 J. E. HIGHT, R. POLLOCK, "Income Distribution Effects of Higher Education Expenditure in California, Florida and Hawaii", *JHR*, Summer, 1973, pp. 318-30.

   The authors show that the income distribution effects of higher education are different in the three American states irrespective of whether the Hansen-Weisbrod or the Pechman method is used to allocate the family tax burden associated with educational expenditures.

549 W. Z. HIRSCH, *Financing First-Level and Second-Level Education in the USA.* Financing Educational Systems: Specific Case Studies 3. Paris: UNESCO-IIEP, 1973. Pp. 49.

   A discussion of the problems raised by decentralised financing of American schools.

550 M. ZYMELMAN, *Financing and Efficiency in Education. Reference for Administration and Policymaking.* Boston: M. Zymelman, 1973. Pp. 314.

   Produced as part of a project sponsored and funded by A.I.D., it is difficult to see for whom this book is written: it is a "manual", in the true sense of the word, in that it is set out in a series of notes and contains not so much as a single reference to the literature. The context is largely American but there are also many references to LDC's. The first half of the book is devoted to finance, with judicious chapters on student loans and vouchers, and the second half is in fact about educational planning issues, with a heavy emphasis on the projections of educational expenditures.

551 K. E. BOULDING, M. PFAFF, A. PFAFF, eds., *Transfers in an Urbanized Economy. Theories and Effects of the Grants Economy.* Belmont, California: Wadsworth Publishing Company, 1973, pp. 203-302.

   This volume contains, among other things, five excellent articles on inter-fiscal grants to education in the United States: (1) B. W. Brown, "State

Grants and Inequality of Opportunity in Education", pp. 208-25; (2) T. Muller, "Income Redistribution Impact of State Grants to Public Schools: A Case Study of Delaware", pp. 226-45; (3) C. Waldauer, "External Effects of Education Grants on Tax Base-Sharing Municipal Governments", pp. 246-57; (4) D. L. Phares, "Impact of Spatial Tax Flows as Implicit Grants on State-Local Tax Incidence: With Reference to the Financing of Education", pp. 258-75; and (5) D. O. Porter, D. C. Warner, "How Effective are Grantor Controls?: The Case of Federal Aid to Education", pp. 276-302.

552   S. G. PEITCHINIS, "Equality and Inequality of Opportunity: The Financing of Post-Secondary Education in Canada", *AJHE*, December, 1973, pp. 64-75.

Summarizes his integrated student assistance system, consisting of a combination of unconditional grants, loans, conditional grants, and scholarships, which was incorporated in the Canadian Council of Ministers of Education's report on the financing of post-secondary education.

1974

553   E. G. WEST, "Differential Versus Equal Student Subsidies in Post-Secondary Education: A Current Canadian Dispute", *HE*, February, 1974, pp. 25-42.

A closely reasoned attack on the arguments of the Ontario Commission on Post-Secondary Education.

554   A. Wolf, "Educated by Voucher", *NS*, April 4, 1974, pp. 12-14.

A journalistic account of the Alum Rock Experiment in California.

555   M. L. EYSENBACH, "Voucher Plans, Voting Models; and the Efficiency of Local School Finance", *JPE*, July/August, 1974, pp. 863-72.

Explores the implications of educational voucher plans for voting behaviour and hence the size of school tax support in the context of a Michigan state study.

556   E. COHN, *Economics of State Aid to Education*. Lexington, Mass.: D. C. Heath & Co., 1974. Pp. 160.

The book is basically concerned with the ways in which state aid can be used to improve resource allocation in local school districts in the USA. After a history of state aid to American education and a description of the present system, the author constructs a simultaneous equation model to estimate the effect of state aid on school size, enrolments, etcetera. The penultimate chapter discusses the finance of higher education, unrelated to the rest of the book.

1975

557   M. NERLOVE, "Some Problems in the Use of Income-Contingent Loans for the Finance of Higher Education", *JPE*, February, 1975, pp. 157-83.

A theoretical discussion of income-contingent repayment programmes for students in higher education, illustrated by the Yale Tuition Postponement Option and other American loan schemes.

558 J. F. CREAN, "The Income Redistributive Effects of Public Spending on Higher Education", *JHR*, Winter, 1975, pp. 116-23.

An attempt to reconsider the redistributive effects of public spending on higher education in the light of an intergenerational-transfer model of the costs and benefits of higher education. The author illustrates his argument with reference to Canadian data.

(c) PRODUCTIVITY AND EFFICIENCY

The educational system may be conceived of as a kind of processing industry in which certain inputs like teachers, buildings, and equipment are applied for the purpose of processing a raw material (students) into a finished product (again, students). Assuming that the educational process aims at definite objectives, the so-called "goals of education", we can inquire whether the inputs are used efficiently to achieve the desired output. In short, we can study the productivity of the educational system like that of any other industry. There are, however, serious conceptual difficulties that have so far barred the way to productivity measurement in education: educational output is difficult to define precisely, the inputs seem to defy standardisation, and the process of transforming inputs into output is more complicated than in the average manufacturing industry. Nevertheless, questions about educational efficiency continue to be asked and some progress is beginning to be made in tackling these problems.

Before and immediately after World War I, there was an intense interest in measuring educational efficiency in the United States. Ayres[559,563], Cooke[560], and Rice[562] provide good examples of the work in that period; the story of the rise of this "cult of efficiency" in American education is well told by Callahan[583]. The theory of productivity measurement of education is discussed by Vaizey[2], Harris[427], Johnson[569], Kershaw and McKean[575,579,873], Clark[588], and Blaug[620]. Blaug and Woodhall[600,624,626] measure *trends* in the productivity of British universities, secondary schools and primary schools. Their measurements have been frequently criticised - see Vaizey[27,459], Johnson[600], Carter[603] - and occasionally imitated: see Hettich[635]. For measurement of productivity in government services in general, see Ridley and Simon[566] and Lytton[576].

There is an extensive, largely American, literature relating the quality of individual schools and school systems to various indices of educational expenditures. Powell[565], Woollatt[567], California and Western Conference[568], Lazersfeld and Thideus[571], Ousview and Castetter[580], and Calkins[592] are some outstanding examples. Using different methods, Hunt[171] and Cartter[607,763] have compared the qualities of universities. More to the point are those authors who attempt direct measurement of the quality of education provided to students, such as the New York State Education Department Quality Project[577], Wasserman[589], Wiseman[597], and Welch[606]. Coleman[1217], abetted by Bowles[272], sparked off a furious debate on "educational production functions", that is, measured relationships between in-school and out-of-school inputs and outputs as revealed by students' scores on achievement tests. For on-going work on educational production functions, see Burkhead and others[614], Katzman[622,634], Raymond[623], Kiesling[628], Conlisk[629], US Department of Health, Education and Welfare[631], Thomas[634], Hanushek[637], Brown[641], and Perl[643], with fundamental criticisms of this whole approach coming from Levin[534,647] and Brown and Saks[650].

Teacher salary scales as connected with teacher efficiency have been studied by Kershaw and McKean[584], Landon and Baird[639], and the Committee on the Utilization of College Teaching Resources[735]. For a review of the literature on class size and teacher effectiveness, see Renshaw[570] and Pennsylvania State University[572].

Ruml[573], Ashby[593], the Hale Committee Report[598], Jamrich[587], OECD[625], Dunworth and Dasey[640], Layard and Jackman[642], Dunworth and Bottomley[648], and Dunworth and Cook[649], Judy[625],[1537], the Committee on College Teaching Resources[735], Williams[747], Deitch[872], Carter[762], and Harris[427] analyse proposals to improve the efficiency of higher education. The location of institutions of higher education, a neglected subject, is discussed by Stretch[594].

Much has been written in recent years on the new teaching aids, like programmed learning and teaching machines, which promise to have a far-reaching effect on educational efficiency. On this subject, see Skinner[581], Ruark[582], UNESCO[590],[591], Shaplin and Olds[595], Carlson[601], Bright[632], Layard[644], and Gee[1902]. IIEP[615] provides some case studies of new educational media in different countries.

A new and significant trend is the increased concern with the application of programme budgeting to education, as witnessed by Williams[608], Hirsch[613], OECD[617], and Burkhead[646].

1909

559   L. P. AYRES, *Laggards in Our Schools*. New York: Russell Sage Foundation, 1909. Pp. 252.

A study of the costs of grade repetition, using an "index of efficiency" based on the speed with which children pass through grades.

1910

560   M. L. COOKE, *Academic and Industrial Efficiency*. Carnegie Foundation for the Advancement of Teaching Bulletin No. 5. New York: Carnegie Foundation, 1910. Pp. 134.

The results of an engineer's examination of efficiency in 8 University Departments of Physics in the USA. Commenting on the striking absence of any gauge of efficiency, comparable to profits on investment, the author proposes to compare the costs of universities in terms of weighted "student hours" as a unit of measurement. He attacks the inefficient use of buildings with tables showing room-utilisation per week in several universities.

1913

561   US Bureau of Education, *Economy of Time in Education*. Report of Committee under the chairmanship of J. H. Baker. Washington: Bureau of Education Bulletin No. 38, 1913. Pp. 105.

The committee concluded that with more efficient use of time, the period of general education could be reduced by 2 years. It compared the distribution of time in American education unfavourably with that of Britain and the Continent. Proposed periods: elementary 6-12, secondary (4+2) 12-18, college 18-20 or 16-20, graduate school 20-24. Contains answers to an opinion-questionnaire and an extensive bibliography.

1915

562 J. M. RICE, *Scientific Management in Education*. London: Harrap, 1915.
     Pp. 282.

   A pioneering work on the subject of educational measurement; his statistical
techniques and some of his reasoning are at fault, but it is an interesting
contribution in its own right. The book collects together a series of articles
published in 1892-93, giving the results of a series of tests in arithmetic
and language administered by the author in 36 different American cities. He
found that the wide divergences between the average scores of different schools
were due not to differences of environment or ability or class size, but to
differences in teaching competence, and that incompetence in teaching was
tolerated because of a mistaken belief that the results are "purely spiritual
in their nature, and incapable of measurement". He calls for scientific standards in the measurement of the results of education.

1920

563 L. P. AYRES, *An Index Number for State School Systems*. New York: Russell
     Sage Foundation, 1920. Pp. 70.

   An attempt to set up an index of educational output for each state and to
compare time trends. It is an interesting early effort, but ignores quality
and frequently begs questions.

1930

564 G. S. COUNTS, *The American Road to Culture. A Social Interpretation of Educa-
     tion in the US*. New York: John Day, 1930. Pp. 194.

   The chapter on "Mechanical Efficiency" attacks the idolatry of efficiency
which the author believes has led to an abandonment of concern with quality
and to an emphasis on trivia.

1933

565 O. E. POWELL, *Educational Returns at Varying Expenditure Levels*. New York:
     Teachers College, Columbia University Press, 1933. Pp. 55.

   An examination of one-teacher schools in New York State to test the hypothesis that educational quality is highly correlated with expenditure. Finds
that output (measured by scores in achievement tests) is always positively
related to current expenditure. The value of this study is limited by rather
crude methods, the small sample, and the sole examination of one-teacher
schools.

1943

566 C. E. RIDLEY, H. A. SIMON, *Measuring Municipal Activities: A Survey of
     Suggested Criteria for Appraising Administration*. Chicago: International
     City Managers' Association, 2nd ed., 1943. Pp. 75.

After a brief discussion of the need for techniques of appraisal and measurement of local government activities, the authors examine in detail a number of units of measurement for public services. Pp. 41-45 deal specifically with the problems of measuring the output and efficiency of education.

1949

567 L. H. WOOLLATT, *The Cost-Quality Relationship on the Growing Edge*. Metropolitan School Study Council Research Study No. 4. New York: Teachers College, Columbia University Press, 1949. Pp. 81.

The book first contains a review of several earlier attempts to investigate the relation between quality of education and level of educational expenditure. The author's own study is confined to schools in New York State with above-average expenditures, from which he concludes that raising the level of expenditure does improve the quality of education; but the definition of "quality" is based on the extent to which schools adopt new educational techniques, and not on the measurable achievement of pupils.

1956

568 California and Western Conference, *Cost and Statistical Study, For the Year 1954-55*. Berkeley: California University Printing Department, 1956. Pp. 129.

A joint study of 10 universities, financed by the Fund for the Advancement of Education, of the factors affecting the costs of higher education. It attempts to provide a measure of inputs which can be used for a comparison of universities, but devises no measure of quality. Describes a method of cost accounting based on a production-function approach. Argues that crude comparisons of total costs or costs per student are useless without accompanying data on differences in the factors affecting expenditures. Found that costs are curvilinear, rather than linear. Further conclusions follow on the importance of such factors as class size and space utilisation.

1957

569 D. G. JOHNSON, "Economics and the Educational System", *SR*, Autumn, 1957, pp. 260-69, reprinted in *PEE*, pp. 374-81.

A popular account of what economics can contribute to the question of efficient operation of an educational system.

1958

570 E. F. RENSHAW, "Will the American Educational System Ever Be Efficient?", *ibid.*, Spring, 1958, pp. 70-79.

A plea for mechanical teachers' aids to overcome the resistance of educationists to larger student-staff ratios.

571 P. F. LAZARSFELD, W. THIDEUS, *The Academic Mind*. Glencoe, Ill.: Free Press, 1958. Pp. 460.

An examination of academic and political freedom for social science teachers in American colleges in the McCarthy era. It contains a few digressions on quality of colleges and teachers, and uses an index of college quality based on size of library, book-student ratio, budget per student, per cent of Ph.Ds, tuition fees, and per cent of graduates taking higher degrees. For the staff, it uses an index of productivity based on publication of articles, books, theses, etc.

572 Pennsylvania State University, *Abstracts and Bibliography of Studies of Class Size*. State College: Pennsylvania State University, 1958. Pp. 55, mimeographed.

An extremely useful bibliography of 160 items and 31 abstracts of the most important articles and books on class size from 1920-58.

1959

573 B. RUML, *Memo to a College Trustee*. *A Report on the Financial and Structural Problems of the Liberal College*. Prepared for the Fund for the Advancement of Education. New York: McGraw-Hill, 1959. Pp. 94.

A proposal to double academic salaries in liberal colleges in the USA by the reorganisation of the curriculum and by altering existing methods of instruction. Pt. 3, pp. 27-45, contains a number of illustrative arithmetical models for colleges of different sizes. Pt. 4, contributed by D. H. Morrison, pp. 45-77, discusses the practical problems that may arise in adopting the Ruml plan. The entire issue of *JHE*, November, 1959, is devoted to a discussion of the Ruml plan.

574 ILO, "The Determination of Teachers' Salaries", *ILR*, July, 1959, pp. 46-64.

The article summarises information collected by ILO on the principles and criteria of rewarding primary and secondary teachers in a number of countries, including some analysis of the implications of the findings.

575 J. A. KERSHAW, R. N. McKEAN, *Systems Analysis and Education*. Research Memorandum. Santa Monica, Calif.: Rand Corp., 1959. RM-2473-FF. Pp. 64.

A preliminary discussion of the possibility of applying "systems analysis" to education, i.e. systematic comparison of the effects of adopting costed alternatives. A current project of the American Institute for Research along similar lines is reviewed.

576 H. D. LYTTON, "Recent Productivity Trends in the Federal Government", *RES*, November, 1959, pp. 341-59; "Public Sector Productivity", *ibid.*, August, 1961, pp. 182-84.

Attempts to determine productivity changes in the government sector: the author defines productivity as output divided by input with both having quantity and quality components. He concentrates on the quantity changes, but draws attention to the fact that, in health and education, quality changes are important. Concludes that in education productivity in the quantity sense has been declining at about 1-1½ per cent p.a.; in the quality sense it has been rising at about the same rate, so that total productivity trends are nil. "This provisional finding of increased medical and educational output quality may help to explain why human capital is improving." He nowhere discusses, however, how to measure either educational quantity or quality.

577 New York State Education Department Quality Measurement Project, *The Assessment of School Quality,* by S. M. Goodman; *Procedures in School Quality Evaluation and School Quality Workbook.* Albany: New York State Education Dept., 1959, 1961-63. Pp. 65, 367.

This very interesting study attempts to measure output by repeated achievement tests to matched pupils in 100 classified schools, and to relate this to variations in input shown by community characteristics and by pupil's educational potential measured by IQ and various socio-economic classifications. The findings show that there is considerable variation in output when these input factors are held constant.

578 G. J. BOYLE, *The Cost of Education Index.* Albany: New York State Education Dept., 1959. Pp. 32, mimeographed.

The author constructs a price index for education in New York State from school finance statistics and the data collected by the US Department of Labour for its Consumer Price Index. He finds that between 1948 and 1957, the Education Index rose by 59 per cent compared with a rise of only 20 per cent in the Consumer Price Index. The greatest part of the increase is attributed to the rising level of teachers' salaries. No attempt is made to isolate improvements in quality. The Index was brought up to date in 1963 by J. Vetro.

1960

579 J. A. KERSHAW, R. N. McKEAN, "How to Make School Decisions: An Outsider's View", *SM*, May, 1960, reprinted in *PEE*, pp. 392-98.

Urges a series of questions a school administrator should consider before choosing among alternative policies, particularly evaluation of true cost, based as far as possible on knowledge of input-output relationships in education, and, where this is non-existent, urges research to elucidate the relationships. Suggests a measure of output based on scores in achievement tests.

580 L. OUSVIEW, W. B. CASTETTER, *Budgeting for Better Schools.* Englewood Cliffs, N.J.: Prentice;Hall, 1960. Pp. 338.

A review of the role of the budget in school administration, the authors believing that quality and expenditure are highly correlated. They suggest various ways in which budget changes might improve efficiency, e.g. merit salary schedules, varying class sizes according to subjects, etc.

1961

581 P. F. SKINNER, *Cumulative Record*. New York: Appleton-Courtney Crofts, 1961,
     pp. 143-183.

       Reprints three articles on "The Science of Learning and the Art of Teaching",
     "Teaching Machines", and "Why We Need Teaching Machines". Extremely clear
     defence of teaching machines as an efficient way of teaching from the point of
     view of experimental psychology.

582 H. C. RUARK, "Technology and Education", *PDK*, June, 1961, reprinted in *PEE*,
     pp. 387-92.

       This article discusses a variety of mechanical aids for teachers, in parti-
     cular, teaching machines, and examines the implications of these for future
     educational policy, concluding that they should no longer be regarded as aids
     to teachers but as capable of performing some of the functions traditional to
     teacher, while leaving him free to develop new and more creative talents.

1962

583 R. E. CALLAHAN, *Education and the Cult of Efficiency. A Study of the Social
     Forces that Have Shaped the Administration of the Public Schools.* Chicago,
     Ill.: Chicago University Press, 1962. Pp. 273.

       This provocative book studies the application of business values and prac-
     tices to American education in the years 1910-29, concluding that the "cult of
     efficiency" had tragic consequences for the American educational system.
     Unfortunately, the meaning of the author's indictment is left somewhat vague,
     particularly in view of his concession that "the tragedy was not inherent in
     the borrowing from business and industry but only in the application". Suffice
     it to say, however, that the book details some striking examples of the abuse
     of economic reasoning.

584 J. A. KERSHAW, R. N. McKEAN, *Teacher Shortages and Salary Schedules*. New York:
     McGraw-Hill, 1962. Pp. 198.

       A model of how economists can help solve the practical problems of education
     at the local level. This book, addressed to American school administrators
     and interested laymen, shows that the shortage of teachers in the USA will
     become more serious in the next decade and that under present-day salary scales
     (pay increases being geared solely to length of training and experience, and
     not to the subject taught) the tax burden to local communities may become
     insupportable. A new salary schedule is proposed which would allow for salary
     supplements to attract scarce teacher-talents. (For a similar proposal in the
     context of English education, see *Strategy for Schools*. A Bow Group Pamphlet.
     London: the Conservative Political Centre, 1964, pp. 100-10.) For a relevant
     research result, see C. Matthis. "The Relationship Between Salary Policies
     and Teacher Morale", *JEP*, 50, 1959, pp. 275-79.

585 UNESCO Institute for Education, Hamburg, *Educational Achievements of 13-Year
     Olds in 12 Countries. Results of an International Research Project 1959-61.*
     Hamburg: UNESCO Institute for Education, 1962. Pp. 68.

The results of a programme of testing the educational attainments of samples of about 1000 13-year olds in 12 countries, with information on the educational and occupational background of the parents.

586   C. S. BENSON, "Teaching Methods and Their Costs. Productivity of Present Educational Systems", *ISSJ*, XIV, 4, 1962, pp. 676-84.

Observations on factor costs in schools and returns from education, mainly with reference to the USA.

587   J. X. JAMRICH, *To Build or Not to Build: A Report on the Utilization and Planning of Instructional Facilities in Small Colleges*. New York: Educational Facilities Laboratories, 1962. Pp. 38.

A study of space utilisation in American colleges, with some suggestion for improving the degree of utilisation.

1963

588   H. F. CLARK, *Cost and Quality in Public Education*. The Economics and Politics of Public Education, No. 5. Syracuse, N.Y.: Syracuse University Press, 1963. Pp. 54.

An outstanding popular discussion of the problem of "efficiency" in education, stressing the almost total failure to investigate the possibilities of improving and increasing the "output" of schools. A review of the literature on the returns to education, pp. 15-25, cites most of the lesser known inter-war items. A great deal of research in the effectiveness of different types of teaching is reviewed and the results of such research are shown to be suspect owing to a failure to allow for "experimental enthusiasm".

589   W. WASSERMAN, *Education Price and Quantity Indexes*. The Economics and Politics of Public Education, No. 12. Syracuse, N.Y.: Syracuse University Press, 1963. Pp. 166.

An original contribution to the literature on measuring the product of the "education industry", quite technical, yet full of concrete illustrations of how to construct indices of educational inputs. The fifth chapter provides a useful review of previous work in this area, showing that even the best studies sometimes ignore changes in the quality of education over time. The appendix demonstrates the possibility of compiling an education price index by linear programming methods.

590   UNESCO, *New Methods and Techniques in Education*. Educ. Stud. & Docs., No. 48. Paris: UNESCO, 1963. Pp. 51.

A review of new educational methods and techniques (programmed learning, television, films, and the like) with an introductory chapter by W. Schramm on the problems of introducing these techniques in underdeveloped countries.

591   UNESCO, *Developments in Audio-Visual Education*. Educ. Stud. & Docs., No. 50. Paris: UNESCO, 1963. Pp. 57.

A collection of papers discussing the use of educational TV and teaching machines in the United Kingdom, USSR, Japan, and France.

592 R. N. CALKINS, *The Unit-Costs of Programmes in Higher Education*. New York: Columbia University, unpublished Ph.D. thesis, 1963.

An analysis of cost data of 145 private Liberal Arts Colleges to determine which characteristics have the greatest influence on cost structures. His comparison of per-pupil unit costs reveals that level of faculty salaries, size of enrolment, curricular emphasis and number of courses offered are the most important variables, in that order of importance. He does not attempt to compare the efficiency of different colleges, but concludes that future unit cost studies should allow for differences in the size and type of colleges.

593 SIR. E. ASHBY, "Investment in Man", *AS*, September, 1963, pp. 203-13.

In this presidential address to the British Association for the Advancement of Science, the author critically examines the current assumptions of national policy in higher education and discusses the concept of efficiency in universities, arguing that efficiency in many cases is low and more research and experimentation is vital.

1964

594 K. L. STRETCH, "Academic Ecology: On the Location of Institutions of Higher Education", *MIN*, Spring, 1964, pp. 320-35.

Considers a neglected aspect of the economics of education with particular reference to the British scene.

595 J. T. SHAPLIN, H. F. OLDS, eds., *Team Teaching*. New York: Harper & Row, 1964. Pp. 430.

A study of the techniques and origins of team teaching in the United States with a chapter on research results by G. Heathers, who criticses those engaged in research for too great an emphasis on evaluation at the expense of research design, and for inadequate controls in evaluation, e.g. failing to allow for the "halo effect". Contains a bibliography and a list of research projects under way.

596 P. SAUNDERS, "Effectiveness of 'The American Economy'"; C. R. McConnell, J. R. Felton, "Evaluation of 'The American Economy'", *AER*, June, 1964, pp. 396-407.

The results of two local studies testing the effectiveness of the nationwide television course "The American Economy" in teaching elementary economics to high school teachers.

597 S. WISEMAN, *Education and Environment*. Manchester: University Press, 1964. Pp. 199.

This interesting book presents the results of four attempts to use multivariate analysis techniques to estimate the influence of socio-economic factors on
educational achievement in secondary schools in the Manchester and Salford
area, concluding that socio-economic variables have a considerable effect on
pupil scores in both attainment and intelligence tests. The book also contains
a useful chapter summarising previous research on school and community characteristics and their relationship to educational output.

598 University Grants Committee, UK, *Report of the Committee on University Teaching Methods (under the chairmanship of Sir E. Hale).* London: HMSO, 1964.
Pp. 173.

Based on surveys of a 1 in 22 sample of university teachers, this report
makes a number of suggestions for improving the quality of teaching in British
universities. See, in particular, the section on the potentialities of audio-
visual aids and teaching machines, pp. 98-102, and the pages on "University
Teaching as a Matter for Training and Study", pp. 103-12, which contrast the
scarcity of British studies on methods of university teaching with the level
of research completed and currently under way in the United States.

599 R. A. WARD, *Operational Research in Local Government.* London: George Allen
& Unwin, 1964, ch. 6, pp. 73-80.

This chapter deals specifically with a study, carried out by the Royal
Institute of Public Administration, of the use of operational research techniques to lower the costs of school transport in Great Britain. It showed
that such techniques could lead to significant economies.

1965

600 M. WOODHALL, M. BLAUG, "Productivity Trends in British University Education,
1938-62", *MIN*, Summer, 1965, pp. 483-98, reprinted in D. C. Rodgers and
H. S. Richlin, *Economics and Education. Principles and Applications.* New York
The Free Press, 1971, pp.121-33. "Comments" by R. Stone and H. G. Johnson,
and "Reply" by Woodhall and Blaug, *MIN*, Autumn, 1965, pp. 95-105.

The article includes a brief discussion of the conceptual problems of defining and measuring educational productivity, and a calculation of an index of
total-factor-productivity for British universities between 1938 and 1962.
This index shows that the input of all factors has risen faster than output,
even when allowance is made for changes in quality.

601 R. O. CARLSON, *Adoption of Educational Innovations.* Eugene, Oregon: Center
for the Advanced Study of Educational Administration, 1965. Pp. 84.

An attempt to explain differences in the rates of adoption and diffusion of
new educational techniques—by examining the extent of team teaching and
language laboratories in two regions of the United States. Previous research
on this subject has concentrated on expenditure per pupil as an explanatory
variable, but this study finds that characteristics of school superintendents
and the "diffusibility" of innovations were more important in explaining variations than level of expenditure. There is an interesting section on unantici-
pated consequences of introducing programmed teaching in schools.

602 H. CORREA, "Planning Educational Curriculum", *KYK*, XVIII, 4, 1965, pp. 685-93.

This paper presents the problem of selecting the best educational curriculum as a quadratic programming problem and then shows how to transform such a problem into an integral linear programming problem.

603 C. F. CARTER, "Can We Get Higher Education Cheaper?", *JMSS*, 1965, pp. 1-14, reprinted in *P-EED*, 2, pp. 326-39.

Attacks the article by Woodhall and Blaug (600) and denies that there is any evidence of inefficiency in British universities. The paper closes with a proposal to give British universities power to borrow on capital account.

1966

604 IIEP, *Symposium on the Qualitative Aspects of Educational Planning*. Paris: UNESCO-IIEP, 1966, mimeographed.

The papers of this conference include: (1) W. A. Lewis, "Economic Aspects of Quality in Education" (pp. 20), which discusses various ways of evaluating educational quality in underdeveloped countries but is sceptical of both cost-benefit analysis and manpower forecasting; (2) W. H. Leff, "A Note on the Quality-Quantity Problem in Education" (pp. 10), which argues the value of a cost-benefit approach to quality without, however, discussing any of the difficulties involved; (3) H. L. Elvin, "The Idea of Quality in Education and the Difficulty of Costing It" (pp. 19), a paper sharply critical of economists' analysis of educational efficiency; (4) R. S. Peters, "Quality in Education" (pp. 28), a philosophical exploration of what we mean by "quality of education", emphasising the multiplicity of criteria that are involved in any educational process; (5) R. Aron, "Sociological Comments on Concepts of Quality and Quantity in Education" (pp. 26), a general discussion of the problem of satisfying possibly conflicting educational objectives; (6) H. Philp, "The Evaluation of Quality in Education" (pp. 14), arguing that quality of education can be measured quantitatively, provided that the various aims of education are clearly defined; (7) T. Husén, "Some Views on Cross-National Assessment of the 'Quality of Education'" (pp. 7), a brief description of an international-comparison study of the achievement of upper-secondary students in mathematics; (8) A. R. Dawood, "Improvement of Quality in Education. Case Study of Secondary Education in India" (pp. 24), a title that speaks for itself; (9) S. A. Shumovsky, "Planification de la qualité de l'instruction des ingénieurs" (pp. 17), a description of engineering education in the Soviet Union; and (10), M. Conlon, "The Concept of Quality in Education" (pp. 10), some random comments on the different approaches of educators and economists to planning.

605 British Broadcasting Corporation, *Educational Television and Radio in Britain: Present Provision and Future Possibilities*. London: BBC, 1966. Pp. 292.

A collection of papers on the future use of TV and radio in education. M. Peston argues in "Educational Needs of the Country: Manpower and Resources, 1966-80", pp. 9-19, that as education becomes increasingly expensive, it will be necessary to substitute capital for labour in teaching. Other authors discuss how television is already used in schools and predict future developments.

606 F. WELCH, "Measurement of the Quality of Schooling", *AER*, May, 1966,
     pp. 379-92; "Comment" by L. R. Martin and A. M. Rivlin, *ibid.*, pp. 393-96.

     A multiple regression analysis of the incomes of rural farm adult males by
     states, amount of schooling, quality of schooling (as measured by four indica-
     tors), age, colour, and farm capital.

607 A. M. CARTTER, *An Assessment of Quality in Graduate Education: A Comparative
     Study of Graduate Departments in 29 Academic Disciplines.* Washington: Ameri-
     can Council on Education, 1966. Pp. 131.

     An attempt to rank 106 American Graduate departments in 29 different sub-
     ject fields on the basis of personal ratings by 4000 scholars. The rankings
     are compared with three earlier studies of graduate schools. For the findings
     in the field of economics, see 763.

608 H. WILLIAMS, *Planning for Effective Resource Allocation in Universities.*
     Washington, D.C.: American Council on Education, 1966. Pp. 78.

     This pamphlet discusses the problem of applying the concept of programme
     budgeting to universities and sketches a procedure for establishing a pro-
     gramme budgeting system in an educational institution.

609 H. F. McCUSKER, Jr., P. H. SORENSEN, "The Economics of Education", *The New
     Media and Education,* eds. P. H. Rossi, B. J. Biddle. Chicago: Aldine Pub-
     lishing Co., 1966, pp. 178-206.

     An analysis of the problem of resource allocation in the American school
     system with a detailed illustrative example of the effects of alternative
     allocation patterns in a representative school district.

610 G. ODDIE, *School Building Resources and their Effective Use: Some Available
     Techniques and their Policy Implications.* Paris: OECD, 1966. Pp. 160.

     A highly technical examination of methods of improving the design and utili-
     sation of school buildings (see also 619).

1967

611 J. HALLAK, ed., *Educational Costs and Productivity.* Paris: UNESCO-IIEP, 1967,
     mimeographed.

     The following papers were presented to this conference: (1) J. Hallak,
     "Efficiency in Education" (pp. 42); (2) Lê Thành Khôi, "Rendement et producti-
     vité de l'enseignement" (pp. 24); (3) F. de Escondrillas, "Guide for a Finan-
     cial Analysis of the Educational System" (pp. 19); (4) J.-P. Gern, "Unit Cost
     Concepts and Statistics Required for an Analysis of Educational Productivity"
     (pp. 31); (5) N. Bodart, "Problems of Measuring Educational Yield in Order to
     Assess Educational Productivity" (pp. 16); (6) M. Woodhall, "Productivity
     Trends in British Secondary Education, 1950-63", a short version of 624
     (pp. 62); (7) N. H. Chau, "Analyse combinée de rendement et de coût" (pp. 16);
     (8) J. Hallak, "Areas for Improved Efficiency in Educational Systems" (pp. 13);

(9) J. D. Cheswass, "Productivity and the Teacher" (pp. 9); (10) R. Poignant, "La rationalisation des programmes de construction des écoles" (pp. 13); and (11) J. Beynon, "Educational Architecture versus Educational Change" (pp. 5).

612 D. R. WITMER, *Unit Cost Studies*. Madison, Wisc.: Board of Regents of State Universities, 1967. Pp. 36.

After a critical review of unit costs studies of American universities, the author analyses unit costs at the University of Wisconsin for 1966-67 in considerable detail.

613 W. Z. HIRSCH, ed., *Inventing Education for the Future*. San Francisco, Calif.: Chandler Publishing Company, 1967. Pp. 353.

A popular collection of articles on educational innovations, among which worth mentioning are A. M. Mood, "The Operations Analysis Program of the U.S. Office of Education", pp. 176-87, and W. Z. Hirsch, "Program Budgeting for Education", pp. 188-219. See also W. Z. Hirsch, "Education in the Program Budget", *Program Budgeting*, ed. D. Novick (Cambridge, Mass.: Harvard University Press, 1967), pp. 180-204, reprinted in *URB*, pp. 306-28.

614 J. BURKHEAD, T. G. FOX, J. W. HOLLAND, *Input and Output in Large-City High Schools*. Syracuse, N.Y.: Syracuse University Press, 1967. Pp. 110.

This study constructs a total-factor-productivity model of American high schools, employing multiple regression analysis to assess the relative weights of the various inputs and the significance of different variables intervening between inputs and output. The model is applied for purposes of making inter-high school comparison to the cities of Chicago and Atlanta, as well as a number of smaller communities in the United States which had participated in Project Talent.

615 *New Educational Media in Action: Case Studies for Planners—I*. Paris: UNESCO-IIEP, 1967. Pp. 203.

This volume consists of six case studies: W. Schramm, "Educational Television in American Samoa", pp. 11-57; S. Wade, "Hagerstown, Maryland: A Pioneer in Closed-Circuit Televised Instruction", pp. 59-82; W. Schramm, "Educational Radio in Thailand", pp. 83-104; W. Schramm, "Ten Years of the Radio Rural Forum in India", pp. 105-33; W. Schramm, "Japan's Broadcast-Correspondence High School", pp. 135-68; and K. Kinane, "Australia's Corresponding Schools, With Supporting Broadcast Programmes", pp. 169-203. (See also 1555, 1556.)

616 B. F. HALEY, "Experiments in the Teaching of Basic Economics", *AER*, May, 1967, pp. 642-52.

A review of experiments in American colleges and universities with the teaching of elementary economics. See also K. Lumsden, "The Effectiveness of Programmed Learning in Elementary Economics", and R. Fels, "A New Test of Understanding in College Economics", *ibid*.

1968

617 OECD, *Budgeting, Programme Analysis and Cost-Effectiveness in Educational Planning.* Paris: OECD, Education and Development, 1968. Pp. 304.

The elven papers presented at this conference consist of: (1) B. Schwartz, "Introduction to Programme Budgeting and Cost-Effectiveness Analysis", pp. 26-55, a useful general discussion of issues at a fairly technical level with a good bibliogrpahy: (2) W. Z. Hirsch, "The Budget as an Instrument for Medium and Long-Range Planning and Programming of Education", pp. 92-106, including an illustrative example of a multi-year educational programme budget for the University of California; (3) H. J. Hartley, "Programme Budgeting and Cost-Effectiveness in Local Schools", pp. 111-27, describing several programme budgets that have been introduced in American school districts; (4) L. Dahl-gaard, "Problems in the Drawing up of a Three-Year Education Budget", pp. 133-41; (5) K. Eide, "Some Financial Instruments and Efficiency Incentives in Educational Policy", pp. 146-86; (6) M. Blaug, "Cost-Benefit and Cost-Effec-tiveness Analysis in Educational Planning", pp. 173-84; (7) J. Froomkin, "Allocation of Resources to Education—Towards a Theory of Subsidy", pp. 201-21; (8) K. Hüfner, E. Schmitz, "The Role of Cost Models in Educational Planning—The Case of the Federal Republic of Germany", pp. 225-47; (9) R. Judy, J. Levine, R. Wilson, J. Walter, "Systems Analysis of Alternative Designs of a Faculty", pp. 252-86, a valuable attempt to apply systems analysis to the Medical School of the University of Toronto; (10) C-F. Hanmer, "Programme Budgeting in Sweden", pp. 291-94; and (11) R. H. Marshall, "Programme Budget-ing in Canada", pp. 295-98. The OECD Secretariat provides a summary record of meeting, pp. 1-6, and J. Vaizey furnishes "A Personal Impression" of the pro-ceedings, pp. 13-8.

618 C. R. BARBER, *Cost Effectiveness of Education.* Occasional Papers 1. Oxford: Oxford College of Technology, Social Science Research Unit, 1968. Pp. 12.

A report of a preliminary attempt to apply cost-effectiveness analysis to a sample of secondary schools in Oxford.

619 G. ODDIE, *Development and Economy in Educational Building. Report on OECD Project in Greece, Portugal, Spain, Turkey and Yugoslavia.* Paris: OECD, 1968. Pp. 134.

The major conclusions of a cost-effectiveness study of educational buildings in the Mediterranean countries.

620 M. BLAUG, "The Productivity of Universities", *MIN*, Spring, 1968, pp. 398-407, reprinted in *P-EED*, 2, pp. 313-25.

An analysis of the concept of university productivity, a review of the author's work in the area, and some further suggestions for measuring univer-sity productivity. The paper was read at the Universities' Conference in 1968; a precis of the other papers at the conference is available in the same issue of *MIN*, pp. 432-36.

621 A. C. KELLEY, "An Experiment with TIPS: A Computer-aided Instructional System for Undergraduate Education", *AER*, May, 1968, pp. 446-57.

Part of a symposium on experiments in teaching economics, which also includes "A Simulation Policy Game for Teaching Macroeconomics", by F. T. Dolbear
and others, pp. 458-68, and "An Experiment with Television in an Elementary
Course", pp. 469-82.

622 M. T. KATZMAN, "Distribution and Production in a Big City Elementary School
     System", *YEE*, Spring, 1968, pp. 201-56.

A multiple regression study which estimates production functions for each
of Boston's 56 school districts by regressing various measures of school output against various measures of school inputs and the socio-economic characteristics of residents of the 56 districts. All the output measures are educational ones: the vocational aims of schools are ignored. See also 634.

623 R. RAYMOND, "Determinants of the Quality of Primary and Secondary Public
     Education in West Virginia", *JHR*, Fall, 1968, pp. 450-70.

Quality is measured by achievement test scores and freshman grade point
averages (for a sample of 5000 students entering West Virginia University)
and the author shows that, among a number of input variables that he examined,
teachers' salaries was most significantly related to educational quality as
just defined.

624 M. WOODHALL, M. BLAUG, "Productivity Trends in British Secondary Education",
     SE, Winter, 1968, pp. 38-59.

Applies their measurement of productivity trends in British university education (600) to British secondary schools.

1969

625 OECD, *Efficiency in Resource Utilization in Education*. Paris: OECD, 1969.
     Pp. 385.

A rather mixed collection of papers, consisting of G. Williams, "Introduc-
tion and Summary of the Discussion", pp. 11-20; R. Lachène, "The Application
of Operational Research to Educational Planning", pp. 33-64; C. C. Abt,
"Design for An Education System Cost-Effectiveness Model", pp. 65-91, reprinted
in *BILD*, pp. 277-317; M. G. Keeney, H. E. Koenig, R. Zemach, "State-Space
Model of Educational Institutions", pp. 99-135; J. Lions, "The Construction of
Timetables for Ontario Schools Using a Computer", pp. 147-60; M. Murray,
G. Svanfeldt, "Admission to School, Colleges and Faculties with Numerous
Classes by Centralised EDP Systems", pp. 173-207; J. S. Folkers, "Research and
Management Aspects of Time-Table Automation for Schools and Universities",
pp. 217-41; R. W. Judy, "Simulation and Rational Resource Allocation in Univer-
sities", pp. 255-85; D. A. C. Heigham, "Two OECD Feasibility Studies on Appli-
cations of Operational Research to Education in England and Wales", pp. 299-
314; D. S. Stoller, "Operation Analysis in the U.S. Office of Education",
pp. 323-24; A. M. Mood, F. D. Weinfeld, "Educational Factors Analysis and the
Educational Opportunities Survey", pp. 327-34; and R. L. Ackoff, "Chairman's
Comment: Toward Strategic Planning of Education", pp. 339-58.

626   M. WOODHALL, M. BLAUG, "Variations in Costs and Productivity of British Primary and Secondary Education", *Economics of Education in Transition,* eds.
K. Hufner, J. Naumann. Stuttgart: Ernst Klett Verlag, 1969, pp. 69-86.

   Attempts to apply their productivity measurement of British tertiary and
secondary education to primary education, with predictable complications.

627   J. A. LAUWERYS, D. G. SCANLON, *The World Year Book of Education 1969.*
Examinations. London: Evans Bros., 1969. Pp. 404.

   The section on "Economic and Social Effects of Examinations" contains, among
other articles, L. Emmerij, "Effects of Examinations on the Economy",
pp. 244-57; H. Leibenstein, "Economics of Skill Labelling", pp. 268-71; and
S. H. Irvine, "Examinations and the Economy: an African Study", pp. 279-90.

628   H. J. KIESLING, *The Relationship of School Inputs to Public School Performance*
in New York State. Santa Monica, Calif.: Rand Corporation, P-4211, 1969.
Pp. 33.

   Extends the author's earlier studies of the relationship between expenditure
per pupil and average achievement performance of pupils in a sample of school
districts in New York State. Additional variables are included in this multiple regression study. Among the interesting findings is a negative relationship between teacher-pupil ratio and pupil performance.

629   J. CONLISK, "Determinants of School Enrollment and School Performance", *JHR,*
Spring, 1969, pp. 140-57.

   This paper is based on aggregated data for children aged 5 through 19 in
the 1960 Census Special Reports on Education (a 5 per cent sample of the
total US population). School performance is defined as being behind or ahead
of one's age group in years of schooling completed. The explanatory variables
are age, colour, sex, rural-urban status, education and income of parents.

630   R. FELS, "Hard Research on a Soft Subject: Hypothesis-Testing in Economic
Education", *SEJ,* July, 1969, pp. 17-29.

   A review of the evidence to date on teaching effectiveness in elementary
economic courses and an agenda of further research that needs to be done.

1970
631   U.S. Department of Health, Education and Welfare, *Do Teachers Make A Difference.*
A Report on Recent Research on Pupil Achievement. Washington, D.C.: Office
of Education, 1970. Pp. 181.

   The best single source for recent American work, largely by economists, on
"educational production functions". Almost every one of the six papers is outstanding; A. M. Mood, "Do Teachers Make a Difference?", pp. 1-24; J. W. Guthrie
"A Survey of School Effectiveness Studies", pp. 25-54; H. M. Levin, "A New
Model of School Effectiveness", pp. 55-78; E. Hanushek, "The Production of
Education, Teacher Quality and Efficiency", pp. 79-99; G. W. Mayeske, "Teacher
Attributes and School Achievement", pp. 100-119; S. Michelson, "The Association
of Teacher Resourceness with Children's Characteristics", pp. 120-68, which
stands out even in this collection. R. M. Gagney and J. S. Colemen close the
volume with brief comments on the conference.

632 L. BRIGHT, *Educational Technology—Practical Issues and Implications. OECD Conference on Policies for Educational Growth. Background Study No. 7.* Paris: OECD, 1970. Pp. 28.

A useful pamphlet on new educational media based largely on American evidence. Unfortunately, the evidence is not actually cited.

633 H. M. LEVIN, "A Cost-Effectiveness Analysis of Teacher Selection", *JHR*, Winter, 1970, pp. 24-33.

Using data derived from the U.S. Office of Education's Survey of Equal Opportunity for the school year 1965-66, the author relates teacher characteristics to student achievement, combining these with data on the costs of teacher training. He finds that recruiting and retraining teachers with high verbal scores is 5-10 times as effective per unit of cost in raising achievement scores as obtaining more experienced teachers.

1971

634 J. A. THOMAS, *The Productive School. A Systems Analysis Approach to Educational Administration.* New York: Wiley & Sons, 1971. Pp. 132.

An effective handbook of management science in education, addressed to American school administrators. Much of the material, indeed virtually all of it, is borrowed from the work of economists.

635 W. HETTICH, *Expenditures, Output and Productivity in Canadian University Education.* Economic Council of Canada Special Study No. 14. Ottawa, Information Canada, 1971. Pp. 123.

An application to Canada of the Woodhall-Blaug method of measuring productivity trends in British university education (see 600). The author shows that productivity in Canadian university teaching has declined over the years 1956 to 1968 and he attributes this principally to the rising real value of students' time.

636 M. T. KATZMANN, *The Political Economy of Urban Schools.* Cambridge, Mass.: Harvard University Press, 1971. Pp. 235.

This is ostensibly another educational production function study, a revised and expanded version of his earlier paper (see 622), but it is actually more than this: it combines the interests of an economist with that of a political scientist and fully lives up to its title. There is a good review of previous studies of "educational production functions", pp. 34-41, a chapter on production in Boston's elementary schools, pp. 45-76, and a particularly interesting chapter on new ideas in restructuring large city school systems, including the notion of tuition vouchers, pp. 160-65.

637 E. HANUSHEK, "Teacher Characteristics and Gains in Student Achievement: Estimation Using Micro Data", *AER*, May, 1971, pp. 280-88.

Some new American evidence on the characteristics of teachers that are liable to produce increases in student scores on achievement tests.

638 R. F. GOLDMAN, W. H. WEBER, H. J. NOAH, "Some Economic Models of Curriculum
     Structure", *TR*, December, 1971, pp. 285-303.

     Presents two analytical models, the first of which considers a school dis-
     trict that seeks to maximize student learning by manipulating teachers'
     salaries and the second of which considers a higher education curriculum with
     a view to maximizing technical progress.

639 J. H. LANDON, R. N. BAIRD, "Monopsony in the Market for Public School Teachers",
     AER, December, 1971, pp. 966-71.

     Applying multiple regression analysis to 1966-67 cross-sectional data on
     136 school districts in the USA, the authors show that teachers' salaries vary
     with the degree of competition among school districts.

1972

640 J. E. DUNWORTH, R. M. DASEY, "Potential Economies in Academic Staff", *UQ*,
     Spring, 1972, pp. 219-30.

     An interesting attempt to estimate potential economies in staff utilisation
     at the University of Bradford and a sustained attack on the concept of the
     staff/student ratio as a basis for allocating staff in British universities.

641 B. B. BROWN, "Achievement, Costs, And the Demand for Public Education", *WEJ*,
     June, 1972, pp. 198-219.

     This paper develops a model of school district behaviour in the USA and
     estimates it with recently developed data from over 5,000 Michigan school
     districts. The results suggest that cognitive achievement is not, in fact,
     an important school objective in the eyes of school administrators.

1973

642 R. LAYARD, R. JACKMAN, "University Efficiency and University Finance", *Essays
     in Modern Economics,* eds. M. Parkin, A. R. Nobay. London: Longman, 1973,
     pp. 170-88.

     The authors begin by speculating on the causes of the inefficiency of uni-
     versities; they then explore the efficiency effects of different ways of pay-
     ing university teachers and of financing universities in the light of the
     assumption that universities are "labour-managed enterprises". See "Discus-
     sion" by M. Blaug, *ibid.*, pp. 189-91.

643 L. J. PERL, "Family Background, Secondary School Expenditure, and Student
     Ability", *JHR*, Spring, 1973, pp. 156-80.

     Data on a *Project Talent* sample of high school students are used to estimate
     the relationship between ability test scores and various educational inputs
     into the school system. The results are roughly speaking anti-Coleman (see
     1217).

644   R. LAYARD, "The New Media and Higher Education", *MIN*, April, 1973, pp. 211-27.

A useful discussion of issues and a review of British and American evidence.

645   J. RAVEN, "The Attainment of Non-Academic Educational Objectives" *IRE*, XIX, 1973, 3, pp. 305-29.

A fascinating, but tendentious, review of obvious and less-than-obvious evidence bearing on the non-cognitive outcomes of schooling in the UK, USA and Ireland, with a few references to other countries. See the severe reply by D. R. Krathwohl and the reply by the author, which expands on the themes of his article, *ibid.*, pp. 330-34, 336-44.

646   J. BURKHEAD, "Economics Against Education", *TCR*, December, 1973, pp. 193-205.

Despite the startling title, this is a useful review of the largely negative results of recent work on educational production functions, as well as a quick review of recent American experience with PPB in education on the state level. The article closes with some perceptive comments on the difficulties of investigating the non-cognitive outcomes of schools.

1974

647   H. M. LEVIN, "Measuring Efficiency in Educational Production", *PF*, January, 1974, pp. 3-24.

A profound attack on past attempts to estimate educational production functions and new empirical material to show that best-practice schools utilise inputs in ways very different from those of average schools.

648   J. DUNWORTH, A. BOTTOMLEY, "Potential Economies of Scale at the University of Bradford", *SEPS*, 8, 1974, pp. 47-55.

Allocates costs per student graduated in 18 disciplines at Bradford University in recent years and shows, for example, that total costs per student can be significantly reduced in certain scientific disciplines without loss of quality.

1975

649   J. DUNWORTH, R. COOK, "University Teaching Accommodation: Its Use and Allocation", *HER*, Spring, 1975, pp. 59-76.

The authors attempt to show how British universities might react constructively to present cuts in finance with particular reference to the use of buildings.

650   B. W. BROWN, D. H. SAKS, "The Production and Distribution of Cognitive Skills within Schools", *JPE*, June, 1975, pp. 571-94.

A new analysis of educational production functions, which places equal
weight on the variance as on the mean of test scores of students, in the light
of which the authors urge a re-assessment of previous results.

(d) TECHNICAL AND VOCATIONAL EDUCATION

This section concentrates on formal technical and vocational education: informal
on-the-job training is largely excluded here, except for apprenticeship programmes
which fall halfway between formal and informal training.

The subject is discussed in its broadest setting by Thomas[652], Rivlin[678], the
National Society for the Study of Education[679], and Fein[699]. There are some good
studies of British technical education, such as Venables[651], Williams[653],
Cotgrove[656], Liepmann[658], and Ashby[746], and there are any number of international
comparisons such as Williams[653,665], the National Joint Advisory Council of the
British Ministry of Labour[654], the Department of Labour in Canada[659], the Oxford
University Department of Education[666], EUSEC[664], McCarthy[700], and Robbins[751].

Clark and Sloan[655,688], Serbein[660], and PEP[731] investigate formal training
schemes in factories. Harbison and Myers[657] write on management training.
Malassis[662] surveys agricultural education in Europe. Government training and retreading programmes, which are of growing importance in all developed countries,
are surveyed and assessed by Gordon[673], Martin[674], Hoos[675], Somers and Stromsdorfer[672,676], Young[680], Hall[686], Levitan and Siegel[687], Bateman[691], Sewell[692],
Corazzini[696], Page[693], Sisco[694], Rosen and Dunlop[873], Lees and Chiplin[701],
Mukherjee[702], Hardin and Borus[703], Hamermesh[705], Holtman[706], Smith[707], Pettman[710],
[720], Barsby[711], Somers and Stromsdorfer[712,713], Hartley and Mancini[717], Zymelman[718],
Gunderson[719], Woodhall[721], Hartley[722], and Ziderman[723,725]. There are further
references in the section, "Measurement of the Returns". Traditional apprenticeship programmes, on the other hand, appear to have lost their former appeal: see
Williams[653,665], Liepmann[658], Strauss[677], Blum[681], ILO[685], Farber[697], and Woodward
and Anderson[726].

Further guides to the literature are provided by Benge[1889], Beard[1892], UNESCO[1893],
and the Office of Education, USA[1894]. The International Vocational Training
Information and Research Centre of the International Labour Office periodically
issues fairly detailed abstracts of the literature on technical education in all
languages which can be consulted in any library under the title "CIRF Abstracts".

1955

651 P. F. R. VENABLES, *Technical Education. Its Aims, Organisation and Future
Development*. London: Bell, 1955. Pp. 645.

On the organisational and curricula side this is clearly the book on technical education in the UK. It analyses the institutional structure at all levels
and includes 5 chapters by other authors on engineering, building, art, women's
subjects, and commerce. The appendix contains a complete list of institutions
and courses. See also the author's *Sandwich Courses for Training Technologists
and Technicians* (London: Max Parrish, 1959), which applies the same treatment
to post-1956 developments in British technical education. (See also 661.)

1956

652   L. G. THOMAS, *The Occupational Structure and Education*. Englewood Cliffs,
N.J.: Prentice-Hall, 1956. Pp. 502.

An amazingly early analysis by an educationist of the occupational structure
of the American labour force with a view to improving the quality of vocational
placement counselling. Includes an uneven review of the American literature
up to 1954 on the determinants of occupational incomes, the measurement of
occupational prestige, and the range in occupational qualifications.

1957

653   G. WILLIAMS, *Recruitment Into Skilled Trades*. London: Routledge & Kegan
Paul, 1957. Pp. 216.

A select sample of engineering, building, motor vehicle, and printing firms
were interviewed to obtain data on apprenticeship and other training schemes
in the UK. The British system of training is compared with US, French and
Dutch practices in the last chapter. Some information on the wages of trainees is furnished.

1958

654   National Joint Advisory Council, Ministry of Labour and National Service,
Training for Skill. London: HMSO, 1958. Pp. 36.

The council, under the chairmanship of R. Carr, reviews Britain's provisions
for technical and vocational training, based on replies received from over
200 trade unions and employers' associations. Practices in Britain are contrasted with those in foreign countries. The study concludes with a list of
practical recommendations designed to improve the training system.

655   H. F. CLARK, H. S. SLOAN, *Classrooms in the Factories. An Account of Educational Activities Conducted by American Industry*. Institute of Research,
Farleigh Dickinson University. New York: Farleigh Dickinson University,
1958. Pp. 139.

This study, based on a questionnaire sent to 500 of the largest American
industrial corporations, reveals a surprising amount of formal education provided by business firms (296 of the firms, employing over 6 workers, reported
educational activities of some kind). Most of the book is, unfortunately,
descriptive and no effort was made to find out how much this kind of education
costs.

656   S. F. COTGROVE, *Technical Education and Social Change*. London: Allen &
Unwin, 1958. Pp. 220.

A readable account of technical education in England and Wales, placed in a
historical setting. Deals with recruitment of students, the curriculum of
technical schools, the demand for technicians and technologists, reviews
changing policies in technical education, and concludes with some practical
recommendations.

1959

657   F. H. HARBISON, C. A. MYERS, *Management in the Industrial World. An Inter-*
      national Analysis. New York: McGraw-Hill, 1959, ch. 5, pp. 87-116.

      The chapter on "The Development of Managerial Resources" is directly con-
      cerned with the role of education in creating high-talent manpower, but the
      12 country studies in this book also touch repeatedly on this theme.

1960

658   K. LIEPMANN, *Apprenticeship. An Enquiry into its Adequacy under Modern Condi-*
      tions. London: Routledge & Kegan Paul, 1960. Pp. 204.

      Based on a survey of the engineering, printing and building industry in the
      Bristol district, this book reviews the apprenticeship problem and concludes
      with a plea for governmental regulation.

659   Department of Labour, Canada, *Acquisition of Skills.* Research Program on
      the Training of Skilled Manpower, Report No. 4. Ottawa: Department of
      Labour, 1960. Pp. 67.

      A study of the education and training of a sample of 800 qualified tool and
      die makers, sheet metal workers, floor moulders, draughtsmen, and electronic
      technicians in 75 firms located in Toronto and Montreal. The central aim of
      the study was to determine where and how workers acquired their skills; also
      investigated were the opinions of workers about their training, and the effect
      of technological change on training requirements.

1961

660   O. N. SERBEIN, *Educational Activities of Business.* Washington, D.C.:
      American Council of Education, 1961. Pp. 180.

      A stratified random sample of about 1600 firms supplied data for this study,
      which ostensibly covers the whole range of business personnel and all phases
      of educational effort within business, but, in point of fact, seems to deal
      largely with formal service training for managers and executives (but see
      ch. 5, pp. 64-75). The usual difficulties were experienced in obtaining
      reliable expenditure figures for training and education (see pp. 9-10). The
      book concludes with an interesting case study: the educational activity of
      the IBM Company (ch. 7, pp. 90-103).

661   P. F. R. VENABLES, W. J. WILLIAMS, *The Smaller Firm and Technical Education.*
      London: Max Parrish, 1961. Pp. 223.

      Gives results of an inquiry among small firms in building and engineering
      industries to estimate the extent of education and training programmes in
      firms and discusses the costs of training in such firms. See, particularly,
      ch. 3, "Manpower and Educational Requirements", pp. 45-70.

1962

662   L. MALASSIS, *Intellectual Investment in Agriculture for Economic and Social
      Development*. OECD Documentation in Agriculture and Food, No. 60. Paris:
      OECD, 1962. Pp. 151.

         A general discussion of the role of research, education and information in
      the agricultural sector with reference to educational planning in the develop-
      ed countries of Europe. A useful source of data on agricultural education
      and extension services in various Western European countries.

663   J. R. DALE, *The Clerk in Industry. A Survey of the Occupational Experience,
      Status, Education and Vocational Training of a Group of Male Clerks Employed
      by Industrial Companies*. Liverpool: University Press, 1962. Pp. 118.

         The results of a survey of 200 clerks employed by 5 companies in the Liver-
      pool area, and a survey of clerical training in 14 firms.

664   The Conference of Engineering Societies of Western Europe and the USA (EUSEC),
      Report on Education and Training of Professional Engineers. Brussels: EUSEC,
      1962. Pp. 76, 83, 89.

         This report represents the first attempt to present a comprehensive and
      accurate comparison of national systems of engineering education and training
      in 15 European countries and the United States. Vol. I contains the raw data
      on a country-by-country basis, Vol. II summarises the data under various
      headings, and Vol. III provides an international glossary of terms used in
      engineering education. The importance of these findings for manpower forecasts
      that make use of the method of international comparisons is self-evident.

1963

665   G. WILLIAMS, *Apprenticeship in Europe: The Lesson for Britain*. London:
      Chapman & Hall, 1963. Pp. 208.

         Examines craft apprenticeship systems in UK, Germany, Holland, France,
      Italy, Switzerland, Sweden, and Belgium, and brings out the unique features
      of the British system. Proposes national training scheme with smaller period
      of apprenticeship varying in length with the skill required; apprentice would
      be indentured to an Apprenticeship Authority, not to an individual firm.

666   Oxford University Department of Education, *Technology and the Sixth Form Boy.
      A Study of Recruitment to Higher Scientific and Technological Education in
      England and Wales*. Oxford: Oxford University Department of Education, 1963.
      Pp. 58.

         The main object of this study was to test the validity of the assumption
      that applied as opposed to pure science in Britain is attracting the less able
      student. The evidence from a sample of 121 schools and almost 1500 pupils
      as well as comparisons with the situation in Holland, Germany, and France
      support the popular assumption. A brief introduction to this volume by
      A. D. C. Peterson, pp. 1-3, sums up the major findings and their implications.

667   J. WELLENS, *The Training Revolution*. London: Evans Bros., 1963. Pp. 136.

   The book deals on a popular level with industrial training, apprentice
schemes, and formal education for industry in Great Britain. The author criticises the present system as inadequate. He believes strongly in manpower
planning, assuming that it is a simple process to calculate manpower needs for
industry: "If society needs 5000 chemical engineers over a stated period it
should make available student places to provide this number . . . no more,
no less"; "The current 'laissez-faire' practice tends to produce student
places in response to student demand. The planned entry method produces student places against the demands of the economic situation . . . student demand
is not a reliable guide to economic need. And when the old method fails to
achieve its purpose anyway, what point is there in defending it?" (p. 103).

1964

668   G. VENN, T. J. MARCHESE, Jr., *Man, Education and Work. Post-secondary Vocational and Technical Education*. Washington, D.C.: American Council on Education, 1964. Pp. 184.

   A popular book on American vocational education, full of alarm about the
growing shortage of technically trained manpower. The book includes a useful
bibliography.

1965

669   H. CORREA, "Optimum Choice Between General and Vocational Education", *KYK*,
XVIII, 1, 1965, pp. 107-16.

   A simple linear-programming formulation of the choice between general and
vocational education, employing their respective costs and expected yields
(see 682).

670   E. W. STROMSDORFER, "Labor Force Adjustment to Structural Displacement in a
Local Labor Market", *ILRR*, January, 1965, pp. 151-65.

   A theoretical analysis from the human capital viewpoint, together with case
study in the St. Louis metropolitan area.

671   T. W. SCHULTZ, "Reflections on Teaching and Learning in Colleges of Agriculture", *JFE*, February, 1965, pp. 17-22.

   A plea for more careful consideration of what is meant by effective college
education, with particular reference to the teaching of agricultural science.

672   G. G. SOMERS, E. W. STROMSDORFER, "A Benefit-Cost Analysis of Manpower Retraining", *Proceedings of the Seventeenth Annual Meeting of the Industrial Relations
Research Association*, 1965. Pp. 14, reprinted in *WYK I*, pp. 385-96.

   An analysis of the findings of a survey of trainees and non-trainees in
Western Virginia, relating the gains in employment and earnings to the costs

of the retraining programme. This is a preliminary version of a forthcoming
book to be edited by G. G. Somers: *Retraining of the Unemployed: Case Studies
of the Current Experience*.

673 M. S. GORDON, *Retraining and Labor Market Adjustment in Western Europe*.
Department of Labor, Manpower Automation Research Monograph No. 4. Washington,
D.C.: Government Printing Office, 1965. Pp. 226.

  A broad review by an economist of government training programmes in Europe
since the war. The closing chapter sums up the lessons of the European experience for the United States.

674 V. MARTIN, *Accelerated Vocational Training for Adults*. Manpower and Employment Studies. Paris: OECD, 1965. Pp. 132.

  This comparative study of the methods and aims of AVT in four countries in
Western Europe (France, Great Britain, The Netherlands, and Belgium) argues
the case rather than to survey the existing scene. The bulk of the book is
devoted to a detailed discussion of AVT syllabuses and the training of AVT
instructors.

675 I. R. HOOS, "Retraining in the United States: Problems and Progress", *ILR*,
November, 1965, pp. 410-26.

  This article describes some of the general issues that were raised in an
ongoing research project on American retraining programmes. Four case studies
of training courses, provided respectively by the Federal Government, a private firm, a trade union, and a state employment office under the Manpower
Development and Training Act, are discussed by way of illustration.

676 G. G. SOMERS, "Retraining: An Evaluation of Gains and Costs", *Employment
Policy and the Labor Market*, ed. A. M. Ross. Berkeley and Los Angeles:
California University Press, 1965, pp. 271-98.

  A cost-benefit study of such American retraining programmes as the 1962
Manpower Development and Training Act, the 1961 Area Development Act, and the
1962 Trade Expansion Act, including a useful theoretical discussion of the
nature of the costs and benefits of retraining both to society and to the
individual.

677 G. STRAUSS, "Apprenticeship: A Evaluation of the Need", *Employment Policy
and the Labor Market*, ed. A. M. Ross. Berkeley and Los Angeles: California
University Press, 1965, pp. 299-333.

  This article demonstrates the relative unimportance of apprenticeship training in the United States, even in the building trades where current apprenticeship training is concentrated. The author denies the need for a vastly
expanded apprenticeship programme.

678 A. M. RIVLIN, "Critical Issues in the Development of Vocational Education",
Unemployment in a Prosperous Economy, eds. W. G. Bowen, F. H. Harbison.
Princeton, N.J.: Princeton University, 1965, pp. 153-67.

A general discussion of present knowledge about the three main questions to be answered about training: (1) how much training should the labour force have?; (2) where should training for work occur?; and (3) who should pay the cost?

679 National Society for the Study of Education, 64th Yearbook, Pt. 1: *Vocational Education*. Chicago, Ill.: Chicago University Press, 1965. Pp. 301.

A collection of papers on various aspects of vocational education, both in schools and in higher education. Chapters of particular interest are: E. Ginzberg, "Social and Economic Trends", pp. 19–38, which calls for greater co-ordination between the various agencies providing vocational training, and more emphasis on training for older workers, to promote mobility and combat obsolescence; G. F. Arnstein, "The Technological Context of Vocational Education", pp. 39–63, which examines the likely influence of automation on future job requirements; and J. C. Swanson, E. G. Kramer, "Vocational Education Beyond the High School", pp. 168–87, which gives an outline of all the possible avenues of vocational training for adults in the United States.

680 J. T. YOUNG, *Technicians Today and Tomorrow*. London: Pitman, 1965. Pp. 222.

This book describes the methods by which technicians are now being educated and trained in Britain and tries to assess their relevance to present and future requirements. The first chapter on "Defining the Technician" and the fourth chapter on the Industrial Training Act of 1962 are particularly valuable. The book includes a comprehensive bibliography on technical education in Britain with brief annotations.

681 J. BLUM, *A Study of Skill Acquisition and Development*. Paris: OECD, 1965. Pp. 97, mimeographed.

The national OECD Mediterranean Regional Project reports generally different sources of skill development other than the formal educational system. This preliminary methodological paper, however, focuses on the informal sources: adult education programmes, apprenticeship-training programmes, and on-the-job training schemes. It reviews some of the latest empirical evidence from the United States on methods of skill acquisition, spells out the implications of these findings for educational planning, maps out research projects in the MRP countries, and concludes with a questionnaire that was used in Spain to obtain necessary data on vocational training.

682 A. J. CORAZZINI, E. BARTELL, "Problems of Programming an Optimum Choice Between General and Vocational Education", *KYK*, XVIII, 4, 1965, pp. 700-4; "Reply" by H. Correa, *ibid.*, XIX, 3, 1966, pp. 521-23.

Extremely critical comments on Correa's paper (669).

1966

683 P. W. MUSGRAVE, "Constant Factors in the Demand for Technical Education: 1860-1960", *BJES*, May, 1966, pp. 173-87, reprinted in *Sociology, History and Education*, ed. P. W. Musgrave. London: Methuen, 1970, pp. 143-57.

A historical survey of public requests in Britain for increased technical education for economic or social reasons. Argues that the two main constants have been pressure of foreign competition and the work of a few prominent industrialists or educationists.

684 P. W. MUSGRAVE, "The Educational Profiles of Management in Two British Iron and Steel Companies With Some Comparisons, National and International", *BJIR*, July, 1966, pp. 201-12.

The title of this article is self-explanatory. It demonstrates that the proportions of various levels of management in the labour force of different countries vary considerably (see also 1339).

685 International Labour Office, *European Apprenticeship: Effects of Educational, Social and Technical Development on Apprenticeship Training Practices for Eight Countries.* Geneva: ILO, 1966. Pp. 276.

The eight countries are Austria, Czechoslovakia, Denmark, France, Western Germany, The Netherlands, Switzerland, and the United Kingdom. This book is an encyclopaedia of information on the organisation of training and the finance of apprenticeship programmes in the countries concerned.

686 R. T. HALL, *The Industrial Training Act, 1964*. Human Resources Development, Fellows' Reports. Paris: OECD, 1966. Pp. 316.

A survey of occupational training and technical education in Great Britain. Argues that industrial training boards, similar to those set up by the 1964 Act in Britain, could usefully be set up in the MRP countries to co-ordinate training programmes.

687 S. A. LEVITAN, I. H. SIEGEL, eds., *Dimensions of Manpower Policy: Programs and Research*. A Volume Commemorating the Twentieth Anniversary of the W. E. Upjohn Institute for Employment Research. Baltimore, Md.: The John Hopkins Press, 1966. Pp. 299.

A collection of essays on current manpower problems in the United States, such as the recent growth of federal manpower programmes, the poverty war, unemployment compensation, and vocational education in depressed areas.

688 H. F. CLARK, H. S. SLOAN, *Classrooms on Main Street*. New York: Teachers College Press, Columbia University, 1966. Pp. 162.

A study of the origins and development of American trade and vocational schools outside the formal educational system. A separate section deals with business schools and employers' opinions of them.

689 Central Training Council, Commercial and Clerical Training Committee, UK, *Training for Commerce and the Office*. London: HMSO, 1966. Pp. 139.

The so-called Hunt Report surveys existing training arrangements in Britain for those in clerical and commercial operations under 21 years of age—demonstrating the neglect of in-service training for office staff in Britain—as well as similar training arrangements in Denmark, France, and Western Germany. The Report conclueds with a series of recommendations designed to improve training facilities.

690 J. E. GERSTL, S. P. HUTTON, *Engineers: The Anatomy of a Profession*. London: Tavistock Publications, 1966. Pp. 229.

Based on a sample survey of the membership of the Institution of Mechanical Engineers. Detailed information is provided about the social origins, education, work setting, and careers of British mechanical engineers; little evidence about salaries, however, is given.

1967

691 W. BATEMAN, "An Application of Cost-Benefit Analysis to the Work-Experience Program", *AER*, May, 1967, pp. 397-408, reprinted in *WYK I*, pp. 397-408.

An interesting example of CBA in the assessment of an American retraining scheme.

692 D. O. SEWELL, "A Critique of Cost-Benefit Analysis of Training", *MLR*, September, 1967, pp. 409-21, reprinted in *WYK I*, pp. 45-51.

A useful critique of the use of CBA to evaluate manpower training schemes.

693 G. T. PAGE, "Canada's Manpower Training and Education: Federal Policy and Programs", *CERD*, December, 1967, pp. 283-98.

A description of Federal Government activity in the field of manpower planning in Canada, including the Technical and Vocational Training Act, the Manpower Mobility Assistance Program, and various research projects carried out by the Department of Manpower and Immigration.

694 N. A. SISCO, "Canada's Manpower Training and Education: A View from Ontario", *ibid.*, pp. 299-304.

A criticism of the Federal Manpower policy on the grounds that it draws a rigid distinction between training, which is a federal responsibility, and education, which is the responsibility of the States. The author argues that education and training policy must be highly co-ordinated and that the present division of responsibility in Canada will prevent this.

695 H. L. WILENSKY, "Careers, Counseling, and the Curriculum", *JHR*, Winter, 1967, pp. 19-40.

A general discussion of career counselling in the light of the dangers of premature vocationalism in schools.

696 A. J. CORAZZINI, "When Should Vocational Education Begin?", *ibid.*, pp. 41-50, reprinted in *WYK II*, pp. 163-74.

A cost-benefit comparison of two competing vocational training programmes in the State of Massachusetts.

697 D. J. FARBER, "Apprenticeship in the United States: Labor Market Forces and
     Social Policy", *ibid.*, pp. 70-90; "Discussion" by A. H. Belitisky, J. Barbash,
     ibid., pp. 90-96; see also H. G. Foster, "Apprenticeship: Market or Power
     Forces", *ibid.*, Spring, 1967, pp. 244-47.

   The article attempts to show that participation in apprenticeship programmes
   responds to short-run changes in the American economy. The comments criticise
   the author's approach and take up the role of labour unions in apprenticeship.

1968

698 E. E. ROBINSON, *The New Polytechnics*. London: Cornmarket Press, 1968.
     Pp. 200.

   A passionate plea for the expansion of polytechnics, if necessary at the
   expense of universities, and an excellent source of information about the
   recent growth of the "public" part of British higher education.

699 R. FEIN, "Brookings Institution Conference on Vocational Education: Intro-
     duction", *JHR*, Summer, 1968, III, Supplement, pp. 1-16.

   This valuable introduction summarises the papers and discussions at the
   conference. The rest of the supplement consists of five papers, one by a
   psychologist and four by economists, all of which are of outstanding quality;
   (1) M. J. Lewis, "Implications of Two Views of Vocational Guidance", pp. 17-31;
   (2) G. G. Somers, "The Response of Vocational Education to Labor Market
   Changes", pp. 32-58; (3) M. K. Taussig, "An Economic Analysis of Vocational
   Education in the New York City High Schools", pp. 59-87; (4) A. J. Corazzini,
   "The Decision to Invest in Vocational Education: An Analysis of Costs and
   Benefits", pp. 88-120; and (5) J. J. Kaufman, "Occupational Training Needs
   for Youth", pp. 121-40. The general conclusions of the empirical studies by
   Taussig and Corazzini is that secondary vocational education in the United
   States yields very low rates of return.

700 M. C. McCARTHY, *The Employment of Highly Specialised Graduates: A Comparative
     Study in the United Kingdom and the United States of America*. Department of
     Education and Science, Science Policy Studies 3. London: HMSO, 1968. Pp. 36.

   A fascinating comparison, not so much of the employment of scientists and
   engineers in the two countries, as of their education and training, America
   providing generalised and Britain specialised first degrees in the two fields.
   The emphasis of the argument is on educational policies that will make manpower forecasts unnecessary.

1970

701 D. LEES, B. CHIPLIN, "The Economics of Industrial Training", *LBR*, April,
     1970, pp. 29-41.

   An economic analysis of the British Industrial Training Act of 1964. The
   authors conclude that industrial training boards have no basis in economic
   logic and that the levy/grant system is poorly designed to repair any alleged
   deficiencies in training by British industry.

702 S. MUKHERJEE, *Changing Manpower Needs. A Study of Industrial Training Boards.*
London: PEP Broadsheet 523, 1970. Pp. 123.

   An excellent review of the accomplishments to date of Industrial Training
Boards in Britain, with a chapter on the Becker-Mincer theory of training, a
separate evaluation of the engineering, electricity supply and iron and steel
boards, and a recommendation to establish a Manpower Commission in Britain
(established in fact a year later).

1971

703 E. HARDIN, M. E. BORUS, *The Economic Benefits and Costs of Retraining.*
Lexington, Mass.: Heath Lexington Books. 1971, Pp. 235.

   This is a thorough regression analysis of the costs and benefits of a
government training programme in the State of Michigan. The programme is
shown to be profitable both to individuals and to society, and the pay-off
is found to be inversely related to the length of training courses. A useful
appendix (pp. 231-35) compares these findings to those of other studies.

704 P. B. DOERINGER, M. J. PIORE, *Internal Labor Markets and Manpower Analysis.*
Lexington, Mass.: D.C. Heath & Co., 1971. Pp. 214.

   This is an important book which develops the vital distinction between the
internal promotion-and-transfer system of an enterprise and the external
labour market of conventional economics. Although it is based on a study of
blue-collar workers in American manufacturing, the argument readily lends
itself to an extension to white-collar workers. The final chapters derive
some radically new policy recommendations with respect to problems of race
and poverty. The last chapter throws new light on the question of structural
unemployment and retraining programmes.

705 D. S. HAMERMESH, *Economic Aspects of Manpower Training Programs. Theory and
Policy.* Lexington, Mass.: Heath Lexington Books, 1971. Pp. 145.

   This book attempts to construct some simulatable models in terms of which
specific manpower training programmes can be evaluated. It contains a particularly interesting chapter (ch. 4) on shifting the Phillips Curve through
manpower training programmes.

706 A. G. HOLTMAN, "Joint Products and On-the-Job Training", *JPE*, July/August,
1971, pp. 929-31.

   In reply to Eckaus' criticisms of Becker's classic analysis of investment in
on-the-job training, the author shows that (a) workers pay for general training in a perfect market even when it is provided as a joint product with output; and (b) when markets are not perfect, general training provided as a
joint product will be underproduced.

707 R. E. SMITH, "The Opportunity Cost of Participating in a Training Program",
JHR, Fall, 1971, pp. 510-18.

The paper presents an anlytical model which is used to estimate the earnings foregone by training in a manpower programme. The model is used to estimate the costs of a training scheme under the Manpower Development Training Act.

1972

708 J. G. SCOVILLE, *Manpower and Occupational Analysis: Concepts and Measures.* Lexington, Mass.: D. C. Heath and Company, 1972. Pp. 136.

The first full-length study by an economist of occupational classification schemes, their uses and abuses. Most of the material relates to the United States but there is some discussion of ILO's ISCO. The heart of the book is chapter 3, which offers an "economic theory of jobs" around the concept of job design. The author goes well beyond Becker's theory of training by attempting to integrate technological constraints, job design turnover, recruitment, promotion, job evaluation and the sharing of training costs between workers and management. Chapter 4 examines some empirical evidence bearing on the theory.

709 D. M. BELLANTE, "A Multivariate Analysis of a Vocational Rehabilitation Program", *JHR*, Spring, 1972, pp. 226-41.

A critique of an earlier article by Conley (see 252) which estimated cost-benefit relationships for particular categories of disabled persons, using regression analysis. Unlike Conley, the author finds that high-productivity groups benefit most per unit of cost from the provision of rehabilitation services.

710 B. O. PETTMAN, "In Partial Defence of the Industrial Training Boards: Some Criticisms Examined", *BJIR*, July, 1972, pp. 224-39.

Considers criticisms of the British ITA emanating from the "Becker School of Human Capital Theory", and argues that the Becker analysis is subject to so many qualifications that its implications for ITA are by no means obvious.

711 S. L. BARSBY, *Cost-Benefit Analysis and Manpower Programs.* Lexington, Mass.: D. C. Heath & Co., 1972. Pp. 224.

This study reviews a large number of cost-benefit analyses of manpower training and retraining programmes in the United States. Includes a useful bibliography on recent American literature.

712 G. G. SOMERS, E. W. STROMSDORFER, "A Cost-Effectiveness Analysis of In-School and Summer Neighborhood Youth Corps: A Nationwide Analysis", *JHR*, Fall, 1972, pp. 446-59.

This paper evaluates the extent to which the in-school and summer NYC programmes in the United States have prevented high school dropouts and improved their labour market performance. It is an exercise in cost-effectiveness rather than cost-benefit analysis because benefits are measured by current earnings and by current unemployment.

713 E. W. STROMSDORFER, *Review and Synthesis of Cost-Effectiveness Studies of Vocational and Technical Education*. Colombus, Ohio: ERIC Clearinghouse on Vocational and Technical Education, 1972. Pp. 143

A superb review of the American cost-benefit literature on vocational training and retraining programmes, preceded by a long introduction on the methodological issues in the estimation of costs and benefits. The author concludes cautiously in favour of vocational as against academic programmes. Includes a complete bibliography as well as a bibliography of bibliographies.

714 D. O. PARSONS, "Specific Human Capital: An Application to Quit Rates and Layoff Rates", *JPE*, November/December, 1972, pp. 1120-43.

Distinguishing between worker-owned and firm-owned human capital acquired as a result of investment in "specific" training, the paper explores the optimal sharing of such investments between firms and workers. Certain predictions of the model with respect to quit and layoff rates are then tested on American manufacturing data.

1973

715 M. J. PIORE, "Fragments of a 'Sociological' Theory of Wages", *AER*, May, 1973, pp. 377-84.

An important article which essentially explores the implications of the concept of socialisation as applied to labour training rather than to formal education.

716 D. J. BROWN, "Resources in Advanced FE—A Critique of the Pooling Committee's Work", *HER*, Summer, 1973, pp. 35-44.

A critical review of some recent exercises by the so-called "Pooling Committee" and another fascinating glance at the strange method of financing AFE colleges in Britain.

717 K. HARTLEY, P. MANCINI, "The Industrial Training Act and the Hotel and Catering Industry: A Case Study", *IRJ*, Summer, 1973, pp. 37-44.

An interesting attempt to apply the Becker distinction between general and specific training to a single industry. Although the results suggest that the ITA has raised the quality of training in the industry, no evidence is found to substantiate the "poaching hypothesis".

718 M. ZYMELMAN, *Cost Effectiveness of Alternative Learning Technologies in Industrial Training—A Study of In-Plant Training and Vocational Schools*. Washington, D.C.: IBRD, Bank Staff Working Paper 169, 1973. Pp. 95, mimeographed.

An extremely useful but, alas, incomplete review of the literature, appraising vocational training schemes and off-the-job-in-plant training programmes. Includes a mini-handbook for evaluators of training programmes.

719 M. GUNDERSON, "Determinants of Individual Success in On-the-Job Training",
     JHR, Fall, 1973, pp. 472-84.

        This study utilizes data on individual trainees in the USA and demonstrates
     the importance of company and training programme characteristics for determin-
     ing success.

1974

720 B. O. PETTMAN, "Industrial Training in Great Britain", *IJSE*, I, 1, 1974,
     pp. 63-83.

        A useful outline of developments in industrial training since the war, up
     to about 1973. Includes a survey of the reactions of a sample of firms in
     the Humberside area to the training proposals of the 1972 Consultative Docu-
     ment.

721 M. WOODHALL, "Investment in Industrial Training: An Assessment of the Effects
     of the Industrial Training Act on the Volume and Costs of Training, *BJIR*,
     March, 1974, pp. 71-90.

        A survey of the literature on the British Industrial Training Act and an
     attempt to estimate the scale and total costs of all forms of in-service
     training of employees in Britain.

722 K. HARTLEY, "Industrial Training and Public Policy: From Industrial Training
     Boards to the State Manpower Bank", *Economic Policies and Social Goals*,
     ed. A. J. Culyer. London: Martin Robertson, 1974, pp. 113-37.

        A critique of the ITBs in Britain with a proposal to set up a State Manpower
     Bank to overcome the imperfections of the capital market in respect of train-
     ing.

723 W. D. HYDE, Jr., *Metropolitan Proprietary Schools: A Study of Functions and
     Economic Responsiveness*. Washington, D.C.: US Department of Health, Educa-
     tion and Welfare, National Institute of Education, 1974. Pp. 203.
        A descriptive study with some original data of private schools in American
     cities.

1975

724 A. ZIDERMAN, A. WALDER, "Trade Unions and the Acceptability of G.T.C. Trainees:
     Some Survey Results", *BJIR*, March, 1975, pp. 78-85.

        Evidence on the attitudes of trade unions to government trained workers in
     Merseyside and London.

725 A. ZIDERMAN, "Costs and Benefits of Manpower Training Programmes in Great
     Britain", *ibid.*, July, 1975, pp. 223-44.

        A cost-benefit analysis of government training centres in Britain, paying
     particular attention to the employment-unemployment aspects of the benefits.
     The study revealed very high rates of return to GTC's.

726 N. WOODWARD, T. ANDERSON, "A Profitability Appraisal of Apprenticeships",
     ibid., July, 1975, pp. 245-56.

     An interesting attempt to apply cost-benefit analysis to a particular
     apprenticeship scheme in the British shipbuilding industry.

(e) HIGHER EDUCATION

In the nature of the case, this section is not self-contained, and further references on higher education in developed countries will be found in almost all the
other sections. Thorp[744] provides a convenient bird's eye view of research in the
economics of higher education, and Rivlin[745] summarises results up to 1962. The
world-wide educational explosion produced a new interest in the 1960's in the problems of planning the future expansion of higher education: on the United States,
see Havighurst[737], Orcutt and others[739], Jaffe and Adams[756], Porter[766], Cartter[767],
and Folger[783]; on Great Britain, see Robbins[751], and Moser and Layard[759]; on Germany, see Edding[753], and Wissenschaftsrat[758]. In this connection, it is important
to get a clear view of the socio-economic characteristics of university and college
students: information on both inflows and outflows in the United States and Great
Britain will be found in Havemann and West[728], Berdie[729], Kelsall[733,751], Bowles[750],
Robbins[751], Harris[752] , Nam and Cowhig[755], Schwartz[764], the International Study
Admissions[770], Kelsall and others[797], Barber[800], Roper[1171], and Hollinshead[1173].
The special question of graduate students is discussed by Berelson[738], Mooney[784],
Robinson[778], and Rudd and Hatch[785].
The 1960's mood of expansion, however, has now grown sour: recent projections
in many countries imply a massive surplus of graduates in the 1980's: see
Cartter[772,820], Feldman and Hoenack[789], Department of Education and Science[793],
von Zur-Muehlen[818], Williams[836], Armitage[837], and Dresch[849].
Questions of university efficiency are discussed by Williams[747], Harris[752],
Carter[762], Levy[789], Fielden[791], Bottomley and others[812,832], Legg[829], Lumsden[842],
Layard and Verry[846], and Dunworth and Cook[850]. There is a rich literature on the
existing and potential sources of finance of higher education, including Hungate[732],
Harris[734,736,752], Millett[734], Rivlin[741], Economist Intelligence Unit[750], Danière[761]
Carter and Williams[748,751], Robbins[751,771,813], Devons[751], Caine[751], Peacock and
Wiseman[751], the Joint Economic Committee[789], Hartman[815], Nerlove[815], and
Morris[833,848]. See also the section on "Costs and Finance".
Caplow and McGee[740], Brown[769], Bibby[806], and Williams, Blackstone and Metcalf[841]
analyse the labour market for academics.
Robbins[751] is the best source for international comparisons of systems of higher
education.

1940

727 League of Nations. International Institute of Intellectual Co-operation,
     *The Future of Graduates: The Investigation and Forecasting of Opportunities
     for Intellectual Employment*. Paris: International Institute of Intellectual
     Co-operation, 1940. Pp. 170.

     This report examines the need for vocational guidance for graduates at a
     time of considerable intellectual unemployment, and recommends the establish-
     ment of national centres to forecast the career opportunities for graduates.
     The statistical requirements of such policies are set out in detail and
     examples given of some specific studies of graduate employment in various

European countries. There is a country-by-country bibliography which shows
what sorts of educational and occupational statistics were available in the
1930's.

1952

728 E. HAVEMANN, P. S. WEST, *They Went to College. The College Graduate in
America Today*. New York: Harcourt Brace, 1952. Pp. 277.

   A popular account, based on a survey conducted by *Time* magazine in 1947,
dealing with the economic, social, and political characteristics of the college
graduate population in the USA. For a summary of the findings by one of the
authors, see *Class, Status and Power. A Reader in Social Stratification*,
eds. R. Bendix, S. M. Lipset (London: Routledge & Kegan Paul, 1954),
pp. 465–80.

1954

729 R. F. BERDIE, *After High School—What?* Minneapolis: Minnesota University
Press, 1954. Pp. 240.

   A thorough study of student-inflow into American universities and colleges,
based on interviews with 25,000 students. Includes chapters on "Parental
attitudes Toward College", by B. Willerman and "Socio-Economic Status and
After-High-School Plans" by W. L. Layton.

1956

730 PEP, *Graduate Employment. A Sample Survey*. London: PEP, 1956. Pp. 300.

   This book, based on a survey of men who took first degrees at British universities in the academic year 1949–50, traces their careers in the 4 years
following graduation up to 1954, relating their academic record to their occupational choices and 4-year age-earning profiles. The broad conclusions of
the study are conveniently summarised in a final chapter, pp. 239–54.

1957

731 PEP, *Graduates in Industry. The Second Report on the Study of Industry and
the University Graduate*. London: PEP, 1957. Pp. 261.

   This work is based on two surveys: one of 47 industrial enterprises which
recruited graduates, and the other of some 600 graduates who had found employment in industry. It analyses the reasons some firms recruited graduates,
their views on the suitability of university education for the needs of industry, the methods used to select graduates, and the factors governing the
amount and type of training given to graduate employees. The conclusions of
the study are summarised in a final chapter, pp. 211–31.

732 T. L. HUNGATE, *A New Basis for Support of Higher Education. A Study of Current Practices, Issues and Needed Change*. New York: Teachers College,
Columbia University, 1957. Pp. 65.

An outstanding study of interstate differences in financing in the USA. The appendices provide useful data on interstate differences in methods and practices of financing higher education in the USA.

733 R. K. KELSALL, *Report on An Inquiry into Applications for Admissions to Universities*. Committee of Vice-Chancellors and Principals of the Universities of the United Kingdom. London: Association of Universities of the British Commonwealth, 1957. Pp. 32.

A study of the numbers, educational and social background, financial assistance received, and career intentions of all students who applied for admission in 1955-56 to a full-time course at British universities and colleges, except Oxford and Cambridge. There is a two-page summary of the findings, pp. 22-23.

1959

734 D. M. KEEZER, ed., *Financing Higher Education 1960-70*. The McGraw-Hill Book Company 50th Anniversary Study of the Economics of Higher Education in the United States. New York: McGraw-Hill, 1959. Pp. 304.

A collection of a dozen papers by various American authorities, including "An Economist's Overview of Higher Education" by P. H. Coombs, pp. 12-35; "Financing of Higher Education: Broad Issues" by S. E. Harris, pp. 35-79; "The Role of Student Charges", by J. D. Millett, pp. 162-83; "Government Support of Higher Education", pp. 183-220; "Potentialities of Educational Establishments Outside the Conventional Structure of Higher Education", by H. F. Clark, pp. 257-74; and several articles dealing with the management and efficient operation of universities and colleges.

735 Committee on Utilization of College Teaching Resources, *Better Utilization of College Teaching Resources*. *A Summary Report*. Fund for the Advancement of Education. New York: FAE, 1959. Pp. 63.

The findings of a programme of grants to some 60 American colleges and universities to explore methods of economising on teachers. Among the conclusions is that the size of classes can be significantly increased without harmful effects on students through better training of teachers and the wider use of mechanical aids.

1960

736 S. E. HARRIS, ed., *Higher Education in the United States. The Economic Problems*. Cambridge, Mass.: Harvard University Press, 1960. Pp. 252.

A large number of contributors, including a few economists, address themselves to the issues of the proper level of tuition fees and government aid, costing, finance, investment of endowed funds, and the like. The article by K. Deitch "Some Observations on the Allocation of Resources in Higher Education", pp. 192-99, is reprinted in *UNESCO-REED*, pp. 802-10.

737 R. J. HAVIGHURST, *American Higher Education in the 1960's*. Columbus, Ohio:
     Ohio State University Press, 1960. Pp. 92.

   A projection of college enrolment by 1975 and a brief discussion of the factors influencing present enrolment trends.

738 B. BERELSON, *Graduate Education in the United States*. New York: McGraw-Hill,
     1960. Pp. 346.

   Based on a number of questionnaire-surveys of institutions of higher learning and of business firms employing professional and technical personnel, this
book describes and discusses the system of American postgraduate education.
For our purposes, the most valuable sections are those on the socio-economic
characteristics of graduate students, pp. 129-53, and on the problems of
recruiting competent teachers, pp. 44-93.

1961

739 G. H. ORCUTT, M. GREENBERGER, J. KORBEL, A. M. RIVLIN, *Micro-analysis of
     Socio-economic Systems: A Simulation Study*. New York: Harper & Bros.,
     1961, pp. 257-85.

   A section of this pioneering book on constructing a computable model of the
US Household Sector deals with "The Demand for Higher Education", in the
course of which the authors give an excellent review of the literature up to
1960 on college-going and on methods of projecting college enrolment.

740 T. CAPLOW, R. J. McGEE, *The Academic Marketplace*. New York: Science Editions,
     Inc., 1961. Pp. 262.

   Based on a sample of 10 major American universities, this book analyses the
nature of the labour market for American academics via a quantitative study
of faculty mobility.

741 A. M. RIVLIN, *The Role of the Federal Government in Financing Higher Education*.
     Washington, D.C.: Brookings Institution, 1961. Pp. 179.

   An outline of the history of federal programmes and the current status of
federal support. Particularly interesting is ch. 8, "The Case for Government
Subsidies to Higher Education", which rejects the Friedman argument (see 1256)
and discusses which levels of higher education should be most heavily subsidised.

1962

742 A. COLLIN, A. M. REES, J. UTTING, *The Arts Graduate in Industry*. London:
     Acton Society Trust, 1962. Pp. 100.

   This study of the utilisation of male arts graduates in manufacturing industry is based on a questionnaire survey of 172 business firms. It covers recruitment policies, types of training received, job patterns and salaries
after training, and the attitudes and expectations of the graduates themselves.

743 Nottingham University, *1962 Graduate Employment Survey. Based on Information Supplied by Nottingham Graduates of 1950 to 1958.* Nottingham: Careers and Appointments Board, 1962. Pp. 15

   Based on a postal questionnaire to 1000 graduates of the years 1950-58 chosen at random. Includes information on salaries.

744 W. L. THORP, "101 Questions for Investigation", *EHE*, pp. 345-57.

   Six topics make up 101 questions which, the author feels, cover the subject of the economics of higher education. A compendium of research topics.

745 A. M. RIVLIN, "Research in the Economics of Higher Education: Progress and Problems", *ibid.*, pp. 357-87.

   An incomplete but illuminating survey of recent research in (1) investment in education and the returns of such investment; (2) supply and demand for manpower; and (3) methods of financing higher education.

1963

746 E. ASHBY, *Technology and the Academics. An Essay on Universities and the Scientific Revolution.* London: Macmillan, 1963. Pp. 118.

   A series of 5 lectures, 3 of which are devoted to tracing the gradual acceptance of scientific and technical education in British universities in the nineteenth century. The last two essays deal with the current problem of the relationship between the universities and the social and economic order in which they function.

747 B. R. WILLIAMS, "Capacity and Output of Universities", *MS*, May, 1963, pp. 185-202.

   A careful attempt to analyse the notion of low plant loads in British universities and to spell out the implications of various proposals to eliminate excess capacity: increases in plant hours of work, a longer university year, increases in staff-student ratios, and improved management.

748 C. F. CARTER, B. R. WILLIAMS, "Proposals for Reform in University Finance", *ibid.*, September, 1963, pp. 255-61.

   The authors' recommendations to the Robbins Committee: a new system of teaching grants, research grants, and capital grants.

749 C. CRAIG, *The Employment of Cambridge Graduates.* University of Cambridge Appointments Boards. Cambridge: Cambridge University Press, 1963. Pp. 102.

   An inquiry into the 1961 occupations of Cambridge graduates of 1952 and 1953, the salaries they have attained, the satisfactions they derive from their occupations, and how they have progressed to their present positions. The quality of this work makes it a kind of a model of how follow-up studies of students ought to be conducted and presented.

750 F. BOWLES, *Access to Higher Education. The International Study of University Admissions*, I. Paris: UNESCO-IAU, 1963. Pp. 212.

The first major project of a joint research programme of UNESCO and the International Association of Universities, covering all types of institutions engaged in higher education in 13 countries around the world. The chief finding of the study is that the selection patterns of different countries can be classified into two basic types (see Bowles' summary 873). The book includes a valuable analysis of international patterns of "Financial Aid to Students", prepared by the Economist Intelligence Unit, London, England, pp. 179-212.

751 *Higher Education. Report of the Committee under the Chairmanship of Lord Robbins 1961-63.* London: HMSO, 1963. Cmnd. 2154. Pp. 335.

The committee advocated an increase of about 80 per cent in the number of students in full-time education in Great Britain over the next 10 years, justifying that expansion by a forecast of the demand for higher education. The report includes a historical survey of the growth of higher education in Great Britain, some striking international comparisons, and a wealth of data on the characteristics of the British student population, the internal structure of British institutions of higher education, and the finance and administration of universities and training colleges. Five appendices of statistics were published with the report: App. 1, *The Demand for Places in Higher Education* (pp. 342) deals with the factors influencing entry to higher education, the pool of ability, and the estimates of future places; App. 2 (A), *Students and Their Education* (pp. 342) provides basic data on university students, wastage and student performance, and problems of student finance; App. 2 (B), *Students and Their Education* (pp. 623) gives the results of various surveys on the social and educational backgrounds of students, on their career intentions, on the content of courses, on methods of teaching, and on professional and adult education; App. 3, *Teachers in Higher Education* (pp. 259) is a compendium of information on student-staff ratios, qualifications of teachers, mobility, salaries, methods of teaching, and so forth; App. 4, *Administrative, Financial and Economic Aspects of Higher Education* (pp. 166) is concerned, among other things, with the cost of higher education and the number of people with higher education in Great Britain; App. 5, *Higher Education in Other Countries* (pp. 306) surveys the picture in Australia, Canada, France, Germany, the Netherlands, New Zealand, Sweden, Switzerland, the United States, and the USSR. All the appendices were prepared under the direction of C. A. Moser, with the aid of P. R. G. Layard and E. White. In addition to the 5 appendices, there are 7 volumes of oral and documentary *Evidence* (Pt. One, Vols. A-F, and Pt. Two) from 31 individuals and 90 organisations (the full list is given in the *Report*, pp. 303-12). The evidence and the discussions covered every aspect of the committee's work and only those directly relevant to the economics of education are listed here: S. Caine on university finance (Vol. A, pp. 138-74); C. F. Carter, B. R. Williams on an "open door" policy in higher education, on technical education, and on new methods of finance (Vol. D, pp. 1324-46); D. V. Glass, J. W. B. Douglas on the "pool of ability" (Vol. D, pp. 1398-1404); E. Devons on finance and administration (Vol. F, pp. 1770-90); The Ministry of Education on the demand for higher education and a critical view of present provisions (Vol. F, pp. 1882-1956); The Treasury on the economic and financial issues in the future expansion of higher education and the problem of controlling university expenditures (Vol. F, pp. 1956-2018); J. Floud on the "pool of ability" (Pt. Two, pp. 45-58); R. K. Kelsall on university selection policies (Pt. Two, pp. 99-102); N. Malleson on student wastage (Pt. Two, pp. 117-24); A. T. Peacock, J. Wiseman on the economic criteria for allocating resources to higher education (Pt. Two, pp. 129-39); A. R. Prest on student loans (Pt. Two, pp. 139-53); and

P. E. Vernon on the "pool of ability" with a brief history of the concept (Pt. Two, pp. 170–78).

The *Robbins Report* has received a great deal of comment but not as yet a full-scale critique. See, however, the symposia in *UQ*, March, 1964; *Forum*, Summer, 1964, particularly the papers by M. Trow and J. E. Floud; and *The Technologist*, I, 2, 1964, particularly the paper by M. H. Peston (pp. 19–25).

1964

752 S. E. HARRIS, "General Problems in Education and Manpower", *OECD-EAHE*, pp. 11-95.

The author briefly summarises the papers in the rest of the volume, reports on the discussions at the meeting of the OECD Study Group in the Economics of Education in Paris, 1962, and provides additional material on a number of topics: admissions and tests; the demand for higher education; the internal efficiency of higher education; financing higher education; returns on investment in education; education and growth; education and manpower; and some quantitative problems.

753 F. EDDING, "The Planning of Higher Education in the Federal Republic of Germany", *ibid*. *OECD-EAHE*, pp. 153-76.

A review of planning experience since the end of the war, a survey of current problems, and an enrolment projection for 1980.

754 S. G. RAYBOULD, *University Extra-Mural Education in England 1945-62; A Study of Finance and Policy*. London: Michael Joseph, 1964. Pp. 207.

An account of the development of part-time adult education provided by the universities with an examination of the present system of finance, under which the extra-mural courses of universities receive special ear-marked grants from the UGC. The author concludes that this leads to a waste of resources and urges that both the courses and the staffing policies of the extra-mural departments should be revised. There is a statistical appendix.

755 US Department of Agriculture, *Characteristics of School Dropouts and High School Graduates Farm and Nonfarm 1960*. Agricultural Report No. 65. Washington, D.C.: Department of Agriculture, 1964. Pp. 31.

This report analyses the socio-economic status of high school dropouts and graduates as revealed by the 1960 Census of Population. See also C. B. Nam, J. D. Cowhig, *Factors Related to College Attendance of Farm and Nonfarm High School Graduates 1960*. Series Census ERS (P-27), No. 32. Washington, D.C.: U.S. Bureau of Census, 1962. Pp. 34. (See also 764.)

756 A. J. JAFFE, W. ADAMS, "College Education for the U.S. Youth: The Attitudes of Parents and Children", *AJES*, July, 1964, pp. 669-84.

Bringing together all the evidence from past public opinion polls, the authors show that parents and children have quite different attitudes to college attendance. They discuss the implications of this finding for the forecasting of college enrolments.

757 M. KENDALL, "Those Who Failed", *UQ*, September, 1964, pp. 398-406; *ibid*.,
     December, 1964, pp. 69-77.

   Two articles presenting data on the subsequent careers of two small samples
of students who failed to obtain their degrees, or who did not complete their
university courses. The samples are compared with a control group of successful graduates, but the value of the statistical material is limited by the
low response rate of the failures, and the fact that their ages are not
standardised.

758 WISSENSCHAFTSRAT, *Abiturienten und Studenten. Entwicklung und Vorschätzung
     der Zahlen 1950 bis 1980*. Tübingen: Mohr, 1964. Pp. 205.

   Projections of future enrolments in "higher education" in the Federal Republic of West Germany (see p. 17 for definition of "higher education"). There
are 80 pages of text, followed by 125 pages of statistical tables.

759 C. A. MOSER, P. R. G. LAYARD, "Planning the Scale of Higher Education in
     Britain: Some Statistical Problems", *JRSS*, Series A, Vol. 127, Pt. 4, 1964,
     pp. 473-513, partly reprinted in *P-EED*, 1, pp. 287-317.

   In the first section of the paper, the authors (respectively Statistical
Advisor and Senior Research Officer to the Robbins Committee) discuss the
nature of the enrolment projections that formed the basis for the committee's
recommendations. In the final section, they review British work on the forecasting of high quality manpower and touch on the general problems raised by
manpower planning. The vigorous discussion on the paper when it was read before the Royal Statistical Society includes valuable contributions from
R. Stone, H. E. Bishop, T. Barna, and J. E. Floud.

760 B. N. RODGERS, *Careers of Social Science Graduates. A Follow-up Study of
     Those Completing Social Science Course at British Universities in 1950, 1955
     and 1960*. Occasional Papers on Social Administration, No. 11. Welwyn, Herts:
     Social Administration Research Trust, 1964. Pp. 75.

   This study follows up the careers of 55 per cent of all students completing
social science courses in 24 British University Social Studies Departments in
the years cited, with particular attention to their employment patterns,
salaries earned and further training received (the title of the pamphlet is
misleading because social science in this context means almost exclusively
social work). There is a convenient summary of findings, pp. 45-9.

761 A. DANIÈRE, *Higher Education in the American Economy*. New York: Random House,
     1964. Pp. 206.

   This book applies the standard tools of modern welfare economics to the
problem of financing higher education in America. It assumes little prior
knowledge of these tools and the style is easy to follow, even for a non-
economist. Nevertheless, it breaks new ground on a number of questions and,
in the words of the preface by S. E. Harris, "the book is clearly one of the
major works on the economics of higher education". The author's fundamental
thesis—cost-covering tuition fees coupled with a loan programme at subsidised
interest rates—is developed in ch. 8, pp. 102-24. Other notable chapters are
ch. 4, pp. 33-47, one of the best expositions in the literature of the inherent

imperfections in the market for educated people; ch. 6, pp. 56-80, on efficient pricing of research activities in universities; and ch. 12, pp. 168-99,
which extends the analysis to primary and secondary education along Friedman-
Peacock-Wiseman lines. (See 1256, 1268.)

1965

762 C. F. CARTER, "The Economics of Higher Education", *MS*, January, 1965, pp. 1-16

A general discussion of those problems of resource allocation within universities in which economic analyis can be helpful. Some alternative estimates
of per-pupil costs are produced for British universities, which differ from
both UGC and Robbins estimates; the author argues that the latter are misleadingly based on average instead of marginal costs.

763 A. M. CARTTER, "Economics of the University", *AER*, May, 1965, pp. 481-95.

An attempt to relate the quality of graduate faculties of American universities to some indicators of costs and size. The article opens with a plea
for more study of the economics of higher education.

764 M. A. SCHWARTZ, *The United States College-Educated Population: 1960*.
Chicago, Ill.: National Opinion Research Center, University of Chicago,
Report No. 102, 1965. Pp. 171.

This report analyses various economic, demographic, and personal characteristics of college-educated individuals enumerated in the 1960 Census of Population.

765 S. WARKOV, J. MARSH, *The Education and Training of America's Scientists and
Engineers: 1962*. Chicago, Ill.: National Opinion Research Center, University of Chicago, Report No. 104, 1965. Pp. 187.

This report focuses primarily on the education and training of persons classified as scientists and engineers in the 1960 Census, covering such areas as
their fields of study, levels of educational attainment, occupations, salaries
and outside income, and selected personal characteristics.

766 R. C. PORTER, "A Growth Model Forecast of Faculty Size and Salaries in U.S.
Higher Education", *RES*, May, 1965, pp. 191-97.

A Harrod-Domar-type model is used to forecast faculty size and salaries
over the period 1960-78. The model demonstrates that there is a determinate
relationship between the birthrate and faculty size in higher education via
successive enrolment rates in primary, secondary, and tertiary education.

767 A. M. CARTTER, "A New Look at the Supply of College Teachers", *TER*, Summer,
1965, pp. 267-77.

A review of demand and supply projections of American college teachers over
the last 15 years showing that the repeated warnings of impending shortages

were based on faulty reading of the data. The article concludes with some suggestions for improving knowledge of the current stock of college teachers.

768 "Higher Education", *RER*, October, 1965, pp. 247-371.

Essay-reviews of the literature for the 5-year period since October, 1960, under nine headings. See, particularly, J. I. Doi, "Organization and Administration, Finance and Facilities", pp. 347-61, and C. R. De Burlo, "Government and Education", pp. 361-70.

769 D. G. BROWN, *The Market for College Teachers—An Economic Analysis of Career Patterns Among Southeastern Social Scientists*. Chapel Hill, N. Carol.: University of North Carolina Press, 1965. Pp. 301.

Based on interviews with 150 economists, sociologists, and historians at the eighteen largest colleges and universities in the South-east of the United States, this book describes and analyses the imperfections that characterise the market for academic social scientists.

770 The International Study of University Admissions, *Access to Higher Education, II: National Studies*. Paris: UNESCO-IAU, 1965. Pp. 648.

This volume complements 750 and is a striking example of the growing interest in comparative education. It includes twelve country-studies: (1) "Brazil" by an institution known as CAPES, pp. 15-56; (2) "Chile" by E. Orellana and E. Grassau, pp. 59-86; (3) "France" by M. Debeauvais, *et al.*, pp. 89-169; (4) "India" by K. G. Saiyidain and H. C. Gupta, pp. 173-237; (5) "Japan" by D. Hidaka, pp. 241-80; (6) "New Zealand" by G. W. Parkyn, pp. 283-333; (7) "Senegal" by F. Bowles, pp. 337-47; (8) "Republic of South Africa", by R. G. MacMillan, pp. 351-94; (9) "U.S.S.R." by V. A. Kitaitzev, pp. 397-435; (10) "U.A.R." by E.S. M. El Said, pp. 439-88; (1) "U.K." by J. A. Lauwerys, pp. 491-589; and (12) "U.S.A." by E. D. West, pp. 593-648. Each chapter includes a description of current admission policies in relation to secondary education and a thorough review of the socio-economic characteristics of students enrolled in institutions of higher education around 1960. In most cases, a country bibliography is included.

1966

771 LORD ROBBINS, *The University in the Modern World, and Other Papers in Higher Education*. London: Macmillan, 1966. Pp. 157.

Eight papers on higher education in Great Britain, including two speeches to the House of Lords complaining of the government's failure to adopt some of the key recommendations of the Robbins Report, and a significant address delivered at Harvard University in 1964, elaborating on the arguments of the Report concerning long-term manpower forecasting and student loans.

772 A. M. CARTTER, "The Supply of and Demand for College Teachers", *JHR*, Summer, 1966, pp. 22-39.

A review of recent American forecasts and a new projection, indicating the likelihood of a buyers' market in the early 1970's.

773 G. FLEUG, *Financial Aspects of University Education in the Republic of Ireland*.
     Human Resources Development, Fellows' Reports. Paris: OECD, 1966. Pp. 65.

        A study in the finance of higher education in Ireland carried out in 1964.

774 S. WALD, *Individual Demand for Higher Education in Greece*. Human Resources
     Development, Fellows' Reports. Paris: OECD, 1966. Pp. 93.

        A study undertaken within the MRP in 1964.

775 E. L. WHEELWRIGHT, ed., *Higher Education in Australia*. Melbourne: F. W.
     Cheshire, 1966. Pp. 134.

        A survey of university and technical education in Australia, including a
     chapter on "Supply and Demand" by A. R. Hall, with comments by P. H. Karmel,
     "Problems of University Expansion" by H. Stretton, and "The Social Role of
     Higher Education" by S. Encel, which discusses such topics as the forecasting
     of demand for university places, the finance of higher education and the real
     costs of higher education in Australia.

776 H. GLENNERSTER, *The Graduate School: A Study of Graduate Work at the London
     School of Economics*. Edinburgh: Oliver & Boyd, 1966. Pp. 200.

        A study based on several surveys of the nature of postgraduate instruction
     at the LSE. Chs. 10 and 11 are particularly recommended as models of univer-
     sity cost analysis by type of course.

777 D. F. HENDRY, "Survey of Student Income and Expenditure at Aberdeen University
     1963-64 and 1964-65", *SJPE*, November, 1966, pp. 363-76.

        Based on a 10 per cent random sample of undergraduates. Income and expendi-
     ture were compared in the two years, and the differential spending patterns
     of resident students and of those living at home were analysed.

778 A. J. ROBINSON, "The Bladen Commission and Graduate Education", *CJEPS*,
     November, 1966, pp. 520-25.

        Considers the implications of the Bladen Report on *Financing Higher Educa-
     tion in Canada* (1965) for graduate education, contrasting the policy of expand-
     ing Canadian graduate schools with alternative methods of providing teachers
     for undergraduate expansion.

1967

779 E. W. BRAITHWAITE, "Education, Social Change and the New Zealand Economy",
     NZJE, 2, 1, 1967, pp. 32-62.

        A discussion of the role of universities in New Zealand's economic growth.
     The author applies a Harbison-Myers-type index of human resource development
     and finds that New Zealand ranks just after the United States.

780 J. H. G. OLIVERA, "Die Universität als Produktionseinheit", *WA*, 98, 1, 1967, pp. 50-63.

A broad discussion of universities as production units, including an estimate of the production function of the University of Buenos Aires and a calculation of the income elasticity of demand for university education from data for 72 countries.

781 A. B. MAUDELSTAMM, R. C. BLITZ, "Summer Employment of Students: A Local Study", *IR*, May, 1967, pp. 339-52.

The article reports on a 1963 survey of student summer activity conducted among students at three high schools and three colleges in Nashville, Tennessee. It emerged that age was of great importance, sex and parents' income were moderately important, and race, grade point average, and religion were of virtually no importance in predicting the students' summer incomes.

782 R. CAMPBELL, B. N. SIEGEL, "The Demand for Higher Education in the United States, 1919-64", *AER*, June, 1967, pp. 482-94, reprinted in *ROG*, pp. 78-90.

A path-breaking paper which demonstrates that, for a given population, enrolment demand in the United States has varied positively with income, positively with the consumer price index, and negatively with the costs of education.

783 J. K. FOLGER, "The Balance Between Supply and Demand for College Graduates", *JHR*, Spring, 1967, pp. 143-69; "Comments" by M. A. Trow and A. Rivlin, *ibid.*, pp. 169-75.

The author concludes that the supply of American college graduates is more than likely to be adequate to meet demand in the next decade.

1968

784 J. D. MOONEY, "Attrition Among Ph.D. Candidates: An Analysis of a Cohort of Recent Woodrow Wilson Fellows", *ibid.*, Winter, 1968, pp. 47-62.

A study of the determinants of Ph.D. dropouts in the United States with a discussion of the policy implications for graduate study.

785 E. RUDD, S. HATCH, *Graduate Study and After*. London: Weidenfeld & Nicholson, 1968. Pp. 229.

The results of a survey of all postgraduate students in England, Scotland, and Wales who started their higher degrees in the academic year 1957-58. The main conclusion of the study is that postgraduate education in Britain is now overexpanded and unduly biased towards pure science. Chapter 6 on salaries, pp. 111-44, reaches strong results ("employers in Britain do not put any value on Ph.D") on the basis of earnings 4-6 years after leaving university, even though American evidence (p. 141) suggests that it takes 20 years for Ph.Ds to reap their full rewards. For a summary of the book, see E. Rudd, "The Rate of Economic Growth, Technology and the Ph.D", *MIN*, Spring, 1968, pp. 366-87.

786   R. P. MACK, "Economic Processes in Economic Change", *AER*, May, 1968, pp. 40-54

      The last half of this article contains a useful discussion of the nature of
the demand for higher education and an interpretation of the history of enrolments in American higher education.

787   H. H. JENNEY, "Pricing and Optimum Size in a Nonprofit Institution: The
      University", *ibid*., pp. 270-83.

      A series of caveats on the pricing policies and optimal size of liberal arts
colleges in the United States.

788   T. W. SCHULTZ, "Resources for Higher Education: An Economist's View", *JPE*,
      May/June, 1968, pp. 327-47.

      A penetrating discussion of the planning of higher education, largely with
reference to American higher education.

1969

789   Joint Economic Committee, 91st Congress of the United States, *The Economics
      and Financing of Higher Education in the United States. A Compendium of
      Papers*. Washington, D.C.: U.S. Government Printing Office, 1969. Pp. 683.

      This major collection of 24 papers on US higher education opens with a long
paper by R. E. Bolton, "The Economics and Public Financing of Higher Education
An Overview", pp. 11-104, which reviews basic data, lucidly analyses the arguments for public aid to higher education, and then canvasses the pros and cons
of various loans and scholarship programmes. This is followed by an examination of the case of California by W. Lee Hansen and B. A. Weisbrod, "The
Search for Equity in the Provision and Finance of Higher Education", pp. 107-2
a theoretical argument by N. Singer and P. Feldman, "Criteria for Public
Investment in Higher Education", pp. 124-34; D. Segal, "'Equity' versus 'Efficiency' in Higher Education", pp. 135-44, which presents new measures of the
inequality of educational opportunity in the US; R. H. Berls, "Higher Educa-
cation Opportunity and Achievement in the United States", pp. 145-204, a detailed analysis of *Project Talent* data, and "An Exploration of the Determinants of Effectiveness in Higher Education", pp. 207-60, a fascinating summary
of the literature on the quality of American undergraduate education; H. H.
Jenny, R. G. Wynn, "Short-Run Cost Variations in Institutions of Higher Learning", pp. 261-94, a preliminary empirical analysis of 31 private colleges;
F. K. Levy, "Sources of Economies of Scale in Universities", pp. 295-302, a
theoretical examination of potential sources of economies of scale in universities; R. W. Tyler, "The Changing Structure of American Institutions of
Higher Education", pp. 305-20; K. A. Simon, "The Planning of US Higher Education: Projections of Enrollment, Degrees, Staff, and Expenditures to 1977-78"
pp. 321-56, an example of simplistic trend projections; A. M. Cartter, R. L.
Farrell, "Academic Labour Market Projections and the Draft", pp. 357-74, a
continuation of earlier articles by the senior author; P. Feldman, S. A.
Hoenack, "Private Demand for Higher Education in the United States", pp. 375-
95, an important article which estimates the demand for higher education with
a cross-section sample of State averages, using such independent variables as
tuition rates, earnings, test scores and education of parents: W. G. Bowen,
"Economic Pressures on the Major Private Universities", pp. 399-439, a new

version with later data of the author's Carnegie Commission pamphlet (see 518);
H. H. Jenny, G. R. Wynn, "Expenditure Expectations for Private Colleges",
pp. 440-64; S. E. Harris, "Financing Higher Education: An Overview", pp. 467-
506; J. H. Stauss, "Endowment as a Source of Increased Revenue", pp. 507-29;
S. J. Mushkin, "A Note on State and Local Financing of Higher Education",
pp. 530-40; A. M. Rivlin, J. H. Weiss, "Social Goals and Federal Support of
Higher Education—the Implications of Various Strategies", pp. 543-55;
A. Danière, "The Benefit and Costs of Alternative Federal Programs of Financial Aid to College Students", pp. 556-98, an important effort to evaluate
loans programmes; C. Kerr, "Federal Aid to Higher Education Through 1976",
pp. 599-617; H. R. Bowen, "Tuitions and Student Loans in the Finance of Higher
Education", pp. 618-31; M. Clurman, "Does Higher Education Need More Money?",
pp. 632-51; J. R. Zacharias, "Educational Opportunity Through Student Loans:
An Approach to Higher Education Financing", pp. 652-64; and R. A. Freeman,
"Federal Assistance to Higher Education Through Income Tax Credits", pp.665-83.

790 H. GALPER, R. M. DUNN, Jr., "A Short-Run Demand Function for Higher Education
     in the United States", *JPE*, September/October, 1969, pp. 765-77.

     The authors estimate a demand function for American higher education, using
     multiple regression analysis with distributed lags, with high school enrol-
     ments, family income and the size of the armed forces as the only independent
     variables. Surprisingly enough, they obtain an excellent fit on 1925-65 data.

791 J. FIELDEN, *Analytical Planning and Improved Resource Allocation in British
     Universities. A Critical Evaluation of American PPBS and its Potential in
     Great Britain.* London: University of London, 1969. Pp. 69.

     A level-headed evaluation of the role of PPBS in some American universities
     and a sound discussion of how output budgeting might be gradually introduced
     in British universities. Includes a number of specimen reports from American
     universities and an excellent bibliography.

1970

792 J. M. BUCHANAN, N. E. DEVLETOGLOU, *Academia in Anarchy. An Economic Diagnosis.*
     New York: Basic Books, Inc., 1970. Pp. 187.

     This provocative book applies some elementary notions of economic analysis
     to the problem of student unrest in an American context.

793 Department of Education and Science, *Student Numbers in Higher Education in
     England and Wales. A Projection, Wtih Some Discussion of Its Cost Implica-
     tions.* Education Planning Paper No. 2. London: HMSO, 1970. Pp. 50.

     Robbins-type projections for 1971, 1976 and 1981, together with an attempt
     to cost these projections at the three bench-mark years. See the editorial
     in *HIR*, Autumn, 1970, pp. 3-8, for a scathing critique of this study.

794 G. WEATHERSBY, M. C. WEINSTEIN, *A Structural Comparison of Analytical Models
     for University Planning,* Ford Foundation Research Program in University Admini-
     stration. Berkeley, California: Office of the Vice-President, University of
     California, Berkeley, 1970. Pp. 45, mimeographed.

The Ford Foundation Research Program in University Administration at Berkeley
has by now produced a whole series of interesting monographs on American
university management problems, of which this is one of the most useful: it
provides a framework for comparing the best known university planning models
currently available and includes an extensive bibliography. (See also 826.)

795 A. J. CULYER, "A Utility-Maximising View of Universities", *SJPE*, November,
     1970, pp. 349-68.

     From an unspecified utility function and an assumption that universities
     act to maximise utility subject to constraints, the author rolls out an almost
     endless series of predictions about how universities will be run, which are
     confirmed by casual observation of universities.

796 R. K. KHANNA, A. BOTTOMLEY, "Costs and Returns on Graduates of the University
     of Bradford", *AER*, Winter, 1970, pp. 56-70.

     The rate-of-return calculations reported in this article are based on the
     amalgamation of several small sample surveys on the earnings side. The cost
     figures for Bradford University however, are carefully done and are based on
     the use of staff diaries to measure staff time inputs.

797 R. K. KELSALL, A. POOLE, A. KUHN, *Six Years After. First Report on a National
     Follow-up Survey of Ten Thousand Graduates of British Universities in 1960.*
     Higher Education Research Unit, Department of Sociological Studies, Sheffield
     University, 1970. Pp. 103.

     The title of this book is self-explanatory. It consists largely of 2 × 2
     tables with an explanatory text, covering such topics as subject of degree,
     class of degree, social class background (confirming the Robbins figure of
     25 per cent working class), employment patterns, earnings in crude bands,
     overseas employment, etcetera. There is a continuous stress on sex differ-
     ences and an entire chapter is devoted to women, containing the first hard
     evidence we have for Britain on the marriage patterns of educated women.

798 B. LAWRENCE, G. WEATHERSBY, V. W. PATTERSON, *Outputs of Higher Education:
     Their Identification, Measurement and Evaluation.* Boulder, Colorado: Western
     Interstate Commission for Higher Education, 1970. Pp. 130.

     A series of brief, largely but not exclusively, philosophical papers on the
     problem of measurement of the outputs of higher education by F. E. Balderston,
     J. Vaizey, C. W. Churchman, A. C. Enthoven, A. W. Astin, and others. The
     collection includes a selective bibliography.

1971

799 W. I. GARMS, "A Benefit-Cost Analysis of the Upward Bound Program", *JHR*,
     Spring, 1971, pp. 206-20; "Comment" by P. Christoffel, M. B. Celio, *ibid.*,
     Winter, 1973, pp. 110-114; "Reply" by Garms, *ibid.*, pp. 115-18.

     The UB programme is designed to find able high school students who are
     unlikely to go to college because of poverty. The author analyzes the private

and social benefits of the programme by making plausible assumptions about resulting lifetime incomes. In this way, he manages to bracket the likely rate of return to the programme.

800   C. R. BARBER, *The First Years After Graduation From Colleges of Technology and Polytechnics. Report of an Investigation of the Careers of Both College Graduates and HND Holders.* Oxford: Oxford Polytechnic Social Science Research Unit, Occasional Paper III, 1971. Pp. 22.

   Despite its small sample, its modest response rate and the limited focus on recent graduates, this is the first piece of evidence to show that the products of the non-university sector of British higher education tend to earn no less than university graduates.

801   V. ONUSHKIN, ed., *Planning the Development of Universities - I.* Paris: UNESCO-IIEP, 1971. Pp. 318.

   A disappointing volume, consisting of a perfectly traditional piece by the Soviet editor on "Some Methodological Aspects of Planning the Development of Universities", pp. 13-28, a summary report of what was apparently a not very exciting discussion, pp. 29-60, a case study of the University of Leningrad by four Soviet authors (interesting if one will only read between the lines), and a case study of the University of Sussex by three British authors.

802   R. KLINOV-MALUL, "Enrolments in Higher Education as Related to Earnings", *BJIR*, March, 1971, pp. 82-91.

   An attempt to estimate the elasticity of enrolments in British universities by fields of study to prospective incomes in these fields (as indicated by data from the Cornmarket Careers Surveys). The attempt failed and the author's discussion of the reasons for the failure is worth serious study.

803   G. BROSAN, C. CARTER, R. LAYARD, P. VENABLES, G. WILLIAMS, *Patterns and Policies in Higher Education.* London: Penguin Education Special, Penguin Books, 1971. Pp. 186.

   This book of essays includes a projection of higher education enrolments up to 1980, as well as an interesting essay on "Meeting the Cost Restraint", by R. Layard and G. Williams. In addition, there are essays by G. Brosan, C. Carter and P. Venables on the Binary Policy and on the relationship between universities and polytechnics in the 1970's.

804   L. S. MILLER, *Demand for Higher Education in the United States,* Stony Brook Working Papers No. 34. Stony Brook, New York: Economic Research Bureau, State University of New York, 1971. Pp. 124.

   The first to estimate demand functions which include measures of student's scholastic aptitudes. Reviews previous studies and proceeds to combine sample observations from two states (Mass. and Calif.). The results show significant differences between low and high achievers.

805   P. LEWIS, "Finance and the Fate of the Polytechnics", *HIR*, Summer, 1971, pp. 23-34.

Probably the first coherent account of the precise methods of financing the non-university sector of British higher education. See also P. Lewis, R. Allemano, "Fact and Fiction About the Pool", *ibid.*, Spring, 1972, pp. 202-32.

806   J. BIBBY, "University Expansion and the Academic Labour Market", *HER*, Autumn, 1971, pp. 23-43.

An interesting attempt to show that British academic salary differentials do reflect market pressures despite uniform scales throughout British universities.

807   F. A. SLOAN, "The Demand for Higher Education: The Case of Medical School Applicants, *JHR*, Fall, 1971, pp. 466-89.

This must be the first successful attempt to estimate a demand function for a particular type of professional training. The author shows that the demand for medical education in the United States is negatively related to tuition fees, positively related to higher expected incomes in medicine, negatively related to higher expected incomes in competing professions, and positively related to the supply of medical education.

1972

808   T. BURGESS, ed., *Planning for Higher Education*. London: Cornmarket Press, 1972. Pp. 185.

This book consists of 16 articles on British higher education which appeared in past issues of *HIR*, together with an introduction by the editor of the journal in his characteristically pungent manner. Some of the 16 articles are listed elsewhere in this bibliography: Ahamad (1105), Maglen and Layard (268) and Hinchliffe (301).

809   P. TAUBMAN, T. WALES, *Mental Ability and Higher Educational Attainment in the 20th Century*. New Jersey: McGraw-Hill for Carnegie Commission on Higher Education and NBER, 1972. Pp. 47.

An analysis of the "pool of ability" for US college education since 1900: a fuller version of 333.

810   G. GARB, "The Economics of a University System Without Degrees", *WEJ*, March, 1972, pp. 57-64.

The author considers the economic effects of abolishing the certification function of universities and decides, after some discussion, that the effect would be beneficial.

811   D. METCALF, "Pay in University Teaching and Similar Occupations", *AE*, 4, 1972, pp. 145-57.

A comparison of the present value of lifetime earnings in a number of occupations in Britain which are competitive with university teaching. The author concludes that, on balance, what differences there are are compensating and not real differences.

812   J. A. BOTTOMLEY, and OTHERS, *Costs and Potential Economies. Studies in Insti-*
      tutional Management in Higher Education. University of Bradford. Paris:
      OECD, Centre for Educational Research and Innovation, 1972. Pp. 431.

      This is a study of average costs per student and of incremental costs at
      one British university, distinguishing incremental costs arising from the
      expansion of enrolments, from changing the structure of courses, from increas-
      ing the teaching load of staff, and from intensive utilisation of buildings.
      The authors adduce evidence of excess capacity in almost all the relevant
      dimensions. For a summary of the book, see J. Dunworth, A. Bottomley,
      "Economy in Academe", *HER*, Summer, 1973, pp. 25-34.

813   Lord Robbins, "Reflections on Eight Years of Expansion in Higher Education",
      HE, May, 1972, pp. 229-34.

      A brief comment by the Chairman of the Robbins Report, chiefly notable for
      the author's conversion to the idea of a student loan scheme.

814   G. B. WEATHERSBY, F. E. BALDERSTON, "PPBS in Higher Education Planning and
      Management: Part I An Overview", *HE*, May, 1972, pp. 191-206.

      A useful bird's eye of the spread of PPBS through American higher education.

815   T. W. SCHULTZ, ed., *Investment in Education: The Equity-Efficiency Quandary*,
      Workshop at the University of Chicago 1971, *JPE*, Pt. II, May/June, 1972.
      Pp. 292.

      An important collection of eleven papers, some with multiple comments, on
      US higher education, mixing theoretical, empirical and policy-oriented essays.
      It begins with a wide-ranging essay by the editor, "Optimal Investment in
      College Instruction: Equity and Efficiency", pp. 2-30, to which A. O. Krueger
      adds comments. There follows an empirical paper by B. R. Chiswick and
      J. Mincer, "Time-Series Changes in Personal Income Inequality in the United
      States from 1939, with Projections to 1985", pp. 34-66, which received sharp
      critical comments by M. J. Bowman and T. Johnson, and a subsequent "Comment"
      by A. S. Schwartz and D. O. Parsons *ibid.*, September/October, 1974,
      pp. 1027-32, with a "Reply" by Chiswick and Mincer; Z. Griliches and W. H.
      Mason, "Education, Income and Ability", pp. 74-103, employ new evidence to
      argue that ability is not an important determinant of earnings; P. Taubman
      doubts that they have achieved their objective. J. C. Hause, "Earnings Pro-
      file: Ability and Schooling", pp. 108-38, extends his earlier work along
      lines directly contradictory to Griliches and Mason. The commentary by
      B. A. Weisbrod makes a stab at settling the disagreement.
      At this point we get two papers on the finance of higher education:
      R. W. Hartman, "Equity Implications of State Tuition Policy and Student Loans",
      pp. 142-71, with comments by D. M. Windham and L. Tweeten, and M. Nerlove.
      "On Tuition and the Costs of Higher Education: Prolegomena to a Conceptual
      Framework", pp. 178-218. We return to earnings functions with a paper by
      S. Bowles, "Schooling and Inequality from Generation to Generation",
      pp. 210-51, which produces a panoply of arguments and some evidence to suggest
      that social class has been underestimated in past studies of the determinants
      of earnings; G. S. Becker pours cold water on Bowles' empirical results. A
      series of papers on finance bring the volume to a close: J. A. Pechman,
      "Note on the Intergenerational Transfer of Public Higher-Education Benefits",
      pp. 256-59; W. Lee Hansen, "Equity and the Finance of Higher Education",
      pp. 260-73, with comments by O. H. Brownlee and F. Welch; H. G. Johnson,
      "The Alternatives Before Us", pp. 280-89; and E. F. Denison, "Some Reflections",
      pp. 290-92.

816   D. METCALF, J. BIBBY, "Salaries of Recruits to University Teaching in Britain",
      HE, August, 1972, pp. 287-98.

      The application of multiple regression analysis and multiple classification
      analysis yielded few if any surprising results: rather like using a hammer
      to crack a small nut (see also 841).

817   J. CUTT, *Program Budgeting and Higher Education*. Department of Accounting and
      Public Finance, Monograph No. 1. Canberra: Australian National University,
      1972. Pp. 144.

      An excellent review of the largely American literature, dealing in fact with
      any and all attempts at university model building rather than with PPB as
      such.

818   S. OSTREY, *Canadian Higher Education in the Seventies*. Ottawa: Economic
      Council of Canada, 1972. Pp. 310.

      A splendid collection of papers presented at a 1971 Conference sponsored
      by the Economic Council. H. L. Handa and M. L. Skolnik lead off with a valu-
      able survey of "Empirical Analysis of the Demand for Education in Canada",
      pp. 5-44, which includes American evidence as well. There follows a paper by
      D. Sewell, "Educational Planning Models and the Relationship Between Education
      and Occupation", pp. 45-74, which brings together Canadian empirical evidence
      to reject both manpower forecasting and rate-of-return analysis. A standard
      forecast by M. von Zur-Muehlen predicts a rising surplus of Canadian Ph.D's
      in the 1970s, "The Ph.D. Dilemma in Canada: A Case Study", pp. 75-132.
      D. A. Dodge, "Occupational Wage Differentials, Occupational Licensing, and
      Returns to Investment in Education: An Exploratory Analysis", pp. 133-76,
      argues that the usual estimates of rates of return in Canada would be reduced
      by about 30 per cent if they were standardised for occupation. W. Hettich,
      "Consumption Benefits of Education", pp. 177-98, is a brave attempt to quantify
      the consumption benefits of education, which turn out to raise the usual esti-
      mates of rates of return by about 20 per cent. D. A. A. Stager surveys costs
      and expenditures in Canadian education in "Allocation of Resources in Canadian
      Education", pp. 199-238. R. M. Stamp examines the long, steady push towards
      a vocational orientation in Canadian education: "Vocational Objectives in
      Canadian Education: An Historical Overview", pp. 239-64. D. A. A. Stager's
      second paper on the "Economics of Continuing Education in the Universities",
      pp. 265-90, makes a case for part-time recurrent education. Lastly, M. Oliver
      discusses the issues raised by "Financing Higher Education in Quebec: Some
      Questions", pp. 291-302.

819   A. DANIÈRE, "The Economics of Higher Education", *AAAPS*, November, 1972,
      American Higher Education, pp. 58-70.

      A brief review of trends in the literature, away from rate-of-return analysis
      to questions of the distribution of education among different social groups
      and from naive productivity theories of the effects of education to screen-
      ing hypotheses and the like.

820   A. M. CARTTER, "Faculty Needs and Resources in American Higher Education",
      ibid., pp. 71-87.

      A multi-valued forecast of excess supply in American academic labour
      markets by 1975 or thereabouts.

1973

821 D. METCALF, "Some Aspects of University Teachers' Labour Market in the UK",
     Essays in Modern Economics, eds. M. Parkin, A. R. Nobay. London: Longman,
     1973, pp. 192-211.

     The author first discusses some general features of the British academic
     labour market, such as uniform salary scales, uniform staffing ratios and
     tenure arrangements, and then moves on to develop and illustrate a simple
     model of faculty salary differentials. See "Discussion" by B. A. Corry,
     pp. 212-14 (see also 841).

822 G. WILLIAMS, "University Recruitment 1968/9 and 1970/1", *UQ*, Spring, 1973,
     pp. 172-99.

     A study of the characteristics of recruits to British university posts
     in 1970/71, showing that the emerging surplus of graduates has attracted more
     applicants per vacancy than in 1968/69 but that universities have failed to
     take advantage of this fact by paying less for age and qualifications.

823 C. F. CARTER, "Costs and Benefits of Mass Higher Education", *HE*, May, 1973,
     pp. 206-13.

     A counter-blast at rate-of-return analysis partly on grounds of the inherent
     imperfections of labour markets but principally because the "vocational pur-
     poses of higher education are incidental and secondary"; it is not clear
     whether the eloquent statement of purposes in this paper is descriptive or
     prescriptive.

824 D. A. KATZ, "Faculty Salaries, Promotions, and Productivity at a Large Univer-
     sity", *AER*, June, 1973, pp. 469-77.

     An interesting attempt to quantify the principal determinants of faculty
     salaries and promotions, applied by way of illustration to a single American
     university, demonstrating that quality of teaching plays little role in the
     reward system.

825 A. FREIDEN, R. J. STAAF, "Scholastic Choice: An Economic Model of Student
     Behavior", *JHR*, Summer, 1973, pp. 396-404.

     Applying standard demand theory to the student's choice of subject in college,
     the authors manage to successfully predict the pattern of subject changes in
     a typical American college.

826 Ford Foundation Program for Research in University Administration, *Final
     Report, October 1973*. Berkeley: University of California, 1973. Pp. 67.

     This is a final summary of the activities of the programme over the five-
     year period 1968-73. Copies of the 42 monographs produced by the programme
     will henceforth be available from the Center for Research in Management
     Science, 26 Barrows Hall, University of California, Berkeley, California,
     94720.

827   G. PSACHAROPOULOS, "A Note on the Demand for Enrollment in Higher Education",
      ECON, 121, 5, 1973, pp. 521-25.

      A new estimate of the demand function for higher education in Hawaii and a
      critique of the Campbell-Siegel estimate for the USA (see 782).

828   L. C. SOLMON, P. J. TAUBMAN, *Does College Matter? Some Evidence on the Impacts
      of Higher Education*. New York: Academic Press, 1973. Pp. 415.

      This excellent collection of American papers starts off with an incisive
      introduction by Taubman, contrasting the economist's and sociologist's approach
      to the benefits of higher education, followed by: (1) L. C. Solmon, "School-
      ing and Subsequent Success. The Influence of Ability, Background, and Formal
      Education", pp. 13-34; (2) A. Ellison, B. Simon, "Does College Make a Person
      Healthy and Wise? A Social-Psychiatric Overview of Research in Higher Educa-
      tion", pp. 35-64; (3) D. Wolfle, "To What Extent Do Monetary Returns to Edu-
      cation Vary With Family Background, Mental Ability, and School Quality?",
      pp. 65-74; (4) L. C. Solmon, "The Definition and Impact of College Quality",
      pp. 77-101, with discussions by R. M. Hauser and A. W. Astin; (5) A. W. Astin,
      "Measurement and Determinants of the Outputs for Higher Education", pp. 107-28,
      an outstanding contribution to a well-worn topic; (6) R. M. Hauser, "Socio-
      economic Background and Differential Returns to Education", pp. 129-46;
      (7) C. Kaysen, "New Directions for Research", pp. 147-50; (8) B. R. Chiswick,
      "Schooling, Screening, and Income", pp. 151-58, an examination of the screen-
      ing hypothesis; and (9) E. B. Page, "Effects of Higher Education. Outcomes,
      Values, or Benefits", pp. 159-73. After several papers on non-economic issues,
      we come back to public expenditures on higher education with (1) R. W. Hartman,
      "The Rationale for Federal Support for Higher Education", pp. 271-92; (2)
      D. S. Mundel, "Whose Education Should Society Support?", pp. 293-316;
      (3) R. B. Freeman, "On Mythical Effects of Public Subsidization of Higher
      Education. Social Benefits and Regressive Income Redistribution", pp. 321-28;
      and (4) W. Lee Hansen, "On External Benefits and Who Should Foot the Bill",
      pp. 329-34. Lastly, there are a series of general papers by (1) F. Machlup,
      "Perspectives on the Benefits of Postsecondary Education", pp. 353-64;
      (2) A. Danière, "Economics of Higher Education. The Changing Scene", pp. 365-
      80, a longer version of 819; (3) M. J. Bowman, "Selective Remarks and Some
      Dicta", pp. 381-92; (4) C. A. Anderson, "Interdisciplinary Research on Out-
      comes of Higher Education", pp. 393-402; and (5) L. C. Solmon, "Perquisites
      for Further Research on the Effects of Higher Education", pp. 403-9.

829   K. LEGG, "Economic Student Group Populations in Universities", *HE*, November,
      1973, pp. 423-38.

      A study of economies of scale in British undergraduate and post-graduate
      courses.

830   H. GREENAWAY, G. WILLIAMS, eds., *Patterns of Change in Graduate Employment*.
      London: Society for Research into Higher Education, 1973. Pp. 154.

      Nine papers on the employment prospects of British graduates, including 3
      excellent papers by G. Williams, "First Employment of University Graduates",
      pp. 25-34, "The Economics of the Graduate Labour Market", pp. 41-58, and
      "Graduate Employment in Europe", pp. 141-54, as well as E. G. Whybrew "Trends
      in the Labour Market for Highly Qualified Manpower", pp. 35-40, and G. C. G.
      Wilkinson, J. D. Mace, "Manpower Forecasting and Qualified Engineers",
      pp. 123-40, another version of "Shortage or Surplus of Engineers: A Review
      of Recent UK Evidence", *BJIR*, XI, 1, 1973, pp. 105-23.

1974

831 S. LOFTHOUSE, "Thoughts on 'Publish or Perish'", *HE*, February, 1974, pp. 59-80.

   A thorough review of American and British evidence to test the dependence
of university salaries on publications. The author argues that, despite
appearances, salaries do not ultimately depend critically on publications.

832 A. BOTTOMLEY, J. DUNWORTH, "Rate of Return on University Education with Economies of Scale", *ibid.*, February, 1974, pp. 91-102; "Comment" by D. Verry,
ibid., April, 1974, pp. 231-33, and "Reply" by Dunworth and Bottomley, *ibid.*,
November, 1974, pp. 469-71.

   Cost data for Bradford University and earnings data for British university
graduates in general are combined to calculate rates of return on various
assumptions about space and staff utilisation.

833 A. MORRIS, "Flexibility and the Tenured Academic", *HIR*, Spring, 1974,
pp. 3-25.

   An attempt to spell out a package of reallocation devices for coping with
the prospective reduction in the rate of university expansion in Britain in
the 1970's.

834 W. McMAHON, "Policy Issues in the Economics of Higher Education and Related
Research Opportunities in Britain and the United States", *HE*, April, 1974,
pp. 165-86.

   A peculiar mixture of under-reported data and *ad hoc* comparisons between
the two countries, together with repeated promises of the breakthroughs in
the economics of education that are just around the corner.

835 S. BROVENDER, "On the Economics of a University: Toward the Determination of
Marginal Cost of Teaching Services", *JPE*, May/June, 1974, pp. 657-64.

   Outlines a practical method of determining the marginal costs of teaching
services in a university department and illustrates the method with reference
to the University of Pittsburgh.

836 G. WILLIAMS, "The Events of 1973-74 In a Long Term Planning Perspective",
HEB, 3, 1, Autumn, 1974, pp. 17-51.

   An analysis of the recent deceleration in the growth of British higher education, suggesting that long term trends will soon be re-established.

837 P. ARMITAGE, "Facing Facts and Jumping to Conclusions", *HE*, Autumn, 1974,
pp. 3-17.

   Cast doubts on the current belief in the UK that the demand for higher education is declining. In the course of the argument, the author reviews the
basis of the standard projections of birth rates and leaving rates at age 16.

838 A. M. YOUNG, "Labor Market Experience of Recent College Graduates", *MLR*,
October, 1974, pp. 33-40.

A Special Labor Force Report on 800,000 1972 college graduates in the USA,
which examines the methods by which graduates looked for jobs, the relationship of their jobs to their major fields of study, their earnings, and their
own assessment of the career potential of their jobs.

839 J. PRATT, T. BURGESS, *Polytechnics: A Report*. London: Pitman Publishing,
1974. Pp. 250.

This is an interesting, although unconvincing, indictment of the British
for failing to plan the development of the polytechnics. Ch. 4 by P. Lewis
and M. Locke deals specifically with finance and salaries but the whole book
may be recommended as an example of a case study in educational planning.

840 J. EMBLING, *A Fresh Look at Higher Education*. *European Implications of the
Carnegie Commission Reports*. Amsterdam: Elseviers Scientific Publishing
Co., 1974. Pp. 263.

This is an ideal source for those who want to become acquainted with the
Carnegie Reports and it also provides a splendidly written review of institutional changes in European educational systems, emphasizing the UK. Some
chapters, such as 1, 6, 7, and 8 are directly relevant to our theme, examining
as they do the role of higher education, the use of resources, graduate employment and recurrent education.

841 G. WILLIAMS, T. BLACKSTONE, D. METCALF, *The Academic Market Place*. *Economic
and Social Aspects of a Profession*. Amsterdam: Elseviers Scientific Publishing Co., 1974. Pp. 566.

This is the first book of any kind to examine the labour market for British
university academics and it is certainly the first book to do so from a multi-
disciplinary point of view. About half of the chapters deal with the economic
aspects and the rest examine the sociological aspects. It is based on several
surveys, including a 10 per cent sample of university teachers, covering their
socio-economic characteristics as well as their values and attitudes. From our
point of view, chs. 10-14 are of central concern, including as they do an
earnings function, a study of alternative salaries and an analysis of wage
dispersion, incorporating previously published papers 811, 816, 822.

842 K. G. LUMSDEN, ed., *Efficiency in Universities: The La Paz Papers*. Amsterdam:
Elseviers Scientific Publishing Co., 1974. Pp. 278.

A collection of eleven papers of extremely high quality. We begin with a
general "Survey of the Issues" by R. Attiyeh, pp. 3-18. There follows:
(1) H. G. Johnson, "The University and the Social Welfare: A Taxonomic
Exercise", pp. 21-49, an anlysis of the objectives of the major interest groups
involved in the management of universities; (2) K. J. Arrow, "Higher Education
as a Filter", pp. 51-74, reprinted from 370; (3) D. V. T. Bear, "The University as a Multi-Production Firm", pp. 77-111; (4) G. C. Archibald, "On the
Measurement of Inputs and Outputs in Higher Education", pp. 113-30;
(5) R. Attijeh, K. G. Lumsden, "Educational Production and Human Capital Formation", pp. 131-45; (6) R. Layard, "The Cost-Effectiveness of the New Media in
Higher Education", pp. 149-73, reprinted from 644; (7) K. G. Lumsden, "The
Information Content of Student Evaluations of Faculty and Courses", pp. 175-
204, a fascinating analysis of questionnaire responses in Stanford's Graduate

School of Business; (8) M. W. Reder, "A Suggestion for Increasing the Efficiency of Universities", pp. 207-15, a proposal for a two-tiers system of
fees; (9) P. H. Cootner, "Economic Organization and Inefficiency in the Modern
University", pp. 217-39; and (10) W. C. Brainard, "Private and Social Risk
and Return to Education", pp. 241-65.

843 M. S. GORDON, ed., *Higher Education and the Labor Market*, Carnegie Commission
on Higher Education. New York: McGraw-Hill, 1974. Pp. 630.

A superb volume of 14 essays with an introduction and conclusion by the
editor. They are in order: (1) M. S. Gordon, "The Changing Labor Market for
College Graduates", pp. 27-82; (2) R. Freeman, "The Implications of the Changing Labor Market for Members of Minority Groups", pp. 83-110; (3) D. L. Adkins,
"The American Educated Labor Force: An Empirical Look at Theories of its
Formation and Composition", pp. 111-46, an essay which contrasts the neoclassical "technogenic" with the "sociogenic" model of human capital formation;
(4) D. E. Kaun, "The College Dropout and Occupational Choice", pp. 147-94;
(5) V. L. Rawlins, L. Ulman, "The Utilization of College-Trained Manpower in
the United States", pp. 195-236, one of the best formulations in the literature of the theory of "credentialism"; (6) S. Haber, "The Professions and
Higher Education in America: A Historical View", pp. 237-80; (7) A. M. Cartter,
"The Academic Labor Market", pp. 281-308; (8) J. W. Garbino, "Creeping Unionism
and the Faculty Labor Market", pp. 309-32; (9) R. S. Eckaus, A. E. Safty,
V. D. Norman, "An Appraisal of the Calculations of Rates of Return to Higher
Education", pp. 333-72; (10) L. C. Thurow, "Measuring the Economic Benefits
of Education", pp. 373-418, an exposition of the so-called "job competition
model"; (11) M. W. Reder, "Elitism and Opportunity in US Higher Education",
pp. 419-26; (12) R. W. Hartman, "Financing the Opportunity to Enter the
'Educated Labor Market'", pp. 427-52; (13) W. Fogel, D. J. B. Mitchell,
"Higher Education Decision Making and the Labor Market", pp. 453-502, with
new evidence on students' knowledge of occupational earnings profiles; and
(14) C. M. Stevens, "Medical Schools and the Market for Physicians' Services",
pp. 503-54.

1975

844 H. L. HANDA, M. L. SKOLNIK, "Unemployment, Expected Returns, and the Demand
for University Education in Ontario: Some Empirical Results", *HE*, February,
1975, pp. 27-44.

An empirical analysis of the private demand for tertiary education in
Ontario, showing that the effect of youth unemployment on enrolments is very
weak, but that the effect of expected earnings on enrolment demand is positive
and strong. The impact of these findings is somewhat weakened by the inadequacies of the data that was used.

845 M. L. LEE, D. W. STEVENS, R. L. WALLACE, "A Conspicuous Production Theory of
Resource Allocation in Higher Education, *ibid.*, pp. 77-86.

A utility-maximising model of universities, different in important respect
from Culyer's earlier effort (see 795).

846 P. R. G. LAYARD, D. W. VERRY, "Cost Functions for University Teaching and
Research", *EJ*, March, 1975, pp. 55-74.

An econometric analysis of the recurrent costs in Britain of undergraduate
and postgraduate teaching and research cross-classified by subjects.

847 S. CHRISTENSEN, J. MELDER, B. A. WEISBROD, "Factors Affecting College Attendance", *JHR*, Spring, 1975, pp. 174-88.

A test of a sophisticated consumption-model which finds that both price and
income elasticities of demand for higher education in the USA are extremely
low.

848 A. MORRIS, "Separate Funding of University Teaching and Research", *HIR*, Spring,
1975, pp. 42-58.

A useful discussion of alternative ways of financing British universities,
with particular reference to the financing of research.

849 S. DRESCH, "Demography, Technology, and Higher Education: Toward a Formal
Model of Educational Adaptation", *JPE*, June, 1975, pp. 535-70.

An ambitious attempt to integrate a demographic model of enrolments with
an explicit production-function model of the demand side. The model is applied
to American higher education and concludes with a projection of a massive decline in college enrolments in the next two or three decades.

850 J. E. DUNWORTH, W. R. COOK, *Incentives to the Efficient Use of Resources in
Universities*. Bradford: University of Bradford School of Social Sciences,
1975. Pp. 198.

A study of current methods of financing British universities with a detailed
proposal for basing future finance on "academic units" with complete responsibility for allocating funds among all alternative uses.

851 W. E. BECKER, Jr., "The University Professor as a Utility Maximizer and Producer of Learning, Research and Income", *JHR*, Winter, 1975, pp. 107-15.

Using an explicit professorial decision-making model, the author explores
alternative ways of raising teaching quality at major American universities.

852 V. STOIKOV, *The Economics of Recurrent Education and Training*. Geneva: ILO,
1975. Pp. 115.

An extension of the earlier article (356) into a full-fledged economic analysis of lifelong, recurrent education, appraised on equity as well as efficiency
grounds. Ch. 2 analyses the efficiency case in cost-benefit terms. Ch. 3
discusses the effects of education on income distribution. Ch. 4, a pivotal
chapter in the book, reviews the evidence on deterioration and obsolescence
of human capital. Ch. 5 provides examples of recurrent education. Ch. 6
discusses financial instruments for achieving recurrent education, and ch. 7
applies the argument to poor countries.

4. EDUCATIONAL PLANNING

Educational planning at the primary and secondary levels turns essentially on accurate forecasts of expected enrolments, grounded in turn on accurate demographic forecasts. Beyond the compulsory school-leaving age, however, the problem becomes more complicated: the demand for further and higher education varies with every change in the character of educational provision below and above the legal school leaving age, as well as with changes in the social and economic climate. Furthermore, there is no reason why the educational authorities should adapt themselves passively to the private demand for extra education; it is within their power to manipulate that demand to satisfy a wide range of social objectives.

On the one hand, educational planning seems easy since it deals with a well-defined "industry" using fairly simple "production" techniques. On the other hand, the "period of production" of education is so long that all forecasts must look at least 10 years ahead, which makes educational planning particularly difficult. Furthermore, there is little consensus in most countries on the objectives of education, with the result that some educational plans are drawn up to satisfy the manpower needs of a growing economy, others to satisfy the rising consumer demand for additional education, still others to guarantee equality of educational opportunity at whatever cost, and perhaps the greatest number of all to fulfil more than one goal with no attention to consistency.

The International Bureau of Education[864], the Canadian Dominion Bureau of Statistics[869], and Fletcher[1682] give a review of educational planning activity around the world in the early 1960's. For examples of actual planning from individual countries, see Crowther[855], the National Union of Teachers[863], and Robbins[751], Vaizey and Knight[874], Plowden[885], Department of Education and Science[909], and Hughes and others[911] on the United Kingdom; Edding and Albers[856], and Widmaier[886] on Germany; Svennilson, Elvin, and Edding[859] on Western Europe; OECD[870], Gass[886], Parnes[886], and Hollister[886] on the Mediterranean countries; and OECD[882,890,894], [908,915,1081] on Sweden, The Netherlands, Austria, Germany and the UK.

Surveys of educational planning in various developed countries are provided by D'Hoogh[432], the International Association of Universities[857], Poignant[860,867], Moberg[860], Haas[867], Artigas[867], the Canadian Dominion Bureau[869], Fletcher[1682], Skorov[1688], Edding[886], and Corbett[887]. There are further references in UNESCO[1904] and Wheeler[1906]. See also section B4 on "Educational Planning" below.

General theoretical discussions are found in Parnes[862,867], Lyons[867], Edding[867], UNESCO[1747], Anderson and Bowman[871,886], Miner[886], Coombs[886], Blaug[891], Hegelheimer[899], Debeauvais[902], Hüfner[906], Ambruster and Bodenhöfer[913], von Weizzäcker[916], and Layard[918]. OECD[888], Correa[904] provide statistical handbooks. IIEP[883] discusses the problems of training the next generation of educational planners.

1953   (a) GENERAL TREATMENTS

853 E. GINZBERG, D. W. BRAY, *The Uneducated*. New York: Columbia University Press,
     1953. Pp. 246.

     This valuable study moves from a review of educational developments in
     America to a review of the facts about illiteracy discovered during World War
     II. The second section of the book presents a unique body of case materials
     designed to reveal the ability of the poorly educated to perform effectively
     in a military organisation once they have acquired literacy. Ch. 9 deals with
     the experience of southern industry in employing the uneducated. Ch. 10
     treats the problems of uneducated migrants. The book concludes with a plea
     for federal assistance to the poorer states to help them improve their
     educational systems.

1959

854 E. E. MUNTZ, "Education and Scarcity in the Top Level Labour Force in the
     United States", *JES*, October, 1959, pp. 105-23.

     One economist's recommendations for repairing the present educational im-
     balance in the USA.

855 Ministry of Education, *15 to 18. A Report of the Central Advisory Council
     for Education, under the Chairmanship of G. Crowther*. London: HMSO, 1959,
     I, II. Pp. 519, 240.

     A detailed discussion of the economic case for raising the school-leaving
     age from 15 to 16 (chs. 5, 12), with a proposal to provide compulsory part-
     time education for all young persons of 16 and 17 who are not in full-time
     education. Vol. II includes the results of a social survey on the socio-econo-
     mic aspects of secondary education in Great Britain.

1960

856 F. EDDING, W. ALBERS, *Die Schulausgaben 1960/1970. Versuch einer Vorausschät-
     zung des Bedarfs der allgemeinbildenden und der berufsbildenden Schulen und
     der Möglichkeiten seiner Finanzierung*. Frankfurt: Mund, 1960. Pp. 159.

     Forecasts of probable expansion of primary and secondary education in West
     Germany over the next 10 years and a review of possible sources of extra
     finance.

1961

857 International Association of Universities, *Some Economic Aspects of Educational
     Development in Europe*. Paris: International Universities Bureau, 1961.
     Pp. 144.

     The proceedings of a conference held at Bellagio, Italy in 1960, containing
     a set of "Background Notes" by J. Vaizey, two brief general articles by
     P. H. Coombs and M. Debeauvais, as well as general articles on educational
     planning in Yugoslavia, Germany, and France.

858 J. VAIZEY, M. DEBEAUVAIS, "Economic Aspects of Educational Development",
     EES, pp. 37-49.

     The consensus of opinion of the economists attending the 1960 seminar of
     the International Association of Universities about the contribution that
     educational planning can make to economic growth.

1962

859 I. SVENNILSON, H. L. ELVIN, F. EDDING, *Policy Conference on Economic Growth
     and Investment in Education, II*. Paris: OECD, 1962. Pp. 126. Excerpts
     reprinted in *UNESCO-REED*, pp. 841-58.

     Chs. 1 and 2 provide a general discussion of issues in educational planning.
     Ch. 3 serves as a useful comparison of educational attainments in various OECD
     countries, together with targets for 1970.

860 OECD, *Policy Conference on Economic Growth and Investment in Education, IV*.
     Paris: OECD, 1962. Pp. 58.

     Three papers on educational planning in Europe: R. Poignant on "France",
     S. Moberg on "Sweden", and M. Elazar on "Yugoslavia", with valuable data on
     the 3 countries.

861 J. R. GASS, R. F. LYONS, *Policy Conference on Economic Growth and Investment
     in Education, V*, "International Flow of Students". Paris: OECD, 1962.
     Pp. 41.

     A study of the emigration and immigration of students in OECD countries.

862 H. S. PARNES, *Forecasting Educational Needs for Social Economic Development*.
     Paris: OECD, 1962. Pp. 113. Excerpts reprinted in *UNESCO-REED*, pp. 861-63.

     This volume sets forth the rationale underlying the Mediterranean Regional
     Project (comprising Turkey, Yugoslavia, Greece, Italy, Spain, and Portugal)
     and, without describing the specific planning techniques that will be utilised
     by each country, presents a systematic discussion of the various steps in
     educational planning. Ch. 2 covers manpower forecasting; chs. 3 and 4 trans-
     late such forecasts into educational requirements; ch. 5 takes up demand plan-
     ning in education; and ch. 6 touches on the question of costing. (See also
     870.)

863 National Union of Teachers, *Investment for National Survival*. London: NUT,
     1962. Pp. 42.

     A proposal by an independent committee on the expenditures needed for future
     educational development in the UK. An appendix by J. Vaizey and S. Pratt
     presents the statistical basis for the 1980 projection.

864 IBE-UNESCO, *Educational Planning. Research in Comparative Education*—XXV
     International Conference on Public Education. Geneva: IBE-UNESCO, 1962.
     Pp. 193.

This comparative Study of 75 countries, based on an IBE questionnaire, shows that only some 30 countries have provision for organised general planning of education. The first chapter presents a quick review of the results.

1963

865 G. H. BANTOCK, *Education in an Industrial Society*. London: Faber & Faber, 1963. Pp. 238.

A solid but verbose rationalisation of the conservative, elitist view of British education with suggestions for a suitable curriculum tailored to the needs of the "intellectually inferior" majority (the author's phrase). See, in particular, pp. 86-7, protesting against such phraseology as "education as an investment" or even "education as a social service".

866 J. VAIZEY, "Forecasts and Projections", *The Control of Education*. London: Faber & Faber, 1963, pp. 99-142.

A review of forecasts the author made at various times (1953, 1954, 1958, 1959, 1960) of enrolment and educational expenditures in the UK, all of which underestimated the actual figures because of erroneous population and price forecasts. In the light of this fact, the author discusses the value of these types of forecasts.

1964

867 H. S. PARNES, ed., *Planning Education for Economic and Social Development*. Paris: OECD, 1964. Pp. 270. Excerpts reprinted in *P-EED*, *1*, pp. 274-86.

Twenty-one lectures presented in 1962 at an OECD Training Course for Human Resource Strategists. Three broad subjects were covered: education and economic growth; the manpower requirements approach to educational planning; and the formulation and costing of educational targets. Under the first heading, S. G. Kelley speaks on "The Role of Incentives in Human Resource Planning", pp. 27-37; J. Vaizey pours cold water on the rate-of-returns approach to the economic contribution of education, concluding that "education, as such, has historically-speaking probably been more opposed to growth than it has supported it", pp. 39-47; J. W. Saxe comments along similar lines; R. F. Lyons addresses himself to "Criteria and Methods for Assessing an Educational System", pp. 57-65. Under the second heading, H. S. Parnes contributes an excellent defence of the manpower-forecasting approach, followed by a list of the successive steps in ascertaining the required expansion of the educational system, pp. 73-84; M. Debeauvais discusses "Methods of Forecasting Long-Term Manpower Needs", arguing for a broad occupational classification into 6 levels corresponding to their respective educational requirements, pp. 85-96; W. Beckerman differentiates "forecasts" from "projections" and discusses various ways of measuring labour productivity by way of estimating future manpower needs of a given sector of the economy, pp. 97-112; N. Novacco goes over the same grounds in the light of Italian experience, pp. 113-22; S.-O. Döös carefully distinguishes between the industrial, occupational, and educational dimensions of manpower and elaborates on the second of these, pp. 123-37; N. Erder describes the methods that have been used in Turkey to estimate future manpower requirements by occupations, pp. 139-46; H. S. Parnes

comes back to the educational dimension, emphasising that it is impossible
to associate each occupational category uniquely with a different level and
type of required education, pp. 147-57; and, lastly, there is the paper by
Tinbergen and Correa, reprinted from *KYK* (see 1778). Under the third heading
H. L. Elvin comments on the adaptation of an educational system to the cultural
characteristics of a society and then moves on to analyse specific ways of
remedying a teacher shortage, pp. 171-93; Yugoslav, French and Spanish planning experience are discussed in turn by H. Haas, R. Poignant, and J. T. Artigas, pp. 195-231; F. Edding discusses the calculation of the costs of a recommended programme of educational expansion, pp. 233-44; and R. F. Lyons deals
with the practical problem of how to formulate and present an educational
plan, pp. 245-49. The volume closes with a statement of some selected research
proposals by participants in the course, pp. 261-70.

868   M. DEBEAUVAIS, "La traduction des objectifs d'emploi en objectifs d'éducation",
      TM, janvier-mars, 1964, pp. 83-105.

      An exposition of methods of translating employment objectives into educa-
      tional objectives, illustrated by French data.

869   Dominion Bureau of Statistics, Education Division, *Education Planning and the
      Expanding Economy*. Ottawa: Queen's Printer and Controller of Stationery,
      1964. Pp. 72.

      A useful survey of the work on educational planning that is currently being
      carried out in leading countries and in international organisations. Half of
      the volume is devoted to a detailed review of educational planning in Canada.
      Includes a brief bibliography.

870   OECD, The Mediterranean Regional Project, *Yugoslavia; Italy; Greece; Spain;
      Portugal; Turkey*. Paris: OECD, 1964. Pp. 143, 212, 195, 135, 308, 189.

      In 1960, the OECD, in co-operation with 6 Mediterranean countries, instituted
      a programme of studies of the educational requirements for economic growth.
      The programme has now concluded its first phase of operation with the prepara-
      tion of long-range manpower and educational output requirements by 1975 for
      each of the 6 countries. For the initial methodological approach of MRP see
      862. For a description of the methods that were employed and a presentation
      of some of the more general findings, see *The OECD Observer No. 8, February,
      1964*, pp. 1-12.

871   D. ADAMS, ed., *Educational Planning*. Syracuse, N.Y.: Syracuse University
      Press, 1964. Pp. 157.

      This valuable collection of papers starts off with a penetrating critique of
      the manpower approach to educational planning by C. A. Anderson and M. J.
      Bowman: "Theoretical Considerations in Educational Planning", pp. 4-47 (see
      also 886). This is followed by: H. S. Parnes, "Assessing the Educational
      Needs of a Nation", pp. 47-67; K. Eide, "Organization of Educational Planning",
      pp. 67-82; B. Hayward, "The Implemented Educational Plan", pp. 82-103; two
      papers on educational planning in Thailand by W. J. Platt, pp. 103-27; and
      C. S. Brembeck, pp. 127-53.

1965

872 S. E. HARRIS, K. M. DEITCH, A. LEVENSOHN, eds., *Challenge and Change in
     American Education*. Berkeley, Calif.: McCutchan Publishing Corp., 1965.
     Pp. 346.

    This volume is drawn from papers and discussions at a seminar held at
Harvard University Graduate School of Public Administration in 1961-62. Among
the 16 papers, the following deserve special mention: M. Yudelman and A. Curle
on the Karachi, Addis Ababa, and Santiago Plans, pp. 103-12; C. S. Benson on
solutions for the teacher shortage in the United States, pp. 169-74; H. S.
Conrad on differential financial aid to university students by subject of
specialisation, pp. 177-80; O. Eckstein on state and local investment in
educational investment, pp. 205-20. There is an introduction by S. E. Harris,
commenting on all the papers in this volume, pp. 1-37. K. M. Deitch contributes an excellent series of commentaries on the various sessions, summarising
and interpreting the discussions.

873 S. E. HARRIS, A. LEVENSOHN, *Education and Public Policy*. Berkeley, Calif.:
     McCutchan Publishing Corp., 1965. Pp. 347.

    This volume is the third of a series based on seminars given at Harvard.
Among the 16 papers, the following deserve special mention: P. H. Coombs and
D. Riesman on educational planning, pp. 99-113; F. Bowles on college admissions
in different countries, pp. 167-78; J. A. Kershaw on productivity measurement
in schools and colleges, pp. 185-92, reprinted in *P-EED*, 2, pp. 305-12;
J. C. Estey and H. Goldthorpe on student aid in American higher education,
pp. 253-76; H. Rosen and J. Dunlop on the Manpower Development and Training
Act, pp. 301-8; and E. F. Denison, R. M. Solow, and O. Eckstein on Denison's
Sources of Economic Growth, pp. 327-42. There is a discussion of "Womanpower
and Education", pp. 317-27, an introduction by S. E. Harris, commenting on all
the papers in this volume, pp. 1-15, and summaries by A. Levensohn of the
discussions at each seminar.

874 J. VAIZEY, R. KNIGHT, "Education", *The British Economy in 1975*, by W. Becker-
     man *et al*. National Institute of Economic and Social Research. Cambridge:
     Cambridge University Press, 1965, pp. 460-97.

    A comprehensive statistical picture of what the British educational system
might look like in 1975, on the assumption that certain outstanding inadequacies
in the system are overcome: pp. 460-65 give a quick review of these inadequacies. See also in the same volume: W. Beckerman, "Britain's Comparative
Growth Record", pp. 24-25, which denies that Britain's comparatively slow
growth rate in recent years is· due to the character of its educational system.
This volume was published in the same week as *The National Plan* (London: HMSO,
1965. Cmnd. 2764), which projects a target national product by 1970. A few
pages in the plan are devoted to education, pp. 192-201; most of the figures
differ from the implied 1970 figures in *The British Economy in 1975*, including
the estimate of the total school population. See also R. Caves *et al.*,
Britain's Economic Prospects (Washington, D.C.: The Brookings Institution,
1968), pp. 416-27.

875 M. S. GORDON, ed., *Poverty in America*. San Francisco: Chandler Publishing
     Company, 1965. Pp. *65.

The current poverty debate in America cuts across a number of issues in the economics of education: the educational characteristics of the unemployed, the payoff from training and retraining, manpower forecasting as a method of preventing poverty, and the like. This volume will introduce the reader to the discussion. See, particularly, R. A. Gordon, "An Economist's View of Poverty", pp. 3-12; H. P. Miller, "Changes in the Number and Composition of the Poor", pp. 81-102; R. J. Lampman, "Income Distribution and Poverty", pp. 102-15; H. P. Minsky, "The Role of Employment Policy", pp. 175-201; M. S. Gordon, "Poverty and Income Maintenance for the Unemployed", pp. 253-65; K. Davis, "Some Demographic Aspects of Poverty in the United States", pp. 299-332; and F. Machlup, "Strategies in the War on Poverty", pp. 445-65. See also B. A. Weisbrod's introduction to *The Economics of Poverty: An American Paradox* (Englewood Cliffs, New Jersey: 1965), pp. 1-28.

876 B. A. WEISBROD, "Preventing High School Dropouts", *Measuring Benefits of Government Investment*, ed. R. Dorfman. Washington, D.C.: The Brookings Institution, 1965, pp. 117-49.

A brilliant analysis of the high school dropout problem in the United States in a cost-benefit framework, accompanied by a case study evaluating the costs and benefits of the Dropouts Prevention Programme of the St. Louis Public Schools. F. Machlup, M. S. March, and H. P. Miller comment on Weisbrod's paper, pp. 149-72.

877 W. D. HALLS, *Society, Schools and Progress in France*. London: Pergamon Press, 1965, ch. 4, pp. 51-74.

The fourth chapter in this book provides an easy introduction to post-war educational planning in France.

878 CED, *Raising Low Incomes Through Improved Education*. A Statement on National Policy by the Research and Policy Committee of the Committee of Economic Development. New York: CED, 1965. Pp. 48.

An interesting attempt to formulate a national educational policy for the United States along what might be called "liberal" lines.

1966

879 H. CORREA, "More Schools or Better Schools?", *SPE*, III, 2, 1966, pp. 123-41.

A simple exposition of the linear-programming approach to educational investment decisions.

880 S. J. MUSHKIN, "Resource Requirements and Educational Obsolescence", *IEA-EE*, pp. 463-79.

This paper advances the interesting notion of one-year sabbatical leaves with pay for everyone at some time in his working life for purposes of "retreading". The scheme would be financed by a 1.5 per cent payroll tax shared between the government, the employer, and employees: in the United States, such a tax would provide for one year's re-education for one million people each year, not quite enough, however, to cover the whole labour force of 70 million in less than 50 years.

881 E. SMOLENSKY, "Investment in the Education of the Poor: A Pessimistic Report",
     AER, May, 1966, pp. 370-78.

     An interesting analysis of increased schooling as an anti-poverty policy
     under conditions of full and less than full employment, concluding with some
     pessimistic comments on the efficacy of this policy under present conditions.
     See the comments of A. M. Rivlin, *ibid*., pp. 396-8.

882 OECD, Education Investment and Planning Programme, *Educational Policy and
     Planning in Sweden*. Paris: OECD, 1966. Pp. 386.

     This volume provides a description of Swedish educational planning at all
     levels. See pp. 407-27 on Swedish experiences with manpower forecasting.

883 IIEP, *Workshop on Training Educational Planning Personnel*. Paris: UNESCO-
     IIEP, 1966, mimeographed.

     A collection of papers prepared for participants in the IIEP workshop:
     R. F. Lyons, "Problem of Training Educational Personnel" (pp. 14); A. C. R.
     Wheeler, "Perspectives d'avenir concernant les besoins et les ressources en
     personnel de planification de l'enseignement et les moyens nécessaires à sa
     formation" (pp. 43); J. Bousquet, "Training of Educational Planning Specialists
     in Developing Countries" (pp. 10); P. R. Hanna, "The Training of Educational
     Planning Personnel at Stanford, California, U.S.A." (pp. 7); J. Hartley,
     "The Training of Educational Planning Personnel in the Diploma Course in Edu-
     cational Administration for Overseas Students at the University of Reading
     (England) Institute of Education" (pp. 5); M. M. Leherpeux, "The Training
     of Experts in Educational Planning and Administration at the National Pedagogic
     Institute, Paris, France" (pp. 55); N. H. Chau, "The Organization of Training
     in Educational Planning at the Institute for the Study of Economic and Social
     Development, Paris" (pp. 2); R. F. Butts, "Program of Training for Education
     and International Affairs at Columbia University, New York, U.S.A." (pp. 6);
     R. Delprat, "Programme de l'enseignement de la section 'Planification de
     l'éducation et des resources humaines' à l'Institut international de recherche
     et de formation en vue de développement harmonisé à Paris, France" (pp. 6);
     C. Watson, "Courses for the Training of Educational Personnel at the Ontario
     (Canada) Institute for Studies in Education" (pp. 22); M. Kotí Ková, "Formation
     en matière de planification de l'éducation à l'université de Prague, Tchéco-
     slovaquie" (pp. 6); R. K. Kapur, "The Proposed Programme of Work for the
     Seventh Course for Educational Planners at the Asian Institute of Educational
     Planning in New Delhi, India" (pp. 9); and J. D. Cheswass, "Draft Summary of
     the Outcome of the Seminar on Statistics and Methodology for Professors of
     Educational Planning (Statistics)" (pp. 7).

884 G. L. MANGUM, ed., *The Manpower Revolution: Its Policy Consequences. Excerpts
     from Senate Hearings Before the Clark Sub-Committee*. New York: Anchor Books,
     Doubleday & Co., 1966. Pp. 580.

     The Senate Sub-Committee on Employment and Manpower of the Committee on
     Labor and Public Welfare, under the chairmanship of Senator J. S. Clark, con-
     ducted hearings in 1963 and 1964 "Relating to the Training and Utilization of
     the Manpower Resources of the Nation". This volume reprints excerpts of the
     record of these hearings, published originally in ten parts under the general
     title, *The Nation's Manpower Revolution*. It provides an excellent introduc-
     tion to recent American debates on structural unemployment, the impact of

automation, the war on poverty, and the concept of "an active manpower policy".
The articles most relevant to our purpose are: H. Goldstein, "Projections of
the Labor Force of the United States", pp. 15-33; C. C. Killingsworth, "Auto-
mation, Jobs and Manpower: The Case for Structural Unemployment", pp. 97-117;
W. W. Heller, "The Case for Aggregate Demand", pp. 117-47; Sub-committee Findings, "The Manpower Revolution", pp. 235-67; W. H. Miernyk, "British and
Western European Labor Market Policies", pp. 359-71; C. G. Uhr, "Recent Swedish
Labor Market Policies", pp. 371-81; "Education and the Manpower Revolution:
Questions Submitted to the Department of Health, Education, and Welfare",
pp. 382-95; and, lastly, a statement of the Sub-Committee's majority policy
recommendations, pp. 451-553.

1967

885   Department of Education and Science, UK, *Children and their Primary Schools*.
A Report of the Central Advisory Council for Education (England). London:
HMSO, 1967, I, II. Pp. 555, 633.

   Most of the Plowden Report is outside the purview of the economics of education. But see Vol. 1, ch. 5, "Educational Priority Areas", pp. 50-68, on the
question of regional inequalities in educational opportunities, and ch. 31,
pp. 341-52, on the costs and priorities of the main recommendation. See also
the "Note of Reservation on Parental Contribution to the Costs of Nursery
Education", pp. 487-89; and "A Suggestion on the Supply and Training of
Teachers", pp. 493-95. Vol. 2 contains 14 special surveys and studies that
were carried out for the Plowden Committee, including a 1964 National Survey
of Parental Attitudes, pp. 93-178, analysed with the aid of multiple regression techniques by G. F. Peaker, pp. 179-221; a study of post-war trends in
the standards of reading of 11-year-olds by G. F. Peaker, pp. 260-89; a survey
of Manchester schools by S. Wiseman, pp. 347-400; and an analysis of variations
in local provision of social services by B. P. Davies, pp. 617-33.

886   J. A. LAUWERYS, G. Z. BEREDAY, M. BLAUG, eds., *World Yearbook of Education
1967. Educational Planning*. London: Evans Bros., 1967.

   A collection of papers on educational planning problems in both developed
and developing countries. There are several general papers by (1) C. A.
Anderson, M. J. Bowman, "Theoretical Considerations in Educational Planning",
pp. 11-37, a shortened version of 871, reprinted in *P-EED 1*, pp. 351-82, and
BILD, pp. 193-211; (2) J. Miner, "The Relationship of Educational and Economic
Planning", pp. 38-56; (3) P. H. Coombs, "What Do We Still Need to Know About
Educational Planning?", pp. 57-72; and (4) J. D. Cheswass, "The Basic Data
Needed for Educational Planning", pp. 73-86. These are followed by three
papers exemplifying the "social-demand approach" to educational planning:
(5) J. Floud, "The Robbins Report and the Reform of Higher Education in
Britain", pp. 87-99; (6) F. Edding, "Educational Planning in Western Germany",
pp. 100-116; and (7) S. Sacks, "Historical Trends and Present Patterns in Educational Expenditure", pp. 117-38. The next section consists of six papers on
"the manpower-requirements approach": (8) J. R. Gass, "The Evolution of
OECD's Approach to Educational Planning in Developed Countries", pp. 139-48;
(9) H. S. Parnes, "The OECD Mediterranean Regional Project in Retrospect",
pp. 149-60; (10) R. G. Hollister, "A Technical Evaluation of OECD's Mediterranean Regional Project: Methods and Conclusions", pp. 161-69, reprinted in
P-EED, 1, pp. 338-47; (11) H. P. Widmaier, "Educational Planning in Western
Germany: A Case Study", pp. 170-95, a shortened version of 1060; (12) J. K.

Folger, "Scientific Manpower Planning in the United States", pp. 196-218;
(13) N. De Witt, "Educational and Manpower Planning in the Soviet Union",
pp. 219-39. Four papers provide examples of "the cost-benefit approach":
(14) G. Hunter, "Primary Education and Employment in the Rural Economy with
Special Reference to East Africa", pp. 242-56; (15) A. Callaway, "Unemployment Among School Leavers in an African City", pp. 257-72; (16) E. Rado,
"Manpower Planning in East Africa", pp. 273-98; and (17) J. A. Smyth, N. L.
Bennett, "Rates of Return on Investments in Education: A Tool for Short-Term
Educational Planning, Illustrated with Ugandan Data", pp. 299-322.

Section V is a miscellany confined to underdeveloped countries: (18) R.
Jolly, "Educational Planning in Zambia", pp. 324-40; (19) S. Shukla, "Training
Educational Planners for Developing Countries", pp. 341-46; (20) Lê Thành Khôi,
"Problems of Educational Planning in French-Speaking Africa", pp. 347-57;
(21) M. Debeauvais, "The Development of Education in Latin America Since the
Santiago Plan", pp. 358-74; (22) G. Benveniste, "The New Educational Technolo-
gies and the Developing Countries", pp. 375-81; (23) H. M. Phillips, "Trends
in Educational Expansion in Developing Countries", pp. 382-96. Lastly, there
are two papers on "models of the educational system": (24) H. Correa, "Models
and Mathematics in Educational Planning", pp. 398-422; and (25) P. Armitage,
C. S. Smith, "A Computable Model of the Educational System: Illustrated with
British Data", pp. 423-40, a brief version of 941.

887 A. CORBETT, *Much Ado About Education. A Critical Survey of the Fate of the
     Major Educational Reports*. London: Council for Educational Advance, 1967.
     Pp. 31.

     A beautiful introduction to the evolution of educational planning in Great
     Britain since 1959 by way of a review of the reports of Crowther, Albermarle,
     Newsom, Robbins, and Plowden.

888 OECD, *Methods and Statistical Needs for Educational Planning*. Paris: OECD,
     1967. Pp. 358.

     After an introductory chapter, the demand-for-places and the manpower-fore-
     casting approaches are discussed in some detail in chs. 2, 3, 4, and 5. Ch. 6
     develops a set of tabulations out of the conclusions of the previous chapters.
     Chs. 7 and 8 consider the question of data collection. Ch. 9 deals with inter-
     national comparisons. The final chapter discusses proposals for future work.
     Several annexes deal with data-collection experience in various OECD Member
     Countries.

889 D. K. FOLEY, "Resource Allocation and the Public Sector", *YEE*, Spring, 1967,
     pp. 45-102.

     Includes a section on the nature of public goods, the problems of resource
     allocation for planning public goods, and a brief discussion of education as
     a public good.

890 OECD, *Manpower and Social Policy in the Netherlands*. Reviews of Manpower and
     Social Policies. Paris: OECD, 1967. Pp. 301.

     The standard format of these reports includes a review of economic trends
     in the country, a summary of labour market policies, and a report by the OECD
     examiners commenting on the national policies of the country.

891 M. BLAUG, "Approaches to Educational Planning", *EJ*, June, 1967, pp. 262-88,
     reprinted in *WYK I*, pp. 468-96.

     An attempt to integrate the three leading current approaches to educational
     planning, emphasising the need to develop "educational flexibility" and "an
     active manpower policy". The paper is marked by an excessively condemnatory
     attitude towards manpower forecasting and fails in the final analysis to indi-
     cate an operational method of integrating the three approaches.

892 R. POIGNANT, *Les plans de développement de l'éducation et la planification
     économique et sociale*. Principes de la planification de l'éducation 2.
     Paris: UNESCO-IIEP, 1967. Pp. 55.

     Ostensibly directed to general issues, this is really a French view of edu-
     cational planning, highly coloured by the experiences of educational planning
     in post-war France. That is to say, educational planning in this pamphlet
     seems to consist of nothing else than analysis of educational expenditures in
     a national income framework, supplemented by demand-for-places projections.

893 F. EDDING, S. N. JENSEN, H. ULSHOEFER, eds., *Internationales Seminar über
     Bildungsplanung*. Berlin: Institut für Bildungsforschung in der Max-Planck
     Gesellschaft, 1967. Pp. 317.

     The papers and discussions of a conference organised in Berlin in 1966.
     G. Kade, K. Bahr, and H. Riese provide general background papers on educational
     planning; M. O'Donoghue, F. Halden, J. Binon and K. Grohmann, and J. Steindl
     describe educational planning in Ireland, Sweden, France, and Austria respec-
     tively. B. von Mutius and H.-P. Widmaier discuss educational planning in
     Western Germany. F. Edding, K. Bahr, E. Schmitz, and G. Oddie address them-
     selves to cost analysis and problems of educational finance. Educational
     models and statistics are analysed by G. Williams, H. Kullmer, and C. G. von
     Weizsäcker. M. O'Donoghue and K. Bahr sum up. The volume includes a biblio-
     graphy, some statistics on German education, and a description of the work of
     the Berlin Institut für Bildungsforschung.

894 OECD, *Educational Policy and Planning*. *Netherlands*. Paris: OECD, 1967.
     Pp. 272.

     This document provides a description of educational planning in The Nether-
     lands in the context of current flows of students through the various levels
     of the educational system. Ch. 7, pp. 79-110, contains a succinct review of
     Dutch experience in forecasting the demand for doctors, engineers, and all
     university graduates.

895 A. HEGELHEIMER, "On the Economic Approaches to Educational Planning in the
     Federal Republic of Germany", *GER*, 5, 4, 1967, pp. 336-43.

     A brief review of the work of Widmaier and Riese (1060, 1076) on long-term
     educational planning in Western Germany.

1968

896 R. E. LAVE, Jr., D. W. KYLE, "The Application of Systems Analysis to Educational Planning", *CER*, February, 1968, pp. 39-56.

   An excellent general statement of the applicability of "the interdisciplinary approach called Systems Analysis" to educational planning.

897 R. G. SPIEGELMAN, "A Benefit/Cost Model to Evaluate Educational Programs", *SPS*, 1968, pp. 443-60.

   A study of Title I of the Elementary and Secondary Education Act, designed to reduce the number of school dropouts, using data for youngsters aged 12-19 in Oakland, California. One of the principal benefits of the programme which the author tries to estimate is the lower cost of law enforcement as a result of reductions in the dropout rate.

898 H. J. HARTLEY, *Educational Planning-Programming-Budgeting: A Systems Approach.* New York: Prentice-Hall, 1968. Pp. 290.

   A book that substitutes taxonomy for analysis and quotations for original ideas. A few examples of programme budgeting applied to American school systems are mentioned along the way.

899 A. HEGELHEIMER, "Bidungsökonomie und Bildungsplanung. Eine Kritische Untersuchung der Ansätze zu einer ökonomischen Theorie der Bildungspolitik", *ZAK*, Zweites Heft, 1968, pp. 93-133.

   A review of current approaches to educational planning, coming down in favour of a dynamic programming approach. A notable feature of the article is the presentation of age-education-earnings profiles for Western Germany, based on 1964 cross-section data.

900 D. R. EVANS, "The Use of Graphical Analysis in Education Planning", *CER*, June, 1968, pp. 139-48.

   A number of illustrations are used to exemplify the advantages of graphical techniques in analysing and projecting the growth of educational systems.

901 H. RIESE, "Theorie der Bildungsplanung und Struktur des Bildungswesens", *KON*, 5/6 Heft, 1968, pp. 262-98.

   This article reviews the controversy between different approaches to educational planning in the light of the institutional context of Western Germany. The author argues that all the approaches point to educational reforms designed to increase the flexibility of education in Western Germany. An English summary is appended.

1969

902 K. HÜFNER, J. Naumann, eds., *Bildungsökonomie—eine Zwischenbilanz. Economics of Education in Transition.* Stuttgart: Ernst Klett Verlag, 1969. Pp. 275.

This Festschrift volume for Friedrich Edding begins with a review of Edding's contributions by H. Becker, pp. 17-23. This is followed by the editors' summary of contributions, pp. 39-50. The contributions themselves consist of 16 papers, of which five are in German, two in French, and the rest in English. The titles are (1) R. Poignant, "Reflexions sur la notion d'efficacité dans le domaine de l'enseignement", pp. 53-67; (2) M. Woodhall, M. Blaug, "Variations in Costs and Productivity of British Primary and Secondary Education", pp. 69-85; (3) T. Husèn, "Some Views on Cross-National Assessment of the 'Quality of Education'", pp. 87-95; (4) M. J. Bowman, C. A. Anderson, "Relationships Among Schooling, 'Ability', and Income in Industrialized Societies", pp. 97-119; (5) H. Riese, "Das Ertags-Kosten-Modell in der Bildungsplanung", pp. 123-38; (6) M. Kaser, "Some Macroeconomics of Education", pp. 139-53; (7) C. G. von Weizsäcker, "Vorlänfige Gedanken zur Theorie der Manpower-Bedarfs—schätzung", pp. 155-66; (8) H. P. Widmaier, "Zur Planung von Sozial-investitionen", pp. 167-82; (9) P. Streeten, "Economic Development and Education", pp. 183-98; (10) M. Debeauvais, "La planification de l'éducation: suggestions pour une réevaluation critique", pp. 199-211; (11) J. R. Gass, "Reflections on Equality, Quantity and Quality in Education", pp. 215-22; (12) F. H. Harbison, "Education and Economic Development in Advanced Countries", pp. 223-29; (13) E. S. Lee, "Education and Migration in the United States", pp. 231-36; (14) P. Menke-Glückert, "Mögliche Zukünfte europäischer Bildungssysteme", pp. 239-51; (15) B. Lutz, "Sozio-ökonomische Bildungsforschung in der Sackgasse?", pp. 253-58; and (16) T. Balogh, "Education and Agrarian Progress in Developed Countries", pp. 259-68. The book closes with a list of Edding's publications to date.

903 S. BOWLES, *Planning Educational Systems for Economic Growth*. Cambridge, Mass.: Harvard University Press, 1969. Pp. 245.

This long-awaited book reproduces the author's published linear programming model for Northern Nigeria (see 1787), together with a new comparison for Greece of the results of a manpower-requirements study, a rate-of-return analysis and a linear programming model. The book also includes an estimate of the elasticity of substitution between more and less educated labour, based on a cross-section regression for 11 countries (see 81).

904 H. CORREA, *Quantitative Methods of Educational Planning*. Scranton, Pa.: International Textbook Co., 1969. Pp. 242.

An attempt at a practical handbook of quantitative methods for educational planning using only the simplest mathematics, and illustrating the argument as it goes along with exercises about a country called "Plainland". Despite valiant efforts, the book does not altogether avoid the criticism of being a "cook book"; see, for example, ch. 7, pp. 119-32 on "Manpower Needs".

905 W. K. RICHMOND, *The Education Industry*. London: Methuen & Co., 1969. Pp. 237.

A lively popular book on the ills of the British educational system and how they can be cured by systems analysis, cost-effectiveness analysis, and all that. There are chapters on The New York Quality Measurement Project and on Swedish work in educational planning at the micro-level.

906 K. HÜFNER, *Traditionelle Bildungsökonomie und System-Orientierte Bildungsplanung*. Berlin: Institut für Bildungsforschung in der Max Planck Gessellschaft, 1969. Pp. 201.

As the title, *Traditional Economics of Education and Systems-Oriented Educational Planning*, makes clear, the author looks forward to a wider, interdisciplinary approach to educational planning than has hitherto been the case. The first two chapters review the work of Becker, Schultz and Denison; later chapters discuss the various elements of systems analysis and attempt to show how they can be applied to education.

907 C. A. ANDERSON, "Some Heretical Views on Educational Planning", *CER*, October, 1969, pp. 260-75.

A brilliant, scathing critique of UNESCO's *Educational Planning* (see 1747) with cogent remarks on both the nature of educational planning and the training of educational planners.

1970

908 OECD, *Manpower Policy in the United Kingdom*.   Reviews of Manpower and Social Policies No. 7.   Paris: OECD, 1970.   Pp. 230.

This study ranges all over the map, from employment promotion in development areas to reforms of industrial relations and the attempts at an incomes policy. It is entirely descriptive and dodges the question whether all the bits and pieces that exist really hang together as a consistent policy.

909 Department of Education and Science, *Output Budgeting for the Department of Education and Science. Report of a Feasibility Study*.   London: HMSO, 1970. Pp. 170.

This booklet discusses the problems of adopting a programme budget for education in the United Kingdom and sketches such a budget to illustrate its feasibility. The quality of the discussion is remarkably lucid (see, for example, pp. 20-29 on the concept of costs, and pp. 43-46 on the measurement of output).

910 M. WOODHALL, *Cost-Benefit Analysis in Educational Planning*.   Fundamentals of Educational Planning 13.   Paris: UNESCO-IIEP, 1970.   Pp. 48.

A useful practical handbook on rate-of-return analysis for educational planners.

911 H. HUGHES, D. C. BENN, T. BLACKSTONE, D. DOWNES, H. GLENNERSTER, S. HATCH, *Planning for Education in 1980*.   Fabian Research Series 282.   London: Fabian Society, 1970.   Pp. 32.

A balanced outline of a British education plan for 1980 from the starting point that "planning should be used to achieve greater social equality". All the proposals are costed and the pamphlet is also a mine of information about present-day facilities and expenditures.

912 J-P. JALLADE, *Educational Planning Methods. OECD Conference on Policies for Educational Growth*.   Background Study No. 8.   Paris: OECD, 1970.   Pp. 57, mimeographed.

Yet another attempt to review and synthesize various approaches to educational planning, no better and no worse than earlier efforts. The synthesis proposed by the author borrows a little from all approaches.

1972

913 W. AMBRUSTER, H-J. BODENHÖFER, "Manpower Approach versus Cultural Approach in Educational Planning", *BILS*, 9, 1972, pp. 52-74.

A rejection of all quantitative approaches to educational planning and an attempt to sketch a new methodology based on the somewhat vague concept of the "innovative efficiency" of educated labour.

914 D. BIRLEY, *Planning and Education*. London: Routledge & Kegan Paul, 1972. Pp. 152.

This is a book about the British scene, addressed to local education officers. Two-thirds of it is devoted to an exposition of PPB as applied to local education authorities.

915 Federal Government of Germany, *Educational Policy and Planning*. *Germany*. Paris: OECD, 1972. Pp. 294.

This background report on all aspects of German education is more descriptive than previous publications in this OECD series. It is a useful reference work but contains little that is new or surprising.

916 C. C. von Weiszäcker, "Problems in the Planning of Higher Education", *HE*, November, 1972, pp. 391-408.

Outlines three "ideal type" educational planning models (the numerus clausus model, the laissez-faire model and the market model) and argues in favour of the latter, with particular reference to higher education in Germany.

917 I. R. HOOS, *Systems Analysis in Public Policy. A Critique*. Berkeley, California: University of California Press, 1972, pp. 147-73.

A slam-bang, no-holds-barred critique of systems analysis, management science, programme budgeting, cost-benefit analysis, etcetera, etcetera. Ch. 6 is specifically devoted to applications in education and health.

918 R. LAYARD, "Economic Theories of Educational Planning", *Essays in Honour of Lord Robbins*, eds. M. H. Peston, B. A. Corry. London: Weidenfeld and Nicolson, 1972, pp. 118-49.

An important, thought-provoking paper, which seeks to combine first rate-of-return analysis and manpower forecasting and then rate-of-return analysis and the so-called social-demand approach, concluding with some comments on "sociological" models of the demand for education.

1973

919 R. CARR-HILL, O. MAGNUSSEN, *Indicators of Performance of Educational Systems*.
     Paris: OECD, 1973. Pp. 104.

     An interesting attempt to derive a list of output-indicators of educational
     systems for purposes of evaluating their performance. Chapter 4 is specifi-
     cally concerned with economic indicators and other chapters cover political
     and social indicators. Chapter 2 on the meaningfulness of selecting goal-
     indicators marks a new sophistication in the discussion of these issues in
     OECD-type publications.

1974

920 G. FOWLER, ed., *Output Measurement and Education*. London: Chartered Insti-
     tute of Public Finance and Accountancy, 1974. Pp. 110.

     A collection of six papers presented at a Bristol conference on educational
     output measurement to an assembly of local authorities' officers. The titles
     are: I. C. R. Byatt, "Output Measurement with Particular Reference to Edu-
     cation"; B. Rodmell, "Output Budgeting and the DES"; J. L. Davies, "The
     Refinement of the Conceptual Framework of Output Measurement"; R. Aitken,
     "Output Budgeting for the Local Education Authority"; K. Ollerenshaw, "The
     Education Budget in the Broader Local Authority Financial Context; and
     P. Armitage, "Planning for Change".

921 L. EMMERIJ, *Can the School Build a New Social Order?* Amsterdam: Elseviers
     Publishing Company, 1974. Pp. 220.

     The answer appears to be: yes, if we opt for recurrent education. Be that
     as it may, the first few chapters of this book provide a very readable account
     of the "explosion" of educational planning in the 1960's, focussed on the
     European scene. Chapters 9 and 10, in particular, summarize recent European
     evidence on family background, school inputs, educational achievement, and
     personal earnings. The final recommendation of a radical policy shift towards
     recurrent education is sketched only briefly.

1975

922 L. N. EDWARDS, "The Economics of Schooling Decisions: Teenage Enrollment
     Rates", *JHR*, Spring, 1975, pp. 155-73.

     Tests on economic model of high school enrolments on 1960 census data for
     states; the model is corroborated for white but refuted for black teenagers.

(b) MATHEMATICAL MODELS

The growing interest in linear and dynamic programming models in economic planning made it almost inevitable that sooner or later someone would apply similar
notions to educational planning. The Correa-Tinbergen-Bos model[4,1736,1778,1779]
was the first of such efforts, although it was a "mechical" rather than a "maximising" model. In recent years, there has been a reaction away from such ambitious

attempts to link education explicitly to the rest of the economy in favour of mathematical models of educational systems treated as self-contained dynamic structures.
Moser and Redfern[923,929,930], Stone[924,925,937,945], Widmaier[931,933,1060], Smith and
Armitage[928,932,941,943,946], Psacharopoulos[939], Thonstadt[928,1090], and Williams[947]
illustrate the development of computable student-flow models, involving probabilis-
tic transition proportions. Chance[927], Bénard[928,944,953,1790], Holtman[935], and
Bowles[903] exemplify the linear-programming approach to educational models.
Correa[886,928], David[926], OECD[940], and Bénard[953] provide surveys of the literature
to date. Fox, Sengupta, and others[932,934,950] exemplify recent work on micro-
modelling of educational institutions. For other references, see the section on
"Mathematical Models" in Part B below.

1965

923 C. A. MOSER, P. REDFERN, "Education and Manpower: Some Current Research",
     *Models for Decision. Proceedings of a Conference on Computable Models in
     Decision Making,* ed. C. M. Berners-Lee. London: English Universities Press,
     1965, pp. 71-84.

     After a brief discussion of a research project on the use of qualified man-
     power in British industry, now under way at the Unit, the article goes on to
     sketch a computable model of the British educational system using the method
     of storing continuous records of a sample of students on magnetic tape.

924 R. STONE, "A Model of the Educational System", *MIN*, Winter, 1965, pp. 172-87,
     reprinted in R. Stone, *Mathematics in the Social Sciences and Other Essays.*
     Cambridge, Mass.: MIT Press, 1966, ch. 9, and *BILD,* pp. 152-69.

     A sketch of a computable model of the British educational system in the
     form of a system of input-output accounting matrices along similar lines to
     the author's model of the British economy. Comprehension of this article
     requires a fairly sophisticated knowledge of matrix algebra.

1966

925 R. STONE, "Input-Output and Demographic Accounting: A Tool for Educational
     Planning", *MIN*, Spring, 1966, pp. 365-81.

     Develops his earlier article in a dynamic framework, replacing the usual
     fixed input coefficients by fixed input-output transition probabilities.
     This type of model, the author argues, enables us to deal with the leading
     factors involved in educational planning.

926 R. G. DAVIS, *Planning Human Resource Development. Educational Models and
     Schemata.* New York: Rand McNally & Co., 1966. Pp. 334.

     This is a somewhat disjointed work, marred by a studious effort to achieve
     at least one flippancy per page. It will be useful, however, to the practical
     educational planner as a reference work to models, techniques, and computa-
     tional methods. Its chief features are a devastating account of how to carry
     out a Parnes-like manpower forecast, pp. 33-63, a clear explanation of one or
     two computable models of educational systems, pp. 86-90, an exposition of

linear programming techniques applied to education, pp. 151-63, and a detailed
chapter on educational cost formulas, pp. 167-218. The book includes an
excellent bibliography.

927 W. A. CHANCE, "Long-Term Labor Requirements and Output of the Educational
     System", *SEJ*, April, 1966, pp. 417-29.

   This paper presents a simplified Leontief-type model linking projections of
future labour requirements to the output of the educational system, and illustrates the argument with a representative linear programming solution of the
model. The paper closes with a few judicious self-critical comments.

1967

928 OECD, Education and Development, Technical Reports, *Mathematical Models in
     Educational Planning*. Paris: OECD, 1967. Pp. 290.

   This volume consists of eight papers with an introductory essay by R. Stone:
"A View of the Conference", pp. 7-20; H. Correa, "A Survey of Mathematical
Models in Educational Planning", pp. 21-94; Forecasting Institute of the
Swedish Central Bureau of Statistics, "Projection Models of the Swedish Edu-
cational System", pp. 95-124; T. Thonstad, "A Mathematical Model of the Nor-
wegian Educational System", pp. 125-58; P. H. Armitage and C. Smith, "The
Development of Computable Models of the British Educational System and their
Possible Uses", pp. 159-206, reprinted in *P-EED*, 2, pp. 202-37; J. Bénard,
"General Optimization Model for the Economy and Education", pp. 207-44;
C. C. von Weizäcker, "Training Policies Under Conditions of Technical Progress:
A Theoretical Treatment", pp. 245-58; P. Alper, "Introduction of Control Con-
cepts in Educational Planning Models", pp. 259-74; and P. L. Dressel, "Comments
on the Use of Mathematical Models in Educational Planning", pp. 275-90. See
the article review by M. Blaug, *MIN*, Autumn, 1967, pp. 43-47.

929 C. A. MOSER, P. REDFERN, "A Computable Model of the Educational System in
     England and Wales", *Bulletin of the 35th (1965) Session of the International
     Statistical Institute*. Belgrave: ISI, 1967, pp. 693-700.

   A briefer version of 923 and some indications of the current status of the
model.

930 P. REDFERN, *Input-Output Analysis and its Application to Education and Man-
     power Planning*. HM Treasury, Centre for Administrative Studies Occasional
     Paper No. 5. London: HMSO, 1967. Pp. 10.

   An input-output model of the British educational system for the year 1963,
drawing on 923.

931 H. P. WIDMAIER, B. FREY, "Wachstrumstheorie und Bildungsökonomik", *ZAK*, 13, 3,
     1967, pp. 129-83.

   An attempt to weave together the demand-for-places and the manpower-forecasting approaches to educational planning with the aid of an explicit input-
output model of the educational system (derived from the senior author's work
in a German Länder).

932 P. ALPER, P. H. ARMITAGE, C. S. SMITH, "Educational Models, Manpower Planning and Control", *ORQ*, July, 1967, pp. 93-103.

An elaboration of 928 by Armitage and Smith to show how the various current approaches to educational planning might be integrated with the aid of control theory.

933 H. P. WIDMAIER, "Rationale Grudlagen der Bildungspolitik", *SZNA*, 6, 4, 1967, pp. 277-328.

A general discussion of the process of educational planning, stressing the role of educational models as illustrated by Swiss data.

1968

934 K. A. FOX, J. K. SENGUPTA, "The Specification of Econometric Models for Planning Educational Systems: An Appraisal of Alternative Approaches", *KYK*, XXI, 4, 1968, pp. 665-94.

A discussion of some recent mathematical models of the educational planning process.

935 A. G. HOLTMANN, "Linear Programming and the Value of an Input to a Local Public School System", *PF*, 4, 1968, pp. 429-40.

Develops a prototype short-term planning model for a high school district, using linear programming and applies it to a Detroit school district, using 1963-64 data.

936 Y. PLESSNER, K. A. FOX, B. C. SANYAL, "On the Allocation of Resources in a University Department", *METRO*, September-December, 1968, pp. 256-71.

An ingenious parametric linear programming model of the department of Economics at Iowa State University. The model determines the optimum number of students in each degree programme, the allocation of staff between teaching, research and administration, the allocation of teaching time between graduate and undergraduate courses, and the optimum allocation of resources to new faculty.

937 R. STONE, G. STONE, J. GUNTON, "An Example of Demographic Accounting: The School Ages", *MIN*, Winter, 1968, pp. 185-212.

The educational model, expounded in previous papers (924, 925), is here applied to the school population of England and Wales in the years 1960-65 for illustrative purposes.

1969

938 P. N. V. TU, "Optimal Educational Investment Program in an Economic Planning Model", *CJE*, February, 1969, pp. 52-64.

A balanced-growth model of educational expansion which maximises the present value of future consumption over a finite time horizon.

939 G. PSACHAROPOULOS, *Enrollment Projections for Higher Education in the State of Hawaii, 1969-1980*. Honolulu: University of Hawaii, 1969. Pp. 158.

An application of a Markov chains student-flow model to project enrolments up to 1980.

940 OECD, Directorate for Scientific Affairs, *Report on the Findings of the Survey of Educational Models in OECD Countries*. Paris: OECD, 1969. Pp. 75, mimeographed.

This report is based on a questionnaire study of educational model builders in the member countries. Some 120 models are tabulated under various headings and about a dozen models are discussed in some detail. See also *Study of One Mathematical Model of the Education System* (Paris: OECD, 1969. Pp. 25, mimeographed) and *Directory of Current Educational Models in OECD Member Countries* (Paris: OECD, 1969. Pp. 90, mimeographed).

941 P. ARMITAGE, C. SMITH, P. ALPER, *Decision Models for Educational Planning*. London: Allen Lane The Penguin Press, 1969. Pp. 124.

An expansion of the earlier article by Armitage and Smith (928) in an effort to extend a Markov chains model of educational supply into a genuine decision model incorporating the planner's "objective function". The book closes with an illustrative discussion of the decision to raise the school-leaving age in Britain (pp. 90-109).

942 H. CORREA, "Flows of Students and Manpower Planning: Application to Italy", *CER*, June, 1969, pp. 167-79.

A modification of the Correa-Bos-Tinbergen model with applications to Italy and Spain to show the consequence of modifications.

1970

943 P. ARMITAGE, C. PHILLIPS, J. DAVIES, "Towards a Model of the Upper Secondary School System", *JRSS*, Series A, June, 1970, pp. 166-92, reprinted by HERU, No. 38.

The paper gives an excellent account of the latest stages of the Moser-Redfern supply model, centering on the problem of subject classification in the context of explaining the choices of subject for G.C.E. O- and A-levels.

944 J. BÉNARD, "Intersectoral Optimization and Development of the Educational System", *Contributions to Input-Output Analysis*, eds. A. P. Carter, A. Brody. Amsterdam: North-Holland Publishing Company, 1970, I, pp. 320-43.

Extends his earlier linear programming model of the educational system in the context of a country's over-all economic activities, the outputs of the educational system being treated as inputs into other sectors and the problem being that of consistent, balanced growth of all sectors, including the educational one.

1971

945   R. STONE, *Demographic Accounting and Model-Building*.   Paris: OECD, 1971.
      Pp. 125.

      This is a new and more detailed exposition of the author's earlier sugges-
      tions for a student flow model (see 925, 937), but the proposal is extended
      here to encompass the demand side and indeed to link us eventually with a
      broader set of economic accounts. The argument is occasionally illustrated
      with data drawn from British educational statistics.

946   P. ARMITAGE, A. CRAMPIN, *Raising the School Leaving Age, Comprehensive Reor-
      ganization and the Demand for Higher Education*. London: Higher Education
      Research Unit, London School of Economics, 1971. n.p.

      A work of some 200 pages in which alternative projections are made of
      student numbers in British higher education up to 1980 on the basis of various
      assumptions about the effects of the higher school leaving age in 1973 and
      the continued comprehensivisation of secondary schools in the 1970's. The
      resulting numbers suggest that the official D.E.S. projections could be off
      the mark by as much as 50,000 students in 1980.

1972

947   G. WILLIAMS, "Computable Models for Planning Education", *Contemporary Problems
      in Higher Education. An Account of Research,* eds. H. J. Butcher, E. Rudd.
      London: McGraw-Hill, 1972, pp. 372-81.

      Summarizes work on student-flow models in Britain over the last decade.

948   R. D. LAMSON, J. H. POWELL, "An Improved Model for Determining the Input Cost
      of University Outputs", *SEP*, June, 1972, pp. 273-81.

      A general input-output technique model for higher education, together with
      some comments on the inherent limitations of such models.

949   P. ARMITAGE, C. S. SMITH, "Controllability: An Example", *HE*, Autumn, 1972,
      pp. 55-66.

      A simple example of the application of control theory to educational plan-
      ning, namely, a two grade university teachers' model.

950   K. A. FOX, J. K. SENGUPTA, T. K. KUMAR, B. C. SANYAL, *Economic Analysis for
      Educational Planning: Resource Allocation in Nonmarket Systems*. Baltimore:
      John Hopkins Press, 1972. Pp. 376.

      A mathematically sophisticated collection of 9 essays by 4 authors, focussed
      on the problem of developing micro-models of educational institutions. Al-
      though the last three chapters are ostensibly concerned with empirical appli-
      cations, the tone and flavour of the book remains excessively abstract and
      more concerned with setting up models than with putting them to work.

1973

951   J. BÉNARD, "Les modèles d'optimation économique de l'éducation", *REP*, janvier-
      fevrier, 1973, pp. 114-30.

      Sums up the present state of his linear programming, intersectoral optimiza-
      tion model of the French economy (see 928).

952   J. N. JOHNSTONE, H. PHILP, "The Application of a Markov Chain in Educational
      Planning", *SEP*, June, 1973, pp. 283-94.

      An application of a student-flow model to the New South Wales State Govern-
      ment education system for the period 1947 to 1961.

953   J. BÉNARD, "Les modèles d'optimation·économique en éducation", *REP*, mai-juin,
      1973, pp. 433-81.

      Reviews the work of Adelman, Bowles and Benard in the area of paediometric
      modelling and compares this type of model with rate-of-return analysis, man-
      power forecasting and the social-demand approach.

(c) MANPOWER FORECASTING

   Educational planning is as old as public education itself: over a hundred years
ago, some of the American states went in for decennial reviews of local educational
needs. What is new about educational planning in our own day is the degree to
which more and more countries are subordinating the expansion of the educational
system to the prospective demand of government and industry for highly qualified
manpower, a prospective demand which is forecast with ever more sophisticated techniques. Sparked off by various United Nations special organisations, and by
American foreign aid programmes, the interest in manpower planning and forecasting
has now spread around the world and received official endorsement almost every-
where in both developed and underdeveloped countries. The very different atmos-
phere in which these problems were discussed before World War II is illustrated by
the League of Nations[727] and Kotschnig[955].
   The literature is, surprisngly enough, rather thin on the theoretical side.
Parnes[862,867,871], Tinbergen[1007], Bombach[1013], Mehmet[1035], Hollister[1039], and
Crossley[1101] between them just about complete the short course in the theory and
methodology of manpower planning in poor countries. Boulding[964] alone voices fundamental objections to the whole approach, and Anderson and Bowman[871,886], Blaug[891]
and Ahamad and Blaug[1113] give a critical review of the implicit assumptions of manpower forecasters. The discussion of manpower problems is often bedevilled by
misleading concepts of "shortages" which ignore trends in earnings and the state
of the labour market. Vaizey[2,1819], Reder[968], Blank and Stigler[970], Lee Hansen[1064],
Arrow and Capron[986], Jewkes[989], Bowman[1003], Thompson[1175], Thomas[1116], Cain and
others[1119] all address themselves to this question.
   Once manpower needs have been more or less accurately forecast, there remains the
still controversial question of translating these manpower demands into the desired
supply of educational output. The controversy between Parnes and Debeauvais[867] is
very illuminating on this score, but see also Debeauvais[867], International Labour
Office[980], Goldstein[1062,1067], and Eckaus[1017]. The Oxford University Department
of Education[666], the Institution of Chemical Engineers[1023], the Institution of
Mechanical Engineers[1026], Wolfle[1175], Cole[1180], Zapoleon[1190], and McCormick[1110]

take up the associated problem of how students choose to study science and engineering, an important aspect of educational-cum-manpower planning in a country like Great Britain, where students find it difficult to change subjects after the age of 16.

For some quantitative examples of manpower forecasts, see the OECD Mediterranean Regional Project[870,1031] on Portugal, Spain, Italy, Greece, Turkey, and Yugoslavia, the Committee on Scientific Manpower[956,969,1033,1057] and the Cambridge Growth Project[1005,1021] on Great Britain, Martinoli[992], Novacco[867], and Birtig[1125] on Italy, Vermot-Gauchy[994,1001,1036] on France, Scheidemann and Gassert[977], Widmaier[1060], and Riese[1076] on Germany, the Belgian Ministry of Education[979] on Belgium, and Jaffe and Carleton[965], Wolfle[1175], the National Science Foundation[996], [1006], Colm and Lecht[1015], Folger[886] and Goldstein and Swerdloff[1067] on the United States.

Jaccard[972], McCrensky[981], the International Bureau of Education[984], and Grégoire[1062], and Williams[1103] review manpower research and policies in recent years throughout Western Europe; for individual countries, there are the studies of Payne[993], Peacock[1002], and Moser and Layard[759] on Great Britain, Folger and others[1100] on the United States, Fourastié[1007], Vimont[1014,1098], and Poignant[860,867] on France, de Wolff[1007], OECD[894], and Ruiter[1030] on the Netherlands, Döös[1007], OECD[882], and Sandgren[1030] on Sweden, Bahr[1009], and Ambruster[1107] on Great Britain, France, and Germany, Auerhan[1024] and the International Labour Office[1799] on Eastern Europe, and the valuable OECD Country Reviews[999]. There is also the quite definitive anthology by Ahamad and Blaug[1113].

Despite two decades of intensive research on patterns of manpower utilisation, very little is known about the way individual firms make use of educated people: the bulk of the research has been aggregative on the level of entire sectors of the economy or, at best, particular industries. Layard, Ager, and others[306], Bright[983], Hill and Harbison[985], Benson and Lohnes[987], Barkin[1073], Keys and Wright[1056], Blaug and others[1072], Gascoigne[1077], Boon[1415], Diamond and Bedrosian[1097], d'Hugues[1114], and Mace and Taylor[1127] indicate the rich harvest that might be reaped by firm studies.

1931

954 H. F. CLARK, *Economic Theory and Correct Occupational Distribution*. New York: Bureau of Publications, Teachers College, Columbia University, 1931. Pp. 176.

Attempts to show the need for manpower planning—here called "planned occupational distribution"—by contrasting what economists have said about "correct occupational distribution" with the actual situation in the USA. The argument is somewhat superficial and the book now has only historical value.

1937

955 W. M. KOTSCHNIG, *Unemployment in the Learned Professions. An International Study of Occupational and Educational Planning*. London: Oxford University Press, 1937. Pp. 347.

A study of the social and economic factors that produced excess supply of professional manpower in the interwar years.

1946

956 Report of a Committee (under the chairmanship of Sir A. Barow) appointed by the Lord President of the Council, *Scientific Manpower*. London: HMSO, 1946. Cmd. 6824. Pp. 26.

   An estimate of the numbers and distribution of professionally trained scientists in Great Britain, and a call for doubling the supply by 1955.

1949

957 S. E. HARRIS, *The Market for College Graduates and Related Aspects of Education and Income*. Cambridge, Mass.: Harvard University Press, 1949. Pp. 207.

   In this book the author argues the imminence of an excess of college graduates in the USA, a viewpoint which he has since abandoned. The essential analyses and conclusions are presented in the first 75 pages; the rest of the book contains most of the documentation and supporting statistics. Many useful tables and charts are included.

1951

958 A. J. JAFFE, C. D. STEWART, *Manpower Resources and Utilization. Principles of Working Force Analysis*. New York: John Wiley, 1951. Pp. 532.

   A good source of information on the structural characteristics of the American labour force in the first half of this century; the book has nothing to say, however, on the educational background of the labour force.

959 PEP, *Manpower. A Series of Studies of the Composition and Distribution of Britain's Labour Force*. London: PEP, 1951. Pp. 102.

   One section of this volume, pp. 77-102, summarised on pp. 20-25, deals with current trends in the education and training of wage-earners.

1952

960 J. BURTLE, "Input-Output Analysis as an Aid to Manpower Policy", *ILR*, May, 1952, pp. 600-26.

   An excellent brief primer in input-output analysis with a discussion of its application to manpower planning.

1953

961 National Manpower Council, *A Policy for Scientific and Professional Manpower*. New York: Columbia University Press, 1953. Pp. 263.

   A statement of recommendations and a long section of "Facts and Issues About Scientific and Professional Manpower" in the USA, with particular attention to engineers, physicists, teachers, and physicians. Includes a bibliography.

1954

962 National Manpower Council, *A Policy for Skilled Manpower*. New York: Columbia
University Press, 1954. Pp. 299.

A statement of recommendations and a long section of "Facts and Issues About
Skilled Manpower" with particular attention to vocational education in America.
Includes a bibliography.

963 W. HABER, F. H. HARBISON, L. R. KLEIN, G. L. PALMER, eds., *Manpower in the
USA: Problems and Policies*. Industrial Relations Research Assn., Public.
No. 11. New York: Harper & Bros., 1954. Pp. 225.

A popular survey of American manpower planning in the form of 16 articles
on various topics: occupational and geographic distribution of employment,
1910-50; patterns of labour mobility; military manpower policy; economic controls for manpower mobilisation, and the like.

964 K. BOULDING, "An Economist's View of the Manpower Concept", National Manpower
Council, *Proceedings of a Conference on the Utilization of Scientific and
Professional Manpower*. New York: Columbia University Press, 1954, pp. 11-33.

"I find the whole manpower concept repulsive, disgusting, dangerous, fascis-
tic, communistic, incompatible with the ideals of a liberal democracy and
unsuitable company for the minds of the young." After a précis of the classic
theory of human resource allocation à la Adam Smith modified by Pigou, Boulding
concedes that some government interference may be in order. R. MacIver summarises the conference's discussion of Boulding's paper. The rest of this
volume includes specialised papers on manpower planning in engineering, medicine, and teaching.

965 A. J. JAFFE, R. O. CARLETON, *Occupational Mobility in the United States, 1930-
1960*. New York: King's Crown Press, 1954. Pp. 105.

This book attempts to forecast the future male manpower supply by occupation
in the United States on the basis of knowledge of changes in the supply of manpower in the decades 1930-50. Models of "cohort work experience" are fitted
to the 1930-50 data and then extrapolated to the 1960's.

1955

966 National Manpower Council, *Improving the Work Skills of the Nation. Proceedings of a Conference on Skilled Manpower*. New York: Columbia University
Press, 1955. Pp. 203.

The conference was designed to encourage implementation of the recommendations of the Council's *Policy for Skilled Manpower* (1954). This volume of
conference papers includes, among others, E. Ginzberg and H. David, "The Problem of Skill Development", pp. 3-12; C. C. Brown, "The Investment in Manpower",
pp. 12-21; C. Faust, "Our Secondary Schools and National Manpower Needs",
pp. 21-36; G. B. Baldwin, "Automation and the Skills of the Labour Force",
pp. 83-95; and K. R. Kunze, "Industry's Training Effort in Improving the Work
Skills of the Nation", pp. 99-118.

967   C. H. COPEMAN, *Leaders of British Industry. A Study of the Careers of More Than a Thousand Public Company Directors.* London: Gee, 1955. Pp. 173.

This study, confined to the directors of public joint stock companies, contains some interesting evidence of the educational attainment of the leaders of British industry. In the penultimate chapter, pp. 128-48, the author contrasts his results with those of several American studies, concluding that "All the American executives (in a 1925 *Fortune* survey) had a high school education, as against 89 per cent of the British directors who had some secondary education; 81 per cent of the Americans went to college, and 65 per cent graduated. This compares with 63 per cent of British directors who had some further education after secondary schooling, and 36 per cent who went to university. Postgraduate studies were undertaken by 22.1 per cent of the American executives as against 7 per cent of the British directors." See also "The Anatomy of the Board", *The Director*, January, 1965, pp. 86-91, which gives the findings of a survey of 10,000 members of the Institute of Directors of Great Britain, showing the academic qualifications of members of the Board by age, type of school attended, size of company, and sector of the economy.

968   M. W. REDER, "The Theory of Occupational Wage Differentials", *AER*, December, 1955, pp. 833-54.

This interesting article attempts to explain cyclical and secular variations in skill differentials by analysing the phenomenon of upgrading of workers relative to the jobs for which they are hired. In the course of the argument, the author touches on the economics of on-the-job training, p. 836, and the effect of rising levels of education on trends in wage differentials associated with skill, pp. 844-45.

1956

969   Advisory Council on Scientific Policy, Committee on Scientific Manpower, *Scientific and Engineering Manpower in Great Britain.* London: HMSO, 1956. Pp. 27.

A report on the number and distribution of scientists and engineers employed in Great Britain and a study of the likely trend in the demand for scientific and engineering manpower in 1959. See also by the same committee, *Scientific Engineering Manpower in Great Britain 1959* (London: HMSO, 1959, Cmd. 902. Pp. 48), which showed that the numbers who had completed their professional training increased more rapidly than was estimated in 1956; *Scientific and Technological Manpower in Great Britain 1962* (London: HMSO, 1962. Cmd. 2146. Pp. 59) carried the same exercise forward to 1965 on the basis of improved statistics; *The Long-Term Demand for Scientific Manpower* (London: HMSO, 1961. Cmd. 1490. Pp. 25) considered the likely demand for and supply of scientists and technologists in 1970. See also the 17 annual reports by the Advisory Council on Scientific Policy which review problems with respect to scientific research and the utilisation of scientific manpower that have arisen in the course of the year.

1957

970   D. M. BLANK, G. J. STIGLER, *The Demand and Supply of Scientific Personnel.* New York: National Bureau of Economic Research, 1957. Pp. 200.

A test of the notion of "shortages" of scientific personnel, illustrated
with reference to engineers, chemists, mathematicians, and physicists in the
USA. Appendices include data on numbers and education of engineers with projections to 1970. See also W. Lee Hansen, "The 'Shortage' of Engineers", *RES*,
August, 1961, pp. 251-56, which quarrels with Blank's and Stigler's findings
about engineers, particularly for the decade of the 1950's.

971 C. F. CARTER, B. R. WILLIAMS, *Industry and Technical Progress*. London:
Oxford University Press, 1957, ch. 9, pp. 87-108.

A discussion of the nature of the current shorages of scientists and technologists in British industry. See also the authors' *Science in Industry*
(London: Oxford University Press, 1959), ch. 11, pp. 122-35, which contains
proposals for changes in the educational system to relieve these shortages.

972 P. JACCARD, *Politique de l'emploi et de l'éducation*. Paris: Payot, 1957.
Pp. 256.

A popular explanation of the means by which countries like the United States,
France, Switzerland, the United Kingdom, and the USSR are recasting their
school systems to meet forecasts of manpower needs. A later work by the same
author, misleadingly entitled *Sociologie de l'éducation* (Paris: Payot, 1962.
Pp. 256), highlights the nature of the reforms which should enter into sound
educational plans.

973 Syndicat général de la construction électrique, *Enquête sur les besoins en
techniciens dans les industries de la construction électrique*. Paris: SGCE,
1957. n.p.

A forecast of requirements of highly qualified manpower in the French electrical engineering industry, based on fixed input-coefficients and various
assumptions about the future growth of output. The coefficients are derived
from the results of an inquiry of 85 firms employing 120,000 workers.

974 C. A. QUATTLEBAUM, *Development of Scientific, Engineering and Other Professional
Manpower (With Emphasis on the Role of the Federal Government)*. Joint Committee on Atomic Energy. Washington, D.C.: US Government Printing Office,
1957. Pp. 172.

The first 30 pages of this booklet rapidly review the leading considerations
entering into the technical manpower development problem in the United States.
There follows a history of federal participation in manpower development,
pp. 31-55, a digest of relevant statistics and opinions, pp. 55-87, and lastly,
a thorough review of current federal contributory programmes to promote the
training of scientists and engineers, pp. 87-118.

975 National Manpower Council, *Womanpower*. New York: Columbia University Press,
1957. Pp. 371.

A general discussion of the determinants of the female labour participation
rate in America with 2 chapters dealing with trends in secondary and higher
education for girls, pp. 167-220.

976 OEEC, *The Problem of Scientific and Technical Manpower in Western Europe, Canada, and the USA*. Paris: OEEC, 1957. Pp. 220.

   A questionnaire was sent to the 17 member countries to ascertain the disparities between demand and supply for scientists and engineers. A table conveniently summerises the 1956 position in the countries concerned. (See also 1012.)

977 K. FR. SCHEIDEMANN, H. GASSERT, *Technischer Nachwuchs Bestand 1956, Bedarf bis 1970 und Deckung des Bedarfs*. Bonn: Bundesministeriums des Innern, 1957. Pp. 39.

   An estimate of the stock of engineers in West Germany in 1956, a projection of the supply of engineers in 1970, and a sketch of likely trends in supply up to 1980.

978 D. J. BROWN, F. H. HARBISON, *High-Talent Manpower for Science and Industry*. Princeton, N.J.: Industrial Relations Section, Research Report No. 95, Princeton University Press, 1957. Pp. 97.

   Contains two essays which lay down a series of propositions about the development of high-talent manpower in the USA and elsewhere.

1958

979 Ministère de l'instruction publique, Belgique, *Premier livre blanc sur les besoins de l'économie belge en personnel scientifique et technique qualifé*. Brusselles: Puvrez, 1958. Pp. 517.

   An official forecast of high-quality-manpower needs of the Belgian economy in the coming decades.

980 ILO, *International Standard Classification of Occupations*. Geneva: ILO, 1958. Pp. 236; rev. ed., 1968. Pp. 355.

   An indispensable reference work for manpower planners, particularly for international comparisons of manpower structures. Occupations are defined in terms of the work to be performed and the duties to be carried out, with occasional reference to particular educational qualifications. The introduction to the work contains several warnings on the use of educational requirements for different occupations as a classificatory device, pp. 3, 4, 6 (see pp. 9-10 in new edition).

981 E. McCRENSKY, *Scientific Manpower in Europe. A Comparative Study of Scientific Manpower in the Public Service of Great Britain and Selected European Countries*. London: Pergamon Press, 1958. Pp. 188.

   A popular discussion of the salaries and other employment conditions of scientists and engineers in professional public service in Western Europe, with a survey of research organisations and a comparison of personnel practices in Russia and the United States.

982   E. GINZBERG, *Human Resources: The Wealth of a Nation*.   New York: Simon &
      Schuster, 1958.   Pp. 183.

      A short popular book based on the research that has been conducted by the
      Conservation of Human Resources Project since 1950.   Particular attention is
      given to wastes of human resources due to unemployment, inadequate training,
      and sex and race discrimination.   A bibliography is included.

983   J. R. BRIGHT, "Does Automation Raise Skill Requirements?", *HBR*, July-August,
      1958, pp. 85-97, reprinted in *PEE*, pp. 66-81.

      Based on a close study of 13 plants, this article denies the popular belief
      that automation necessarily results in an upgrading of work-force skill
      requirements.   As the author shows, automation of an enterprise often tends
      to reduce the skill and training required of the work force in that enterprise.

1959

984   IBE, *Training of Technical and Scientific Staff.   Measures to Increase Facili-
      ties*.   XXIInd International Conference on Public Education.   Geneva: IBE-
      UNESCO, 1959.   Pp. 300.

      A survey of what has been done since 1950 to increase the supply of quali-
      fied scientists and technicians in different countries around the world.   The
      findings of the survey are summarised on pp. 11-49.

985   S. E. HILL, F. H. HARBISON, *Manpower and Innovation in American Industry*.
      Princeton, N.J.:   Industrial Relations Section, Research Report No. 97,
      Princeton University Press, 1959.   Pp. 85.   Excerpts reprinted in *UNESCO-REED*,
      pp. 724-29.

      Based on empirical data drawn from 50 American companies.   Demonstrates that
      increased demand for high-talent manpower in recent years has been due to the
      rate and character of innovations.

986   K. J. ARROW, W. M. CAPRON, "Dynamic Shortages and Price Rises: The Engineer-
      Scientist Case", *QJE*, May, 1959, pp. 292-309, reprinted in *P-EED*, 1, pp. 318-37.

      The authors argue that the "shortage" of engineers and scientists in the USA
      in recent years is not evidence of a failure of the price mechanism but rather
      the result of a dynamic market adjustment to rising demand.   They test this
      notion with empirical data, criticising the Blank-Stigler approach.

987   C. S. BENSON, P. R. LOHNES, "Skill Requirements and Industrial Training in
      Durable Goods Manufacturing", *ILRR*, July, 1959, pp. 540-53.

      Based on a stratified random sample of manufacturing plants in Massachusetts,
      this study attempts to demonstrate that skill requirements vary systematically
      not only with the type of process employed but also with the character of the
      firm's product market.   Shortages of skilled workers are typically met by
      training, overtime work, and job dilution.   The article suggests the sort of
      research that needs to be done to establish a firm basis for manpower fore-

casting. The same sample was also used to question personnel officers about
the kind of education they prefer their workers to have.

988   C. S. BENSON, P. R. LOHNES, "Public Education and the Development of Work
      Skills", *HER*, Spring, 1959, pp. 137-50.

      A restatement of 987.

1960

989   J. JEWKES, "How Much Science?", *EJ*, March, 1960, pp. 1-16.

      The author argues that it is at present impossible to say whether we suffer
      from a shortage of scientists and technologists and, he concludes, that for a
      long time to come the tests of a nation's needs for science will be based
      largely on judgement and common sense.

990   J. LAUWERYS *et al.*, *Supply, Recruitment and Training of Science and Mathematics
      Teachers*. Paris: OECD, 1960. Pp. 46.

      An estimate of the gap between the demand and supply of qualified full-time
      science and mathematics teachers at the secondary level in OECD member-coun-
      tries and a set of short-term and long-term recommendations for closing the
      gap.

991   H. DAVID, ed., *Education and Manpower*. New York: Columbia University Press,
      1960. Pp. 326.

      A volume of reprinted sections of various publications of the National Man-
      power Council with introductory essays by H. David and E. Ginzberg.

992   G. MARTINOLI, *Trained Manpower Requirements for the Economic Development of
      Italy—Targets for 1975. The Role of Education in Italian Economic Develop-
      ment*. Rome: SVIMEZ (Associazione per lo Sviluppo dell'Industria nel Mezzo-
      giorno), 1960. Pp. 59.

      A discussion of the implications of the 1975 targets for Italian education.

993   G. L. PAYNE, *Britain's Scientific and Technological Manpower*. London: Oxford
      University Press, 1960. Pp. 466.

      The aim of this book is to survey current data on the expected demand and
      supply of scientists and engineers in Great Britain. Addressed to an American
      audience, the book also provides descriptions of secondary education, univer-
      sities, and technical education, with constant comparisons of British and
      American experience. A glossary of terms and a bibliography conclude this
      very useful book.

994   OEEC, Office for Scientific and Technical Personnel, *Forecasting Manpower Needs
      for the Age of Science*. Paris: OEEC, 1960. Pp. 141. Excerpts reprinted in
      UNESCO-REED, pp. 759-73.

Account of a Conference on Forecasting Techniques that met in The Hague in 1959, consisting of 3 general papers by E. I. Schmidt, P. H. Coombs and H. Goldstein, 3 technical papers by S. Moberg, M. Vermot-Gauchy and P. de Wolff, brief reports on forecasting experiences in the UK, Yugoslavia, Italy, India, Japan, and Holland, a statement of future work in forecasting by OEEC, a list of institutions concerned with forecasting in the member countries, and a bibliographical check list.

1961

995 Department of Labour, Canada, *Engineering and Scientific Manpower Resources in Canada. Their Earnings, Employment and Education, 1957.* Professional Manpower Bulletin No. 9, Manpower Resources Division of the Economics and Research Branch. Ottawa: Department of Labour, 1961. Pp. 106.

A report based on a mail questionnaire to 23,000 university graduates in Canada, contains detailed figures on the earnings and occupational characteristics of engineers and scientists in Canadian industry, answering such questions as: how do salaries vary with length of experience and level of education?; what kind of employers pay highest salaries?; and what kinds of work are performed by engineers and scientists with different course specialities? See also other bulletins in the series on the employment prospects of scientists and engineers in Canada, particularly Bulletin No. 14 on *Employment and Earnings in the Scientific and Technical Professions, 1959-1962* (Ottawa: Department of Labour, 1963. Pp. 24).

996 National Science Foundation, *The Long-Range Demand for Scientific and Technical Personnel. A Methodological Study.* Prepared for NSF by the US Department of Labor. Washington, D.C.: Government Printing Office, 1961. Pp. 70.

To date the most comprehensive and systematic attempt at a quantifications of the future demand for scientists and engineers in the USA, particularly with reference to the chemical and electrical industries. Describe methods for projecting the future supply of scientists and engineers and proposes measures to close the gap between expected demand and supply.

1962

997 W. LEE HANSEN, "Educational Plans and Teacher Supply", *CER*, October, 1962, pp. 136-41.

A useful discussion of why American and British teacher forecasts have gone wrong with a brief review of the factors influencing changes in the demand and supply of teachers. See the revised version in 1335.

998 S. COTGROVE, "Education and Occupation", *BJS*, XIII, 1962, pp. 33-42.

A popular article on the question whether British education adequately prepares people for their occupational roles.

999 OECD, *Country Reviews, Policies for Science and Education.* Paris: OECD, 1962.

Country reviews are carried out periodically in each of the OECD member countries as a means of assessing current progress in educational planning, with special reference to the supply of high-level manpower. The standard procedure for the reviews is for 2 or 3 experts from other member countries to visit the country under review, report their findings and draw up a list of questions which are then debated at a special plenary meeting of the OECD Committee for Scientific and Technical Personnel. So far 5 reviews of this kind have been published: *Yugoslavia* (pp. 62); *Norway* (pp. 53); *Denmark* (pp. 61); *Sweden* (pp. 74); *Greece* (pp. 62). Along similar lines, there is also *Higher Education and the Demand for Scientific Manpower in the USA* (1963, pp. 101), *Scientific Policy in Sweden,* (1964, pp. 66), *Training of Technicians in Ireland* (1964, pp. 112), and *Training of and Demand for High-Level Scientific and Technical Personnel in Canada* (1966, pp. 136). In every case, valuable data is included in the reviews.

1000   National Advisory Council on the Training and Supply of Teachers, *The Demand for and Supply of Teachers 1960-80. Seventh Report.* London: HMSO, 1962. Pp. 30.

Analyses the current and projected shortage of teachers in Great Britain and outlines various proposals that might remedy the situation. (See also 1028.)

1963

1001   M. VERMOT-GAUCHY, "Ière partie: La planification à long terme vers de nouvelles méthodes d'étude"; "IIe partie: Expansion économique et besoins en personnels qualifiés perspectives 1959 à 1975"; "IIIe partie: L'éducation et la formation", *Bulletin SEDEIS. Futuribles.* Paris: Société d'études et de documentation économiques, industrielles et sociales, 1963. Pp. 44, 48, 54.

A detailed educational plan for France, with particular reference to highly qualified manpower. (See also 1036.)

1002   A. T. PEACOCK, "Economic Growth and the Demand for Qualified Manpower", *DBR,* June, 1963, pp. 3-19.

The author warns against the pitfalls in the manpower-forecasting approach and calls for more study of the relative rates of return to various forms of higher education in Great Britain. The argument is illustrated by the work of the Advisory Council on Scientific Manpower (969) and of NEDC.

1003   M. J. BOWMAN, "Educational Shortage and Excess", *CJEPS,* November, 1963, pp. 446-62.

An illuminating clarification of the various meanings of "shortage" or "excess" of manpower, with special attention to teacher shortage and excess.

1004   S. E. HARRIS, "The Need for More Information on Investment in Human Capital", *OECD-RF,* pp. 228-40.

Despite its title, this paper deals mostly with unsettled questions in manpower planning but, along the way, it touches on a number of other unsettled questions in the economics of education.

1005   A. BROWN, C. LEICESTER, G. PYATT, "Output, Manpower and Industrial Skills in
       the UK, 1948-1970", *ibid.*, pp. 240-60.

       The 1970 job forecasts of the Cambridge Growth Project of the Department
       of Applied Economics at Cambridge.

1006   National Science Foundation, *Scientists, Engineers, and Technicians in the
       1960's: Requirements and Supply.* Washington, D.C.: National Science Foun-
       dation, 1963. Pp. 68.

       Detailed projections of both demand and supply of scientific and technical
       manpower up to 1970 were made, using the methodology outlined in an earlier
       publication by NSF. (See 996.) The projections are based on explicit assump-
       tions about economic growth, enrolment rates, and the extrapolation of past
       trends. The conclusion is that if present trends continue, demand will ex-
       ceed supply throughout the decade, and the booklet closes with a discussion
       of the likely adjustments in utilisation of manpower and on-the-job training
       that will be made to bring demand and supply into balance. There is a strik-
       ing absence of any discussion of the effect of changes in salary differentials
       on demand and supply. (See also 1019.)

1007   OECD, *Employment Forecasting. International Seminar on Forecasting Techniques,
       Brussels, June 4-7, 1962. Final Report.* Paris: OECD, 1963. Pp. 112.

       This volume contains an exposé of the various methods of manpower forecast-
       ing and planning by J. Tinbergen, pp. 9-21, an excellent paper reviewing
       Swedish experience with long-term manpower forecasting by S.-O. Döös,
       pp. 24-58, a review of French manpower forecasts by J. Fourastié, pp. 59-78,
       and a review of Dutch techniques of forecasting by P. de Wolff, pp. 79-103.

1008   *Manpower Report of the President and A Report on Manpower Requirements,
       Resources, Utilization, and Training, by the United States Department of
       Labor.* Washington, D.C.: 1963. Pp. 204, 135.

       The Manpower Development and Training Act of 1962 provides that the Secre-
       tary of Labor shall report to the President on America's manpower problems
       and that the President shall transmit a Manpower Report to Congress. This
       report, the first of its kind, brings together in one volume virtually all
       the statistical data now available on current manpower needs in the United
       States. See particularly the summary of findings, pp. 3-9, the data on the
       rising educational levels of the labour force, pp. 12-13, the facts on pro-
       ductivity trends by industries, pp. 67-73, the projection of employment trends
       in major occupational groups, pp. 99-105, and the projection of future man-
       power supplies, pp. 105-10. See also the 1964 version of the same report
       (pp. 279) and an accompanying *Report of the Secretary of Labor on Manpower
       Research and Training under the Manpower Development and Training Act* (Wash-
       ington, D.C.: US Government Printing Office, 1964. Pp. 193). Similar
       reports have been published every year since (see 1095).

1009   K. BAHR, *Die Ermittlung des Nachwuchsbedarfs an technischen Führungskräften.
       Eine international vergleichende Untersuchung.* Berlin: Hermann Luchterhand
       Verlag, 1963. Pp. 129.

       A valuable review of recent efforts to forecast manpower in developed countries. Among the publications that are critically scrutinised are 969, 1001 and several official German studies not mentioned in this bibliography.

1010   International Bureau of Education, *Shortage of Primary Teachers*.   XXVIth International Conference on Public Education. Geneva: IBE-UNESCO, 1963. Pp. 191.

This survey of the supply of teachers to primary schools in 83 countries reveals a staff shortage in three-quarters of the countries. The introduction to the book provides a convenient summary of the general findings about the causes of the shortage and the various measures taken to combat it.

1011   M. D. STEUER, M. D. GODFREY, "Skill Categories and the Allocation of Labour", *BJIR*, December, 1963, pp. 228-40.

The authors analyse the problem of optimum allocation of labour by firms among skill categories such as operative, craftsman, etc., when the work force is fixed and output can be raised only by upgrading workers. From the fact that the wages of a worker depend on the skill category to which he is assigned, they deduce by graphic arguments that profit-maximising frims will misallocate labour by placing too many men in unskilled jobs. The paper concludes with some tentative findings of the authors' ongoing research on skill mix proportions in American manufacturing in the post-war years.

1964

1012   OECD, *Resources of Scientific and Technical Personnel in the OECD Area. Statistical Report of the Third International Survey on the Demand for and Supply of Scientific and Technical Personnel*. Paris: OECD, 1964. Pp. 293.

The objectives of this survey were to determine the changes in the employment prospects of scientists and technicians in the various sectors of the economies of member countries since the second OECD survey in 1956. A wealth of data is presented for individual countries, for groups of countries like the whole of Western Europe contrasted with Canada and the USA, and for small and large developed countries contrasted with developing countries. For the most part the figures are allowed to speak for themselves without any serious attempt at interpretation. This study exemplifies once again the need for more internationally comparable data.

1013   G. BOMBACH, "Long-Term Requirements for Qualified Manpower in Relation to Economic Growth", *OECD-EAHE*, pp. 201-21; revised version as "Manpower Forecasting and Educational Policy", *SE*, Fall, 1966, pp. 343-74, reprinted in *WYK I*, pp. 435-57, and *BILD*, pp. 67-95.

A brilliant discussion of the methodology of manpower forecasting in developed countries, showing how it has been done and suggesting how it might be done better. It is a summary of a longer study which the author prepared for OECD.

1014   C. VIMONT, "Methods of Forecasting Employment in France and Use of These Forecasts to Wrok Out Official Educational Programmes", *OECD- EAHE*, pp. 223-46

    A review of French experience with employment forecasting and with trans-
lating these forecasts into educational requirements.

1015   National Academy of Sciences, *Toward a Better Utilization of Scientific and
       Engineering Talent. A Programme for Action.* Report of the Committee on
       Utilization of Scientific and Engineering Manpower. Washington, D.C.:
       NAS, 1964. Pp. 153.

    The report contains a review of the facts and a number of practical recom-
mendations designed to improve the utilisation of scientists and engineers
in the United States, irrespective of current shortages or surpluses. The
report is followed by 9 study papers among which are: F. H. Harbison, "Toward
the Development of a Comprehensive Manpower Policy", pp. 65-70, which sets
out the machinery for the development of a national manpower programme in
America; G. Colm, L. A. Lecht, "Requirements for Scientific and Engineering
Manpower in the 1970's", pp. 71-82, differing in its estimates from previous
forecasts by ± 100,000; A. M. Ross, "How Do We Use Our Engineers and Scientists?", pp. 83-98; A. O. Gamble, "Proposals for Development of An Improved
Manpower-Related Information Programme", pp. 99-112; and P. W. Cherington,
"Case Studies on Utilization of Scientists and Engineers on Titan II and
NTDS Development Studies", pp. 121-35.

1016   V. STOIKOV, "The Allocation of Scientific Effort: Some Important Aspects",
       QJE, May, 1964, pp. 307-24.

    This paper analyses the optimum allocation of scientists and engineers
between teaching and research so as to maximise the magnitude of research
findings produced in a given period of time. Surprisingly enough, it is
shown that an optimal allocation over the next 10 or 20 years requires that
the fraction of graduating scientists and engineers entering teaching in the
USA be increased considerably.

1017   R. S. ECKAUS, "Economic Criteria for Education and Training", *RES*, May, 1964,
       pp. 181-90; see "Comment" by D. A. Ross, *ibid.*, February, 1966, pp. 103-5.

    After some critical remarks on the rate-of-return approach, alleging that
there exist no prices in the "markets" for education and educated labour that
reflect real demand and supply influences, the author sketches a method of
national manpower planning, using American data on the owrk-traits required
in different occupations. (See also 1070.)

1018   National Science Foundation, *American Science Manpower 1962. A Report of the
       National Register of Scientific and Technical Personnel.* Washington, D.C.:
       NSF, 1964. Pp. 155.

    This report analyses the education, employment, scientific specialisation,
and other characteristics reported by about 215,000 American scientists in
1962, approximately 90 per cent of America's total stock of natural scientists.

1019   National Science Foundation, *Scientific and Technical Manpower Resources.
       Summary Information on Employment, Characteristics, Supply, and Training.*
       Washington, D.C.: NSF, 1964. Pp. 184.

This superb volume presents all the existing information in the United
States on cu-rent trends in the distribution of scientific manpower, by sectors and occupations, pp. 4-77, the educational attainments and age-specific
earnings of scientific manpower, pp. 77-123, the present rate of output of
new scientists, engineers, and technicians, pp. 123-61, and a review of short-
term and long-term forecasting of the demand for such personnel, pp. 161-71.
The work includes bibliographical references and a list of American organisations concerned with scientific and engineering manpower information.

1020 Engineering Manpower Commission of Engineers Joint Council, *Demand for
      Engineers, Physical Scientists and Technicians—1964; The Placement of Engineer*
      ing Graduates—1964; Professional Income of Engineers—1964. New York: EJC,
      1964. Pp. 80, 20, 80.

      The first is a questionnaire-survey of current employment patterns in 543
      companies and agencies employing about 40 per cent of the total number of
      degree-holding engineers and about 20 per cent of the physical scientists and
      technicians in the United States. The second is designed to measure the
      speed with which new engineering graduates are committed to employment. The
      third study presents data on the earnings of 230,000 engineering graduates
      by types of employer, level of supervision, and years of work experience.

1021 C. LEICESTER, "Economic Growth and the School Leaver", *CRAC*, Summer, 1964,
      pp. 9-15.

      An attempt to estimate the needs of British manufacturing industry by
      1970, assuming a 4 per cent growth rate in the economy, and to translate
      these manpower requirements into educational requirements by subjects of
      specialisation. But see the effective criticsm by G. Jones, "The Needs of
      Industry.", *ibid.*, Autumn, 1964, pp. 7-12.

1022 J. K. FOLGER, C. B. NAM, "Trends in Education in Relation to the Occupational
      Structure", *SE*, Fall, 1964, pp. 19-34.

      Using American Census data for 1940, 1950, and 1960 for men of prime work-
      ing age, the authors demonstrate a moderate but declining association between
      education and occupation, and raise some problems for further research.

1023 The Institution of Chemical Engineers, *The Choice of Chemical Engineering at*
      University or Technical College. London: ICE, 1964. Pp. 53.

      This valuable quantitative inquiry, based on a random sample of first-year
      students of chemistry and mechanical engineering, was designed to throw
      light on the circumstances leading science school-eavers in 1963 to choose
      chemical engineering for study in higher or further education in the United
      Kingdom. The results of the study are conveniently summarised on pp. 2-5.

1024 J. AUERHAN, *Lectures on the Labour Force and Its Employment*. Geneva:
      International Institute for Labour Studies, 1964. Pp. 42.

      Three lectures by a Czech manpower expert on "Estimation of Manpower Require-
      ments for Economic Development", "Planning of Education to Meet Expected
      Requirements of Manpower", and "Planning of Training to Meet Expected Require-
      ments of Manpower", with particular reference ot the experiences of Czecho-

slovakia. Manpower planning by the so-called "ratio of saturation", as used
in the USSR and other Eastern European countries, is explained in some detail.

1025   National Manpower Council, *Government and Manpower. A Statement by the
       National Manpower Council With Background Chapters by the Council Staff.*
       N.Y.: Columbia University Press, 1964. Pp. 470.

   This volume deals with the dual role of federal, state, and local governments in the United States as consumers and producers of high-quality manpower. Pt. One, "A Statement by the National Manpower Council", pp. 9-87,
contains a discussion of the structure of the labour force in the public
sector as well as a review of labour market and manpower policies. The background chapters, which make up Pt. Two, present information on governments
as major employers, their competitive positions in the labour market, and the
impact of public policies upon manpower utilisation in the areas of health,
education, science, technology, and defence. Accompanying this book is the
proceedings of a conference on government and manpower, entitled *Public
Policies and Manpower Resources* (New York: Columbia University Press, 1964.
Pp. 260¼, including a paper by S. E. Harris on "The Relationship of Economic
Resources to Policy", pp. 194-235, and a summary of "Conference Findings"
by H. David, pp. 237-50.

1026   Institution of Mechanical Engineers, *Engineering Education and CAreer Patterns.*
       A Conference Arranged by the Education and Training Group. London: IME,
       1964. Pp. 95.

   The conference papers include one by S. P. Hutton and J. E. Gerstl,
"Engineering, Education and Careers", pp. 1-16, reporting on a survey of the
education, training and career patterns of a sample of the members of the
Institution of Mechanical Engineers (see 690, 1026) and an essay by B. T.
Turner on "The Effective Use of Engineers in the Changing Industrial Environment", pp. 16-39. The discussion, reprinted in this volume, produced some
interesting contributions.

1965

1027   Ministry of Labour, UK, Manpower Studies No. 2, *The Metal Industries. A
       Study of Occupational Trends in the Metal Manufacturing and Metal Using
       Industries.* London: HMSO, 1965. Pp. 98.

   This report by the Manpower Research Unit of the Ministry of Labour discusses occupational trends in more than 300 large and medium-sized metal firms
throughout Great Britain. Firms were also asked the extent to which they took
a systematic forward look at their future manpower requirements: it appears
that only 1 out of 4 British firms make some sort of forecast for more than
2 years ahead, and only 1 out of 40 do so for all categories of workers,
p. 20.

1028   National Advisory Council on the Training and Supply of Teachers, *The Demand
       for and Supply of Teachers, 2963-1986. Ninth Report.* London: HMSO, 1965.
       Pp. 98.

   A forecast of the teacher shortage in Great Britain up to 1986, on the
assumption that the current pattern of school attendance continues unchanged,

subject to the rise in the school-leaving age to 16 in 1970-71. The volume
includes 50 pages of supporting material and a sharply dissenting note by
E. E. Robinson, endorsed by C. F. Carter and J. Vaizey.

1029   B. DUNCAN, "Dropouts and the Unemployed", *JPE*, April, 1965, pp. 121-35.

   This interesting paper reviews the record of change in educational attainment in the United States since the turn of the century, and links this to
changes in the employment situation. It demonstrates that since the end of
World War II fluctuations about the trend towards higher rates of school
attendance for boys have varied inversely with the state of the job market;
when jobs are scarce, young men remain at high school; when jobs are plenti-
ful, the dropout rate accelerates.

1030   OECD, Human Resources Development, *Manpower Forecasting in Educational Planning*. Paris: OECD, 1965. Pp. 185.

   This report of the joint EIP/MRP Meeting that was held in 1965 includes
papers by: H. S. Parnes, "Scope and Methods of Human Resource and Educational
Planning", pp. 15-35, which give the author's latest reflections on the man-
power-forecasting approach to educational planning; L. Sandgren "Estimates
of Manpower Reuqirements in the Light of Educational Planning in Sweden",
pp. 37-43; R. Ruiter, "Manpower Forecasts and Educational Planning in the
Netherlands", pp. 45-56, which highlights the growing disenchantment in
Holland with manpower forecasting; M. O'Donoghue, "The Manpower/Educational
Activities of the Irish E.I.P. Team", pp. 57-69; J. Steindl, "The Role of
Manpower Requirements in the Educational Planning Experience of the Austria
E.I.P. Team", pp. 71-81; G. Bombach, "Forecasting Requirements for Highly
Qualified Manpower as a Basis for Educational Policy", pp. 83-133, a reprint
of 1013 with some new introductory remarks; R. Hollister, "Summary of the
Technical Evaluation of the M.R.P. Experience", pp. 135-50 (see 886, 1039),
and a very interesting Verbatim Record of the discussions, pp. 151-85.

1031   OECD, Country Reports, *The Mediterranean Regional Project. An Experiment in
Planning by Six Countries*. Paris: OECD, 1965. Pp. 39.

   A description of MRP and a summary of the main findings together with some
statistical tables.

1032   N. M. MELTZ, *Changes in the Occupational Composition of the Canadian Labour
Force, 1931-1961*. Economics and Research Branch, Department of Labour,
Canada, Occasional Paper No. 2. Ottawa: Queen's Printer, 1965. Pp. 136.

   This work is a thorough analysis of the significant changes in occupational
composition over the 30 years period, including an explicit discussion of the
implication of the analysis for techniques of forecasting manpower requirements. The author suggests that manpower forecasts of the Parnes-type ought
to be supplemented by relative earnings data in a particular way (see
pp. 107-9). See also the interesting technique employed in ch. 5, pp. 35-50,
for distinguishing between the effects of changes in the supply of a skill
and changes in the demand for that skill.

1033   Committee on Manpower Resources for Science and Technology, UK, *A Review of
the Scope and Problems of Scientific Manpower Policy*. Cmnd. 2800. London:
HMSO, 1965. Pp. 17.

A summary of the current work of the committee and a useful list of research projects presently under way in Great Britain bearing upon scientific manpower policy.

1034 J. SCOVILLE, "The Development and Relevance of U.S. Occupational Data", *ILRR*, October, 1965, pp. 70-80.

Traces the history of the American census of occupations and shows that the problems posed by modern manpower and labour market research call for a drastic overhauling of the census.

1035 O. MEHMET, *Methods of Forecasting Manpower Requirements, with Special Reference to the Province of Ontario*. Ottawa, Canada: Queen's Printer, 1965. Pp. 57.

A useful survey of existing methods, such as "the econometric method" (input-output analysis), "the productivity method" (the OECD-MRP approach), "the trend projection method", "the employers' survey method", "the interarea comparisons method", and "the elasticity of factor substitution method", (more a suggestion than a description of an existing method). A separate chapter considers the translation of manpower forecasts into forecasts of educational requirements. The subtitle of the book is only relevant to ch. 10, pp. 52-57. A good bibliography is included.

1036 M. VERMOT-GAUCHY, *L'éducation nationale dans la France de 1975*. Monaco: Futuribles, Éditions du Rocher, 1965. Pp. 332.

After a preliminary historical section on the growth of higher education in France, the book turns to detailed forecasts of the demand for highly qualified manpower over the next decade by means of estimates of sectoral labourproductivity coefficients. This section incorporates and develops materials previously published by the author (see 994, 1001). These forecasts of demand are then related to the likely supply of educated manpower up to 1975.

1037 Economics and Research Branch, Department of Labour, Ottawa, *Skilled and Professional Manpower in Canada, 1945-1965*. Ottawa: Department of Labour, 1965. Pp. 112.

This study contains a discussion of the sources of specialised manpower in Canada, an analysis of shortages in selected occupational groups in 1956, and, lastly, an estimate of prospective requirements for skilled manpower over the decade 1955-65 in which a forecast of probable net immigration figures heavily.

1038 *Active Manpower Policy. The Final Report and Supplement to the Final Report of the International Management Seminar on Active Manpower Policy, Brussels, 14-17 April 1964*. Paris: OECD, Manpower and Social Affairs Directorate, Social Affairs Division, 1965. Pp. 166, 207.

The Final Report consists of two essays prepared for the seminar: W. E. Bakke, "An Active and Positive Manpower Policy", pp. 127-43, and L. Aarvig, "Active Manpower Policy. The Attitude and Role of Employers and Thier Organisations", pp. 145-56, and a text which weaves together the material from the country-studies in the *Supplement*. By an "active manpower policy" is meant the integrated provision by the public authorities of local employment exchanges, occupational counselling services, manpower forecasting information, public works programmes in depressed areas, vocational training and retraining schemes, and a system of unemployment compensationa and relocation payments.

1966

1039 R. G. HOLLISTER, *A Technical Evaluation of the First Stage of the Mediterranean Regional Project*. Paris: OECD, 1966. Pp. 146.

This outstanding study analyses the methods of estimating manpower and educational requirements that were used in the six MPR country-studies. It develops new techniques—such as "sensitivity analysis" and "sources-of-change analysis"—for evaluating such estimates: see, particularly, the conclusions of the study, pp. 59–64. An appendix presents comparative statistics for the six MRP countries (see also 886).

1040 OECD, Documentation in Agriculture and Food, *Trained Manpower for Tomorrow's Agriculture*. Paris: OECD, 1966. Pp. 243.

This work is subtitled "A Report on Pilot Studies in France and Sweden on Projecting Future Needs for People with Agricultural Training and on Planning the Educational Investment Required to Meet Those Needs" and applies the OECD-MRP approach to the agricultural sector. The French pilot study is by L. Malassis, pp. 13–63; that on Sweden is by G. Ericsson and F. Petrini, pp. 63–143. W. N. T. Roberts follows the two pilot studies with a comparative analysis of their projection methods, pp. 143–72. The volume concludes with a convenient summary chapter, pp. 177–85.

1041 S. WICKHAM, "Future Demand for Vocational Skills at Different Levels", *ILR*, February, 1966, pp. 99–117.

This paper discusses the problems involved in basing vocational training programmes on manpower forecasts as illustrated by French experience. The French Planning Commission now makes use of an occupational classification comprising six training levels, corresponding to four basic skills. These are projected forward by a combination of techniques. The author presents some of the preliminary forecasts and comments briefly on them.

1042 B. C. ROBERTS, J. H. SMITH, eds., *Manpower Policy and Employment Trends*. London: G. Bell & Sons, 1966. Pp. 137.

This series of lectures on British labour markets given at the London School of Economics in 1964 includes a general paper by J. R. Crossley: "Forecasting Manpower Demand and Supply", pp. 15–25, and another one on "Essential Statistics for Manpower Forecasting", pp. 25–35; G. G. C. Routh, "The Changing Pattern of Employment Since 1900", pp. 35–47, with material drawn from his book; C. Freeman, "Research, Technical Change and Manpower Forecasting", pp. 47–63; P. R. G. Layard, "Manpower Needs and the Planning of Higher Education", pp. 63–89, reproducing the second half of 759; J. H. Smith, "The Analysis of Labour Mobility", pp. 89–98; N. Sear "The Future Employment of Women", pp. 98–111; and B. C. Roberts, J. L. Hirsch, "Factors INfluencing Hours of Work", pp. 111–37.

1043   K. EIDE, "Educational Developments and Economic Growth in OECD Member Coun-
       tries", *IEA-EE*, pp. 174-202.

       This paper consists of three unconnected parts: the first part analyses
       the situation with respect to highly qualified manpower in the OECD areas in
       1959; the second discusses various approaches to educational planning; and
       the third reviews the work of OECD in the manpower area.

1044   R. TRAJTENBERG, *The Change in the Educational Content of the Labour Force.
       A Second Stage Analysis on the Sources of Change.* Paris: OECD, 1966.
       Pp. 39, mimeographed.

       This paper pursues the method of analysis proposed in 1039, breaking down
       the matrix of the educational distribution of the labour force by occupation
       into its various components.

1045   OECD, Directorate for Scientific Affairs, *The Education and Utilisation of
       Highly Qualified Personnel—An Analysis of Census Data.* Paris: OECD, 1966.
       Pp. 75, mimeographed.

       A valuable document that summarises a great deal of census information
       relevant to the testing of Tinbergen-type and Parnes-type models. A healthy
       sceptical air pervades the commentary on the data.

1046   OECD, Directorate for Scientific Affairs, *Lectures and Methodological Essays
       on Educational Planning. Lectures given at the Human Resources Development
       Training Course, 1964.* Paris: OECD, 1966. Pp. 306.

       The lectures, given at a course for OECD Human Resource Fellows, consist
       of C. A. Myers, "The Role of Education in Economic Growth", which reproduces
       material from 1352; F. H. Harbison, "Strategies for Human Resource Develop-
       ment", which illustrates some of the problems of planning by case-studies
       of Nyasaland, Colombia, China, and Egypt; S. Mardin, "Social Factors Affect-
       ing Educational Reforms", dealing with the social demand for education in
       Turkey; J. Vaizey, "Financial and Policy Implications ofEducational Plans",
       which predicts a period of financial stringency for education in most coun-
       tries in the 1970's and discusses methods of financing educational expansion;
       L. Tabah, "Demographic Aspects of Educational Planning", which deals with
       population trends in developing countries; and J. Tinbergen, "Projections of
       Output and Employment", which describes in outline the Correa-Tinbergen model
       (see 1736). The second part of the volume consists of five more detailed
       methodological papers: L. J. Emmerij and H. H. Thies, "Projecting Manpower
       Requirements by Occupation"; J. L Blum, "Skill Acquisition and Development";
       H. S. Parnes, "Labour Force Mobility"; C. Van Dijk, "The Operating Costs of
       Education"; and H. H. Thies, "Regional Aspects of Educational Planning".
       These papers give detailed information of some of the work done by MRP teams.

1047   J.-P. JALLADE, *Contribution à une planification à moyen terme de l'enseigne-
       ment en Espagne.* Human Resources Development, Fellows' Reports. Paris:
       OECD, 1966. Pp. 130.

       A study of manpower needs in Spain up to 1971, carried out in 1964.

1048   L. G. VASSILION, *Esquisse d'un plan d'éducation pour le Péloponnèse*. Human
       Resources Development, Fellows' Reports. Paris: OECD, 1966. Pp. 122.

       A study of Greek education in the light of manpower needs, carried out in
       1964.

1049   Human Resources Development, Fellows' Reports, *Manpower and Education*.
       Paris: OECD, 1966.

       This volume includes a number of studies carried out in 1963 or 1964 by
       some of OECD's Human Resources Development Fellows: V. Morris, "High Level
       Manpower in OECD Countries", an attempt to measure stocks of high-level man-
       power in the OECD area (pp. 40); A. M. Grant, "Changing Occupational Patterns
       and Their Relation to Technological Development. Report on a Research Pro-
       ject Performed Within the M.R.P." (pp. 36); D. P. Sanders and others, "Edu-
       cational Preparation of Skilled Manpower" (pp. 70); T. N. Chirikos, "Mobility
       of Scientific and Engineering Personnel in Greece" (pp. 35); and L. Srdić,
       "Economic Activity and Educational Background of the Norwegian Female Labour
       Force" (pp. 44).

1050   B. W. WILKINSON, *Studies in the Economics of Education*. Economics and
       Research Branch, Department of Labour, Canada: Occasional Papers, No. 4.
       Ottawa: Queen's Printer, 1966. Pp. 148.

       In the opening chapter, the author reviews all the existing approaches to
       assessing the economic value of education and comes down in favour of the
       manpower-planning approach. Ch. 2 analyses net Canadian emigration to the
       United States in absolute numbers and in estimated human capital values.
       Ch. 3 translates the US Dictionary of Occupational Titles into an estimate
       of Canadian labour requirements by occupations, using 1961 Canadian census
       figures, in the style of Eckaus' work (see 1017).

1051   Netherlands Economics Institute, *The Educational Structure of the Labour
       Force: A Statistical Analysis*. Rotterdam: NEI, 1966. Pp. 169.

       An attempt to present information on the educational characteristics of
       the labour force in as many countries as possible, with a discussion of
       various techniques for estimating the educational structure of the labour
       force when direct data are lacking. The relation between highly qualified
       manpower and various economic variables is analysed by means of least-square
       regression techniques.

1052   G. B. MARCH, ed., *Occupational Data Requirements for Educational Planning:
       Proceedings of a Conference at the University of Wisconsin*. Wisconsin:
       Center for Studies in Vocational and Technical Education, 1966. Pp. 165.

       This collection of papers, and the discussion which followed them, reveals
       important differences of opinion among the participants on the importance
       and value of manpower data and projections for educational planning. R. N.
       Evans argues the need for better occupational data, pp. 1-18, but participants
       questioned the costs involved, and argued that a more pressing need was for
       analysis of existing data. B. Weisbrod speaks of the difficulty of defining
       manpower "needs" in the absence of data on rates of return, pp. 33-40, and
       also questions the distinction between vocational and rates of return,

pp. 33-40, and also questions the distinction between vocational and non-vocational education. D. A. Schon describes the extent of forecasting within US government departments, pp. 42-51. S. G. Kelley reviews the work of MRP, pp. 60-83, and W. J. Platt describes the use of international comparisons of the educational stock of the labour force, pp. 84-101. Some interesting comments on these papers were made by W. G. Bowen, H. S. Parnes, and F. Harbison, pp. 105-13. Finally, S. A. Levitan surveys manpower and occupational data in the US, but denies that occupational projections should be given top priority, pp. 126-38. M. L. Joseph also argues that manpower forecasters should not attempt to make longer and more detailed forecasts of manpower needs without more research into questions of substitutability, and the role of wage adjustments in the labour market, pp. 161-65.

1053 R. A. LESTER, *Manpower Planning in a Free Society*. Princeton, N.J.: Princeton University Press, 1966. Pp. 227.

This book is aimed primarily at improving manpower planning and manpower policies in the United States, setting forth a programme of action designed to realise the purposes of Title I of the Manpower Development and Training Act of 1962. It includes, however, useful comparisons with Europe, as, for example, in ch. 3 on "A New Concept of the Employment Service", pp. 45-85. See also the discussion on cost-benefit analysis of training schemes, ch. 7, pp. 172192.

1054 "A Symposium: Manpower Projections", *ILRR*, May, 1966, pp. 1-85.

This symposium is made up of five useful articles largely based on American experience: (1) G. L. Mangum, A. L. Nemore, "The Nature and Function of Manpower Projections", pp. 1-17; (2) H. Goldstein, "Projections of Manpower Requirements and Supply", pp. 17-28; (3) V. Darmstadter, "Manpower in a Long-Term Economic Projection Model", pp. 28-59; (4) P. E. Haase, "Technological Change and Manpower Forecasts", pp. 59-72; and (5) R. Ferber, K. Sasaki, "Labor Force and Wage Projections in Hawaii", pp. 72-85.

1055 V. KLEIN, "The Demand ofr Professional Womanpower", *BJS*, June, 1966, pp. 183-97.

An attempt to forecast the demand for highly trained women in Great Britain, based on a questionnaire sent to 70 professional organisations, with a detailed breakdown of the existing structure of female professional participation. Argues that the reserve of professional womanpower is limited, since already the proportion of married women working is considerably higher in the professions than in unskilled occupations.

1056 B. A. KEYS, H. H. WRIGHT, *Manpower Planning in Industry. A Case Study*. Staff Study No. 18. Economic Council of Canada. Ottawa, Canada: Queen's Printer, 1966. Pp. 43.

A survey of 17 large companies employing 5 per cent of the total Canadian work force, emphasising anticipated shifts and trends in manpower requirements rather than utilisation of present skills. The survey highlights the general absence of manpower planning at the firm level in Canada.

1057 Committee on Manpower Resources for Science and Technology, UK, *Report on the 1965 Triennial Manpower Survey of Engineers, Technologists, Scientists and Technical Supporting Staff.* London: HMSO, 1966. Cmnd. 3103. Pp. 64.

This pamphlet shows the distribution of certain types of highly qualified manpower by sector of employment in the British economy in 1965, with a forecast based on employers' opinions for 1968. Ch. 4 distinguishes between "demand" and "need" and compares earlier forecasts with the actual results. See also the Committee's *Interim Report of the Working Group on Manpower Parameters for Scientific Growth* (London: HMSO, 1966. Cmnd. 3102. Pp. 38). Both documents are reviewed in *Nature,* October 15, 1966.

1058 K. GALES, R. C. WRIGHT, *A Survey of Manpower Demand Forecasts for the Social Services.* London: The National Council of Social Service, 1966. Pp. 95.

A review of recent British work, much of it official, on demand forecasting for teachers, doctors, dentists, medical auxiliaries, social workers, health visitors, probation officers, etcetera. Unfortunately, the review is spoiled by a fiarly naive view of the concept of "needs": for example, in some cases, government itself is both employer and provider of educational facilities; in other cases, it fulfils only the latter function, in consequence of which ti is in no position to define "needs".

1059 D. H. GRAY, *Manpower Planning. An Approach to the Problem.* London: Institute of Personnel Management, 1966. Pp. 54.

What this pamphlet is about is manpower planning in the individual enterprise. It has no relevance, therefore, to educational planning.

1060 H. P. WIDMAIER, *Bildung in neuer Sicht. Schriftenreihe des Kulturministeriums Baden-Württemberg zur Bildungsforschung Bildungsplanung Bildungspolitik.* Baden-Württemberg: Neckar-Verlag, 1966. Pp. 300.

A forecast of the demand for highly qualified manpower by 1981 in one of the Länder of Western Germany, using the MRP-approach of OECD. By the use of a model of the entire educational system, this forecast becomes the basis of a projection for all levels of the educational system in Baden-Württemberg over the next 15 years. (See also 886.)

1061 J. G. SCOVILLE, "Education and Training Requirements for Occupations", *RES,* November, 1966, pp. 387-94.

Applies Eckaus' method (1017) of estimating the education and training requirements of industries to the component occupations of an industry.

1062 OECD, *Organisational Problems in Planning Educational Development.* Paris: OECD, 1966. Pp. 109.

A somewhat amorphous collection of papers, including pieces of N. Erder, "Some Administrative Problems in Educational Planning", pp. 13-23; R. Poignant on "The Roles of Educational Plans in Economic and Social Development Programmes", pp. 23-37, chiefly with reference to France; a careful and exhaustive review of the relationship between "Manpower Requirements and Educational Organisation" by H. Goldstein, pp. 37-51; S. J. Mushkin, "Resource Requirement

and Educational Obsolescence", pp. 51-65; and "Some Reflections on Centrali-
zation versus Decentralization in Education", pp. 65-75, illustrated by Dutch
educational problems, by W. Brand. R. Grégoire's "Summary Report of the
Discussion" provides an admirable precis of the various contributions, stressing that few current educational plans in Europe are, in fact, based on manpower forecasts.

1967

1063 **Commonwealth Education Liaison Committee,** *Education and Training of Techni-*
      cians: Report of an Expert Conference, 1966. London: HMSO, 1967. Pp. 326.

    A collection of speeches and papers delivered at a conference on the train-
ing of technicians in Commonwealth countries, which includes several discussions of the problems of forecasting demand for technicians and of planning technical education to meet manpower needs. See the speech by Sir W.
Jackson on technical training in Britain, pp. 19-26, and a paper by L. S.
Chandrakant on manpower planning in India, pp. 29-52.

1064 **W. LEE HANSEN,** "The Economics of Scientific and Engineering Manpower", *JHR*,
      Spring, 1967, pp. 191-215.

    This paper begins by defining some of the issues in the current American
debate on manpower shortages and then proposes rate-of-return analysis as a
way of providing new insights into these issues. See the attached comments
by C. A. Moser and D. Brown, pp. 215-20. In another "Comment", *ibid.*, Spring,
1968, pp. 246-52, L. O. Bumas reasserts the standard definition of "shortage"
in terms of vacancy statistics and supplies some supporting evidence.

1065 **C. A. ANDERSON,** "The Adaptation of Education to a Mobile Society", *ibid.*,
      pp. 221-48.

    The author argues that America's educational system is capable of respond-
ing adequately to any demands of high-level manpower that are likely to
materialise in the next few decades, and therefore denies the need to gear
educational expansion to manpower forecasts. See the attached comments by
C. B. Nam and R. Hollister, pp. 248-53.

1066 **OECD,** *Policy Conference on Highly Qualified Manpower.* Paris: OECD, 1967.
      Pp. 361.

    This meeting on the utilisation of highly educated manpower in the member
countries was held in Paris in September, 1966. The volume opens with a
section that contains (1) a statement of the terms of reference of the meeting; (2) reports from the two study groups; (3) a general report by
R. Grégoire; and (4) a series of conclusions and recommendations, pp. 11-49.
This is followed by extracts from the dozen principal reports presented:
(1) A. Page, "Adaptation of the Supply of Scientific and Technical Personnel
to the Needs of the Economy: French Experience", pp. 53-116; (2) H. Folk,
"The Response of Higher Education to Economic Needs", pp. 117-44, a particularly valuable contribution to the literature; (3) L. Levine "Some Aspects
of the Operation of the Labour Market for Highly Qualified Personnel",
pp. 145-54; (4) R. Cain, "The Programme of Postcensal Studies of Professional
and Technical Manpower in the United States", pp. 155-78; (5) E. Thorsrud,

"A Social Research Approach to the Education and Utilisation of Engineers",
pp. 179-200; (6) F. Halden, "The Evolution of the Tasks and Functions of
Engineers", pp. 201-10; (7) J. R. Orr, "A Study of Engineering Responsibility
Levels in the United Kingdom", pp. 211-26; (8) M. Blaug, M. H. Peston, and
A. Ziderman, "The Utilisation of Qualified Manpower in Industry", pp. 227-88
(see also 1072); (9) M. Chapuy, "In-Career Training of Highly Qualified Per-
sonnel in a Large Public Enterprise", pp. 289-314; (10) J. K. Wolfe, "Continu-
ing Education for Engineers and Scientists", pp. 315-32; (11) G. J. Spence,
"The Growth and Co-ordination of Scientific and Technical Manpower Studies
in the United Kingdom", pp. 333-41; and (12) Department of Citizenship and
Immigration, Canada, "Recent Institutional Changes for Improved Manpower
Utilisation", pp. 341-50.

1067 H. GOLDSTEIN, S. SWERDLOFF, *Methods of Long-Term Projection of Requirement*
      for and Supply of Qualified Manpower. UNESCO Statistical Reports and Studies
      Paris: UNESCO, 1967. Pp. 48.

        An excellent review, together with a useful bibliography, of the status of
      employment forecasting in the United States. Despite its title, however,
      the discussion on the demand side stops short of the translation of occupa-
      tional into educational requirements.

1068 R. A. GORDON, ed., *Toward a Manpower Policy*. N.Y.: John Wiley, 1967.
      Pp. 372.

        A collection of papers and "discussions" on America's manpower problems,
      including G. L. Mangum, "The Emergence of a National Manpower Program",
      pp. 11-34; (2) P. Arnow, "What Are Our Manpower Goals?", pp. 41-57; (3)
      L. C. Thurow, "The Role of Manpower Policy in Achieving Aggregative Goals",
      pp. 71-103; (4) J. A. Kershaw, "The Need for Better Planning and Coordina-
      tion", pp. 117-32; (5) Employment Service Task Force, "Placement and Coun-
      selling. The Role of the Employment Service", pp. 143-73; (6) D. S. Bushnell
      "The Value of Vocational Education", pp. 193-205; (7) G. G. Somers, "Our
      Experience with Retraining and RelocationP, pp. 215-36; (8) B. Olsson,
      "Labor-Market Policy in Modern Society", pp. 249-71; (9) C. A. Myers, "The
      Role of the Employer in Manpower Policy", pp. 285-300; and (10) R. A. Lester,
      "The Role of Organized Labor", pp. 317-32. J. T. Dunlop sums up, pp. 355-72.
      Unfortunately, the book lacks an index.

1069 R. D. ROBINSON, *High-Level Manpower in Economic Development. The Turkish*
      Case. Cambridge, Mass.: Center for Middle Eastern Studies, Harvard Univer-
      sity Press, 1967. Pp. 134.

        An excellent descriptive account of Turkish problems in high-level manpower
      development, both on the demand and on the supply side, with a useful biblio-
      graphy.

1070 M. A. HOROWITZ, I. L HERRNSTADT, "More Doubts About Average Training Times
      Computed from GED and SVP Levels", *RES*, November, 1967, pp. 638-40.

        Cogently argues that GED levels (see 1017) straddle more than one conven-
      tional school level and cannot be translated into equivalent years of
      schooling. (See also 1088.)

1071   R. R. NELSON, M. J. PECK, E. D. KALACHECK, *Technology, Economic Growth and Public Policy.* Washington, D.C.: The Brookings Institution, 1967, chs. 6-7, pp. 113-50.

   These chapters on the effects of technical change on employment trends in the American economy—automation, structural unemployment, and all that—are extremely relevant to issues of manpower and educational planning. "The Educational Problem" is specifically discussed, pp. 142-45.

1072   M. BLAUG, M. H. PESTON, A. ZIDERMAN, *The Utilisation of Educated Manpower in British Industry.* London: Oliver & Boyd, 1967. Pp. 103.

   A pilot study of the utilisation problem in six Britih firms (summarised in 1066).

1073   S. BARKIN, ed., *Technical Change and Manpower Planning. Co-ordination at Enterprise Level.* Industrial Relations Aspects of Manpower Policy 4. Paris: OECD, 1967. Pp. 287.

   A series of 29 case studies—1 in Austria and Canada respectively, 4 in France, 4 in Western Germany, 3 in Norway, 7 in Sweden, 6 in the United Kingdom, and 3 in the United States—of the manpower impact of dramatic technical and economic change on individual enterprises. Each country chapter is introduced by the editor, conveniently summarising the main points of the country's case studies.

1074   G. JONES and others, *Perspectives in Manpower Planning. An Edinburgh Group Report.* London: Institute of Personnel Management, 1967. Pp. 93.

   This pamphlet is largely concerned with manpower planning at the level of the individual firm, but there are some references to national manpower forecasting and a strangely inconclusive final chapter on "Manpower and Eduation". Ch. 8, "Manpower and Training", pp. 75-84, is a useful account and criticism of the Industrial Training Act.

1075   Ministry of Labour, UK, *Electronics. Manpower Studies No. 5.* London: HMSO, 1967. Pp. 72.

   This pamphlet contains, among other things, a forecast of occupational requirements in the industry by 1970, based on a survey of employers' opinions.

1076   H. RIESE, *Die Entwicklung des Bedarfs an Hochschulabsolventen in der Bundesrepublic Deutschland.* Wiesbaden: Steiner, 1967. Pp. 156. Partly reprinted in *BILD*, pp. 132-51.

   A Parnes-type forecast of the demand for university graduates in Western Germany by 1981. Owing to the lack of occupational statistics in Western Germany before 1961, much of the forecast is based upon fairly arbitrary extrapolations.

1968

1077 M GASCOIGNE, "Manpower Forecasting at the Enterprise Level: A Case Study",
      BJIR, March, 1968, pp. 94-106.

         An interesting attempt to conduct a post-mortem on the short-term manpower
      forecasts of an unnamed UK company, showing that even estimates for only 2
      years ahead were inaccurate up to 20 per cent. An attempt to fit simple
      Cobb-Douglas production functions gave statistically insignificant results.

1078 N. DeWITT, *Manpower Guidelines for Educational Policy Planning in the State
      of California*. Consultant's Report prepared for the State Committee on
      Public Education. Berkeley, Calif.: State Committee on Public Education,
      1968. Pp. 75, mimeographed.

         A manpower-forecasting analysis of desirable future trends in Californian
      state education. Includes an extensive bibliography of largely unpublished
      owrk on education in the State of California.

1079 M. J. PECK, "Science and Technology", *Britain's Economic Prospects*, ed. R. E.
      Caves *et al*. Washington, D.C.: The Brookings Institution, 1968, pp. 448-84.

         An unconvincing attempt, based on comparisons with the USA, to show that
      Britain's economic problems are aggravated by a shortage of engineers. The
      nub of the difficulty has to do with the fact that the American definition
      of "engineer" is by function, whereas the British one is by education.

1080 L. A. LECHT, *Manpower Requirements for National Objectives in the 1970's*,
      Washington, D.C.: National Planning Association, 1968. Pp. 471.

         An interesting attempt to make forecasts for satisfying not just economic
      objectives, but also widely shared social and cultural goals. Over half of
      the book consists of American data not easily accessible elsewhere.

1081 OECD, *Educational Policy and Planning, Austria*. Directorate for Scientific
      Affairs, OECD. Paris: OECD, 1968. Pp. 434.

         A full-scale educational plan for Austria with projections up to 1980, and
      a series of manpower forecasts largely based on comparisons with the USA
      and Western European countries.

1082 E. GINZBERG, *Manpower Agenda for America*. N.Y.: McGraw-Hill, 1968. Pp. 250

         A collection of short speeches and addresses delivered over the last two
      years, drawing on the work of the Center for the Conservation of Human
      Resources, which the author has directed since the 1940's.

1083 OECD, *Training, Recruitment and Utilisation of Teachers. Country Case-
      Studies. Primary and Secondary Education. Denmark, Italy and Luxemberg*.
      Paris: OECD, 1968. Pp. 205, 189, 31.

         These are descriptive studies that include forecasts of requirements up to
      1980.

1084 OECD, *Training, Recruitment and Utilisation of Teachers. Country Case-
Studies. Primary and Secondary Education. Austria, Greece and Sweden.*
Paris: OECD, 1968. Pp. 127, 121, 133.

The same comments apply here as above.

1085 Department of Employment and Productivity, *Company Manpower Planning.*
Manpower Papers No. 1. London: HMSO, 1968. Pp. 54.

A simple exposition of some standard techniques for planning the utilisation and recruitment of manpower at the level of the individual firm. Includes a useful annotated bibliography.

1086 A. G. HOLTMANN, "The 'Shortage' of School Teachers and the Principle of
Equal Net Advantage", *JEI*, June, 1968, pp. 211-18.

An interesting analysis of the concept of "manpower shortages" with special
reference to the situation of teachers in the United States.

1087 A. J. JAFFE, J. FROOMKIN, *Technology and Jobs. Automation in Perspective.*
N.Y.: Frederick A. Praeger, 1968. Pp. 284.

A major study of the so-called "manpower revolution" in the United States
caused by the growth of "automation". The authors show that there is little
basis for the popular notion that technical change in the United States
suddenly became more capital-intensive in the 1950's, leading to vast changes
in the skill composition of specific industries and to drastic increases in
the demand for more educated workers. The book includes international comparisons of labour productivity trends and a look at probable future labour
force trends in the United States.

1088 S. A. INFE, "The Use of the *Dictionary of Occupational Titles* as a Source of
Estimates of Educational and Training Requirements", *JHR*, Summer, 1968,
pp. 363-75.

An explanation of the scales of functional or performance requirements for
occupations developed for the revised American 1965 *Dictionary*, published in
1966 as a *Supplement to the Dictionary*.

1969

1089 V. A. RICHARDSON, "A Measurement of the Demand for Professional Engineers",
BJIR, March, 1969, pp. 52-70.

An attack on the work of the UK Committee on Manpower Resources for Science
and Technology, and an attempt to show that the Committee's claim of an
existing "shortage" of engineers in the UK are denied by recent trends in
the salaries for engineers.

1090 T. THONSTADT, *Education and Manpower: Theoretical Models and Empirical Applications.* London: Oliver & Boyd, 1969. Pp. 162.

This book joins a Markov-chain model of the Norwegian educational system to numerical estimates of manpower requirements in Norway in 1960. The final chapter develops a multisector dynamic model of the school system under the special case of uniform growth.

1091   E. J. DEVINE, "Manpower Shortages in Local Government Employment", *AER*, May, 1969, pp. 538-45; "Comment" by W. H. Oakland, *ibid.*, pp. 563-67.

A brave attempt to analyse shortages of nurses, policemen and teachers in the United States, making use of the theory of simple monopsony.

1092   B. AHAMAD, *A Projection of Manpower Requirements by Occupation in 1975.* Department of Manpower and Immigration, Canada. Ottawa: Queen's Printer, 1969. Pp. 315.

This study consists of a number of alternative projections of occupational requirements in 1975 by each of the five economic regions of Canada. The method used is in essence that of Parnes in the MRP project, except that the growth of output and employment are themselves projected rather than being taken as given at the outset of the exercise.

1093   US Department of Labor, *Manpower Report of the President, Including a Report on Manpower Requirements, Resources, Utilization and Training.* Washington, D.C.: US Government Printing Office, 1969. Pp. 253.

Pt. I of this seventh manpower report of the president reviews the American employment situation since 1960 and presents some porjections up to 1975. Pts. II and III discuss several distinct problem areas in the manpower field.

1094   L. A. LECHT, *Manpower Needs for National Goals in the 1970's.* New York: Praeger, 1969. Pp. 181.

This book projects the manpower requirements by 1975 for the acheivement of a set of sixteen national goals. The goals are first translated into expenditure projections and then are in turn converted to value-added projections for 86 industries. Input-output tables are used to turn the value-added forecasts into employment and occupation forecasts.

1095   J. G. SCOVILLE, *The Job Content of the U.S. Economy 1940-1970.* New York: McGraw-Hill, 1969. Pp. 144.

This study classifies 200-odd occupations in the American economy into five job families, based in part on a regression of earnings on the training and aptitude requirements of different jobs. The regression coefficients are viewed as estimates of the market values of skills and abilities, and occupations are classified using these weights (pp. 24-7). The book includes an analysis of the changes in job content between 1940 and 1960 (ch. 3), as well as a projection of job content up to 1970 (ch. 4).

1970

1096   British Committee on Chemical Education, *Report of the Committee on Enquiry
       into the Relationship Between University Courses in Chemistry and the Needs
       of Industry*. London: Royal Institute of Chemistry, 1970. Pp. 337.

       This report, based on group discussions, depth interviews and postal ques-
       tionnaires, effectively refutes the Swann Report, at least as far as chemists
       are concerned. It finds that there is no serious dissatisfaction on the part
       of employers with the quality of graduates presenting themselves for indus-
       trail posts, nor any sign of a shortage of chemists, nor any tendency for
       post-graduate chemists to scorn employment in industry.

1097   D. E. DIAMOND, H. BEDROSIAN, *Hiring Standards and Job Performance*. US
       Department of Labor. Manpower Research Monograph 18. Washington, D.C.:
       US Government Printing Office, 1970. Pp. 35.

       A study using the technique of job-analysis of ten skilled and unskilled
       occupations in the New York and St. Louis area, showing that the vast major-
       ity of firms did not possess job descriptions for the low-skill occupations
       and that education made little or no difference to job performance.

1098   C. VIMONT, "Comparison des previsions d'emploi par profession du Ve plan et
       de l'evolution réelle de l'emploi de 1962 a 1968", *PDP, Numero Special*,
       Fevrier, 1970, pp. 9-18.

       The Fifth French Plan involved a comprehensive manpower forecast, the
       first venture of this kind in France, for the period 1962-70. The results of
       the sample census of 1968 provides a check on the accuracy of this forecast.
       The author, after a detailed comparison of prediction with outcome for each
       of the 17 occupational categories, concludes that the demand for engineers,
       draughtsmen and certain service occupations was badly underestimated, but
       that in all other cases, the deviations of the predictions from actual out-
       comes stem from the overestimate of economic growth in the 1960's and not
       from the manpower forecasting methods themselves. See also earlier articles
       by the author in *POP*, 1966, nos. 3, 5, on these methods. It may be noted
       that the entire issue of this *Numero Special* is devoted to problems of man-
       power planning in France.

1099   M. ZYMELMAN, *The Relationship Between Productivity and the Formal Education
       of the Labor Force in Manufacturing Industries*. Harvard University, Graduate
       School of Education, Center for Studies in Education and Development, Occa-
       sional Papers No. 5. Cambridge, Mass.: CSED, 1970. Pp. 124.

       Employing the data gathered by Horowitz, Zymelman and Herrnstadt ( ) the
       author re-examines the fit between occupation and education over the census
       decade 1950-1960 in the US, Canada, the UK and Japan, comparing both within
       and between countries. He produces the striking finding that the education
       of unskilled workers, domestic servants and cleaners has risen in all four
       countries over the decade by about 5 per cent.

1100   J. K. FOLGER, H. S. ASTIN, A. E. BAYER, *Human Resources and Higher Education.
       Staff Report of the Commission on Human Resources and Advanced Education*.
       New York: Russell Sage Foundation, 1970. Pp. 475.

This is an important source book on higher education in the U.S.A. It contains a number of reviews of evidence such as ch. 2 on the market for college graduates, ch. 4 on manpower demand and supply in seven selected professions, ch. 5 on the demand for higher education, ch. 7 on mobility of high-level manpower, ch. 9 on the education of women, ch. 10 on talent development among underprivileged groups, and ch. 11 on brain drain. The concluding chapter on manpower planning abandons the hope of forecasting "manpower requirements" and focusses instead on "active manpower policies".

1101 J. R. CROSSLEY, "Theory and Methods of National Manpower Policy", *SJPE*, June, 1970, pp. 127-46.

The paper falls into two parts: the first discusses the practice of manpower forecasting in the light of linear growth theory, linear programming, and all that; the second discusses data needs in the field of forecasting in the British context.

1102 D. HARTUNG, R. NUTHMANN, W. D. WINTERHAGER, *Politologen im Beruf. Zur Aufnahme und Durchsetzung neuer Qualifikationen im Beschäftsgungssystem.* Stuttgart: Ernst Klett Verlag, 1970. Pp. 250.

This fascinating study looks at graduates in political science in Western Germany (a category that did not exist at all in Germany until 1950) over the period 1961 to 1969. Among its findings are that (1) the average earnings of all political science graduates employed in 1969 was hardly different from that of university graduates as a whole, although the dispersion of earnings was apparently greater, and (2) the proportion of graduates employed who held positions closely related to the knowledge content of their qualifications was only about one-third.

1103 G. WILLIAMS, *Educational Policies, Plans and Forecasts During the Nineteen-Sixties and Seventies. OECD Conference on Policies for Educational Growth. Background Study No. 5.* Paris: OECD, 1970. Pp. 46.

An interesting review of the experiences of OECD member countries with supply and demand forecasting in the field of education.

1104 D. E. YETT, "The Chronic 'Shortage' of Nurses: A Public Policy Dilemma", *Empirical Studies in Health Economics,* ed. H. E. Klarman. Baltimore: John Hopkins Press, 1970, pp. 357-89.

A discussion of a famous policy question in the American context.

1105 B. AHAMAD, "A Post Mortem on Teacher Supply Forecasts", *HIR*, Summer, 1970, pp. 21-40.

An excellent review of teacher supply forecasts in Britain since 1965. (See also 1113.)

1971

1106 Department of Trade and Industry, UK, *Persons with Qualifications in Engineering, Technology and Science 1959 to 1968.* Studies in Technological Manpower No. 3. London: H.M.S.O., 1971. Pp. 134.

    This volume summarizes data from past triennial surveys and presents new evidence from both the 1966 Census of Population and the latest triennial survey of 1968. Among the interesting findings are rising unemployment rates for engineers and scientists.

1107 W. AMBRUSTER, *Arbeitskräftebedarfsprognosen also Grundlage der Bildungsplanung. Eine Kritische Analyse.* Berlin: Max-Planck-Institut für Bildungsforschung, 1971. Pp. 210.

    This is undoubtedly *the* German book on manpower forecasting. It contains a bird's eye review of manpower forecasting in Austria, Sweden, the Netherlands, Ireland and Germany (pp. 48-83), followed by a long critical discussion of methods, procedures and results. The author's attitude to his subject is dispassionate and it is not clear how he views the future development of manpower forecasting.

1108 Council for Scientific Policy, UK, *Report of the Working Group on Biological Manpower.* London: H.M.S.O., 1971. Cmnd. 4737. Pp. 137.

    This report attempts to assess current shortages or surpluses of biological manpower, a task which it virtually abandons owing to the varied employment of biologists. Much evidence is given of the substitutability of biologists for other kinds of life scientists. The report nicely illustrates the difficulties of applying the manpower-requirements approach to a particular category of scientists.

1109 M. ZYMELMAN, *A Manual of Manpower Planning Methods.* Harvard University Graduate School of Education. Center for Studies in Education and Development. Occasional Papers No. 7. Cambridge, Mass.: CSED, 1971. Pp. 64.

    This is a handbook of practical methods at the national, regional and enterprise level for making employment-by-occupation forecasts. Unfortunately, it places rather heavy reliance on the author's own work (see 1099) in which the productivity of labour of an industry is made a function solely of the occupational structure of that industry.

1972

1110 K. McCORMICK, "Models and Assumptions in Manpower Planning in Science and Technology", *The Sociological Review Monograph 18, The Sociology of Science,* ed. P. Halmos. Keele: University of Keele, 1972, pp. 147-86.

    An examination of British evidence relating to the career choices of British students and the utilisation of highly qualified manpower in British industry. The author weaves a middle ground between the "science lobby" (Jackson Committee, Dainton, Swann, etcetera) and "marketeers, like Blaug".

1111 B. AHAMAD, K. F. N. SCOTT, "A Note on Sensitivity Analysis in Manpower Forecasting", *JRSS*, 135, 3, 1972, pp. 385-92.

Using Canadian data, the authors estimate confidence intervals for a manpower forecast by assuming that a known probability distribution of the employ-
ment-by-industry and employment-by-occupation vectors.

1112 M. L. SKOLNIK, C. S. SMITH, "Selecting an Optimal Set of Manpower Requirements
When Skill Substitution Is Possible", *BJIR*, November, 1972, pp. 256-69.

An interesting article which attempts to set out the conditions under
which both employers and the educational authorities would both choose the
same optimal set. Some British evidence is adduced to show that these conditions are seldom met with in the real world.

1113 B. AHAMAD, M. BLAUG, eds., *The Practice of Manpower Forecasting. A Collection
of Case Studies*. Amsterdam: Elsevier Scientific Publishing Company, 1972.
Pp. 345.

This book consists of ten country studies with an introduction and conclusion by the editors. There are five case studies dealing with forecasts for
all occupations: (1) B. Ahamad, "Canada", pp. 26-47; (2) K. Gannicott,
M. Blaug, "The United States", pp. 48-76; (3) G. Psacharopoulos, "France",
pp. 77-105; (4) M. Blaug, "Thailand", pp. 106-30 (see also "A Post-Mortem of
Manpower Forecasting in Thailand", *JDS*, Winter, 1971); and (5) K. Hinchliffe,
"Nigeria", pp. 131-56. This is followed by five case studies dealing with
forecasts for single occupations: (1) M. Woodhall, "Engineers in India",
pp. 157-200; (2) K. Gannicott, "Engineers in Sweden", pp. 201-39; (3) K.
Gannicott, M. Blaug, "Scientists and Engineers in Britain", pp. 240-60 (see
also "Manpower Forecasting Since Robbins: A Science Lobby in Action", *HIR*,
Autumn, 1969); (4) B. Ahamad, "Teachers in England and Wales", pp. 261-84
(see also 1105); and (5) B. Ahamad, "Doctors in the United States, Britain
and Canada", pp. 285-309.

1973

1114 P. d'HUGUES, G. PETIT, F. RERAT, *Les emplois industriels. Nature. Formation.
Recrutement*. Cahiers du centre d'etudes de l'emploi 4. Paris: Presses
universitaires de France, 1973. Pp. 515.

This study of the jobs held by qualified workers in a sample of 100 manufacturing establishments in France attempts to compare the match between education and occupation in the light of recent changes in skill labelling prac
tices. The findings of the study cast serious doubt on the traditional occupational categories that are employed in official French surveys of manpower
(English summary, pp. 491-502).

1115 R. B. THOMAS, "On the Definition of 'Shortages' in Administered Labour Markets",
MS, June, 1973, pp. 169-86.

An interesting essay on teacher shortages in Britain, disaggregated by subject specialisation and by type of school.

1116 R. B. THOMAS, "Post-War Movements in Teachers' Salaries", *IRJ*, Autumn, 1973,
pp. 13-27.

Tests a simple market model of the determination of teachers' pay in Britain and shows that it has some explanatory power despite the administered nature of the labour market for teachers

1117 Cahiers du centre d'études de l'emploi, *L'analyse de l'emploi par region et département, Les attitudes de travailleurs et des employeurs à l'égard de l'emploi; Les bouchés professionels des étudiants*. Paris: Presses universitaires de France, 1973, 3 vols. Pp. 215, 166, 145.

The first two volumes consist of 8 essays with English summaries by 12 authors on such topics as manpower forecasts for French manufacturing by region; short-run output-employment functions in several French manufacturing industries; employers' attitudes towards the employment of women and older people, etcetera. The third volume by P. Vrain is devoted to a major survey of 12,000 licentiates in political science, economics and law with a view to analysing the factors that determine their educational and occupational careers (English summary, Vol. 3, pp. 133-38).

1118 G. PSACHAROPOULOS, "An Input-Output Model for the Assessment of Labor Skill Requirements", *HE*, November, 1973, pp. 461-74.

The paper applies an interindustry model to past data for Greece to reveal the sensitivity of manpower forecasts to the various critical steps that are involved in its use.

1119 G. G. CAIN, R. B. FREEMAN, W. LEE HANSEN, *Labor Market Analysis of Engineers and Technical Workers*. Baltimore: John Hopkins University Press, 1973. Pp. 88.

A useful discussion and literature review of the demand for and supply of engineers in the American context (indeed, there is not a single reference to the vast European literature on the subject), supplemented by an estimate of the earnings function for engineers in 1962. A final chapter reviews American experience with engineering manpower forecasts.

1974

1120 S. R. TIMPERLEY, *Personnel Planning and Occupational Choice*. London: Allen & Unwin, 1974. Pp. 236.

This sociological study is based on a survey of 1970 graduates of the University of Liverpool, supplemented by a survey of graduates employed in eight companies located in the North of England. The analysis of these two surveys in chs. 3 and 4 is preceded by a descriptive survey of recent sociological literature on occupational choice. The final chapter draws some practical lessons for company manpower planning. The author seems unaware of the literature in the economics of education, or in labour economics for that matter.

1121 J. S. WABE, *Problems in Manpower Forecasting*. Westmead: Saxon House, D.C. Heath, 1974. Pp. 287.

A series of theoretical papers on the problems of national manpower forecasting, presented at a 1973 conference sponsored by the UK Engineering

Industry Training Board. While extremely competent throughout, the papers
have a dated quality, reflecting the preoccupations of the 1960's rather than
the 1970's. The eight papers are: (1) J. S. Wabe, "Issues in Manpower Forecasting", pp. 1-16; (2) J. S. Wabe, "Practical Difficulties in a Manpower
Forecasting Exercise", pp. 17-60; (3) D. L. Bosworth, G. J. Evans, R. M.
Lindley, "Mechanistic Manpower Models", pp. 61-84; (4) G. J. Evans, J. S Wabe,
"Testing a Demand Explanation of the RAS Model", pp. 85-96; (5) G. J. Evans,
"The Labour Market Mechanism and the Hoarding of Manpower", pp. 97-152;
(6) D. L. Bosworth, "Production Functions and Skill Requirements", pp. 153-96;
(7) C. J. Roberts, "The Demand for Manpower: Employment Functions", pp. 197-
238; and (8) R. M. Lindley, "Manpower Movements and the Supply of Labour",
pp. 239-82.

1122 R. COLLINS, "Where Are Educational Requirements for Employment Highest?", *SE*,
Fall, 1974, pp. 419-42.

A suggestive neo-Marxist, sociological analysis of employment in the San
Francisco Bay Area, showing that the service-oriented nature of certain business enterprises produces abnormally high demands for educated labour.

1123 J. S. WABE, D. L. BOSWORTH, G. J. EVANS, R. M. LINDLEY, C. J. ROBERTS,
Manpower Forecasting for the Engineering Industry, Occasional Paper No. 4.
Watford: Engineering Industry Training Board, 1974. Pp. 61.

A report on the activities of the Manpower Planning Unit at the University
of Warwick in the field of employment forecasting for the British engineering
industry. The first part throws light on changes in the occupational mix of
the industry in recent years and on measuring the phenomenon of labour hoarding. The last part discusses the theoretical problem of estimating short-run
employment functions.

1124 M. A. HOROWITZ, *Manpower and Education in Franco Spain*. Hamden, Conn.: The
Shoe String Press, 1974. Pp. 164.

A rather traditional but invaluable reference book, full of data on manpower and education. Ch. 6 reviews previous attempts in Spain to forecast
manpower requirements and concludes that Spain has yet to make a major effort
at manpower planning.

1125 G. BIRTIG, *Universita e Occupazione Previsioni Sull'Offerta e ladomanda di
laureati al 1978*. Milano: Opera Universitaria dell'Universitaria degli
Studi di Milano, Quaderno 11, 1974. Pp. 90.

Although focussed on the problem of graduate unemployment in Italy, this
slim book is, in fact, a compendium of Italian educational data (expenditures,
enrolments, pupil-teacher ratios, drop outs, etcetera). It includes a single-
valued manpower forecast for university graduates up to 1978, based on widely
accepted sectoral employment growth rates, showing an excess of university
graduates over the next five years.

1975

1126 R. B. FREEMAN, "Supply and Salary Adjustments to the Changing Science Manpower
Market: Physics, 1948-1973", *AER*, March, 1975, pp. 27-39.

Develops a simple recursive model and uses it to estimate the future state of physics manpower, yielding strikingly different results from those obtained by standard manpower-forecasting methods.

1127 J. D. MACE, S. M. TAYLOR, "The Demand for Engineers in British Industry: Some Implications for Manpower Forecasting", *BJIR*, July, 1975, pp. 175-94.

A case study of 500 engineers in 12 British firms is used to reject the manpower-requirements approach to educational planning.

1128 M. BLAUG, "The Uses and Abuses of Manpower Planning", *NS*, July 31, 1975, pp. 174-76.

A comment on the recent speeches of a British minister, demanding that higher education be geared increasingly to manpower requirements.

5. BRAIN DRAIN AND INTERNATIONAL TRADE

We have touched elsewhere on the factors determining the internal migration of labour in a country: see section on "The Measurement of Returns". Here we are largely concerned with the international migration of labour. Johnson[1130] and Grubel and Scott[1133] mark the beginning of a debate that raged on in the 1960's. Employing the traditional tools of welfare economics and rejecting the ideology of nationalism, Johnson and Grubel and Scott attempted to shift the burden of proof to those who claimed that "brain drain" involves a redistribution of income from poor to rich countries. Thomas[1140], Patinkin[1145], Aitken[1133], Jolly and Seers[1167], and Sen[1169] criticise their argument; for a rebuttal, see Johnson[1140,1142] and Scott[272,1140]. Berry and Soligo[1152] attempt to pose the problem afresh. Adams and Dirlam[1145] and Oldham[1147] review policy proposals with respect to brain drain. The latest proposal is a special income tax on brain drainers: see Bhagwati and Dellafar[1164] and Bhagwati and Hamda[1170]. For evidence on the magnitude of recent brain drain, see WHO[1132], Grubel and Scott[1134,1135,1139], Grubel and McAlpin[1149], Thomas[1140], US Congres[1141], the Jones Report[1143], Niland[1156], and Gupta[1168]. Dedijer and Svenningson[1921] supply further references for individual countries.

Ever since the so-called Leontief Paradox in international trade theory, there have been many attempts to show that the human-capital-intensity of a country's export industries is crucial in explaining trade flows between nations. Kenen[272], Baldwin[1158], Lowinger[1161], Lubitz[1162], Fareed[1163], and Keesing[1435] illustrate these developments in trade theory.

1962

1129   L. A. SJAASTAD, "The Costs and Returns of Human Migration", *JPE*, Suppl., October, 1962, pp. 80-93, reprinted in *KIK*, pp. 457-76, and *RLMA*, pp. 253-65.

   An able review and discussion of the evidence about internal migration from the standpoint of human capital theory.

1965

1130   H. G. JOHNSON, "The Economics of the 'Brain Drain': The Canadian Case", *MIN*, Spring, 1965, pp. 299-312.

   This article neatly debunks some current shibboleths about the emigration of highly qualified manpower from countries like Canada and the United Kingdom.

1966

1131   S. P. AWASTHI, "Brain Drain from Developing Countries: An Exercise in Prob-
       lem Formulation", *MJ*, April-June, 1966, pp. 80-98.

       A general discussion of how brain drain might be investigated in developing
       countries, with some useful references to the literature.

1132   Pan American Health Organization, WHO, *Migration of Health Personnel, Scien-
       tists, and Engineers from Latin America*.   Report prepared by the PAHO Sub-
       committee on Migration for the PAHO Advisory Committee on Medical Research.
       Washington, D.C.:   WHO, 1966.   Pp. 118.

       A report on brain drain from Latin America, concentrating on physicians,
       with chapters on the characteristics of educated migrants, the causes of
       migration, and the appropriate remedies for Latin American brain drain.

1133   H. G. GRUBEL, A. D. SCOTT, "The International Flow of Human Capital", *AER*,
       May, 1966, pp. 268-75, reprinted in *P-EED*, 2, pp. 241-49, and *KIK*, pp. 477-84.
       "Comment" by B. A. Weisbrod, *ibid.*, pp. 277-80, and N. D. Aitken, *ibid.*,
       June, 1968, pp. 539-45, and "Reply" by Grubel and Scott, *ibid.*, pp. 545-48.

       Some preliminary results of a forthcoming study on the US balance of trade
       in human capital from foreign student exchange and the immigration of scien-
       tists and engineers, followed by a theoretical re-assessment of the brain
       drain argument.

1134   H. G. GRUBEL, A. D. SCOTT, "The Immigration of Scientists and Engineers to
       the United States, 1949-61", *JPE*, August, 1966, pp. 368-79.

       The first to present time series on total US immigration of scientific man-
       power related to statistics on the US output of first degrees in various
       disciplines, together with calculations of the present capital value of these
       migrants to the United States.

1135   H. G. GRUBEL, A. D. SCOTT, "The Cost of US College Student Exchange Programs",
       JHR, Fall, 1966, pp. 81-99.

       A cost-benefit analysis of the foreign college student programme from the
       viewpoint of the United States, showing that the US in recent years has de-
       rived an annual benefit of $16m. a year from the programme.

1136   A. E. GOLLIN, ed., *The International Migration of Talent and Skills*.   Pro-
       ceedings of a Workshop and Conference Sponsored by the Council on International
       Educational and Cultural Affairs of the US Government.   Washington, D.C.:
       Department of State, USA, 1966.   Pp. 165.

       A verbatim report of the discussions at the conference which ranged far and
       wide on the issue of brain drain.   The participants included such well-known
       authorities as C. A. Anderson, M. J. Bowman, H. G. Grubel, G. L. Payne, and
       D. Wolfle.   The volume includes a useful bibliography, pp. 151-55.

1137   B. THOMAS, "From the Other Side: A European View", *AAAPS*, September, 1966, pp. 63-72.

       A discussion that starts from the United States 1965 Immigration Act and ends up with a full-scale treatment of the current brain drain from the developing world (see also 1140).

1138   X. ZOLOTAS, *International Labour Migration and Economic Development*. Bank of Greece Papers No. 21. Athens: Bank of Greece, 1966. Pp. 62.

       The first part of this pamphlet looks at the problems of measuring the economic effects of migration; the author criticises Grubel and Scott for their "cavalier treatment of the losses from the 'brain drain'". Pt. II gives an analysis of post-war emigration from Greece and discusses various ways of limiting emigration, including increased investment in Greek technical education.

1967

1139   H. G. GRUBEL, A. D. SCOTT, "The Characteristics of Foreigners in the U.S. Economics Profession", *AER*, March, 1967, pp. 131-45.

       Continuing their analysis of brain drain with the aid of American statistics, the authors analyse the characteristics of foreign-born economists in the United States by country of origin, educational qualifications, and earnings.

1140   B. THOMAS, "The International Circulation of Human Capital", *MIN*, Summer, 1967, pp. 479-506; "Comments" by H. G. Johnson, A. Scott, *ibid.*, Autumn, 1967, pp. 105-16, reprinted in *P-EED*, 2, pp. 250-301.

       After a review of the available evidence on the magnitude of brain drain and a critique of Grubel and Scott on the welfare economics of migration, the author sketches a dynamic shortage model in which the Federal Space Program of the United States is said to constitute the major pull in recent years, producing brain drain out of Europe, Asia, and Latin America.

1141   Research and Technical Programs Subcommittee of the Committee on Government Operations, 90th US Congress, 1st Session, *The Brain Drain Into the United States of Scientists, Engineers, and Physicians*. Washington, D.C.: US Government Printing Office, 1967. Pp. 110.

       Although the bulk of this pamphlet contains statistics, there are some interesting pages on the share of the developing countries in the scientific brain drain, and the variety of conflicting views on brain drain in the United States and elsewhere.

1142   H. G. JOHNSON, "Some Economic Aspects of Brain Drain", *PDR*, Autumn, 1967, pp. 379-411.

       A careful discussion of the possible sources of loss from brain drain, with due attention to the developing countries, suggesting that little net loss is to be expected. The paper concludes with some proposals for compensation payments to countries suffering loss from brain drain. Three technical appendices are included.

1143 Committee on Manpower Resources for Science and Technology, UK, *The Brain Drain. Report of the Working Group on Migration*. London: HMSO, 1967. Cmnd. 341-7. Pp. 125.

This volume marshalls all the available data on the emigration and immigration of British scientists, engineers, and technologists such as it is, and concludes without much analysis that the net outflow now constitutes a serious loss to the United Kingdom. A number of solutions are canvassed and rejected and the report concludes that "the right solution is to create more challenging opportunities, particularly in industry, for talented people." The appendix contains some interesting quantitative and qualitative evidence as well as brief but useful bibliography.

1144 S. BARKIN, "The Economic Costs and Benefits and Human Gains and Disadvantages of International Migration", *JHR*, Fall, 1967, pp. 495-516.

A purely theoretical discussion of brain drain from the point of view of the individual, the firm, and the whole economy.

1968

1145 W. ADAMS, ed., *The Brain Drain*, New York: Macmillan, 1968. Pp. 273.

The papers presented at this 1967 conference consisted of (1) a useful "Introduction" to the problem by W. Adams, pp. 1-8; (2) S. Dedijer, "'Early' Migration", pp. 9-28; (3) B. Thomas, "'Modern' Migration", pp. 29-49; (4) C. Iffland, H. Rieben, "The Multilateral Aspects: The US, Europe, and the 'Poorer' Nations", pp. 50-67; (5) H. G. Johnson, "An 'Internationalist' Model", pp. 69-91, another version of 1142; (6) D. Patinkin, "A 'Nationalist' Model", pp. 92-108; (7) K. E. Boulding, "The 'National' Importance of Human Capital", pp. 109-19; (8) E. Oteiza, "A Differential Push-Pull Approach", pp. 120-34; (9) C. P. Kindleberger, "Study Abroad and Emigration", pp. 135-55; and 6 country studies, namely, France, Greece, The European Common Market, Africa, India, and the entire developing world, by R. Mosse, G. Coutsoumaris, J. Houssiaux, R. K. A. Gardiner, V. M. Dandekar, and H. Myint respectively. W. Adams and J. B. Dirlam sum up in "An Agenda for Action", pp. 247-64.

1146 R. BLANDY, "'Brain Drains' in an Integrating Europe", *CER*, June, 1968, pp. 180-93.

This paper examines the migration statistics of France and Switzerland, and attempts to test the hypothesis that brain drain into these two countries will soon increase as a consequence of high levels of overall migration within Europe.

1147 C. H. G. OLDHAM, ed., *International Migration of Talent From and To the Less-Developed Countries*. Ditchley Park, Enstone: Ditchley Foundation, 1968. Pp. 29.

A report of a conference on brain drain, chiefly interesting for its policy proposals and an appendix on the data required to measure the magnitude of brain drain.

1148   S. KANNAPPAN, "The Brain Drain and Developing Countries", *ILR*, July, 1968, pp. 1-26.

A useful and balanced article on the welfare gains and losses of brain drain from developing countries, concluding that the net advantage of world transactions in human skills is favourable to the developing countries.

1149   H. G. GRUBEL, M. B. McALPHIN, "Austrian, German and Swiss Economists in the United States", *KYK*, XXI, 2, 1968, pp. 299-312.

Extending the earlier article by Grubel and Scott on foreigners in US economics (1139), this paper presents a detailed analysis of the characteristics of economists who were born or educated in Germany, Austria, or Switzerland.

1969

1150   E. J. MISHAN, "Migration Fallacies", *Twenty-One Popular Economic Fallacies*. London: Allen Lane The Penguin Press, 1969, pp. 183-211.

A cogent estimate of the loss to Britain of brain drain and a criticism of the official estimates of the Jones Report (1143).

1151   E. G. WEST, "Welfare Economics and Emigration Taxes", *SEJ*, July, 1969, pp. 52-59.

Takes the debate on brain drain one step further out of the Paretian-welfare context in the Buchanan-Tullock world of the "calculus of consent".   In the light of Buchanan-Tullock considerations, the author discusses the question of an emigration tax and criticizes the earlier work of Grubel and Scott (1133).

1152   R. A. BERRY, R. SOLIGO, "Some Welfare Aspects of International Migration", *JPE*, September-October, 1969, pp. 778-94.

A terse theoretical statement of the conditions under which "brain drain" imposes a loss to the outflow country in a neoclassical world.

1153   G. C. DORAI, "A Cost-Benefit Analysis of the International Flow of Students", *IEJ*, October-December, 1969, pp. 234-49.

An analytical discussion of the elements of a cost-benefit analysis of the international flow of students, with some empirical illustrations drawn from the Indian context.

1970

1154 K. V. NAGARAJAN, "Brain Drain: A Preliminary Survey", *IEJ*, January-March, 1970, pp. 324-42.

   A rather superficial survey, both of the evidence and the theories invoked in the brain drain debate.

1155 S. SHENOY, "The Movement of Human Capital", *Economic Issues in Immigration*. London: Institute of Economic Affairs, 1970, pp. 45-64.

   Another very general discussion with some statistical data.

1156 J. R. NILAND, *The Asian Engineering Brain Drain. A Study of International Relocation into the United States from India, China, Korea, Thailand and Japan*. Lexington, Mass.: D.C. Heath & Co., 1970. Pp. 181.

   An important study of brain drain of engineers from five Asian countries, based on American data and a detailed survey of a sample of foreign engineering students. The book focusses on five issues: the magnitude of the drain; the nature of their mobility patterns; the reasons that govern their decision to relocate; and the policy implications of the drain. The major conclusion of the book is that the character of brain drain varies so much from one national group to another that each country's drain should be treated as a special case.

1157 S. BOWLES, "Migration as Investment: Empirical Tests of the Human Investment Approach to Geographical Mobility", *RES*, November, 1970, pp. 356-62.

   After estimating the present value of the expected income gain from moving out of the South in the U.S.A., the author shows that it predicts migration better than conventional measure of regional differences in current incomes; schooling increases and age reduces the probability of moving; and blacks and whites respond differently to differences in expected incomes.

1971

1158 R. E. BALDWIN, "Determinants of the Commodity Structure of US Trade", *AER*, March, 1971, pp. 126-46.

   This article serves both as an excellent review of recent work on the Hecksher-Ohlin theory and a demonstration of the education-intensity of US exports.

1159 G. LABER, R. X. CHASE, "Interprovincial Migration in Canada as a Human Capital Decision", *JPE*, July/August, 1971, pp. 795-804.

   This paper develops a regression model containing only two independent variables—the expected value of earnings differentials and a distance variable—which succeeds remarkably well in explaining almost two-thirds of the variation in interprovincial migration of labour in Canada.

1160 Y. COMAY, "Influences on the Migration of Canadian Professionals", *JHR*,
      Summer, 1971, pp. 333-44.

      This article employs multiple regression analysis to analyse the determin-
      ants of migration between Canada and the United States. US education turned
      out to be the most important single determinant of the decisions of Canadians
      to seek full-time employment in America (see also 1165).

1161 T. C. LOWINGER, "The Neo-Factor Proportions Theory of International Trade:
      An Empirical Investigation", *AER*, September, 1971, pp. 675-81.

      An investigation of Brazil's physical and human capital endowments relative
      to her main trading partners in an effort to demonstrate the role of skill-
      intensity of a country's export industries.

1162 R. LUBITZ, "A Note on United States Direct Investment and Human Capital",
      JPE, September/October, 1971, pp. 1171-75.

      Demonstrates a negative relationship between the human capital outflow in
      US direct investment and the human capital endowments of the receiving coun-
      tries. Unfortunately, the data underlying the rest are somewhat dubious.

1972

1163 A. E. FAREED, "Human Capital Intensity of US Trade", *EJ*, June, 1972,
      pp. 629-40.

      Re-examines the HC-intensity of US foreign trade in 1951 with the aid of
      the 1947 input-output table and shows that US exports were more HC-intensive
      than its import replacements.

1164 Y. COMAY, "The Migration of Professionals: An Empirical Analysis", *CJE*,
      August, 1972, pp. 419-29.

      Uses regression analysis to explain the migration of scientists and engin-
      eers migrating from Canada to the US. Earnings turn out to be of little
      explanatory value (see 1160).

1165 R. G. MYERS, *Education and Emigration. Study Abroad and the Migration of
      Human Resources*. New York: David McKay, 1972. Pp. 423.

      A case study of Peruvian students in the United States in the context of a
      general analysis of the problem of brain drain with special reference to non-
      returning students.

1166 R. JOLLY, D. SEERS, "The Brain Drain and the Development Process", *Rich and
      Poor Countries*, ed. G. Ranis. London: Macmillan, 1972, pp. 365-79.

      A discursive attack on any and all "neoclassical" apologies for brain drain
      and a general argument that inequality within and between countries promotes
      brain drain.

1167 J. BHAGWATI, W. DELLALFAR, "The Brain Drain and Income Taxation", *WD*, I,
      1-2, 1973, pp. 94-101.

      Contains the interesting proposal to levy an income tax on brain drainers
      after their arrival in the host country, together with estimates of the pro-
      ceeds of such a tax if the host country in question were the US.

1973

1168 M. L. GUPTA, "Outflow of High-Level Manpower from the Philippines. With
      Special Reference to the Period 1965-71", *ILR*, February, 1973, pp. 167-91.

      A good factual account of the sharp rise in the Filippino brain-drain since
      1965, concluding with a few pages on the possible costs and benefits of brain-
      drain to the Philippines.

1169 A. K. SEN, "Brain Drain: Causes and Effects", *Science and Technology in
      Economic Growth,* ed. B. R. Williams. London: McMillan, 1973, pp. 323-41.

      An ingenious attack on Johnson (see 1142) and an argument to the effect that
      the magnitude of loss from brain drain cannot be considered without bringing
      in the social welfare function of a country.

1974

1170 J. BHAGWATi, K. HAMDA, "The Brain Drain, International Integration of Markets,
      Professionals and Unemployment. A Theoretical Analysis", *JDE*, 1 (1974),
      pp. 1-24.

      The first issue of this new journal opens with an important critique of the
      Grubel-Scott-Johnson let-us-not-worry-about-brain-drain- analysis and attempts
      to build a non-neoclassical two-sector model of an LDC to express the welfare
      loss of brain drain.

6. SOCIAL MOBILITY AND RESERVES OF TALENT

Anyone wishing to know what the sociology of education is about can read standard texts like Musgrave[1215], and Havighurst and Neugarten[1221], or, better still, the classic bibliographical essay by Floud and Halsey[1188]. Here we are concerned with only part of the field, namely, the social class determinants of dropouts and admissions at various stages of the educational system, the environmental influences on educability, and the relations between educational attainment and occupational choice.

Floud[1174], Floud and others[1178], Floud and Halsey[1196], Crowther[855], Ministry of Education[1176], Glass[1192], Furneaux[1201], Robbins[751], and Douglas[1235] analyse the educational performance of English secondary school students in relation to their social class origins; Douglas[1211] covers the same grounds for primary school pupils. Kelsall[1209], Furneaux[1201], Himmelweit[1209,1219], Robbins[751], Floud[1219], and Knight[1225] look at the selection process at the university level. Little and Westergaard[1225] and Halsey[1254] review all the British evidence to date on class differentials in educational opportunity, and Vaizey[1225] draws some significant conclusions from the British data. The story is more or less the same in other countries: for France, see Peyre[1196], Ferrez[1200], Girard and Pressat[1205], Laderriere[1225], and Eicher and Mingat[1254]; for Germany, see Müller[1179] and Pfaff and Fuchs[1254]; for The Netherlands, see Ruiter[1224]; for Sweden, see Ruin[1225]; for the whole of Europe, see Sohlman[1240], Nam[1241], and OECD[1254]; and for the United States, see Sexton[1203], Sussman[1225], Coleman[1217], Bowles and Levin[1231], Lyle[1220], Nam and others[1230], Masters[1238], and Levin and others[1254]. Jencks' *Inequality*[329] has started the argument all over again. For some reactions to Jencks, see Jencks[1250] and Levine[1252].

An enormous literature has accumulated on the so-called "pool of ability" which was said to place a ceiling on the number of highly educated people that could be produced even under the most favourable circumstances. Aspects of the subject are covered by Cole[1180], Zapoleon[1190], Miner[1183], Halsey[1200], Furneaux[1201], Glass[1202], Little[1209], Carter[1206], Vernon[1209,1219], Project Talent[1210], Husèn[1225], and, perhaps definitively, by Robbins[751].

From a number of international comparisons of patterns of social and occupational mobility, see Havighurst[1189], Lipset and Bendix[1191], Svalastoga[1194], Bolte[1195], Anderson[1199], and Duncan and Hodge[1207]. Ginzberg and others[1172], Rosenberg[1185], Department of Education and Science[1223], Musgrave[1224], Slocum[1226], Miller[1254], and the masterful study by Blau and Duncan[1229], followed by Duncan and others[1248] have looked at the various social, economic, and psychological characteristics of occupational choice.

1949

1171 E. ROPER, *Factors Affecting the Admission of High School Seniors to College.* Washington, D.C.: American Council on Education, 1949. Pp. 312.

The data in this study were gathered in 1947 by personal interviews with a
representative sample of 10,000 high school seniors in order to determine
the socio-economic characteristics that make high school graduates admissible
to institutions of higher learning in the United States. The findings with
respect to the demand for college education are summarised on pp. xiv-xxviii;
the findings with respect to the supply of places are summarised on
pp. xxviii-lii.

1951

1172   E. GINZBERG, S. W. GINSBURG, S. AXELRAD, J. L. HERMA, *Occupational Choice.*
An Approach to a General Theory. New York: Columbia University Press, 1951.
Pp. 271.

   This book, based on a detailed analysis of a limited number of case studies,
develops the notion that occupational choice is a temporal process, not a
unique decision. The findings do not lend themselves to a neat summary, but
the influence of parents and their education is emphasised. An appendix
reviews previous literature on the subject.

1952

1173   B. S. HOLLINSHEAD, *Who Should Go to College.* Published for the Commission
on Financing Higher Education. New York: Columbia University Press, 1952.
Pp. 190.

   A readable general account of the "pool of ability" in the USA, the motives
for entering college, the characteristics of the college population, and the
factors that might be manipulated to increase college attendance. The book
includes a memorandum by R. J. Havighurst and R. R. Rodgers on "The Role of
Motivation in Attendance at Post-High-School Educational Institutions",
pp. 135-85, containing a case study of a mid-western community and a summary
of the literature pertinent to the subject.

1954

1174   J. E. FLOUD, "The Educational Experience of the Adult Population of England
and Wales as at July 1949", *Social Mobility in Britain,* ed. D. V. Glass.
London: Routledge & Kegan Paul, 1954, pp. 98-141.

   A pioneering study of the role of education in preserving the class structure of Britain, based on a random sample of the adult population. In the
same volume, see also H. T. Himmelweit, "Social Status and Secondary Education Since the 1944 Act: Some Data for London", pp. 141-60, and J. R. Hall,
D. V. Glass, "Education and Social Mobility", pp. 291-308. (See also 1178.)

1175   D. WOLFLE, *America's Resources of Specialized Talent. A Current Appraisal
and a Look Ahead.* The Report of the Commission on Human Resources and
Advanced Training. New York: Harper & Bros., 1954. Pp. 332.

   A path-breaking book on manpower projection for specialised professional
occupations. Stresses flexibility of both demand for and supply of specialised

professions. Particularly noteworthy are chs. 6 and 7 which analyse the
potential supply, relating intelligence, ability, desire, grades, and various
socio-economic indicators to the numbers entering and graduating from colleges
The book closes with proposals for improving the utilisation of the potential
supply. Most of ch. 6 is reprinted in *EES*, pp. 216-40. (See also 140.) For
an article review of the book, protesting against Wolfle's definition of
"shortage" having nothing to do with the earnings of various kinds of manpower, see P. Thompson, "Manpower Allocation and the Pricing Process", *JPE*,
October, 1955, pp. 441-46. See the author's subsequent views in "Forecasting
Surpluses and Shortages in Key Occupations", *AAAPS*, September, 1959,
pp. 29-37.

1176 Ministry of Education, UK, *Early Leaving: A Report of the Central Advisory
Council for Education*. London: HMSO, 1954. Pp. 99.

An examination of the factors that influence the age at which pupils leave
English secondary schools, with a discussion of policies to reduce premature
leaving among grammar-school pupils of high ability. A sample survey of
secondary school pupils shows the influence of home background, financial
factors, and job-opportunities on the decision whether to leave school at
15, the minimum leaving age.

1955

1177 W. L. WARNER, J. C. ABEGGLEN, *Occupational Mobility in American Business and
Industry*. Minneapolis: Minnesota University Press, 1955. Pp. 315.

A study of the American business élite based on a questionnaire submitted
to almost 18,000 businessmen. Includes a review of previous studies and a
useful selected bibliography of "the literature on status, occupations and
occupational mobility". The principal findings of the book are conveniently
summarised, pp. 23-37. With respect to education, it was found that business
leaders as a group are better educated than the general population and, indeed
that education is now one of the chief avenues to business leadership.

1956

1178 J. E. FLOUD, A. H. HALSEY, F. M. MARTIN, *Social Class and Educational Opportunity*. London: Heinemann, 1956. Pp. 152.

Carries further the 1949 study by comparing a prosperous residential district in southern England with an industrial county borough in the north.
Concludes that, despite "formal equality of opportunity", the chances of
children of equal ability entering grammar schools are still dependent on
their social origins; size of family emerges as the crucial single index of
the influence of home environment on educational success.

1179 K. V. MÜLLER, *Begabung und soziale Schichtung in der hochindustrialisierten
Gesellschaft*. Schiftenreihe des Instituts für empirische Soziologie. Colonge
Westdeutscher Verlag, 1956. Pp. 135.

A study of occupational mobility as related to educational output in
Western Germany in the early 1950's.

1180 C. C. COLE, Jr., *Encouraging Scientific Talent. A Study of America's Able Students Who are Lost to College and Ways of Attracting Them to College and Science Careers.* Princeton, N.J.: College Entrance Examination Board, 1956. Pp. 259.

   Reviews all the available American sources to data on the demand and supply of science graduates, and on the factors encouraging or discouraging the production of scientists, with an analysis of the incidence of college-going among different groups in the population, concluding with a series of recommendations for attracting students with scientific ability to take up careers in science. The book includes the findings of "A National Study of High School Students and Their Plans", pp. 140-70, as well as a detailed bibliography arranged under a dozen subject headings, pp. 231-56.

1181 J. E. FLOUD, A. H. HALSEY, "English Secondary Schools and the Supply of Labour", *The Yearbook of Education, 1956,* ed. J. A. Lauwerys. London: Evans Bros., 1956, pp. 519-32, reprinted in *EES*, pp. 80-92.

   An analysis of the relationship between educational provision and occupational distribution, i.e. between ability and opportunity, in England.

1957

1182 C. A. ANDERSON, "The Social Status of University Students in Relation to Type of Economy: An International Comparison", *Transactions of the Third World Congress of Sociology.* London: International Sociological Association, 1957, V, pp. 51-63.

   A comparison of the social composition of university students in 24 countries in relation to income levels in the countries.

1183 J. B. MINER, *Intelligence in the United States. A Survey with Conclusions for Manpower Utilization in Education and Employment.* New York: Springer Publishing Co., 1957. Pp. 180.

   Based on a representative sample of the US population, this study investigates the significance of intelligence scores in relation to education, sex, marital status, age, race, occupation, geographical area, religion, class identification, and city size. Chs. 6 and 7 formulate a method for measuring the waste of intellectual resources in education and in employment. The final chapter contains recommendations for eliminating waste. A bibliography of the literature since 1940 is included.

1184 D. E. SUPER, P. B. BACHRACH, *Scientific Careers and Vocational Development Theory. A Review, A Critique and Some Recommendations.* New York: Bureau of Publications, Teachers College, Columbia University, 1957. Pp. 135.

   This monograph attempts to summarise what research has shown to be the characteristics of scientists, mathematicians, and engineers. It includes a comprehensive bibliography.

1185 M. ROSENBERG, *Occupations and Values.* Glencoe, Ill.: Free Press, 1957. Pp. 158.

An exhaustive analysis of occupational choices and values, based on a sample of 6000 college students from 11 universities in the United States.

1958

1186 R. M. STEPHENSON, "Stratification, Education, and Occupational Orientation: A Parallel Study and Review", *BJS*, March, 1958, pp. 42-53.

Compares the US and the UK and finds little difference in patterns of educational choice upon graduation from secondary schools.

1187 E. de S. BRUNNER, S. WAYLAND, "Occupation, Labor Force Status and Education", *JES*, 1958, reprinted in *EES*, pp. 55-67.

The patterns of occupational distribution by levels of education in the USA, noting differences between races, sexes, and regions.

1188 J. E. FLOUD, A. H. HALSEY, "The Sociology of Education", *CS*, VII, 3, 1958, pp. 165-93, 201-35.

An excellent history of the sociology of education, a discussion of its related branches, and a selected bibliography in French and English. See also J. E. Floud, "The Sociology of Education", *Society. Problems and Methods of Study*, ed. A. T. Welford *et al.* (London: Routledge & Kegan Paul, 1962), pp. 521-42.

1189 R. J. HAVIGHURST, "Education, Social Mobility and Social Change in Four Societies. A Comparative Study", *IRE*, IV, 1958, pp. 167-86.

The four societies are America, Great Britain, Australia, and Brazil. The author draws some basic conclusions about the role of education in social mobility in the closing pages of the article.

1190 M. W. ZAPOLEON, *The Identification of Those with Talent For Science and Engineering and Their Guidance in Elementary and Secondary Schools.* Washington, D.C.: The President's Committee on Scientists and Engineers, 1958. Pp. 57.

A review of the existing American literature on the subject with a bibliography and a list of current research. The bulk of the text summarises the major findings of research on identification and prediction of talent, and on motivation and vocational choice.

1959

1191 S. M. LIPSET, R. BENDIX, *Social Mobility in Industrial Society.* London: Heinemann, 1959. Pp. 309.

This famous sociological study includes a thorough review of comparative data on social mobility in advanced countries, as well as a case study of

Oakland, Calif., for purposes of demonstrating the hypothesis that the pattern of social mobility does not differ significantly between mature industrialised countries. The relationship between educational opportunities and intergenerational and interoccupational mobility is discussed at several places in the book, pp. 91-101, 189-92, 227-60. (See also 1440.)

1192 D. V. GLASS, "Education", *Law and Opinion in the Twentieth Century*, ed. M. Ginsberg. London: Stevens, 1959, pp. 319-46.

A review of the development of English secondary and university education since 1900, emphasising the influence of the social structure on the educational system, which summarises recent findings and refers to much of the interwar literature on the inequality of educational opportunity among social classes.

1193 N. GROSS, "The Sociology of Education", *Sociology Today. Problems and Prospects*, eds. R. K. Merton *et al.* New York: Basic Books, 1959, pp. 128-53.

An attempt to assess the current status of this branch of American sociology, with copious reference to the literature.

1194 K. SVALASTOGA, *Prestige, Class and Mobility.* Copenhagen: Gyldendals, 1959. Pp. 466.

The report of a sample survey on the influence of occupation and education on social mobility in Denmark in 1953-54, concluding that education is playing an increasingly important role in the mobility process. Compares social mobility in England and Denmark using recent British findings.

1195 K. M. BOLTE, *Sozialer Aufstieg und Abstieg. Eine untersuchung über Berufsprestige und Berufsmobilität.* Stuttgart: Ferdinand Enke, 1959. Pp. 253.

A study of the prestige rankings of occupations as related to occupational mobility in Western Germany from 1927 to 1953, with a useful bilingual bibliography.

1196 P. NAVILLE *et al.*, *École et Société.* Recherches de sociologie du travail No. 5. Paris: Librairie Marcel Rivière, 1959. Pp. 131.

A collection of essays on educational opportunity and social class in France, including an analysis by C. Peyre of social and regional variations in secondary school attendance, pp. 6-33, an examination by P. Naville of the social origins of pupils taking technical or vocational training, pp. 34-58, and a paper by J. E. Floud and A. H. Halsey on the relation between education and occupational choice, pp. 59-73, which is partly reprinted in 1181.

1197 National Science Foundation, *Scientific Manpower 1958. Papers of the Seventh Conference on Scientific Manpower.* Washington, D.C.: US Government Printing Office, 1959. Pp. 87.

The report, the third in a series of annual summaries of developments in the field of scientific manpower utilisation, includes a symposium on "Demographic and Sociological Aspects of Scientific Manpower", containing 4 papers:

W. F. Ogburn, "A Factor Affecting the Supply of Intellectuals", pp. 62-67;
M. Trow, "Some Implications of the Social Origins of Engineers", pp. 67-75;
H. S. Becker, "An Analytical Model for Studies of the Recruitment of Scien-
tific Manpower", pp. 75-80, and T. Parsons, "Professional Training and the
Role of Professions in American Society", pp. 80-87.

1960

1198 P. DE WOLFF, "Intellectual Resources and the Growth of Education", *Forecasting Manpower Needs for the Age of Science*. Paris: OEEC, 1960, pp. 89-101.

Reviews Dutch work on the "pool of ability" in The Netherlands.

1961

1199 C. A. ANDERSON, "A Skeptical Note on the Relation of Vertical Mobility to
Education", *AJS*, 1961, reprinted in *EES*, pp. 164-79.

Using British and American data, the author shows that education may well
be much less important in explaining vertical mobility in developed countries
than is usually thought: most of the mobility is explainable by variations
in ability and associated motivation.

1200 A. H. HALSEY, ed., *Ability and Educational Opportunity*. Paris: OECD, 1961.
Pp. 211.

This book is concerned with the major obstacles to the use of potential
human abilities in education, i.e. class stratification, cultural inequalities, urban-rural differences, etc., with particular reference to the OEEC
member countries. A. H. Halsey reviews the findings of the conference.
D. Wolfle writes on the "pool of ability". J. Ferrez discusses "Regional
Inequalities in Educational Opportunites" in France. J. E. Floud takes up
"Social Class Factors in Educational Achievement". T. Husén analyses "Educational Structure and the Development of Ability", and P. de Wolff and
K. Härnqvist present the results of an attempt to measure "Reserves of Ability in Sweden and Holland". The book closes with some comparative educational
statistics presented by J. Vaizey and a bibliography of the relevant literature in several European countries.

1201 W. D. FURNEAUX, *The Chosen Few. An Examination of Some Aspects of University
Selection in Britain*. London: Oxford University Press, 1961. Pp. 245.

A thorough study of the student-selection process of British universities,
based on data from a sample of 12,000 school leavers and 2000 university
students gathered in the decade 1950-60. The book includes an analysis of
"the pool of ability", ch. 4, pp. 41-51, and of socio-economic status and
type of school as determinants of educational attainments and educational
goals, ch. 5, pp. 51-74, as well as an appraisal of university selection techniques, ch. 7, pp. 84-101. Most of the details and some of the data are rele-
gated to the second part of the book and a summary of the main conclusions is
given in the opening pages, pp. xxi-xxvi. (See also 1209.)

1202 D. V. GLASS, *Differential Fertility, Ability and Educational Objectives. Problems for Study*. London: Godfrey Thompson Lecture Fund, 1961. Pp. 27.

Reviews recent work on "the pool of ability" in Great Britain and concludes with a discussion of its implications for the future expansion of higher and further education.

1203 P. C. SEXTON, *Education and Income. Inequalities of Opportunity in Our Public Schools*. New York: Viking Press, 1961. Pp. 298.

A study addressed to the layman of a single large, northern, urban public-school system, dealing with the economic, racial and sexual barriers to equality of educational opportunity.

1204 A. N. LITTLE, "'Will More Mean Worse?' An Inquiry into the Effects of University Expansion", *BJS*, December, 1961, pp. 351-63.

An attempt to test the restrictionist hypothesis that an expansion of university intake can take place only at the expense of university standards via the admission of less able students. The hypothesis is not definitely rejected by the results of the test but the evidence suggests that the extreme fears of the restrictionists are not justified. (See also 1209.)

1962

1205 A. GIRARD, R. PRESSAT, "Deux études sur la démocratisation de l'enseignement: I. L'origine sociale des élèves de 6e. II. Résultats d'une enquête dans l'Académie de Bordeaux", *POP*, janvier-mars, 1962, pp. 10-29.

Brings up to date earlier studies, published in the same journal between 1953 and 1955, of the social background of students in French secondary education.

1206 C. F. CARTER, "The Economic Use of Brains", *EJ*, March, 1962, pp. 1-12.

A plea for research into the factors affecting the supply of high ability and its distribution between occupations. The author concludes that "we need further evidence before it will be safe to suppose that there is plenty of high ability available, at present running to waste, and easily conserved."

1963

1207 O. D. DUNCAN, R. W. HODGE, "Education and Occupational Mobility. A Regression Analysis", *AJS*, May, 1963, pp. 629-44.

Analysing a sample of 1000 males in the city of Chicago, the authors conclude that education seems now to be a more important determinant of occupational status than father's occupation. The article briefly reviews previous findings and defends regression analysis as a powerful new technique for analysing occupational mobility.

1208   J. BEN-DAVID, "Professions in the Class System of Present-Day Societies.
A Trend Report and Bibliography", *CS*, XII, 3, 1963-64, pp. 247-330.

A thorough review of the literature on the social mobility of professional
people, with special emphasis on the role of education, and a representative
selection of the sociological literature since 1950 in English, French and
German dealing with professionals and intellectuals.

1209   P. HALMOS, ed., *SRM No. 7: Sociological Studies in British University Education*. Keele: Keele University, 1963. Pp. 204.

P. E. Vernon, "The Pool of Ability", pp. 45-59, is his Memorandum submitted
to the Robbins Committee (see 751). W. D. Furneaux develops the arguments
of his book *The Chosen Few* (1201) in a paper entitled "The Too Few Chosen,
and the Many That Could Be Called", pp. 59-79. R. K. Kelsall, "University
Student Selection in Relation to Subsequent Academic Performance: A Critical
Appraisal of the British Evidence", pp. 99-117, is his Memorandum submitted
to the Robbins Committee (see 751). J. G. H. Newfield summarises some of the
results of a national survey of the careers of university students: "Some
Factors Related to the Academic Performance of British University Students",
pp. 117-31. A. N. Little deals with "Some Myths of University Expansion",
pp. 185-99. T. S. Simey closes the volume with "The Sociology of University
Education. A Note on Research Priorities", pp. 199-204.

1964

1210   Project Talent Office, *Project Talent. The Identification, Development, and
Utilization of Human Talents*. Pittsburgh: Project Talent Office, Pittsburgh
University, 1960-64.

(i)   J. C. FLANAGAN, F. B. DAVIS, J. T. DAILEY, M. P. SHAYCROFT, D. B. ORR,
I. GOLDBERG, C. A. NEYMAN, Jr., *Designing the Study* (1960).

(ii) J. C. FLANAGAN *et al.*, "Design for a Study of American Youth", *The
Talents of American Youth*. Boston: Houghton Mifflin, 1962, I.

(iii) J. C. FLANAGAN *et al.*, *Studies of the American High School* (1962).

(iv) M. F. SHAYCROFT *et al.*, *Studies of a Complete Age Group—Age 15* (1963).

(v)   G. R. BURKETT, *Selected Pupil and School Characteristics in Relation
to Percentage of Negroes in School Enrolment* (1964).

(vi) J. C. FLANAGAN *et al.*, *The American High-School Student* (1964).

The first two reports describe the basic plans for the study which was to
survey available talent in the USA, to identify interests, aptitudes, and
background factors, to analyse factors affecting vocational choice, to determine the effectiveness of various types of educational experience, and to
study procedures for realising individual potential. A battery of tests was
administered in 1960 to a nationally representative sample of 450,000 students
in grades 9-12 in about 1350 secondary schools. Data obtained included aptitude and achievement test scores, family social and economic background, personal background, plans and aspirations, school and community characteritics,
etc.; the third report summarises much of this information about American
high schools, using the school as the unit of measurement. The fourth report
presents the findings for a sample of 15-year-olds. The fifth report presents the facts in relation to Negro enrolment. The sixth major publication

in the series provides all the information that was gathered on the characteristics of high-school students. The pages of the reports are not consecu-
tively numbered but they average about 300-500 pages. For a brief review of
the major results of Project Talent, see J. T. Dailey, "Education and Emergence from Poverty", *JMF*, November, 1964, pp. 430-34. (See also 1216.)

1211 J. W. B. DOUGLAS, *The Home and the School. A Study of Ability and Attainment
in the Primary School*. London: Macgibbon & Kee, 1964. Pp. 189.

   The results of a follow-up study of a national sample of over 5000 children
living in Great Britain, analysing the determinants of their achievements
in primary schools, up to and including the 11+ secondary selection examination.

1212 E. GINZBERG, J. L. HERMA, *Talent and Performance*. New York: Columbia
University Press, 1964. Pp. 265.

   A study of the careers of talented graduates, based on a sample of 340 men
who received fellowships for graduate or professional training at Columbia
University between 1944 and 1950.

1213 C. A. ANDERSON, P. J. FOSTER, "Discrimination and Inequality in Education",
SE, Fall, 1964, pp. 1-19.

   This paper deals with the possible fallacies in interpreting statistical
inequalities in data on educational opportunities, concluding with a typology
of differential treatments of students with respect to education.

1214 A. N. LITTLE, J. WESTERGAARD, "The Trend of Class Differentials in Educational
Opportunity in England and Wales", *BJS*, December, 1964, pp. 301-17.

   Marshals all the available British evidence on social class determinants of
educational opportunity in recent years and concludes that while social inequalities in educational opportunity have been diminishing somewhat since
1944, this is merely a continuation of a long-term trend. (See also 1225.)

1965

1215 P. W. MUSGRAVE, *The Sociology of Education*. London: Methuen, 1965. Pp. 278.

   It is not for an economist to pass judgement on a textbook in the sociology
of education, but why must sections devoted to the economics of education,
pp. 102-30, so invariably lack both accuracy in reporting and clarity of
exposition?

1216 *Progress Towards the Goals of Project Talent*. Bulletin No. 4, 1965. US
Dept. of Health, Education, and Welfare, Office of Education. Washington,
D.C.: US Government Printing Office, 1965. Pp. 11

   A brief description of some of the preliminary results of Project Talent
(see 1210) with particular reference to patterns of ability and career choices.

1966

1217   J. S. COLEMAN *et al.*, *Equality of Educational Opportunity*. US Department of
       Health, Education, and Welfare. Washington, D.C.: Government Printing
       Office, 1966. Pp. 737.

       A comprehensive account of regional and racial differences in the distribu-
       tion of educational resources in the US, with a study of the influence of
       school and home environment on pupil achievement. The effects of school de-
       segregation programmes on Negro and White pupils are examined in detail.
       (See 1231 and 1243.)

1967

1218   D. PYM, "'Technical' Change and the Misuse of Professional Manpower: Some
       Studies and Observations", *OP*, January, 1967, pp. 1-16.

       A good example of the psychologist's approach to the utilisation question:
       malutilisation is defined from the point of view of the worker and his feel-
       ing that his IQ talents are or are not being fully utilised.

1219   J. E. MEADE, A. S. PARKES, eds., *Genetic and Environmental Factors in Human
       Ability*. London: Oliver & Boyd, 1967. Pp. 242.

       This symposium held by the Eugenics Society in 1965 included two sessions
       on "The Nature and Meaning of Intelligence Tests" and on "Selection of
       Higher Education". Under the first heading, P. E. Vernon, "Development of
       Current Ideas about Intelligence Tests", pp. 3-14, and D. Pidgeon, "Intelli-
       gence Testing and Comprehensive Education", pp. 42-52, discuss the historical
       impact of IQ testing on English education, while B. B. Bernstein and
       D. Young, "Some Aspects of the Relationship Between Communication and Per-
       formance in Tests", pp. 15-23, and H. T. Himmelweit, "Social Background,
       Intelligence, and School Structure: An Interaction Analysis", pp. 24-41,
       describe research projects. Under the second heading, there is a general
       paper by J. Floud, "Principles and Procedures of University Selection",
       pp. 55-63, and two papers on the problems of selection policies by J. Drever
       and L. Hudson, concluding with some provocative comments by Lord Robbins,
       pp. 100-1; S. Wiseman, "Environmental and Innate Factors and Educational
       Attainment", pp. 64-80, belongs more properly under the first heading.

1220   J. R. LYLE, "Research on Achievement Determinants in Educational Systems:
       A Survey", *SPS*, I, 1967, pp. 143-55.

       A review of American literature since 1960 on achievement determinants in
       public elementary and secondary school systems. The succinct conclusion of
       the review is: "Out-of-school factors are far more significant than in-
       school factors.... Experience of the teacher seems to...be more important as
       an output determinant than class size or teacher formal education, for dis-
       tricts with relatively small ranges of variation in expenditures," p. 153.

1221   R. J. HAVIGHURST, B. L. NEUGARTEN, *Society and Education*. Boston: Allyn &
       Bacon, 3rd ed., 1967. Pp. 538.

A popular American textbook in the sociology of education with a comprehensive bibliography. The treatment of economic issues is decidedly superficial.

1222 A. H. HALSEY, "The Sociology of Education", *Sociology: An Introduction.* New York: John Wiley, 1967, pp. 381-434.

A broad discussion of the subject, with particular reference to developing countries.

1223 Department of Education and Science, UK, *Scientists and Engineers and their Choice of Jobs. 1956-59.* London: HMSO, 1967. Pp. 129.

Deals with the factors affecting the choice of job of science and engineering graduates, the sources of information available to them and the recruitment policies of major employers. No details are given of the earnings of the sample, but the importance of salary as a factor influencing choice is discussed.

1224 P. W. MUSGRAVE, "Towards a Sociological Theory of Occupational Choice", *SOR*, March, 1967, pp. 33-47.

After briefly reviewing previous attempts, the author sketches a new theory of socialisation focused on occupational choice. See the critique by M. A. Coulson, E. T. Keil, D. S. Riddell, J. S. Struthers, *ibid.*, November, 1967, pp. 301-22.

1225 OECD, Study Group in the Economics of Education, *Social Objectives in Educational Planning.* Paris: OECD, 1967. Pp. 309.

This conference concentrates on one of the social objectives of educational planning, namely, the equalisation of educational opportunities among the principal social groups and geographical regions of OECD countries. C. A. Anderson contributes a review of research results on the determinants of the private demand for education: "Sociological Factors in the Demand for Education", pp. 31-48; a brief thought-provoking paper by J. Vaizey considers "Some Dynamic Aspects of Inequality", pp. 49-52; T. Husèn summarises Swedish research on the intrusion of social factors into the selective process: "The Effect of School Structure Upon Utilization of Ability: The case of Sweden and Some International Comparisons", pp. 53-66; N. R. Ramsøy, "The Clientele of Comprehensive Schools in the United States", pp. 67-84; R. Ruiter, "The Past and Future Inflow of Students into the Upper Levels of Education in The Netherlands", pp. 85-148; J. Westergaard, A. Little, a revised version of 1214, pp. 215-32; O. Ruin, "The Selection Process in the Swedish Educational System", pp. 233-52; P. Laderriere, "Regional Inequalities of Opportunity in French Education", pp. 253-86. B. Hayward reviews "Unequal Social Participation in Education: the OECD Programme and Implications for Policy", pp. 303-9; S. J. Mushkin looks at "Educational Policies for the Culturally Disadvantaged Child" in the United States, pp. 287-302. Lastly, there is the conference's only major research paper: "Trends in University Entry: An Inter-Country Comparison" by R. Knight, pp. 149-213. See also L. Sussman, "Summary Review by the Rapporteur", pp. 15-30.

1226 W. L. SLOCUM, *Occupational Careers: A Sociological Perspective.* Chicago, Ill.: Aldine Publishing Co., 1967. P. 272.

This book ably summarises recent work on the sociology of occupational choice and occupational mobility. The relationship between education and occupation, while discussed in several places in the book, is treated separately in one chapter. The focus of the discussion throughout is almost entirely on the United States.

1227 C. A. ANDERSON, *The Social Context of Educational Planning*. Fundamentals of Educational Planning 5. Paris: UNESCO-IIEP, 1967. Pp. 35.

A characteristically scintillating essay, emphasising the exaggerated expectations in most countries of what schools can contribute to national development. There are some sharp comments on the manpower-forecasting approach.

1228 A. PEARSE, ed., "Social Functions of Education", *ISSJ*, XIX, 3, 1967, pp. 313-429.

Six of the papers presented at a Round-table on the Sociology of Education held in 1966. Among the most relevant are (1) A. Pearse, "Introduction: Sociologists and Education", pp. 313-24; (2) A. E. Gollin, "Foreign Study and Modernization: The Transfer of Technology Through Education", pp. 359-77 (3) P. Heintz, "Education as an Instrument of Social Integration in Underdeveloped Societies", pp. 378-86; and (4) A. Solari, N. Campiglia, and S. Prates, "Education, Occupation and Development", pp. 404-15, which include a case-study of Montevideo, Uruguay, that tests the hypothesis of upgrading in the course of economic development. The six articles are rounded off by an unsatisfactory selected bibliography in the sociology of education, 1958-66, pp. 416-29.

1229 P. M. BLAU, O. D. DUNCAN, *The American Occupational Structure*. New York: John Wiley, 1967. Pp. 520

This is undoubtedly the most sophisticated study of occupational mobility ever published. It is based on evidence collected from a representative sample of over 20,000 American men in 1962, divided into 17 occupational categories, and reviews and discusses virtually all available data on American occupational structure. Successive chapters look at historical trends in occupational structure, current patterns and movements, models of the stratification process, inequalities in opportunities between Negroes and Whites, geographical mobility, rural-urban mobility, marriage and fertility patterns across occupations, with a final chapter on "conditions of occupational success". See, particularly, the role of education in the determinants of upward mobility, pp. 401 ff., and the superiority of the United States over other countries in providing upward mobility for the working class, pp. 432-4. Oddly enough, however, the basic definition of "occupation" as measured by the Census is nowhere discussed in the book.

1968

1230 C. B. NAM, A. L. RHODES, R. E. HERRIOTT, "School Retention by Race, Religion, and Socioeconomic Status", *JHR*, Spring, 1968, pp. 171-90.

A national study of the relationship of race, religion, socio-economic status, and area of residence to the probability of finishing high school in the United States. The article includes a good bibliography on the high-school dropout problem.

1231   S. BOWLES, H. M. LEVIN, "The Determinants of Scholastic Achievements—An
       Appraisal of Some Recent Evidence", *ibid*., Winter, 1968, pp. 3-24.

    This is a critique of Coleman (1217) questioning the adequacy of the data,
the type of statistical analysis used, and the interpretation of the results.
The central attack is on the basic thesis of Coleman's study, namely, that
there is no simple and strong relationship between standard "quality" inputs
into schools—expenditure on buildings, equipment, teachers' pay, etc.—and
output as measured by achievement tests; furthermore, the social composition
of the student body of a school is more influential than the home background
of students in determining individual achievement. For a vigorous reply and
a restatement of the argument, see J. S. Coleman, "Reply to Bowles and Levin",
ibid., Spring, 1968, pp. 237-46.

1232   B. DAVIES, *Social Needs and Resources in Local Services. A Study of Varia-
       tions in Standards of Provision of Personal Social Services Between Local
       Authority Areas*. London: Michael Joseph, 1968. Pp. 341.

    This book applies correlation analysis and occasionally regression analysis
to some 500 statistical series to assess the degree to which local authority
provision of social services in Great Britain achieves "territorial justice".
Ch. 12, pp. 260-85, is devoted to primary and secondary education, where the
author adopts "equality of educational opportunity" as the criterion of
"justice". The conclusions of the education chapter are perhaps less interesting than those of other chapters.

1233   C. JENCKS, "Social Stratification and Higher Education", *HER*, Spring, 1968,
       pp. 277-316.

    Concerned as it is with the effect of higher education on social mobility
in the United States, the article is, among other things, a valuable summary
of recent American research on the relationship between education and occupation (see also 1236).

1234   Schools Council, Enquiry 1, *Young School Leavers. Report of an Enquiry
       Carried Out for the Schools Council by the Government Social Survey*.
       London: HMSO, 1968. Pp. 386.

    A study, based on a sample of young school leavers in Great Britain, of
school objectives and school subjects from the points of view of students,
parents and teachers. It includes valuable material on the jobs and career
prospects of 15-year-old leavers.

1235   J. W. B. DOUBLAS, J. M. ROSS, H. R. SIMPSON, *All Our Future. A Longitudinal
       Study of Secondary Education*. London: Peter Davies, 1968. Pp. 241.

    This book, a sequel to *The Home and The School* (1211), follows the sample
of 5000 boys and girls born in 1946 through the first 5 years of secondary
schooling. Most of its findings related to the persistence of social class
differences in educational opportunity. The striking discovery that the
major differences in test performance are established by the age of 8, if not
by the age of 5, is perhaps insufficiently emphasised by the authors.

1236 C. JENCKS, D. RIESMAN, *The Academic Revolution*. New York: Doubleday & Co.,
      1968. Pp. 580.

      A fascinating history of American higher education, and a running socio-
      logical commentary on the rise of academic professionalism in the United
      States. Ch. 3, pp. 61-154, is a later version of 1233, arguing that mass
      higher education has had no measurable effect on equality of opportunity in
      American society. Ch. 6, pp. 257-90, deals with the financing of public and
      private colleges. There are excellent chapters on Catholic and Negro
      colleges, and a useful closing chapter on graduate education.

1969

1237 T. HUSÈN, *Talent, Opportunity and Career. A Twenty-Six Year Follow-up of
      1,500 Individuals*. Stockholm: Almqvist & Wiksell, 1969. Pp. 309.

      This unique Swedish longitudinal study looks, among other things, at the
      relationship between education, social class, native ability and earnings and
      by means of two-way tables concludes that social class is somewhat more
      important than education in affecting earnings (pp. 152-60).

1238 S. H. MASTERS, "The Effect of Family Income on Children's Education: Some
      Findings on Inequality of Opportunity", *JHR*, Spring, 1969, pp. 158-75.

      This paper uses the 1/1000 sample of the 1960 Census to estimate the prob-
      abilities of retardation and dropping out for children from different family
      backgrounds. The determinants of the retardation and dropout rates also
      investigated with particular emphasis on Negro children. This sort of
      article succeeds in making non-Americans blush over the paucity of their own
      census data.

1970

1239 E. F. DENISON, "An Aspect of Inequality of Opportunity", *JPE*, September/
      October, 1970, pp. 1195-1202.

      A powerful plea for a new view of equality of educational opportunity which
      would deliberately give more education to the less able. The author crudely
      estimates expenditures on higher education in the USA by level of student
      abilities and sketches a programme for redistributing funds from the more to
      the less able.

1240 A. SOHLMAN, *Differences in School Achievement and Occupational Opportunities:
      Explanatory Factors. A Survey Based on European Experience. OECD Conference
      on Policies for Educational Growth. Background Study No. 10*. Paris: OECD,
      1970. Pp. 68, mimeographed.

      A fascinating survey of evidence on the relations between home background
      factors and educational achievement, between in-school factors and educational
      achievement, and between educational achievement and occupational success.

1241   C. NAM, *Group Disparities in Educational Participation. OECD Conference on Policies for Educational Growth. Background Study No. 4.* Paris: OECD, 1970. Pp. 279.

   This study collects all the available evidence for OECD member countries and develops some new quantitative measures of equality or inequality of educational access and participation by region and social class. Over half of the document is given over to the presentation of data. In general, the study demonstrates the persistence of regional and social disparities in the 1950's and 1960's despite the educational explosion of these countries.

1242   L. C. SOLMON, "A Note on Equality of Educational Opportunity", *AER*, September, 1970, pp. 768-71.

   A brief note to emphasize the role of foregone earnings in the social demand for education.

1243   G. G. CAIN, H. W. WATTS, "Problems in Making Policy Inferences from the Coleman Report", *ASR*, 35 (2), 1970, pp. 228-49.

   This repeats much of their earlier criticisms. There is a reply by J. S. Coleman and D. J. Aigner.

1971

1244   H. P. TUCKMAN, "High School Inputs and Their Contribution to School Performance", *JHR*, Fall, 1971, pp. 490-509; see "Comment" by J. Hambor, L. Phillips, H. L. Votey, *ibid.*, Spring, 1973, pp. 260-63.

   This article examines the consequences of a change in several school inputs when interaction effects between in-school and out-of-school factors are present. The sample comprises 1,000 public high schools in America surveyed by the Bureau of Census during the 1965-66 school year.

1245   H. M. LEVIN, J. W. GUTHRIE, G. B. KLEINDORFER, "School Achievement and Post-School Success: A Review", *RER*, 41 (1), 1971, pp. 1-16.

   A comprehensive review of the American evidence relating education to lifetime earnings, occupational attainment, political participation, social mobility, school choice and social deviance.

1246   L. DONALSON, "Social Class and The Polytechnics", *HIR*, Autumn, 1971, pp. 44-68.

   Shows that the social class composition of students in some British technical colleges is no better than it is in most British universities. A valuable source for availabe information on the social class composition of students in British higher education.

1247   S. BOWLES, "Unequal Education and The Reproduction of the Social Division of Labor", *RRPE*, Fall/Winter, 1971, pp. 1-30.

A subtle exposition of the Marxist argument that schooling in capitalist societies is inherently inegalitarian. The argument is couched with reference to the United States but generalises easily.

1972

1248 O. D. DUNCAN, D. L. FEATHERMAN, B. DUNCAN, *Socioeconomic Background and Achievement*. New York: Seminar Press, 1972. Pp. 284.

This monumental follow-up study of Duncan and Blau (see 1229) once again uses path analysis to look at both the antecedents of occupational status, such as intelligence, family background, and education, and the consequences, such as personal earnings. For that reason, its findings are frequently of relevance to the economics of education: see, in particular, pp. 91-102.

1249 A. J. CORAZZINI, D. J. DUGAN, H. G. GRABOWSKI, "Determinants and Distributional Aspects of Enrollment in US Higher Education", *JHR*, Winter, 1972, pp. 39-59.

The authors develop a demand and supply enrolment model and then test by means of regression analysis first on a national sample and then on a special sample of Boston high school seniors. Family income emerges strongly as a critical variable affecting demand.

1973

1250 C. JENCKS, "Inequality in Retrospect", *HER*, February, 1973, pp. 138-64.

This is Jencks' reply to the battery of critics brought together in this issue of *HER* and, although he concedes little, it adds much to an understanding of his book. Of all his critics, the most relevant to our purpose is L. Thurow, "Proving the Absense of Positive Associations", *ibid.*, pp. 106-12, who explains away the apparent inconsistency between Jencks' results and those of human capital theorists.

1251 A. KUHN, A. POOLE, P. SALES, H. P. WYNN, "An Analysis of Graduate Job Mobility", *BJIR*, March, 1973, pp. 124-42.

An analysis of the mobility of British university graduates by length of service for a cohort of 1960 graduates, extending the book by Kelsall and others (see 797).

1252 D. M. LEVINE, "Educational Policy After Inequality", *TCR*, December, 1973, pp. 149-79.

A compendium review of objections to Jencks' book (329), with emphasis on the conflicts between Jencks and the human-capital school (pp. 169-72).

1974

1253   C. R. HILL, F. P. STAFFORD, "Allocation of Time to Preschool Children and
        Educational Opportunity", *JHR*, Summer, 1974, pp. 323-41.

        One of the first studies to demonstrate the widely-held belief that high-
        status mothers devote more time to preschool child care than do low-status
        mothers. The authors are unable, however, to link these class differences
        in time investments devoted to preschool children to the subsequent cognitive
        achievement of these children.

1975

1254   OECD, *Seminar on Education, Inequality and Life Chances*. Paris: Directorate
        for Social Affairs, Manpower and Education, 1975 (processed).

        This OECD seminar, held in January, 1975, resulted in 16 papers of uneven
        quality by economists and sociologists: (1) OECD Secretariat, "Education,
        Inequality and Life Chances—The Major Policy Issues" (pp. 27), a nice state-
        ment of the issues; (2) OECD Secretariat, "Inequalities in the Distribution
        of Education Between Countries, Sexes, Generations and Individuals" (pp. 86),
        a few pages of text and a mass of figures; (3) OECD Secretariat, "Inequality
        in the Distribution of Personal Income (pp. 53); (4) OECD Secretariat, "In-
        equality of Educational Opportunity By Social Origin in Higher Education",
        (pp. 19), with a Discussion Paper by I. B. Kravis (pp. 18) commenting on
        (2), (3), and (4); (5) J-C. Eicher, A. Mingat, "Education and Equality in
        France" (pp. 85), which includes, among many other interesting results, pre-
        liminary estimates of rates of return to educational investment in France by
        the social origin of individuals, plus a discussion paper by R. Boudon
        (pp. 12); (6) S. M. Miller, "Social Mobility and Equality" (pp. 45), which
        summarizes sociological work on social mobility in a number of countries:
        (7) N. Keyfitz, "Equality of Opportunity and Social Mobility. A Survey of
        Methods of Analysis" (pp. 39); (8) N. R. Ramsøy, "On Social Stratification
        in a Temporal Framework" (pp. 22); (9) A. H. Halsey, "Education and Social
        Mobility in Britain Since World War II" (pp. 73), with a comment by A. K.
        Sen (pp. 6); (10) T. Watanabe, "Income Inequality and Economic Development:
        A Study on (sic) Japanese Case" (pp. 32); (11) M. Pfaff, G. Fuchs, "Education,
        Inequality and Life Income: A Report on the Federal Republic of Germany"
        (pp. 110), with a comment by P. Wiles (pp. 17) and R. Layard (pp. 4);
        (12) T. Husèn, "Strategies for Educational Inequality" (pp. 58), with a com-
        ment by K. Eide (pp. 13); (13) M. Woodhall, "Distributional Impact of Methods
        of Educational Finance" (pp. 51), which canvasses a variety of financial
        issues in respect of higher education in OECD countries, with a comment by
        G. Williams (pp. 4); (14) B. A. Okner, A. M. Rivlin, "Income Distribution
        Policy in the United States" (pp. 53), with a comment by J. Mincer (pp. 13);
        (15) A. Lindbeck, "Inequality and Redistribution Policy Issues. Principles
        and Swedish Experience" (pp. 210), with a comment by R. Bentzel (pp. 11) and
        R. Neild (pp. 12); (16) J. Tinbergen, "Education, Inequality and Life Chances:
        Report on the Netherlands" (pp. 38), with a comment by J. Pen (pp. 6); and
        (17) OECD Secretariat, "Education, Inequality and Life Chances", (pp. 10).

7. THE POLITICS OF EDUCATION

When Friedman[1256] in 1955 published his proposal to encourage private education by means of state-financed educational vouchers, he started a controversy which even now has not run its full course. Wiseman[1259] spelled out the implications of a free market for British education and was promptly criticised by Horobin and Smyth[1260]. Since then, Peacock and Wiseman[1268] have re-stated their case, and West[1271,1273,1277] has carried it still further, working out in considerable detail how it might be introduced in Great Britain. In America, vouchers are now part of the radical programme for education: see Areen and Jencks[1278] and section A3b on "Public and Private Finance" above. For a variety of adverse comments on educational vouchers, see Benson[1], Vaizey[2], Miner[433], Rivlin[741], Blaug[1274], and Robinson[1276]. Tiebout[1257] suggests a way around the problem. The same argument has come up in medical care, as Lees[1282] makes clear. Musgrave[1258] make valuable background reading for this debate. Stubblebine[190] and Pauly[507] supply supporting ammunition drawn from welfare economics for the voucher argument.

The issue of federal aid to education, a controversial one in the United States, is canvassed from various angles by Munger and Fenno[1262], Sufrin[1263,1264], Orlans[1265], and the US Congress Subcommittee on Education[1267]. Bailey and others[1261] study the same question at the state level.

1937

1255 G. A. N. LOWNDES, *The Silent Social Revolution. An Account of the Expansion of Public Education in England and Wales 1895-1935*. London: Oxford University Press, 1937, ch. 11, pp. 235-49.

   The last chapter of this very readable history states the economic case for public education: "Ideally no doubt the provision of education for the whole population as a right requries no justification or at least no justification relying upon the social and economic return likely to be experienced by the community. Unfortunately, however, the average Englishman is more ready to open his heart to such an ideal than his purse."

1955

1256 M. FRIEDMAN, "The Role of Government in Education", *Economics and the Public Interest*, ed. R. E. Solo. New Brunswick, N.J.: Rutgers University Press, 1955, pp. 123-44, revised in M. Friedman, *Capitalism and Freedom*. Chicago Ill.: Chicago University Press, 1963, pp. 85-108, reprinted in *UNESCO-REED*, pp. 881-93, and *PEE*, pp. 132-43.

A plea for more private provision of education with a plan whereby the
central government would furnish vouchers to parents, redeemable for a specified maximum sum per child per year in any "approved" educational institution
of their own choice.

1956

1257 C. M. TIEBOUT, "A Pure Theory of Local Expenditures", *JPE*, October, 1956,
pp. 416-25.

The economic case for local operation and finance of social services based
on the notion that services provided by local rather than by central governments furnish an element of consumer choice by virtue of the freedom to
choose residence. See also the author's "An Economic Theory of Fiscal Decentralization", *Public Finances: Needs, Sources, Utilization,* ed. J. M.
Buchanan (Princeton, N.J.: Princeton University Press, 1961), pp. 79-96, and
"Comments" by B. A. Weisbrod, pp. 131-32.

1959

1258 R. A. MUSGRAVE, *The Theory of Public Finance. A Study in Public Economy*.
New York: McGraw-Hill, 1959, ch. 1, pp. 3-27, exceprts reprinted in *PEE*,
pp. 96-104.

Essential background reading to questions of educational finance and the
economic case for public education. Develops the distinction between "private wants", "social wants" and "merit wants", pointing out that education
does not fall exclusively into any of the 3 categories. Emphasises that
arguments about public or private finance should not be confused with the
issue of public or private provision.

1259 J. WISEMAN, "The Economics of Education", *SJPE*, February, 1959, pp. 48-58,
reprinted in *P-EED,* 2, pp. 360-72.

Shows that the fact that education yields public as well as private benefits provides a case for state assistance to parents, not direct provision
of education by the State. Sketches an educational system for Great Britain
in the light of this conclusion. (See also 1268.)

1960

1260 G. W. HOROBIN, R. L. SMYTH, "The Economics of Education: A Comment", *SJPE*,
February, 1960, pp. 69-74, reprinted in *UNESCO-REED*, pp. 895-900, and "Reply"
by J. Wiseman, *ibid.*, pp. 75-76, reprinted in *P-EED*, 2, pp. 373-81.

A valuable reply to the arguments of Friedman and Wiseman in favour of private education. Develops the economic case for state education along existing lines.

1962

1261 S. K. BAILEY, R. T. FROST, P. E. MARSH, R. C. WOOD, *Schoolmen and Politics.
A Study of State Aid to Education in the Northeast*. The Economics and Politics of Public Education, No. 1. Syracuse, N.Y.: Syracuse University Press,
1962. Pp. 111.

   A study by 4 political scientists of the political forces influencing state
   aid to education in the north-eastern part of the United States. Argues the
   case that government aid to public schools can only be understood as the out-
   come of conflicting political forces.

1262 F. J. MUNGER, F. R. FENNO, Jr., *National Politics and Federal Aid to Education*. The Economics and Politics of Public Education, No. 3. Syracuse,
N.Y.: Syracuse University Press, 1962. Pp. 193.

   An important study of American education as a subject of political controversy. After a brief survey of the history of unsuccessful attempts to ap-
   prove a long-term federal aid programme for elementary and secondary education in the USA, this book reviews issues of federal aid to education, organi
   sations for and against federal aid, results of public opinion polls, the
   positions of the two major political parties, the action of various president
   the role of the Office of Education and of House and Senate Committees on
   Education, concluding with an appraisal of future prospects of increasing
   federal educational assistance.

1263 S. C. SUFRIN, *Issues in Federal Aid to Education*. The Economics and Politics
of Public Education, No. 4. Syracuse, N.Y.: Syracuse University Press,
1962. Pp. 64.

   A rapid review of the problem of taxable capacity and the difficulties in
   administering federal aid. The final chapter looks at the Congressional
   Debate over the Public School Assistance Act of 1961, illustrating the deep-
   seated American fear of centralisation of education.

1963

1264 S. C. SUFRIN, *Administering the National Defense Education Act*. The Economic
and Politics of Public Education, No. 8. Syracuse, N.Y.: Syracuse University Press, 1963. Pp. 76.

   A review of the administrative problems of the National Defense Education
   Act of 1958, largely with respect to elementary and secondary schools. Useful for the glimpse it affords of American attitudes to central control of
   education.

1265 H. ORLANS, *The Effects of Federal Programs on Higher Education. A Study of
36 Universities and Colleges*. Washington, D.C.: The Brookings Institution,
1963. Pp. 361.

   An attempt to evaluate the educational and administrative impact of Title X
   of the National Defense Education Act of 1958 upon selected departments at
   36 American universities and colleges. A convenient quick summary of the
   principal conclusions is found on pp. 293-94.

1266 R. M. PARISH, "The Economics of State Aid to Education", *ER*, September, 1963,
      pp. 292-305.

      The author justifies Australian state aid to private schools on grounds of
      expediency, having previously argued that the government ought to encourage
      investment in education. In a subsequent comment, H. F. Lydall takes excep-
      tion to the argument, *ibid.*, June, 1964, pp. 260-68.

1267 US Congress Subcommittee on Education, *The Federal Government and Education*.
      Washington, D.C.: US Government Printing Office, 1963. Pp. 178.

      An overall summary of all federal support for education, including expendi-
      ture on schools, universities, student grants, government-sponsored research
      and foreign aid. A brief section on projected manpower needs points to cri-
      tical shortages of highly trained manpower in almost every sector, with
      "little relief in sight". The report concludes that although the Federal
      Government is heavily involved in the education system, "there is little
      evidence of a well-co-ordinated programme" and makes proposals for greater
      co-ordination and in particular the setting up of a Joint Congressional
      Committee on Education to provide an overall picture of federal educational
      activities and education needs.

1964

1268 A. T. PEACOCK, J. WISEMAN, *Education for Democrats*. London: Institute of
      Economic Affairs, 1964. Pp. 69.

      The Friedman-Wiseman proposal for the private provision but public finance
      of education, worked out in greater detail and with special attention to the
      British scene. For a brief popular version of the Peacock-Wiseman thesis,
      see E. G. West, "Parents' Choice in Education", *Rebirth of Britain. A Sym-
      posium of Essays* (London: Pan Books, 1964), pp. 171-87.

1965

1269 W. E. LAIRD, D. L. SCHILSON, "Financing Investment in Education", *JGE*, April,
      1965, pp. 55-62.

      The authors recommend a Friedman-type voucher system for education, on the
      grounds that this would increase national investment in education by tapping
      new sources of revenue, and also that it would increase the range of consumer
      choice. Veterans' aid schemes after World War II and the Korea War are quoted
      as showing the feasibility of the voucher system.

1270 R. HARRIS, A. SELDON, *Choice in Welfare 1965. Second Report on an Enquiry
      Conducted by Mass-Observation Into the Extent of Knowledge and Preference in
      State and Private Provision for Education, Health Services and Pension.*
      London: Institute of Economic Affairs, 1965. Pp. 89.

      An interesting second attempt to combine the techniques of market research
      and opinion polling to discover how well informed a national sample of British
      married men were about the finance of the social services, including education

how many of them might prefer private alternatives to state services, and how far they might use private welfare services if their costs were other than they are. The findings are full of surprises and certainly do not suggest a consensus in favour of extending state services in all directions.

1271   E. G. WEST, *Education and the State. A Study in Political Economy*. London: The Institute of Economic Affairs, 1965. Pp. 242.

This is an unusually provocative and important book, combining, at one and the same time, an argument for fostering private education in modern Britain by means of a Friedman-Peacock-Wiseman voucher scheme, a sketch of a reinterpretation of the history of education in nineteenth-century Britain, and a series of notes on the treatment of education by the great economists of the past. The discussion moves simultaneously on all three fronts, which makes for fascinating, if sometimes a little confusing reading. This is a book that will delight some and infuriate others.

1966

1272   A. FISHLOW, "The American Common School Revival: Fact or Fancy", *Industrialization in Two Systems*, ed. H. Rosovsky. New York: John Wiley, 1966, pp. 40-67.

A careful analysis of the spread of publicly supported schools in the decades before the Civil War (1840-1860), emphasising the unequal regional extension of schooling throughout the United States.

1967

1273   E. G. WEST, "The Political Economy of American Public School Legislation", *JLE*, October, 1967, pp. 101-28.

A fascinating account of the fight to secure free, compulsory schooling in the State of New York in the nineteenth century by one who views with scepticism the arguments that were voiced then and now in favour of free, state-provided education.

1274   *Institute of Economic Affairs, Education: A Framework for Choice*. London: Institute of Economic Affairs, 1967. Pp. 101.

This contains, among other things, a critique by M. Blaug of West (1271), "Economic Aspects of Vouchers for Education", pp. 21-48, and a reply by E. G. West, "Dr. Blaug and State Education: A Reply", pp. 49-86.

1275   P. MERANTO, *The Politics of Federal Aid to Education in 1965: A Study in Political Innovation*. Syracuse, N.Y.: Syracuse University Press, 1967. Pp. 144.

This extremely interesting study demonstrates the accumulation of relatively minor and apparently unrelated incremental changes that finally culminated in the passage of the Elementary and Secondary Education Act in 1965, which for the first time significantly extended federal aid to education in the United States.

1968

1276 G. ROBINSON, "The Voucher System of Education Finance and Independence in
      Education", *SEA*, January, 1968, pp. 31-40.

      After a brief review of the earlier debate on education vouchers in Great
      Britain in the 1920's, the author moves on to consider the recent proposals
      of Peacock and Wiseman in the light of the status differences that exist in
      English education.

1277 E. G. WEST, *Economics, Education and the Politician*. London: Institute of
      Economic Affairs, 1968. Pp. 76.

      Another powerful defence of education vouchers, with a practical proposal
      for their introduction in Britain: local authorities that have failed to
      provide primary education in accordance with the 1944 Act should be forced to
      issue vouchers to the parents concerned spendable on any primary school what-
      soever within a 7-mile radius.

1972

1278 M. CARNOY, ed., *Schooling in a Corporate Society. The Political Economy of
      Education in America*. New York: David McKay Co., 1972. Pp. 303.

      This collection of 14 essays provides an excellent introduction to the
      radical critique of education, most of the authors being members of the Union
      of Radical Political Economics. There are two fine essays by S. Bowles
      (see 815 and 1247) as well as a piece on vouchers by J. Areen and C. Jencks
      (see 539 and 542). Thereafter, we have M. Raskin, "The Channeling Colony";
      M. Reich, "Economic Theories of Racism"; P. Blair, "Job Discrimination and
      Education"; S. Michelson, "Rational Income Decisions of Blacks and Everybody
      Else", an important contribution to the discussion on the private demand for
      education; T. Ribich, "The Case for 'Equal Opportunity'"; S. Michelson, "The
      Political Economy of Public School Finance", which is in part concerned with
      the nineteenth century history of Massachusetts education; M. Carnoy, "Is
      Compensatory Education Possible?", who also contributes a rousing introduc-
      tion to the volume; H. Levin, "The Case for Community Control of Schools";
      B. B. Stretch, "The Rise of the 'Free School'"; P. Brenner, "Political Know-
      ledge and Experience in Elementary Education"; and, finally, an excerpt from
      I. Illich's *Deschooling Society*.

1279 K. E. BOULDING, "The Schooling Industry as a Possibly Pathological Section of
      the American Economy", *RER*, Winter, 1972, pp. 129-43.

      A sparkling, provocative essay in a style we have come to expect from the
      author.

1974

1280 A. BRETON, "Student Unrest and the Yield on Human Capital", *CJE*, August, 1974,
      pp. 434-48.

Another attempt to exploit the theory of human capital to account for student unrest, in this case, the cyclical and seasonal character of student protest movement. The thesis is that excess supply of higher education generates student unrest as a mechanism for reducing public expenditure on higher education, lest excess supply reduce the returns on human capital that students have come to expect.

8. THE ECONOMICS OF HEALTH

The economics of human resources consists, of course, of much more than the economics of education: apart from the economics of migration, the principal complement is health economics. The following section is highly selective and merely designed to suggest some of the parallels in economic analyses of education and health. For a general review of the field, see Mushkin[1283] and Klarman[1290,1297]. Mushkin[1283,1284] and Weisbrod[1281,1284,1291] measure human capital formation in health in the United States. Weisbrod[1281], Mushkin[1283], Klarman[1290,1297], Jewkes and Jewkes[1285], Wiseman[1286], and Axelrod[1289] discuss the application of cost-benefit analysis to health expenditures. Arrow[1287] and Lees[1282,1294] raise the fundamental issues of externalities and Pareto-optimality. Fein[1295], Peacock and Shannon[1296], and Feldstein[1298] write on the doctor shortage. Cooper and Culyer[1302] and Culyer[1303,1307] discuss the assessment of the National Health Service.

1961

1281 B. A. WEISBROD, *Economics of Public Health. Measuring the Economic Impact of Diseases*. Philadelphia: Pennsylvania University Press, 1961. Pp. 127.

   A valuable little book addressed to the layman. It develops the argument that medical care is a "public good" and evaluates the social benefits of eliminating three specific diseases. Estimates are presented for illness-induced output losses and for treatment costs; the concept of human capital is employed to measure the value of human resources destroyed by each disease.

1282 D. S. LEES, *Health Through Choice. An Economic Study of the British Health Service*. London: Institute for Economic Affairs, 1961. Pp. 62.

   This attack on the collective provision and public finance of medical care in Great Britain suggests analogies to the state provision and finance of education, some of which the author himself explores. See also *Monopoly or Choice in Health Services: A Symposium of Contrasting Approaches* (London: Institute for Economic Affairs, 1964. Pp. 56.)

1962

1283 S. J. MUSHKIN, "Health as an Investment", *JPE*, Suppl., October, 1962, pp. 129-57, partly reprinted in *KIK*, pp. 380-92.

   A comprehensive but somewhat badly organised survey of recent American work in the field of the economics of health.

1963

1284 S. J. MUSHKIN, B. A. WEISBROD, "Investment in Health: Lifetime Health Expendi ture on the 1960 Work Force", *KYK*, XVI, 4, 1963, pp. 583-99, reprinted in *WYK I*, pp. 296-308.

Measures the stock of health capital in the US labour force by treating health expenditures made for or by members of the labour force throughout their lifetime as investment in human beings: the figure for 1960 is $204 b., which is 38 per cent of the estimated $535 b., of educational capital in the 1957 labour force.

1285 J. and S. JEWKES, *Value for Money in Medicine*. Oxford: Basil Blackwell, 1963. Pp. 61.

The pamphlet casts doubt on the proposition that increased expenditures on British health services would be a sound economic investment from a social point of view.

1286 J. WISEMAN, "Cost-Benefit Analysis and Health Service Policy", *SJPE*, 1963, reprinted in *Public Expenditure. Appraisal and Control*, eds. A. T. Peacock, D. J. Robertson. Edinburgh: Oliver & Boyd, 1963, pp. 128-45, and *KIK*, pp. 433-52.

This article briefly describes available studies of investment in health and goes on to raise some serious doubts about the policy implications that are usually drawn from this type of cost-benefit analysis. With minor adjust- ment, these doubts are equally relevant for the rate-of-return approach to the economic value of education.

1287 K. J. ARROW, "Uncertainty and the Welfare Economics of Medical Care", *AER*, December, 1963, pp. 941-70.

An important contribution which argues that the special characteristics of the medical-care market can be explained as responses to the nonmarketability of information about risks.

1964

1288 A. JUDEK, *Medical Manpower in Canada*. Ottawa: Queen's Printer for the Royal Commission on Health Services, 1964. Pp. 413.

A well-informed study of the socio-economic characteristics of Canadian physicians (despite its title, the book deals only with physicians). The author forecasts Canada's requirements for doctors on the basis of a constant ratio of physicians to population. Nevertheless, the book contains an excel- lent, succint discussion of the forces that have historically produced a rise in the productivity of physicians.

1965

1289   S. J. AXELROD, ed., *The Economics of Health and Medical Care*. Ann Arbor,
       Mich.: University of Michigan, 1965. Pp. 321.

       An excellent collection of articles about health problems in the United
       States and the developing countries.

1290   H. E. KLARMAN, *The Economics of Health*. New York: Columbia University Press,
       1965. Pp. 200. Excerpts reprinted in *KIK*, pp. 420-32.

       Undoubtedly the best introduction to the field of health economics. Cer-
       tain sections of the book, such as "Distinctive Economic Characteristics",
       "The Case for Intervention", "Costs and Benefits of Health Programs", "What
       Can We Afford to Spend", and the entire chapter on "Supply of Personnel",
       pp. 10-20, 47-56, 74-102, 162-77, are directly related to issues in the
       economics of education. The book includes an unusually comprehensive biblio-
       graphy. (See 1311). See also the author's "Present Status of Cost-Benefit
       Analysis in the Health Field", *AJPH*, November, 1967, pp. 287-95, reprinted
       in *WYK I*, pp. 148-53.

1966

1291   B. A. WEISBROD, "Investing in Human Capital", *JHR*, Summer , 1966, pp. 5-22,
       reprinted in *URB*, pp. 71-88.

       A broad survey of American findings on investment in health and education
       with particular attention to some of the author's own work on the external
       benefits of education.

1292   R. J. LAMPMAN, "Towards an Economics of Health, Education and Welfare",
       ibid., pp. 45-54.

       Reviewing Schultz (104) and Klarman (1290), the author sketches a framework
       to integrate work on health, education, and welfare.

1293   The Office of Health Economics, *Medical Manpower*. London: OHE, 1966.
       Pp. 32.

       A pamphlet that reviews the present structure of medical personnel in
       Great Britain and concludes with some cogent comments on the concept of a
       shortage of medical manpower.

1967

1294   D. LEES, "Efficiency in Government Spending Social Services: Health", *PF*,
       1-2, 1967, pp. 176-89.

       A vigorous defence of the author's previous arguments for re-establishing
       a medical care market in Britain, in the course of which he reviews the exter-
       nal benefits issue once again.

1295   R. FEIN, *The Doctor Shortage. An Economic Diagnosis.*   Washington, D.C.:
       The Brookings Institution, 1967. Pp. 199.

       This model study offers, perhaps for the first time, a forecast of the
       likely "demand" rather than "need" for doctors in the USA in 1980, together
       with a forecast of the likely supply, after making adequate allowances for
       possible sources of increased productivity. Startlingly different conclusions
       are produced from those usually encountered in this literature (see, for
       example, pp. 134-40).

1968

1296   A. T. PEACOCK, J. R. SHANNON, "The New Doctors' Dilemma", *LBR*, January, 1968,
       pp. 26-38.

       A criticism of the recent projections of the future of the British National
       Health Services by the National Institute for Economic and Social Research
       (D. Paige, K. Jones, *Health and Welfare Services in Britain in 1975.* London:
       NIESR, 1966), particularly of the projected "shortage" of 8800 doctors by
       1980.

1969

1297   H. E. KLARMAN, "Economic Aspects of Projecting Requirements for Health Man-
       power", *JHR*, Summer, 1969, pp. 360-76.

       A superb survey of the literature on manpower forecasting in the field of
       health services largely with reference to the USA and Canada.

1970

1298   M. S. FELDSTEIN, "The Rising Price of Physicians' Services", *RES*, May,
       1970, pp. 121-33.

       This paper develops and tests a dynamic model of the pricing of doctors'
       services in the USA and shows that American doctors have discretionary con-
       trol over both price and quantity, which they have exercised to maintain a
       permanent state of excess demand.

1299   C. W. BAIRD, "A Proposal for Financing the Purchase of Health Services",
       JHR, Winter, 1970, pp. 89-105; see also "Comment" by J. H. Weiss and "Reply",
       ibid., Winter, 1971, pp. 123-29.

       After reviewing the arguments for externalities in health care and conclud-
       ing that "health care is different", the author outlines his proposal to make
       medical expenses in the USA deductible, not from gross income as they now are,
       but from net income, thus sharing the cost among all taxpayers.

1971

1300 P. WING, M. S. BLUMBERG, "Operating Expenditures and Sponsored Research at
      US Medical Schools: An Empirical Study of Cost Patterns", *ibid*., Winter,
      1971, pp. 75-102.

    This paper estimates programme costs for four-year US medical schools and
shows that sponsored research induces additional nonsponsored expenditures.
Some evidence for a U-shaped average cost curve is produced.

1301 C. T. STEWART, Jr., "Allocation of Resources to Health", *ibid*., pp. 103-22;
      see "Comment" by E. Meeker, *ibid*., Spring, 1973, pp. 257-59.

    An important article which begins by developing a fourfold classification
of resources devoted to health, then tests the effects of certain treatment
variables on life expectancy for all nations in the Western Hemisphere, and
concludes with certain broad comments on the misallocation of medical
resources in the USA and in the developing countries.

1302 British Medical Association, *Health Services Financing*. London: British
      Medical Association, 1971. Pp. 603.

    This outstanding study contains a recommendation for a new system of financ-
ing health services in Britain. It includes a series of valuable country
studies on health finance, of which the most useful from our standpoint are:
(1) M. H. Cooper, A. J. Culyer, "An Economic Assessment of Some Aspects of
the Organisation of the National Health Service", pp. 187-250; (2) J. Wiseman,
A. T. Peacock, "Alternative Sources of Finance of Medical Care: The Public
Sector", pp. 251-72; (3) A. Seldon, "Private Expenditure as a Source of
Finance for Medical Care in Britain", pp. 273-308; and (4) J. Buchanan,
C. M. Lindsay, "The Organisation and Financing of Medical Care in the United
States", pp. 535-85.

1303 A. J. CULYER, "The Nature of the Commodity 'Health Care' and Its Efficient
      Allocation", *OEP*, July, 1971, pp. 189-211.

    An excellent discussion of the special characteristics of medical care as
a commodity and its implications for policy. The author takes the view that
an itemization of the peculiar characteristics of medical care tells us
nothing about the most efficient method of producing or allocating it.

1972

1304 M. GROSSMAN, "On the Concept of Health Capital and the Demand for Health",
      JPE, March/April, 1972, pp. 223-55.

    Develops a model of the demand for the commodity "good health", which views
as a durable capital stock that produces an output of "healthy time" as a
function of age. The model predicts variations in health and medical care
among individuals in terms of variations in the demand and supply curves of
health capital.

1305   A. G. HOLTMANN, "Prices, Time and Technology in the Medical Care Market",
       JHR, Spring, 1972, pp. 179-90.

       Develops the comparative static implications of Becker's time allocation
       model as applied to the demand for medical care. The argument has perhaps
       some analogies in the economics of education.

1306   I. GARFINKEL, "Equal Access, Minimum Provision, and Efficiency in Financing
       Medical Care", *ibid.*, pp. 242-49.

       Carefully develops the different economic implications of equal access
       versus equal minimum provision as objectives for a medical care programme.

1307   A. J. CULYER, "On the Relative Efficiency of the National Health Service",
       KYK, XXV, 2, 1972, pp. 266-87.

       A largely theoretical paper, assessing the British National Health Service
       in the light of modern welfare economics. The paper concludes that all
       "health care delivery systems" fall short of the optimal conditions of wel-
       fare economics but nothing can be said *a priori* about how various systems
       perform relatively to one another.

1973

1308   R. J. RUFFIN, D. E. LEIGH, "Charity, Competition and the Pricing of Doctors'
       Services", *JHR*, Spring, 1973, pp. 212-22.

       This paper develops a charity-competition model of price discrimination in
       medicine, in oppostion to the Kessel model of discriminating monopoly.

1309   R. T. MICHAEL, "Education and the Derived Demand for Children", *JPE*, March/
       April, 1973, Supplement, *New Economic Approaches to Fertility*, pp. 128-64.

       Develops a model relating education of husband and wife on the use of birth
       control devices and tests the model on American data. See "Comment" by
       M. G. Reid, *ibid.*, pp. 165-67; also Y. Ben-Porath, "Economic Analysis of
       Fertility in Israel: Point and Counterpoint", *ibid.*, pp. 216-18.

B: DEVELOPING COUNTRIES
1. GENERAL SURVEYS

There is no single satisfactory introduction to the economics of education applied to underdeveloped countries, although Lê Thành Khôi in French[1321] comes as near as anyone to providing it. Possibly, conditions of different countries are too diverse and the issues too controversial to yield principles which would command general assent. A glance at the relevant chapters in some textbooks on economic development, such as Lewis[1310], Enke[1315], Kindleberger[1317], Bruton[1318], and particularly Meier[1695] and Higgins[1753] makes a good beginning. Vaizey[2,1314] touches on all the leading issues and other standard textbooks like Blaug[15] include chapters on the special problems of underdeveloped countries. Hodgkin[1311], Curle[1316], Coombs[1557], and Harbison[1324] provide quick popular guides. Hunter[1312,1320] is excellent on African education.

1955

1310   W. A. LEWIS, *The Theory of Economic Growth*. London: Allen & Unwin, 1955, ch. 4. pp. 183-200.

   A brief but cogent discussion of the role of education and training in economic development.

1957

1311   R. A. HODGKIN, *Education and Change. A Book Mainly For Those Who Work in Countries Where Education Is Part of a Process of Rapid Social Change*. London: Oxford University Press, 1957. Pp. 150.

   A book for laymen on the role of education in fostering social change, mixing the sociological with the anthropological approach.

1962

1312   G. HUNTER, *The New Societies of Tropical Africa. A Selective Study*. London: Oxford University Press, 1962, ch. 10, pp. 237-72.

   One of the best brief introductions to educational and manpower problems in tropical Africa.

1313 C. KERR, J. T. DUNLOP, F. H. HARBISON, C. A. MYERS, *Industrialism and Industrial Man. The Problems of Labor and Management in Economic Growth.* London: Heinemann, 1962. Pp. 317.

An attempt to present a systematic discussion of labour economics in a historical perspective. The authors touch repeatedly on education as a factor in the formation both of an industrial work force and a political élite dedicated to modernisation (see particularly pp. 36-39, 118-19, 286-87). For a précis of the argument by the authors, see *ILR*, March, 1955, pp. 223-36.

1963

1314 J. VAIZEY, "Some of the Main Issues in the Strategy of Educational Supply", *OECD-EGIE, III,* pp. 51-70, reprinted in an enlarged version in J. Vaizey, *The Control of Education.* London: Faber & Faber, 1963, pp. 35-89.

A general discussion of educational problems in underdeveloped countries, full of incisive comments on a large number of topics: manpower planning, rural education, private education, women's education, planning assistance, overseas students, and teachers' supply.

1315 S. ENKE, *Economics for Development.* Englewood Cliffs, N.J.: Prentice-Hall, 1963, chs. 21-22, pp. 385-415.

This is the first of the dozen or so recent American college textbooks on economic development to deal explicitly, and at some length, with educational investment in poor countries. The approach adopted by the author is that of raising questions instead of attempting to provide answers.

1316. A. CURLE, *Educational Strategy for Developing Societies. A Study of Educational and Social Factors in Relation to Economic Growth.* London: Tavistock Publications, 1963. Pp. 180.

A chatty, impressionistic book which touches on all the questions that arise in educational planning in underdeveloped countries. See also the author's *The Role of Education in Developing Societies* (Accra: Ghana University Press, 1961. Pp. 33), and "Some Aspects of Educational Planning in Underdeveloped Areas", *HER*, Summer, 1962. pp. 292-300.

1965

1317 C. P. KINDLEBERGER, *Economics Development.* New York: McGraw-Hill, 2nd ed., 1965, ch. 6, pp. 104-17.

A new chapter on investment in human capital in underdeveloped countries, too brief to be adequate but indicative of the new trend in thinking about economic development.

1318 H. J. BRUTON, *Principles of Development Economics.* Englewood Cliffs, N.J.: Prentice-Hall, 1965, ch. 12, pp. 205-41.

Ch. 12 on "The Training of Labor" presents a manpower-requirements approach
to educational planning and an analysis of on-the-job training inspired by
Becker. The discussion is not very systematic but many shrewd comments are
made, as it were, in the margins.

1966

1319 J. W. HANSON, C. S. BREMBECK, eds., *Education and the Development of Nations*.
New York: Holt, Rinehart & Winston, 1966. Pp. 529.

Reprints some 50 articles and papers, covering the entire spectrum of attitude to the role of education in social and economic development. Most of
the contributions are rather superficial. There are only 7 or 8 items on
the economics of education proper. Useful bibliographical references, particularly to minor pieces in educational journals, are to be found scattered
through the book: pp. 8-9, 42-43, 74-75, 98-99, 114-15, 158-59, 187-89,
223-24, 247-48, 273-74, 301-2, 347-49, 397-400, 444-46, 463-64, 496-98,
509-10.

1967

1320 G. HUNTER, *The Best of Both Worlds? A Challenge on Development Policies in
Africa*. London: Oxford University Press, 1967. Pp. 132.

Ch. 4, pp. 96-118, is devoted explicitly to education but earlier chapters
on employment and the rural economy are also relevant. On balance, this
highly readable book is a development of the author's earlier works on manpower in East Africa, particularly 1578.

1321 LÊ THÀNH KHÔI, *L'industrie de l'enseignement*. Paris: Editions de minuit,
1967. Pp. 419.

This is an attempt at a definitive textbook of the economics of education,
focused on planning problems in developing countries. In some respects it
falls short of its aims of expounding relevant economic theory, but it is
nevertheless an improvement on what is available in English between the
covers of one book: it covers a wide range of literature in both French and
English and is well documented with facts and figures.

1969

1322 H. J. NOAH, ed. and transl., *The Economics of Education in the USSR*.
New York: Frederick A. Praeger, 1969. Pp. 227.

A translation of 24 papers which were presented at a Soviet conference
on the economics of education in 1964. The Russian version, which appeared
in 1966, edited by V. A. Zhamin, was the first substantial publication of a
newly founded Scientific Research Laboratory for Problems of the Economics
of Education at the Moscow State Pedagogical Institute. The papers fall
roughly into three groups: (1) observations on the scope and significance
of the economics of education; (2) reports on work-in-progress attempting to
measure the contribution of education to the productivity of labour in

particular enterprises; and (3) summaries of completed research on special aspects of educational planning. The authors include such well-known names as V. A. Zhamin, I. I. Kaplan, and V. E. Komarov.

1971

1323 D. ADAMS, ed., *Education in National Development*. London: Routledge & Kegan Paul, 1971. Pp. 234.

After an interesting introduction, we get papers by P. Foster, J. Vaizey, D. Rogers, R. A. Cox, E. H. Reimer, M. Zymelman, R. M. Bjork, R. G. Myers, L. G. Thomas and H. Correa. Two papers stand out in this collection: R. M. Bjork, "Population, Education and Modernization", pp. 118-45, a superb review of the evidence on the relationship between education and fertility control, concluding that developing countries cannot expect to significantly reduce birth rates by educational expansion; and R. G. Myers, "Emigration, Education and Development", pp. 146-78, which is particularly strong on the problem of measuring loss of or gain from brain drain.

1973

1324 F. H. HARBISON, *Human Resources and the Wealth of Nations*. New York: Oxford University Press, 1973. Pp. 173.

A popular book which goes beyond Harbison and Myers (see 1352) in taking account of the ILO World Employemnt Programme. Includes a selected bibliography which, unfortunately, appears to be years out of date.

1974

1325 M. J. BOWMAN, "Perspectives on Education and Development", *INDR*, September, 1974, pp. 425-34, reprinted in *WYK I*, pp. 3-7.

A bird's-eye guide to the literature.

2. THE ECONOMIC CONTRIBUTION OF EDUCATION

(a) *Historical Comparative Material*

The historical-comparative method offers rich possibilities in illuminating the relationship between education and economic growth, but so far it has hardly begun to be applied to this range of problems. Perhaps the most interesting result to date is the finding of Anderson[1335] about the 40 per cent bottleneck: apparently all the now advanced countries achieved 40 per cent literacy rates before their Rostowian "take-offs". See also Peaslee[1359] for similar findings about primary education.

Webb[1327], Altick[1327], and Kahan[1335] provide some of the raw material for Anderson's conclusion. West[1343,1344,1345] provides an iconoclastic view of education in the British industrial revolution. Saville[1330], Jefferson[1333], and Musgrave[1339] contend that the key to Britain's industrial decline is to be found in the neglect of technical education. Bowman[1331] argues the crucial significance of land-grant colleges in America's industrial growth. The Ministry of Education, Japan[1332,1336]; Passin[1334], and Emi[1340] discuss the important case of Japan. Kerr and others[1313] represent an ambitious attempt to describe something like a typical pattern for the historical emergence of a modern labour force.

1928

1326   A. MAYHEW, *The Education of India. A Study of British Educational Policy in India, 1835-1920.* London: Faber & Guryer, 2nd ed., 1928. Pp. 306.

    A classic of its kind and full of material on a much-neglected topic; the lasting economic contribution, or lack of contribution, of the education provided by the colonial powers to their colonies.

1950

1327   R. K. WEBB, "Working Class Readers in Early Victorian England", *ENHR*, IV, 1, 1950, pp. 333-51.

    This article collects a wealth of source material on literacy in Great Britain in the days of the Industrial Revolution. This material is incorporated in the author's full-length study: *The British Working Class Readers, 1790-1848: Literacy and Social Tension* (New York: Oxford University Press, 1955). For further evidence of education and literacy in Britain in the first half of the nineteenth century see R. D. Altick, *The English Common*

Reader. A Social History of the Mass Reading Public 1800-1900 (Chicago, Ill.:
Chicago University Press, 1957), particularly chs. 7-8, pp. 141-88.

1959

1328 F. MUSGROVE, "Middle-Class Education and Employment in the Nineteenth
Century", *EHR*, August, 1959, pp. 99-112.

Drawing on the evidence of novelists, social commentators, and the findings
of the School Inquiry (Taunton) Commission of 1868, the author tries to show
that the rapid growth of middle-class education in the second quarter of the
century was not matched by the expansion of middle-class employment. H. J.
Perkin denied Musgrove's entire argument in "A Critical Note", *ibid.*, XIV,
1, 1961, pp. 122-30, which drew "A Rejoinder" from Musgrove, *ibid.*, XIV, 2,
1961, pp. 320-29. The material utilised by Musgrove also appears in a
different context in the author's study of *The Migratory Elite* (London:
Heinemann, 1963).

1960

1329 W. R. BRICKMAN, "A Historical Introduction to Comparative Education", *CER*,
February, 1960, pp. 6-13.

A sketch of the literature and the statistical information available for a
comparative study of educational systems in the nineteenth century, suggesting the possibility of a historial approach to the economic value of education.

1961

1330 J. SAVILLE, "Some Retarding Factors in the British Economy Before 1914",
YBESR, May, 1961, pp. 51-59.

Considers attitudes to education, and particularly technical education, as
one of the causes of the climacteric which occurred in the 1870's.

1962

1331 M. J. BOWMAN, "The Land-Grant Colleges and Universities in Human-Resource
Development", *JEH*, 1962, pp. 523-46, reprinted in *UNESCO-REED*, pp. 634-50.

An analysis of the contribution made by land-grant colleges, with their
heavy bias towards vocational education, to American economic growth in the
nineteenth century.

1963

1332 Ministry of Education, Japan, *Japan's Growth and Education. Educational
Development in Relation to Socio-Economic Growth. The 1962 White Paper on
Education.* Tokyo: Ministry of Education, 1963. Pp. 243.

Estimates the stock of educational capital since 1905, measures the spread of education in Japan, reviews historical data on educational expenditures, assesses the average level of education of the labour force, and compares Japan's achievements with those of other countries. All in all, a remarkable volume and without doubt the authoritative work on Japanese education. (See also 1336.)

1964

1333 C. JEFFERSON, "Worker Education in England and France, 1800-1914", *CSSH*, April, 1964, pp. 345-66.

After summarising J. F. C. Harrison's recently published book *Learning and Living, 1790-1960, A Study in the History of the English Adult Education Movement* (1961), the author traces the history of the same movement in France, and concludes by contrasting prevailing attitudes to worker education in the two countries.

1965

1334 H. PASSIN, *Society and Education in Japan*. New York: Teachers College, Columbia University, 1965. Pp. 347.

A development of his earlier essay (1335), this book provides valuable background reading to more economically oriented surveys of the history of Japanese education, such as 1332. Half of the book consists of original documents.

1966

1335 C. A. ANDERSON, M. J. BOWMAN, eds., *Education and Economic Development*. London: Frank Cass, 1966. Pp. 436.

This volume consists of papers presented at a conference in 1963 under the auspices of the Comparative Education Center of the University of Chicago. A few of these are reprinted in *UNESCO-REED* and have been mentioned above. The complete table of contents is as follows: A Kahan, "Russian Scholars and Statesmen on Education as an Investment"; A. Harberger, "Investment in Man versus Investment in Machines: The Case of India"; H. Leibenstein, "Shortages and Surpluses in Education in Underdeveloped Countries: A Theoretical Foray"; W. Lee Hansen, "Human Capital Requirements for Educational Expansion: Teacher Shortages and Teacher Supply"; M. J. Bowman, "From Gilds to Infant Training Industries", reprinted in *Sociology, History and Education*, ed. P. W. Musgrave, London: Methuen, 1970, pp. 158-61; R. J. Storr, "The Growth of American Education"; P. J. Foster, "The Vocational School Fallacy in Development Planning", reprinted in *P-EED*, 1, pp. 396-423; R. I. Crane, "Technical Education and Economic Development in India Before World War I"; C. R. Wharton, "Education and Agricultural Growth: The Role of Education in Early Stage Agriculture"; F. H. Harbison, "The Prime Movers in Innovation"; T. Hägerstrand, "Quantitative Techniques for Analysis of the Spread of Information and Technology"; S. Rottenberg, "The International Exchange of Knowledge"; A. Kahan, "The 'Hereditary Workers' Hypothesis and the Development of a Factory Labor Force in 18th and 19th Century Russia" and "Determinants of the Incidence of Literacy in Rural 19th Century Russia", reprinted in *Sociology, History and Education,* ed. P. W. Musgrave, London: Methuen, 1970, pp. 96-100; R. Blitz, "Some Observations Concerning the Chilean Educational System and its Relation to Economic Growth"; C. A. Anderson, "Patterns and Variability in the Distribution and Diffusion of Schooling" and "The Educational Preconditions of Development: Notes from History"; A. Kahan, "Social Structure, Public Policy, and the Development of Education and the Economy in Czarist Russia"; W. H. G. Armytage, "The Interrelation Between Economic Growth and Developments in Education in England 1588-1805"; H. Passin, "Portents of Modernity and the Meiji Emergence"; and R. Easterlin, "Some Notes Concerning the Evidence of History".

1336 Japanese National Commission for UNESCO, *The Role of Education in the Social and Economic Development of Japan.* Tokyo: Ministry of Education, 1966. Pp. 429.

A historical survey of the development of education and its contribution to industrialisation and economic growth in Japan since 1868. Reproduces and expands material from 1332.

1337 A. FISHLOW, "Levels of Nineteenth-Century American Investment in Education", *JEH*, December, 1966, pp. 418-36.

Estimates the total resource costs of American private and public education in the last half of the nineteenth century and compares these magnitudes to contemporary European expenditures and to present-day educational efforts. An important article full of penetrating observations.

1967

1338 M. SANDERSON, "Education and the Factory in Industrial Lancashire, 1780-1840", *EHR*, August, 1967, pp. 266-79.

A fascinating account of the rise and fall of privately provided factory schools in the heyday of the industrial revolution.

1339 P. W. MUSGRAVE, *Technical Change, The Labour Force and Education. A Study of the British and German Iron and Steel Industries. ·1860-1964.* Oxford: Pergamon Press, 1967. Pp. 286.

The main aim of this study is to examine the ways in which British and German education responded in the past to the "needs" of a particular industry. The meaning of "need" is discussed in the first chapter, after which the book settles down to straight-forward economic history.

1340 K. EMI, "Economic Development and Educational Investment in the Meiji Era", *UNESCO-REED,* pp. 94-106.

An interesting article which demonstrates the strategic role of foreign teachers and experts in Japanese education in the latter half of the nineteenth century.

1968

1341 R. S. SCHOFIELD, "The Measurement of Literacy in Pre-Industrial England, Literacy in Traditional Societies", ed. J. Goody. Cambridge: Cambridge University Press, 1968, pp. 311-325.

  This paper discusses the problem of measuring literacy in the preindustrial era and should be read as a gloss on the work of Webb and Altick on the nineteenth century (see 1327).

1969

1342 M. SAUNDERSON, "The Universities and Industry in England, 1919-1939", *YBESR*, May, 1969, pp. 39-65.

  An interesting historical article on the links between industry and the universities in the inter-war period. Sect. IV (pp. 49-57) reports on the problem of graduate unemployment in the 1930's and on the appearance of man-power shortages and surpluses in different fields.

1970

1343 E. G. WEST, "Resource Allocation and Growth in Early Nineteenth-Century British Education", *EHR*, XXIII, 1, 1970, pp. 68-95.

  Another effort by the author to show that there was ample provision of education long before the British state assumed a monopoly of it. The article contains the surprising finding that the percentage of national income devoted to primary and lower secondary education in the United Kingdom was about the same in 1833 as in 1933.

1971

1344 J. S. HURT, "Professor West on Early Nineteenth-Century Education", *EHR*, November, 1971, pp. 624-32; E. G. West, "The Interpretation of Early Nineteenth-Century Education Statistics", *ibid.*, pp. 633-42.

  The author denies West's finding that private education in England virtually exploded in the first quarter of the nineteenth century. In his reply, West restates his case and amplifies it in certain respects.

1975

1345 E. G. WEST, *Education and the Industrial Revolution*. London: B. T. Batsford, 1975. Pp. 275.

  This book incorporates the author's earlier papers (49, 50, 1344) and carries the iconoclastic story down to 1890 or thereabouts.

(b) INTERNATIONAL COMPARISONS

The international-comparisons approach is one of the best developed techniques for assessing the economic contribution of education, held up until recently, however, by paucity and sheer lack of data. The earlier section under the same title in Part A covered some of the ground in the form of simple correlations between educational expenditures and GNP per head, across countries, and within countries. The necessity to pay strict attention to the lags involved in the relationship between education and economic growth is exemplified by the findings of Bowman and Anderson[1348]. Failure to take account of these lags spoils much of the results of Harbison and Myers[1352], results which are subject to other criticisms as well: see Bowman[1352], Sen[1357], and Williams[1782]. Far more complicated interconnections between education and growth are explored by Curle[1349], McClelland[1358], and Bennett[1360].

The UN[1346], Galenson and Pyatt[1351], and Baster and Subramanian[1354] employ multivariate analysis with the aid of a wide array of social and economic indicators, of which educational provision is only one factor. Layard and Saigal[1840], followed by Horowitz and others[1356,1362], and Jallade and Emmerij[1369,1373] use cross-section country data to analyse the effect of the educational and occupational structure of the labour force on income per head, in an effort to develop tools to improve manpower forecasting in poor countries.

Banks and Textor[1347], Russett and others[1353], and Harbison and others[1370] illustrate the kind of raw data that is available for international comparisons.

1961

1346   UN, *Report on the World Social Situation, with Special Reference to the Problem of Balanced Social and Economic Development*.   New York: UN, 1961. Pp. 98.

   This pioneering study applies rank-correlation techniques to analyse the relationship between economic growth and such factors as medical care, nutrition, housing, education, wages, and social security in 74 countries around the world. The work contains an excellent discussion of the inherent limitations of this sort of approach to the sources of economic growth.

1963

1347   A. S. BANKS, R. B. TEXTOR, *A Cross-Polity Survey*.   Cambridge, Mass.:   The MIT Press, 1963.   Pp. 118, 199.

   This book rates 115 separate political entities in 57 different social, economic, and political characteristics, some quantitative and some qualitative. The bulk of the book is taken up by tables showing the degree of association between variables taken two at a time. The findings are complex and difficult to assimilate.

1348   M. J. BOWMAN, C. A. ANDERSON, "Concerning the Role of Education in Development", *Old Societies and New States. The Quest for Modernity in Asia and Africa*, ed. C. Geertz.   Glencoe, Ill.:   Free Press, 1963, pp. 247-80, reprinted in *UNESCO-REED*, pp. 113-31.

Perhaps the best effort to date to see what can be learned from correlations between income and education around the world. The results are briefly reviewed in 826 but they are only fully developed here.

1349 A. CURLE, *"Education, Politics and Development"*, CER, February, 1964, pp. 226-45.

An interesting attempt to test some generally held notions about various relationships between a country's level of economic, political, and educational development by means of quantitative indicators.

1350 W. A. LEWIS, "Secondary Education and Economic Structure", *SES*, June, 1964, pp. 219-33.

This paper attempts to derive a linear relationship between the percentage of males aged 25 and over who left school at 15 or later and the ratio of persons engaged in all non-agricultural industries to the stock of persons aged 15 and over, using data for 27 countries in recent decades. On the basis of this relationship, the author analyses the various enrolment rates that correspond to different levels of economic structure. In the closing section of the paper, he contrasts the situation in Jamaica in 1960 with the situation in England and Wales in 1950.

1351 W. GALENSON, G. PYATT, *The Quality of Labour and Economic Development in Certain Countries. A Preliminary Study.* Geneva: ILO, 1964. Pp. 116.

This study of the quality of the labour force (calorie intake, education, health, and social security) as a factor in the promotion of economic growth develops a number of regression equations from a simple model of the growth process and derives some tentative conclusions about the weights of the elements determining labour force quality from least square estimates of these equations for 52 countries. There is an interesting chapter on available data for this kind of international comparison, pp. 52-69, and a final chapter on "Possible Extensions of the Study", pp. 79-85.

1352 F. H. HARBISON, C. A. MYERS, *Education, Manpower and Economic Growth. Strategies of Human Resource Development.* New York: McGraw-Hill, 1964. Pp. 229. Partly reprinted in *P-EED*, 2, pp. 13-60.

The authors develop a composite index for ranking 75 countries into four levels of human resource development, in the light of which they analyse appropriate policies and strategies of human resource development, stressing the role of informal as well as formal education. The basic chapter on "Quantitative Indicators of Human Resource Development", pp. 23-49, is reprinted and discussed in *IEA-EE*. Chs. 4-6, pp. 49-131, deal with the developing countries. Ch. 7, pp. 137-71, deals with the problems of developed countries. The discussion is drawn together in ch. 8, pp. 173-89. Ch. 9 on "Establishing Human Resource Targets", pp. 189-209, is full of sensible comments on manpower planning. The book closes with a chapter on the "Integration of Human Resource and General Development Planning", pp. 209-25. See the authors' brief summary of the book's conclusions: "Education and Employment in the Newly Developing Economies", *CER*, June, 1965, pp. 5-11. See the reviews by M. J. Bowman, *JPE*, October, 1966, pp. 315-17, reprinted *P-EED*, 2, pp. 61-66, and K. M. Deitch, *PDK*, January, 1965, pp. 242-44. (See also 1370.)

1353 B. M. RUSSETT, H. R. ALKER, Jr., K. W. DEUTSCH, H. D. LASWELL, *World Hand-book of Political and Social Indicators*. New Haven, Conn.: Yale University Press, 1964. Pp. 373.

This basic reference work provides quantitative data for 133 countries of 75 indicators of social, economic, and political development in recent years, including a dozen or so indicators of the development of human resources. In the last section of the book, trends and patterns in the data are analysed from several points of view.

1965

1354 N. BASTER, M. SUBRAMANIAN, *Aspects of Social and Economic Growth*. Report No. 1. Geneva: UN Research Institute for Social Development, 1965. Pp. 47.

This preliminary study of patterns of social and economic development in both developed and underdeveloped countries carries on the work begun in the 1961 UN Report (1346). It calculates rank correlation coefficients between various indicators of economic growth and selected social indicators from the fields of education and health for 18 countries in the years of 1950 to 1960. The authors stress the tentative character of their conclusions, pp. vii–viii, 3, 44–47.

1355 Ministry of Education, Japan, *Educational Standards in Japan 1964. The 1964 White Paper on Education*. Tokyo: Ministry of Education, 1965. Pp. 222.

This is an up-to-date version of a previous publication with the same title for the year 1959. Its purpose is to compare the quantity and quality of educational provision in Japan in 1964 with that of the USA, the UK, West Germany, France, and the USSR in the same year. The volume also contains a number of intra-Japanese comparisons between prefectures in 1960, relating education to prefectural income, sectoral distribution of the labour force, and the like, as well as the results of national surveys of scholastic achievement in elementary and lower secondary schools.

1966

1356 M. A. HOROWITZ, M. ZYMELMAN, I. L. HERRNSTADT, *Manpower Requirements for Planning. An International Comparison*. Boston, Mass.: Department of Economics, Northeastern University, 1966, I, II. Pp. 225, 165.

Data from 19 countries on the occupational composition of the labour force, cross-classified by industry and by educational attainments, and ranked by output per head. Linear regression analysis showed that the occupational structure of an industry is related to the productivity of labour in that industry, both between states in the United States and between countries around the world. Vol. 1, ch. 3, pp. 10–19, contains a useful discussion of the shortcomings of occupational censuses, and Vol. 1, ch. 5, pp. 39–47, presents a step-by-step description of the use of the data for purposes of projecting manpower requirements.

1357 A. K. SEN, "Economic Approaches to Education and Manpower Planning", *IDR*,

April, 1966, pp. 1-23, partly reprinted in *P-EED*, 2, pp. 67-75.

A rigorous critique of the Correa-Bos-Tinbergen model, Denison's growth model, and the Harbison-Myers composite index. Indeed, pp. 9-11 contain one of the most effective criticisms of the Harbison-Myers study (1352) yet published.

1358   D. C. McCLELLAND, "Does Education Accelerate Economic Growth?", *EDCC*, April, 1966, pp. 257-78.

An important article that relates secondary school enrolments and the stock of educated adults to measures of electricity consumption in different countries around the world. It also looks at the interaction between achievement-motivation, as measured by McClelland's *n*-achievement test, educational levels, and economic growth, showing that in the 1950's achievement motivation was negatively associated with rapid expansion of secondary education but positively associated with rapid expansion of higher education. In the final pages of the paper, the author calculates the average productivity of higher education, where the numerator of the productivity figure refers to GNP per head of 3-4 years later; this productivity is misleadingly called "a rate of return".

1967

1359   A. L. PEASLEE, "Primary School Enrolments and Economic Growth", *CER*, February, 1967, pp. 57-68.

A study of correlations between primary school enrolments and per capita income since 1850, concluding that the 34 richest countries today all achieved primary school enrolments of over 10 per cent before their "take-offs" and that no country has ever achieved significant economic growth within the last hundred years without first attaining the 10 per cent level.

1360   W. S. BENNETT, Jr., "Educational Change and Economic Development", *SE*, Spring, 1967, pp. 101-14.

Simple correlation analysis of unlagged relationships between educational levels and economic indicators for 69 countries, showing that economic development is only slightly related to general secondary education but closely related to vocational secondary education. A non-linear relationship between economic development and the ratio of vocational to general education is demonstrated, suggesting that vocational education increases up to a level of $500 GNP per head and then declines as per capita GNP increases.

1361   M. J. BOWMAN, "The 'Fit' Between Education and Work", *Cross-National Conference*, New York: Lake Mohank, 1967. Pp. 31, mimeographed.

An interesting review of work on international comparisons of the relationship between occupational structure and labour productivity, 1356 and 1369, and a discussion of the author's calculations of the rate of return on investment in education in Japan in 1961.

1362   M. ZYMELMAN, *The Relationship Between Productivity and the Formal Education of the Labor Force in Manufacturing Industries.* Camb., Mass.: Center for Studies in Education and Development, Harvard University, 1967. Pp. 131, mimeographed.

This carries further the work of 1356 in analysing the productivity of labour in three-digit occupations in the manufacturing sector of about a dozen countries. The study makes a valuable contribution to our understanding of the relationship between occupation and education.

1968

1363 A. O. KRUEGER, "Factor Endowments and *Per Capita* Income Differences Among Countries", *EJ*, September, 1968, pp. 641-58.

The paper shows that if all countries are subject to the same constant-return-scale aggregate production function, educational attainment, age structure, and urban-rural distribution account for more than half the difference in income levels between the United States and the less developed countries (see also 103).

1969

1364 W. ASHER, J. E. SHIVELY, "The Technique of Discriminant Analysis: A Reclassi-fication of Harbison and Myers' Seventy-Five Countries", *CER*, June, 1969, pp. 180-86.

An attempt to use multiple-discriminant analysis to group 75 countries into Harbison and Myer's four categories of national development (see 1356). The analysis showed that one factor, consisting of a high ratio of educational expenditure to national income, enrolment in primary and secondary schools and the age structure of the population basically distinguishes the groupings of countries.

1365 H. J. NOAH, M. A. ECKSTEIN, *Toward a Science of Comparative Education.* London: Collier-Macmillan, 1969. Pp. 222.

This plea for an empirically oriented science of comparative education contains an exercise in the testing of hypotheses about the relationship between education and economic growth. The reader is taken by stages through the formulation of the problem, the selection of appropriate indicators, the collection of relevant data, the statistical manipulation of the data, and the drawing of conclusions from the results (Pt. III, pp. 125-80).

1366 M. A. ECKSTEIN, H. J. NOAH, *Scientific Investigations into Comparative Educa-tion. An Anthology Illustrating the Strategy and Tactics of Comparative Education.* London: The Macmillan Co., 1969. Pp. 428.

This valuable collection of readings reprints many articles found elsewhere in this bibliography (Correa 942, Carnoy 1445, Paterson 441, Bennett 1360, McClelland 1358, Curle 1349) and many more besides, illustrating the efforts of economists, sociologists, psychologists and political scientists in the field of international comparisons.

1367 F. EDDING, D. BERSTECHER, *International Developments of Educational Expenditure 1950-1965.* UNESCO Statistical Reports and Studies. Paris: UNESCO, 1969. Pp. 125.

This is a study of trends in educational outlays of 35 UNESCO Member States, and follows earlier UNESCO publications on the same subject. Some cautious conclusions (pp. 57-8, 77) are drawn on the basis of the data. A succinct summary of the findings is given on pp. 79-80.

1368 E. E. HAGEN, O. HAWRYLYSHYN, "Analysis of World Income and Growth, 1955-1965", *EDCC*, October, 1969, pp. 1-96.

An ambitious comparison of growth rates in developed and underdeveloped countries over a 10-year period, which includes an attempt to measure the effect of formal education on the quality of labour. Education does not emerge as making a significant contribution to the explanation of variance in growth between countries but the authors candidly admit the inadequacies of their measures (pp. 69-73, 90-93).

1970

1369 J-P. JALLADE, C. CRONER, L. EMMERIJ, *Occupational and Educational Structures of the Labour Force and Levels of Economic Development—Possibilities and Limitations of an International Comparison Approach.* Paris: OECD, 1970. Pp. 321.

The most ambitious and sophisticated attempt so far to find systematic relationships across 53 countries between the occupational and educational composition of the labour force, on the one hand, and levels of economic development, on the other. The study includes an evaluation of previous work (ch. 2) and a conclusion (ch. 24) which marks the first notice of rate-of-return analysis in an OECD publication. The main results of the study are succinctly reviewed in ch. 23. The volume also includes four comments on the study: (1) M. J. Bowman, "Education and Manpower Planning Revisited", pp. 259-82, a brilliant critique of the intellectual framework of the man-power-forecasting approach; (2) M. Blaug, "Comments", pp. 283-86; (3) J. Maton, "The Elasticities of the OECD Study as Parameters of Log-Linear Models", pp. 287-308; and (4) J. Steindl, "Skilled Manpower and Growth", pp. 309-18 (see also 1373).

1370 F. H. HARBISON, J. MARUHNIC, J. R. RESNICK, *Quantitative Analysis of Modernization and Development.* Princeton, N.J.: Industrial Relations Section, Princeton University, 1970. Pp. 224.

This is a "do-it-yourself" book of comparative statistics for 112 countries, the data taking the form of economic, cultural, health and nutrition, human resource development (stocks, flows, and expenditures) and demographic indicators. The data are analysed in terms of simple correlation and regression coefficients, as well as by a new composite-ranking method (ch. 2). Ch. 6 recalculates the Harbison-Myers human resource index (1352) in the light of 1965 data.

1371 K. BIEDA, "The Pattern of Education and Economic Growth, *ER*, September, 1970, pp. 368-83.

This paper applies international comparison to *differences* in enrolments by subjects and *differences* in the growth rates of various countries, using a variety of lags between the two variables. The most striking finding is the consistently high product—moment correlation coefficient between the number of students in social sciences at the tertiary level and the rate of economic growth.

1372 V. N. KOTHARI, "Disparities in Relative Earnings Among Different Countries", *EJ*, September, 1970, pp. 605-616.

The "different countries" in the title are in fact the city of Bombay and the United States. Comparisons are made in terms of human-capital considerations.

1971

1373 J.-P. JALLADE, L. EMMERIJ, *Occupational and Educational Structures of the Labour Force and Levels of Economic Development. Further Analyses and Statistical Data*. Paris: OECD, 1971. Pp. 127.

This companion volume to 1369 adds little that is new to the story. Annex A on the problems of measuring occupation and education across countries, however, stands on its own as an interesting contribution.

1374 M. SELOWSKY, "Labor Input Substitution in the Study of Sources of Growth and Educational Planning", *Studies in Development Planning*, ed. H. B. Chenery Cambridge, Mass.: Harvard University Press, 1971, pp. 386-402.

This extends the author's earlier work (see 85) and calculates rates of return in Chile, Mexico and Colombia on various growth and substitutability assumptions.

1972

1375 G. PSACHAROPOULOS, "The Economic Returns to Higher Education in Twenty-Five Countries", *HE*, May, 1972, pp. 141-58.

Compares private and social rates of return to levels of education in 25 countries and contrasts them with rates of return to physical capital and with incomes per head.

1376 G. PSACHAROPOULOS, "The Profitability of Higher Education: A Review of the Experience in Britain and the United States", *Contemporary Problems in Higher Education. An Account of Research*, eds. H. J. Butcher, E. Rudd. London: McGraw Hill, 1972, pp. 361-71.

A competent review of published evidence for both countries.

1377 G. PSACHAROPOULOS, K. HINCHLIFFE, "Further Evidence on the Elasticity of Substitution Among Different Types of Educated Labor", *JPE*, July/August, 1972, pp. 786-92.

Re-examines Bowles' earlier results (see 81) in the light of a larger sample of countries, divided into poor and rich. Finds considerably lower elasticities than Bowles did.

1378 W. BECKERMAN, "Human Resources and Economic Development: Some Problems of Measurement", *ISSJ*, XXIV, 4, 1972, pp. 723-43.

After considering difficulties with international comparisons in this area, the author goes on to recommend rate-of-return studies in the field of human resource development.

1974

1379 S. PANITCHPAKDI, *Educational Growth in Developing Countries. An Empirical Analysis.* Rotterdam: Rotterdam University Press, 1974. Pp. 176.

The author estimates a model which explains the growth of education by such factors as population transition proportions between levels of education, per capita income, earnings of educated people, etcetera, and tests the model by "cross-section" regressions using data from different periods for single countries as the observations. Unfortunately, the exposition of the model as an example of "demand-and-supply analysis" is either obscure or misleading, and sometimes both. The final chapter complicates the model by introducing Adelman-Morris socio-political indicators.

(c) CASE STUDIES AND SPECIAL PROBLEMS

This section is frankly in the nature of a potpourri; it could hardly be anything else, given the amorphous state of the subject at present. As Lewis[1403], Benham[1387], and Kaser[1389] reveal, there is no consensus either among scholars or among planners about the role of education in economic development. A few writers have tried their hand at a theoretical treatment, such as Schultz[1401,1412], Svennilson[1405], Anderson[1406], Johnson[1410], Leibenstein[1335], and Bottomley[1433].

Because of her low level of development, African education poses particular difficulties. There is a rich literature on the role of education in promoting social and occupational mobility in English- and French-speaking Africa, of which examples are Richards[1380], Sofer[1381], McCulloch[1382], UNESCO[1389], Ardener and Warnington[1390], Schwab[1398], Foster[1335,1420], Clignet and Foster[1437], Callaway[1408], Berg[1418], Goldthorpe[1426], and Coleman[1429]. Blaug[1419], Lê Thành Khôi[1424], Foster[1691], and Wharton[1335] are concerned in more general terms with the provision of education designed to accelerate the transformation of African subsistence economies into fully fledged exchange economies.

Easterlin on Israel[1394], Jolly on Cuba[1414,1485], Havighurst on Brazil[1422,1431], Myers[1427] and Carnoy[1445,1446,1447] on Mexico, Friedlander on Puerto Rico[1430], Nairn on Thailand[1441], Nalla Gounden on India[1444], Knight on Uganda[1448,1457], Heijnen and Dubbeldam on Tanzania[1456,1469], Blaug, Layard and Woodhall on India[1459], Thias and Carnoy on Kenya[1461], Dougherty on Colombia[1478], Gannicott on Taiwan[1493] and Myrdal[1454] on almost the whole of Asia provide case studies on special problems. Foster and Sheffield[1507] is excellent on rural development.

1954

1380 A. I. RICHARDS, ed., *Economic Development and Tribal Change. A Study of
      Immigrant Labour in Buganda.* Cambridge: Heffer, 1954. Pp. 301.

         Five contributors survey labour migration in Uganda from every point of
      view. Some sample survey material on the educational standards of migrants
      is presented. This study bears out the notion of significant tribal differ-
      ences in occupations, schooling, and receptivity to cultural change.

1955

1381 C. and R. SOFER, *Jinja Transformed. A Social Survey of a Multi-Racial Town-
      ship.* East African Studies, No. 4. Kampala, Uganda; 1955, pp. 42-48.

         Presents the results of a stratified sample of the African population of
      Jinja, Uganda, including the distribution by educational standards; includes
      a correlation analysis of earnings and education.

1956

1382 M. McCULLOCH, *A Social Survey of the African Population of Livingstone.*
      Rhodes-Livingstone Papers, No. 26. Manchester: Manchester University Press,
      1956. Pp. 82.

         Presents the educational histories of a random sample of the population of
      Livingstone, Zambia, relating these to the distribution of occupations and
      to monthly earnings. Education and wage differences prove to be correlated
      with membership of particular tribes.

1383 UNESCO, *The Social Implications of Industrialization and Urbanization: Five
      Studies of Urban Populations of Recent Rural Origin in Cities of Southern
      Asia.* Calcutta: UNESCO, 1956. Pp. 268.

         Five studies of Bangkok, Bombay, Dacca, Delhi, and Dyakarta, the last two
      of which contain material on the educational standards of migrants as related
      to the causes of labour migration.

1384 K. A. BUSIA, "Education and Social Mobility in Economically Underdeveloped
      Countries", *Transactions of the Third World Congress of Sociology.* London:
      International Sociological Association, 1956, V, pp. 81-83.

         Reviews findings to date of the relationship between education and economic
      development in Africa.

1957

1385 W. A. LEWIS, "Consensus and Discussions on Economic Growth: Concluding
      Remarks to a Conference", *EDCC*, October, 1957, pp. 75-80.

         Touches briefly on education and concludes that no consensus emerged during the conference on the priority of education among social expenditures or on the priority of certain types of education as against others.

1958

386 B. BENEDICT, "Education Without Opportunity. Education, Economics, and Communalism in Mauritius", *HR*, November, 1958, pp. 315-31.

A social anthropologist considers the economic and political reasons for the recent educational explosion in this relatively isolated island.

1959

387 F. BENHAM, "Education and Economic Development in Underdeveloped Countries", *IA*, April, 1959, pp. 181-88.

A leading economist attacks the "illusion" of universal primary education in underdeveloped countries in the near future and denies that educational expenditures are very profitable investment for most underdeveloped countries in the world today.

388 C. SHOUP and others, *The Fiscal System of Venezuela. A Report*. Baltimore: John Hopkins Press, 1959, ch. 15, pp. 406-24.

Makes a rough estimate of the rate of return on investment in education, and calculates the cost of achieving universal primary education in 5 years.

1960

389 M. KASER, "Needs and Resources for Social Investment", *ISSJ*, XXII, 3, 1960, pp. 409-33.

Able report of the discussion of a conference on the direct and indirect returns of social investment, mostly health and education, with many references to the literature. No consensus emerged on the measurement of social outlays or on the implications of the results of such measurement.

390 S. and E. ARDENER, W. A. WARMINGTON, *Plantation and Village in the Cameroons*. London: Oxford University Press, 1960, pp. 64-67, 248-61.

An outstanding analysis of the economic and educational background of migratory labour on plantations in the Cameroons, employing two samples, one of which was randomly drawn. Ch. 8 supplies general material on the influence of education on the expenditure patterns of African workers.

391 V. THOMPSON, R. ADLOFF, *The Emerging States of French Equatorial Africa*. London: Oxford University Press, 1960, ch. 18, pp. 277-301.

A thorough review of educational developments in the republics of Chad, Central Africa, Gabon, and the Congo (Brazzaville), with a comprehensive bibliography.

1392 P. J. FOSTER, "Comparative Methodology and the Study of African Education",
      CER, October, 1960, pp. 110-17.

      Reviews and queries some popular generalisations about the role of African
      education in promoting social and economic development in Africa and pleads
      for more case-studies with a comparative bias.

1393 E. MARCUS, "Large-Scale Investment and Development—The Dilemma of the Gabon
      Republic", *EDCC*, October, 1960, pp. 64-74.

      The author considers the complementary between investment in physical
      capital and human capital, particularly on-the-job training, in the context
      of one of the most backward African countries.

1961

1394 R. A. EASTERLIN, "Israel's Development: Past Accomplishments and Future
      Problems", *QJE*, February, 1961, pp. 63-86.

      Attributes Israel's remarkable growth in recent years to the high quality
      of its labour force as measured by the level of educational attainment. "It
      is no exaggeration to say that in 1948 the educational level of the Jewish
      population in Israel was close to the highest in the world.

1395 R. KLINOV-MALUL, "Profitability of Investment in Education", *Fifth Report
      1959 and 1960*. The Falk Project for Economic Research in Israel. Jerusalem:
      FPERI, 1961, pp. 138-46.

      Preliminary results of a study based on a random sample of Israeli house-
      holds. The findings about the rate of return at various levels of education
      are particularly interesting, owing to the relatively low proportion of per-
      sons in Israel with primary education and the extremely high proportion with
      secondary and higher education. (See also 205.)

1396 Y. GRUNFELD, "The Measurement of Educational Capital in Israel", *Fifth
      Report 1959 and 1960*. The Falk Project for Economic Research in Israel.
      Jerusalem: FPERI, 1961, pp. 146-50.

      Preliminary results of a study which reveals a sharp fall in the per capita
      stock of educational capital in 1951 due to an increase in immigration from
      Asia and Africa. (See also 1421.)

1397 D. C. McCLELLAND, *The Achieving Society*. Princeton, N.J.: D. Van Nostrand
      Co., 1961, pp. 413-17.

      This bold and stimulating attempt to trace the sources of economic growth
      to what might be called the Protestant Ethic, as measured by the n-Achievement
      Test, does not hold out high hopes of stimulating n-Achievement by specific
      educational policies. For a summary of the book by the author, see B. F.
      Hoselitz, W. E. Moore, eds., *Industrialization and Society*. (Paris: UNESCO,
      1963), pp. 74-96.

1398 W. B. SCHWAB, "Social Stratification in Gwelo", *Social Change in Modern Africa*, ed. A. Southall. London: Oxford University Press, 1961, pp. 126-45.

An interesting study of the occupational aspirations of adults and school-children in sample survey taken in the fourth largest town in Rhodesia.

1962

1399 K. L. NEFF, *Education and the Development of Human Technology*. US Department of Health, Education and Welfare, Office of Education. Bulletin No. 20. Washington, D.C.: Government Printing Office, 1962. Pp. 34.

A brief discussion of the functional role of education in economic develop-ment, followed by terse comments on specific problem areas such as literacy, vocational training, teacher training, education of women, part-time and correspondence education, and team teaching.

1400 UNECA, *Economic Bulletin for Africa, II, 2, June, 1962*. Addis Ababa, Ethiopia: UNECA, 1962, chs. 5, 6, pp. 82-101.

A rapid but incisive discussion of what we know about the contribution of education and other social services to economic development.

1401 T. W. SCHULTZ, "Investment in Human Capital in Poor Countries", *Foreign Trade and Human Capital*, ed. P. D. Zook. Dallas: Southern Methodist University Press, 1962, pp. 3-15.

Argues that the importance of accumulating human capital explains many of the puzzles and paradoxes of the economies of underdeveloped countries.

1402 J. K. GALBRAITH, *Economic Development in Perspective*. Harvard University Press, 1962, ch. 4, pp. 46-59.

In a very brief chapter, Galbraith endorses the view that education is a form of investment—in terms far stronger than is warranted by the evidence—and concludes that much education in underdeveloped countries like India is wasteful.

1403 W. A. LEWIS, "Education and Economic Development", *SES*, June, 1961, pp. 113-27, and *ISSJ*, XIV, 4, 1962, pp. 685-700, and *OECD-EGIE, III*, pp. 35-49, reprinted in *UNESCO-REED*, pp. 135-45.

Reviews problems of education in Africa and expresses an algebraic measure of absorptive capacity with respect to secondary education. Concludes with cogent observations on realistic educational planning in Africa.

1404 M. J. BOWMAN, C. A. ANDERSON, "The Role of Education in Economic Development", *Development of the Emerging Countries. An Agenda for Research*. Washington, D.C.: Brookings Institution, 1962, pp. 153-81.

Presents preliminary results of an original research project (see 1348) and lists additional topics on which research is needed.

1963

1405 I. SVENNILSON, "The Concept of Economic Growth", *Proceedings of the Eleventh International Conference of Agricultural Economists. The Role of Agriculture in Economic Development*. London: Oxford University Press, 1963, pp. 18-29.

Tries to show how different parameters related to growth may be included in a collective decision-making model, using education as an example of such a parameter.

1406 C. A. ANDERSON, "The Impact of the Educational System on Technological Change and Modernization", *Industrialization and Society*, eds. B. F. Hoselitz W. E. Moore. Paris: UNESCO, 1963, pp. 259-78, reprinted in *UNESCO-REED*, pp. 901-14.

In this free-wheeling essay, the author outlines the major policy implications of the "sociological" view of the role of education in promoting growth in underdeveloped countries. See also W. E. Moore, "Industrialization and Social Change", *ibid.*, particularly, pp. 343-45.

1407 M. J. BOWMAN, W. W. HAYNES, *Resources and People in East Kentucky: Problems and Potentials of a Lagging Economy*. Baltimore: John Hopkins Press, 1963. Pp. 448.

An analysis of the problems of the East Kentucky region in the United States that lays great stress on the role of population, migration, and education; see especially chs. 11-13.

1408 A. CALLAWAY, "Unemployment Among African School Leavers", *JDS*, I, 3, 1963, pp. 351-71, reprinted in *Education and Nation-Building in Africa*, eds. L. G. Cowan *et al*. New York: Frederick Praeger, 1965, pp. 235-56.

An authoritative discussion of the recent emergence of the phenomenon of unemployed school leavers in West Africa.

1409 H. M. BURNS, *Education and the Development of Nations*. Center for Development Education. All-University School of Education. Syracuse, N.Y.: Syracuse University Press, 1963. Pp. 112.

This is a collection of non-technical papers which discuss the role of education in promoting social and economic progress in underdeveloped countries. Among them are: D. K. Adams, "On the Nature of Development Education" pp. 5-12; V. M. Barnett, Jr., "The Role of Education in Economic Development", pp. 13-28; and D. C. McClelland, "Changing Values for Progress", pp. 60-78.

1964

1410 H. G. JOHNSON, "Towards a Generalised Capital Accumulation Approach to Economic Development", *OECD-RF*, pp. 219-25, reprinted in *P-EED*, 1, pp. 34-44.

A clarifying Fisherian generalisation of the human-capital approach.

1411   R. CLIGNET, "Éducation et aspirations professionnelles", *TM*, janvier-mars, 1964, pp. 61-83.

   A discussion of the influence of education on professional aspirations in underdeveloped countries, based on some sample surveys taken in French West Africa. (See 1437.)

1412   T. W. SCHULTZ, *Transforming Traditional Agriculture*.   New Haven, Conn.: Yale University Press, 1964. Pp. 212.

   In this book, Schultz argues, among other things, that "investment in farm people" constitutes a neglected source of growth in low-income countries. See particularly ch. 12, pp. 175-207, which reproduces material previously published by the author.

1413   H. CORREA, "Quality of Education and Socio-Economic Development", *CER*, June, 1964, pp. 11-17.

   This unclassifiable article uses the grades obtained by students from 12 different Latin-American countries attending 4 international institutions in Santiago to measure the quality of education offered in the country of origin. The resulting ordinal index of educational quality is then correlated with various statistical indicators to demonstrate that the quality of education is more a result of determinants outside the educational system than of inputs in the educational system itself.

1414   R. JOLLY, "Education", *Cuba.   The Economic and Social Revolution*, ed. D. Seers. Durham, N.C.:   North Carolina University Press, 1964, pp. 161-283.

   An excellent appraisal of the economic implications of Cuba's recent efforts in both formal and informal education. See, particularly, the succinct analysis of the educational picture before Castro, pp. 161-74, the discussion of literacy campaigning under Castro, pp. 190-219, and the review of Cuban attempts at manpower planning, pp. 267-74. A fascinating appendix to the book, pp. 346-70, discusses the political content of Cuban education since 1959.

1415   G. K. BOON, *Economic Choice of Human and Physical Factors of Production. An Attempt to Measure the Micro-Economic and Macro-Economic Possibilities of Variation in Factor Proportions of Productions*. Amsterdam: North-Holland Publishing Co., 1964. Pp. 331.

   This book attempts to clarify the problem of choice of technique in underdeveloped countries; all the empirical data, however, is drawn from developed countries, in most cases from The Netherlands, and there is little systematic theoretical discussion of the problem. Chs. 3 and 11 refer specifically to the impact of labour training costs on the choice adopted. The author points out that as each technique requires a specific type of skill, comparisons between techniques must take into account the capital requirements for training in addition to physical capital requirements. He derives various empirical generalisations: capital-intensive industries tend to be education-intensive industries; the size of the firm is positively related to the use of highly educated manpower; capital-labour ratios are positively related to the ratio of human to physical capital; and so forth, pp. 92-98.

1416 W. L. TAYLOR, *Reflections on the Economic Role of Education in Underdeveloped Countries*. London: Oxford University Press, 1964. Pp. 31.

An inaugural lecture given in the University College of Rhodesia and Nyasaland in April, 1963, containing some tentative estimates of future enrolments in Central Africa.

1417 C. A. ANDERSON, "Economic Development and Post-Primary Education", *Post-Primary Education and Political and Economic Development,* eds. D. C. Piper, T. Cole. Durham, N.C.: Duke University Press, 1964, pp. 3-26.

Apart from this directly relevant essay, the volume includes a series of papers on secondary and higher education in Africa and Asia by American sociologists and political scientists.

1418 E. J. BERG, "Socialism and Economic Development in Tropical Africa", *QJE*, November, 1964, pp. 549-74.

This fascinating article throws doubt on the effectiveness of the socialist model in Africa, owing to the scarcity of managerial manpower, the inappropriateness of the socialist approach to the agricultural problems of subsistence economies, and the constraints of external market forces on internal economic policies. See, particularly, pp. 560-62.

1965

1419 M. BLAUG, *The Role of Education in Enlarging the Exchange Economy in Middle Africa: The Engish Speaking Countries*. Paris: UNESCO, 1965. Pp. 63, mimeographed.

The purpose of this study is to investigate the role of education in the transformation of an economy based on self-sufficient subsistence agriculture to an economy based on market transactions, with particular reference to the English-speaking countries of Africa south of the Sahara and north of the Republic of South Africa. It analyses the nature of the problem, reviews the existing evidence, particularly quantitative evidence, proposes future research to fill the gaps in current knowledge, and concludes with a few policy proposals based on what we now know about the interrelationship between education and economic development in an African context.

1420 P. J. FOSTER, *Education and Social Change in Ghana*. London: Routledge, 1965. Pp. 322.

A study of the impact of education on social and economic change in Ghana. The first half of the book is devoted to the history of Ghanaian education in the colonial period; the second half deals with the contemporary scene and includes the results of social surveys of secondary school pupils conducted by the author. The book is highly provocative and attacks a number of current myths about the relationship between educational and economic development. See the book review by S. G. Week, *HER*, Summer, 1966, pp. 369-74.

1421 Bank of Israel, "Investment in Education and Human Capital in Israel", *Bank of Israel Bulletin*, No. 23, March, 1965, pp. 3-27.

Presents estimates of the stock of education embodied in the Israeli labour force in 1961-63 and annual investments in education in Israel since 1948.

1422 R. J. HAVIGHURST, "Secondary Schooling and Socio-Economic Structure in Brazil", *SES*, March, 1965, pp. 106-18.

Reports on a number of surveys designed to reveal the economic and social impact of secondary schooling in Brazil. (See also 1431.)

1423 V. A. ZHAMIN, "Economics of Education", *SOV*, June, 1965, pp. 49-57.

The article describes research activities in the economics of education in the West, indicates some works forthcoming in the Soviet Union, and closes with an agenda for further research.

1424 LÊ THÀNH KHÔI, "Dimension historique de l'éducation", *TM*, avril-juin, 1965, pp. 335-57.

General comments on the treatment of education in the history of economic thought and on the role of education in the underdeveloped countries today.

1425 T. D. WILLIAMS, "Some Economic Implications of the Educational Explosion in Ghana", *The Education Explosion. World Year Book of Education 1965*, eds. G. Z. F. Bereday, J. A. Lauwerys. London: Evans Bros., 1965, pp. 479-95.

Contains, among other things, an interesting sceptical discussion of the tendency of Ghanaian education to produce unemployable school leavers.

1426 J. E. GOLDTHORPE, *An African Elite. Makerere College Students 1922-1960*. Nairobi: Oxford University Press, 1965. Pp. 109.

The work offers a short account of the history of Makerere College in the context of the development of education in East AFrica, followed by a detailed study of the origins of Makerere students in respect of tribe, parents' literacy, kinsmen's education, kinsmen's occupation, and other aspects of family backgrounds. The most interesting part of the book, however, deals with the career experiences of Makerere graduates, including their earnings in the 1950's.

1427 C. N. MYERS, *Education and National Development in Mexico*. Industrial Relations Sections, Department of Economics, Princeton University. Princeton, N.J.: Princeton University, 1965. Pp. 147.

This important contribution presents a regional analysis of the relationship between education and economic growth in Mexico since 1920. Among the author's more striking conclusions is that education appears to have increased rather than narrowed the regional disparities in Mexican economic growth. See also pp. 110-34, which traces some of the adaptive practices that have evolved, without benefit of planning or central direction, to bridge the most important manpower gaps in the Mexican economy.

1428 H. N. PANDIT, "Nature and Dimensions of Unemployed Educated Manpower in
      India, 1953 to 1964", *MJ*, October 1965-March 1966, pp. 119-76.

      An examination of the nature and dimensions of educated unemployment in
      India with the help of data collected by different agencies at different
      bench-mark dates.

1429 J. COLEMAN, ed., *Education and Political Development*. Princeton, N.J.:
      Princeton University Press, 1965. Pp. 620.

      This collection of essays on the role of education in promoting political
      and social change includes several which touch on the economic contribution
      of education in developing countries. For instance, F. X. Sutton, "Education
      and the Making of Modern Nations", pp. 51-74, examines the part played by
      education in the growth of African nationalism; M. Debeauvais provides a
      description of "Education in Former French Africa", pp. 75-91; H. Passin's
      chapter on Japan repeats much of the material in his book (1334). B. H.
      Hoselitz, in "Investment in Education and its Political Impact", and W. J.
      Platt, "Conflicts in Educational Planning", introduces the reader to some of
      the economic literature. J. Coleman, in his introduction to each section
      stresses the need for educational planners and economists to consider the
      political implications of their policies.

1430 S. L. FRIEDLANDER, *Labor Migration and Economic Growth: A Case-Study of
      Puerto Rico*. Cambridge, Mass.: MIT Press,1965. Pp. 181.

      This study of the effects of migration on the economy of Puerto Rico
      includes an interesting attempt to quantify improvements in the quality of
      the labour force, caused by both emigration of unskilled workers and invest-
      ment in education, and an attempt to measure the contribution of these
      improvements to economic growth since 1948. Using a Cobb-Douglas production-
      function, the author concludes that about 50 per cent of additional output
      can be attributed to the improved quality of the labour force.

1431 R. J. HAVIGHURST, J. R. MOREIRA, *Society and Education in Brazil*. Pittsburgh:
      University of Pittsburgh Press, 1965. Pp. 257.

      This is a study of the past and present role of education in Brazilian
      society with some attention to the economic value of education in the sense
      both of expected earnings from additional education and in future require-
      ments of qualified manpower.

1966

1432 A. PESHKIN, "Education in the Developing Nations: Dimensions of Change:,
      CER, February, 1966, pp. 53-66.

      A general discussion of the role of education in promoting social and
      economic development, with a review of recent research.

1433 A. BOTTOMLEY, "Optimum Levels of Investment in Education and Economic Develop-
      ment", *ZGS*, April, 1966, pp. 237-46, reprinted in *WYK-I*, pp. 458-67.

A brief theoretical note on the costs of and returns to education in developing countries. The references to the literature are somewhat dated.

1434 V. N. KOTHARI, "Factor Cost of Education in India", *IEJ*, April-June, 1966, pp. 631-47.

An estimate of the total resource cost of Indian education, including earnings foregone, for the years 1950-51, 1956-57 and 1959-60. (See also 1443.)

1435 D. B. KEESING, "Labor Skills and Comparative Advantage", *AER*, May, 1966, pp. 249-59.

An attempt to demonstrate that skill differences between countries constitute a persistent source of differences in comparative advantage and hence, of observed trade patterns. But see H. G. Johnson's comments, pp. 280-82.

1436 J. P. ARLES, "Manpower Mobilisation and Economic Growth: An Assessment of Moroccan and Tunisian Experience", *ILR*, July, 1966, pp. 1-22.

The author assesses the cost-benefit relationship of some North African schemes to utilise unemployed or underemployed manpower in special development projects.

1437 R. CLIGNET, P. J. FOSTER, *The Fortunate Few: A Study of Secondary Schools and Students in the Ivory Coast*. Chicago, Ill.: Northwestern University Press, 1966. Pp. 242.
An extension of Foster's work on Ghana (1420) to a French-speaking country. The book examines the pattern of recruitment into secondary schools, analyses students' job expectations, and examines the relation between the output of secondary schools and demand in the labour market. This book takes its place beside Foster's study of Ghana as a major contribution to our knowledge of the social and economic role of formal education in Tropical Africa.

1438 V. A. ZHAMIN, "The Economic Effects of Popular Education in the USSR", *IEA-EE*, pp. 324-34.

In this very enigmatic paper, Professor Zhamin of the Association of Soviet Economic Scientific Institutions discusses methods currently in use in the USSR to measure the economic value of education. Unfortunately, the example given, pp. 328-31, seems to make no sense: either some passages have been left out or the translation has distorted the meaning of the original.

1439 M. RASHID, "Absorption of the Educated", *ibid.*, pp. 398-421.

This article manages to discuss the problem of graduate unemployment in Pakistan without a single reference to earnings.

1440 N. J. SMELSER, S. M. LIPSET, "Social Structure, Mobility and Development", *Social Structure and Mobility in Economic Development*, eds. N. J. Smelser, S. M. Lipset. London: Routledge & Kegan Paul, 1966, pp. 1-51.

A broad view of the evidence, half of which is devoted to the impact of education on social and economic development in low-income countries.

1441 R. C. NAIRN, *International Aid to Thailand. The New Colonialism?* New Haven: Yale University Press, 1966. Pp. 228.

This profound and disturbing book consists of a devastating analysis of the effects of two major United Nations field programmes in Thailand: the Cha Cheong Sao Educational Pilot Project, an attempt at curriculum reform in Thai primary education, and the Thailand UNESCO Fundamental Educational Center, a community development project. By way of contrast, the author also considers three comparable bilateral aid operations in Thailand.

1442 V. N. KOTHARI, ed., *Investment in Human Resources.* Indian Economic Association Conference. Bombay: Popular Prakashan, 1966. Pp. 102.

Of the 22 papers read at this Indian Economic Conference, 9 are reprinted here, of which the most noteworthy are (1) P. R. Panchmukhi, "Measurement of Educational Outputs", pp. 71-85, which uses Principal Component Analysis to construct an index of educational output for India for 1950-60, then divides this index by an index of educational expenditures, revealing a decline in the productivity of Indian education over the decade; and (2) M. T. Patel, I. Ali, "Investment in Human Resources in a Tribal Village of Madhya Pradesh", pp. 83-93.

1967

1443 B. SINGH, *Education as Investment.* Meerut, India: Meenakshi Prakashan, 1967. Pp. 236.

A collection of 17 papers were given at an Indian symposium at Lucknow University in 1966. Most of them go over well-worn ground. But see (1) V. K. R. V. Rao, "Education as Investment", pp. 4-17, which accepts the general idea of the rate-of-return approach but objects to quantifying it; (2) S. Merrett, "Refashioning the Concept of Investment in Education", pp. 33-45, which does not quite seem to live up to its title; (3) R. C. Young, "Educational Planning and Economic Criteria in India's Context", pp. 79-101; (4) K. Mukerji, N. Krishnarao, "Education and Economic Development in India Between 1951 and 1961: An Empirical Investigation", pp. 102-9, an interstate comparison between enrolment ratios at all levels of education and both absolute per capita income and the rate of growth of per capita income over the decade 1951-61; (5) V. N. Kothari, "Returns to Education in India", pp. 126-40, an ingenious rate-of-return calculation for the city of Bombay, based on admittedly inadequate data collected in 1956; (6) I. Z. Husain, "Returns to Education in India: An Estimate", pp. 141-56, another rate-of-return calculation which is vitiated, however, by taking account of only 3-4 years of employment; (7) J. N. Sinha, "Educational Planning for Optimum Manpower Supplies", pp. 157-67, a regression analysis of the relationship between educational densities and income per head across Indian States; (8) J. C. Saigal, "The Use of International Comparisons in Manpower Forecasting", pp. 172-84; and (9) B. Singh, "Resource Constraints on Education in India", pp. 185-205.

1444 A. M. NALLA GOUNDEN, "Investment in Education in India", *JHR*, Summer, 1967, pp. 347-58.

The fist to calculate social rates of return to educational investment in India from national survey data; these are compared with Harberger's estimates of rates of return to physical capital (1335). In addition, the paper estimates human capital formation from 1950-61 and compares these with physical capital formation over the same period.

1445 M. CARNOY, "Rates of Return to Schooling in Latin America", *ibid*., pp. 359-74.

The article summarises the author's own results for Mexico and compares these with Shoup's results for Venezuela (1338), Camacho's results for Colombia, previously only available in Spanish, and Harberger and Selowsky's unpublished results for Chile, and discusses several implications of these comparisons.

1446 M. CARNOY, "Earnings and Schooling in Mexico", *EDCC*, July, 1967, pp. 408-19.

Multiple regression analysis of a non-random sample of urban male wageearners taken in Mexico in 1963. Variables other than age and years of schooling, such as father's occupation, industry of employment, and city of residence, added little to the explanation of Mexican earnings differentials.

1447 M. CARNOY, "Aspects of Labor Force Mobility in Latin America", *JHR*, Fall, 1967, pp. 517-37.

This paper estimates the rates of return to migrants between Colombia and Mexico, by age at migration, and by number of years of schooling of migrants.

1448 J. B. KNIGHT, "The Determination of Wages and Salaries in Uganda", *BOUIES*, 29, 3, 1967, pp. 233-64.

An important article on wage and salary structure in a developing country, with considerable attention to the effect of education on salaries, pp. 251-63. (See also 1457.)

1449 J. VAIZEY, "Education and the Irish Economy", *IJE*, Winter, 1967, pp. 113-23.

A popular article on the role of education in Irish growth.

1450 S. M. LIPSET, A. SOLARI, *Elites in Latin America*. New York: Oxford University Press, 1967. Pp. 531.

A number of essays in this volume refer explicity to the impact of higher education on social and economic development, apart from the manipulation of access to higher education by the political elites of Latin America. There is, first of all, a long essay by S. M. Lipset, "Values, Education and Entrepreneurship", pp. 3-60, particularly pp. 40-49. This is followed by D. Ribiero, "Universities and Social Development", pp. 343-81; L. Scherz-Garcia, "Relations Between Public and Private Universities", pp. 382-407; K. N.

Walker, "Political Socialization in Universities", pp. 408-30; A. Solari, "Secondary Education and the Development of Elites", pp. 457-83; and A. Gouveia, "Education and Development: Opinions of Secondary School Teachers", pp. 484-513.

1451   H. LEIBENSTEIN, *Rates of Return to Education in Greece. A Discussion of Results and Policy Implications*. Development Advisory Service, Economic Development Report No. 94. Cambridge, Mass.: Center for International Affairs, Harvard University, 1967. Pp. 62, mimeographed.

The most interesting part of this pioneering paper is not the rate-of-return calculations it produces—the first ever for Greece—but the fascinating discussion of the policy implications of the results.

1452   G. E. HURD, T. J. JOHNSON, "Education and Social Mobility in Ghana", *SE*, Winter, 1967, pp. 55-79; "Comments" by P. J. Foster, *ibid.*, Winter, 1968, pp. 111-15; "Reply" by Hurd and Johnson, *ibid.*, pp. 115-21.

The authors argue that Ghanaian secondary and higher education, is élitist and highly selective. Foster disagrees in part, at least in terms of emphasis. The disagreement leads to a useful discussion of the concept of élitism in the African context.

1968

1453   N. H. LEFF, *The Brazilian Capital Goods Industry 1929-1964*. Cambridge, Mass.: Harvard University Press, 1968, ch. 3, pp. 41-87.

Discusses trends in the demand and supply of skilled labour over the 25-year period, calculates rates of return to engineering education in recent years and shows, generally, how this industry has successfully competed in world markets with a less-than-average educated labour force. Studies of this kind for other industries in underdeveloped countries would do much to illuminate the role of education in the development process.

1454   G. MYRDAL, *Asian Drama. An Inquiry into the Poverty of Nations*. New York: Pantheon, 1968, III, chs. 32-33, pp. 1651-1828.

Ch. 32 of this highly controversial book provides an excellent survey of adult literacy problems in Central and South-east Asia around 1963. Ch. 33 covers the school system and the leading educational problems of the area. These chapters are full of neatly presented data and provocative recommendations.

1455   M. KASER, "Soviet Boarding Schools", *SS*, July, 1968, pp. 94-105.

A fascinating account of the Soviet policy of expanding boarding education in the late 1950's.

1456   J. D. HEIJNEN, *Development and Education to the Mwanza District (Tanzania). A Case Study of Migration and Peasant Farming*. Amsterdam: Centre for the Study of Education in Changing Societies and the University of Utrecht, 1968. Pp. 171.

This superb study of a cotton-growing district along Lake Victoria was
designed to assess the effects of primary education on agricultural development. The principal conclusions are that even 8 years of primary education
seem to have little effect on productivity and that the great majority of
school leavers, contrary to popular mythology, do not display strong resistance against farming as an occupation. This bald summary does not, however,
do justice to the analysis drawn together in the last chapter of the book.

1457   J. B. KNIGHT, "Earnings, Employment, Education and Income Distribution in
Uganda", *BOUIES*, November, 1968, pp. 267-97.

A continuation of an earlier article (see 1448) and an attack on Smyth and
Bennett (see 886), for attempting to base educational planning in Uganda on
calculations of the rate of return on educational investment.

1969

1458   J. G. WILLIAMSON, "Dimensions of Postwar Philippine Economic Progress", *QJE*,
February, 1969, pp. 93-109.

Applies a Denison-model to the Philippines and shows that about one-tenth
of aggregate Philippino growth from 1955 to 1965 is "explained" by investment
in education.

1459   M. BLAUG, R. LAYARD, M. WOODHALL, *The Causes of Graduate Unemployment in
India*. London: Allen Lane The Penguin Press, 1969. Pp. 312.

This study develops a dynamic surplus model of Indian labour markets and
tests it by estimating the private rate of return on investment in years of
schooling. The book also develops new estimates of the social rate of return
on educational investment in India, concluding that Indian higher education
is badly over-expanded. After a review of the evidence on labour markets
from both the demand and supply side, including the phenomenon of brain
drain, the last chapter of the book canvasses possible cures for graduate
unemployment.

1460   R. JOLLY, ed., *Education in Africa: Research and Action*. Nairobi: East
Africa Publishing House, 1969. Pp. 313.

The 19 papers in this volume were presented to a UK conference in 1968.
Among the most relevant to our concerns were: (1) C. M. O. Mate, "Addis
Ababa in Retrospect: An Evaluation of Experience Since the 1961 Conference",
pp. 3-28, which is followed by some UNESCO documents, reviewing the achievement of Addis Ababa targets up to 1965; (2) R. Jolly, "Costs and Confusions
in African Education: Some Implications of Recent Trends", pp. 47-62, which
reflects on the rapid rise in African wages and salaries in recent years;
(3) A. C. Mwingira, "Education for Self Reliance: The Problems of Implementation", pp. 65-80, which discusses Tanzania's new educational policies;
(4) P. J. Foster, "Education for Self Reliance: A Critical Evaluation",
pp. 81-102, a hard-hitting critique of Nyerere's programme; (5) J. A. Anderson, "The Harambee Schools: The Impact of Self Help", pp. 103-34; (6)
J. Silvey, "Unwillingly from School: The Occupational Attitudes of Secondary
School Leavers in Uganda", pp. 135-54; (7) G. Hunter, "Education for the
Rural Community", pp. 155-68; and (8) L. Brown, "Education for Adults in
African societies", pp. 169-88.

1461 H. H. THIAS, M. CARNOY, *Cost-Benefit Analysis in Education. A Case Study on Kenya*. Washington, D.C.: IBRD, No. EC-173, 1969. Pp. 225.

This study includes a multiple regression of earnings on age, sex, education and a host of socio-economic variables, based on a labour force survey conducted by the authors, various calculations of the private and social rate of return on investment in years of schooling, an analysis of educational production functions in Kenyan primary and secondary schools, and projections of rates of return based on various alternative assumptions about future wage-employment relationships.

1462 R. H. STROUP, M. B. HARGROVE, "Earnings and Education in Rural South Vietnam", *JHR*, Spring, 1969, pp. 215-24.

A multiple regression analysis using dummy variables of income data for 3,000 rural households in South Vietnam. Separate regressions are run for personal earnings and household income, as well as for eight occupational earnings categories. In all cases, the regression coefficient for education is significant and relatively large.

1463 J. D. DE VORETZ, "Alternative Planning Models for Philippine Educational Investment", *PEJ*, VIII, 2, 1969, pp. 99-116.

This paper contrasts the results that are derived from a rate-of-return analysis, a manpower forecast and the application of a linear programming model to Philippine education. It is a summary of a doctoral dissertation and in this brief form it is not always intelligible.

1464 E. A. TAN, "Implications of Private Demand for Education on Manpower Planning", *ibid.*, pp. 117-29.

This is a theoretical formulation of the demand for education, coupled with alternative models of schools-as-firms. The title of the paper only applies to the concluding comments, not to the body of the text.

1465 J. G. WILLIAMSON, D. J. DE VORETZ, "Education as an Asset in the Philippine Economy", *Philippine Population in the Seventies*, ed. M. B. Concepcion. Manila: Community Publishers, 1969, pp. 133-68.

After reviewing their Denison-type measurement of the contribution of education to Philippine economic growth, also available elsewhere (see 1458), the authors present rate-of-return estimates for 1966.

1466 D. C. McCLELLAND, D. G. WINTER, *Motivating Economic Achievement. Accelerating Economic Development Through Psychological Training*. New York: The Free Press, 1969. Pp. 415.

This book, following up McClelland's earlier work (see 1397), reports the results of a field experiment conducted in India which was designed to test the effects of psychological training on entrepreneurs in a developing country. The first two chapters give a succinct account of the evidence lying behind the concept of achievement drive as a crucial element in the growth process. The findings of the field experiment are summed up in

chapter 7.   Chapter 8 provides some fascinating case studies. Although the
sample was small and the results difficult to interpret, this is an important
and perhaps seminal book.

1467 CESO, *Primary Education in Sukumaland, Tanzania. A Summary Report of a
Study of Education in Changing Societies*. Groningen: Wolters-Noordhoff
Publishing, 1969. Pp. 147.

This book contains the findings of an interdisciplinary team of CESO which
studied primary education in the Mwanza District of Sukumaland, Tanzania in
1965/66. The report covers both the strictly educational factors as well
as the interaction between schools and the economy, the social structure and
the political community. A chapter by J. F. De Jongh, pp. 8-28, summarizes
the principal results. From our point of view, the most directly pertinent
chapter is 3, pp. 29-41, by J. D. Heijnen.

1468 CESO, *Educational Problems in Developing Countries*. Groningen: Wolters-
Noordhoff Publishing, 1969. Pp. 155.

Among the more relevant of the nine papers in this volume are (1) P. J.
Foster, "Secondary Education: Objectives and Differentiation", pp. 71-96,
based on his own work in Ghana and Nigeria, and W. K. Medlin, "The Role of
Education in Social Development: The School as an Agent of Modernization in
a Traditional Muslim Society", pp. 120-42, dealing with the Soviet Republic
of Uzbekistan. The introduction to the volume by J. F. De Jongh, pp. 4-13,
summarizes the contents of all the papers.

1970

1469 L. F. B. DUBBELDAM, *The Primary School and the Community in Mwanza District,
Tanzania*. Groningen: Wolters-Noordhoff Publishing, 1970. Pp. 199.

This study grew out of the main CESO study (see 1487) and is largely based
on a special sample survey of teachers and parents in the district. Of particular interest are the author's findings about parental expectations in the
district, pp. 148-52.

1470 J. K. HINCHLIFFE, "A Comparative Analysis of Education Development in Ghana
and The Western Region of Nigeria", *NJESS*, March, 1970, pp. 103-13.

A variety of comparisons, including rates of return, enrolments, costs and
expenditures, lead to the conclusion that the two educational systems have
been developing along broadly similar paths since 1960 but that the rate of
development has been much more intense in Ghana.

1471 O. D. HOERR, *Education, Income and Equity in Malaysia*. Economic Development
Report No. 176. Center for International Affairs. Cambridge, Mass.:
Harvard University, 1970. Pp. 52, mimeographed.

A regression analysis of earnings in West Malaysia, followed by rate-of-
return calculations and a discussion of their implications for policy. The
raw data is transformed at the outset of the exercise in such a way that the
final results are somewhat difficult to interpret.

1472   D. H. CLARK, P. E. FONG, "Returns to Schooling and Training in Singapore",
       MER, October, 1970, pp. 79-103.

       Calculates both rates of return and present values for the year 1966 and
       discusses their implications in the light of changes that are now taking
       place in Singapore's educational system.

1473   J. D. CONROY, "The Private Demand for Education in New Guinea: Consumption
       or Investment", *ER*, December, 1970, pp. 497-516.

       An interesting article which collates existing evidence for New Guinea to
       show that private demand for education is largely motivated by investment con-
       siderations. The closing pages of the article discuss the imminent problem
       of educated unemployment in New Guinea.

1474   A. JOZEFOWICZ, *Unemployment Among the Educated Youth*. National Commission on
       Manpower and Education. Research Study No. 5, Karachi: Planning Commission,
       Government of Pakistan, 1970. Pp. 128.

       This pioneering study is, unfortunately, limited to unemployed registrants
       and, even so, much of the information collected is either inadequately analyse
       or else not tabulated at all. Nevertheless, this study is a gold-mine of
       information of unemployment in West and East Pakistan, provided the reader is
       prepared to ignore the numerous unsupported inferences drawn by the author.

1475   W. P. FULLER, *Education, Training and Productivity: A Study of Skilled
       Workers in Two Factories in South India*. Palo Alto, Calif.: Stanford Inter-
       national Development Education Center, School of Education, Stanford Univer-
       sity, 1970. Pp. 130.

       A multiple regression analysis of the effect of education and training on
       the productivity (as measured by efficiency ratings) of some 600 turners,
       millers and grinders in two large firms in Bangalore. The chief finding that
       neither amount of education or training had much effect on efficiency, but
       that type of training did have a definite effect, is somewhat marred by the
       peculiar measure of efficiency used in this study.

1476   N. BENNETT, "Primary Education in Rural Communities: An Investment in Ignor-
       ance", *JDS*, July, 1970, pp. 92-103.

       The author raises a series of provocative questions about primary education
       in developing countries and complains about the lack of evidence to answer
       any of them. His survey of research results, however, hardly begins to cover
       the available literature.

1477   M. CARNOY, "The Quality of Education, Examination Performance and Urban-Rural
       Income Differentials in Puerto Rico", *CER*, October, 1970, pp. 335-49.

       The author demonstrates that socio-economic background explains less of
       urban-rural income differences in Puerto Rico than quality of education and
       that quality of education only becomes a powerful determinant of earnings
       differences after primary education. The methods employed to demonstrate
       these results involve some difficult transformations of the data.

1971

1478 C. R. S. DOUGHERTY, "The Optimal Allocation of Investment in Education",
Studies in Development Planning, ed. H. B. Chenery. Cambridge, Mass.:
Harvard University Press, 1971, pp. 270-92.

In this important paper, the author projects rates of return to educational
investment in Colombia, using a CES production function to trace out the
wage-implications of changing enrolments. He concludes that Colombia should
accelerate the rate of growth of primary and secondary education over the
next 10 years and cut back the growth of higher education.

1479 G. S. SAHOTA, "The Distribution of Tax Burdens Among Different Education
Classes in Brazil", *EDCC*, April, 1971, pp. 438-60.

An estimate of the legal and actual tax burden distribution among families
by education levels, including all-level government taxes, social security
contributions and special taxes classified by city size. This must be the
first study of this kind of the precise gap in a country between private and
social returns from education.

1480 M. HERSHKOWITZ, Z. SUSSMAN, "Growth, Induced Changes in Final Demand, Educational Requirements, and Wage Differentials", *RES.*, May, 1971, pp. 169-75.

Presents a simple model of the effects of rising income per head on consumption patterns and via these on "average educational requirements in terms of
years of schooling". The model is tested on Israeli data and the results
show that economic growth in the context of the Israeli economy tends to have
a neutral effect on educational requirements.

1481 A. N. DANIELSEN, K. OKACHI, "Private Rates of Return to Schooling in Japan",
JHR, Summer, 1971, pp. 391-97.

Calculates the private rate of return in Japan in 1966 and compares the
results with those for the United States in 1959.

1482 A. K. SEN, "The Aspects of Indian Education", *Aspects of Indian Economic
Development*, ed. P. Chaudhuri. London: Allen & Unwin, 1971, pp. 144-59.

A far-ranging discussion of rate-of-return studies of Indian education,
followed by an analysis of the special problems of medical and primary education.

1483 M. BLAUG, *Summary of the Rate of Return to Investment in Education in Thailand*. Bangkok: The Ford Foundation, 1971. Pp. 16.

A summary of multiple regression analysis of earnings, a new study of educational costs, and calculations of the rate of return in Thailand, all for
1970.

1484 M. CARNOY, "Class Analysis and Investment in Human Resources: A Dynamic
Model", *RRPE*, Fall/Winter, 1971, pp. 56-81.

After some irrelevant rhetoric, the author develops a model of development
stages in rates of return to levels of education. He finds little evidence,
however, to confirm his hypotheses but argues persuasively that different
"alpha coefficients" for successive levels of education significantly alter
unadjusted rates of return.

1485 J. LOWE, N. GRANT, T. D. WILLIAMS, *Education and Nation-Building in the
Third World*. Edinburgh: Scottish Academic Press, 1971. Pp. 264.

This popular book contains a dozen interesting articles, of which two or
three fall clearly within our scope, namely, (1) T. D. Williams, "The Demand
for Education", pp. 26-59 and (2) T. D. Williams, "The Efficiency of Education", pp. 60-83, both of which are survey articles, and (3) R. Jolly,
"Contrasts in Cuban and African Educational Strategies", pp. 210-31, which
draws heavily on his chapters in *Cuba: The Economic and Social Revolution*
(see 1414).

1486 R. M. SUNDRUM, "Manpower and Educational Development in East and Southeast
Asia: A Summary of Conference Proceedings", *MER*, October, 1971, pp. 78-90.

The whole of this issue is devoted to a paper presented at an Asian Manpower Conference in Singapore in 1971. The volume includes, among the papers
most relevant to the economics of education, W. Lockwood, "Employment, Technology and Education in Asia", pp. 6-24; H. Oshima, "Labour Absorption in
East and Southeast Asia", pp. 75-77; Y. B. De Witt, "Fitting the Manpower
Plan to The Overall Development Plan", pp. 159-71; G. Castillo, "Education
for Agriculture", pp. 172-93; and D. H. Clark, "Manpower Planning in Singapore", pp. 194-210.

1972

1487 Central Council for Education, Japan, *Basic Guidelines for the Reform of
Education*. Tokyo: Ministry of Education, Japan, 1972. Pp. 219.

Apart from the basic report, "Fundamental Policies and Measures for the
Overall Expansion and Development of School Education", this volume also contains "Analysis and Evaluation of the Development of Education and Its Future
Problems in Japan", pp. 73-217, which is a mine of information on Japanese
salaries, educational standards, parental attitudes to education, as well as
international comparisons of unit costs and educational expenditures.

1488 I. G. TIRADO, "Programme Budget Proposals for the Department of Education in
Puerto Rico", *CS*, January, 1972, pp. 60-72.

A critique of the budget accounts of the Puerto Rican ministry of education
and an attempt to recast the 1969 budget into a PPB format.

1489 D. C. ROGERS, "Student Loan Programs and the Returns to Investment in Higher
Levels of Education in Kenya", *EDCC*, January, 1972, pp. 243-59.

This paper calculates the private rate of return on educational investment
in Kenya from government salary scales and then recalculates these on the
assumption of various loan schemes. The author argues that a loan scheme to
cover the total costs of higher education would be perfectly feasible in
Kenyan conditions.

1490 M. CARNOY, "The Rate of Return to Schooling and the Increase in Human Resources in Puerto Rico", *CER*, February, 1972, pp. 68-86.

A rate-of-return analysis for Puerto Rico based on earnings functions with some attempt to predict likely future changes in rates of return.

1491 A. CHAKRAVARTI, "The Social Profitability of Training Unskilled Workers in the Public Sector in India", *OEP*, March, 1972, pp. 111-23.

Calculates the social rate of return on training schools by using world prices to calculate costs and benefits, as recommended by Little and Mirrlees.

1492 S. PAUL, "An Application of Cost-Benefit Analysis to Management Education", *JPE*, March/April, 1972, pp. 328-46.

A cost-benefit analysis of the two-year postgraduate programme of the Indian Institute of Management at Ahmedabad based upon assumed age-earnings profiles. The results yield a social rate of return of at least 13 per cent.

1493 K. GANNICOTT, *Rates of Return to Education in Taiwan, Republic of China*. Taipei: Planning Unit, Ministry of Education, 1972. Pp. 63.

An excellent example of the use of multi-regression analysis to investigate the interrelationships between family background, age, education, occupation and sector of activity, on the one hand, and personal earnings on the other, after which private and social rates of return are calculated by holding non-educational variables constant.

1494 E. R. RADO, "The Relevance of Education for Employment", *JMAS*, X, 3, 1972, pp. 459-75.

A hard-hitting article on the role of education in the employment problem of Tropical Africa.

1495 G. E. SKOROV, "The Developing Countries: Education, Employment, Economic Growth", *SOV*, August, 1972, pp. 5-64.

These are excerpts of a book published in Moscow in 1971 by a well-known Soviet authority on education in developing countries. The excerpts, together with a Soviet review of the book, pp. 65-70, succeed admirably in conveying the flavour of Soviet discussions on these questions.

1496 A. O. KRUEGER, "Rates of Return to Turkish Higher Education", *JHR*, Fall, 1972, pp. 482-99.

Using data on earnings-by-occupation, the author converts these to earnings-by-education by assuming certain occupation-education equivalences. She shows that the Turkish case is anomalous in some respects, in that private rates of return increase with educational attainment.

1497 L. EMMERIJ, "Education and the World Employment Programme", *HE*, November, 1972, pp. 483-96.

A commentary on three ILO reports, dealing with Colombia, Ceylon and Kenya and what was learned about the relationship between education and unemployment.

1973

1498 K. HINCHLIFFE, "Manpower Planning and Occupational Choice in Nigeria", *WAJE*, February, 1973, pp. 165-72.

An interesting study of career choice among some 250 male students at Ahmadu Bello University from which the author draws strong and somewhat misleading conclusions.

1499 E. O. EDWARDS, M. P. TODARO, "Educational Demand and Supply in the Context of Growing Unemployment in Less Developed Countries", *WD*, March-April, 1973, 107-17.

Challenges the belief that more education is desirable in LDC's and attempts to explain the continuously rising private demand for education in the face of growing educated unemployment. Concludes with some strong policy recommendations for the LDC's as well as donor agencies.

1500 P. J. RICHARDS, "Job Mobility and Unemployment in the Ceylon Urban Labour Market", *OBES*, Vol. 35, 1, 1973, pp. 49-59.

In this extremely interesting analysis of 800 male saleworkers employed in Colombo textile stores, the author canvasses a number of explanations for the fact that the urban unemployed in a country like Ceylon are largely young and relatively highly educated. He concludes that Ceylonese employers have a marked preference for maturity and work experience and place a low value on mere certification.

1501 J. BHAGWATI, "Education, Class Structure and Income Equality", *WD*, I, 5, 1973, pp. 21-36.

A protest against "the calculation of dubious numbers, masquerading as rates of return to education undifferentiated by social class and caste", with particular reference to India. The paper presents a wide variety of socioeconomic evidence to suggest the class distribution bias of educational provision in India.

1502 G. PSACHAROPOULOS, G. WILLIAMS, "Public Sector Earnings and Educational Planning", *ILR*, July, 1973, pp. 43-57.

Estimates earnings functions for public sector employees in Iran in 1971, calculates rates of return to investment in education, and in the light of these comments on the policy instruments available to the Iranian government for affecting the general structure of salaries in the economy.

1503 M. BLAUG, *Education and the Employment Problem of Developing Countries.* Geneva: ILO, 1973. Pp. 189.

After considering the nature of the employment problem of poor countries
and the practical lessons of the economics of education, the author goes on
to discuss both traditional and radical solutions to educated unemployment
in developing countries.

1974

1504 G. USWATTE-ARATCHI, "University Admission in Ceylon: Their Economic and
      Social Background and Employment Expectations", *MAS*, 8, 3, 1974, pp. 289-318.

      An analysis of the results of a survey of all Ceylonese university students
      admitted in the year 1967. Among the fascinating findings are those on
      parental incomes and occupations, showing a systematic relationship between
      family origins and fields of study. Questions on employment expectations
      showed an overwhelming desire to enter the civil service.

1505 S. C. GOEL, "Education and Economic Growth in India", *CE*, June, 1974,
      pp. 147-58.

      A Harbison-Myers type inquiry into the statistical relationship between
      levels of educational expenditure and levels of economic development in
      India, 1950-71. The paper leans heavily for some of its arguments on income
      distribution effects unsupported by evidence.

1506 S. G. FIELDS, "The Private Demand for Education in Relation to Labour Market
      Conditions in Less-Developed Countries", *EJ*, December, 1974, pp. 906-25.

      An attempt to explain the demand for education in LDC's in the face of
      educated unemployment. Three models are developed — the bumping model, the
      stratification model, and the pooling model — and their results compared.
      The concluding arguments draw some policy implications.

1507 P. FOSTER, J. R. SHEFFIELD, eds., *Education and Rural Development*, The
      World Year Book of Education, 1974. London: Evans Brothers, 1973. Pp. 417.

      A good collection of 20 papers (surprisingly good for a World Year Book of
      Education whose quality has been steadily falling for years; fortunately,
      this is the last of the series). The editors start off with a superb intro-
      duction, which in 11 pages "says it all". Of the 20 papers, the most note-
      worthy for our purposes are: (1) C. A. Anderson, "Effective Education for
      Agriculture", pp. 31-49; (2) T. W. Schultz, "The Education of Farm People:
      An Economic Perspective", pp. 50-68; (3) A. W. Wood, "Developing Educational
      Alternatives: Some New Ways for Education in Rural Areas", pp. 137-49;
      (4) E. R. Watts, "The Educational Needs of Farmers in Developing Countries",
      pp. 150-62; (5) R. Evenson, "Research, Extension and Schooling in Agricultural
      Development", pp. 163-84; (6) G. Hunter, "A Comment on Educational Reform and
      Employment in Africa", pp. 278-82; (7) J. A. Anderson, "The Formalization
      of Non-Formal Education: Village Polytechnics and Prevocational Youth Train-
      ing in Kenya", pp. 283-301; (8) G. T. Castillo, "Education for Agriculture",
      pp. 311-36; (9) B. R. Harker, "The Contribution of Schooling to Agricultural
      Modernization: An Empirical Analysis", pp. 350-71; and (10) D. P. Chaudhri,
      "Rural Education and Agricultural Development: Some Empirical Results from
      Indian Agriculture", pp. 372-86.

3. THE ECONOMIC ASPECTS OF EDUCATION

(a) *Costs and Finance*

Martin and Lewis[1508], The Netherlands Economic Institute[500], and Blot and Debeauvais[500,1516] take up the determinants of national educational expenditures. Okigbo[1520] writes on criteria for public expenditures on education. Additional finance for educational expansion in Asia and Latin America is treated by Löbel[1647], Wolfe[1688], UNESCO-ECLA[1664], and UNESCO[1531]. The Pakistan Ministry of Education[1513] and Hicks[1531] canvass new sources of revenue for the finance of education. Prest[500] discusses the relationship between modes of provision and modes of finance. These and other administrative aspects of educational finance are analysed for India by Misra[1514], for the USSR by Noah[1527], for Africa and Asia by a series of IIEP monographs[1522-26,1528,1529,1532,1534-37,1539], capped by the summary volume of Coombs and Hallak[1538]. Jallade[1541] attempts to measure the total redistributive effects of public expenditures on education in a particular country. Goode[500], Phillips[1521] Higgins[1531], Tobias[1531], Schultz[1663], Williams[1675], Ewers[1688], Benveniste[1688], Coombs and Bigelow[1698], and Cerych[1707,1728,1729] are all concerned one way or the other with external financial aid to education. Tinbergen[1693] contributes "ten commandments of educational assistance" to the discussion.

1956

1508 A. MARTIN, W. A. LEWIS, "Patterns of Public Revenue and Expenditure", *MS*, September, 1956, pp. 203-44.

Seeks to discover the appropriate level and distribution of public revenues and expenditures, including expenditure on education, in underdeveloped countries by an international comparison. See also T. N. Wang, "Some Problems of International Comparison of Public Social Expenditure", *IER*, February, 1955, pp. 23-52.

1960

1509 G. KIMBLE, *Tropical Africa, II. Society and Polity*. New York: Twentieth Century Fund, 1960, ch. 16, pp. 93-159.

An excellent survey of formal and informal education in British, French, Portuguese, and Belgian territories.

1961

1510   W. BRAND, "The Financing of Education", *Conference of African States on the Development of Education in Africa. Final Report*. Addis Ababa: UNESCO, 1961, pp. 31-45.

   Brief general discussion of educational costs by way of an estimate for Tropical Africa.

1511   UNESCO, *Manual of Educational Statistics*. Paris: UNESCO, 1961; 2nd ed., 1965. Pp. 241.

   This manual, ostensibly addressed to government officials responsible for the collection of educational statistics, is a reference indispensable to anyone making international comparisons of educational standards and facilities. After an introductory chapter on the history of efforts to achieve international standardisation of educational statistics, the book discusses and illustrates the special problems of statistics of illiteracy, educational attainment, institutional levels and types of education, and, lastly, educational finance.

1512   N. GINSBURG, *Atlas of Economic Development*. Chicago, Ill.: Chicago University Press, 1961, pp. 38-46.

   Useful maps of the world are presented, showing the "Percentage of Adults Literate", "Proportion of Children 5-14 in Primary School", "Percentage of Total Population in Secondary and Higher Education", all based on UNESCO 1958-59 data.

1513   Ministry of Education, Pakistan, *Report of the Commission on National Education*. Karachi: Government of Pakistan Press, 1961. Pp. 369.

   Although most of this volume is concerned with the specific problems of Pakistan education, some of the Committee's recommendations have wider implications, such as the suggestion that half of the costs of universal primary education should be met by additional earmarked taxes, that private industry should be taxed to support technical and vocational education, and that 5-7 per cent of the costs of all major development projects should be paid to the Ministry of Education.

1962

1514   A. MISRA, *Educational Finance in India*. London: Asia Publishing House, 1962. Pp. 616.

   A comprehensive study of educational finance in India since 1700, with a detailed evaluation of existing practices. The book includes a valuable bibliography and a long appendix of statistics on educational finance in India.

1964

1515 O. P. F. HORWOOD, "The Financing of Higher Education in South Africa, with
      Particular Reference to the Universities", *SAJE*, September, 1964, pp. 159-86.

         A useful source of information on methods of financing higher education
      in the Republic of South Africa.

1965

1516 D. BLOT, M. DEBEAUVAIS, "Les dépenses d'éducation dans le monde. Une analyse
      statistique", *TM*, arvil-juin, 1965, pp. 443-63.

         A multiple regression analysis of the relationship between educational
      expenditures and GNP in 95 countries, which is then applied to evaluate the
      targets of the 3 regional educational plans for Asia, Africa, and Latin
      America.

1517 LÊ THI NAM TRÂN, "Les dépenses publiques de l'éducation dans les pays du
      plan Karachi", *ibid.*, pp. 531-51.

         A critical analysis of the 1960-61 data of educational expenditures in the
      Karachi Plan countries.

1518 NGUYÊN HUU CHAU, "Les coûts de l'éducation. Essai de justification d'une
      analyse économique", *ibid.*, 1965, pp. 421-43.

         An international comparison of per pupil educational costs and a discussion
      of the accounting problems of interpreting such data.

1519 LÊ THÀNH KHÔI, "Sur l'intérêt d'une présentation fonctionnelle du budget de
      l'éducation nationale: la Tunisie", *ibid.*, pp. 463-79.

         An analysis of the structure of Tunisia's educational budget.

1966

1520 P. N. C. OKIGBO, "Criteria for Public Expenditure on Education", *IEA-EE*,
      pp. 479-97.

         After a rapid review of the difficulties in cost-benefit analysis applied
      to African countries, the author turns to the Correa-Tinbergen approach (1778)
      and illustrates its application to Nigerian data.

1521 H. M. PHILLIPS, "International Aid for Educational Development in the Form
      of Technical Assistance and Real Resources", *ibid.*, pp. 564-91.

         A review of the figures of international aid for education to underdeveloped
      countries in recent years.

1522 J. D. CHESWASS, *Educational Planning and Development in Uganda*. African
      Research Monographs No. 1. Paris: UNESCO-IIEP, 1966. Pp. 97.

        This study is mis-titled: what it really deals with is educational admini-
      stration and cost-accounting in Uganda. It describes the rules-of-thumb used
      by Ugandan planners to calculate future enrolments, capital and recurrent
      costs per place, staff ratios and required teacher-training facilities, and
      the like.

1523 J. F. THORNLEY, *The Planning of Primary Education in Northern Nigeria*.
      African Research Monographs No. 2. Paris: UNESCO-IIEP, 1966. Pp. 41.

        A detailed account of the administrative problems raised by the growth of
      primary education in Nigeria, with particular emphasis on cost analysis of
      educational programmes.

1524 J. HALLAK, R. POIGNANT, *Les aspects financiers de l'enseignement dans les
      pays africains d'expression francaise*. Monographies africaines No. 3.
      Paris: UNESCO-IIEP, 1966. Pp. 76.

        A useful description of the structure of educational finance in 14 French-
      speaking African countries. No significant relation was found in 1961 be-
      tween public expenditures on education and GDP per head across the 14 coun-
      tries.

1525 J. B. KNIGHT, *The Costing and Finance of Educational Development in Tanzania*.
      African Research Monographs No. 4. Paris: UNESCO-IIEP, 1966. Pp. 80.

        A valuable contribution to cost analysis of education, illustrating the
      technique of projecting unit costs by major categories of expenditures
      throughout the educational system.

1526 J. HALLAK, R. POIGNANT, *Les aspects financiers de l'éducation en Côte-d'Ivoire*.
      Monographies africaines No. 8. Paris: UNESCO-IIEP, 1966. Pp. 44.

        This monograph gives further details of the structure of educational finance
      in one French-speaking African nation.

1527 H. J. NOAH, *Financing Soviet Schools*. Studies of the Russian Institute,
      Columbia University. New York: Teachers College Press, 1966. Pp. 291.

        The first comprehensive study of Soviet educational finance, including
      estimates of total real expenditures on education in the USSR since 1940,
      showing that general education has been favoured in recent years at the
      expense of specialist training. An important chapter on teachers' salaries
      demonstrates that Soviet teachers are not particularly well paid.

1967

1528 J. VAIZEY, J. D. CHESWASS, *The Costing of Educational Plans*. Fundamentals of
      Educational Planning 6. Paris: UNESCO-IIEP, 1967. Pp. 63.

A brief introduction by J. Vaizey leads up to a description by J. D. Chewass of the costing of an educational plan in a typical African country.

1529 P. GUILLAUMONT, D. GARBE, P. VERDUN, *Les dépenses d'enseignement au Sénégal.* Monographies africaines 5. Paris: UNESCO-IIEP, 1967. Pp. 51.

A standard analysis of the costs and finance of Senegalese education by levels of education, nature of costs, and source of finance.

1530 M. BOTTI, *Recherches sur les coûts de l'enseignement primaire à Madagascar et dans huit pays francophones d'Afrique.* Paris: SEDES, 1967. Pp. 101.

An analysis of unit costs in primary education in the French Cameroons, Dahomey, Gabon, Madagascar, Mali, Mauritania, Niger, Senegal, and Togo. The volume includes about 50 tables.

1531 UNESCO, *Investment in Education.* *Regional Technical Assistance Seminar on Investment in Education.* Paris: UNESCO, 1967. Pp. 446.

In addition to the proceedings and conclusions of the seminar, this report includes 13 country papers on the economic and financial difficulties of implementing the Karachi Plan, as well as a number of essays by international consultants emphasising the problem of raising additional revenue to finance investment in education. B. Higgins, the rapporteur of the seminar, contributes an excellent paper on "Financing Investment in Education", touching on the physical and monetary bottlenecks to educational expansion, the advisability of calculating rates of return to investment in education, new sources of domestic finance, and the role of foreign aid. M. Debeauvais writes on the "Determination of Objectives in the Regional Planning of Education", furnishing new estimates of the costs of implementing the Karachi Plan, based on improved educational statistics for 1960-61. M. I. Makhmoutov writes on "Problems of Financing Investment in Education in USSR". F. Edding furnishes what is, in fact, a short manual on the techniques of cost analysis and cost planning, illustrated by Irish, British, and German data, under the title "Problems of Expanding Investment in Education". "Problems of Expanding Education, With Special Reference to the Process of Revenue Raising, Centrally and Locally, For Educational Purposes" are discussed by Mrs. U. Hicks. G. Tobias analyses the implications of the acceptance by the IBRD since 1962 of the propriety of extending long-term credits to low-income countries for educational expansion: "Problems in International Financing of Education".

1968

1532 A. CALLAWAY, A. MUSONE, *Financing of Education in Nigeria.* African Research Monographs No. 15. Paris: UNESCO-IIEP, 1968. Pp. 150.

A superb reconstruction of financial flows and unit costs at every level of the Nigerian educational system in all regions over an 11-year period 1952-63. The volume includes a valuable bibliographical essay on educational planning in Nigeria since independence.

1969

1533 J. HALLAK, *The Analysis of Educational Costs and Expenditures*. Fundamentals
of Educational Planning 10. Paris: UNESCO-IIEP, 1969. Pp. 70.

    Another general discussion of the problem of educational costing, with
some striking examples largely drawn from developing countries.

1972
1534 J. HALLAK, M. CHEIKHESTANI, H. VARLET, *The Financial Aspects of First-Level
Education in Iran*. Financing Educational Systems: Specific Case Studies 1.
Paris: UNESCO-IIEP, 1972. Pp. 58.

    A comparative analysis of unit costs and sources of finance of three types
of primary education in Iran: ordinary public schools, Education Corps
schools and private schools. The study also attempts a cost-effectiveness
evaluation of the Education Corps schools.

1535 J. HALLAK, *Financing and Educational Policy in Sri Lanka (Ceylon)*. Financing
Educational Systems: Country Case Studies 1. Paris: UNESCO-IIEP, 1972.
Pp. 159.

    This is more than an educational finance study. It is, in fact, a study
of educational planning in Ceylon with particular reference to costs and
methods of finance.

1536 T. N. CHAU, *Population Growth and Costs of Education in Developing Countries*.
Paris: UNESCO-IIEP, 1972. Pp. 313.

    The emphasis in this study is on the effect of demographic growth on the
development and costs of primary education and teacher training. It consists
of four case studies on Ceylon, Colombia, Tanzania and Tunisia by J. Hallak,
T. N. Chau, F. Caillods and C. Tibi, as well as a general chapter synthesiz-
ing the findings of the case studies by T. N. Chau.

1537 P. H. COOMBS, J. HALLAK, eds., *Educational Cost Analysis in Action: Case
Studies for Planners - I, II, III*. Paris: UNESCO-IIEP, 1972. Pp. 360, 271,
346.

    These 3 volumes consist of 27 case studies on the diverse uses of cost and
cost-benefit analysis in educational planning, complementing the book on the
same theme by the two editors (see 1538). Volume I consists of (1) N. Bennett,
"Tanzania: Planning for Implementation", pp. 13-36; (2) J. Cheswass, "Tanzania: Factors Influencing Change in Teachers' Basic Salaries", pp. 39-76;
(3) J. Alles, and others, "Ceylon: Costing First- and Second-Level General
Education", pp. 79-117; (4) D. Chuprunov, L. Tul'chinskii, "USSR: Economic
Planning and the Financing of Higher Education", pp. 121-140; (5) V. I. Basov,
"USSR: Estimating the Annual Budget Requirements of the Educational System",
pp. 143-63; (6) C. Tibi, "France: The Use of Capital Costs in Educational
Planning — The Case of the Fifth French Plan", pp. 167-205; (7) H. W. Reiff,
"Thailand: Educational Cost Analysis", pp. 209-63; (8) H. W. Reiff, "Thai-
land: The Use of Cost Analysis in Estimating the Total Cost of an Educational
Plan and Testing its Feasibility", pp. 267-96; (9) J. Auerhan, E. S. Solomon,
"Asia: Cost Analysis in an Asian Model of Educational Development", pp. 299-
329; and (10) L. Arrigazzi, "Chile: Evaluating the Expansion of a Vocational

Training Programme", pp. 333-60, an evaluation of a World Bank exercise in cost-benefit analysis applied to vocational training.

Volume II consists of (1) T. N. Chau, "Ivory Coast: The Cost of Introducing a Reform in Primary Education", pp. 11-61; (2) T. N. Chau, J. Hallak, P. H. Coombs, "Madagascar: The Role of Cost Analysis in the Introduction and Implementation of the 1962 Reform of Primary Education", pp. 63-93; (3) O. Magnussen, "Norway: The Use of Educational Cost Models in Planning the Extension of Compulsory Education", pp. 95-129; (4) R. M. Durstine, B. M. Hudson, "Barbados: Marginal Costs for Marginal Decisions — The Case of Team Teaching", pp. 131-67; (5) K. Podolski, "Poland: The Role of Cost Analysis in Planning a Teacher-Training Programme", pp. 169-91; (6) R. C. Fachin, "Brazil: Costing an Expansion Programme for Secondary Education in Rio Grande do Sul", pp. 193-215; (7) M. Woodhall, "India: The Use of Cost-Benefit Analysis as a Guide to Resource Allocation in Education", pp. 217-45; and (8) M. Woodhall, "Colombia: The Use of Cost-Benefit Analysis to Compare the Rates of Return at Different Educational Levels", pp. 247-71.

Volume III consists of (1) N. Bennett, "Uganda: Educational Cost Evaluation", pp. 11-65; (2) J. Cheswass, J. Hallak, "Uganda: Behaviour of Non-Teacher Recurring Expenditures", pp. 67-103; (3) N. Bennett, "Uganda: The Use of Cost Evaluation in the Planning of Makerere University College", pp. 105-45; (4) M. Woodhall, "United Kingdom: The Use of Cost Analysis to Improve the Efficiency of School Building in England and Wales", pp. 147-77; (5) J. B. Levine, R. W. Judy, R. Wilson, "Canada: Comprehensive Analytical Methods for Planning in University Systems — Planning a New Health Sciences Education Complex", pp. 179-225; (6) J. Proust, "Morocco: Costs of Public Secondary Education — Analysis of the Results of a Governmental Survey", pp. 227-69; (7) L. Arrigazzi, J. de Simone, "Chile: Improving Efficiency in the Utilization of Teachers in Technical Education", pp. 271-301; (8) J. Zhamin, B. Remennikov, "USSR: Comparative Costs and Efficiency of Full-Time and Part-Time Education", pp. 303-13; and (9) L. Faluvegi, "Hungary: Programming Annual Current and Capital Expenditures During the Planning Period", pp. 315-46.

1538   P. H. COOMBS, J. HALLAK, *Managing Educational Costs*. New York: Oxford University Press, 1972. Pp. 288.

A companion volume to 27 case studies carried out by UNESCO-IIEP (1537), which is addressed to "non-economists, in particular ... people who actually run educational systems". The first six chapters illustrate the type of problems that are encountered in costing educational systems, leading up to the last five chapters, the core of the book, entitled "doing your own cost analysis". The book includes a brief, annotated bibliography.

1973

1539   J. E. ANDERSON, *Organization and Financing of Self-Help Education in Kenya*. Financing Educational Systems: Specific Case Studies 4. Paris: UNESCO-IIEP, 1973. Pp. 70.

An analysis of the organisation and financing of harambee schools at the first and second level in Kenya.

1974

1540   P. WILLIAMS, "Lending for Learning: An Experiment in Ghana", *MIN*, July,
       1974, pp. 326-45.

       An analysis of the short-lived students loans scheme introduced by the
       Busia Progress Party Government in Ghana in 1971. The author concludes by
       drawing some lessons from this experiment for Africa as a whole.

1541   J-P. JALLADE, *Public Expenditures on Education and Income Distribution in
       Colombia*. World Bank Staff Occasional Papers No. 18. Baltimore: John
       Hopkins University Press, 1974. Pp. 74.

       The first attempt in the literature to measure the total redistributive
       effects of public expenditures on education in a developing country. The
       author concludes that the net effect of public financing of education in
       Colombia is equalising, most of that effect deriving from the public financ-
       ing of primary education.

1542   C. TIBI, *Aspects financiers du système de prêts aux étudiants en Colombie*.
       Financement des systèmes éducatifs: études de cas spécifiques 5. Paris:
       UNESCO-IIEP, 1974. Pp. 61.

       An analysis of the financial aspects of student loan schemes in Colombia.
       Contrast this with Jallade's more ambitious study of the same subject (1559).

(b) PRODUCTIVITY AND EFFICIENCY

So pressing have been the demands on educational authorities in underdeveloped
countries that questions of dropouts, retardation, inappropriate curricula, poor
deployment of teachers, and the like have been generally neglected. There is,
therefore, very little to report in this area of research and study. Maleche[1544],
Elkan[1545], Blot[1550], UNESCO[1554], and the Agricultural Economics Research Centre,
Delhi University[1559] indicate how the problem of wastage might be investigated in
primary and secondary schools: Kamat and Deshmukh[1549] deal with the same problem
in higher education. Jones[1561,1562], the UK Colonial Office[1543], Evans[1546],
FAO[1598], Blaug[1503], Balogh[1665], Foster[1335], and Dumont[1572,1576,1580] write on the
vexed question of infusing a rural bias in African education. Callaway[1408,1547],
[1580] and Hollander[1802] comment on the associated problem of unemployable school
leavers. Beeby[1553] analyzes the causes of low teacher quality in developing countries.
   The use of audio-visual techniques and programmed learning as instruments for
improving the efficient utilisation of scarce teacher resources in poor countries
are discussed by Komoski and Green[1551], UNESCO[1602], Neurath[1606], de Sola Pool[1607],
Benveniste[886], IIEP[1555,1556], and Schramm[1616].

1953

1543   UK, Colonial Office, *African Education, A Study of Educational Policy and
       Practice in British Tropical Africa*. London: Oxford University Press, 1953.
       Pp. 186.

Includes the Jeffery Report on West Africa, the Binns Report on East Africa, and the Proceedings of a conference held in Cambridge in 1952 which formed a complete cross-section of the educational world of British Africa. A popular version of this volume with a great many quotations has been published by J. M. Campbell, *African History in the Making* (London: Edinburgh House Press, 1956. Pp. 120.

1960

1544 A. J. MALECHE, "A Study of Wastage in Primary Schools in Uganda", *Conference Papers 1960. East African Institute of Social Research*. Kampala, Uganda: EAISR, 1960. Pp. 19, mimeographed.

Working with the school registers of a sample of grant-aided primary schools in Uganda, the author presents a statistical analysis of the causes of retardation and wastage. See also a further study of "Wastage Among School Leavers in West Nile—1959 and 1960", *Conference Papers 1962* (pp. 19, mimeographed) and a paper summarising previous research on wastage at EAISR by F. K. Kamoga, "Future of Primary Leavers in Uganda", *Conference Papers 1963* (pp. 16, mimeographed).

1545 S. ELKAN, "Primary School Leavers in Uganda", *CER*, October, 1960, pp. 102-10.

A study of the causes of wastage at entry to secondary schools in Uganda in 1957, based on a sample of over 1000 children.

1962

1546 P. C. C. EVANS, "Western Education and Rural Productivity in Tropical Africa", *AF*, October, 1962, pp. 313-23.

A thorough refutation of the oft-repeated charge that Western-type schooling in Africa is inherently anti-rural and some positive recommendations for infusing a rural idiom into African education.

1547 A. C. CALLAWAY, "School Leavers in Nigeria", *The Nigerian Political Scene*, eds. R. O. Tilman, R. T. Cole. Durham, N.C.: Duke University Press, 1962, pp. 220-38.

A constructive analysis of the problems created by a surplus of primary school leavers in Eastern and Western Nigeria. Urges creation of village-level agricultural plans designed to train and integrate young farmers into a village agricultural economy.

1548 FAO, *African Survey. Report on the Possibilities of African Rural Development in Relation to Economic and Social Growth*. Rome: FAO, 1962, pp. 123-35.

This authoritative report is highly critical of the state of agricultural education in Tropical Africa and submits a set of recommendations to improve it.

1963

1549   A. R. KAMAT, A. G. DESHMUKH, *Wastage in College Education. Two Studies About the Students of the University of Poona*. Poona: Gokhale Institute of Politics and Economics, 1963. Pp. 202.

   This statistical study of dropouts and retardation in higher education in India consists of 2 parts; the first considers a 3-year entry of students at one of the colleges of the University of Poona, and the second analyses the failures in the pre-degree examination of the university. The authors provide a brief statement of the limitations of the first of these, p. 119.

1964

1550   D. BLOT, *Les déperditions d'effectifs scolaires: analyse théorique et applications*. Paris: IEDES, 1964. Pp. 50, mimeographed.

   The first part of this monograph develops a rather complicated mathematical model of the problem of wastage and retardation in an educational system in a typical developing country. The second part attempts to apply this model to the primary schools of Morocco.

1551   P. K. KOMOSKI, E. J. GREEN, *Programmed Instruction in West Africa and the Arab States*. Educ. Stud. & Docs., No. 52. Paris: UNESCO, 1964. Pp. 32.

   A report on workshops in programmed instruction conducted in Jordan and Nigeria. The pamphlet is introduced with a note on programmed instruction by W. Schramm.

1966

1552   S. MERRETT, "Earnings, Work, Study and The Gestation Period of the Argentine Engineering Student", *BOUIES*, 28, 2, 1966, pp. 117-31.

   A multiple regression analysis of the effects of student's age, social class, employment, and net earnings on academic performance in the Faculty of Engineering of the University of Buenos Aires in 1964. Students in this study are pictured as time-adjusters, adjusting their hours of work to their demand for earnings and trading off hours of study and leisure against working hours.

1553   C. E. BEEBY, *The Quality of Education in Developing Countries*. Cambridge, Mass.: Harvard University Press, 1966. Pp. 139.

   This important book emphasises the lack of education and training of teachers as the principal bottleneck for educational development in low-income countries. Ch. 4, the core of the book, sketches a stage-theory of educational development in terms of the characteristics of teachers found at various phases of educational development. Ch. 2, entitled "Economists and Educators", discusses the biases that economists and educators respectively bring to educational planning.

1967

1554 UNESCO, "The Problem of Educational Wastage", *Bulletin of the UNESCO Regional Office for Education in Asia*, 1, 2, 1967. Pp. 68.

      A survey of the causes of drop-outs and repetition in Asian primary education with a review of selected studies in different countries and an excellent bibliographical check-list.

1555 W. SCHRAMM, P. H. COOMBS, F. KAHNERT, J. LYLE, *The New Media: Memo to Educational Planners*. Paris: UNESCO-IIEP, 1967. Pp. 175.

      An important book based on 23 case studies from 17 countries, designed to develop guidelines for the developing countries. There are chapters on the different uses of the new media, the evaluation of their effectiveness, the variability in their costs, and, finally, the way in which they can be integrated into educational plans.

1556 IIEP, *New Educational Media in Action: Case Studies for Planners—II, III*. Paris: UNESCO-IIEP, 1967. Pp. 226, 198.

      The second volume of case studies contains four studies from Africa (Niger, the Ivory Coast, Togo, and Algeria), two from Latin America (Peru and Colombia), one from the Middle East (Lebanon), and one from the United States; ranging all the way from evaluations of educational television for in-school instruction in Niger to the use of radio with rural forum groups in Togo. The third volume includes ten case studies from six countries (Italy, Niger, New Zealand, Honduras, Nigeria, and the United States).

1557 P. H. COOMBS, *The World Education Crisis—A Systems Analysis*. International Conference on the World Crisis in Education, Williamsburg, Virginia, October, 1967. Paris: UNESCO-IIEP, 1967. Pp. 212, 969 (Technical Annex).

      This is not really an example of "systems analysis" but simply a well-informed discussion of the educational explosion around the world, concentrating on rising unit costs, its causes and remedies. "Education is a mass-production, labour-intensive industry, still in the handicraft stage" (p. 48)—this sentence is a good example both of the main theme of the book and its pungent style. The Technical Annex is a useful compilation of data drawn from a large variety of sources.

1969

1558 H. N. PANDIT, *Measurement of Cost, Productivity and Efficiency of Education*. Delhi: National Council of Educational Research and Training, 1969. Pp. 434.

      This collection of 32 papers, prepared for a 1967 conference of Indian economists and educators, includes a number of valuable empirical studies, as well as some sound discussions of policy issues. Since the quality of the papers is highly uneven, I will only mention that the following struck me as making a definite contribution to the literature: (1) D. L. Sharma, "Unit Costs of Education, Our Knowledge, Gaps and Our Need", pp. 27–41; (2) K. R. Shah, "Private Costs of Elementary Education", pp. 57–74; (3) K. R. Shah, "Expenditure on Professional School Education in India, 1950–51 to 1960–61",

pp. 75-91; (4) R. Datt, "Unit Costs of Education—A Case Study of Haryana
Colleges", pp. 92-113; (5) A. R. Kamant, "Efficiency of Education",
pp. 123-30; (6) D. Hajela, B. D. Tikkiwal, "Wastage in Education and Measures
to Prevent It", pp. 146-163; (7) Q. V. Khan, "Efficiency Coefficients for
School Stage Education", pp. 164-72; (8) R. D. Srivastava, "Cost Reduction
in Primary School Buildings", pp. 173-196; (9) P. R. Panchamu Khi, "Economic
Analysis and Planning of Education Industry", pp. 215-43; (10) M. S. Ramanujam, "Planning Models for Optimum Allocation of Resources in Education",
pp. 244-59; (11) I. Z. Husain, "Returns Approach to Educational Planning",
pp. 280-93; (12) V. R. and P. R. Panchamukhi, "Socio-Economic Variables and
Urban Incomes", pp. 306-36; (13) D. P. Chaudhri, "Education of Farmers and
Productivity", pp. 337-48; (14) B. Ramamoorthy, M. S. Prakasa Rao, "Terminali-
zation Approach to Pre-University Education", pp. 356-74; (15) R. C. Sharma,
"Benefit-Cost Analysis of Educational Projects: A Review of Researches",
pp. 393-415.

1971

1559 Agricultural Economics Research Centre, University of Delhi, *Primary Education in Rural India. Participation and Wastage.* Bombay: Tata McGraw-Hill
Publishing Co., 1971. Pp. 86.

  A serious attempt to statistically distinguish the in-school and out-of-
school factors producing wastage in Indian rural elementary schools.

1972

1560 H. W. R. HAWES, *Planning the Primary School Curriculum in Developing Countries.*
Fundamentals of Educational Planning 17. Paris: UNESCO-IIEP, 1972. Pp. 50.

  A minor masterpiece. After explaining why curriculum reform usually fails
(in Africa), the author describes the process of constructing a new curriculum.

(c) TECHNICAL AND VOCATIONAL EDUCATION

  The controversy between the proponents of technical education and general education was fought out a long time ago in the developed countries. Strangely enough,
the underdeveloped countries have shown little interest in resurrecting this controversy and until recently appeared to be content with a strong academic bias in
the curriculum. As the International Labour Office[1564], and UNESCO[1565] will show,
relatively few resources are devoted in most underdeveloped countries to technical
and vocational schools, and certainly the syllabi of Asian and African primary and
secondary schools are singularly lacking in vocational emphasis. The reason may
be, as Staley[1582] argues, that there is much confusion as to what is meant by
"vocational education". As the introduction to the previous section indicated, a
number of authors have seized upon the neglect of agricultural science as the most
prominent example of the excessively general education now provided for students
in Asian, African, and Latin American schools. See Zolotas[1567] and Alisbah and
Berry[1569] for further thoughts along these lines. The whole question of the role of
education in rural development is thoroughly canvassed once again by Sheffield[1579],
IIEP[1580], Griffiths[1581], and Foster and Sheffield[1507].

1922

1561   T. J. JONES, ed., *Education in Africa: A Study of West, South, and Equatorial
       Africa, by the African Education Commission, Under Auspices of the Phelps-
       Stokes Fund.* New York: Phelps-Stokes Fund, 1922, pp. 16-38, 57-80.

       The first comprehensive investigation of Africa's educational problems,
       emphasising the need for agricultural education of the sort offered by Negro
       schools in the American South. For an appreciation of the historical impact
       of this Report, see J. J. Shields, Jr., *The Reports of the Phelps-Stokes
       Fund on Education in Africa and the Formation of a Theory of Community Develop-
       ment by the British* (Phelps-Stokes Fund Occasional Papers, No. 4. N.Y.:
       PSF, 1961. Pp. 10).

1925

1562   T. J. JONES, ed., *Education in East Africa: A Study of East, Central and
       South Africa by the Second African Education Commission Under Auspices of the
       Phelps-Stokes Fund.* New York: Phelps-Stokes Fund, 1925, pp. 46-76, 335,402.

       A concern for rural education marks the second Phelps-Stokes Report as it
       did the first. Parts of this book and of the previous volume are conveniently
       reprinted in *Phelps-Stokes Reports on Education in Africa,* ed., L. J. Lewis
       (London: Oxford University Press, 1962. Pp. 213).

1957

1563   P. M. HAUSER, ed., *Urbanization in Asia and the Far East.* Tension and Tech-
       nology Series. Paris: UNESCO, 1957, ch. 7, "Problems of Manpower and
       Productivity".

       Some data and discussion of the role of rural education in economic develop-
       ment.

1958

1564   ILO, *African Labour Survey.* Geneva: ILO, 1958, pp. 170-217.

       A review of the problems, achievements and prospects of technical and voca-
       tional education in English and French-speaking Africa south of the Sahara.
       See also ch. 3, pp. 89-105, on "Community Development". In addition, this
       authoritative book provides a superb discussion of the problems of economic
       development in Africa.

1959

1565   UNESCO, *Secondary Technical and Vocational Education in Underdeveloped Coun-
       tries.* Educ. Stud. & Docs. Paris: UNESCO, 1959. Pp. 34.

       After a general discussion of the contribution of technical and vocational
       education to economic growth, detailed figures are presented and analysed for

Ghana, Brazil, and the Philippines. The study was prepared for UNESCO by
the Economist Intelligence Unit in London.

1566 E. A. TIRYAKIAN, "Occupational Satisfaction and Aspiration in an Underdeveloped
Country: The Philippines", *EDCC*, July, 1959, pp. 431-44.

As with similar surveys in Africa, it was found that a very small percentage of respondents wanted their children to follow agricultural pursuits.

1960

1567 X. ZOLOTAS, *Economic Development and Technical Education*. Bank of Greece,
Papers and Lectures No. 4. Athens: Bank of Greece, 1960. Pp. 60.

An opening section on the role of technical education in economic development leads up to a description of post-war shortages of skilled manpower in
Greece, concluding with a series of recommendations for expanding technical,
particularly agricultural and commercial education. A short appendix estimates the cost of the suggested reforms.

1568 A. KAHAN, "The Economics of Vocational Training in the USSR", *CER*, October,
1960, pp. 75-83.

A review of the history of Soviet efforts to tailor vocational training to
the manpower needs of the Soviet economy.

1962

1569 B. ALISBAH, A. BERRY, "Priorities in Economic Development", *JIA*, XXVI, 2,
1962, pp. 172-82.

Argues in favour of agricultural investment as complementary to industrial
investment, and stresses the advantages of technical education even if it
comes at the expense of general literacy education.

1963

1570 S. G. SHAPOVALENKO, ed., *Polytechnical Education in the USSR*. UNESCO Monographs on Education—III. Paris: UNESCO, 1963. Pp. 433.

This volume by a number of Soviet educationists reviews Marist-Leninist
ideas on polytechnical education, Soviet experience with technical and vocational education in the years 1917-58, and then goes on to explain and defend
the 1958 reform of technical education in the USSR, illustrating its implications for the teaching of a number of individual subjects. Includes the text
of the 1958 reform and a Russian bibliography.

1571 OECD, Documentation on Agriculture and Food, *Higher Education in Agriculture.
Report of the 1962 Conference*. Paris: OECD, 1963. Pp. 187.

Eleven papers on the content of higher agricultural education in both developed and developing countries and two papers on American and French experience in providing assistance for the establishment of institutions of higher agricultural education in developing countries. (See also 1575.)

1964

1572 R. DUMONT, "Le développement agricole, spécialement tropical, exige un enseignement totalement repensé", *TM*, janvier-mars, 1964, pp. 13-39, reprinted in English in *UNESCO-REED*, pp. 664-74.

A strong plea for a rurally biased curriculum associated with school farms in underdeveloped countries, in imitation of what the author takes to be the Soviet example. (See also 1576.)

1573 A. CALLAWAY, "Nigeria's Indigenous Education: the Apprentice System", *ODU*, July, 1964, pp. 1-18.

A valuable description of apprenticeship practices in Ibadan.

1965

1574 A. CALLAWAY, "From Traditional Crafts to Modern Industries", *ibid*., July, 1965, pp. 28-51.

A further description of apprenticeship training in the traditional handi-craft industry of urban Nigeria.

1575 OECD, Documentation in Food and Agriculture, *Agricultural Education at University Level*. Paris: OECD, 1965. Pp. 260.

Reports from all the member states on the general situation of higher agri-cultural education in their own countries and on their contribution to higher education in agriculture in developing countries.

1576 R. DUMONT, *Developpement agricole africain*. Paris: Presses universitaires de France, 1965. Pp. 223.

A full-scale treatment of Dumont's proposals for making schools the axis of rural development in Africa. While much of this book is full of wisdom, its general thesis smacks of what Foster has criticised under the lable of "the vocational school fallacy in economic development".

1966

1577 P. K. DAS,"Manpower Implications of Employee Development in an Undertaking", *MJ*, April-June, 1966, pp. 7-18.

An interesting analysis of the role of on-the-job training as an ingredient of work experience and effective job-performance in India.

1578 G. HUNTER, *Manpower, Employment and Education in the Rural Economy of Tanzania*.
      African Research Monographs No. 9. Paris: UNESCO, IIEP, 1966. Pp. 40.

   This study is concerned with the bulk of the Tanzanian population, who have
   received either no or at best very little formal education, and their opportunities for productive employment in the rural economy. The author proposes
   various ways of expanding informal agricultural and vocational education so
   as to maximise the economic contribution of these uneducated youngsters.
   (See also 1580.)

1967

1579 J. R. SHEFFIELD, *Education, Employment and Rural Development*. Nairobi:
      East African Publishing House, 1967. Pp. 499.

   This is the report of a conference held at Kericho, Kenya, in 1966 to discuss rural development in the light of the Kenya Development Plan. Apart from
   a summary of the conference conclusions, the book includes twenty-four papers,
   covering topics such as employment policy, agricultural development, educational planning and finance, education in rural areas, and the problem of
   unemployment of secondary school leavers. While primarily about problems in
   Kenya, several of the papers draw on experience in other East African countries and India.

1968

1580 UNESCO-IIEP, *Manpower Aspects of Educational Planning*. *Problems for the
      Future*. Paris: UNESCO-IIEP, 1968. Pp. 264.

   This is an important book, not so much for the papers it contains as for
   the "colloquy" it provides—a verbatim report of the discussion among the
   participants at the symposium. It deals with three much neglected aspects of
   manpower planning: (1) employment opportunities for the educated; (2) the
   role of education in agricultural development; and (3) the implementation of
   manpower plans. The collection opens with an interesting "Highlights of the
   Symposium", pp. 15-54, by G. Skorov, which plants enough questions to keep
   ten symposia busy. F. Harbison contributes "A Systems Analysis Approach to
   Human-Resource Development Planning", pp. 57-78, which attempts to go beyond
   a limited manpower-requirements approach and illustrates the argument with
   reference to Nigeria. G. Skorov, "The Absorptive Capacity of the Economy",
   pp. 107-12, and G. Hunter, "Manpower and Educational Needs in the Tradiational
   Sector, with Special Reference to East Africa", pp. 161-80, write on Tanzanian problems. V. K. R. V. Rao, "Educational Output in Relation to Employment
   Opportunities, with Special Reference to India", pp. 113-23, and A. Callaway,
   "Unemployment Among School Leavers in an African City", pp. 124-39, describe
   the problem of educated unemployment in India and Nigeria. R. Dumont restates
   his views on "African Agriculture and its Educational Requirements",
   pp. 181-94. R. L. Thomas, "Implementing a Manpower Programme in a Developing
   Country", pp. 211-36, discusses his work on manpower forecasting in Tanzania
   and, finally, R. Jolly analyses "Employment, Wage Levels, and Incentives" in
   Africa, pp. 237-48.

1581   V. L. GRIFFITHS, *The Problems of Rural Education*. Fundamentals of Educationa
       Planning 7. Paris: UNESCO-IIEP, 1968. Pp. 38.

       The thesis of this pamphlet is, to put it baedly, "that in backward rural
       areas the schools cannot be made a main instrument of progress", p. 11. The
       author concludes with a sketch of a workable plan for improving primary edu-
       cation in rural areas.

1970

1582   E. STALEY, *Planning Occupational Education and Training for Development*.
       New Delhi: Orient Longmans, 1970. Pp. 188.

       This popular book on vocational and technical education in developing coun-
       tries marks a healthy antidote to dominant trends in this brand of literature.
       After a preliminary bow to quantitative manpower forecasting, the author gets
       down to cases in ch. 3 on "Curriculum Design" and ch. 4 on "Institutional
       Choices", advocating comprehensive secondary education and in-service train-
       ing rather than expansion of strictly vocational schools. Unfortunately,
       much of the evidence cited by the author refers to the US, not to developing
       countries themselves.

1583   M. ALEXANDER-FRUTSCHI, *Issues in Occupational Education and Training.
       Account of an International Workshop at Stanford University*. New Delhi:
       Orient Longmans, 1970. Pp. 301.

       A readable account by the editor of a two-week conference, interlarded by
       occasional verbatim reporting and the reproduction of speeches from some of
       the participants. The purpose of the conference was to discuss the import
       of Staley's book on occupational education and training (see 1582).

1584   C. A. ANDERSON, "University Planning in an Underdeveloped Country: A Commen-
       tary on the University of East Africa Plan, 1967-70", *MIN*, VII, 1-2, 1970,
       pp. 36-51.

       A devastating critique of higher education planning in East Africa.

1972

1585   D. H. CLARK, "New School Leavers in Singapore", *HE*, November, 1972, pp. 449-62

       Using the results of a tracer study, the author shows that vocational secon-
       dary school graduates fared no better in Singapore labour markets than aca-
       demic secondary school graduates. The paper also calculates income/cost
       ratios for types of post-secondary schools in Singapore.

1975

1586   J. M. RITZEN, J. B. BALDERSTON, *Methodology for Planning Technical Education.
       With a Case Study of Polytechnics in Bangladesh*. New York: Praeger Publish-
       ers, 1975. Pp. 161.

An extremely interesting study of the costs and benefits of the polytechnic system in Bangladesh, including a tracer study of polytechnic graduates, emphasizing the nature of graduate unemployment and the determinants of earnings. A mathematical model of the system is developed, incorporating a manpower forecast, and the model is solved with the aid of quadratic programming.

(d) INFORMAL EDUCATION

By "informal education" we mean simply all education provided outside formal institutions and not leading in any way to a recognised qualification, or, broadly speaking, adult education, literacy programmes, agricultural extension, and community development.

The literature on community development is long on description and short on analysis and evaluation. For the descriptive side, see Thompson[1592], Dube[1594], du Sautoy[1595], Henry[1597], Batten[1598], Kimble[1509], and the International Labour Office[1564]. Neisser[1590], Belshaw[1596], Tinker[1601], Center for International Studies, MIT[1600], and Blaug[1419] attempt some analysis and the UN[1599] provides a few serious efforts to evaluate the effectiveness of community development projects in India and South-east Asia.

Johnston and Mellor[1603], UNESCO[1608], Wharton[1335], Schultz[1412] and Montgomery[1632] complete the list on agricultural extension. It seems to be particularly difficult to obtain any descriptions or statistics of agricultural extension in underdeveloped countries.

In the early post-war years, community development and adult literacy were always considered together as "mass education" or "fundamental education". Later, the two were separated and literacy work came to be somewhat neglected until it was revived by UNESCO's World Campaign for Universal Literacy. The original statement of UNESCO's campaign[1609] contained an economic section which is given more fully in Debeauvais and Lê Thành Khôi[1611]. After the criticisms of Curle[1610] and others, UNESCO abandoned the campaign and replaced it by the World Experimental Literacy Programme[1618]. UNESCO[1613,1614], the Pakistan National Study Group[1617], Jeffries[1630], Smyth[1637] and Simmons[1638] throw additional light on the nature of UNESCO's new campaign. Williams[1592] argues that literacy can be taught by radio. Bertelson[1621], Blaug[1625], and Holtmann[1633] analyse priorities in adult education and the trade-off between schooling for children and literacy for adults. Smith[1605] gives a novel reason for worrying about literacy. Anderson[1335] and Taira[1634] consider the historical record of literacy at early stages of development. Jolly[1414] supplies some fascinating evidence on Cuba. Fougeyrollas and others[1627], King[1628], Sheffield and Diejomaoh[1636] and Coombs[1639] provide some of the first hard data on total expenditures on informal education in Africa. Ahmed[1640] attempts a more general, textbook-type treatment.

For further bibliographical references on informal education in all its aspects, see UNESCO[1881-84,1887], Mayer[1888], Alexander-Frutschi[1905], Couch[1900,1909], Literacy International Committee[1935], and Nussbaum[1934].

1943

1587 UK, Colonial Office, *Mass Education in African Societies*. Advisory Committee on Education in the Colonies. London: HMSO, 1943. Pp. 63.

Coining a new term, this report was the first major study to place what UNESCO was shortly to call "fundamental education" in the foreground of educational policy in Africa.

1950

1588 G. FLORES, "A Study on Functional Literacy for Citizenship in the Philippines" *QBFE*, July, 1950, pp. 24-28.

   An attempt to discover how many years of primary education are required to provide an adult with functional literacy.

1953

1589 M. READ, "Recent Developments in Adult Education", *Symposium on Popular Education*. Organised by the Afrika-Institute-Studiecentrum. Leiden: Universitaire Pars Leiden, 1953, pp. 50-74.

   Reviews experience with adult literacy campaigns in various British territories in Africa.

1955

1590 C. S. NEISSER, "Community Development and Mass Education in British Nigeria", *EDCC*, July, 1955, pp. 352-66.

   A sociological analysis of 4 community development projects in Nigeria.

1591 N. L. WILLIAMS, "Teaching to Read by Radio", *FAE*, October, 1955, pp. 147-53.

   Description of a Malaya literacy training project, showing that it is possible to teach illiterates to read in 75 half-hour broadcasts without further teaching assistance.

1592 T. D. THOMPSON, *Domasi Community Development Scheme 1949-54*. Zomba, Nyasaland: Government Printing Office, 1955, pp. 70-80.

   An account of the so-called "Kwaca schools" which are mass education centres.

1956

1593 C. MADGE, "Education in a Peasant Society", *Yearbook of Education, 1956*, ed. J. A. Lauwerys. London: Evans Bros., 1956, pp. 545-55.

   A general discussion with illustrative material from Thailand.

1957

1594 S. C. DUBE, "Some Problems of Communication in Rural Community Development", *EDCC*, January, 1957, pp. 129-46.

   A description of an educational experiment aimed at creating a desire for change in a group of Indian villages in Uttar Pradesh. Demonstrates that the effectiveness of a dozen different methods varied widely due to the form of the media, the content of the communication, and the character of the agents

of change. See also the author's remarkable book, from the anthropological
point of view: *India's Changing Villages—Human Factors in Community Development* (New York: Cornell University Press, 1958. Pp. 230).

1958

1595 P. DU SAUTOY, *Community Development in Ghana*. London: Oxford University
Press, 1958. Pp. 209.

   A popular account of the history of community development in Ghana since
1948. The administration of mass literacy campaigns is described in great
detail.

1596 H. BELSHAW, Chairman, *Report of the Mission to Survey Community Development
in Africa*. New York: UN, 1958. Pp. 178.

   A general account of community development work in Africa based on a visit
to English and French-speaking East and West Africa. See, in particular,
ch. 4 on the relationship between "Formal Education and Community Development".

1959

1597 N. B. HENRY, ed., *Community Education. Principles and Practice from World-
Wide Experience*. The Fifty-Eighth Yearbook of the National Society for the
Study of Education, I. Chicago, Ill.: Chicago University Press, 1959.
Pp. 417.

   An anthology of essays on the nature and purpose of community development,
reports on some representative projects, and descriptions of training centres
for community development workers in different countries. See, particularly,
W. S. Gray, "World Literacy: Its Status and Problems". The book includes a
list of "Selected Readings on Community Education", pp. 405-13.

1598 T. R. BATTEN, *School and Community in the Tropics*. London: Oxford University
Press, 1959. Pp. 177.

   A popular book for teachers and extension workers mainly illustrated by
work in the Philippines.

1960

1599 UN, *Community Development and Economic Development. A Study of the Contribution of Rural Community Development Programmes to National Economic Development in Asia and the Far East*. Bangkok: UN, 1960. Pp. 113, 100.

   A statistical and descriptive record of achievements in the 1950's. Pt. IIa,
A Case Study of the Ghosi Community Development Block. Uttar Pradesh, India
(Bangkok: UN, 1960. Pp. 100), contrasts 6 villages with and 6 villages with-
out community development projects. For previous attempts to evaluate the

effectiveness of community development work in Asia, see the report by
H. Belshaw, J. B. Grant, *Report of the Mission on Community Organization
and Development in South and South-east Asia* (New York: UN, 1953. Pp. 167)
and *Report of a Community Evaluation Mission in India* (New York: UN, 1959.
Pp. 101) by M. J. Coldwell, R. Dumont, and M. Read.

1600 *Community Development and National Change. Summary of a Conference Sponsored
by the Center for International Studies, MIT.* Cambridge, Mass.: MIT, 1960.
Pp. 70.

This volume is a useful source for provocative ideas and suggestions on
community development, many of them voiced by leading American economists.

1961

1601 H. TINKER, "Community Development: A New Philosopher's Stone?", *IA*, July,
1961, pp. 309-22.

An assessment of the actual functioning of CD programmes in the Philippines,
Thailand, and Malaya. Valuable as a sceptical account which argues that
there is a sharp gap between theory and practice in each of the 3 countries.

1602 UNESCO, *Report of a Meeting on Educational Broadcasting in Tropical Africa.*
Paris: UNESCO, 1961. Pp. 12.

Some 50 delegates attended this meeting and discussed the possibilities of
making more effective use of radio for educational purposes in Africa.
Covers the present situation, prospects, and makes policy recommendations.

1603 B. F. JOHNSTON, J. W. MELLOR, "Agriculture in Economic Development", *AER*,
September, 1961, pp. 566-93.

A brilliant review of the role of agriculture in economic development with
a brief but careful discussion of the influence of extension-education programmes on agricultural productivity.

1604 J. P. LEAGANS, *India's Experience With Training in Extension Education for
Community Development.* Ford Foundation. New York: State College of
Education, 1961. Pp. 24.

A brief but comprehensive review of the work undertaken in India to train
rural development personnel.

1962

1605 R. S. SMITH, "Population and Economic Growth in Central America", *EDCC*,
January, 1962, pp. 134-50.

The author defends programmes to raise literacy rates in underdeveloped
countries by citing the need to control human fertility on the grounds that

"no large population has ever experienced a major downtrend in fertility before achieving a very substantial measure of literacy and urbanization."

1606 P. NEURATH, "Radio Farm Forums as a Tool of Cultural Change in Indian Villages", *ibid.*, April, 1962, pp. 275-83.

Reviews Indian experience with the teaching of agricultural science by radio.

1963

1607 I. DE SOLA POOL, "The Role of Communication in the Process of Modernization and Technological Change", *Industrialization and Society*, eds. B. F. Hoselitz, W. E. Moore. Paris: UNESCO, 1963, pp. 279-99.

A discussion of the use of mass media to promote attitudes favourable to social and economic development, with particular reference to societies with low literacy rates.

1608 UNESCO, *Social Research and Problems of Rural Development in South-East Asia*. Technology and Society Series. Paris: UNESCO, 1963. Pp. 268.

Eighteen papers on agricultural extension and community development work in Asia.

1609 UNESCO, *World Campaign for Universal Literacy*. Paris: UNESCO, 1963. Pp. 84. Excerpts reprinted in *UNESCO-REED*, pp. 152-56, 675-79.

A report of a proposed 10-year campaign to bring literacy to two-thirds of the 500 million illiterates in the member states of UNESCO at a total cost of about $2 b. The Report includes a new survey of illiteracy with replies from 67 countries and a fairly detailed analysis of the cost and financing of such a campaign.

1610 A. M. TANG,"Research and Education in Japanese Agricultural Development, 1880-1938", *ESQ*, February and May, 1963, pp. 27-41, 91-99.

A pioneering study on the historical effects of agricultural research and extension in Japan, using a Denison-type analysis of the unexplained "residual" in Japanese agriculture over the 60-year period.

1964

1611 A. CURLE, *World Campaign for Universal Literacy: Comment and Proposal.* Center for Studies in Education and Development, Graduate School of Education, Harvard University, Occasional Papers, No. 1. Cambridge, Mass.: CSED, 1964. Pp. 40.

An excellent critique of the current World Campaign for Universal Literacy sponsored by UNESCO. The author recommends concentrating on the literacy of the labour force, rather than of the whole population.

1612 M. DEBEAUVAIS, LÊ THÀNH KHÔI, "Les relations de l'alphabétisation et du
      développement économique", *TM*, *Études*, 1964, pp. 7-50.

      An excellent analysis of the costs and possible methods of financing a
      world literacy campaign, prepared in 1962 for UNESCO's World Campaign for
      Universal Literacy.

1613 UNESCO, "The Cost and Finance of Adult Literacy Programmes in Africa",
      *Regional Conference on the Planning and Organization of Literacy Programmes
      in Africa, Abidjan, March 1964*. Paris: UNESCO, 1964. Pp. 12, mimeographed.

      Outlines the nature of cost-benefit analysis of literacy campaigns, costs
      a campaign for Africa, and considers alternative methods of financing it.

1614 UNESCO. *Outline Handbook on the Organization and Financing of Adult Literacy
      and Adult Education Programmes*. Sirs-el-Layyan: Arab States Training Centre
      for Education for Community Development, 1964. Pp. 112.

      This work constituted the basic document for discussion at the Arab States
      Regional Conference on the Planning and Organization of Literacy Programmes,
      convened in Cairo in 1964, which adopted a resolution launching a 15-year
      literacy campaign for all Arab states.

1615 UNESCO, *Final Report*. *Regional Conference on the Planning and Organization
      of Literacy Programmes in the Arab States, Alexandria, United Arab Republic,
      October 1964*. Paris: UNESCO, 1965. Pp. 59.

      This formal document discusses the planning and financing of literacy cam-
      paigns, the content and teaching methods of literacy courses, the character
      of UNESCO's World Experimental Literacy Programme, and the cost of the new
      Arab Literacy Campaign.

1616 W. SCHRAMM, *Mass Media and National Development: The Role of Information in
      the Developing Countries*. Stanford, California: Stanford University Press,
      and Paris: UNESCO, 1964. Pp. 333.

      A study of the impact of mass communication on economic and social change,
      which includes a discussion of the use of mass media in formal education and
      adult literacy campaigns and the costs of improving methods of communication
      in developing countries.

1617 National Study Group, *Report on Adult Literacy and Adult Education in Pakistan*.
      Karachi: Ministry of Education, Pakistan, 1964. Pp. 125.

      The report of a Study Group in Pakistan on regional pilot projects designed
      to carry out the principles of UNESCO's new World Experimental Literacy Pro-
      gramme. Expressing agreement with the views of UNESCO's International Commit-
      tee of Experts, the Report attempts to spell out its implications for a coun-
      try like Pakistan. Annexes 2-5, pp. 77-119, give examples of several mock-
      projects with detailed estimates of their probable costs. See also a similar
      but less detailed Report of an Indian National Study Group, *Adult Literacy
      and Adult Education* (New Delhi: Ministry of Education, India. Pp. 37).

1618 UNESCO, General Conference, Thirteenth Session, Programme Commission, *World Literacy Programme*. Paris: UNESCO, 1964. Pp. 23 (13C/PRG/4).

This important document describes UNESCO's new intensive, selective approach to "functional literacy" campaigns, replacing the World Campaign for Universal Literacy by the Experimental World Literacy Programme.

1619 P. PHIPPS, *Reading By Adults in Uganda. A Report on a Survey of Reading Habits of Educated Adults and an Investigation of Library and Bookshop Facilities*. Kampala: East African Institute of Social Research, Makerere University College, 1964. Pp. 87, mimeographed.

This fascinating pioneer study of the reading habits of educated people in Uganda (5 or more years of formal schooling) is based on a stratified random sample of 600 adults. A convenient summary of the main findings is found on pp. 58-64, 77-79.

1965

1620 IEDES, *Le rôle de l'éducation dans le passage de l'économie de subsistance à l'économie de marché: l'Afrique tropicale d'expression française*. Paris: UNESCO, 1965. Pp. 42, mimeographed.

This study, directed by Lê Thành Khôi, forms a companion piece to 1419. After a description of the subsistence economies and educational systems of French-speaking Africa, the author demonstrates statistically that enrolment ratios are directly related to the degree of "commercialisation". He concludes, however, that education has had no significant influence on economic growth in French Africa. The last third of the monograph deals with the potential role of informal education in the transition to an exchange economy.

1621 C. G. WIDSTAND, ed., *Development and Adult Education in Africa*. Uppsala: Scandinavian Institute of African Studies, 1965. Pp. 97.

These proceedings of a seminar held in Uppsala in October, 1964, include, among others, excellent papers by P. Bertelsen, on "Problems of Priorities in Adult Education", pp. 22-39, and by A. Callaway on "Adult Education and Problems of Youth Unemployment", pp. 39-57, as well as several pieces on the role of mass media in adult education.

1622 P. G. H. HOPKINS, "The Role of Adult Education in Economic Development", *Economic Development in Africa*, ed. E. F. Jackson. Oxford: Basil Blackwell, 1965, pp. 51-71.

After ridiculing rate-of-return analysis of education and repudiating any and all economic criteria for assessing educational expenditures, the author concludes: "Even if we cannot assign 'notional monetary values', we can declare confidently that adult education pays dividends and big ones; and that it must be given high priority by any nation interested in its economic, social, and political development."

1966

1623 F. M. ROGERS, W. HERZOG, "Functional Literacy Among Colombian Peasants",
      EDCC, January, 1966, pp. 190-203.

         A study, based on 250 interviews, of the correlates of functional literacy
      among Colombian farmers. Higher positive correlations were obtained between
      functional literacy, self-defined abilities, and years of formal schooling
      received.

1624 R. BLANDY, M. NASHAT, "The Education Corps in Iran: A Survey of its Social
      and Economic Aspects", *ILR*, May, 1966, pp. 521-30.

         The authors describe the activities of the special army corps of teachers
      in Iran, created in 1963 to spread literacy in rural areas using the prin-
      ciples of the "community school", and give a favourable assessment of its
      effectiveness.

1625 M. BLAUG, "Literacy and Economic Development", *SR* , Fall, 1966, pp. 393-415.

         This paper discusses the role of time preference in allocating resources
      to adult literacy campaigns in poor countries, analyses the nature of the
      economic benefits of literacy in industry and agriculture, and concludes
      with a discussion of UNESCO's new World Experimental Literacy Programme.

1626 L. MALASSIS, *Economic Development and the Programming of Rural Education*.
      Paris: UNESCO, 1966. Pp. 59.

         A discussion of the relationship between education and agricultural develop-
      ment and the problems of planning education in rural areas. The author
      emphasises that educational strategy must be integrated with community devel-
      opment and agricultural extension programmes to be effective in predominantly
      agricultural economies.

1967

1627 P. FOUGEYROLLAS, F. SOW, F. VALLADON, *L'éducation des adultes au Sénégal*.
      Monographies africaines No. 11.   Paris: UNESCO-IIEP, 1967. Pp. 46.

         A very sketchy description of current Senegalese activities in the field of
      adult education with a brief review of the background since independence.

1628 J. KING, *Planning Non-Formal Education in Tanzania*. African Research Mono-
      graphs No. 16. Paris: UNESCO-IIEP, 1967. Pp. 40.

         A valuable description of the magnitude and character of Tanzania's efforts
      in the fields of community development, adult literacy, agricultural exten-
      sion, and in-service training, together with a discussion of the difficulties
      of integrating these services into the planning of formal education.

1629 J. J. SHIELDS, Jr., *Education in Community Development*. New York: Frederick
      A. Praeger, 1967. Pp. 127.

A pedestrian description of the educational component of community development programmes, supported by the United States Agency for International Development.

1630 C. JEFFRIES, *Illiteracy: A World Problem*. London: Pall Mall Press, 1967. Pp. 204.

A popular book which succeeds admirably in describing the recent conversion of the UNESCO Universal Literacy Programme into the UNESCO World Experimental Programme, replacing mass campaigns in "rudimentary literacy" by selective, intensive campaigns in "functional literacy". Several chapters deal with the organisation of literacy programmes and the development of follow-up reading material. The book includes a brief but excellent bibliography.

1631 H. SCHUMAN, A. INKELES, D. H. SMITH, "Some Social Psychological Effects and Noneffects of Literacy in a New Nation", *EDCC*, October, 1967.

Structured interviews with some 200 rural cultivators and some 400 urban factory workers in East Pakistan yielded some important findings on the specific effect of literacy on values and attitudes.

1632 G. MONTGOMERY, "Education and Training for Agricultural Development", *Agricultural Development and Economic Growth*, eds. H. M. Southworth, B. F. Johnson. Ithaca, N.Y.: Cornell University Press, 1967, pp. 147-79.

A general survey of the literature (with an excellent bibliography on agricultural extension) focussed on developing countries.

1970

1633 A. G. Holtmann, "Cost-Benefit Analysis in Adult Literacy Programmes", *Third Meeting of the Panel for the Evaluation of Experimental Literacy Projects, Teheran*. Paris: UNESCO, 1970. Pp. 19, mimeographed.

A good paper on cost-benefit analysis as such, but bearing only marginally on the concrete problems of applying it to adult literacy programmes.

1971

1634 K. TAIRA, "Education and Literacy in Meiji Japan: An Interpretation", *EEH*, Summer, 1971, pp. 371-94.

A fascinating attempt to estimate literacy rates in nineteenth century Japan, concluding that Meiji Japan started out in 1860 with literacy rates of 35 per cent for men and 8 per cent for women, reaching 75 and 68 per cent respectively by 1900.

1635 W. ELKAN, "Out-of-School Education and Training for Primary-School Leavers in Rural Kenya: A Proposal", *ILR*, September, 1971, pp. 205-16.

A discussion of informal education in Kenya and a proposal to introduce basic training in the use of tools in existing Youth Centres.

1972

1636 J. R. SHEFFIELD, V. P. DIEJOMAOH, *Non-Formal Education in African Development*.
New York: African-American Institute, 1972. Pp. 258.

A useful account of some 40 out-of-school projects all over Africa, with
extensive descriptions of five of them. The book also includes a useful
annotated bibliography on informal education prepared by C. Gilpin.

1637 J. RYAN, ed., *Planning Out-of-school Education for Development*. Paris:
UNESCO-IIEP, 1972. Pp. 269.

A collection of 13 papers plus 7 rapporteur's reports of a 1971 conference
on the subject of non-formal education. Three general papers by A. Callaway,
C. A. Anderson and P. H. Coombs lead off the debate, followed by 3 papers on
the role of the communications media in non-formal education, 3 papers evaluating the World Experimental Literacy Projects in Iran (with a fine paper by
J. A. Smyth) and papers on specific non-formal projects in different countries.

1638 J. L. SIMMONS, *Towards an Evaluation of Literacy and Adult Education in a
Developing Country*. Cambridge, Mass.: Harvard University, Graduate School
of Education, 1972. Pp. 172.

A path-breaking cost-benefit analysis of adult literacy courses in Tunisia,
revealing that the costs of producing a literate in this way vastly exceed
the costs per completed student in primary schools and that many of the
expected benefits of literacy courses have failed to accrue.

1974

1639 P. H. COOMBS, M. AHMED, *Attacking Rural Poverty. How Nonformal Education Can
Help*. Baltimore: John Hopkins University Press, 1974. Pp. 292.

An eminently sensible and penetrating popular book on rural development,
agricultural extension, nonformal education and training, etcetera, constructe
on the basis of 25 case studies of programmes in 15 developing countries.
See, in particular, ch. 8, "A Critique of Agricultural Education" and ch. 11,
"The Economics of Nonformal Education".

1975

1640 M. AHMED, *The Economics of Nonformal Education. Resources, Costs and Benefits*. New York: Praeger Publishers, 1975. Pp. 122.

A useful book for non-economists by the junior author of a principal source
on the subject of nonformal education (1639). The author is sceptical of
both cost-benefit and cost-effectiveness analysis, indeed of all economic
analysis, of educational problems but provides no real alternative other than
a vaguely specified systems analysis. Illustrations of some nonformal educational activities in certain developing countries are provided but what is
lacking is a single example of how a nonformal educational project might be
appraised.

4. EDUCATIONAL PLANNING

However remarkable has been the recent growth of interest in educational planning in developed countries, the whole-hearted endorsement of educational planning in all underdeveloped countries in the last 10 years is without precedent in the history of public education. Without a single exception, every ministry of education in poor countries around the world is today engaged in executing short-term educational plans and drawing up long-term ones. UNESCO[1686],[1904] and Wheeler[1906] give a quick overview of the scope and intensity of this activity. Harbison[1660],[1677], [1693], Platt[1654],[1671], Phillips[1672],[1693], Vaizey[1314],[1816], Griffiths[1674], and Blaug[15] serve as introductions to the subject. UNESCO[1511], Brolin[1735], and Cheswass[986],[1751] canvass the statistical needs for educational planning, and IIEP[1703] indicates the gap in current knowledge of key variables involved in the planning process.

An interesting new development in this field is that of regional educational planning: see UNESCO[1531],[1659],[1668], Lê Thi Nam Trân[1517], and Yudelman and Curle[872] on the Karachi Plan; UNESCO[1661],[1662],[1678] and de Coster and Georgis[1676] on the Addis Ababa Plan; and the Organisation of American States[1664], Vera[1684], Moreira[1685],[1688], and Debeauvais[886] on the Santiago Plan. Country case studies are provided in the planning volumes of the International Bank for Reconstruction and Development[1642],[1643],[1645],[1646],[1649],[1657],[1658],[1666],[1667],[1680]. In addition, there is the work of the Pakistan Planning Commission[1652], the Indian Planning Commission[1653], and Ministry of Education, India[1724]; The Presidential Commission to Survey Philippine Education[1764], Harbison and Ibrahim[1644], the UAR Ministry of Education[1669], and Hamdy[1808] on the United Arab Republic; Hunter[886],[1681],[1824], Rado[886], Symth and Bennett[886], and Williams[1706] and Smyth[1761] on East Africa and the ILO Ceylon report[1767]. The Soviet Union is a fascinating special case: see DeWitt[886],[1655],[1850], Kahan[1508], Shapovalenko[1570], Fletcher[1682], Skorov[1688],[1693], Nozhko[1686], Noah[1743], IIEP[1746], and Movsovic[1890]. Orleans[1656] and Chu-Yuan Cheng[1835] on China provide additional material on the communist approach to educational planning.

For further reading suggestions, see UNESCO[1884], Alexander-Frutschi[1905], and Wheeler[1906].

(a) GENERAL TREATMENTS

1954

1641 UNESCO, *Compulsory Education in South Asia and the Pacific.* Paris: UNESCO, 1954. Pp. 157.

A country-by-country discussion of the problems faced in introducing compulsory universal primary education. Includes a short reading list.

1955

1642 IBRD, *The Economic Development of Nigeria*. Report by the Intern. Bank for
      Reconstr. and Devlpment. Baltimore: John Hopkins Press, 1955, ch. 3,
      pp. 69-75; ch. 21, pp. 560-604.

      A plan for educational expansion related to a general plan for economic
      development in Nigeria.

1957

1643 IBRD, *The Economic Development of Jordan*. Report by the Intern. Bank for
      Reconstr. and Devlpment. Baltimore: John Hopkins Press, 1957, ch. 6,
      pp. 297-323.

      A brief description of education in Jordan, followed by a series of policy
      recommendations.

1958

1644 F. H. HARBISON, I. A. IBRAHIM, *Human Resources for Egyptian Enterprises*.
      New York: McGraw-Hill, 1958. Pp. 230.

      An attempt to outline the labour problems of industrialisation in Egypt.
      Ch. 5 contains a useful sketch of the Egyptian educational system. Ch. 6
      appraises Egypt's manpower situations.

1959

1645 IBRD, *A Public Development Programme for Thailand*. Report by the Intern.
      Bank for Reconstr. and Devlpment. Baltimore: John Hopkins Press, 1959,
      ch. 6, pp. 175-98.

      A rapid review of educational problems in Thailand and a costed development
      programme.

1646 IBRD, *The Economic Development of Malaya*. Report by the Intern. Bank for
      Reconstr. and Devlpment. Baltimore: John Hopkins Press, 1959, ch. 9,
      pp. 317-99.

      A fairly detailed description of the educational system and a development
      programme for the Federation and for Singapore, treated separately.

1960

1647 M. DEBEAUVAIS, ed., "Colloque international sur la planification de l'éduca-
      tion et ses problèmes économiques et sociaux", *TM*, janvier-juin, 1960,
      pp. 27-251.

      Reports and proceedings of a conference held in Paris in 1959, with an
      introduction and a summing-up by the editor. The papers are grouped under

3 headings: economic factors, sociological factors, and pedagogic factors.
Under the first heading, C. Bettelheim, H. L. Elvin, B. F. Hoselitz, and
J. Vaizey deal in general terms with the problems of underdeveloped countries,
while F. V. Garmonov writes on the USSR, W. Ozga on Poland, and A. M. Karden,
with J. E. Naraghi on Iran. An article by E. Löbel on "Problems of Financing
Education" is reprinted in *UNESCO–REED*, pp. 826–33.

1648 J. C. SHEARER, *High-Level Manpower in Overseas Subsidiaries. Experience in
Brazil and Mexico*. Princeton, N.J.: Industrial Relations Section, Princeton
University, 1960. Pp. 159.

Based on background interviews with 52 American corporations, this study
poses the question: do American firms adequately develop and utilise domestic high-level manpower resources in their Brazilian and Mexican subsidiaries?
The author gives a strong negative answer to this query, thereby illuminating
the influence of foreign investment on the educational systems of underdeveloped capital-importing countries.

1649 IBRD, *The Economic Development of Libya*. Report by the Intern. Bank for
Reconstr. and Devlpment. Baltimore: John Hopkins Press, 1960, ch. 13,
pp. 252–75.

An educational plan for the 1960's.

1650 T. R. BATTEN, *Problems of African Development*. London: Oxford University
Press, 3rd ed., 1960. Pp. 140, 152.

A book addressed to the layman by the ex-Vice Principal of Makerere College,
East Africa. Vol. 1 describes the African economy and its problems of development. Vol. 2 deals with social developments, including education. On a
popular level, this is one of the best introductions available to problems of
economic and educational planning in Africa.

1651 F. PARKER, *African Development and Education in Southern Rhodesia*. Kappa
Delta Phi, International Education Monographs No. 2. Columbus, Ohio: Ohio
State University Press, 1960. Pp. 164.

A popular account of the history of educational policy for Africans in
Southern Rhodesia with a final chapter on current problems and an appendix
on the present structure (1957) of African education.

1652 Pakistan Planning Commission, *The Second Five-Year Plan (1960-65)*. Karachi:
Government of Pakistan, 1960, ch. 14, pp. 337-55, ch. 16, pp. 369-80.

Summarises educational progress under the first five-year plan and indicates
the educational targets and programmes to achieve these targets of the second
five-year plan. See also *The First Five-Year Plan (1955-60)* (Karachi:
Government of Pakistan, 1957), ch. 27, pp. 539-90.

1653 India, Planning Commission. *Third Five-Year Plan: A Draft Outline*. New
Delhi: Government of India Press, 1960, pp. 98-108, 132-39.

The relevant pages give an outline of the educational provisions within the
third five-year plan and discuss the manpower requirements to be satisfied by
1965.

1961

1654   W. J. PLATT, *Toward Strategies of Education*. International Industrial
       Development Center. Stanford Research Institute. Menlo Park, Calif.: SRI,
       1961. Pp. 37.

       A general and rather unsystematic discussion of educational strategy in
       underdeveloped countries with some interesting graphic devices for illustrat-
       ing different types of policies, pp. 17-23.

1655   N. DeWITT, *Soviet Professional Manpower. Its Education, Training and Supply*.
       National Science Foundation. Washington, D.C.: Government Printing Office,
       1955. Pp. 400.

       _____, *Education and Professional Employment in the USSR*. National Science
       Foundation. Washington, D.C.: Government Printing Office, 1961. Pp. 856.

       After a preliminary study, the later book, taking into account the Educa-
       tional Reform of 1958, constitutes the most authoritative examination of
       Soviet education yet available. It includes some notable USA-USSR comparisons
       (see particularly pp. 37, 438-48, 452-56, 472-78), a mass of current and
       historical data, and a complete listing of primary and secondary sources.
       See also the author's "Soviet and American Higher Education: Magnitude,
       Resources and Costs", *OECD-EAHE*, pp. 133-52, which contains additional mater-
       ial on the real resource costs of education in the USSR. (See 886, 1740,
       1850.)

1656   L. A. ORLEANS, *Professional Manpower and Education in Communist China*.
       National Science Foundation. Washington, D.C.: Government Printing Office,
       1961. Pp. 260.

       Exemplifies the chaotic state of Chinese educational statistics. Some of
       the striking features of Chinese communist education are brought out by
       citations from official sources: the incredible expansion of both formal and
       informal education, the frightening decline in quality, and the extreme flexi-
       bility of the Chinese approach, going so far as to rely heavily on private
       finance. Chs. 1-5 deal with the educational system. Chs. 6-8 cover problems
       of professional manpower.

1657   IBRD, *The Economic Development of Venezuela*. Report by the Intern. Bank
       for Reconstr. and Devlpment. Baltimore: John Hopkins Press, 1961, ch. 14,
       pp. 320-57.

       A description of the Venezuelan educational system and a list of policy
       recommendations.

1658   IBRD, *The Economic Development of Tanganyika*. Report by the Intern. Bank for
       Reconstr. and Devlpment. Baltimore: John Hopkins Press, 1961, ch. 15,
       pp. 301-21.

       An able review of Tanganyika's educational problems and a series of pro-
       prosals for expanding education in the next decade.

1659 UNESCO, *The Needs of Asia in Primary Education. A Plan for the Provision of Compulsory Primary Education in the Region.* Educ. Stud. & Docs. No. 41. Paris: UNESCO, 1961. Pp. 60.

A collection of resolutions and recommendations adopted in connection with the Karachi Plan, including some regional statistical data.

1660 UNESCO, *Conference of African States on the Development of Education in Africa.* Final Report. Addis Ababa: UNESCO, 1961. Pp. 64.

A general review of educational problems, culminating in a series of resolutions. See, in particular, F. H. Harbison, "The Process of Educational Planning", pp. 47-54, a useful little manual of educational planning.

1661 UNESCO, *Conference of African States on the Development of Education in Africa. Outline of a Plan for African Educational Development.* Addis Ababa: UNESCO, 1961. Pp. 27.

The conference adopted a short-term plan for 1961-66, a long-term plan for 1961-80, and made various recommendations designed to achieve the proposed targets.

1662 UNESCO, *Meeting of Ministers of Education of African Countries Participating in the Implementation of the Addis Ababa Plan.* Paris: UNESCO, 1962. Pp. 223.

Contains educational data for 1950-60 for all participating countries. See also *First Session of the Conference of Ministers of Education of African Countries Participating in the Implementation of the Addis Ababa Plan. Review of Recent Trends in Expenditures for Education in Africa* (Paris: UNESCO, 1964. Pp. 47).

1663 T. W. SCHULTZ, "US Endeavors to Assist Low-Income Countries Improve Economic Capabilities of Their People", *JFE*, December, 1961, pp. 1068-77.

After some introductory remarks on human capital, the author discusses the implications for American educational assistance of underinvestment in human capital in low-income countries.

1962

1664 OAS, Inter-American Economic and Social Council, *Provisional Report of the Conference on Education and Economic and Social Development in Latin America. Santiago, Chile, March, 1962.* Washington, D.C.: ECLA, 1962. Pp. 285.

Report of a conference jointly sponsored by UNESCO, ECLA, and OAS, summarising the discussions and reviewing the conclusions and recommendations formulated by the participants, pp. 1-105. Included are two valuable annexes prepared by UNESCO and ECLA on "The Demographic, Economic, Social and Educational Situation in Latin America", pp. 155-238, and "A Basis for an Estimate of Educational Targets for Latin America and Financial Resources Needed to Meet Them", pp. 259-85.

1665 T. BALOGH, "Misconceived Educational Programmes in Africa", *UQ*, June, 1962, pp. 243-49.

The author sketches the outlines of a rurally biased educational system for
Africa. See also the same writer: "The Problem of Education in Africa",
TCR, Fall, 1962, pp. 526-52.

1666   IBRD, *The Economic Development of Uganda*. Report by the Intern. Bank for
       Reconstr. and Devlpment. Baltimore: John Hopkins Press, 1962, ch. 12,
       pp. 343-74.

       A review of the present situation and a list of policy recommendations.

1667   IBRD, *The Economic Development of Kenya*. Report by the Intern. Bank for
       Reconstr. and Devlpment. Baltimore: John Hopkins Press, 1962, ch. 8,
       pp. 210-57.

       As is usual with IBRD economic survey missions, the chapter on education
       is a valuable review of educational problems in relation to manpower needs.

1668   UNESCO, *Report of Meeting of Ministers of Education of Asian Member States
       Participating in the Karachi Plan. Tokyo, April 2-11, 1962*. Bangkok:
       UNESCO, 1962. Pp. 88.

       A review of the progress made in implementing the Karachi Plan of 1960 for
       attaining compulsory free primary education by 1980 in the 17 Asian member
       states. UNESCO contributed a survey of "The Economic Implications of the
       Plan of Educational Development in Asia", pp. 59-69, reprinted in *UNESCO-REED*,
       pp. 148-50, 784-85, 917-24. UNECAFE contributed a brief treatment of "Some
       Considerations on the Relationship of Educational Planning to Economic and
       Social Development in the ECAFE Region", pp. 71-76.

1669   UAR, Ministry of Education, *Educational Planning in the United Arab Republic*.
       Cairo: Ministry of Education, 1962. Pp. 24.

       A description of educational planning efforts in the UAR under the five-
       year educational plan, 1960-65.

1670   J. TINBERGEN, H. C. BOS, "The Global Demand for Higher and Secondary Educa-
       tion in the Underdeveloped Countries in the Next Decade", *OECD-EGIE, III*,
       pp. 71-81.

       Owing to lack of knowledge of manpower-output ratios in underdeveloped coun-
       tries, this projection for 1970 is based on desirable increases in income per
       head and the expansion of education required to meet these desirable targets.
       The interesting discussion that followed this and other papers concludes with
       "ten commandments of educational assistance", pp. 96-97.

1671   W. J. PLATT, *Conflicts in Educational Planning*. Menlo Park, Calif.: Stan-
       ford Research Institute, 1962. Pp. 24.

       A discursive discussion of the conflicting goals of educational plans in
       underdeveloped countries.

1672 H. M. PHILLIPS, "Economic and Social Aspects of the Planning of Education", *ISSJ*, XIV, 4, 1962, pp. 706-19, reprinted in *UNESCO-REED*, pp. 926-35.

A general but thorough discussion geared to underdeveloped countries.

1673 H. MYINT, "The Universities of Southeast Asia and Economic Development", *PA*, Summer, 1962, pp. 116-28.

An illuminating analysis of the problems of higher education throughout South-east Asia in relation to opportunities in the labour market for both secondary school and university graduates.

1674 V. L. GRIFFITHS, *Educational Planning*. The New African Library. London: Oxford University Press, 1962. Pp. 118.

An excellent popular introduction for "the many people in all kinds of positions who want to have some say in national educational policy"; it assumes no prior knowledge of education or economics.

1963

1675 P. WILLIAMS, *Educational Assistance. A Factual Survey of the Government and Private Contribution to Overseas Development Through Education and Training*. London: Overseas Development Institute, 1963. Pp. 125.

Pt. III of a five-part survey of British aid to developing countries. Includes a long chapter on overseas students in Britain. The author concludes with some personal reflections on the quality of Britain's educational aid.

1676 S. De COSTER, P. GEORIS, *Ascension sociale et enseignement dans les états et dans les territoires de l'Afrique moyenne*. Brussels: Cemubac, 1963. Pp. 180.

A critique of the Addis Ababa Plan from the point of view of the effect of education on social mobility, and via mobility on economic change. The book deals at some length with Ghana and Chad as special cases of the general argument. A brief bibliography is attached.

1677 I. LUBLIN, C. DOLLARD, eds., *Human Resources. Training of Scientific and Technical Personnel. Science, and Technology, and Development*. XII. United States Papers Prepared for the United Nations Conference on the Application of Science and Technology for the Benefit of the Less Developed Areas. Washington, D.C.: US Government Printing Office, 1963. Pp. 204.

Twenty-one short papers by various American experts such as F. H. Harbison on "High-Level Manpower Development and Economic Growth"; P. M. Hauser on "Population and Labour Force Resources as Factors in Economic Development"; S. L. Wolfbein on "Manpower Projections and Techniques", mostly in the United States; J. I. Saks, E. C. McVoy, on "Techniques of Manpower Assessment" with reference to Turkey; and C. H. Ewing on "Skilled Manpower Training to Support Industrial Growth in a Developing Nation", namely Thailand. The last 10 papers are devoted to the proper content of science and mathematics teaching in primary, secondary, and tertiary education in underdeveloped countries.

1678   UNESCO, *The Development of Higher Education in Africa*. Report of the Confer-
       ence on the Development of Higher Education in Africa, Tananarive, 3-12
       September, 1962. Paris: UNESCO, 1963. Pp. 339.

       The conference, a follow-up of the Addis Ababa meeting of 1961, considered
       the special problems involved in planning the expansion of all types of post-
       secondary education in Africa in the next 2 decades. This volume includes
       the Report of the Conference, pp. 17-83, and several Background Papers:
       "The Staffing of Higher Education in Africa", by Sir A. Carr-Saunders *et al.*,
       pp. 91-155 (also 1810); "The Financing of Higher Education in Africa", by
       J. Tinbergen *et al.*; "Inter-African Co-operation", by R. L. Weeks, pp. 213-23;
       as well as useful statistics on higher education in Africa, pp. 223-73, and
       a complete list of African institutions of higher education, pp. 273-309.

1679   M. DEBEAUVAIS, "The Balance Between Different Levels of Education", *IEA-CEE*,
       pp. 523-47.

       An important contribution to a planning model of educational pyramids,
       chiefly with reference to underdeveloped countries.

1680   IBRD, *The Economic Development of Spain*. Report by the Intern. Bank for
       Reconstr. and Devlpment. Baltimore: John Hopkins Press, 1963, ch. 18,
       pp. 389-99.

       The first IBRD mission report on a European country. Reviews the measures
       for educational expansion proposed by the OECD Mediterranean Regional Project.

1681   G. HUNTER, *Education For a Developing Region. A Study in East Africa*.
       London: Allen & Unwin, 1963. Pp. 119.

       A brilliant informed contribution to educational planning in Africa.
       Ostensibly designed to forecast the supply of overseas students in the coming
       years, it reviews the facts and sketches in the likely expansion of education
       in East Africa in the next 10 years.

1682   B. A. FLETCHER, "The Planning of Education", *Researches and Studies*, Univer-
       sity of Leeds Institute of Education, April, 1963, pp. 9-52.

       A useful review of educational planning experiences in the USSR and other
       Eastern European countries, France, the UK (pre-Robbins,) Sweden, Holland,
       and Africa.

1683   O. R. PACHECO, *Some Aspects of Educational Planning in Puerto Rico*. Hato Rey:
       Department of Education, Commonwealth of Puerto Rico, 1963. Pp. 55.

       A general survey of Puerto Rican education focused on the basic problems
       and issues involved in planning educational expansion in the coming years.
       It includes a discussion of changes in occupational structure, pp. 24-26,
       a calculation of the rate of return on investment in extra education—about
       75 per cent, pp. 27-29, and a review of Puerto Rican manpower studies,
       pp. 31-35.

1684 O. VERA, "The Educational Situation and Requirements in Latin America",
Social Aspects of Economic Development in Latin America, eds. E. de Vries,
J. M. Echavarria. Paris: UNESCO, 1963, I, pp. 279-307.

An able summary of the educational situation and the outstanding educational
problems of Latin America with illustrative data.

1685 J. R. MOREIRA, "Education and Development in Latin America", *ibid.*, pp. 308-44.

This article concentrates on the differences in educational provision within Latin America and suggests some explanations.

1686 UNESCO, *Elements of Educational Planning.* Educ. Stud. & Docs., No. 45,
Paris: UNESCO, 1963. Pp. 42.

A quick review of principles, methods and techniques of educational planning with extracts from some current plans in Asia, Africa, and Latin America.
(See also 1660, 1664, 1668.)

1964

1687 Afro-Anglo-American Program in Teacher Education. *Conference on the African
University and National Educational Development.* Lake Mohouk, N.Y.: 1964.n.p.

This publication consists of 10 brief papers and discussion reports, includ-
ing F. Harbison, "The African University and Human Resource Development: an
Economist's View" (pp. 11); R. F. Butts, "The African University and Human
Resource Development: an Educationist's View" (pp. 16); L. J. Lewis, "Educa-
tional Research and National Development", (pp. 9); and A. J. Lewis, "The
African University Co-operating with Other Agencies in the Interest of
National Educational Development" (pp. 14).

1688 IIEP, *Problems and Strategies of Educational Planning in Latin America.*
First Seminar of the International Institute of Educational Planning, Paris,
1964. Paris: IIEP, 1964. Pp. 117.

H. Correa, in a paper entitled "Have Economic Plans Paid Enough Attention
to Education in Latin America?", shows that educational bottlenecks in
Colombia and Ecuador threaten the fulfilment of current economic targets.
M. G. Louri writes on "Structure and Problems of Educational Development in
Latin America", and constructs a typological classification of Latin American
educational systems. S. F. Martin replies in the negative to the question
"Has Educational Planning Paid Enough Attention to Economic Factors?".
M. Wolfe considers "Financial Bottlenecks to Educational Development in Latin
America". L. M. Bravo discusses "The Changing Role of Education at Different
Stages of Economic Development", with particular reference to Mexico. R. F.
Lyons reviews the "Policy Implications of the OECD Mediterranean Regional
Project". Practical suggestions for "Planning Educational Innovation" are
canvassed by G. Benveniste. T. Balogh complains of the failure to create
the institutional conditions for effective agricultural education in a brief
paper on "Land-Tenure, Education and Development". C. D. Ewers addresses
himself to "Project Analysis and Programming for International Financing".
And G. Benveniste follows this up in "Current Problems and Issues in External

Aid for Education". "Possible Criteria for External Aid to Education" are
weighed by L. Cerych. J. R. Moreira provides a review of current efforts in
"Educational Planning in Latin America", based on a questionnaire distributed
to the delegates at the UNESCO Santiago meeting of 1963. R. Grégoire deals
with "The Organizational Principles for Effective Educational Planning".
Lastly, G. Skorov and R. Poignant survey respectively "Administrative Aspects
of Educational Planning in the USSR" and "Educational Planning Practice in
France". (See also 1721.)

1689 R. JACOBS, "The Inter-Disciplinary Approach to Educational Planning", *CER*,
      June, 1964, pp. 17-28.

      A discussion of the interdisciplinary contributions of economists, sociolo-
      gists, anthropologists, political scientists, and educators to educational
      planning in newly developing countries.

1690 I. DEBLÉ, "Les Rendements Scolaires dans les pays d'Afrique d'expression
      francaise", *TM*, *Études*, 1964, pp. 53-105.

      A contribution to the methodology of educational planning in poor countries,
      illustrated with reference to a sample of schools in the republics of Mali
      and the Ivory Coast.

1691 P. J. FOSTER, "Status, Power, and Education in a Traditional Community",
      SR, 72, 2, 1964, pp. 158-82.

      A study of attitudes to education in Fanti village in southern Ghana,
      typical of subsistence economies with little enthusiasm for education. The
      article develops a political interpretation of the lack of interest in educa-
      tion, in the course of which the author throws doubts on various competing
      interpretations of the demand for education in Middle Africa.

1692 T. BALOGH, "The Economics of Educational Planning: Sense and Nonsense",
      CE, October, 1964, pp. 5-18.

      After reiterating the essence of his earlier piece with P. P. Streeten
      (see 165), the author offers some sound guide lines to educational planning
      in underdeveloped countries. (See also 1711, 1734.)

1693 UNESCO, *Economic and Social Aspects of Educational Planning*. Paris: UNESCO,
      1964. Pp. 264.

      This handbook opens with an excellent review by H. M. Phillips of the basic
      features of educational planning and the 5 or 6 different approaches to it
      that are current in the literature, pp. 15-57. This is followed by a brief
      paper on "Human Resource Development and National Planning" by F. H. Harbison,
      which touches skilfully on the conflict between the economic and the humanis-
      tic attitude to educational planning, pp. 59-68. Another essay by Harbison
      deals with procedures for estimating future manpower requirements, pp. 111-30,
      duplicating ch. 9 of 1352. R. Diez-Hochleitner writes on educational planning
      in general, including the organisational, administrative, and financing
      aspects, pp. 85-98. A. Sauvy provides a brief analysis of "Social Factors in
      Educational Plans", particularly the effect of education on social stratifi-

cation, pp. 99-110. G. Skorov discusses the "Manpower Approach to Educational
Planning: Methods Used in the Centrally Planned Economies", illustrating the
techniques employed in the USSR, pp. 131-46. "Statistical Analysis and
Quantification in Educational Planning" by E. S. Solomon describes methods of
quantifying and costing educational plans, with examples from African and
Latin American experience, pp. 147-64. K. Brolin shows what are the "Statistics Needed for Educational Planning", filling a long-neglected gap in the
literature, pp. 223-42. A long paper by J. Tinbergen develops the manpower
approach he has outlined in other works with particular attention to the question of plan revisions after observation of actual developments; an appendix
contains some practical rule-of-thumb methods for planners, pp. 165-222.
Similar practical considerations motivate the essay by C. D. Ewers on "Project Analysis and Programming for International Financing", pp. 243-54.
Lastly, there is a long "Selected Bibliography", particularly useful for its
coverage of Soviet literature, pp. 255-64.

1694 Symposium on Education and Development, *CER*, June, 1964, pp. 5-40.

The symposium consists of the following five papers: (1) F. H. Harbison,
C. A. Myers, "Education and Employment in the Newly Developing Economies",
pp. 5-10; (2) H. Correa, "Quality of Education and Socio-economic Development", pp. 11-16; (3) R. Jacobs, "The Interdisciplinary Approach to Educational Planning", pp. 17-27; (4) R. Heifetz, "Manpower Planning: A Case
Study from Puerto Rico", pp. 28-36, reprinted from *ILR* (1116); and (5) H. H.
Smythe, N. Sasidhorn, "Educational Planning in Thailand", pp. 37-40.

1695 G. M. MEIER, ed., *Leading Issues in Development Economics*. New York: Oxford
University Press, 1964, pp. 266-85.

These pages reprint 1404 and 1798, and a brief note by H. Myint on "Investment in Social Infrastructure", together with some introductory remarks by
the editor and a bibliography.

1965

1696 H. MYINT, "Education and Economic Development", *SES*, March, 1965, pp. 8-21.

An incisive essay on educational strategies in underdeveloped countries.

1697 J. P. NAIK, *Educational Planning in India*. Bombay: Allied Publishers,
1965. Pp. 197.

Eight somewhat repetitious essays on various aspects of Indian educational
planning. They are addressed to the general reader but can be recommended
even to specialists for their many shrewd comments.

1698 P. H. COOMBS, K. W. BIGELOW, *Education and Foreign Aid*. Cambridge, Mass.:
Harvard University Press, 1965. Pp. 74.

This book comprises two papers: one by P. H. Coombs on "Ways to Improve
United States Foreign Educational Aid", pp. 3-40, a useful discussion of the
strengths and weaknesses of America's bilateral educational aid, and another

by K. W. Bigelow on "Problems and Prospects of Education in Africa",
pp. 43-74, making many of the same points as does Coombs in the context of
African education.

1699 L. CERYCH, "Vers une stratégie de l'aide extérieure à l'éducation", *IRE*, XI,
      1, 1965, pp. 34-49.

      Suggests some quantitative and qualitative criteria that ought to govern
      external aid to education in developing countries. (See also 1707.)

1700 U. K. HICKS, "The Economics of Educational Expansion in Low-Income Countries"
      TBR, March, 1965, pp. 3-30.

      A general article on the problem of an appropriate educational pyramid in
      developing countries, with particular reference to West Africa and South-east
      Asia.

1701 E. R. RADO, R. JOLLY, "The Demand for Manpower: An East African Case Study",
      JDS, April, 1965, pp. 226-51. Partly reprinted in *P-EED*, 2, pp. 76-97.

      In this important contribution, the authors marshal data to cast doubt on
      Harbison's rule of thumb about the growth of educated manpower in developing
      countries and to confirm an equation laid down by Tinbergen (see 500). The
      equation is fitted to East African data and the authors spell out the man-
      power implications for Uganda.

1702 F. V. BENNETT, S. A. HALL, U. S. LUTWAMA, E. R. RADO, "Medical Manpower in
      East Africa: Prospects and Problems", *EAMJ*, April, 1965, pp. 149-62.

      An excellent example of manpower forecasting in the field of health services
      using the method of international comparisons.

1703 IIEP, *Educational Planning: an Inventory of Major Research Needs*. Paris:
      IIEP, 1965. Pp. 53.

      This somewhat bizarre document presents an agenda of research topics deserv-
      ing of investigation, under such headings as "Educational Costs and Effi-
      ciency", "Financing Education", "Teachers", "Manpower Aspects", "The Planning
      Process", and "International Aspects of Educational Planning". Despite the
      title, the discussion of needed research is more or less confined to the
      underdeveloped countries.

1704 M. S. HUQ, *Education and Development Strategy in South and Southeast Asia*.
      Honolulu: East-West Center Press, 1965. Pp. 286.

      The focus of this study is four countries, India, Pakistan, Indonesia, and
      the Philippines, but material on the USA, Japan, and the USSR is also includ-
      ed. The author attempts both to describe educational planning problems in
      each of the four countries and to convey recent findings in the economics,
      sociology, and psychology of education. The result is somewhat confusing.
      Still, much of the material presented in this book is not easily available
      elsewhere.

1966

1705 Overseas Development Institute, *Aid to Education: An Anglo-American Appraisal.*
Report of a Ditchley Foundation Conference. London: ODI, 1966. Pp. 52.

   The report of the conference, prepared by P. Williams, reviews British and
American aid policies and sketches a programme for Anglo-American co-operation in educational aid to developing countries.

1706 P. WILLIAMS, *Aid in Uganda—Education.* London: Overseas Development Institute, 1966. Pp. 152.

   An excellent survey of the leading issues in Ugandan educational development, emphasising the problems of cost and finance, and a careful review of
past patterns of educational aid and the potential scope of future assistance.

1707 L. CERYCH, *Problems of Aid to Education in Developing Countries.* New York:
Frederick A. Praeger, 1966. Pp. 213.

   A thorough policy-oriented discussion of external aid to education, reviewing the estimates of the UNESCO regional plans, followed by a detailed analysis of the role of external aid at different levels of the educational system,
concluding with suggestions for a rational aid policy.

1708 R. L. MEIER, *Development Planning.* London: McGraw-Hill, 1966. Pp. 420.

   This textbook on the practical problems of development planning in poor
countries breaks new grounds in devoting about a quarter of the total coverage to educational planning.

1709 W. K. RICHMOND, *Educational Planning: Old and New Perspective.* London:
Michael Joseph, 1966. Pp. 256.

   The book is chiefly concerned with contrasting methods of educational planning in Hungary and Czechoslovakia with the absence of planning, or what the
author describes as a "Micawberish weakness for muddling through", in England.
There is, however, a brief section on measuring the economic returns to education, which gives a very unsatisfactory picture of the state of the subject.
The author declares that "to say that the precise nature of the relationship
between expenditure and returns in education is as yet dimly understood is
a prize understatement," without, however, citing a single study of this
relationship.

1710 J. R. CARTER, *The Legal Framework of Educational Planning and Administration
in East Africa.* African Research Monographs No. 7. Paris: UNESCO-IIEP,
1966. Pp. 32.

   This brief monograph throws light on a dark corner of educational planning:
the legal and administrative framework for implementing educational plans
with particular reference to the delicate balance between central and local,
public and private decision-making.

1711 T. BALOGH, "Stagnation Through Education", *The Economics of Poverty*. London:
      Weidenfeld & Nicholson, 1966, pp. 101-7.

      An all-out attack on the human investment revolution in economic thought
      and on "the fashionable conventional wisdom in the field of educational plan-
      ning and policy in poor countries". Much of it reproduces 1692.

1712 *Education and the South African Economy*. The Second Report of the 1961
      Education Panel. Johannesburg: Witwatersrand University Press, 1966.
      Pp. 152.

      An argument for rapid expansion of secondary and higher education in South
      Africa, particularly for the non-white population, in order to maintain a
      5 per cent rate of economic growth. The argument is chiefly based on inter-
      national comparisons of occupational and educational structure, and on an
      analysis of racial differences in educational attainments in South Africa.

1713 W. Y. ELLIOT, ed., *Education and Training in the Developing Countries: The
      Role of U.S. Foreign Aid*. New York: F. A. Praeger, 1966. Pp. 399.

      A collection of thirty papers describing and assessing American contribu-
      tions to educational programmes in Africa, Asia, and Latin America. There is
      some examination of general problems of educational planning in underdeveloped
      countries, and of the roles of the US government, universities, and private
      foundations, in providing financial and technical assistance, as well as dis-
      cussion of specific subjects such as the Ashby Report in Nigeria, pp. 108-32,
      and training needs in India, pp. 231-41.

1714 B. A. LIU, *Estimating Future School Enrolment in Developing Countries. A
      Manual of Methodology*. Statistical Reports and Studies. Paris: UNESCO,
      1966. Pp. 156.

      Apart from a discussion of the kinds of methods generally employed in most
      countries, this monograph includes three case studies of enrolment projection
      in Colombia, Philippines, and the Sudan and illustrative examples of actual
      projections in New Zealand, France, and the United States.

1715 E. R. RADO, "Manpower, Education, and Economic Growth", *JMAS*, IV, 1, 1966,
      pp. 83-94.

      An expert discussion of current thinking about educational planning in low-
      income countries in the guise of a review of 1352 and 1824.

1716 *UN Economic Survey of Asia and the Far East 1965*. Hongkong: UN Publications,
      1966, P. I, pp. 7-154, particularly, chs. 1, 3, 4, pp. 7-27, 67-154; also
      issued as *Economic Bulletin for Asia and the Far East*, XIV, 4, March, 1966.
      Bangkok: UN Publications, 1966, pp. 7-154.

      After a brief but interesting review of recent work in the economics of
      education, ch. 2 of the Survey consists of a bird's-eye view of education and
      training in Asian countries around 1963, leaning heavily on the *Asian Model*
      (1786). Ch. 4 contains a case study of a rural works programme in East Paki-
      stan, a remarkably succinct description of the growth of Japanese education
      in the early stages of its industrialisation, and a review of manpower fore-
      casts in Taiwan, India, Malaysia, and Pakistan.

1717 G. H. LALVANI, "Ingredients of Manpower Planning", *MJ*, April-June, 1966,
pp. 19-46.

A general description of an "active manpower policy" in a typical developing country.

1718 B. O. UKEJE, *Education for Social Reconstruction*. Lagos: Macmillan (Nigeria),
1966. Pp. 184.

A study of the Nigerian education system, with an analysis of the role of
education in promoting social, political, and economic development. The
author makes a number of recommendations about the expansion of education to
meet manpower needs, the balance between different levels of education and
the content of the curriculum in Nigeria. The book includes a bibliography.

1719 A. CURLE, *Planning for Education in Pakistan. A Personal Case Study*.
London: Tavistock Publications, 1966. Pp. 208.

A personal account of the author's experiences as an educational adviser
to the Government of Pakistan. It includes material on Pakistan's educational
progress and a fascinating description of how the chapter on education in
Guidelines for the Third Five-Year Plan came to be written. (See also 1744.)

1720 A. MADDISON, *Foreign Skills and Technical Assistance in Economic Development*.
Development Centre Studies. Paris: OECD, 1966. Pp. 104.

This pamphlet gathers some data on the flow of technical assistance to the
developing countries, on the basis of which the author makes a number of concrete recommendations to both the recipients and the donors of aid to maximise the effectiveness of technical assistance. The work includes a useful
bibliography.

1721 R. F. LYONS, ed., *Problems and Strategies of Educational Planning. Lessons
from Latin America*. Paris: IIEP, 1966. Pp. 111.

This volume includes thirteen papers, including P. H. Coombs, "Some Reflec-
tions on Educational Planning in Latin America", pp. 3-13; J. A. Mayobre,
"The Economic Background to Educational Planning in Latin America", pp. 13-19;
M. Wolfe, "Social and Political Problems of Educational Planning in Latin
America", pp. 19-28; S. Lourné, "Education for Today or Yesterday?", pp. 28-41;
R. Diez-Hochleitner, "A Regional Overview", pp. 45-50; M. H. Carrere, "Some
Aspects of Educational Planning in Latin America", pp. 53-57; R. Grégoire,
"Conditions for Effective Educational Planning", pp. 57-63; T. Balogh, "Land
Tenure, Education and Development in Latin America", pp. 67-73; M. Wolfe,
"Some Notes on Rural Educational Policies", pp. 73-76; A. Chaparro, "Education
and Training for Agricultural Development", pp. 76-82; C. T. Bernheim,
"Regional Co-operation at University Level", pp. 82-88; R. F. Lyons, "The
Role of Cost Analysis in Educational Planning", pp. 88-91; and, lastly,
G. Benveniste, "Highlights of the Seminar", pp. 95-111 (see also 1688).

1722 T. D. WILLIAMS, "Educational Development in Ghana and Guatemala: Some Problems in Estimating 'Levels of Educational Growth'", *CER*, October, 1966,
pp. 462-69.

Drawing on material from Ghana and Guatemala, this article suggests that
the ranking of countries adopted by Harbison and Myers into four levels of
development may depend very heavily on the time the data is collected and may
therefore give misleading information, particularly since their index is used
for purposes of long-range planning.

1723   W. A. LEWIS, *Development Planning. The Essentials of Economic Policy.*
London: George Allen & Unwin, 1966.

A guide to the techniques of development planning. Some of the author's
well-known papers on educational planning (see 1350, 1403) are skilfully
woven into the text: see, particularly, pp. 104-10, 222-34.

1724   Ministry of Education, India, *Report of the Education Commission 1964-66.
Education and National Development.* Delhi: Ministry of Education, 1966.
Pp. 692.

This massive report culminates in a series of recommendations, such as
reducing the rate of growth of enrolments in secondary and higher education,
vocationalising secondary education, introducing manual work and production
experience as integral parts of general education at all levels of the educational system, developing high-quality, pace-setting institutions at all
levels but particularly in higher education, imparting an agricultural bias
into primary and secondary curricula, and so on. From our point of view,
the most important chapters in the book are: ch. 5, pp. 89-107, based on
the manpower forecasts of the Planning Unit of the Indian Statistical Institute, which in turn are based on a sectoral version of the Tinbergen regression (500): ch. 6, pp. 108-43, on equalisation of educational opportunities;
ch. 14, pp. 348-68, on agricultural education; and ch. 19, pp. 464-87, on
educational finance and unit costs. See also the valuable "Minute of Supple-
mentation", by R. A. Gopalaswami, pp. 517-78, with a different set of manpower
forecasts, emphasising the problem of educated unemployment. Various supplementary volumes to the Report are promised but have not yet appeared. For a
potted version of the Report, see J. C. Aggarwal, *Major Recommendations of
the Education Commission (1964-66)* (Delhi: Arya Book Depot, 1966. Pp. 168).
(See also 1865.)

1725   V. K. R. V. RAO, *Education and Human Resource Development.* Bombay: Allied
Publishers, 1966. Pp. 220.

Six general essays addressed to the lay reader by a member of the Indian
Planning Commission responsible for educational planning.

1726   C. A. MYERS, "Human Resources and World Economic Development: Frontiers for
Research and Action", *ILR*, November, 1966, pp. 435-48.

A free-wheeling commentary on current issues in human resource development.

1967

1727   A. C. MWINGIRA, S. PRATT, *The Process of Educational Planning in Tanzania.*
African Research Monographs No. 10. Paris: UNESCO-IIEP, 1967. Pp. 102

A useful description in considerable detail of the actual process of planning in Tanzania as exemplified by the new 5-year development plan for education 1964-69.

1728   L. CERYCH, *L'aide extérieure et la planification de l'éducation en Côte-d'Ivoire.* Monographies africaines No. 12. Paris: UNESCO-IIEP, 1967. Pp. 48.

A valuable estimate of the total amount and distribution of external aid for education in the Ivory Coast in recent years. Particularly interesting is the discussion in ch. 3 of the case for sending students to study abroad.

1729   L. CERYCH, *The Integration of External Assistance with Educational Planning in Nigeria.* African Research Monographs No. 14. Paris: UNESCO-IIEP, 1967. Pp. 78.

This repeats the Ivory Coast Study but traces the pattern of external aid in somewhat greater detail. See, in particular, ch. 5 on "Transfers of Foreign Models".

1730   C. E. BEEBY, *Planning and the Educational Administrator.* Paris: UNESCO-IIEP, 1967. Pp. 36.

A general essay on the working relationships between educational authorities and educational planners.

1731   F. HARBISON, *Educational Planning and Human Resource Development.* Paris: UNESCO-IIEP, 1967. Pp. 34.

This pamphlet consists of two essays: (1) "Priorities and Choices in Human Resource Development", pp. 11-22, a general discussion of the kinds of choices that face all educational planners in low-income countries; and (2) "Systems Analysis Approach to Human Resource Development Planning", pp. 25-34, a brief attempt to divorce educational planning from purely quantitative forecasts.

1732   G. W. ROBERTS, "A Note on School Enrolment in Trinidad and Tobago, 1960", *SES*, June, 1967, pp. 113-26.

A dynamic student-flow model of primary education, applied to Trinidad and Tobago.

1733   W. A. LEWIS, "Planning Public Expenditure", *National Economic Planning,* ed. M. F. Millikan. New York: National Bureau of Economic Research, 1967, pp. 201-27.

A summary of a few chapters of the author's *Development Planning* (1723), drawing on his work about educational planning in Jamaica.

1734   T. BALOGH, "The Economics of Educational Planning: Sense and Nonsense", *The Teaching of Development Economics. Its Position in the Present State of Knowledge,* eds. K. Martin, J. Knapp. London: Frank Cass, 1967, pp. 85-105.

Although the title of this article is identical to the author's 1692, the content draws on the author's other articles on educational planning, but manages to exceed all of these in vituperativeness and downright misrepresentations—a not inconsiderable feat. After demolishing the entire subject with the notable exception of the manpower-forecasting approach—the only approach to educational planning currently in use in developing countries—the author comes down in favour of "serious political-sociological study ... of traditional educational patterns" and long-term forecasting of manpower requirements.

1735 M. BLAUG, *A Cost-Benefit Approach to Educational Planning in Developing Countries*. Report No. EC-157. Washington, D.C.: IBRD, 1967. Pp. 41.

An attempt to show the relevance of rate-of-reutrn analysis to educational planning in poor countries, particularly with respect to reforms of the salary structure.

1736 J. TINBERGEN, *Development Planning*. World University Library. London: Weidenfeld & Nicholson, 1967, pp. 125-48.

A useful simplified account of the so-called Correa-Tinbergen-Bos model of education. (See 1778, 1779.)

1737 E. GINZBERG, H. A. SMITH, *Manpower Strategy for Developing Countries. Lessons from Ethiopia*. New York: Columbia University Press, 1967. Pp. 188.

An enlarged version of an AID report which specifically disavows quantitative manpower forecasting and relies instead on an analysis of the current situation, stressing the need to create new jobs and to utilise the existing stock of manpower more efficiently. The book concludes with some general recommendations to the Ethiopian government.

1738 M. ZYMELMAN, "An Analog Simulation of an Elementary School System in a Developing Country—Some Policy Implications", *CER*, June, 1967, pp. 149-70.

Describes the use of an analogue computer to solve a non-linear model of elementary education in Costa Rica. The results indicate a steady deterioration of the student-staff ratio and the article concludes with some policy recommendations to stabilise the ratio.

1739 A. C. R. WHEELER, *The Organization of Educational Planning in Nigeria*. African Research Monographs No. 13. Paris: UNESCO-IIEP, 1967. Pp. 68.

A study of educational administration in Nigeria.

1740 A. B. SHAH, ed., *Education, Scientific Policy and Developing Societies*. Bombay: Manaktalas, 1967. Pp. 506.

A collection of articles, previously published in *MIN*, mainly dealing with scientific and university policy in Africa and Asia, but also including Stretch (594) and A. King, "Higher Education, Professional Manpower and the State: Reflections on Education and Professional Employment in the U.S.S.R." (a review of 1655).

1741 Education and World Affairs, Committee on Education and Human Resource
      Development, *Nigerian Human Resource Development and Utilization*. A Final
      Report Prepared for USAID. New York: Education and World Affairs, 1967.
      Pp. 200.

      This work marks a significant break in African educational planning with
      the quantitative-manpower-forecasting approach. It appears to have been
      written by a seven-man task force under the chairmanship of F. H. Harbison.
      The Nigerian labour force is allocated to three sectors—a modern sector, an
      intermediate sector, and a subsistence sector—and the entire argument is con-
      ducted in terms of the differential demands of the three sectors for educated
      manpower. Some forecasts are made, but the recommendations are more concerned
      with ensuring the maximum response of the educational system to the demands
      of the labour market. The study includes a terse description of the employ-
      ment problems of Nigeria, the Nigerian educational system, the finance of
      Nigerian education, and an excellent bibliography of government and general
      sources.

1742 W. J. PLATT, P. H. SORENSON, *Planning for Education and Manpower in Micro-
      nesia*. Menlo Park, Calif.: Stanford Research Institute, 1967. Pp. 212.

      This is an educational plan, roughly similar in methodology to the MRP
      exercise, for the Trust Territories of the Pacific Islands.

1743 H. J. NOAH, "Economics of Education in the Soviet Union", *PC*, July-August,
      1967, pp. 42-52.

      An extremely well-informed article on the problems facing Soviet educational
      planners and a description of the growing interest in the USSR in the econo-
      mics of education.

1968

1744 A. CURLE, *Educational Planning: The Adviser's Role*. Fundamentals of Educa-
      tional Planning 8. Paris: UNESCO-IIEP, 1968. Pp. 28.

      A short version of the author's book on Pakistan (1737).

1745 R. H. P. KRAFT, ed., *Education and Economic Growth*. Tallahassee, Flo.:
      Educational Systems Development Center, Florida State University, 1968.
      Pp. 189.

      The nine papers in this volume were originally delivered at a conference
      held in 1967. They consist of: (1) R. H. P. Kraft, "Introduction: Educa-
      tion and Economic Growth", pp. 2-8; (2) H. Correa, "An Optimum Enrolment
      Policy for Developing Countries", pp. 9-19; (3) N. DeWitt, "Problems of Edu-
      cational Planning in Developing Countries", pp. 20-41; (4) R. G. Davis, "On
      the Development of Educational Planning Models at Harvard, CSED: An Alge-
      braic History of Activity in One Small Place", pp. 42-84; (5) R. W. Jastram,
      "A Systems Approach to Educational Organization", pp. 86-111; (6) R. H. P.
      Kraft, "Inter-Firm Correlations: The Contribution of Educationally Heavy
      Inputs to Increasing Profitability", pp. 112-29; (7) F. Edding, J. Naumann,
      "A Systems Look at Educational Planning", pp. 130-60; (8) I. Sobel, "A
      Strategy of Human Resource Development", pp. 161-75; and (9) J. Naumann,
      "Summary", pp. 176-87.

1746 K. NOZHKO, E. MONOSZON, J. ZHAMIN, V. SEVERTSEV, *Educational Planning in the USSR. With Observations of an IIEP Mission to the USSR Headed by R. Poignant.* Paris: UNESCO-IIEP, 1968. Pp. 295.

The Soviet work that forms the core of this study runs to 200 pages; it is the longest and, unfortunately, the dullest account of Soviet educational planning that is available in English. The observations of the IIEP Mission that follow it must be judged in political terms: there are frequent indications of an unwillingness by the Soviet authorities to co-operate wholeheartedly in getting at the facts, pp. 246, 256, 258, 284, 287, and the pages on Soviet manpower forecasting are a model of diplomatic writing, pp. 256–78. See also the calculation of the Soviet ratio of educational expenditures to national income, pp. 284–86.

1747 UNESCO, *Educational Planning. A Survey of Problems and Prospects.* Paris: UNESCO, 1968. Pp. 197.

This document, prepared for the International Conference on Educational Planning, held in Paris, August, 1968, consists in part of critical comments on educational planning over the past decade and for the rest of a discussion of the problems with which educational planning will have to deal in the next 10 years. Chs. 2, 3, 4, pp. 30–69, contain some fascinating information on the character of educational planning around the world, based on a special survey carried out for this conference.

1748 "International Development Education", *RER*, June, 1968, pp. 201-304.

A series of bibliographical essays on the literature for the 6-year period 1962–68, of which the most relevant are: (1) D. P. Sanders, P. S. Barth, "Education and Economic Development", pp. 213–30; (2) H. W. Weiler, "Education and Social Development", pp. 243–63; (4) T. N. Chirikos, A. C. R. Wheeler, "Concepts and Techniques of Educational Planning", pp. 264–76; and (5) S. Spaulding, "Research on Content, Methods, and Techniques in Education for Development", pp. 277–92.

1749 OECD, *Education, Human Resources and Development in Argentina. Methodological Problems and Statistical Data.* Paris: OECD, 1968. Pp. 293.

This is the second of the OECD volumes on Argentina (see 1857), consisting of a series of technical annexes. Among the most interesting of these are Annexes D–I, pp. 63–132, exemplifying the paediometric model adopted in the main report, Annex K, pp. 149–74, presenting a tabulation of the labour force by sector, occupation, and education, and Annex Q, pp. 269–87, on "sources-of-change analysis" of the date of Annex K.

1750 "Organization of Educational Planning in the Asian Region", *Bulletin of the UNESCO Regional Office for Education in Asia,* September, 1968, pp. 1-204, i-xxxv.

A country-by-country review of the machinery and process of educational planning in 19 Asian countries, in so far as it can be pieced together from public documents. A valuable, partly annotated bibliography of official documents is also included.

1751 J. D. CHESWASS, *Methodologies of Educational Planning for Developing Countries, I. Text; II. Tables.* Paris: UNESCO-IIEP, 1968. Pp. 106,84.

The aim of this manual is to teach educational administrators in developing countries how to make projections of student enrolments, teachers supply, and expenditures without the use of computers. Fully worked out arithmetical examples are provided drawn from a hypothetical developing country.

1752 R. G. HARPER, S. WUDHIPREECHA, *Educational Planning at the Local Level.* Education in Thailand Series 7. Bangkok: Ministry of Education, 1968. Pp. 33.

An interesting description of the implementation of educational plans at the county level based on a special survey of primary schools in twelve selected counties. The survey revealed some surprising variation between schools (see p. 33).

1969

1753 B. HIGGINS, *Economic Development. Principles, Problems and Policies.* New York: W. W. Norton & Co., 2nd ed., 1969, ch. 19, pp. 405-45.

There is a long chapter in this new edition on educational planning which comes down in favour of rate-of-return analysis and includes an ingenious diagrammatic model of the education "industry".

1754 Japanese National Commission for UNESCO, *National Statements on Educational Goals, Aims and Objectives in the Asian Countries.* Tokyo: Japanese National Commission for UNESCO, MEEAO/Final Report, Appendix 6, 1969. n.p., mimeographed.

A country-by-country listing of educational objectives as culled from official documents, supplemented by a commentary from the national authorities. Fourteen Asian countries are included. An interesting document for considering the question whether clearly stated operational aims are in fact ever laid down for any educational system. See also the *Final Report* (pp. 12) of the Meeting of Experts on Educational Goals, Aims and Objectives in Asia.

1755 T. N. CHAU, *Demographic Aspects of Educational Planning.* Fundamentals of Educational Planning 10. Paris: UNESCO-IIEP, 1969. Pp. 84.

Discusses the demographic foundation of educational plans and provides guidelines to the various techniques for analysing the structure of a population.

1756 A. CURLE, *The Professional Identity of the Educational Planner.* Fundamentals of Educational Planning 11. Paris: UNESCO-IIEP, 1969. Pp. 50.

The author argues against special programmes to train educational planners, urging instead that existing courses in educational administration should be broadened to encompass human resource development.

1757 G. Z. F. BEREDAY, *Essays on World Education: The Crisis of Supply and Demand.*
New York: Oxford University Press, 1969. Pp. 359.

A collection of rather superficial papers, prepared for the International
Conference on Education held in Williamsburg in 1967. The main paper of the
conference, *The World Education Crisis* by Coombs, appeared in 1968 (see 1557).
Among the authors of the 17 papers are such well-known names as F. Edding,
L. Cerych, F. Bowles, T. Husèn, G. Z. F. Bereday, W. Schramm, C. E. Beeby,
P. Idenburg and C. Kerr. The book closes with an inocuous set of recommenda-
tions for "'Enlarging' Education", pp. 312-59.

1758 G. C. RUSCOE, *The Conditions for Success in Educational Planning.* Fundamentals of Educational Planning 12. Paris: UNESCO-IIEP, 1969. Pp. 45.

A brief but useful discussion of the administrative context of successful
educational planning, with particular reference to Latin American conditions.

1970

1759 H. N. PANDIT, "Economic Approaches to Investment Decision-Making in Education",
IDER, January, 1970, pp. 1-54.

Another attempt to sum up where we stand. The author takes no position
and metes out justice to all.

1760 A. W. SHURCLIFF, "Manipulating Demand and Supply of High-Level Manpower",
ILR, February, 1970, pp. 133-48.

A free-wheeling essay on active manpower policies in developing countries
and the need to improve the utilization of high-level manpower by government
action.

1761 J. SMYTH, "The Political Economy of Educational Planning in Uganda", *CER*,
October, 1970, pp. 350-62.

Tracing the history of educational planning in Uganda to show how little
impact systematic planning had on actual educational decisions in Uganda
since 1940.

1762 P. DALIN, "Planning for Change in Education: Qualitative Aspects of Educational Planning", *IRE*, XVI, 4, 1970, pp. 436-49.

A broad discussion of the problem of changing educational systems with
illustrations drawn widely from a number of European countries.

1763 G. PSACHAROPOULOS, "Estimating Shadow Rates of Return to Investment in Education", *JHR*, Winter, 1970, pp. 34-50.

The author calculates shadow rates of return as solutions to the dual of a
linear programming model for the Greek economy as a whole. He finds a ranking of social rates that are inverse to the ranking of private rates, even
after incorporating alternative input vectors in the model. The article is a
summary of a thesis and is difficult to follow in this compressed version.

1764 *Education for National Development. New Patterns, New Directions.* Manila:
Presidential Commission to Survey Philippine Education, 1970. Pp. 285.

This education survey report is in some sense the first comprehensive
assessment of the educational system that has ever been carried out in the
Philippines. It marshalls a great deal of interesting data and is unique in
frankly admitting that the educational system is badly overexpanded. The
recommendations, however, apart from stressing quality rather than quantity,
tend to be somewhat *ad hoc* and untouched by a consistent underlying philosophy.

1971

1765 R. M. MORGAN, C. B. CHADWICK, eds., *Systems Analysis for Educational Change:
The Republic of Korea.* Gainesville, Florida: University of Florida Press,
1971. Pp. 200.

A comprehensive investigation of the Korean educational system, including
a manpower forecast, a new rate-of-return exercise, and suggested strategies
for introducing educational innovations.

1766 C. D. ROWLEY, *The Politics of Educational Planning in Developing Countries.*
Fundamentals of Educational Planning 15. Paris: UNESCO-IIEP, 1971. Pp. 56.

The author admits that he has only a "superficial knowledge" of "the expert
literature on educational planning" (p. 11). Unfortunately, his experiences
are also confined to few countries and to special countries at that. In consequence, this pamphlet hardly begins to do justice to its title.

1767 ILO, *Matching Employment Opportunities and Expectations. A Programme of
Action for Ceylon. Report. Technical Papers.* Geneva: ILO, 1971. Pp. 251.

This is the first pilot study in Asia under the ILO World Employment Programme, written by a team headed by D. Seers. It contains a chapter on education but, more significantly, a chapter on labour markets which is fully
integrated with the discussion of educational issues. Chapters 5-8 and 17-22
of the *Technical Papers* analyse the structure of employment and earnings in
relation to educational opportunities.

1768 OECD, *Reviews of National Policies for Education. Japan.* Paris: OECD, 1971.
Pp. 162.

Apart from the usual Examiners' Report and Questions, this volume contains
several papers, among which are "The Financing of Higher Education: A Very
Tentative Proposal" by P. Dore, pp. 115-24, and "The Social and Economic
Issues of Japanese Educational Policy" by B. Hayward, pp. 153-62.

1769 C. HOU-CHAU, *Planning Education for a Plural Society.* Fundamentals of Educational Planning 16. Paris: UNESCO-IIEP, 1971. Pp. 65.

A valuable account of educational problems in Malaysia.

1972

1770 M. CARNOY, H. THIAS, "Educational Planning with Flexible Wages: A Kenyan
      Example", *EDCC*, April, 1972, pp. 438-73.

      A dense paper, largely based on their book (see 1461) but substantially
      rewritten. It reports rates of return on educational investment in Kenya
      and then uses crude production function estimates to project future demand
      for educated labour. Wages and employment by education are then calculated
      on the basis of various assumptions about the supply of educated personnel.

1973

1771 H. M. PHILLIPS, *Planning Educational Assistance for the Second Development
      Decade*. Fundamentals of Educational Planning 18. Paris: UNESCO-IIEP, 1973.
      Pp. 75.

      A level-headed review of the problems of educational aid to developing
      countries.

1772 W. D. CARTER, *Study Abroad and Educational Development*. Fundamentals of
      Educational Planning 19. Paris: UNESCO-IIEP, 1973. Pp. 49.

      An analysis of subsidized foreign study as an integral element in a develop-
      ing country's educational plan.

1773 K. R. McKINNON, *Realistic Educational Planning*. Fundamentals of Educational
      Planning 20. Paris: UNESCO-IIEP, 1973. Pp. 45.

      A discussion of the organisational aspects of educational planning in the
      context of a case study of a plan drawn up for Papua and New Guinea.

1974

1774 G. M. COVERDALE, *Planning Education in Relation to Rural Development*. Funda-
      mentals of Educational Planning 21. Paris: UNESCO-IIEP, 1974. Pp. 37.

      A plea for a common curriculum in the primary schools of both town and
      country, reflecting in both cases the daily lives of children in content and
      points of reference.

1775 C. TIBI, *Développement économique et aspects financiers de la politique
      d'éducation en Tunisie*. Financement des systèmes éducatifs: études de cas
      nationales 2. Paris: UNESCO-IIEP, 1974. Pp. 213.

      After a description of the economy and educational system of Tunisia, the
      author proceeds to project enrolments, educational costs and educational
      expenditures up to 1980, including some loosely conceived projections of
      manpower demands. His aim is to provide a strategy of educational expansion,
      rather than a carefully designed plan.

1975

1776   G. PSACHAROPOULOS, "The Macro-Planning of Education: A Clarification of
       Issues and a Look Into the Future", *CER*, June, 1975, pp. 214-24.

       A child's guide to recent controversies in the field of educational plan-
       ning, with particular reference to developing countries, and a forecast of
       likely future developments in the planning field.

(b) MATHEMATICAL MODELS

   Little more need be said about the use of mathematical models in educational
planning beyond what was said in the earlier section A 4b above. The *fons et origo*
of educational models, the Correa-Tinbergen-Bos model[4],[1778],[1779],[1782] with popular
versions by OECD[1046] and Tinbergen[1736], is really a special case, namely, a
"balanced growth" model of the educational system. In recent years, there has in
fact been much more interest in dynamic student-flow models: examples for poor
countries are furnished by Moorthy and Thore[1777] and UNESCO[1786]. Adelman[1783],
Bowles[1787] and Versluis[1790] have applied linear programming models to educational
planning decisions in Argentina, Nigeria and Peru.
   For further references, see Johnstone[1931].

1959

1777   S. K. MOORTHY, S. A. O. THORE, "Accelerator Theory in Education", *IDR*,
       February, 1959, pp. 57-69, reprinted in *UNESCO-REED*, pp. 791-98.

       Presents a simple model showing that growth at one level of education en-
       tails accelerated growth at all higher levels, via the number of teachers
       produced by higher levels, and tests this notion with the aid of Indian data.
       In the closing section of the article, the authors attempt to integrate the
       national education budget with the national capital investment budget.

1962

1778   H. CORREA, J. TINBERGEN, "Quantitative Adaptation of Education to Accelerated
       Growth", *KYK*, XV, 4, 1962, pp. 776-85.

       Simplified version of the Correa model, solved by plugging in plausible
       values for certain coefficients. The model assumes: (1) there is a fixed
       reflationship between level II and III graduates and physical output; (2) all
       three levels of education last 6 years each; (3) all level II teachers are
       level III graduates; (4) there is full employment; (5) output grows at a
       constant exponential; (6) capital and educated labour are complementary
       factors; and (7) educated labour is perfectly substitutable between broad
       classes of occupations.

1964

1779 H. F. McCUSKER, Jr., *An Approach for Educational Planning in the Developing Countries*. Prepared for the Symposium on the Possibilities of Operations Research in Developing Countries, June, 1963. Menlo Park, Calif.: SRI, 1963. Pp. 23.

An application of the Correa-Tinbergen model to Taiwan and a comparison of its results with those obtained from manpower forecasts.

1780 J. TINBERGEN, H. C. BOS, "A Planning Model of Educational Requirements of Economic Development", *OECD-RF*, pp. 147-70, reprinted in *P-EED*, 2, pp. 125-51, and *BILD*, pp. 96-131.

An extension of the Tinbergen-Correa model involving more complicated basic equations, including additional labour-demand equations, and wastage equations. T. Balogh delivered a damning condemnation of this type of work (see 1780). A. K. Sen offered a constructive critique, pointing out the analogies in the Tinbergen-Bos model to a capital-requirements model, pp. 170-80, reprinted in *P-EED*, 2, pp. 152-67, while G. Bombach commented in general terms on the Tinbergen paper, pp. 188-98.

1781 T. BALOGH, "Education and Economic Growth. Comments on Professor Tinbergen's Planning 'Model'", *KYK*, XVII, 2, 1964, pp. 261-73; "Reply" by J. Tinbergen, *ibid.*, pp. 274-75, reprinted in *OECD-RF*, pp. 180-88, and T. Balogh, *The Economics of Poverty*. London: Weidenfeld & Nicholson, 1968, pp. 87-97.

This critique of the Correa-Tinbergen model denies the possibility of discovering any numerical relationship between education and economic growth. The reply admits Balogh's practical objections but defends the notion of stable relations between economic variables and education.

1965

1782 OECD, Education and Development, Technical Reports, *Econometric Models of Education. Some Applications*. Paris: OECD, 1965. Pp. 99.

This volume consists, first of all, of a reprint of the paper by Tinbergen and Bos: "A Planning Model For the Educational Requirements of Economic Development" (see 1779). This is followed by three detailed statistical applications of the model for Spain, Turkey, and Greece by L. J. Emmerij, J. Blum, and G. Williams respectively, concluding with a few pages of comment by Tinbergen and Bos appraising their own model in the light of these case-studies.

1966

1783 I. ADELMAN, "A Linear Programming Model of Educational Planning: A Case Study of Argentina", *The Theory and Design of Economic Development*, eds. I. Adelman, E. Thorbecke. Baltimore, Md.: The John Hopkins Press, 1966, pp. 385-412; "Comment" by S. Bowles, *ibid.*, pp. 412-17.

A lucid description of a four-period, 20-year dynamic programming model of Argentinian education, which simultaneously optimises educational investment and investment in real capital, combining elements of the manpower-require-ment and cost-benefit approaches to educational planning. The comments by Bowles draw attention to some of the weaknesses of the model.

1784 S. COHEN, *Planning Models of Educational Requirements for Economic Develop-ment As Applied to Yugoslavia.* Rotterdam: Netherlands Economic Institute, Division of Balanced International Growth, Publication No. 35/66, 1966. Pp. 36.

An application of the Correa-Tinbergen-Bos model to Yugoslavia in which a number of complications are successively added to the original model. The volume concludes with a comparison of the results to those for Spain, Turkey, and Greece.

1785 J. VERSLUIS, *Mathematical Models of Educational Planning.* Rotterdam: Netherlands Economic Institute, Division of Balanced International Growth, Publication No. 36/66, 1966. Pp. 74.

A thorough review of the current status of the Correa-Tinbergen-Bos model.

1786 UNESCO, *An Asian Model of Educational Development. Perspectives for 1965-80.* Paris: UNESCO, 1966. Pp. 126.

An educational model of Asian countries—that is, Member States participat-ing in the Karachi Plan, or, all Asian countries except Japan, mainland China, Australia, and New Zealand—which is used to project up to 1980 (1) the shape of educational pyramids, (2) the stock of teachers required, (3) the level of costs and expenditures, and (4) the output of particular types of skilled man-power. This is followed by a long discussion of Asia's educational problems in the next decade and a half. The book is also a valuable reference for country data relating to the year 1964.

1967

1787 S. BOWLES, "The Efficient Allocation of Resources in Education", *QJE*, May, 1967, pp. 189-219, reprinted in *P-EED*, 2, pp. 168-201.

A linear programming model of education in Northern Nigeria, with an objec-tive function given by the increment in discounted net lifetime earnings attributable to additional years of education, a number of obvious endogenous and exogenous constraints, and a set of instrument variables defined so as to reflect the actual policy instruments available to the government. One of the interesting results of the model is that the optimum enrolments in various schools differ considerably from Nigerian educational plans based on the man-power-requirements approach.

1969

1788 D. J. DE VORETZ, "A Dynamic Programming Model for the Philippine Educational Sector", *Philippine Population in the Seventies,* ed. M. B. Conception. Manila: Community Publishers, 1969, pp. 169-86.

This paper sets out a linear programming model for an educational system, but no attempt is made to plug in the parameter values for the Philippines.

1970

1789   I. WERDELIN, *On a Quantitative Educational Plan for Elementary Education in Iraq*. Beirut: Regional Centre for Planning and Administration in the Arab Countries, 1970. Pp. 114.

A dynamic student-flow model for Iraqi primary education which seeks to satisfy certain enrolment targets by 1980.

1974

1790   J. BÉNARD, J. VERSLUIS, *Employment Planning and Optimal Allocation of Physical and Human Resources*. Geneva: ILO, 1974. Pp. 118.

This booklet consists of two papers with more or less self-explanatory titles: (1) J. Versluis, "A Linear Programming Model for Simultaneous Economic, Manpower and Educational Planning. A Case Study for Peru"; and (2) J. Bénard, "Full Employment and the Optimal Allocation of Material and Human Resources in a Dual Developing Economy". For a non-technical description of these models, see R. Olivier, Y. Sabolo, "Simultaneous Planning of Employment, Production and Education", *ILR*, April, 1973.

(c) MANPOWER FORECASTING

Harbison and Myers[1352], Harbison[1798], Debeauvais[1817], Paukert[1818], and Jolly and Rado[1812] state the case for manpower forecasting and planning in the context of low-income countries. Hunter, Rado and Lloyd[1809] and Ginzberg[1876] provide brief introductions to the field. Instructions on how to go about forecasting manpower will be found in the methodological manuals of the Organisation of American States[1805], Agency for International Development[1807], Nozhki[1815], and Srivastava[1821]. The most popular method of projecting manpower needs in poor countries is that of following "manpower growth paths", that is, by assuming that all poor countries will sooner or later use manpower in the same way that it is now being used in rich countries. We have already seen many examples of this method; for others, see Harbison[1794,1801] and Heifetz[1800], with Hollister[1820] providing a thorough critique of the approach. Another method frequently employed is that of extrapolating manpower-output ratios, which, in some of its variants, turns into the method of estimating manpower growth paths. Fogg[1803], Bennett and others[1702], and Zschock[1863] are examples of this second method. The third method, which has not yet caught on, is econometric forecasting, that is, estimating the manpower-income function from cross-section data about various countries with the aid of multiple-regression techniques. All the work in this area stems from the pioneer efforts of Tinbergen[500,1778,1779]. Ministry of Education, India[1724], Burgess and others[1865], Hunter[1861] and the ILO Colombia Report[1873] supply examples of this method.

   Harbison and Myers[1824] is a valuable collection of country case studies of educational planning based on the manpower approach. See also OECD's Mediterranean Regional Project applied to Latin America[870,1749,1825]. Blaug[1735] and Cash[1836] provide fundamental critiques of the manpower-forecasting approach. For post-mortems of past forecasts in Africa, see Skorov[1844], Rado[1859], and particularly Jolly and Colclough[1878].

1956

1791   Planning Commission, India, *Report of the Engineering Personnel Committee.*
       New Delhi: Planning Commission, 1956. Pp. 83.

    A manpower forecast for engineers over the second Five-Year Plan period,
1956-61.

1958

1792   Ministry of Education, Japan, *Demand and Supply for University Graduates.*
       Tokyo: Mininstry of Education, 1958. Pp. 69.

    This pamphlet consists, first of all, of a historical survey of the demand
and supply of graduates by faculties since 1912, and secondly, of an analysis
of the present distribution of graduates in different industrial sectors with
a 5-year projection of the distribution to 1960. Much of the data presented
is not analysed or discussed in any way.

1960

1793   W. BRAND, *Requirements and Resources of Scientific and Technical Personnel
       in Ten Asian Countries.* UNESCO Statistical Reports and Studies. Paris:
       UNESCO, 1960. Pp. 31.

    After reviewing the methodology of manpower planning, the author describes
the methods of manpower forecasting utilised in India, Burma, the Philippines,
Thailand, China, Korea, Japan, Ceylon, Turkey, and Vietnam, and concludes
with recommendations for future research.

1794   E. ASHBY, Chairman, *Investment in Education. The Report of the Commission on
       Post-School Certificate and Higher Education in Nigeria.* Nigeria: Federal
       Ministry of Education, 1960. Pp. 140.

    F. H. Harbison contributes a survey of high-level manpower needs in Nigeria
and projects an educational plan to fulfil these needs by 1980. See also
J. N. Archer, *Educational Development in Nigeria, 1961-70. A Report on the
Phasing and Cost of Educational Development on the Basis of the Ashby Com-
mission Report on Post-School Certificate and Higher Education in Nigeria*
(Lagos: Federal Government Printer, 1961. Pp. 137).

1961

1795   B. HAYWARD, *The Future of Education in Puerto Rico—Its Planning.* Hato Rey,
       Puerto Rico: Departamento de Instrucción Pública, 1961. Pp. 45, mimeographed.

    A projection to 1975 of school enrolment and of the funds available for
education in Puerto Rico.

1796   Ministry of Labour and Employment, India, *Educational and Technical Training
       Requirements of Production Process Workers in the Cotton Textile Industry.*
       New Delhi: Ministry of Labour, 1961. Pp. 80.

An interesting attempt to define the minimum and optimum educational qualification for occupations typically filled by craftsmen and operatives in the
Indian cotton textile industry. Employers' opinions in five large enterprises
were surveyed and compared with current hiring standards. The results are
summarised on pp. 1-8.

1797 Ministry of Labour and Employment, Government of India, *Report on the Pattern
of Graduate Employment*. Fariband: Government of India Press, 1961. Pp. 95.

The 1960 all-India survey of graduate employment was intended to provide
data for the country as a whole similar to that obtained in a 1958 survey of
the employment of Delhi University graduates (Ministry of Labour and Employment, Government of India, *Employment Survey of the Alumni of Delhi University*. Delhi: Government of India Press, 1962. Pp. 198). The sample taken
included 22,500 graduates from all Indian universities except Delhi graduated
in 1954, or about a quarter of the total number of Indian graduates. Unfortunately, the low response rate to the postal questionnaire (37 per cent)
throws some doubt on the findings. See also Ministry of Labour and Employment, Government of India, *Employment of Matriculates. A Case Study* (Delhi:
Government of India, 1963. Pp. 83), a survey of employment of 1954 school
leavers in 4 districts in India with a response rate of 50 per cent.

1962

1798 F. H. HARBISON, "Human Resources, Development Planning in Modernising Economies", *ILR*, May, 1962, pp. 435-58, and *OECD-EGIE, III*, pp. 9-32, reprinted
in *WYK II*, pp. 214-47.

Makes a strong case for manpower planning in underdeveloped countries and
develops some central considerations of manpower planning strategy. Concludes
with a plea for the training of "strategists in human resource development".

1799 ILO "Manpower Planning in Eastern Europe", *ILO*, August, 1962, pp. 3-35.

A review of methods of manpower planning on the national, regional, and
sectorial levels in the Soviet Union and in the Eastern European countries,
with a final section on the optimum utilisation of highly professional manpower.

1800 R. HEIFETZ, "Manpower Planning: A Case Study from Puerto Rico", *ibid.*,
pp. 28-37.

A useful analysis of the assumptions and methods of the report by the
Puerto Rican Committee on Human Resources, *Puerto Rico's Manpower Needs and
Supply* (1957), particularly its use of the education-occupation relationship
found in the USA in 1950 to estimate the future educational needs of the
Puerto Rican labour force.

1801 F. H. HARBISON, "Human Resources and Economic Development in Nigeria",
The Nigerian Political Scene, ed. R. O. Tilman, T. Cole. Durham, N.C.: Duke
University Press, 1962, pp. 198-220.

A succinct discussion of the agenda for educational expansion in Nigeria.
This volume also contains an annotated bibliography of materials on Nigerian
education since 1957, pp. 311-15; for the earlier years, see the bibliography
in J. Coleman, *Nigeria: Background to Nationalism* (Berkeley, Calif.: California University Press, 1958).

1802 A. TAYLOR, ed., *Educational and Occupational Selection in West AFrica*.
London: Oxford University Press, 1962. Pp. 219.

There is more on educational than on occupational selection in Africa in
this volume, and 5 of the 15 articles deal in effect with American and English
experience. An occupational selection, see S. Biesheuvel, "Some Comments on
the Application of Vocational Guidance in West Africa" and "Personality Tests
for Personnel Selection and Vocational Guidance in Africa", pp. 123-27,
139-54; F. R. Wickert, "Some Implications of Decision Theory for Occupational
Selection in West Africa", pp. 127-39; E. D. Hollander, "Observations on the
Labour Market in Ghana", pp. 154-60; and A. Rodger, "Cautions for Personnel
Selectors", pp. 160-67. The volume closes with a report of the discussions
and a set of recommendations, pp. 167-208.

1963

1803 C. D. FOGG, "Manpower Planning", *Managing Economic Development in Africa*,
ed. W. A. Hausman. Cambridge, Mass., 1963, pp. 51-70.

Describes the technique of ratio analysis in forecasting the manpower
requirements of a development plan and reviews the methods used to project
the number of additional teachers needed to fulfil 1980 targets for primary
and secondary education in Eastern Nigeria.

1804 V. R. K. TILAK, "The Future Manpower Situation in India, 1961-76", *ILR*, May,
1963, pp. 435-47.

A semi-official forecast of employment in India by industry and occupation
and a translation of these forecasts into educational requirements.

1805 Organization of American States, *Methodological Meeting of Human Resources.
A Methodology for the Analysis of Human Resources.* Washington, D.C.: OAS,
1963. Pp. 22.

A working document, analysed and discussed by invited experts, presented
at a conference in Mexico City in 1963. It provides a succinct manual of
instruction to manpower forecasters, following the approach of the OECD Mediterranean Regional Project.

1806 K. N. BUTANI, *Manpower Planning in the U.S.S.R.* New Delhi: Institute of
Applied Manpower Research, 1963. Pp. 90.

This detailed but uncritical description of methods and techniques of
Soviet manpower forecasting is based on the author's participation in a one-
month ILO study tour in the USSR in 1963.

1807 Agency for International Development, Department of State, *Techniques for Determining Manpower Skill Needs and Training Requirements*. Washington, D.C.: US Department of State, 1963. Pp. 145.

A handbook of simplified techniques for use in developing countries by manpower advisers. It includes methods for determining current skill needs, for maintaining a continuing programme of manpower reporting, and includes a sample questionnaire to business firms.

1808 M. HAMDY, *Long-Term Manpower Planning Research. Progress Report of the First Round of Research*. Memo. No. 286. Cairo: Institute of National Planning, 1963. Pp. 8.

A brief explanation of the methods and data used in long-term manpower planning in the United Arab Republic. See also M. S. Fahmy, S. Weheba, *A Note on Estimates of Teacher Requirements for the Period 1965-85 by Level and Branch of Education*. Memo. No. 349. (Cairo: INP, 1963. Pp. 38.)

1809 R. ROBINSON, ed., *African Development Planning*. Cambridge: Cambridge University Overseas Studies Committee, 1963. Pp. 148.

These conference papers include, among other things, three excellent pieces by G. Hunter, E. R. Rado, and W. A. Lloyd on the problems of manpower planning in developing countries, pp. 87-111, as well as a forceful summing up of "The Argument of the Conference" with particular attention to the question of stressing primary, rather than secondary and higher education, pp. 24-34.

1810 A. M. CARR-SAUNDERS, *Staffing African Universities*. London: Overseas Development Institute, 1963. Pp. 26.

This pamphlet considers the quantitative needs for expatriate university teachers in Africa and suggests practical ways in which the problem of meeting these needs may be overcome. (See also 1678.)

1811 Joint Thai-USOM Human Resources Study, *Preliminary Assessment of Education and Human Resources in Thailand*. Bangkok: Educational Planning Office, Ministry of Education, 1963. Pp. 195.

This is the document summarised by Platt and Brembeck (see 1319) consisting essentially of a series of manpower forecasts up to 1966 and 1980 for Thailand, based on labour force projections. A fuller version of the document, with an interesting collection of working papers, is also available but virtually unobtainable outside Thailand.

1964

1812 R. JOLLY, E. RADO, "Education in Uganda—Reflections of the Report of the Uganda Education Commission", *EAER*, 1, New Series, 1964, pp. 69-80.

A critique of *Education in Uganda. The Report of the Uganda Education Commission* (Entebbe, Uganda; 1963) from the standpoint of quantitative educational planning geared to forecasts of future manpower requirements.

1813 UCRN Manpower Survey Sub-Committee, *The Requirements and Supplies of High Level Manpower in Northern Rhodesia. 1961-70: The Requirements and Supplies of High Level Manpower in Southern Rhodesia 1961-70.* Salisbury: University College of Rhodesia and Nyasaland Department of Economics. Occasional Papers, Nos. 2, 3, 1964. Pp. 22,22.

    Manpower forecasts for the 2 countries, prepared by W. L. Taylor and D. S. Pearson, following upon preliminary work by E. A. G. Robinson, F. H. Harbison, and G. Seltzer.

1814 Ministry of Labour and Employment, India, *The Iron and Steel Industry (Public Sector). Educational and Technical Training Requirements of Supervisory and Production Process Workers.* Delhi: Manager Government of India Press, 1964. Pp. 460.

    The findings given in this report are based on a special survey of three Indian public steel plants, with the object of assessing both the "minimum" and the "desirable" level of education and training considered necessary by employers for satisfactory performance in each occupation. Most of the report is taken up by tables; the text runs to only 30 pages.

1815 K. G. NOZHKO, *Methods of Estimating the Demand for Specialists and of Planning Specialized Training Within the USSR.* Statistical Reports and Studies. Paris: UNESCO, 1964. Pp. 63.

    After some historical remarks, the author explains in detail the two methods currently employed in the USSR to forecast the demand for high-quality manpower. A closing section discusses long-term educational planning in the USSR. The appendices contain relevant statistics and model forms for estimating the demand for teachers in "general education schools". A brief bibliography of Russian sources is included. (See also 1746.)

1816 J. VAIZEY, "Education in African Economic Development", *Economic Development for Africa South of the Sahara,* ed. E. A. G. Robinson. London: Macmillan, 1964, pp. 340-60.

    A series of spirited and incisive *obiter dicta* on the role of education in an overall strategy for economic development in low-income countries. See, particularly, the opening and closing remarks on "education as investment" and the comments supporting central manpower planning, pp. 340-41, 348-49, 360.

1817 M. DEBEAUVAIS, "Manpower Planning in Developing Countries", *ILR*, April, 1964, pp. 317-39.

    A general discussion of employment forecasting techniques in data-poor underdeveloped countries, preceded by an introduction which stresses the stimulating effect of attempting, however, inadequately, to plan manpower developments in a country.

1818 F. PAUKERT, "The Interdependence of High-level Manpower Planning and Economic Planning", *ibid.*, pp. 339-53.

After discussing the interdependence of the future supply and demand for high-level manpower, the author reviews various methods of gearing manpower planning to general economic planning.

1819 J. VAIZEY, "The Labour Market and the Manpower Forecaster—Some Problems", *ibid.*, pp. 353-71, partly reprinted in *UNESCO-REED*, pp. 700-11.

This article examines the ways in which earnings differentials enter into forecasts of the demand and supply of skilled manpower in underdeveloped countries. Particular attention is paid to three policy problems: the migration of educated people, the unemployment of intellectuals, and the development of appropriate salary structures for economic growth.

1820 R. G. HOLLISTER, "The Economics of Manpower Forecasting", *ibid.*, pp. 371-97.

In this brilliant paper, the author develops the necessary conditions for the existence of "manpower growth paths", that is, manpower utilisation patterns which all economies must follow in the process of development. He concludes that manpower planning based upon such a hypothesis must be regarded with extreme scepticism. He then goes on to explore the possibilities of using knowledge of the present occupational distribution of the labour force for forecasting purposes, in the course of which he cites American and Japanese data to suggest an optimum disaggregation of industries for meaningful manpower planning.

1821 R. K. SRIVASTAVA, *Projecting Manpower Demand. A Review of Methodology*. Delhi: Directorate of Manpower, 1964. Pp. 77, mimeographed.

A useful non-technical presentation of different methods of forecasting manpower demands and a brief review of forecasting experience around the world. The volume includes a lengthy bibliography.

1822 P. KILBEY, "Technical Education in Nigeria", *BOUIES*, May, 1964, pp. 181-95.

Reviews Nigeria's efforts in recent years to provide a system of technical education in the light of projected manpower needs.

1823 S. OKITA, "Manpower Policy in Japan", *ILR*, July, 1964, pp. 45-59.

After a brief historical review of the role of education and training in Japan's development from 1868 to 1940, the author sketches the national manpower development policy that has emerged since the late 1950's.

1965

1824 F. HARBISON, C. A. MYERS, eds., *Manpower and Education. Country Studies in Economic Development*. New York: McGraw-Hill, 1965. Pp. 343.

This volume of essays surveys the experience of 11 countries with educational planning based on manpower forecasts. In each case, the authors analyse the current manpower situation, review the forecasts that have been made and describe the development of the educational system in the light of

manpower needs. M. A. Horowitz writes on Argentina, pp. 1-37; W. F. Whyte
on Peru, pp. 37-73; R. C. Blitz on Chile, pp. 73-108; W. H. Knowles on
Puerto Rico, pp. 108-40; G. B. Baldwin on Iran (the only author in the book
who allows himself some doubts on the practical value of manpower planning),
pp. 140-73; B. Glassburner on Indonesia, pp. 173-202; E. Berg on Senegal,
Guinea, and the Ivory Coast, pp. 232-68; G. Seltzer on Nyasaland, pp. 268-97;
and R. L. Thomas on Uganda, pp. 297-325. In addition, there are two fascinating essays by I. C. Y. Hsü, "The Impact of Industrialization on Higher Education in Communist China", pp. 202-32, and by G. Hunter on "Issues in
Manpower Policy: Some Contrasts from East Africa and Southeast Asia",
pp. 325-43.

1825   OECD, *Problems of Human Resource Planning in Latin America and in the
       Mediterranean Regional Project Countries*. Report on the Seminar held at
       Lima in March, 1965. Paris: OECD, 1967. Pp. 275.

       This seminar was specifically devoted to the theme of the long-term fore-
    casting of manpower requirements, along the lines pioneered by MRP. The
    volume consists, first of all, of a report of the discussions, pp. 29-67,
    and secondly, of four supporting papers: (1) V. L. Urquidi, "Problems of
    Forecasting Manpower Requirements in Latin America", pp. 77-84; (2) C. M.
    Faustor, "Comparative Study of the MRP Report on Spain and the Peruvian
    Experience in Human Resources Planning", pp. 85-102; (3) A. S. Crespo, "Com-
    parative Study of the MRP Report on Greece and the Argentinian Experience in
    Human Resources Planning", pp. 103-22; and (4) Z. Slawinski, "The Structure
    of Manpower in Latin American Evolution During the Past Few Decades and Long-
    term Prospects", pp. 123-74. The volume also contains three OECD documents
    on MRP, already published elsewhere, pp. 175-223, and a useful statistical
    annex on the MRP countries, Peru, and Argentina, pp. 225-75.

1826   M. R. SINHA, ed., *The Economics of Manpower Planning*. Bombay: Asian Studies
       Press, 1965. Pp. 194.

       All of the seven essays in this volume have previously appeared in *ILR*
    (see 1817-20, 1823).

1827   E. G. MALHERBE, "Manpower Training: Educational Requirements for Economic
       Expansion", *SAJE*, March, 1965, pp. 29-51.

       This paper gives a picture of South Africa's present and future manpower
    requirements, as revealed by a recent sample tabulation of the Population
    Census of 1960, compared with the present output of her educational institu-
    tions at different levels, concluding with some constructive proposals to
    reform the Republic's educational system.

1828   Institute of Applied Manpower Research, *Demand and Supply of Engineering
       Manpower (1961-1975). Second Report on Engineering Manpower Survey*.
       New Delhi: IAMR, 1965. Pp. 90.

       A long-term forecast of the demand for engineers in India against the likely
    supply of engineering graduates over the next 15 years. The various assump-
    tions on which the forecast is based are discussed and upper and lower limits
    of the forecast are presented.

1829   F. H. HARBISON, "The Development of Human Resources. An Analytical Outline",
       Economic Development in Africa, ed. E. F. Jackson. Oxford: Basil Blackwell,
       1965, pp. 71-77.

       A succinct summary of the author's concept of a "strategy of human resource
       development" as fully developed in 1798.

1830   USAID/NEC, *Far East Manpower Assessment and Educational Planning Seminar*.
       Manila: National Economic Council, Republic of the Philippines, and USAID,
       1965. Pp. 130.

       After a few brief introductory essays, the bulk of the volume consists of
       country-papers on manpower planning in Taiwan, Korea, the Philippines,
       Thailand, and Vietnam.

1831   UNESCO-IAU, *Higher Education and Development in South-East Asia. Summary
       Report and Conclusions*. Paris: UNESCO, 1965. Pp. 83.

       The report by H. Hayden and the conclusions by J. Lockwood summarise the
       findings of a larger study to be published later surveying the present posi-
       tion and estimating the future needs of higher education in Burma, Cambodia,
       Indonesia, Laos, Malaysia, the Philippines, Thailand, and Vietnam. See,
       particularly, ch. 3, pp. 27-35, on "High-Level Manpower for Development".
       (See also 1861.)

1832   J. Q. LANHOUNMEY, "La planification de l'éducation au Dahomey", *TM*, avril-
       juin, 1965, pp. 405-21.

       An analysis of a recent educational plan for Dahomey.

1833   M. CARTIER, "Planification de l'enseignement et formation professionnelle
       en Chine continentale", *ibid.*, 1965, pp. 511-30.

       A valuable review of educational policies in China since 1949.

1834   Ministry of Education, Ireland, *Investment in Education*. Dublin: Stationery
       Office, 1965. Pr. 8311. Pp. 410.

       An educational plan for Ireland for the next decade, based on the manpower-
       forecasting approach, drawn up by a Survey Team appointed by the Minister for
       Education. Pt. I consists of a description of the existing Irish educational
       system, and a forecast of probably future enrolments and teacher requirements.
       Pt. II considers the patterns of employment of educated people and the social
       determinants of staying on at school, projects the requirements for educated
       manpower by 1971, and calculates the likely manpower deficits by that date.
       Pt. III discusses the efficiency of the educational system at the primary
       and secondary level and examines the structure of educational finance in
       Ireland. Pt. IV examines the various ways of dealing with the forecasted
       manpower deficits, and contains, in addition, an interesting general discus-
       sion of the relationship of education and economic progress in the context of
       a market economy. Throughout the volume there are comparisons to other Euro-
       pean countries, and particularly the United Kingdom.

1835   CHU-YUAN CHENG, *Scientific and Engineering Manpower in Communist China,*
       1949-1963. Washington, D.C.: National Science Foundation, 1965. Pp. 588.

       This book gathers together all available material on the scientific and
       engineering manpower of mainland China. It analyses the Census of 1955 with
       respect to the age, education, occupations, and earnings of scientists and
       engineers, describes government science policy, discusses the history of
       Soviet assistance in developing China's specialised manpower, assesses the
       influence of Western-trained scientists and engineers, and concludes with
       biographical data on 1200 prominent Chinese scientists and engineers. There
       is also an interesting chapter, somewhat outside the purview of the book, on
       the status of social science in Communist China.

1836   W. C. CASH, "A Critique of Manpower Planning and Educational Change in Africa",
       EDCC, October, 1965, pp. 33-48, reprinted in *P-EED,* 2, pp. 98-122.

       A penetrating critique of the assumptions of manpower-forecasting methods
       of the Harbison-type and a sketch of an alternative cost-benefit approach to
       educational planning in Africa.

1837   K. A. BLAKEY, "The Scope for Manpower Analysis in Planning Production in
       Certain African Countries", *ILR,* November, 1965, pp. 380-97.

       A proposal to introduce manpower-analysis and manpower-costing in every
       industrial project in Africa, so as to provide a stimulus for the development
       of specific kinds of technical education and in-training programmes.

1838   R. BLANDY, "Some Questions Concerning Education and Training in the Develop-
       ing Countries", *ibid.,* December, 1965, pp. 476-90.

       This paper draws attention to some of the anomalies that have arisen as a
       result of the manpower-forecasting approach to educational planning in
       developing countries. Among the remedies discussed by the author is the
       adoption of an occupational classification scheme based, not on job-content,
       but on the education and training required for the occupation.

1966

1839   B. SAMAME, "Manpower Problems and Policies in Peru", *ibid.,* February, 1966,
       pp. 127-43.

       A review of current manpower problems in Peru and the work being done by
       the Employment and Human Resources Service of the Peruvian Ministry of
       Labour.

1840   P. R. G. LAYARD, J. C. SAIGAL, "Educational and Occupational Characteristics
       of Manpower: An International Comparison", *BJIR,* July, 1966, pp. 222-67.

       A regression analysis, based on data for over 30 countries, of the relation-
       ship between the productivity of labour and the fraction of various types of
       manpower in the labour force of leading sectors of the economy. The paper
       discusses the implications of the findings for manpower planning.

1841 C. C. ONYEMELUKWE, *Problems of Industrial Planning and Management in Nigeria*. London: Longmans, 1966. Pp. 330.

This study of the problems of industrial expansion in Nigeria includes a chapter on "Manpower Development", pp. 283-312, which discusses Nigeria's future needs for highly trained manpower, and the planning of technical and management education.

1842 H. E. SMITH, ed., *Readings on Economic Development and Administration in Tanzania*. Dar-es-Salaam: Institute of Public Administration, 1966, pp. 425-40.

A short description of the manpower survey conducted in 1964, which provided data on the size of the labour force, numbers unemployed, and occupational distribution, as well as forecasts of the demand and supply of skilled manpower in Tanzania. There is a brief discussion of technical training and the problem of unemployed primary school leavers.

1843 R. L. CLARK, "Manpower in Economic Development", *MJ*, July-September, 1966, pp. 26-39.

Some sharp comments on the manpower-forecasting approach, with comments by I. Sachs, pp. 40-43, S. N. Sinha, pp. 43-54, and P.-Y. Chinchankar and M. V. Namjoshi, pp. 54-95.

1844 G. SKOROV, *Integration of Educational and Economic Planning in Tanzania*. African Research Monographs No. 6. Paris: UNESCO-IIEP, 1966. Pp. 78.

An excellent critical review of the three leading manpower forecasts that have been made in Tanzania in 1962, followed by a discussion of the links between these forecasts and various economic development problems.

1845 Institute of National Planning, *Manpower Planning in the United Arab Republic*. Cairo: INP, 1966. Pp. 97.

The purpose of this booklet is to describe the recent efforts of the UAR in the field of manpower and educational planning. Most of the space is taken up with a detailed review of a long-term MRP-type forecast for 1985, including 63 tables of data, mostly with reference to 1960.

1846 A. B. ARAOZ, "Manpower and Employment in Brazil", *ILR*, April, 1966, pp. 362-83.

After outlining Brazil's employment problems and policies, the author discusses some recent forecasts of manpower requirements in Brazilian industry.

1847 OECD, Directorate for Scientific Affairs and Development Centre, *Long-Term Forecasts Relating to Manpower and Education in Peru (1960-80)*. Paris: OECD, 1966. Pp. 17, mimeographed.

A description of the methods used in a study undertaken in 1965 by the National Planning Institute of Peru and OECD as part of the programme of the Ford Foundation. It represents the latest refinements of the Parnes method of forecasting associated with MRP.

1848 H. M. PHILLIPS, "Science and Technology in Economic Development". *ISSJ* , XVIII, 3, 1966, pp. 325-44.

A discussion of the problems of assessing the returns from investment in scientific research and of forecasting requirements of scientific manpower, particularly in developing countries. Argues that estimates of manpower requirements must be based on adequate information about the present stock of scientific and technical manpower.

1849 Republic of Zambia, *Manpower Report. A Report and Statistical Handbook on Manpower Education, Training and Zambianisation 1965-6.* Lusaka: Government Printer, 1966. Pp. 194.

Based on a complete survey of the Zambian labour force, this report on the manpower problems of Zambia includes forecasts for 1970 and data, the first of its kind for Africa, on annual earnings over the last decade by levels of education.

1850 N. DeWITT, "High-Level Manpower in the U.S.S.R.", *New Directions in the Soviet Economy. Studies prepared for the Sub-Committee on Foreign Economic Policy of the Joint Economic Committee, Congress of the United States. Pt. III: The Human Resources.* Washington, D.C.: US Government Printing Office, 1966, pp. 789-817.

An up-dated version of the analysis presented in the author's earlier book (1655).

1851 H. N. PANDIT, "Supply and Demand for Secondary and Higher Educated Manpower: 1960-61 to 1975-76", *MJ*, July-September, 1966, pp. 37-62.

A useful review of the current situation with respect to Indian manpower stocks. The supply is projected with the aid of linear regressions. The method for projecting demand, however, is not disclosed.

1852 Directorate of Employment, Training and Technical Education, Delhi Administration, India, "Survey of Engineering Graduates of University of Delhi— 1964 Batch", *ibid.*, October-December, 1966, pp. 50-85.

An examination of the employment patterns of the engineering graduate of Delhi University in 1964.

1853 D. SINGH, "Estimating Maintenance Manpower", *ibid.,* 1966, pp. 40-49.

An example of interfirm analysis as a means of forecasting requirements for maintenance staff in the Indian fertiliser industry.

1854 A. S. BHALLA, "Manpower and Economic Planning in the Philippines", *ILR*,
      December, 1966, pp. 550-70.

      A survey article of Philippino manpower problems within the framework of
      overall economic planning in the Philippines.

1855 S. P. WRONSKI, K. S. PANICH, *Secondary Education, Manpower and Educational
      Planning in Thailand*. Bangkok: Educational Planning Office, Ministry of
      Education, Thailand, 1966. Pp. 46.

      This is a digest of a fuller report (*Current and Projected Secondary Edu-
      cation Programs for Thailand: A Manpower and Educational Development Project*.
      Bangkok: Educational Planning Office, Ministry of Education, Thailand, 1966.
      Pp. 257), which contains a forecast of manpower requirements up to 1986,
      based on labour force projections, as well as a brief discussion of the
      results of some special surveys into the educational system of Thailand.

1967

1856 S. P. AGARWAL, S. KUMAR, "Methods of Estimating Stock of Educated Manpower—
      Illustrated with reference to Graduates and above in Arts, Science and
      Commerce", *MJ*, January-March, 1967, pp. 9-46.

      An attempt to explain the methods used to estimate manpower stocks in
      India and to apply them to a manpower category so far ignored in Indian
      studies.

1857 OECD, *Education, Human Resources and Development in Argentina*. Paris: OECD,
      1967. Pp. 465.

      This important volume represents a further development of the OECD Mediter-
      ranean Regional Project: more emphasis is put on the internal "efficiency"
      of the educational system; the forecasts of manpower requirements are accom-
      panied by educational supply projections, based on observed past trends of
      new entrants, dropouts, and repeaters; and all the demand-forecasts and
      supply-projections involve ranges of values rather than single values for the
      critical variables. The author points out that "what has been attempted in
      the present volume is not to elaborate an educational plan. The aim is
      rather to give a quantitative and consistent framework of the past, present
      and future situation of the education system under specified conditions."
      The frequent resort to international comparisons alone makes this a valuable
      reference work.

1858 E. L. KLINGELHOFER, "Occupational Preferences of Tanzanian Secondary School
      Pupils", *JSP*, 72, 1967, pp. 149-59.

      This study tests the hypothesis that pupils' occupational interests in
      Tanzania are unrelated to national needs as revealed by manpower requirements
      forecasts. The sample involved 3500 pupils in 31 secondary schools, and
      African and Asian students were separately analysed.

1859 E. RADO, "Manpower Planning in East Africa", *EAER*, June, 1967, pp. 1-30.

      A revised version of the author's earlier article (886).

1860   E. RADO, "The 1966-71 Uganda Manpower Plan", *JDS*, July, 1967, pp. 451-56.

An interesting note which shows that the wrong assumption about current
marginal rates of substitution between different types of high-level manpower
led to a sizeable overestimate of educational requirements in Uganda's Second
Development Plan.

1861   G. HUNTER, *Higher Education and Development in South-East Asia, Vol. III,
Pt. 1, High Level Manpower.*   Paris: UNESCO-IAU, 1967.   Pp. 184.

This report was submitted in 1964 and a résumé of it can be found in the
first volume of this series, *Director's Report,* Ch. 5.   It consists of two
sections: the first consists of general comments on the position of high-
level manpower in the whole of South-east Asia, and the second consists of
ten individual country-studies (Burma, Thailand, Malaysia, Singapore,
Sarawak, Sabah, Indonesia, Cambodia, South Vietnam, and The Philippines).
The forecasting technique employed by the author is the so-called Harbison
rule-of-thumb: higher educated manpower must grow twice as fast, and secondary educated manpower must grow three times as fast as GNP.

1862   National Economic Development Board, *Methodology on* [sic] *Manpower and Employment
Projections in the Second Plan of Thailand.*   Bangkok: NEDB, Office of the
Prime Minister, 1967.   Pp. 70.

Prepared with the assistance of ILO experts, this document details the
manpower forecasts that entered into Thailand's Second Plan (1967-71).   The
method used, in contrast to earlier forecasts in Thailand, starts from projections of sectoral GDPs rather than from labour force growth rates.

1863   D. K. ZSCHOCK, *Manpower Perspectives of Colombia.*   Princeton, N.J.:   Princeton University Press, 1967.   Pp. 151.

Using time series for the incremental labour-output ratio, and completely
arbitrary assumptions about minimum educational requirements for occupations,
the author forecasts the perspective demand for manpower in Colombia, distinguishing between the separate requirements of the exchange economy and the
subsistence economy in Colombia.

1968

1864   V. E. KOMAROV, ed., "Selections Concerning the Training of Qualified Specialists: Factors Affecting the Demand for Specialists, and Methods of Determining Future Requirements", *UNESCO-REED*, pp. 732-41.

A collection of quotations from leading Soviet books on manpower planning.

1865   T. BURGESS, R. LAYARD, P. PANT, *Manpower and Educational Development
1961-1986.*   London: Oliver & Boyd, 1968.   Pp. 89.

The full report of the manpower forecast that formed the basis of the
Indian Education Commission Report (1724).   The method used is based on
Tinbergen-regression, involving the assumption that educated manpower should
grow at the same rate as projected output.

1866   M. K. BACCHUS, "A Quantitative Assessment of the Levels of Education Required
       in Guyana by 1975", *SES*, June, 1968, pp. 178-96.

       A manpower forecast based on the international-comparisons approach.

1867   S. P. SEN GUPTA, *India's Manpower Requirements—Some Preliminary Estimates*
       (1968-69 - 1978-79). Directorate General of Employment and Training.
       Delhi: Government of India Press, 1968. Pp. 48.

       A 10-year forecast of total employment by sectors and occupations, plus 3
       forecasts of demand for engineers, doctors and scientists. The basic data
       used is somewhat different from those subsequently adopted in the Fourth
       Five-Year Plan and the forecasting methods employed are crude; nevertheless,
       it is interesting to notice that a huge surplus of engineers is predicted by
       1979.

1868   N. BENNETT, C. SENTONGO, J. B. MUKALAZI, A. LUNDI, Ministry of Planning and
       Economic Development, *High Level Manpower Survey, 1967, and Analyses of*
       Requirements, 1967-1981. Entebbe, Uganda: Government Printers, 1968.
       Pp. 53.

       This document contains the results of a survey and a projection based on a
       two-stage technique. First, it is assumed that manpower in three broad
       sectors of the economy should grow as fast up to 1981 as the output of these
       sectors. Next, the existing ratios of the numbers of four types of educated
       manpower should be changed by 1981 in accordance with ruling benefit/cost
       ratios for these four types in 1967. The forecast does not lead to any
       serious shortages by 1971 (p. 25). The last chapter of the study consists
       of a series of recommendations on manpower policies (pp. 29-34).

1869   G. TOBIAS, R. S. QUEENER, *India's Manpower Strategy Revisited 1947-1967*.
       Bombay: N. M. Tripathi Private Ltd., 1968. Pp. 265.

       This thorough review of India's manpower problems, includes a historical
       survey of India's manpower institutions, a review of the characteristics of
       the Indian labour force, an outline of the educational system and other
       training programmes, a discussion of imbalances in six critical manpower
       areas, and, finally, a statement of a recommended manpower strategy for India.

1969

1870   Institute of Applied Manpower Research, *Employment Outlook for Engineers*,
       1969-79. Delhi: I.A.M.R., 1969. Pp. 64.

       A long-term forecast for engineers based on a linear relation between the
       employment of engineers and national income. Despite considerable unemploy-
       ment of engineers in 1969, demand for engineers is predicted to equal supply
       in 1979 if the economy grows at 6 per cent per annum in the 1970's.

1871   R. D. LOKEN, *Manpower Development in Africa*. New York: Praeger, 1969.
       Pp. 153.

       A general, non-technical discussion of manpower planning in Africa in the
       1960's with a case study of Ghana.

1970

1872 A. N. K. NAIR, W. KEDDEMAN, *An Assessment of Ethiopia's Manpower Requirements and Resources for Economic Development 1961-70 EC (1969-1978).* Addis Ababa: Ministry of National Community Development, Imperial Ethiopian Government, 1970. Pp. 103.

  An example of a long-term manpower forecast, combining the international-comparisons approach, to obtain estimates of employment by sector, the sample-survey approach, to derive the occupational distribution of the labour force, and qualitative judgements to equate occupation with education. The resulting numbers appear to be systematically inflated.

1873 ILO, *Towards Full Employment. A Programme for Colombia. Prepared by an Inter-Agency Team Organised by the I.L.O.* Geneva: I.L.O., 1970, ch. 15, pp. 215-37.

  This report, prepared by a committee under the chairmanship of D. S. Seers, contains a chapter by R. Jolly which forecasts the needs for manpower in Colombia by 1985 on the basis of so-called Tinbergen regressions.

1971

1874 S. MERRETT, "The Education-Occupation Matrix: An Indian Case Study", *ILR*, May, 1971, pp. 505-10.

  A discussion of the education-occupation matrix (ten rows by ten columns) in the Indian fertilizer industry. Unfortunately, the occupational categories seem themselves to be defined in educational terms, which make the results difficult to interpret.

1875 O. MEHMET, "Manpower Planning and Labour Markets in Developing Countries: A Case Study of West Malaysia", *JDS*, March, 1971, pp. 277-89.

  A discussion of the fragmented labour markets in West Malaysia, insulated on ethnic lines, in relation to the problems of aggregate manpower forecasting. The paper closes with comments on the policy of employment creation.

1876 E. GINZBERG, *Manpower for Development. Perspectives on Five Continents.* New York: Praeger Publishers, 1971. Pp. 331.

  A popular book, based on field visits to 27 countries, by an author who is described on the dust jacket blurb as "one of the founding fathers of manpower economics". The approach is interdisciplinary and deeply informed by personal observations. Virtually every aspect of manpower economics is discussed but the costs and finance of education are never mentioned.

1972

1877 R. JOLLY, "The Skilled Manpower Constraint", *Constraints on the Economic Development of Zambia,* ed. C. Elliott. Nairobi: Oxford University Press, 1972, pp. 21-56.

After a somewhat confusing attempt to define manpower scarcities, the
author settles down to an attempt to find evidence for manpower scarcities
in the Zambian economy.

1878 R. JOLLY, C. COLCLOUGH, "African Manpower Plans: an Evaluation", *ILR*,
      August/September, 1972, pp. 207-64.

An extremely comprehensive evaluation, not only of African manpower forecasts but also of rate-of-return exercises in Tropical Africa. The authors
draw the conclusion that African manpower plans of the 1960's were misleading,
not only in that they overestimated the demand for skilled manpower but also
in that they led to the neglect of a number of crucial manpower problems.
Nevertheless, they find rate-of-return analysis objectionable on even more
fundamental grounds.

1879 B. D. MABRY, T. P. KOMPOR, "Manpower Imbalances in Thailand", *WEJ*, December,
      1972, pp. 428-48.

A crass Parnes-type manpower and educational forecast for Thailand, showing
that surpluses at all levels of education except the secondary are bound to
emerge by 1976.

C: BIBLIOGRAPHIES

1932

1880 C. ALEXANDER, T. COVERT, *Bibliography on School Finance 1923-1931*. US
      Department of Interior, Office of Education, Bulletin No. 15. Washington,
      D.C.: Government Printing Office, 1932. Pp. 343.

   A fully annotated and highly unselective bibliography of over 4000 American
publications, classified under a variety of headings: school accounting;
buildings; types of schools; higher education; pensions; salaries; state
aid; taxation; and the like. There is a long unannotated section on individual states and a few pages on the economic value of education, pp. 337-40.
See also the supplement by T. Covert, *Selected Bibliography on School Finance
1933 to 1948*. Federal Security Agency, Office of Education, Bulletin No. 14
(Washington, D.C.: Government Printing Office, 1949. Pp. 47).

1952

1881 UNESCO, *Teaching Agriculture: A Selected Bibliography*. Paris: UNESCO,
      1952. Pp. 52.

   A country-by-country annotated list.

1954

1882 UNESCO, *Education for Community Development. A Selected Bibliography*.
      Educ. Stud. & Docs., No. 8. Paris: UNESCO, 1954. Pp. 48.

   Annotated bibliography covering general works on the theory and practice of
community development and descriptive material on individual projects.

1955

1883 UNESCO, *Education Abstracts*. "Training of Fundamental Education", VII, 8,
      October, 1955; "Fundamental Education", VIII, 7, September, 1956; "Long
      Range Educational Planning", IX, 6, July, 1957; "Adult Education in Community
      Development", IX, 8, October, 1959; "Rural Education", 7-8, Sept.-Oct., 1959;
      "Primary Education in Asia", XII, 3, March, 1960; "Educational Planning.
      A Preliminary Listing", XIV, 2, 1962; "Teaching Comparative Education", XV,
      4, 1963. Paris: UNESCO, 1955-63.

Various annotated bibliographies which yield relevant material. Part of
a monthly series of special subjects surveying recent literature.

1956

1884   UNESCO, *Literacy Education. Selected Bibliography.* Paris: UNESCO, 1956.
Pp. 48.

An annotated bibliography of recent material, broken down into "Organizatio
of Literacy Campaigns and Methods of Instruction" and "Materials for Literacy
Teaching".

1885   *Select Annotated Bibliography of Tropical Africa,* compiled by the International African Institute under direction of D. Forde. New York: Twentieth
Century Fund, 1956, sect. V, pp. 1-55.

One section in this well-known annotated bibliography deals specifically
with education.

1886   A. R. MUNSE, E. D. BOOHER, *Selected References on School Finance.* US Department of Health, Education, and Welfare, Office of Education, Circular
No. 462. Washington, D.C.: Government Printing Office, 1956. Pp. 42.

Unannotated listing under the following headings: education and the economy; Federal Government and education; higher education; school buildings;
school business administration; school personnel compensation; state aid to
education; taxation for schools; transportation of pupils; unit costs in
education; and other school finance references.

1887   WHO, *Health Education: A Selected Bibliography.* Educ. Stud. & Docs., No. 19.
Paris: UNESCO, 1956. Pp. 46.

Although most of this annotated bibliography deals with descriptions of
existing health education programmes, other writings in health economics are
also included.

1957

1888   P. MAYER, *Reading List on Rural Conditions and Betterment in the British
Colonies.* London: Oxford University Press, 1957. Pp. 121.

Contains, among other things, a useful reading list on "Rural Education".

1958

1889   R. C. BENGE, *Technical and Vocational Education in the UK: A Bibliographical
Survey.* Educ. Stud. & Docs., No. 27. Paris: UNESCO, 1958. Pp. 51.

A detailed annotated survey of legislation, official publications, bibliographies, and books and articles for England and Wales, Scotland and Ireland.

1890 M. I. MOVSOVIC, *Technical and Vocational Education in the USSR: A Biblio-graphical Survey*. Educ. Stud. & Docs., No. 30. Paris: UNESCO, 1958. Pp. 53.

A comprehensive survey of Soviet sources and publications, including laws and decrees. The three levels of vocational education are discussed separately. There is a list of Soviet periodicals dealing with problems of vocational and technical education.

1891 K. SIMPSON, H. C. BENJAMIN, *Manpower Problems in Economic Development: A Select Bibliography*. Princeton, N.J.: Industrial Relations Section, 1958. Pp. 93.

Annotated materials classified under 6 headings and 40 subheadings.

1959

1892 B. BEARD, ed., *The Effect of Technological Progress on Education. A Classi-fied Bibliography From British Sources 1945-1957*. London: Institution of Production Engineers, 1959. Pp. 141.

A detailed classificatory bibliography of technical education, mostly in the UK, with brief annotations and an index of authors and titles.

1893 UNESCO, *An International Bibliography of Technical and Vocational Education*. Educ. Stud. & Docs., No. 31. Paris: UNESCO, 1959. Pp. 72.

This annotated bibliography covers some 90 countries and includes a certain amount of general information on technical and vocational education. Limited coverage is given to the UK, the USA, and the USSR, because these are covered in 1889, 1890, and 1894.

1894 Office of Education, USA, *Technical and Vocational Education in the USA. A Bibliographical Survey*. Educ. Stud. & Docs., No. 36. Paris: UNESCO, 1959. Pp. 24.

An annotated bibliography in five sections: general works, agricultural education, distributive education, home economics education, and trade and industrial education.

1961

1895 *Education and Development in India and Pakistan: A Select and Annotated Bibliography*. Michigan State University Education in Asia Series I. Michigan: College of Education, 1961. Pp. 221.

A reading guide in the essay style. Other bibliographies are listed on pp. 174, 221. This work is less valuable than it might have been, owing to the failure to apply strict canons of bibliography.

1896   *Education in Emerging Africa.   A Select and Annotated Bibliography.*
       Michigan State University Education in Africa Series, No. 4. Mighigan
       State University: College of Education, 1961. Pp. 153.

          This is the first annotated bibliography devoted exclusively to education
       in Africa. Unfortunately, it follows no consistent principle of annotation:
       the content of the items cited is advertised rather than summarised, usually
       in the language of the relevant author. Standard canons of bibliography are
       violated on almost every page. (See also 1923.)

1962

1897   T. KELLY, *A Select Bibliography of Adult Education in Great Britain.*   London:
       National Institute of Adult Education, 1962. Pp. 126.

          A select bibliography with brief annotations under a variety of headings
       of items published up to the end of 1961. Annual supplements to this useful
       listing appear each September in the *Year Book* of the National Institute of
       Adult Education.

1898   *Educational Investment in Manpower Development.* Princeton, N.J.: Industrial
       Relations Section, *Selected References* No. 108, 1962. Pp. 4.

          A brief annotated list of books and articles on investment in human capital

1899   J. J. SHIELDS, Jr., *A Selected Bibliography on Education in East Africa,
       1941-1961.* Makerere Library Publications, No. 2. Kampala, Uganda: Makerere
       University College, 1962. Pp. 39.

          This supplements other bibliographies and is particularly strong on officia
       publications and articles in East African journals.

1900   M. COUCH, ed., *Education in Africa: A Select Bibliography.   Pt. I: British
       and Former British Territories.* London: University of London Institute of
       Education, Education Libraries Bulletin Supplement 5, 1962. Pp. 61.

          The most comprehensive bibliography available for English-speaking Africa,
       classified by countries, years of publication, and types of education.

1963

1901   K. L. NEFF, *Selected Bibliography on Education in South-East Asia.*   US
       Department of Health, Education, and Welfare, Office of Education.   Washingto
       D.C.: Government Printing Office, 1963. Pp. 16.

          A country-by-country annotated list.

1902   R. D. GEE, *Teachings Machines and Programmed Learning.   A Guide to the Litera-
       ture.* Herts. C.C. 1963. Pp. 37.

          An annotated bibliography of books and articles on teaching machines.

1903 S. M. KATZ, F. McGOWAN, *A Selected List of U.S. Readings on Development.*
Prepared for the UN Conference on the Application of Science and Technology
for the Benefit of the Less Developed Areas. Washington, D.C.: Agency for
International Development, 1963. Pp. 363.

A very selective list of American materials under a large number of subject-
headings with sections on manpower problems and educational planning,
pp. 104–42.

1904 UNESCO, *Bibliography in Educational Planning.* Paris: UNESCO, 1963, mimeographed.

An annotated bibliography with a detailed breakdown for all phases of the
planning process, particularly useful on unpublished reports for particular
countries, most of which are obtainable on application to UNESCO or the relevant Ministries of Education.

1905 M. C. ALEXANDER-FRUTSCHI, ed., *Human Resources and Economic Growth. An
International Annotated Bibliography on the Role of Education and Training
in Economic and Social Development.* Menlo Park, Calif.: Stanford Research
Institute, 1963. Pp. 398.

1150 items are listed under a detailed classificatory scheme. There is a
special section on areas and countries, including Africa and Asia, pp. 283–
328. Some relevant topic headings are: "Culture and the Motivation to
Develop", "Communicating Ideas for Change", "Literacy Education", "Community
Development", and "Rural Education". The bulk of the literature cited is in
the English language.

1964

1906 A. WHEELER, *Educational Planning: A Bibliography.* Paris: UNESCO-IIEP, 1964.
Pp. 131.

(Same item as 1904.) See also the companion-volume: *Educational Planning:
A Directory of Training and Research Institutions* (Paris: UNESCO-IIEP, 2nd
ed., 1968. Pp. 235).

1907 M. KENDALL, *Research Into Higher Education. A Bibliography.* Research Unit
for Student Problems, University of London. London: Research Unit for
Student Problems, 1964. Pp. 45.

Despite its ambitious title, this annotated bibliography is confined to
the question of "what happens to the student, in both academic and nonaca-
demic respects, once he has entered college"; there are few references to non-
English literature.

1908 B. A. YATES, "Educational Policy and Practice in Tropical Africa: A General
Bibliography", *CER*, October, 1964, pp. 215–28.

The purpose of this brief annotated bibliography is to suggest some 130
items—secondary sources and official reports—giving an overall view of the
current problems confronting African education.

1965

1909 M. COUCH, ed., *Education in Africa: A Select Bibliography. Pt. II: French-Speaking Territories (former French and Belgian Colonies); Portuguese and Spanish Territories; Ethiopia and Eritrea; Liberia; and General African References 1962-1964.* London: University of London Institute of·Education, Education Libraries Bulletin Supplement 9, 1965. Pp. 116.

      The most comprehensive bibliography available on French-speaking and Spanish-speaking Africa, classified by countries and years of publication.

1910 M. BLAUG, *Annotated Bibliography on the Role of Education in the Transition from Subsistence to Cash Economies in Middle Africa, South and South-East Asia.* Paris: UNESCO, 1966. Pp. 27, mimeographed.

      This bibliography covers the literature in English that concerns the role of education in encouraging the indigenous population of Africa and Asia to seek wage employment and to sell produce to the market. It is broken down into 6 sections: measurement of the subsistence economy; case studies of subsistence economies in transition; social change and the impact of cash economies; empirical evidence of educational standards in the cash economy; the role of formal education in the transition; and the role of informal education in the transition.

1911 IEDES, *Bibliographie. Rôle de l'éducation dans le passage de l'économie de subsistance à l'économie de marché: l'Afrique tropicale d'expression française.* Préparée par l'Institut d'étude du développement économique et social de l'Université de Paris, sous la direction de Lê Thành Khôi. Paris: UNESCO, 1966. Pp. 24, mimeographed.

      This annotated bibliography covers the relevant literature in French and is divided into five sections: general surveys; society and traditional education; the development and effects of the cash economy; the development and problems of education; education and economic and social development.

1912 G. BARON, *A Bibliographical Guide to the English Educational System.* London: London University, 3rd ed., 1965. Pp. 124.

      An annotated bibliography in the essay style covering every institutional phase of English education.

1913 T. N. CHIRIKOS, *Survey of Current and Recently Completed Research on High-Level Manpower Utilization in the United States.* Paris: OECD, 1965. Pp. 37, mimeographed.

      Prepared for OECD by a member of the Human Resource Development and Educational Planning Project of the College of Commerce and Administration, Ohio State University, this survey classifies research under several headings and provides at the same time a listing of all research organisations in the United States working in the manpower field.

1914 *Sociology of Education Abstracts,* quarterly since 1965. London: University of Liverpool School of Education, up to Vol. 4, 1.

This is a very useful publication that carries fairly detailed abstracts
of a wide array of mostly American and English books and articles, prepared
by a panel of expert abstractors, and classified under a dozen different
headings. Virtually all publications in the economics of education published
in the USA and the UK are included here.

1966

1915 Society for Research into Higher Education, UK, *Research into Higher Education Abstracts*, quarterly since 1966. London: SRHE, up to Vol. 2, 1.

These abstracts are based on a regular survey of almost 200 journals, concentrating on current work in the United Kingdom but with a select coverage
of American publications. The abstracts are classified into nine problem
areas and extensive cross-referencing is provided.

1916 J. P. POWELL, *Universities and University Education: A Select Bibliography*.
The National Foundation for Educational Research in England and Wales,
Occasional Publication No. 14. Slough: NFER, 1966. Pp. 51.

Although this bibliography includes a section devoted to the USA, it is
basically a guide to the literature on the British university system, classified under such headings as: history, aims and functions, teaching methods,
teaching aids, examinations, libraries, academic profession, students, and
study methods.

1917 OECD, *The Educational Factor for Development: Special Annotated Bibliography*.
OECD Library 10, 11. Paris: OECD, 1966, I, II. Pp. 130, 117.

A very uneven bibliography in both French and English, confined to documents published between 1961 and 1966 and available at the OECD Library in
Paris.

1918 K. M. DEITCH, E. P. McLOONE, *The Economics of American Education: A Bibliography. Including Selected Major References for Other Nations*. Bloomington,
Ind.: Phi Delta Kappa, 1966. Pp. 67.

A useful check-list by 13 major headings and sub-headings, including a
section on "Articles Reviewing Important Portions of the Literature".

1967

1919 K. HÜFNER, *Hochschulökonomie und Bildungsplanung*. Studien und Berichte 9A.
Bibliographische Materialien zur Hochschulforschung. Berlin: Institut für
Bildungsforschung in der Max-Planck-Gesellschaft, 1967. Pp. 139.

A comprehensive bibliography of about 750 items on the economics of higher
education that is particularly strong on the American literature. The book
is introduced by a brief bibliographical essay.

1920   UNECA, *Selected Bibliography. Manpower and Training Problems in Economic and Social Development*. Addis Ababa: UNECA, 1967. Pp. 45, mimeographed.

       Particularly useful on African material.

1921   S. DEDIJER, L. SVENNINGSON, eds., *Brain Drain and Brain Gain. A Bibliography on Migration of Scientists, Engineers, Doctors and Students*. Lund, Sweden: Research Policy Programme, Lund, 1967. Pp. 48.

       A useful bibliography classified under: (1) migration in general; (2) history; (3) studies and articles; and (4) news and comments, with an index of authors and countries.

1922   M. WOODHALL, "The Economics of Education", *RER*, October, 1967, pp. 387-98.

       A useful bibliographical essay, covering research during the years of 1963-66.

1968

1923   J. W. HANSON, G. W. GIBSON, eds., *African Education and Development Since 1960: A Select and Annotated Bibliography*. East Lansing, Mich.: Michigan State University, 1968. Pp. 327.

       A list of some 1600 books and articles published between 1960 and 1966 with very detailed but totally uncritical annotations.

1924   T. BRISTOW, B. HOLMES, *Comparative Education Through the Literature*. London: Butterworths, 1968. Pp. 181.

       A bibliographical guide of the essay type, confined to the English literature. Its thorough country and subject index makes it a valuable reference.

1925   K. HÜFNER, "Economics of Higher Education and Educational Planning—A Bibliography", *SEPS*, 2, 1968, pp. 25-101.

       A comprehensive indexed bibliography with a brief introductory essay. (See also 1919.)

1926   Research for Better Schools Inc., *An Annotated Bibliography of Benefits and Costs in the Public Sector*. Philadelphia: RBS, 1968. Pp. 242.

       An excellent annotated indexed bibliography of about 2700 entries, covering education (incorporating almost the whole of the present work) military system evaluation, agriculture, water resources, health, urban renewal, transportation, etc.

1927   A. HEGELHEIMER, "Recent Manpower-Research Projects for Educational Planning and Policy in the Federal Republic of Germany", *GER*, VI, 4, 1968, pp. 334-42.

       A bibliographical essay on the current manpower literature in Western Germany.

1969

1928 OECD, Bibliography. *International Migration of Manpower*. Paris: OECD,
      1969. Pp. 137.

         A partly annotated bibliography under five main headings. Includes author's
      index.

1970

1929 W. D. WOOD, H. F. CAMPBELL, *Cost-Benefit Analysis and the Economics of
      Investment in Human Resources. An Annotated Bibliography*. Kingston,
      Ontario: Industrial Relations Centre, Queen's University, 1970. Pp. 211.

         389 items arranged under eight headings and superbly annotated. Unfortun-
      ately, about half of the items are about cost-benefit analysis as such;
      since there also are sections devoted to health, poverty, and social welfare,
      this leaves only about 100 items devoted to schooling and training. Most of
      the material relates to Canada and the U.S. Section 6 on "Training, Retrain-
      ing and Mobility" is a particularly useful source for references on American
      work.

1930 M. WOODHALL, "The Economics of Education", *Educational Research in Britain 2*,
      ed. H. J. Butcher. London: University of London Press, 1970, pp. 244-57.

         A bibliographical essay, written in 1968 and hence already somewhat out
      of date. The volume also includes essays on "Compensatory Education", "Uni-
      versity Teaching Methods" and "Education for Business and Management".

1971

1931 M. A. JOHNSTONE, "Mathematical Models in Educational Planning: A Biblio-
      graphy", *TAU*, December, 1971, pp. 284-307.

         An annotated bibliography of 107 items in English and French. The models
      are carefully subdivided into several categories.

1972

1932 W. K. RICHMOND, *The Literature of Education. A Critical Bibliography 1945-
      1970*. London: Methuen & Co., 1972. Pp. 206.

         Sparkling bibliographical essays on all branches of educational studies,
      including the economics of education plus selectively-annotated book lists.
      The author's interests are unusually wide, but the annotation soon shows that
      they are not perhaps wide enough for the herculean task he has set himself.
      Oddly enough, the book has no index—a criminal omission.

1933 National Board on Graduate Education, University of Illinois, *An Annotated
      Inter-office Bibliography on Graduate Education*. Champaign, Illinois, Office
      of the Chairman, University of Illinois, 1972. Pp. 30, 25, 14.

An annotated and comprehensive bibliography, largely but not entirely on graduate education in the United States.

1934 M. J. NUSSBAUM, *Adult Literacy in the Developing Countries: A Bibliography*. Bethesda, Maryland: ERIC Document Reproduction Service (P.O. Drawer O), 1972. Pp. 133, mimeographed.

A valuable annotated bibliography, obtainable on request from ERIC.

1935 Literary International Committee, *Literacy Today. A Panorama of Adult Literacy*. New Delhi: LIC, 1972.

This is a bi-monthly journal produced by the Information Service of the Literacy International Committee, A-9, Maharani Bagh, New Delhi-14, which reviews new books and pamphlets about literacy courses around the world. The lists of Books Received make it an invaluable reference source for new works on adult literacy.

1974

1936 P. JOHNSON, J. BIBBY, M. M. McGRORRY, *Ghanaian Education 1957–1972. An Annotated Bibliography*. London: University of London Institute of Education Libraries Bulletin, Supplement 18, 1974. Pp. 139.

A superb, exhaustive annotated bibliography under 16 headings with a subject and author index. See, particularly, Section N, "Educational Planning and Administration".

1975

1937 P. G. ALTBACH, D. H. KELLY, *Higher Education in Developing Nations: A Selected Bibliography 1969–1974*. New York: Praeger Publisher, 1975. Pp. 229.

A continuation of Altbach's first bibliography published by the Harvard Center for International Affairs in 1970. Some 2,400 books and articles in English, French, Spanish and German are listed by continents and countries. There is a bibliography of bibliographies, a subject index, and a listing of agencies concerned with research and publication in the field of higher education.

D: ITEMS RECEIVED TOO LATE FOR CLASSIFICATION

1 Carnegie Commission on Higher Education, *Higher Education: Who Pays? Who Benefits? Who Should Pay? A Report and Recommendations*. New York: McGraw-Hill, 1974. Pp. 190.

   The first half of the book answers the question "who pays?" in great detail. The next section on "who benefits?" reviews American work on rates of return to investment in higher education, and the last section presents a complex package of policy proposals.

2 M. MIKLIUS, "The Distributional Effects of Public Higher Education: A Comment", *HE*, August, 1975, pp. 351-56.

   A critique of the Hansen-Weisbrod measurements on the grounds of ignoring the lifetime distribution of costs and benefits of higher education.

3 K. HINCHLIFFE, "Screening, Deschooling and Developing Countries", *HE*, August, 1975, pp. 305-16.

   After an opening discussion of the screening hypothesis and a review of Reimer's *School is Dead*, the author presents two empirical studies of Northern Nigeria and discusses their implications in the light of screening-cum-deschooling.

4 B. BERNER, "'Human Capital', Manpower Planning and Economic Theory: Some Critical Remarks", *Acta Sociologica*, 17, 3, 1975, pp. 236-55.

   A Marxist critique of human capital theory in a Swedish perspective.

5 D. J. O'KEEFFE, "Some Economic Aspects of Raising the School Leaving Age in England and Wales in 1947", *EHR*, August, 1975, pp. 500-16.

   An analysis of the short-term earnings effects of the 1947 ROSLA, together with a sketch of a cost-benefit analysis of that action.

6 R. MANNING, "Optimal Development of a Skilled Work Force", *QJE*, August, 1975, pp. 504-12.

   A terse, mathematical treatment of the problem of optimal balanced growth, applied to the ratio of skilled to unskilled workers, instead of the ratio of capital to labour.

7 R. B. FREEMAN, "Overinvestment in College Training", *JHR*, Summer, 1975,
   pp. 287-311.

      Further evidence of the decline in the rate of return on higher education in
   America since 1970. Argues that this explains the recent downturn in the fraction of high school graduates going to college.

8 M. CARNOY, D. MARENBACH, "The Return to Schooling in the United States,
   1939-69", *ibid.*, pp. 312-31.

      Estimates rates of return to investment in American schooling in four Census
   years by sex and race and shows that the social rate of return to white high
   school investment declined in the 30-year period.

9 J. G. ATKINSON, "The Value of a B.Ed. Degree", *HER*, Summer, 1975, pp. 60-63.

      Calculates the private rate of return to the new U.K. B.Ed. Degree, based on
   the current pay scales of teachers.

10 J. BHAGWATI, C. RODRIGUEZ, "Welfare-Theoretical Analyses of the Brain Drain",
    JDE, September, 1975, pp. 195-222.

      This paper reviews and synthesizes the earlier theoretical analyses of brain
    drain and develops the Bhagwati-Hamada suggestion of a surtax on the incomes of
    skilled immigrants from the LDC's into the DC's. The whole of this issue of
    JDE is devoted to this question and the Bhagwati-Rodriguez paper is followed
    by four theoretical and two econometric contributions: (1) C. A. Rodriguez,
    "Brain Drain and Economic Growth: A Dynamic Model", pp. 223-48; (2) R. McCulloch
    J. L. Yellen, "Consequences of a Tax on the Brain Drain for Unemployment and
    Income Inequality in Less Developed Countries", pp. 249-64; (3) K. Hamada,
    J. Bhagwati, "Domestic Distortions, Imperfect Information and the Brain Drain",
    pp. 265-80; (4) K. Hamada, "Efficiency, Equality, Income Taxation and the Brain
    Drain: A Second-Best Argument", pp. 281-88; (5) R. E. B. Lucas, "The Supply-
    of-Immigrants Function and Taxation of Immigrants' Incomes: An Econometric
    Analysis", pp. 289-308; and (6) G. Psacharopoulos, "Estimating Some Key Para-
    meters in the Brain Drain Taxation Model", pp. 309-18.

11 L. D. SINGELL, W. J. YORDON, "Incentives for More Efficient Education: The
    Development of a Model", *Incentives and Planning in Social Policy*, eds. B. Stein,
    S. M. Miller. Chicago: Aldine, 1973, pp. 71-92.

      A longitudinal small-sample study in a particular American school district,
    relating pupil achievement scores to various in-school and out-of-school fac-
    tors, on the basis of which the authors draw up a proposal for an experimental
    program to improve the academic performance of slow learners in the first grade.

12 S. S. BELLIN, S. S. BELLIN, "Teacher Incentives Tied to Public Performance: A
    Strategy for Educational Accountability", *ibid.*, pp. 117-48.

      A useful discussion of teacher incentive payment systems in the context of
    American elementary education.

13 E. F. DENISON, *Accounting for United States Economic Growth 1929-1969*.
Washington, D.C.: The Brookings Institution, 1974, pp. 43-7, 219-59.

This book carries the analysis of the *Sources of Economic Growth* (1962)
forward from 1957 to 1969 and reworks many of the earlier calculations. See
ch. 1, pp. 1-8, for a succinct statement of the changes, in particular the
rejection of the "three-fifth assumption" for calculating the labour quality
index by education in favour of standardisation of the principal non-educational
determinants of hourly earnings differentials, leaning heavily on the Wolfle-
Smith and Weisbrod-Karpoff data. Education is now shown to account for 14
per cent of the 3.33 percentage growth rate in the American economy over the
period 1929-69 (p. 132), an estimate that is even higher than the earlier figure
given in the *Sources of Economic Growth*.

14 B. O. PETTMAN, "Industrial Training in Great Britain", *IJSE*, I, 1, 1974,
pp. 63-83.

A useful survey of recent developments, together with a study of Humberside
firms to throw light on their reactions to the levy-grant system. See also
B. O. Pettman, B. Showler, "Government Vocational Training Schemes in Great
Britain, *ibid*., I, 2, 1974, pp. 184-96.

15 M. FISHER, "The Human Capital Approach to Occupational Differentials", *IJSE*,
I, 1, 1974, pp. 40-62.

A largely theoretical and occasionally sceptical review of the human capital
explanation of wage differentials by occupational categories.

16 F. WELCH, "Relationship Between Income and Schooling", *Review of Research in
Education*, eds. F. Kerlinger, J. Carroll. Itaska, Illinois: Peacock, 1974,
pp. 179-201.

An excellent review of recent rate-of-return studies with particular reference to black-white differences, followed by a brief survey of recent studies
on the role of education in agriculture.

17 G. CHAMBERLAIN, Z. GRILICHES, "Unobservables With a Variance-Components Structure: Ability, Schooling, and the Economic Success of Brothers", *IER*, June,
1975, pp. 422-49.

A highly technical econometric article, whose interest for our purposes
resides in the fact that Gorseline's data (131) is reworked to show that there
was little relationship in Indiana in the 1920's between the distribution of
"ability" and the distribution of schooling.

18 S. W. POLACHEK, "Differences in Expected Post-School Investment as a Determinant
of Market Wage Differentials", *IER*, June, 1975, pp. 451-67.

Shows that differences in expected male-female lifecycle labour force participation rates can account for most male-female age-specific wage differentials
even if both groups face the same costs of post-school investment and hence
make post-school investment in response to expected labour force participation,
rather than *vice versa*.

19. A. MAYNARD, *Experiment With Choice in Education*.   London: Institute of Econo-
    mic Affairs, 1975.   Pp. 78.

    The subtitle of this useful pamphlet is self-explanatory: An Analysis of New
    Methods of Consumer Financing To Bring More Resources Into Education By
    Vouchers and Loans.

20 D. W. BRENEMAN, "Manpower Projections in Retrospect", *ER*, 56, 2, 1975 (Educa-
    tional Record), 1975, pp. 132-35.

    A brief review with references of recent American experience.

21 J. TINBERGEN, "Substitution of Academically Trained By Other Manpower", *WA*, 111,
    3, 1975, pp. 466-76.

    Reworks various estimates of the elasticity of substitution between highly
    qualified and less qualified labour to demonstrate that most substitution
    elasticities vary around unity, a figure higher than that found by other authors

22 W. R. CLINE, "Distribution and Development. A Survey of the Literature", *JDS*,
    1, 1975, pp. 359-400.

    Although this survey carries us well beyond our subject, the author includes
    some trenchant remarks on the role of education in certain income distribution
    models, such as those of Mincer and Thurow (pp. 365-68).

23 K. HINCHLIFFE, "Education, Individual Earnings and Earnings Distribution",
    JDS, January, 1975, pp. 149-61.

    Working with lifetime earnings by education rather than mean or median earn-
    ings, the author demonstrates that earnings by education are much less equally
    distributed in Ghana and India than in the United States.

24 S. C. FARBER, "A Labor Shortage Model Applied to the Migration of College Pro-
    fessors", *JHR*, Fall, 1975, pp. 482-99.

    Tests the impact of labour market conditions on the migration behaviour of
    American college professors across seven disciplines. Concludes that an Arrow-
    Capron type of labour shortage model is applicable to the academic labour
    market.

25 J. E. HIGHT, "The Demand for Higher Education in the U.S., 1927-72; The Public
    and Private Institutions", *ibid.*, pp. 512-20.

    Shows that the income elasticity of demand for enrolments is significantly
    greater in the private than in the public sector of American higher education.
    Nevertheless, the ratio of private to public sector enrolments has steadily
    declined over the period 1927-51 because the income effect has been swamped by
    the substitution effect, private tuition rates having risen much faster than
    public tuition rates.

26 A. MAURIZI, "Rates of Return to Dentistry and the Decision to Enter Dental School", *ibid.*, pp. 521-28.

Generates new time series data on the private rate of return to dentistry in the United States and shows that the demand for dental education varies positively with the relative rate of return to dentistry.

27 D. L. MARTIN, "Interest Rates and Occupational Choice", *ibid.*, pp. 537-43.

Explores the hypothesis that the market rate of interest is a determinant of labour supply to occupations offering on-the-job training.

28 M. E. DA SILVA FREIRE, J. J. R. F. DA SILVA, "The Application of Production Function to the Higher Education System—Some Examples from Portuguese Universities", *HE*, November, 1975, pp. 447-60.

An input-output regression analysis of Portuguese university education, using time series data.

29 W. W. McMAHON, "Economic and Demographic Effects on Investment in Higher Education", *SEJ*, January, 1975, pp. 506-14.

Tests a mixed consumption-public-investment model of higher education in the United States and draws some implications from his results for future long-term trends in higher education.

30 J. M. CAMPBELL, T. D. CURTIS, "Graduate Education and Private Rates of Return: A Review of Theory and Empiricism", *EI* (Economic Inquiry), March, 1975, pp. 99-118.

The paper begins with a review of nine studies of the returns to post-graduate education in the United States. This is followed by a discussion of objections to rate-of-return analysis, including the old chestnut about rate-of-return vs. present values. Lastly, the authors present some new evidence, designed to show the extreme instability of rate-of-return calculations applied to the final stages of higher education. Little is made, however, of the factor to which Schultz has drawn attention, namely, part-time earnings of postgraduate students.

31 G. S. FIELDS, "Rural-Urban Migration, Urban Unemployment and Underemployment, and Job-Search Activity in LDCs", *JDE*, 2, 1975, pp. 165-87.

An extension of the Harris-Todaro model to take account, among other things, of employers' preferences for educated people. The author succeeds in building and estimating a rich and plausible model of unemployment in LDC's.

32 S. P. DRESCH, "A Critique of Planning Models for Postsecondary Education", *JHE*, May/June, 1975, pp. 245-86.

After a critique of some American work on this subject in recent years, the author examines two current efforts at a more comprehensive model of American postsecondary education.

33 A. W. NIEMI, Jr., "Sexist Differences in Returns to Educational Investment", *QREB*, Spring, 1975, pp. 17-25.

Calculates sexist and racist differences in private rates of return for the United States in 1960 and 1970 and also considers differences in earnings between men and women and between hlacks and whites over the decade 1960-70.

34 R. W. McMEEKIN, Jr., *Educational Planning and Expenditure Decisions in Developing Countries With a Malaysian Case Study.* New York: Praeger Publishers, 1975. Pp. 195.

A sceptical account of extant approaches to educational planning and a plea for a cost-effectiveness framework. Chs. 4 and 5, the bulk of the book, apply c/e analysis to the Malaysian educational system.

35 J. R. DAVIS, J. F. MORRALL, III, *Evaluating Educational Investment.* Lexington, Mass.: D. C. Heath and Company, 1974. Pp. 112.

Another attempt at a textbook of the human capital approach to education. Ch. 4 on problems of discrimination and ch. 6 on human capital concepts in the theory of international trade differentiate this product from other textbooks of its kind.

36 B. R. CHISWICK, *Income Inequality. Regional Analyses Within a Human Capital Framework.* New York: Columbia University Press, 1974. Pp. 212.

This book contains a number of applications of "the schooling model" to observed cases of intraregional, interregional and international inequalities in the distribution of income: the South versus non-South and Blacks versus Whites in the United States, the United States versus Canada, Mexico, Great Britain, the Netherlands, and Israel, etcetera. Ch. 2, "A Nontechnical Analysis of the Distribution of Income", is a useful, simplified exposition of the human capital explanation of income distribution.

37 R. G. PAULSTON, ed., *Non-Formal Education. An Annotated International Bibliography.* New York: Praeger Publishers, 1972. Pp. 332.

A superb, annotated, cross-classified bibliography. Would it were brought up to date because the real explosion in the literature on non-formal education only has occurred in the last few years.

38 D. O. PARSONS, "Intergenerational Transfers and Educational Decisions", *QJE*, November, 1975, pp. 603-17.

A new American earnings function with better family-background data than is available in most other studies of earnings functions.

39 T. ISHIKAWA, "A Note on the Optimal Spacing Properties in a Simple Jevonial Model of Educational Investment", *ibid.*, pp. 633-42.

A theoretical extension of the Ben-Porath lifecycle theory of human capital, paying particular attention to the problem of the optimal patterns of interruptions of the educational process.

40 G. HOLT, "Human Capital Investment under Constrained Optimization", *QREB*, Spring, 1975, pp. 47-51.

   A brief theoretical note showing how a constraint, such as an admission requirement, qualifies the private optimization rule of human capital theory.

41 W. LEE HANSEN, R. J. LAMPMAN, "Basic Opportunity Grants for Higher Education: Good Intentions and Mixed Results", *Challenge*, 1974, reprinted in *Benefit-Cost and Policy Analysis 1974. An Aldine Annual*, eds. R. Zeckhauser and others. Chicago, Illinois: Aldine Publishing, 1975, pp. 283-91.

   An explanation of the workings of this American government programme with some notes towards an evaluation.

42 G. PSACHAROPOULOS, "Earnings Determinants in a Mixed Labour Market", *Employment Problems and Policies in Developing Countries. The Case of Morocco*, ed. W. van Rijckeghem. Rotterdam: Rotterdam University Press, 1976, pp. 123-44.

   An earnings function fitted to Moroccan data, showing high returns to primary education and foreign-educated labour.

43 H. GINTIS, "Welfare Criteria with Endogenous Preferences: The Economics of Education", *INER* (International Economic Review), June, 1974, pp. 415-30.

   This strange article translates the familiar Marxist objection to taking preferences as given into a bit of mathematics and some quasi-mathematical "theorems", adding remarks on the economics of education along the way.

44 UNESCO, Literacy Division, *The World Experimental Literacy Programme: A Critical Assessment*. Paris: UNESCO Press, 1976. Pp. 198.

   Here at long last is the final evaluation of UNESCO's EWLP (1967-72). Given the pressures on UNESCO and the political sensitivity of the participating countries, this is a surprisingly frank document. It consists of 11 country reports (Algeria, Ecuador, Ethiopia, Guinea, India, Iran, Madagascar, Mali, Sudan, Syria, and Tanzania) followed by a general assessment of the entire programme. In brief, the EWLP proved to be much more expensive than was originally contemplated, although still cheaper than equivalent primary education; no firm evaluative results, and certainly no internationally comparable results, were obtained but qualitative evidence is generally positive. Much of the problem is traced to the conflicting objectives of the original programme: see the penetrating pages, "Why EWLP? The intentions", pp. 115-30.

45 G. PSACHAROPOULOS, *Earnings and Education in OECD Countries*. Paris: OECD, 1975. Pp. 194.

   An invaluable review of the earnings function literature in developed countries (what a pity the half-dozen studies for developing countries were not included). There is a particularly striking chapter on rents in professional earnings (ch. 5) and the difficulty of infering the existence of such rents from earnings data.

46 A. KLEVMARKEN, J. M. QUIGLEY, "Age, Experience, Earnings, and Investments in Human Capital", *JPE*, February, 1976, pp. 47-72.

    Making use of an unique Swedish data source, the authors estimate the separate effects of age and experience on the earnings of engineers with identical educational qualifications.

47 J. L. AZAD, "Financing Institutions of Higher Education in India: The Need for a Realistic Fee Policy", *HE*, February, 1976, pp. 1-8.

    Develops a peculiar proposal to charge full fees to unqualified students, without raising any doubts about how qualified students are now admitted to Indian colleges and universities.

48 G. BURKE, "The Economics of Bonded Service: The Case of Graduate Secondary Teachers in Victoria, Australia", *ibid.*, pp. 35-48.

    A crude cost-benefit calculation of the Australian practice of bonding trained teachers.

49 D. J. DAVIS, "Some Effects of Ph.D. Training on the Academic Labour Markets of Australian and British Universities", *ibid.*, pp. 67-78.

    Discusses the effects of the rising number of Ph.D.s on the staffing of Australian and British universities.

50 R. P. DORE, "Human Capital Theory, the Diversity of Societies and the Problem of Quality in Education", *ibid.*, pp. 79-102.

    An interesting attempt to expand on Wiles' analysis of the economic value of education in the light of the diverse circumstances of developing countries.

51 D. VERRY, B. DAVIES, *University Costs and Outputs*. Amsterdam: Elsevier Publishing Company, 1976. Pp. 277.

    This study uses cross-sectional data to estimate cost functions for British universities and polytechnics by individual faculties in order to throw light on the question of the optimum size of a faculty.

52 H. CORREA, "Quantitative Analysis of the Implementation of Educational Plans in Latin America", *SEPS*, 9, 1975, pp. 247-55.

    This paper defines an index of plan implementation and applies the index to the 1960-70 educational plans of Latin American countries. The author concludes that lack of statistical data and of qualified personnel are the main reasons for failure of implementation.

53 G. S. FIELDS, "Higher Education and Income Distribution in A Less Developed Country", *OEP*, July, 1975, pp. 245-59.

An important paper which first provides various alternative criteria of fiscal equity and then applies these criteria to the case of Kenya. The author concludes that, on all three criteria, higher education in Kenya is financed regressively.

54 A. S. BLINDER, "On Dogmatism in Human Capital Theory", *JHR*, Winter, 1976, pp. 8-22.

This brilliant note shows that work experience is not measured adequately either by age or by age minus the age of leaving school. See also M. N. Rosenzweig, "A Nondogmatic Reply", *ibid*.

55 R. C. EDWARDS, "Individual Traits and Organizational Incentives: What Makes a 'Good' Worker?", *JHR*, Winter, 1976, pp. 51-68.

This paper develops and tests a neo-Marxian model of the firm in order to come to grips with the question of what it is that determines the economic value of an employee to an employer. Some fatal concessions are made along the way to the theory of human capital.

56 F. A. SLOAN, "Real Returns to Medical Education: A Comment"; "Reply" by C. M. Lindsay, *JHR*, Winter, 1976, pp. 118-30.

An important comment on Lindsay's 1973 article with a reply by the author.

57 J. DUNWORTH, R. COOK, "Budgetary Devolution as an Aid to University Efficiency", *HE*, May, 1976, pp. 153-68.

Authors propose a new method of budgetary devolution to academic faculties or departments in the context of British higher education, which they argue will improve the allocation of resources within universities.

58 E. G. WEST, "The Yale Tuition Postponement Plan in the Mid-Seventies", *HE*, May, 1976, pp. 169-76.

An assessment of the income-contingent loan scheme of Yale University with particular reference to the problem of default rates.

59 A. KELLY, "Family Background, Subject Specialization and Occupational Recruitment of Scottish University Students: Some Patterns and Trends", *HE*, May, 1976, pp. 177-88.

A study of the occupational recruitment patterns of Scottish universities in 1970 and 1972 with some attention to the historical trends in these patterns.

60 A. WESTOBY, D. WEBSTER, G. WILLIAMS, *Social Scientists at Work*. Guildford, Surrey: Society for Research into Higher Education, 1976. Pp. 145.

A study of 4,500 social science graduates of British universities who graduated in 1951, 1961, and 1967. Successive chapters study the occupational distribution of these three cohorts, their labour force participation rates, their

family background, their views about the usefulness of their education, and
their earnings from employment. The most interesting result that emerges is
that the trends in salaries by subject studied closely reflect the relative rate
of growth of the supply of graduates in these subjects.

61 C. BROWN, "A Model of Optimal Human-Capital Accumulation and the Wages of
    Young High School Graduates", *JPE*, April, 1976, pp. 299-316.

    This paper re-estimates the parameters of Ben-Porath's model of optimal accu-
    mulation of human capital over the life cycle using data on the wages of young
    high school graduates. The performance of the model is disappointing and the
    estimates of two key parameters are implausible on a priori grounds.

62 C. B. KNAPP, W. LEE HANSEN, "Earnings and Individual Variations in Postschool
    Human Investment", *JPE*, April, 1976, pp. 351-58.

    This paper refines the Mincer-Becker-Chiswick human capital explanation of
    the distribution of earnings to allow for variations in post-school investment
    within age education groups. Allowing for these variations, increases the
    estimated returns to education and reduces those to post-school training.

63 V. A. ZHAMIN, "The Economics of Higher Education", *SE*, November, 1975,
    pp. 5-113.

    The whole issue of this journal is devoted to reprinting the first two sec-
    tions of a 1973 Soviet book of essays on the economics of higher education,
    edited by V. A. Zhamin. The papers reprinted here give a good picture of the
    state-of-the-art in the subject in the USSR. As the editors of the journal
    observe: "On the basis of the evidence of this volume one is forced to con-
    clude that the study of the economics of higher education in the Soviet Union
    has hardly proceeded beyond the level of description of problems, trends, and
    possible solutions".

64 S. D. NOLLEN, "The Economics of Education: Research—Results and Needs", *TCR*,
    September, 1975, pp. 51-77.

    An up-to-date, comprehensive literature survey for the non-economist.

65 D. E. YETT, *An Economic Analysis of the Nurse Shortage*. Lexington, Mass.:
    Lexington Book, 1975. Pp. 324.

    A comprehensive analysis of the labour market for professional nurses during
    the period 1939-69. Ch. 2 examines the concept of a manpower shortage. Ch. 4
    analyzes trends in nurses' salaries. Ch. 5 discusses the effects of the loans
    and scholarship provisions of the Nurse Training Act on the supply of profes-
    sionally trained nurses.

INDEX OF AUTHORS BY ITEM
NUMBERS

Aarrestad, J., 320
Aarvig, L., 1038
Abegglen, J. C., 1177
Abramovitz, M., 62, 417
Abt, C. C., 625
Ackoff, R. L., 625
Adams, D., 871, 1323, 1748
Adams, J., 1748
Adams, D. K., 1409
Adams, W., 756, 1145
Adelman, I., 1783
Adkins, D. L., 843
Adloff, R., 1391
Afro-Anglo-American Program in Teacher
    Education, 1687
Agarwal, S. P., 1724, 1856
Agency for International Development
    (AID), 1807, 1830
Ager, M., 306
Agricultural Economics Research Centre,
    India, 1559
Ahamad, B., 1092, 1105, 1111, 1113
Ahmed, M., 1639, 1640
Aigner, D. J., 1243
Aitken, R., 920, 1133
Albers, W., 856
Albin, P. S., 264
Alexander, C., 1880
Alexander, K., 534
Alexander-Frutschi, M. C., 1583, 1905
Ali, I., 1442
Alisbah, B., 1569
Alker, H. R., Jr., 1353
Allemano, R., 805
Alles, J., 1537
Alper, P., 928, 932, 941
Altbach, P. G., 1937
Altick, R. D., 1327
Aluko, S. A., 502
Ambruster, W., 913, 1107
Anderson, C. A., 135, 828, 871, 886,
    902, 907, 1065, 1136, 1182, 1199,
    1213, 1225, 1227, 1335, 1348, 1404,
    1406, 1417, 1507, 1584, 1637

Anderson, J. E., 1460, 1507, 1537
Anderson, T., 726
Anon, 510
Araoz, A. B., 1846
Archer, J. N., 1794
Archibald, G. C., 842
Ardener, S. and E., 1390
Areen, J., 539, 542, 1278
Arles, J. P., 1436
Armitage, P. H., 837, 886, 920, 928, 932,
    941, 943, 946, 949
Armytage, W. H. G., 1335
Arnow, P., 1068
Arnstein, G. F., 679
Aron, R., 604
Arrigazzi, L., 1537
Arrow, K. J., 261, 341, 370, 842, 986,
    1287
Artigas, J. T., 867
Aschenfelter, O., 237, 304
Ashby, E., 593, 746, 1794
Asher, W., 1364
Astin, A. W., 828
Astin, H. S., 1100
Atkinson, B., 396
Attiyeh, R., 842
Auerhan, J., 1024, 1537
Aukrust, O., 61
Awasthi, S. P., 1131
Axelrad, S., 1172
Axelrod, S. J., 1289
Ayres, L. P., 559, 563

Bacchus, M. K., 1866
Bachrach, P. B., 1184
Bahr, L., 893, 1009
Bailey, D., 312
Bailey, S. K., 1261
Baird, C. W., 1299
Baird, R. N., 639
Bakke, W. E., 1038
Balderston, F. E., 814
Balderston, J. B., 1586

Baldwin, G. B., 966, 1824
Baldwin, R. E., 272, 1158
Balogh, T., 165, 902, 1665, 1688, 1692, 1711, 1721, 1734, 1780, 1781
Bank of Israel, 1421
Banks, A. S., 1347
Bantock, G. H., 865
Barbash, J., 697
Barber, C. R., 618, 800
Barkin, S., 1073, 1144
Barlow, A., 956
Barlow, R., 210, 456
Barna, T., 759
Barnett, V. M. Vr., 1409
Baron, G., 1912
Barsby, S. L., 711
Bartell, E., 682
Barth, P. S., 1748
Barzel, Y., 456
Basov, V. I., 1537
Baster, N., 1354
Bateman, W., 691
Batten, T. R., 1598, 1650
Baumol, W. J., 46, 442
Bayer, A. E., 285, 1100
Bear, D. V. T., 842
Beard, B., 1892
Becker, G. S., 145, 156, 170, 179, 206, 235, 815
Becker, H. S., 902, 1197
Becker, W. E., Jr., 851
Beckerman, W., 867, 874, 1378
Bedrosian, H., 1097
Beeby, C. E., 1553, 1730, 1757
Belitisky, A. H., 697
Bellante, D. M., 709
Belshaw, H., 1596, 1599
Bénard, J., 928, 944, 951, 953, 1790
Ben-David, J., 1208
Bendix, R., 1191
Benedict, B., 1386
Benewitz, M. C., 236
Benge, R. C., 1889
Benham, F., 1387
Benjamin, H. C., 1891
Benn, D. C., 911
Bennett, F. V., 1702
Bennett, N. L., 886, 1476, 1537, 1868
Bennett, W. S., Jr., 1360, 1366
Ben-Porath, Y., 194, 225, 272, 1309
Benson, C. S., 1, 9, 11, 493, 496, 497, 534, 586, 872, 987, 988
Bentzel, R., 1254
Benveniste, G., 886, 1688, 1721
Berdie, R. F., 729
Bereday, G. Z., 1757
Berelson, B., 738
Berg, E. J., 1418, 1824

Berg, I., 265
Bergstrom, T., 456
Berls, R. H., 789
Bernheim, C. T., 1721
Bernstein, B. B., 1219
Berry, R. A., 1152, 1569
Berstecher, D., 1367
Bertelsen, P., 1621
Bertram, G. W., 72
Besen, S. M., 83
Bettelheim, C., 1647
Beynon, J., 611
Bhagwati, J., 1167, 1170, 1501
Bhalla, A. S., 1854
Bibby, J., 288, 806, 816, 1936
Bieda, K., 1371
Biesheuvel, S., 1802
Bigelow, K. W., 1698
Binon, J., 893
Birch, D. W., 362
Birkeli, J., 126
Birley, D., 914
Birtig, G., 1125
Bishop, H. E., 759
Bjork, R.M., 1323
Blackstone, T., 841, 911
Blair, P. M., 316, 1278
Blakey, K. A., 1837
Blandy, R., 55, 1146, 1624, 1838
Blank, D. M., 970
Blau, P. M., 1229
Blaug, M., 15, 27, 60, 182, 209, 224, 250, 311, 393, 430, 499, 600, 617, 620, 624, 626, 642, 891, 902, 928, 1066, 1072, 1113, 1128, 1274, 1369, 1419, 1459, 1483, 1503, 1625, 1735, 1910
Blinder, A. S., 363
Blitz, R. C., 47, 429, 781, 1335, 1824
Blot, D., 500, 1516, 1550
Blum, J., 681, 1046, 1782
Blumberg, M. S., 1300
Blumenthal, T., 213
Bodart, N., 611
Bodenhöfer, H.-J., 226, 913
Bodkin, R. G., 76
Bolte, K. M., 1195
Bolton, R. E., 789
Bombach, G., 1013, 1030, 1780
Bonner, J., 163
Booher, E. D., 1886
Boon, G. K., 1415
Borus, M. E., 180, 245, 703
Bos, H. C., 1670, 1780, 1782
Bosworth, D. L., 1121, 1123
Botti, M., 1530
Bottomley, A., 376, 648, 796, 812, 832, 1433
Boudon, R., 1254

Boulding, K., 534, 551, 964, 1145, 1279
Bousquet, J., 883
Bow Group, 584
Bowen, H. R., 789
Bowen, W. G., 2, 169, 207, 427, 449,
    488, 491, 518, 789, 1052
Bowlby, R. L., 347
Bowles, F., 750, 770, 873, 1757
Bowles, S., 81, 93, 272, 342, 401, 815,
    903, 1157, 1231, 1247, 1278, 1783,
    1787
Bowman, M. J., 7, 8, 14, 16, 21, 32, 35,
    68, 113, 115, 123, 154, 155, 162, 190,
    193, 231, 272, 407, 534, 815, 828,
    871, 886, 902, 1003, 1136, 1325, 1331,
    1335, 1348, 1352, 1361, 1369, 1404,
    1407
Boyle, G. J., 578
Braden, I. C., 382
Brainard, W. C., 842
Braithwaite, E. W., 779
Brand, W., 1062, 1510, 1793
Brandl, J. E., 272
Bravo, L. M., 1688
Bray, D. W., 853
Brazer, H. E., 161, 210, 428, 534
Brembeck, C. S., 871, 1319
Brenner, P., 1278
Breton, A., 1280
Brickman, W. R., 1329
Bridgeman, S., 144
Bright, J. R., 983
Bright, L., 632
Bristow, T., 1924
British Broadcasting Corporation (BBC),
    605
British Committee on Chemical Education,
    1096
British Medical Association, 1302
Brolin, K., 1693
Brook, K., 380
Brosan, G., 803
Brovender, S., 835
Brown, A., 1005
Brown, B. B., 641
Brown, B. W., 551, 650
Brown, C. C., 966
Brown, D. G., 769, 1064
Brown, D. J., 716, 978
Brown, L., 1460
Brown, M., 77
Brownlee, O. H., 815
Brunner, E. de S., 1187
Bruton, H. J., 1318
Buchanan, J. M., 534, 792, 1302
Bumas, L. O., 1064
Burgess, T., 808, 839, 1865
Burkett, G. R., 1210

Burkhead, J., 33, 489, 493, 496, 614,
    646
Burns, H. M., 1409
Burns, J. M., 524, 526
Burston, W. H., 478
Burtle, J., 960
Bushnell, D. S., 1068
Busia, K. A., 1384
Butani, K. N., 1806
Butter, I. H., 217
Butts, R. F., 883, 1687
Byatt, I. C. R., 920

Cahiers du centre d'études de l'emploi,
    1117
Caillods, F., 1536
Cain, G. G., 245, 261, 1119, 1243
Cain, R., 1066
Caine, S., 177, 751
California and Western Conference, 568
Calkins, R. N., 592
Callahan, R. E., 583
Callaway, A., 886, 1408, 1532, 1547,
    1573, 1574, 1580, 1621, 1637
Calvert, J. R., 362
Campbell, H. F., 1929
Campbell, J. M., 1543
Campbell, R., 782
Campiglia, N., 1228
C. A. P. E. S., Brazil, 770
Caplow, T., 740
Capron, W. M., 986
Carleton, R. O., 965
Carlson, R. O., 601
Carlton, F. T., 41
Carnoy, M., 1278, 1366, 1445, 1446, 1447,
    1461, 1477, 1484, 1490, 1770
Carovano, J. M., 504
Carr-Hill, R., 919
Carrere, M. H., 1721
Carroll, A. B., 234
Carr-Saunders, A., 1678, 1810
Carter, C., 803
Carter, C. F., 462, 603, 748, 751, 762,
    823, 971, 1028, 1206
Carter, J. R., 1710
Carter, W. D., 1772
Cartier, M., 1833
Cartter, A. M., 190, 490, 607, 763, 767,
    772, 789, 820, 843
Cash, W. C., 1836
Castetter, W. B., 580
Castillo, G. T., 1486, 1507
Caves, R., 874
Celio, M. B., 799
Central Council for Education, Japan,
    1487
Central Training Council, UK, 689

Cerych, L., 1688, 1699, 1707, 1728, 1729, 1757
Chadwick, C. B., 1765
Chakravati, A., 1491
Chamberlin, N. W., 261
Chance, W. A., 927
Chandrakant, L. S., 1063
Chaparro, A., 1721
Chapuy, M., 1066
Chase, R. X., 1159
Chau, N. H., 611, 883
Chau, T. N., 1536, 1537, 1755
Chaudhri, D. P., 1507, 1558
Cheikhestani, M., 1534
Cheng, Chu-Yuan, 1835
Cherington, P. W., 1015
Chesler, H. A., 245
Cheswass, J. D., 611, 883, 886, 1522, 1528, 1537, 1751
Chiplin, B., 701
Chirikos, T. N., 1049, 1748, 1913
Chiswick, B., 206, 241, 256, 272, 279, 366, 524, 526, 815, 828
Christensen, S., 847
Christoffel, P., 799
Chuprunov, D., 1537
Cipriani, C. J., 233
Clark, D. H., 1472, 1486, 1585
Clark, H. F., 42, 133, 139, 588, 655, 688, 734, 954
Clark, R. L., 1843
Clignet, R., 1411, 1437
Clurman, M., 787
Cochrane, D., 519
Cochrane, J. L., 271
Cohen, S., 1784
Cohen, W. J., 161
Cohn, E., 23, 313, 325, 448, 465, 472, 527, 556
Colberg, M. R., 117
Colclough, C., 1878
Coldwell, M. J., 1599
Cole, C. C., Jr., 1180
Coleman, James, 329, 1801
Coleman, J. S., 631, 1217, 1231, 1243
Coleman, John, 1429
Collin, A., 742
Collins, D., 532
Collins, R., 1122
Colm, G., 1015
Colonial Office, UK, 1543, 1587
Comay, Y., 344, 1160, 1164
Committee for Economic Development (CED), 481, 878
Committee on Education and Human Resource Development, 1741
Committee on Government Operations, USA, 1141

Committee on Manpower Resources for Science and Technology, UK, 1033, 1057, 1143
Committee on Scientific Manpower, UK, 969
Committee on Utilization of College Teaching Resources, 735
Commonwealth Education Liaison Committee, 1063
Conference of Engineering Societies (EUSEC), 664
Conley, R. W., 252
Conlisk, J., 272, 303, 629
Conlon, M., 604
Conrad, A. H., 77
Conrad, H. S., 872
Conroy, J. D., 1473
Cook, R., 649, 850
Cooke, M. L., 560
Coombs, P. H., 734, 857, 873, 886, 994, 1537, 1538, 1555, 1557, 1637, 1639, 1698, 1721, 1757
Cooper, M. H., 1302
Cootner, P. H., 842
Copeman, C. H., 967
Corazzini, A. J., 682, 696, 699, 1249
Corbett, A., 887
Corina, J., 309
Corlett, J., 476
Correa, H., 4, 602, 669, 682, 867, 879, 886, 904, 928, 942, 1323, 1366, 1413, 1688, 1694, 1745, 1778
Corry, B. A., 821
Cotgrove, S. F., 656, 998
Couch, M., 1900, 1909
Coulson, M. A., 1224
Council for Scientific Policy, UK, 1108
Counts, G. S., 564
Coutsoumaris, G., 1145
Coverdale, G. M., 1774
Covert, T., 1880
Cowhig, J. D., 755
Cox, R. A., 1323
Craig, C., 749
Crampin, A., 946
Crane, R. I., 1335
Creamer, D., 161
Crean, J., 332, 558
Crespo, A. S., 1825
Croner, C., 1369
Crosland, C. A. R., 419
Crossley, J. R., 1042, 1101
Cullity, J. P., 453
Culyer, A. J., 521, 795, 1302, 1303, 1307
Curle, A., 872, 1316, 1349, 1366, 1611, 1719, 1744, 1756
Cutt, J., 817

Dahlgaard, L., 617
Dailey, J. T., 1210
Dale, J. R., 663
Dalin, P., 1762
Daly, D. J,, 272
Dancy, K. J., 470
Dandekar, V. M., 1145
Danielsen, A. N., 1481
Danielson, A. L., 263
Danière, A., 289, 761, 789, 819, 828, 872
Darmstadter, V., 1054
Das, P. K., 1577
Dasey, R. M., 640
Datt, R., 1558
David, H., 966, 991, 1025
David, M. H., 161, 167, 428
Davies, B. P., 885, 1232
Davies, J. L., 920, 943
Davis, F. B., 1210
Davis, J. R., 534
Davis, K., 875
Davis, R. G., 926, 1745
Dawood, A. R., 604
Dawson, D. A., 470
Debeauvais, M., 112, 116, 458, 500, 770, 857, 858, 867, 868, 886, 902, 1429, 1516, 1531, 1612, 1647, 1679, 1817
Deblé, I., 1690
De Burlo, C. R., 768
de Coster, S., 1676
Dedijer, S., 1145, 1921
de Escondrillas, F., 611
Deitch, K., 736, 872, 1352, 1918
De Johgh, J. F., 1467, 1468
Dellalfar, W., 1167
Delprat, R., 883
Denison, E. F., 62, 64, 73, 90, 102, 815, 873, 1239
Denton, F. T., 204
Department of Citizenship and Immigration, Canada, 1066
Department of Education and Science (DES), UK, 793, 885, 909, 1223
Department of Employment and Productivity, UK, 1085
Department of Labour, Canada, 659, 995, 1037
Department of Trade and Industry, UK, 1106
Derksen, J. B. D., 502
Deshmukh, A. G., 1549
de Simone, J., 1537
de Sola Pool, I., 1607
Deutsch, K. W., 1353
Devine, E. J., 1091
Devletoglou, N. E., 792

Devons, E., 751
De Voretz, J. D., 1463, 1465, 1788
DeWitt, N., 886, 1078, 1655, 1745, 1850
De Witt, Y. B., 1486
de Wolff, P., 243, 250, 994, 1007, 1198, 1200
D'Hoogh, C., 432, 502
d'Hugues, P., 1114
Diamond, D. E., 1097
Diejomaoh, V. P., 1636
Diez-Hochleitner, R., 1693, 1721
Directorate of Employment, India, 1852
Dirlam, J. B., 1145
Dodge, D. A., 319, 818
Doeringer, P. B., 704
Doi, J. I., 768
Dollard, C., 1677
Dominion Bureau of Statistics, Canada, 869
Donalson, L., 1246
Döös, S.-O., 867, 1007
Dorai, G. C., 1153
Dore, R., 1768
Dougherty, C. R. S., 1478
Dougherty, R. S., 97
Douglas, J. W. B., 751, 1211, 1235
Downes, D., 911
Drees, W., 250
Dresch, S. P., 544, 849
Dressel, P. L., 928
Drever, J., 1219
Dubbeldam, L. F. B., 1469
Dube, S. C., 1594
Dublin, L. J., 132
Due, J. F., 534
Dufty, N. F., 254
Dugan, D. J., 1249
Dumont, R., 1572, 1576, 1580, 1599
Duncan, B., 1029
Duncan, O. D., 152, 377, 1207, 1229, 1248
Dunlop, J. T., 873, 1068, 1313
Dunn, R. M., Jr., 790
Dunworth, J., 376, 640, 648, 649, 812, 832, 850
Durstine, R. M., 1537
duSautoy, P., 1595
Dyck, H. J., 434
Dymond, W. R., 261

Easterlin, R. A., 1335, 1394
Eckaus, R. S., 156, 159, 335, 371, 843, 1017
Eckstein, M. A., 1365, 1366
Eckstein, O., 425, 872, 873
Economic Council of Canada, 188
Economist Intelligence Unit, 750

Edding, F., 5, 418, 436, 438, 500, 753, 856, 859, 867, 886, 893, 1367, 1531, 1745, 1757
Edelson, N. M., 456
Education Panel, South Africa, 1712
Edward E. O., 1499
Edwards, L. N., 922
Eicher, J.-C., 146, 343, 1254
Eide, K., 500, 617, 871, 1043, 1254
Elazar, M., 860
Eliasberg, V. F., 417
Elkan, S., 1545
Elkan, W., 1635
Elliot, W. Y., 1713
Ellis, A. C., 129
Ellison, A., 828
El Said, E. S. M., 770
Elvin, H. L., 604, 859, 867, 1647
Embling, J., 500, 840
Emi, K., 1340
Emmerij, L. J., 243, 250, 627, 921, 1046, 1369, 1373, 1497, 1782
Employment Service Task Force, US, 1068
Encel, S., 775
Engineering Manpower Commission of Engineers Joint Council, USA, 1020
Enke, S., 1315
Erder, N., 867, 1062
Erickson, D. E., 543
Ericsson, G., 1040
Erleckyj, N. E., 77
Estey, J. C., 873
Evans, D. R., 900
Evans, G. J., 1121, 1123
Evans, P. C. C., 1546
Evans, R. N., 1052
Evenson, R., 1507
Ewers, C. D., 1688, 1693
Ewing, C. H., 1677
Eysenbach, M. L., 555

Fachin, R. C., 1537
Fahmy, M. S., 1808
Fallon, P. R., 103
Faluvegi, L., 502, 1537
Farber, D. J., 697
Fareed, A. E., 1163
Farr, G. N., 232
Farrell, R. L., 789
Fase, M. M. G., 262
Faust, C., 966
Faustor, C. M., 1825
Featherman, D. L., 1248
Federal Government of Germany , 915
Fein, R., 190, 699, 1295
Feldman, P., 789
Feldstein, M. S., 474, 1298

Fells, R., 616, 630
Felton, J. R., 596
Fenno, F. R., Jr., 1262
Ferber, R., 1054
Ferman, L. A., 245
Ferrez, J., 1200
Fielden, J., 791
Fields, S. G., 1506
Figa-Talamanca, L., 312
Fine, S. A., 1088
Finegan, T. A., 207
Firestone, O. J., 124
Fisher, A. G. B., 43
Fisher, F. M., 515
Fisher, M. R., 374
Fishlow, A., 1272, 1337
Fitzgerald, R. T., 444
Flanagan, J. C., 1210
Fleisher, B. M., 273
Fletcher, B. A., 1682
Fleug, G., 773
Flores, G., 1588
Floud, J. E., 751, 759, 886, 1174, 1178, 1181, 1188, 1196, 1200, 1219
Fogel, W., 212, 843
Fogg, C. D., 1803
Foley, D. K., 272, 515, 889
Folger, J. K., 121, 783, 886, 1022, 1100
Folk, H., 275, 1066
Folkers, J. S., 625
Fong, P. E., 1472
Food and Agricultural Organisation (FAO), 1548
Ford Foundation Program for Research in University Administration, 826
Forte, F., 500
Foster, H. G., 697
Foster, P. J., 1213, 1323, 1335, 1392, 1420, 1437, 1452, 1460, 1468, 1507, 1691
Fougeyrollas, P., 1627
Fourastié, J., 1007
Fowler, G., 920
Fox, K. A., 934, 936, 950
Fox, T. G., 614
Frank, M., 243, 502
Franke, W., 274
Freeman, C., 1042
Freeman, R. A., 789
Freeman, R. B., 295, 828, 843, 1119, 1126
Freiden, A., 825
Freund, R., 13
Frey, B., 931
Friedlander, A. S., 515
Friedlander, S. L., 1430
Friedman, C. H., 181

Friedman, M., 134, 1256
Froomkin, J., 617, 1087
Frost, R. T., 1261
Fuchs, G., 1254
Fuller, W. P., 1475
Furneaux, W. D., 1201, 1209

Gagney, R. M., 631
Galbraith, J. K., 1402
Galenson, W., 1351
Gales, K., 1058
Gallaway, L. E., 228
Galper, H., 790
Gamble, A. O., 1015
Gannicott, K., 113, 1493
Garb, G., 810
Garbe, D., 1529
Garbino, J. B., 843
Garcia, A., 500
Gardiner, R. K. A., 1145
Garfinkel, I., 1306
Garmonov, F. V., 1647
Garms, W. I., 439, 799
Garner, W. T., 318
Gascoigne, M., 1077
Gass, J. R., 861, 886, 902
Gassert, H., 977
Gee, R. D., 1902
Georis, P., 1676
Gern, J.-P., 611
Gerstl, J. E., 690, 1026
Gibson, G. W., 1923
Gifford, A., 527
Gilman, H. J., 198
Ginsburg, N., 1512
Ginsburg, S. W., 1172
Gintis, H., 24, 296, 401
Ginzberg, E., 539, 679, 853, 966, 982,
    1082, 1172, 1212, 1737, 1876
Girard, A., 1205
Gisser, M., 192
Glass, D. V., 751, 1174, 1192, 1202
Glassburner, B., 1824
Glennerster, H., 419, 463, 511, 514,
    520, 531, 776, 911
Glick, P. C., 137
Godfrey, M. D., 1011
Goel, S. G., 1505
Goffman, I. J., 534
Goldberg, I., 1210
Goldman, R. F., 638
Goldstein, H., 884, 994, 1054, 1062,
    1067
Goldthorpe, H., 873
Goldthorpe, J. E., 1426
Gollin, A. E., 1136, 1228
Goode, R., 486, 500, 503
Gopalaswami, R. A., 1724

Gordon, M. S., 673, 843, 875
Gordon, N. M., 382
Gordon, R. A., 875, 1068
Gorseline, D. E., 131
Gouveia, A., 1450
Grabowski, H. G., 1249
Grant, A. M., 1049
Grant, J. B., 1599
Grant, N., 1485
Grassau, E., 770
Gray, D. H., 1059
Gray, W. S., 1597
Green, E. J., 1551
Greenaway, H., 830
Greenberger, M., 739
Greenwood, M. J., 364
Grégoire, R., 1062, 1066, 1688, 1721
Gribbard, H. A., 245
Griffiths, V. L., 1581, 1674
Griliches, Z., 65, 69, 74, 76, 88, 272,
    378, 815
Grohmann, K., 893
Gross, B. M., 493
Gross, N., 1193
Grossman, M., 1304
Groves, H. M., 150
Grubel, H. G., 1133, 1134, 1135, 1136,
    1139, 1149
Grunfeld, Y., 1396
Guillaumont, P., 1529
Gunderson, M., 719
Gunton, J., 937
Gupta, H. C., 770
Gupta, M. L., 1168
Gustman, A. L., 469
Guthrie, J. W., 631, 1245
Gwartney, J., 304, 330, 398

Haas, H., 867
Haase, P. E., 1054
Haber, S., 843, 963
Haber, W., 963
Hagan, E. E., 1368
Hägerstrand, T., 1335
Hajela, D., 1558
Halden, F., 893, 1066
Hale, E., 598
Haley, B. F., 616
Haley, W. J., 373
Hall, A. R., 775
Hall, J. R., 1174
Hall, R. T., 686
Hall, S. A., 1702
Hallak, J., 34, 611, 1524, 1526, 1533,
    1534, 1535, 1536, 1537, 1538
Halls, W. D., 877
Halmos, P., 1209
Halsey, A. H., 1178, 1181, 1188, 1196,
    1200, 1222, 1254

Hambor, J., 1244
Hamda, K., 1170
Hamdy, M., 1808
Hamermesh, D. S., 705
Handa, H. L., 461, 818, 844
Hanna, P. R., 883
Hanoch, G., 223
Hanson, J. W., 1319, 1923
Hanushek, E., 631, 637
Harberger, A., 261, 1335
Harbison, F. H., 657, 902, 963, 978,
    985, 1015, 1046, 1052, 1313, 1324,
    1335, 1352, 1370, 1580, 1644, 1660,
    1677, 1687, 1693, 1694, 1731, 1741,
    1784, 1798, 1801, 1824, 1829
Hardin, E., 261, 703
Hargrove, M. B., 1462
Harker, B. R., 1507
Härnqvist, K., 1200
Harper, R. G., 1752
Harris, R., 1270
Harris, S. E., 410, 422, 427, 500, 734,
    736, 752, 789, 872, 873, 957, 1004,
    1025
Harrison, B., 328
Hartley, H. J., 617, 883, 898
Hartley, K., 717, 722
Hartman, R. W., 529, 815, 828, 843
Hartung, D., 1102
Harvey, S., 245
Hatch, S., 785, 911
Hause, J. C., 272, 297, 385, 815
Hauser, P. M., 1563, 1677
Hauser, R. M., 828
Havemann, E., 728
Havighurst, R. J., 737, 1173, 1189,
    1221, 1422, 1431
Hawes, H. W. R., 1560
Haworth, C., and J. G., 398
Hawrylyshyn, O., 1368
Hay, K. A. J., 84
Hayden, H., 1831
Haynes, W. W., 1407
Hayward, B., 871, 1225, 1768, 1795
Hebein, F. J., 388
Hegelheimer, A., 895, 899, 1927.
Heifetz, R., 1694, 1800
Heigham, D. A. C., 625
Heijnen, J. D., 1456, 1468
Heinemann, H. N., 292
Heintz, P., 1228
Heller, W. W., 884
Hemphill, H. D., 446
Hendry, D. F., 777
Henry, N. B., 1597
Herma, J. L., 1172, 1212
Herriott, R. E., 1230
Herrnstadt, I. L., 1070, 1356

Hershkowitz, M., 1480
Herzog, W., 1623
Hettich, W., 635, 818
Hickrod, C. A., 538
Hicks, U., 425, 1531, 1700
Higgins, B., 1531, 1753
Hight, J. E., 548
Hildebrand, G. H., 70
Hill, C. R., 1253
Hill, S. E., 985
Himmelweit, H. T., 1174, 1219
Hinchliffe, K., 301, 337, 1113, 1377,
    1470, 1498
Hines, F., 280
Hirsch, J. L., 1042
Hirsch, W. Z., 176, 195, 203, 421, 423,
    452, 494, 549, 613, 617
Hodge, R. W., 1207
Hodgkin, R. A., 1311
Hoenack, S. A., 540, 789
Hoerr, O. D., 1471
Hogan, T., 456
Holland, J. W., 614
Hollander, E. D., 1802
Hollander, S., 56
Hollinshead, B. S., 1173
Hollister, R. G., 261, 286, 287, 886,
    1030, 1039, 1065, 1820, 1826
Holmes, B., 1924
Holtmann, A. G., 214, 272, 285, 310, 345,
    706, 935, 1086, 1305, 1633
Hoos, I. R., 675, 917
Hopkins, P. G. H., 1622
Horobin, G. W., 1260
Horowitz, M. A., 1070, 1124, 1356, 1824
Horwood, O. P. F., 1515
Hoselitz, B. F., 1429, 1647
Hou-Chau, C., 1769
Houssiaux, J., 1145
Houthakker, H. S., 143
Hsü, I. C. Y., 1824
Hu, I.-W., 307
Hudson, B. M., 1537
Hudson, L., 1219
Hufner, K., 51, 617, 902, 906, 1919,
    1925
Hughes, H., 911
Hughes, J. J., 266
Hughes, R. M., 409
Hungate, T. L., 732
Hunt, S. J., 4, 171
Hunter, G., 886, 1312, 1320, 1460, 1507,
    1578, 1580, 1681, 1809, 1824, 1861
Hunter, L. C., 201
Huq, M. S., 1704
Hurd, G. E., 1452
Hurd, M. D., 298
Hurt, J. S., 1344

Husain, I. Z., 1443, 1558
Husèn, T., 604, 902, 1200, 1225, 1237,
    1254, 1757
Hutton, S. P., 690, 1026
Hyde, W. D., 723

Ibrahim, I. A., 1644
Idenburg, P., 1757
Iffland, C., 1145
Ihnen, L. A., 234, 397
Illitch, I., 1278
Inkeles, A., 1631
Institut d'étude du développement
    économique et social (IEDES), 1620,
    1911
Institut national de la statistique
    et des études économiques (INSEE),
    420
Institute of Applied Manpower Research,
    India, 1828, 1870
Institute of National Planning, UAR,
    1845
Institution of Chemical Engineers,
    UK, 1023
Institution of Mechanical Engineers,
    1026
International African Institute, 1885
International Association of Univer-
    sities, 857
International Bank for Reconstruction
    and Development (IBRD), 1642, 1643,
    1645, 1646, 1649, 1657, 1658, 1666,
    1667, 1680
International Bureau of Education
    (IBE), 864, 984, 1010
International Institute of Educational
    Planning (IIEP), 604, 615, 883,
    1556, 1580, 1688, 1703
International Labour Office (ILO),
    574, 685, 980, 1564, 1767, 1799,
    1873
International Study of University
    Admissions, 770
Irvine, S. H. 627

Jaccard, P., 972
Jackman, R., 642
Jackson, W., 1063
Jacobs, R., 1689, 1694
Jacobson, P. B., 187
Jaffe, A. J., 756, 958, 965, 1087
Jallade, J.-P., 912, 1047, 1369,
    1373, 1541
Jallade, L. A., 326
James, H. T., 434, 439
Jamrich, J. X., 587
Japanese National Commission for
    UNESCO, 1336, 1754

Jastram, R. W., 1745
Jefferson, C., 1333
Jeffries, C., 1630
Jencks, C., 329, 539, 542, 1233, 1236,
    1250, 1278
Jenkins, S., 512
Jenness, R. A., 261
Jenney, H. H., 787, 789
Jenning, F. G., 539
Jensen, S. N., 893
Jewkes, J., 989
Jewkes, J. and S., 1285
Johns, R. L., 12, 534
Johnson, D. G., 569
Johnson, E. A. J., 48
Johnson, G. E., 284, 290, 338, 381, 394
Johnson, H. G., 6, 105, 153, 541, 600,
    815, 842, 1130, 1140, 1142, 1145,
    1410
Johnson, P., 1936
Johnson, T., 282, 388, 815, 1452
Johnston, B. F., 1603
Johnstone, D. B., 544
Johnstone, J. N., 952
Johnstone, M. A., 1931
Joint Economic Committee, US Congress,
    789
Joint Thai-USOM Human Resources Study,
    1811
Jolly, R., 506, 886, 1166, 1414, 1460,
    1485, 1580, 1701, 1812, 1877, 1878
Jones, D. J., 306
Jones, G., 1021, 1074
Jones, J. A. G., 242
Jones, T. J., 1561, 1562
Jorgenson, D. W., 74
Joseph, M. L., 1052
Jozefowicz, A., 1474
Judek, A., 1288
Judges, A. V., 412
Judy, R. W., 261, 617, 625, 1537
Juster, F. T., 199

Kade, G., 893
Kahan, A., 172, 1335, 1568
Kahnert, F., 1555
Kalachek, E. D., 1071
Kalton, G., 498
Kamant, A. R., 1558
Kamat, A. R., 1549
Kamoga, F. K., 1544
Kannappan, S., 1148
Kaplan, I. I., 1322
Kapur, R. K., 883
Kardan, A. M., 1647
Karmel, P. H., 430, 775
Karpoff, P., 248
Kaser, M. C., 437, 902, 1389, 1455

Katz, A., 383, 824
Katz, S. M., 1903
Katzman, M. T., 622, 634, 636
Kaufmann, J. J., 232, 699
Kaun, D. E., 843
Kaysen, C., 828
Keat, P. G., 149
Keddeman, W., 1872
Keeney, M. G., 625
Keesing, D. B., 1435
Keezer, D. M., 734
Keil, E. T., 1224
Kelley, A. C., 621
Kelley, D. H., 1937
Kelley, S. G., 867, 1052
Kelly, J. A., 439
Kelly, T., 1897
Kelsall, R. K., 733, 751, 797, 1209
Kendall, M., 757, 1907
Kendrick, J. W., 6
Kenen, P. B., 272
Kerr, C., 789, 1313, 1757
Kershaw, J. A., 575, 579, 584, 873, 1068
Keyfitz, N., 1254
Keys, B. A., 1056
Khan, Q. V., 1558
Khanna, R. K., 796
Kiesling, H. J., 443, 447, 628
Kikier, B. F., 53, 57, 58, 126, 271
Kilbey, P., 1822
Killingsworth, C. C., 884
Kimble, G., 1509
Kinane, K., 615
Kindleberger, C. P., 1145, 1317
King, A., 1740
King. J., 250, 1628
Kitaitzev, V. A., 770
Klarman, H. E., 1290, 1297
Klein, L. R., 963
Klein, V., 1055
Kleindorfer, G. B., 1245
Klevmarken, A., 315
Klingelhofer, E. L., 1858
Klinov-Malul, R., 205, 802, 1395
Kneller, G. F., 10
Knight, J. B., 1448, 1457, 1525
Knight. R., 874, 1225
Knowles, W. H., 1824
Koenig, H. E., 625
Komarov, V. E., 1322, 1864
Komoski, P. K., 1551
Kompor, T. P., 1879
Korbel, J., 739
Kostaman, S. L., 96
Kothari, V. N., 1372, 1434, 1442, 1443
Kotí Kova, M., 883
Kotschnig, W. M., 955

Kraft, R. H. P. 1745
Kramer, E. G., 679
Kratwohl, D. R., 645
Kravis, I. B., 1254
Krishnarao, N., 1443
Krueger, A. O., 170, 272, 815, 1363, 1496
Kuhn, A., 797, 1251
Kullmer, H., 893
Kumar, S., 1856
Kumar, T. K., 950
Kunze, K. R., 966
Kuznets, S., 134
Kyle, D. W., 896

Laber, G., 128, 1159
Laderrière, P., 1225
Ladinsky, J., 229
Laidlaw, B., 473
Laird, W. E., 1269
Lalvani, G. H., 1717
Lambert, R., 514
Lampman, R. J., 875, 1292
Lamson, R. D., 948
Lancelot, W. H., 409
Landon, J. H., 639
Lanhounmey, J. Q., 1832
La Noue, G. R., 542
Lansing, J. B., 227, 482
Lassiter, R. L., Jr., 191, 200
Laswell, H. D., 1353
Lauwerys, J. A., 240, 627, 770, 886, 990
Lave, R. E., Jr., 896
Laveche, R., 625
Lavers, R. J., 505, 511
Lawrence, B., 798
Lawrov, V. V., 502
Layard, P. R. G., 98, 103, 268, 306, 389, 473, 642, 644, 751, 759, 803, 842, 846, 918, 1042, 1254, 1459, 1840, 1865
Layton, W. L., 729
Lazarsfeld, P. F., 571
Lê Thành Khôi, 173, 611, 886, 1321, 1424, 1519, 1612, 1620
Lê Thi Nam Trân, 1517
Leagans, J. P., 1604
League of Nations, 727
Lecht, L. A., 1015, 1080, 1094
Lee, E. S., 902
Lee, M. L., 307, 845
Lees, D. S., 163, 480, 487, 701, 1282, 1294
Lee Hansen, W., 164, 184, 272, 279, 525, 528, 529, 789, 815, 828, 970, 997, 1064, 1119, 1335
Leff, N. H., 1453

Leff, W. H., 604
Legg, K., 829
Leherpeux, M. M., 883
Leibenstein, H., 627, 1335, 1451
Leicester, C., 1005, 1021
Leigh, D. E., 1308
Leite, M. F., 450, 451, 459
Lester, R. A., 1053, 1068
Levensohn, A., 872, 873
Levhari, D., 395
Levin, H. M., 314, 517, 534, 631, 633, 647, 1231, 1245, 12478
Levine, D. M., 1252
Levine, J. B., 617, 1537
Levine, L., 1066
Levine, R. A., 261
Levitan, S. A., 687, 1052
Levy, F. K., 789
Lévy-Garboua, L., 346, 369
Lewis, A. J., 1687
Lewis, H. G., 134
Lewis, L. J., 1562, 1687
Lewis, M. J., 699
Lewis, P., 454, 805, 839
Lewis, W. A., 604, 1310, 1350, 1385, 1403, 1508, 1723, 1733
Leybourne, G. G., 408
Lieberman, M., 415
Liefmann-Keil, E., 502
Liepmann, K., 658
Lindbeck, A., 1254
Lindley, R. M., 1121, 1123
Lindsay, C. M., 305, 354, 1302
Lininger, C., 167
Link, C. R., 349, 398, 406
Lions, J., 625
Lipset, S. M., 1191, 1440, 1450
Literary International Committee, 1935
Lithwick, N. H., 75
Little, A. N., 1204, 1209, 1214, 1225
Liu, B. A., 1714
Liù, T. C., 70
Lloyd, W. A., 1809
Löbel, E., 1647
Locke, M., 839
Lockwood, J., 1831
Lockwood, W., 1486
Lofthouse, S., 831
Lohnes, P. R., 987, 988
Loken, R. D., 1871
Lorimer, T., 482
Lotka, A. J., 132
Louis, L. S., 468
Louri, M. G., 1688
Lourné, S., 1721
Loveless, E., 445
Lowe, J., 1485

Lowinger, T. C., 1161
Lowndes, G. A. N., 1255
Lubitz, R., 1162
Lublin, I., 1677
Lumsden, K. G., 616, 842
Lundi, A., 1868
Lutwama, U. S., 1702
Lutz, B., 902
Lydall, H. F., 244, 1266
Lyle, J. R., 1220, 1555
Lynch, P., 450, 451, 459
Lyons, R. F., 861, 867, 883, 1688, 1721
Lytton, H. D., 576

Mabry, B. D., 1879
Mace, J. D., 830, 1127
Machlup, F., 162, 828, 875, 876
Mack, R. P., 786
Maclennan, B., 509
MacMillan, R. G., 770
Maddison, A., 1720
Madge, C., 1593
Maglen, L., 268
Magnussen, O., 919, 1537
Main, E. D., 238
Makhmoutov, M. I., 1531
Malassis, L., 662, 1040, 1626
Maleche, A. J., 1544
Malherbe, E. G., 1827
Malkiel, B. G., and J. A., 358
Malleson, N., 751
Mancini, P., 717
Mangum, G. L., 259, 884, 1054, 1068
Mann, H., 37
March, G. B., 1052
March, M. S., 876
Marchese, T. J., Jr., 668
Marcus, E., 1393
Marcus, M. J., 176, 203, 452
Mardin, S., 1046
Marsh, J., 765
Marsh, P. E., 1261
Marshall, A., 39
Marshall, F. R., 380
Martin, A., 1508
Martin, F. M., 1178
Martin, L. R., 606
Martin, S. F., 1688
Martin, V., 674
Martinoli, G., 992
Maruhnic, J., 1370
Mason, W. N., 815
Masters, S., 279, 386, 1238
Mate, C. M. O., 1460
Maton, J., 255, 1369
Matthews, R. L., 516
Matthis, C., 584
Maudelstamm, A. B., 781

Maxwell, L., 278
Mayer, P., 1888
Mayeske, G. W., 631
Mayhew, A., 291, 1326
Mayobre, J. A., 1721
McAlpin, M. B., 1149
McCarthy, M. C., 700
McClelland, D. C., 1358, 1366, 1397,
    1409, 1466
McConnell, C. R., 596
McCormick, K., 1110
McCrensky, E., 981
McCulloch, M., 1382
McCusker, H. F., Jr., 609, 1779
McDobald, J. S., 261
McGee, R. J., 740
McGowan, F., 1903
McGrorry, M. M., 1936
McKean, R. N., 425, 575, 579, 584
McKechnie, G. H., 261
McKie, J. W., 190
McKinnon, K. R., 1773
McLoone, E. P., 1918
McMahon, W., 455, 834
McNamara, J. F., 468
McNulty, J. K., 546
McVoy, E. C., 1677
Meade, J. E., 178, 1219
Mechling, J., 289
Medlin, W. K., 1468
Meeker, E., 1301
Mehmet, O., 1035, 1875
Meier, G. M., 1695
Meier, R. L., 1708
Melder, J., 847
Melichar, E., 249
Mellor, J. W., 1603
Melnik, A., 344
Melnik, A. R., 233
Meltz, N. M., 1032
Menke-Glückert, P., 902
Meranto, P., 1275
Merrett, S., 216, 508, 520, 1443,
    1552, 1874
Metcalf, D., 334, 361, 811, 816, 821,
    841
Michael, R. T., 324, 336, 1309
Michelson, S., 631, 1278
Miernyk, W. H., 884
Miller, H. P., 136, 137, 148, 160,
    174, 194, 208, 269, 875, 876
Miller, L. S., 804
Miller, S. M., 1254
Miller, W. L., 52, 122
Millett, J. D., 734
Mills, G., 495
Mincer, J., 142, 157, 270, 272, 377,
    392, 815, 1254

Miner, J., 33, 433, 886
Miner, J. B., 1183
Mingat, A., 1254
Ministry of Education, Belgium, 979
Ministry of Education, India, 1724
Ministry of Education, Ireland, 1834
Ministry of Education, Japan, 1332,
    1355, 1792
Ministry of Education, Pakistan, 1513
Ministry of Education, UK, 484, 855,
    1176
Ministry of Labour and Employment, India,
    1796, 1797, 1814
Ministry of Labour, UK, 1027, 1075
Minsky, H. P., 875
Mishan, E. J., 523, 1150
Misra, A., 1514
Mitchell, D. J. B., 843
Moberg, S., 860, 994
Monoszon, E., 1746
Montgomery, G., 1632
Mood, A. M., 613, 625, 631
Mooney, J. D., 237, 784
Moore, W. E., 1406
Moorthy, S. K., 1777
Moreh, J., 92, 127
Moreira, J. R., 1431, 1685, 1688
Morgan, J. N., 161, 167, 210, 227, 247
Morgan, R. M., 1765
Morgenstern, R. D., 348
Moriguchi, C., 482
Morphet, E. L., 12
Morris, A., 833, 848
Morris, V., 299, 1049
Morrison, D. H., 573
Morse, L. D., 387
Morton, T. E., 382
Moser, C. A., 751, 759, 923, 929, 1064
Mosse, R., 1145
Movsovic, M. I., 1890
Moxham, J., 242
Mukalazi, J. B., 1868
Mukerjee, S., 702
Mukerji, K., 1443
Müller, K. V., 1179
Muller, T., 551
Mundel, D. S., 828
Munger, F. J., 1262
Munse, A. R., 1886
Muntz, E. E., 854
Murphy, J. L., 405
Murray, M., 625
Musgrave, P. W., 683, 684, 1215, 1224,
    1339
Musgrave, R. A., 500, 1258
Musgrove, F., 1328
Mushkin, S. J., 500, 534, 789, 880,
    1062, 1225, 1283, 1284

Musone, A., 1532
Mwingira, A. C., 1460, 1727
Myers, C. A., 657, 1046, 1068, 1313, 1352, 1694, 1726, 1824
Myers, C. N., 1427
Myers, P. J., 392
Myers, R. G., 231, 1165, 1323
Myint, H., 1145, 1673, 1695, 1696
Myrdal, G., 1454

Nagarajan, K. V., 1154
Naik, J. P., 1697
Nair, A. N. K., 1872
Nairn, R. C., 1441
Nalla Gounden, A. M., 1444
Nam, C. B., 121, 755, 1022, 1065, 1230, 1241
Naraghi, J. E., 1647
Nashat, M., 1624
National Academy of Sciences, USA, 1015
National Advisory Council on the Training and Supply of Teachers, UK, 1000, 1028
National Board on Graduate Education, University of Illinois, 1933
National Economic Development Board, Thailand, 1862
National Educational Association, USA, 45, 496
National Joint Advisory Council, UK, 654
National Manpower Council, 961, 962, 966, 975, 1025
National Science Foundation, USA, 197, 996, 1006, 1018, 1019, 1197
National Society for the Study of Education, 679
National Study Group on Adult Literacy, Pakistan, 1617
National Union of Teachers, UK, 863
Naumann, J., 902, 1745
Naville, P., 1196
Neff, K. L., 1399, 1901
Neher, P. A., 84
Neild, R., 1254
Neisser, C. S., 1590
Nelson, R. R., 67, 71, 78, 100, 272, 1071
Nemore, A. L., 1054
Nerlove, M., 378, 557, 815
Netherlands Economic Institute, 500, 1051
Neugarten, B. L., 1221
Neurath, P., 1606
New York State Education Department, 577
Newfield, J. G. H., 1209

Neyman, C. A., Jr., 1210
Nguyên Huu Chau, 1518
Nicholson, J. S., 40
Niland, J. R., 1156
Noah, H. J., 638, 1322, 1365, 1366, 1527, 1743
Norman, V. D., 843
Norris, K., 27, 451, 459
Nottingham University, 743
Novacco, N., 867
Nozhko, K. G., 1746, 1815
Nussbaum, M. J., 1934
Nuthmann, R., 1102

Oakland, W. H., 1091
O'Connell, J. F., 331
Oddie, G., 610, 619, 893
O'Donoghue, M., 19, 502, 893, 1030
Office of Education, USA, 1894
Office of Health Economics, UK, 1293
Ogburn, W. F., 1197
Ogilvy, B. J., 276
Oi, W. Y., 156
Okachi, K., 1481
Okigbo, P. N. C., 1520
Okita, S., 1823, 1826
Okner, B. A., 1254
Oldham, C. H. G., 1147
Olds, H. F., 595
Oliver, M., 818
Olivera, J. H. G., 780
Olivier, R., 1790
Ollerenshaw, K., 920
Olsen, E. O., 537
Olson, E., 460
Olsson, B., 1068
Onushkin, V., 801
Onyemelukwe, C. C., 1841
Orcutt, G. H., 739
Orellana, E., 770
Organisation for Economic Cooperation and Development (OECD), 111, 500, 501, 617, 625, 860, 870, 882, 888, 890, 894, 908, 928, 940, 999, 1007, 1012, 1030, 1031, 1038, 1040, 1045, 1046, 1049, 1062, 1066, 1081, 1083, 1084, 1225, 1254, 1571, 1575, 1749, 1768, 1782, 1825, 1847, 1857, 1917, 1928
Organisation of American States (OAS), 1664, 1805
Organisation of European Economic Cooperation (OEEC), 976, 994
Orlans, H., 1265
Orleans, L. A., 1656
Orlowski, M., 502
Orr, D. B., 1210
Orr, J. R. 1066
Oshima, H., 1486

Ostrey, S., 818
Oteiza, E., 1145
Oulton, N., 390
Ousview, L., 580
Overseas Development Institute (ODI), 1705
Oxford University Department of Education, 666
Ozga, W., 1647

Pacheco, O. R., 1683
Page, A., 1066
Page, D. A., 20
Page, E. B., 828
Page, G. T., 693
Palmer, G. L., 963
Pan American Health Organisation, WHO, 1132
Panchmukhi, P. R., 1442, 1558
Pandit, H. N., 1428, 1558, 1759, 1851
Panich, K. S., 1855
Panitchpakdi, S., 1379
Pant, P., 1865
Parish, R. M., 1266
Parker, F., 1651
Parker, W. N., 190
Parkes, A. S., 1219
Parkyn, G. W., 770
Parnes, H. W., 261, 862, 867, 871, 886, 1030, 1046, 1052
Parsons, D. O., 379, 714, 815
Parsons, T., 24, 1197
Passin, H., 1334, 1335, 1429
Patel, M. T., 1442
Paterson, I. W., 441, 1366
Patinkin, D., 1145
Patterson, V. W., 798
Paukert, F., 1818
Paul, S., 1492
Pauly, M. V., 507
Payne, G. L., 993, 1136
Peacock, A. T., 424, 479, 500, 502, 505, 511, 521, 751, 1002, 1268, 1296, 1302
Peaker, G. F., 885
Pearse, A., 1228
Peaslee, A. L., 1359
Pechman, J. A., 500, 529, 815
Peck, M. J., 1071, 1079
Peitchinis, S. G., 552
Pellegrin, R. J., 187
Peltzman, S., 547
Pen, J., 1254
Pennsylvania State University, 572
Perkin, H. J., 1328
Perl, L. J., 643
Perlman, R., 28

Peshkin, A., 1432
Peston, M. H., 502, 605, 751, 1066, 1072
Peters, R. S., 604
Peterson, A. D. C., 666
Peterson, W. L., 18
Petit, G., 1114
Petrini, F., 1040
Pettman, B. O., 710, 720
Peyre, C., 1196
Pfaff, A. and M., 551
Pfaff, M., 1254
Phares, D. L., 551
Phelps, E. S., 71
Phillips, C., 943
Phillips, H. M., 886, 1521, 1672, 1693, 1771, 1848
Phillips, L., 1244
Philp, H., 604, 952
Phipps, P., 1619
Pidgeon, D., 1219
Pidot, G. B., Jr., 469
Piore, M. J., 704, 715
Pirozynski, Z., 502
Planning Commission, India, 1653, 1791
Planning Commission, Pakistan, 1652
Platt, W. J., 871, 1052, 1429, 1654, 1671, 1742
Plessner, Y., 936
Podolski, K., 1537
Podoluk, J. R., 186
Poignant, R., 611, 860, 867, 892, 902, 1062, 1524, 1526, 1688
Polachnek, S., 377
Political and Economic Planning (PEP), 730, 731, 959
Pollak, W., 534
Pollatschek, M. A., 344
Pollock, R., 548
Poole, A., 797, 1251
Popkin, J., 76
Porter, D. O., 551
Porter, R. D., 766
Post, G., 75
Powell, J. H., 948
Powell, J. P., 1916
Powell, O. E., 565
Prakasa Rao, M. S., 1558
Prates, S., 1228
Pratt, J., 839
Pratt, S., 863, 1727
President's Commi-sion to Survey Philippine Education, 1764
Pressat, R., 1205
Prest, A. R., 196, 499, 500, 751
Project Talent Office, 1210
Proust, J., 1537
Pryke, R., 419

Psacharopoulos, G., 89, 95, 99, 257, 337, 389, 827, 939, 1113, 1118, 1375, 1376, 1377, 1502, 1763, 1776
Public Schools Commission, UK, 513, 514
Pyatt, G., 1005, 1351
Pym, D., 1218

Quattlebaum, C. A., 974
Queener, R. S., 1869

Rado, E., 886, 1494, 1701, 1702, 1715, 1809, 1812, 1859, 1860
Raimon, R. L., 79
Ramamoorthy, B., 1558
Ramanujam, M. S., 1558
Ramsøy, N. R., 1225, 1254
Rao, V. K. R. V., 1443, 1580, 1725
Rashid, M., 1439
Raskin, M., 1278
Ratledge, E. C., 406
Raven, J., 645
Rawlins, V. L., 304, 843
Raybould, S. G., 754
Raymond, R., 399, 623
Raynauld, H., 261
Razin, A., 125
Read, M., 1589, 1599
Reder, M. W., 179, 370, 842, 843, 968
Redfern, M., 280
Redfern, P., 923, 929, 930
Reed, R. H., 269
Rees, A., 179
Rees, A. M., 742
Reich, M., 1278
Reid, G. L., 185, 201
Reid, M. G., 1309
Reiff, H., 1537
Reimer, E. H., 1323
Remennikov, B., 1537
Renshaw, E. F., 147, 190, 317, 427, 483, 570
Rerat, F., 1114
Research for Better Schools Inc., 1926
Resnick, J. R., 1370
Ressenaar, P., 250
Reuber, G., 261
Rhodes, A. L., 1230
Ribich, T. I., 246, 279, 405, 534, 1278
Ribiero, D., 1450
Rice, J. M., 562
Richards, A. I., 1380
Richards, P. J., 1500
Richardson, V. A., 1089
Richlin, H. S., 20
Richmond, W. K., 905, 1709, 1932
Riddell, D. S., 1224
Ridley, C. E., 566

Rieben, H., 1145
Riese, H., 893, 901, 902, 1076
Riesman, D., 138, 873, 1236
Riew, J., 440, 472
Ritzen, J. M., 1586
Rivlin, A. M., 22, 190, 329, 496, 606, 678, 739, 741, 745, 783, 789, 881, 1254
Robbins, L., 46, 751, 771, 813, 1219
Roberts, B. C., 1042
Roberts, C. J., 1121, 1123
Roberts, G. W., 1732
Roberts, W. N. T., 1040
Robertson, D. J., 185
Robinson, A. J., 778
Robinson, E. E., 698, 1028
Robinson, G., 1276
Robinson, R. D., 1069, 1809
Rodger, A., 1802
Rodgers, B. N., 760
Rodgers, R. R., 1173
Rodmell, B., 920
Rogers, D. C., 20, 251, 1323, 1489
Rogers, F. M., 1623
Rolph, E. R., 502
Roose, K. D., 533
Roper, E., 1171
Rosen, H., 873
Rosen, S., 323
Rosenberg, M., 1185
Ross, A. M., 1015
Ross, D. A., 1017
Ross, J. M., 1235
Rosselle, E., 502
Rothschild, M., 365
Rottenberg, S., 1335
Routh, G., 183, 1042
Rowley, C. D., 1766
Rowley, C. K., 522
Roy, A. D., 142
Ruark, H. C., 582
Rudd, E., 536, 785
Ruffin, R. J., 1308
Ruin, O., 1225
Ruiter, R., 243, 1030, 1225
Ruml, B., 413, 426, 573
Ruscoe, G. C., 1758
Russett, B. M., 1353
Ryan, J., 1637
Rymes, T. K., 75

Sabolo, Y., 1790
Sacks, S., 886
Safty, A. E., 843
Sahota, G. S., 1479
Saigal, J. C., 1443, 1840
Saiyidain, K. G., 770
Saks, D. H., 650

Saks, J. I., 1677
Sales, P., 1251
Samame, B., 1839
Sanders, D. P., 1049, 1748
Sanderson, M., 1338
Sandgren, L., 1030
Sanyal, B. C., 935, 950
Sargan, J. D., 306
Sasaki, K., 1054
Sasidhorn, N., 1694
Saunders, P., 596
Saunderson, M., 1342
Sauvy, A., 1693
Saville, J., 1330
Sawhill, I. V., 355
Saxe, J. W., 867
Scanlon, D. G., 627
Scanlon, W. J., 279
Schaffer, H. G., 110
Schaller, H. G., 190
Scheidemann, K. Fr., 977
Scherz-Garcia, L., 1450
Schilson, D. L., 1269
Schmidt, E. I., 994
Schmitz, E., 617, 893
Schofield, R. S., 1341
Schon, D. A., 1052
Schools Council, UK, 1234
Schoota, C., 312
Schramm, W., 615, 1555, 1616, 1757
Schriver, W. R., 347
Schultz, T. W., 22, 104, 106, 107, 108,
   110, 114, 118, 119 141, 162, 190,
   222, 272, 294, 534, 671, 788, 815,
   1401, 1412, 1507, 1663
Schuman, H., 1631
Schwab, W. B., 1398
Schwartz, A., 359
Schwartz, B., 617
Schwartz, M. A., 764, 815
Schwartzman, D., 82, 90
Schweitzer, S. O., 302
Scott, A., 272, 1133, 1134, 1135,
   1139, 1140
Scott, F. K. N., 1111
Scoville, J., 708, 1034, 1061, 1095
Sear, N., 1042
Seers, D., 506, 1166
Segal, D., 789
Segelhorst, E. W., 176, 195
Seldon, A., 1270, 1302
Selowsky, M., 85, 1374
Seltzer, G., 1824
Sen, A. K., 211, 1169, 1254, 1357,
   1481, 1780
Sengupta, J. K., 934, 950
Sen Gupta, S. P., 1867
Senf, P., 500

Sentongo, C., 1868
Serbein, O. N., 660
Sesnowitz, M., 399
Severtsev, V., 1746
Sewell, D. O., 692, 818
Sexton, P. C., 1203
Shah, A. B., 1740
Shah, K. R., 1558
Shannon, J. R., 1296
Shapiro, S., 431
Shaplin, J. T., 595
Shapovalenko, S. G., 1570
Sharma, D. L., 1558
Sharma, R. C., 1558
Sharples, B., 471
Sharshansky, I., 527
Shaw, F., 1
Shaycroft, M. P., 1210
Shearer, J. C., 232, 1648
Sheehan, J., 27, 30, 419, 450, 451, 457,
   459
Sheffield, J. R., 1507, 1579, 1636
Sheldon, R., 456
Shell, K., 515
Shenoy, S., 1155
Shields, J. J., Jr., 1561, 1629, 1899
Shively, J. E., 1364
Shoup, C., 1388
Shukla, S., 886
Shumovsky, S. A., 604
Shurcliff, A. W., 1760
Siegel, B. N., 782
Siegel, I. H., 687
Siegfried, J. J., 293
Silvey, J., 1460
Simey, T. S., 1209
Simmons, J. L., 1638
Simon, B., 828
Simon, H. A., 566
Simon, K. A., 789
Simpson, H. R., 1235
Simpson, K., 1891
Singer, N., 789
Singh, B., 1443
Singh, D., 1853
Sinha, J. N., 1443
Sinha, M. R., 1826
Sirageldin, I., 247
Sisco, N. A., 694
Sjaastad, L. A., 272, 1129
Skinner, P. F., 581
Skolnik, M. L., 86, 818, 844, 1112
Skorov, G., 1495, 1580, 1688, 1693, 1844
Slawinski, Z., 1825
Sleeman, J., 435
Sloan, F. A., 807
Sloan, H. S., 655, 688
Slocum, W. L., 1226

Smelser, N. J., 1440
Smith, C. S., 260, 267, 281, 886, 928, 932, 941, 949, 1112
Smith, D. H., 1631
Smith, H. A., 1737
Smith, H. E., 1842
Smith, J. G., 140
Smith, J. H., 1042
Smith, R. E., 707
Smith, R. S., 1605
Smolensky, E., 881
Smyth, J. A., 886, 1637, 1761
Smyth, R. L., 1260
Smythe, H. H., 1694
Sobel, I., 274, 1745
Society for Research into Higher Education, UK, 1915
Sofer, C. and R., 1381
Sohlman, A., 1240
Solari, A., 1228, 1450
Solie, R. J., 245
Soligo, R., 1152
Solmon, L. C., 828, 1242
Solomon, E. S., 1537, 1693
Solow, R. M., 61, 873
Somers, G., G., 22, 245, 261, 672, 676, 699, 712, 1068
Sorenson, P. H., 609, 1742
Sow, F., 1627
Spaulding, S., 1748
Spence, G. J., 1066
Spence, M., 357, 384
Spengler, J. J., 322
Spiegelman, R. G., 897
Srdić, L., 1049
Srivastava, R. D., 1558
Srivastava, R. K., 1821
Staaf, R. J., 825
Stafford, F. P., 338, 381, 394, 1253
Stager, D. A. A., 319, 818
Staley, E., 1582
Staleman, O. F., 243
Stamp, R. M., 818
Stauss, J. H., 789
Steindl, J., 893, 1030, 1369
Stephenson, R. M., 1186
Steuer, M. D., 1011
Stevons, C. M., 843
Stevens, C. W., 845
Stewart, C. D., 958
Stewart, C. T., Jr., 1301
Stigler, G. J., 202, 411, 970
Stiglitz, J. E., 350, 402
Stoikov, V., 79, 339, 351, 356, 852, 1016
Stollar, D., 534
Stoller, D. S., 625

Stone, G., 937
Stone, R., 600, 759, 924, 925, 928, 937, 945
Storr, R. J., 1335
Strauss, G., 677
Streeten, P. P., 165, 902
Stretch, B. B., 1278
Stretch, K. L., 594, 1740
Stretton, H., 775
Stromsdorfer, E. W., 239, 245, 261, 307, 670, 672, 712, 713
Stroup, R. H., 1462
Strumilin, S. G., 63, 130
Struthers, J. S., 1224
Stubblebine, W. C., 190
Subramanian, M., 1354
Sufrin, S. C., 1263, 1264
Sundrum, R. M., 1486
Super, D. E., 1184
Susna, E., 292
Sussman, L., 1225
Sussman, Z., 1480
Sutton, F. X., 1429
Svalastoga, K., 1194
Svanfeldt, G., 625
Svennilson, I., 859, 1405
Svenningson, L., 1921
Swanson, J. C., 679
Swerdloff, S., 1067
Swift, F. H., 477
Syndicat général de la construction életrique, 973

Tabah, L., 1046
Taira, K., 1634
Tamaske, J. A., 312
Tan, E. A., 1464
Tang, A. M., 1610
Tanzania, Republic of, 20
Taubman, J., 333, 809, 815, 828
Taussig, M. K., 304, 699
Tawney, R. H., 44
Taylor, A., 1802
Taylor, S. M., 1127
Taylor, W. L., 1416
Textor, R. B., 1347
Thias, H. H., 1046, 1461, 1770
Thideus, W., 571
Thomas, B., 242, 484, 1137, 1140, 1145
Thomas, J. A., 434, 634
Thomas, L. G., 652, 1323
Thomas, R. B., 475, 1115, 1116
Thomas, R. L., 1580, 1824
Thompson, P., 1175
Thompson, T. D., 1592
Thompson, V., 1391
Thonstad, T., 928, 1090

Thore, S. A. O., 1777
Thornley, J. F., 1523
Thorp, W. L., 744
Thorsrud, E., 1066
Thurow, L., 17, 80, 87, 219, 272, 843,
    1068, 1250
Tibi, C., 1536, 1537, 1542, 1775
Tickton, S. G., 413, 426
Tiebout, C. M., 1257
Tikkiwal, B. D., 1558
Tilak, V. R. K., 1804
Timperley, S. R., 1120
Tinbergen, J., 94, 101, 250, 867,
    1007, 1046, 1254, 1670, 1678, 1693,
    1736, 1778, 1780, 1781
Tinker, H., 1601
Tirado, I. G., 1488
Tiryakian, E. A., 1566
Tobias, G., 1531, 1869
Todaro, M. P., 1499
Tolles, N. A., 249
Tolley, G. S., 460
Tomaske, J. A., 312
Trajtenberg, R., 1044
Treasury, UK, 751
Trow, M., 751, 783, 1197
Tu, P. N. V., 59, 938
Tuckman, H. P., 1244
Tul'chinskii, L., 1537
Tunes, J. T., 187
Turnbull, P., 391, 404
Turner, B. T., 1026
Turvey, R., 196
Tweeten, L., 280, 815
Tyler, R. W., 789

Uhr, C. G., 884
Ukeje, B. O., 1718
Ulman, L., 843
Ulshoefer, H., 893
United Arab Republic (UAR), 1669
United Nations (UN), 1346, 1599
United Nations Economic, Scientific and
    Cultural Organisation (UNESCO), 590,
    591, 1383, 1511, 1531, 1554, 1565,
    1602, 1608, 1609, 1613, 1614, 1615,
    1618, 1641, 1659, 1660, 1661, 1662,
    1668, 1678, 1686, 1693, 1747, 1750,
    1786, 1831, 1881, 1882, 1883, 1884,
    1893, 1904
United Nations Economic Commission for
    Africa (UNECA), 1400, 1920
United Nations Economic Commission for
    Asia and the Far East (UNECAFE),
    1716
UNESCO Institute fo Education, 585
United States Agency for International
    Development/NAtional Economic Coun-
    cil, USAID/NEC, 1830

United States Bureau of Education, 561
United States Congress Sub-Committee on
    Education, 1267
United States Department of Agriculture,
    755
United States Department of Education,
    Health and Welfare, 631, 1216
United States Department of Labor, 1008,
    1093
University College of Rhodesia and
    Nyasaland Manpower Survey Sub-Committee
    (UCRN), 1813
University Grants Committee (UGC), UK,
    598
University of the State of New York, 20
Urquidi, V. L., 1825
Uswatte-Aratchi, G., 1504
Utting, J., 742

Vaizey, J., 2, 3, 6, 27, 29, 31, 120,
    151, 168, 250, 419, 450, 451, 459, 499,
    500, 513, 617, 857, 858, 863, 866, 867,
    874, 1028, 1046, 1200, 1225, 1314,
    1323, 1449, 1528, 1647, 1816, 1819
Valladon, F., 1627
Van den Haag, E., 138
Van Dijk, C., 1046
Van Straubenzee, B., 512
Varlet, H., 1534
Vassilion, L. G., 1048
Venables, P. F. R., 651, 661, 803
Venn, G., 668
Vera, O., 1684
Verdun, P., 1529
Vermot-Gauchy, M., 994, 1001, 1036
Vernon, P. E. 751, 1209, 1219
Verry, D., 832, 846
Versluis, J., 1785, 1790
Vetro, J., 578
Vickrey, W., 485
Villard, H., 145
Vimont, C., 1014, 1098
Vogelnik, D., 492
von Mutius, B., 893
von Thünen, H., 38
von Weizäcker, C. G., 893, 902, 916, 928
von Zur-Muehlen, M., 818
Vosgerau, H.-J., 189
Votey, H. L., 1244
Vrain, P., 1117
Vuaridel, R., 166

Wabe, J. S., 1121, 1123
Wade, S., 615
Wagner, L., 462
Wald, S., 774
Waldauer, C., 551
Waldén, L. J., 66
Walder, A., 724

Wales, T. J., 333, 353, 809
Walker, K. N., 1450
Wallace, R. L., 845
Wallace, T. D., 397
Wallis, W. A., 528
Walsh, J. R., 132
Walter, J., 617
Wang, T. N., 1508
Ward, A. V., 25, 467
Ward, R. A., 599
Warkov, S., 765
Warmington, W. A., 1390
Warner, D. C., 551
Warner, W. L., 1177
Wasserman, W., 589
Watanabe, T., 1254
Watson, C., 883
Watts, E. R., 1507
Watts, H. W., 1243
Wayland, S., 1187
Weathersby, G., 794, 798, 814
Webb, R. K., 1327
Weber, A. R., 245
Weber, W. H., 638
Week, S. G., 1420
Weeks, R. L., 1678
Weheba, S., 1808
Weiler, H. W., 1748
Weinfeld, F. D., 625
Weinstein, M. C., 794
Weisbrod, B. A., 77, 109, 158, 175,
    215, 248, 261, 279, 525, 529, 789,
    815, 847, 875, 876, 1052, 1133,
    1257, 1281, 1284, 1291
Weiss, J. H., 789, 1299
Weiss, L., 321
Weiss, R. D., 277
Weiss, Y., 300, 308, 327, 395
Welch, F., 91, 221, 253, 367, 372,
    400, 606, 815
Wellens, J., 667
Werdelin, I., 1789
West, E. D., 770
West, E. G., 49, 50, 54, 553, 1151,
    1268, 1271, 1273, 1274, 1277, 1343,
    1344, 1345
West, P. S., 728
West Midland Group, 416
Westergaard, J., 1214, 1225
Westoby, A., 26, 311
Wharton, C. R., 1335
Wheeler, A. C. R., 883, 1739, 1748,
    1906
Wheelwright, E. L., 775
Whipple, D., 360
White, E., 751
White, K., 408
Whybrew, E. G., 830

Whyte, W. F., 1824
Wickert, F. R., 1802
Wickham, S., 1041
Widmaier, H. P., 886, 893, 902, 931,
    933, 1060
Widstand, C. G., 1621
Wilensky, H. L., 695
Wiles, P., 375, 414, 1254
Wilkinson, B. W., 218, 1050
Wilkinson, G. C. G., 830
Willerman, B., 729
Williams, A., 500
Williams, B. R., 464, 747, 748, 751, 971
Williams, G., 653, 665
Williams, G., 391, 404, 625, 803, 822,
    830, 836, 841, 893, 947, 1103, 1254,
    1502, 1782
Williams, H., 608
Williams, J. E., 245
Williams, N. L., 1591
Williams, P., 1540, 1675, 1706
Williams, T. D., 1425, 1485, 1722
Williams, W. J., 661
Williamson, J. G., 321, 1458, 1465
Wilson, G., 454, 514, 520, 521
Wilson, R., 617, 1537
Windham, D. M., 545, 815
Wing, P., 1300
Winter, D. G., 1466
Winterhagen, W. D., 1102
Wise, D. A., 403
Wiseman, J., 190, 424, 479, 500, 502,
    751, 1259, 1260, 1268, 1286, 1302
Wiseman, S., 597, 885, 1219
Wissenschaftsrat, 758
Witmer, D. R., 283, 466, 612
Wolf, A., 554
Wolfbein, S. L., 1677
Wolfe, J. K., 1066
Wolfe, M., 1688, 1721
Wolfle, D., 140, 828, 1136, 1175
Wood, A. W., 1507
Wood, R. C., 1261
Wood, W. D., 261, 1929
Woodhall, M., 25, 340, 535, 600, 611,
    624, 626, 721, 902, 910, 1113, 1254,
    1459, 1537, 1922, 1930
Woodward, N., 726
Woollatt, L. H., 567
Woolfe, R., 514
World Health Organisation (WHO), 1132,
    1887
Wright, H. H., 1056
Wright, R. C., 1056
Wronski, S. P., 1855
Wudhipreecha, S., 1752
Wykstra, R. A., 220
Wynn, H. P., 1251
Wynn, R. G., 789

Yates, B. A., 1908
Yett, D. E., 1104
Youmans, K. C., 290
Young, A. M., 838
Young, D., 1219
Young, J. T., 680
Young, R. D., 1443
Yudelman, M., 872

Zacharias, J. R., 789
Zambia, Republic of, 1849

Zapoleon, M. W., 1190
Zemach, R., 625
Zhamin, V. A., 96, 1322, 1423, 1438,
    1537, 1746
Ziderman, A., 36, 258, 299, 352, 368,
    724, 725, 1066, 1072
Zolotas, X., 1138, 1567
Zsock, D. K., 1863
Zucker, A., 230, 236
Zymelman, M., 550, 718, 1099, 1109,
    1323, 1356, 1362, 1738

INDEX OF CONTINENTS AND COUNTRIES (OTHER THAN US AND UK) BY ITEM NUMBERS

AFRICA, 872, 886, 1145, 1312, 1320, 1383, 1392, 1403, 1418, 1419, 1429, 1460, 1494, 1509, 1516, 1524, 1548, 1560, 1561, 1562, 1564, 1576, 1580, 1584, 1596, 1602, 1613, 1620, 1621, 1636, 1639, 1650, 1660, 1661, 1662, 1678, 1681, 1682, 1686, 1687, 1693, 1700, 1702, 1713, 1740, 1802, 1809, 1810, 1816, 1824, 1836, 1837, 1859, 1878, 1885, 1896, 1899, 1900, 1908, 1909, 1910, 1911, 1923
Algeria, 1556
Argentina, 255, 780, 1552, 1749, 1783, 1824, 1825, 1857
ASIA, 872, 1156, 1454, 1516, 1517, 1531, 1537, 1554, 1563, 1599, 1608, 1639, 1641, 1659, 1668, 1673, 1686, 1693, 1700, 1703, 1713, 1716, 1740, 1750, 1786, 1824, 1901
Australia, 254, 430, 466, 516, 615, 751, 775, 951
Austria, 477, 685, 893, 1030, 1073, 1081, 1084

Bangladesh, 1586, 1631, 1716
Barbados, 1537
Belgium, 255, 432, 674, 979
Brazil, 770, 1161, 1422, 1431, 1453, 1479, 1537, 1565, 1648, 1846
Burma, 1793, 1831, 1861

Cambodia, 1831, 1861
Cameroons, 1390, 1530
Canada, 72, 75, 86, 94, 124, 186, 188, 204, 218, 332, 441, 446, 461, 470, 471, 552, 553, 625, 635, 659, 693, 694, 751, 778, 818, 844, 869, 883, 976, 995, 999, 1012, 1032, 1037, 1050, 1056, 1066, 1073, 1092, 1099, 1111, 1159, 1160, 1165, 1258, 1537
Central Africa, 1391
Chad, 1391, 1676

Chile, 85, 770, 1335, 1374, 1537, 1824
China, 1656, 1793, 1824, 1833, 1835
Colombia, 1374, 1445, 1447, 1478, 1497, 1536, 1537, 1541, 1542, 1556, 1623, 1688, 1714, 1863, 1873
Congo (Brazzaville), 1391
Cost Rica, 1738
Cuba, 1414, 1485
Czechoslovakia, 477, 685, 883, 1024

Dahomey, 1530, 1832
Denmark, 685, 999, 1083, 1194

Ecuador, 1688
Ethiopia, 1737, 1872
Egypt (see United Arab Republic)
EUORPE, 73, 417, 436, 437, 500, 585, 662, 664, 665, 673, 685, 859, 864, 976, 981, 1012, 1053, 1145, 1146, 1369, 1373, 1762

France, 34, 116, 326, 343, 346, 369, 420, 477, 500, 591, 674, 685, 751, 770, 857, 860, 867, 868, 877, 883, 892, 893, 951, 972, 973, 1001, 1007, 1014, 1036, 1040, 1041, 1062, 1066, 1073, 1098, 1113, 1114, 1117, 1145, 1195, 1200, 1205, 1225, 1254, 1537, 1571, 1682, 1688, 1714

Gabon, 1391, 1393, 1530
Ghana, 1420, 1425, 1452, 1470, 1540, 1565, 1595, 1676, 1691, 1722, 1802, 1871, 1936
Greece, 93, 619, 774, 870, 903, 999, 1048, 1049, 1084, 1118, 1138, 1145, 1451, 1567, 1763, 1782, 1825
Guatamala, 1722
Guinea, 1824
Guyana, 1866

Honduras, 1556
Hungary, 502, 1537

419

India, 85, 615, 770, 883, 994, 1113,
    1145, 1326, 1335, 1372, 1383, 1428,
    1434, 1442, 1443, 1444, 1459, 1466,
    1475, 1482, 1491, 1492, 1501, 1505,
    1507, 1514, 1537, 1549, 1558, 1559,
    1577, 1579, 1580, 1594, 1599, 1604,
    1606, 1653, 1697, 1704, 1716, 1724,
    1725, 1777, 1791, 1793, 1796, 1797,
    1804, 1814, 1828, 1851, 1852, 1853,
    1856, 1865, 1867, 1869, 1870, 1874,
    1895
Indonesia, 1383, 1704, 1824, 1831, 1861
Iran, 1502, 1534, 1624, 1637, 1647,
    1824
Iraq, 1789
Ireland, 459, 645, 773, 893, 999,
    1030, 1449, 1531, 1834
Israel, 1394, 1395, 1396, 1421, 1480
Italy, 870, 942, 992, 994, 1083, 1125,
    1556
Ivory Coast, 1411, 1437, 1526, 1537,
    1556, 1690, 1728, 1824

Jamaica, 1350, 1733
Japan, 213, 339, 351, 591, 615, 770,
    994, 1099, 1254, 1332, 1334, 1335,
    1336, 1340, 1355, 1429, 1481, 1487,
    1610, 1634, 1704, 1716, 1754, 1768,
    1792, 1793, 1820, 1823
Jordan, 1551, 1643

Kenya, 1460, 1461, 1489, 1497, 1507,
    1539, 1579, 1635, 1667, 1770
Korea, 1765, 1793, 1830

Laos, 1831
LATIN AMERICA, 657, 872, 886, 1413,
    1450, 1516, 1664, 1684, 1685, 1686,
    1688, 1713, 1721, 1825
Lebanon, 1556
Libya, 1649
Luxemburg, 1083

Madagascar, 1530, 1537
Malawi, 1592, 1824
Malaysia, 1471, 1591, 1601, 1646, 1716,
    1769, 1831, 1861, 1875
Mali, 1530, 1690
Mauritania, 1530
Mauritius, 1386
Mexico, 85, 1374, 1427, 1445, 1446,
    1447, 1648, 1688
Micronesia, 1742
Morocco, 1537, 1550

Netherlands, 94, 243, 250, 256, 262,
    674, 685, 751, 890, 894, 994, 1007,
    1030, 1198, 1200, 1225, 1682

New Guinea, 1473, 1773
New Zealand, 276, 751, 770, 779, 1556,
    1714
Niger, 1530, 1556
Nigeria, 502, 903, 1113, 1408, 1470,
    1498, 1520, 1523, 1532, 1547, 1551,
    1556, 1573, 1574, 1580, 1590, 1642,
    1718, 1729, 1739, 1741, 1787, 1794,
    1801, 1803, 1822, 1841
Norway, 61, 320, 500, 928, 999, 1049,
    1073, 1090, 1537

Pakistan, 1439, 1474, 1513, 1617, 1652,
    1704, 1716, 1719, 1744, 1895
Papua, 1773
Peru, 1166, 1556, 1790, 1824, 1825,
    1839, 1847
Philippines, 1168, 1458, 1463, 1465,
    1565, 1566, 1588, 1598, 1601, 1704,
    1714, 1764, 1788, 1793, 1830, 1831,
    1854, 1861
Poland, 1537, 1647
Portugal, 450, 459, 619, 870

Rhodesia, 1382, 1398, 1416, 1651, 1813

Sabah, 1861
Sarawak, 1861
Senegal, 770, 1529, 1530, 1627, 1824
Singapore, 1472, 1486, 1585, 1861
South Africa, 770, 1515, 1712, 1827
Spain, 619, 867, 870, 1124, 1680, 1782,
    1825
Sri Lanka, 1497, 1500, 1504, 1535, 1536,
    1537, 1767, 1793
Sudan, 1714
Sweden, 297, 315, 535, 751, 860, 882,
    893, 928, 999, 1007, 1030, 1040, 1073,
    1084, 1113, 1200, 1225, 1237, 1254,
    1682
Switzerland, 685, 751, 933, 972

Taiwan, 1495, 1716, 1781, 1830
Tanzania, 1456, 1460, 1467, 1469, 1525,
    1536, 1537, 1578, 1580, 1628, 1658,
    1727, 1842, 1844, 1858
Thailand, 615, 871, 1113, 1383, 1441,
    1483, 1537, 1593, 1601, 1645, 1677,
    1694, 1752, 1793, 1811, 1830, 1831,
    1855, 1861, 1862, 1879
Tobago, 1732
Togo, 1530, 1556
Trinidad, 1732
Tunisia, 1436, 1519, 1536, 1638, 1775
Turkey, 619, 867, 870, 1069, 1496, 1782,
    1793

Uganda, 886, 1380, 1381, 1426, 1448,
  1457, 1460, 1522, 1537, 1544, 1545,
  1619, 1666, 1701, 1706, 1761, 1812,
  1824, 1860, 1868
U.K., U.S.A., items too numerous to be
  indexed
USSR, 63, 96, 130, 172, 591, 604, 751,
  770, 801, 886, 972, 981, 1322, 1335,
  1423, 1438, 1455, 1468, 1527, 1531,
  1537, 1568, 1570, 1647, 1655, 1682,
  1688, 1693, 1704, 1740, 1743, 1746,
  1799, 1806, 1815, 1850, 1890
United Arab Republic, 770, 1614, 1615,
  1644, 1669, 1808, 1845
Uruguay, 1228

Venezuela, 1388, 1445, 1657
Vietnam, 1462, 1793, 1830, 1831, 1861

Western Germany, 5, 13, 453, 477, 500,
  685, 751, 753, 758, 856, 857, 886,
  893, 895, 899, 901, 915, 931, 977,
  1009, 1060, 1073, 1076, 1102, 1107,
  1179, 1195, 1254, 1339, 1531, 1927

Yugoslavia, 492, 619, 857, 860, 867,
  870, 994, 999, 1784

Zambia, 1849, 1877